of the People

In 1500 fewer than three million people spoke English; today English speakers number at least a billion worldwide. This book asks how and why a small island people became the nucleus of an empire 'on which the sun never set'. David Rollison argues that the 'English explosion' was the outcome of a long social revolution with roots deep in the medieval past. A succession of crises from the Norman Conquest to the English Revolution were causal links and chains of collective memory in a unique, vernacular, populist movement. The keyword of this long revolution, 'commonweal/th', has been largely invisible in traditional constitutional history. This panoramic synthesis of political, intellectual, social, cultural, religious, economic, literary and linguistic movements offers a 'new constitutional history' in which state institutions and power elites were subordinate and answerable to a greater community that the early modern English called 'commonweal/th' and we call 'society'.

DAVID ROLLISON is an independent scholar and Honorary Research Associate at the University of Sydney. He is the author of *The Local Origins of Modern Society: Gloucestershire 1500–1800* (1992).

A Commonwealth of the People

Popular Politics and England's Long Social Revolution, 1066–1649

David Rollison

CAMBRIDGE
UNIVERSITY PRESS

CAMBRIDGE UNIVERSITY PRESS
Cambridge, New York, Melbourne, Madrid, Cape Town, Singapore,
São Paulo, Delhi, Dubai, Tokyo

Cambridge University Press
The Edinburgh Building, Cambridge CB2 8RU, UK

Published in the United States of America by Cambridge University Press,
New York

www.cambridge.org
Information on this title: www.cambridge.org/9780521139700

First published 2010

Printed in the United Kingdom at the University Press, Cambridge

A catalogue record for this publication is available from the British Library

Library of Congress Cataloging in Publication data
Rollison, David, 1945–
A commonwealth of the people : popular politics and England's long social
revolution, 1066–1649 / David Rollison.
    p. cm.
Includes bibliographical references.
ISBN 978-0-521-85373-6 (hbk.) – ISBN 978-0-521-13970-0 (pbk.)
1. Great Britain – Politics and government – 1066–1485.   2. Great Britain –
Politics and government – 1485–1603.   3. Great Britain – Politics and
government – 1603–1649.   4. Political culture – Great Britain – History.
5. Popular culture – Great Britain – History.   6. Populism – Great Britain –
History.   7. Community life – Political aspects – Great Britain – History.
8. Collective memory – Political aspects – Great Britain – History.   9. Great
Britain – Social conditions.   10. Social change – Great Britain – History.
I. Title.
DA176.R65   2009
942 – dc22   2009035291

ISBN 978-0-521-85373-6 hardback
ISBN 978-0-521-13970-0 paperback

History is a discipline widely cultivated among nations and races. It is eagerly sought after. The ordinary people aspire to know it. Kings and leaders vie for it. Both the ignorant and the learned are able to understand it. It serves to entertain large, crowded gatherings and brings to us an understanding of human affairs. It shows how changing conditions affected human affairs, how certain dynasties came to occupy an ever wider space in the world until they heard the call and their time was up ... History makes us acquainted with the conditions of past nations as they are reflected in their national character. (Ibn Khaldun)[1]

Even if all of mankind should need to perish ... humanity has been charged with a goal, as the loftiest task for all time to come, of growing together in oneness and commonality so that humanity can confront its impending doom as a united entity. This loftiest of all tasks encompasses the sum total of the ennoblement of humanity. (Friedrich Nietzsche)[2]

---

[1] Ibn Khaldun, *The Muqaddimah, An Introduction to History*, trans. Franz Rosenthal, ed. N.J. Dawood (Princeton 1989), 5.
[2] Quotation from Rudiger Safranski, *Nietzsche: a Philosophical Biography* (London 2003), 105.

Dedicated to the memory of my mother
Pamela Mabel Job (d. 2006)
and James Edward Jones (d. 2007)

Contents

Preface: points of departure

In 1995 the Prime Minister of Australia, Paul Keating, formally announced his support for an Australian Republic. In the course of his speech to the House of Representatives he rejected Monarchy and other formal survivals of empire. His only concession to the European and British past was 'that the Australian republic retain the name "Commonwealth of Australia"'.[1] '"Commonwealth" is a word of ancient lineage which reflects our popular tradition and our Federal system', he said.

More recently a leading Australian novelist, David Malouf, who is of Lebanese-Irish extraction, expanded on Prime Minister Keating's theme. 'Any argument for [a republic] based on the need to make a final break with Britain will fail,' wrote Malouf. This is 'not because people want to preserve the tie but because breaking it is neither here nor there. The republic will be accepted because we need, as a society, to reinforce our bonds with one another, not break our bonds elsewhere':

bonds of affection and concern that celebrate the gift of one another's presence and make the community one, as Federation, a century ago, made the continent and the nation one. And we will use for this notion of *res publica* the good old English word "commonwealth", as our founding fathers did, rather than the Frenchified "republic". Nothing very terrible has ever happened under a commonwealth. The same cannot be said for a republic, as many newer Australians, who are pretty familiar with their own histories if not with ours, have good reason to recall.'[2]

Malouf's words are worth repeating and remembering for the nobility of the sentiments they express, but evocations of tradition ought to make historians – and citizens – prick up their ears. Prime Minister Keating's passing reference was the beginning of this enquiry into the historical meanings of the commonwealth family of words.

---

[1] Paul Keating, 'An Australian Republic – The Way Forward': speech delivered to the Australian House of Representatives, Canberra, 7 June 1995. Text available at australianpolitics.com.

[2] David Malouf, 'Made in England: Australia's British Inheritance', *Quarterly Essay* 12:4 (2003), 27–8.

What's in a name? Australians should continue to call their country a 'commonwealth' because it is a prestigious historical word with appropriate historical associations. What contribution can historical study make to this issue? It was a word I had underlined and queried in sixteenth- and seventeenth-century sources.[3] To provide a starting point for enquiry, I set out to trace it as far back as I could. When was it first used, who by, in what contexts and with what meaning(s)? The exercise would have value for the study of political thought – the subject I was teaching at the time of Paul Keating's speech. It would raise questions about how political words and political languages work, in theory and in practice. Do words matter, or is language 'superstructural', derivative of general political-economic, demographic, ecological and social 'structures'? At the other extreme, is language, the main form of our primary sources, self-contained? Do primary sources ever point to a social reality beyond texts and the conventional discourses they embody and express? Do they point to anything beyond discursive and linguistic acts? Traditionally, historians presume they do.[4]

'Post-structuralist' critique has implications for the way we read primary sources (in this case 'commonwealth' usages). What are they sources of? The problem goes deeper than written sources. Surely, experience tells us that 'people remember what they want to remember, not what actually happened.'

Everyone colours events after his fashion, brews up his own mélange of reminiscences. Therefore getting through to the past itself, the past as it really was, is impossible. What are available to us are only its various versions, more or less credible, one or another of them suiting us better at any given time. The past does not exist. There are only infinite renderings of it.[5]

---

[3] 'The term "commonwealth" came into wide use to refer to a constitutional (and substantial) alternative to "kingdom", and helped make country in the national sense thinkable.' David Rollison, *The Local Origins of Modern Society* (London and New York 1992), 17.

[4] Keith Jenkins, *The Postmodern History Reader* (London and New York 1997) is a useful collection. For accounts which accord with the general approach pursued in this book: Adrian Jones, 'Word *and* Deed: Why a Post-Structuralist History is Needed and How it Might Look', *Historical Journal* 43:2 (2000), 517–41 is a salutary exploration of 'ways to re-assimilate historical studies of discourses with older historiographies of classes, institutions, social structures and ideologies' (517); to the proposition '*either* discourse or structure', Miguel Cabrera, 'Linguistic approach or return to subjectivism? In search of an alternative to social history', *Social History* 24:1 (January 1999), 82–3, answers 'both': for Cabrera, 'The fact that the new history attributes to discourse an active role in the production of meanings does not imply, whatsoever, that it replaces social causality with a kind of linguistic determinism, or that it denies the existence of the real, as is sometimes foolishly supposed'.

[5] Ryszard Kapuscinski, *Travels with Herodotus* (New York 2007), 262.

My generation often calls the discovery of this 'treacherous and complicating' aspect of the human condition 'post-modernist', 'post-colonial' and 'post-structuralist'. For Ryszard Kapuscinski, the 'greatest discovery' of his life-long literary travelling companion, Herodotus, the father of History, was that 'we are never in the presence of unmediated history'. There is only 'history recounted, history as it appeared to someone, as he or she believes it to have been.'[6] Does it point to anything beyond itself? The answer offered in this book is that authenticated archival and archaeological sources provide a field of certainty within which differences of interpretation are inevitable. The Norman Conquest, the deposition of Edward II and the execution of Charles I definitely happened. What they signify is subject to enduring disagreement.[7]

Enquiry into the historical provenance and meanings of the 'commonwealth' words involves investigation of another, past society tackling the same problematic as twenty-first-century countries like Australia: the perennial business of constituting and reconstituting institutions and identities. It would serve as a testing ground for theory debates. Is History necessary? Are our circumstances today not so different from any that have existed in the past that historical studies no longer have any practical relevance to us? How high a priority is the study of past constitutions? Should it not be left to specialists to advise specialist politicians as to the correct and appropriate use of words?

I put it to students that whatever their instinctive responses, these questions should not be answered in advance. I recommended an 'empirical' approach. Always start with an attested primary source. If you want to know what Aristotle, Cicero, John of Salisbury, William Langland, Machiavelli, Shakespeare, Mary Wollstonecraft, Marx, Nietzsche or Michel Foucault thought, read what they wrote and reconstitute their contexts on the basis of other contemporary evidence. The question of what it means for a country to call itself a commonwealth is even more demanding. The amount of time we devote to it will depend on how important we think it is. It becomes more important when we have children and grandchildren who are bound to feel the need for ideas and to ask questions. What should be passed on?

The issues are interdisciplinary. We need to lay prejudices and preconceptions aside and gather information about how (of what) 'Australia'

---

[6] *Ibid.*, 272.

[7] For an account of 'things which are archaeologically and archivally certain', see Ian Mortimer, 'What Isn't History? The Nature and Enjoyment of History in the Twenty-First Century', *History: the Journal of the Historical Association*, 93:4, no. 312 (October 2008), 468–70.

(or whatever country it is that we are seeking to name) is actually 'constituted'. How should we visualize the whole thing: as landscape traversed or mapped from a bird's-eye view? Should we reduce it to institutions, as constitutional studies often do? What are its component parts? Is it an 'imagined community', as Benedict Anderson wrote of all modern nation-states? How is it imagined and by whom? Ethnicity and religious affiliation have always been prominent in private and public discourse in Australia (and many other countries). Is it always so? Were ethnicity and religious affiliation implicated in earlier usages of the commonweal/th words, or did other issues predominate? What about class? Class was an especially lively topic of discussion at the University of Western Sydney, where a higher proportion of students identified themselves as 'working class' than is true of more prestigious (older) universities in more expensive regions of Sydney. What values do the different parts and members of the Australian commonwealth hold dear? And it is clearly crucial for the student of political and constitutional thought to address the nature, distribution and sources of power.

We can be forgiven for sharing the response of Bertolt Brecht's 'worker who reads history': 'So many reports! So many questions!' Arguably, England was the first nation-state in world history. At the beginning of its journey it had a handful of classical literary sources concerning the forms of city-states and empires to compare its own experience with, but the 'kingdom' of England was neither of these. It had no easily comparable predecessor: hence the constant theme of a people trying to make sense of events after they had occurred.

All the disciplines of the human sciences must contribute to this question of how a society is actually constituted, how and why it differs from other human communities – as opposed to how it/they is/are supposed to be. The epigrams at the beginning of this book are intended to invoke two larger contexts of human studies as I conceive them. Ibn Khaldun reminds us that every culture and civilization of which we have any knowledge had a special place for Herodotus's discipline. This book is a study, in Ibn Khaldun's words, of how 'past conditions' (a 'long early modern' period encompassing the fourteenth to seventeenth centuries) created English 'national character' and how both were shaped into a force that 'came to occupy an ever wider space in the world.' Ibn Khaldun laid down a number of principles that apply to the study of early modern England, including the idea that 'producers who delegate security to others, to specialists of government and war, become politically and militarily emasculated.'[8] One of the reasons that the English commonalty

---

[8] Ernest Gellner, *Conditions of Liberty: Civil Society and its Rivals* (London 1994), 64.

was far from politically emasculated in the thirteenth to seventeenth centuries was that it was armed and trained. The patriarchal reference is
intended and unavoidable: this was a reflexively patriarchal culture. I will
touch on Nietzsche in due course.

The people to whom I am most indebted, dead and alive, are in the
footnotes: this is a work of synthesis, and I have tried to make sure
the giants upon whose shoulders my conjectures are based are properly
acknowledged throughout. In the research I tried to follow my own advice
and start with primary sources. An Australian Research Council Large
Grant (2001–3) enabled me to spend two years shuffling between the
Library of the Institute of Historical Research and the British Library.
No praise is too high for the quality of the resources and facilities offered
by these institutions and their staffs. Without the generosity of Paula and
Trevor Hammett, Paul and Britt Clement, and Cathy Shrank, London
would have been beyond our means. Many of the early ideas were tried
out at meetings of Sybil Jack's Sydney Renaissance Society or Andrew
McCrae's early modern symposium at Sydney University, and then at the
biennial conferences of the Australian and New Zealand Association for
Medieval and Early Modern Studies (ANZAMEMS). Since then various
bits and pieces of the story have been presented at seminars and conferences too numerous to list. I hope I listened carefully enough to the
responses, which have been extremely important. I am especially grateful to my fellow members and associates of ANZAMEMS for the critical
encouragement and advice they gave when the project was an infant. The
'school' I most closely identify and associate with is that of Keith Wrightson, his students, and (most recently) their students. I have my own sense
of the limits and possibilities of the ship Peter Laslett launched back in the
1960s, what might loosely be called 'Cambridge reconstitutionalism'; I
am certain, nevertheless, that the most substantial advances in the recent
historiography of the English thirteenth to seventeenth centuries, and of
early modern Europe in general, have been made by social, economic
and demographic historians whose work begins with microstudies using
difficult and previously neglected archives. Sorting the archives of everyday life into coherent histories is not as easy as its practitioners often
make it seem. Conal Condren, Patricia Crawford, Phil Withington, Alex
Shepherd, Andrew McCrae, Michael Bennett, Vivien Brodsky, Charles
Zika, the editorial board of *History Workshop Journal*, anonymous readers
for *Social History*, *Cultural and Social History* and the *William and Mary
Quarterly*, James Holstun, Steve Hindle, Garthine Walker, Pat Hudson,
Simon Middleton, Peter Thompson, Rob Sweeny, Wythe Holt, Keith
Wrightson and Paul Griffiths commented on parts or all of earlier and
succeeding drafts. John Arnold was a valued guide to my early forays into

medieval history and tried his best to correct my Latin. I am especially grateful to Andy Wood for patiently and sympathetically commenting on so many successive drafts, and for many valuable suggestions.

Dafydd Rollison urged me to write down something about the history and politics of industry. By presenting me with two grandsons during the long genesis of this book, Ben and Amanda Rollison reminded me why history matters. The 'English explosion' idea emerged from years of trying to explain to students with no background in English history and historical culture how and why what happened in early modern England was of some significance to their lives. I would like to thank generations of students at Sydney Technical College, the University of New South Wales and the University of Western Sydney for instant feedback that some of my ideas worked, at least as heuristic and mnemonic devices. In Australia, twelve thousand miles from the imperial mother country, it was worth pondering silly questions like 'Why are we doing this in English?' What follows is my answer to that question. My greatest debt, as always, is to my lover, companion and comrade, Christine Rollison.

Introduction: An uncommon tradition

In sum, all actions and habits are to be esteemed good or evil by their causes and usefulness in reference to the commonwealth.[1]

1   A study of social revolution

How swift does evolution have to be before we can call it revolution?[2]

For most of the age of the commonweal – 1381 to 1649 – England's population was less than three million, about a twentieth of its population today and about a sixth of the current population of Australia. It is necessary to imagine the inhabitants of greater Sydney or Newcastle-upon-Tyne in 2008 dispersed unevenly across the landscape of England in hamlets, villages, market towns and boroughs, provincial capitals, regional capitals like York, Bristol, Southampton, Norwich, Canterbury and the twin-cities on the Thames, London and Westminster, which were firmly, by the fourteenth century, the national capitals. This was the locale of the long social revolution that is the subject of this book. It was a 'country' just about small enough to be known, experienced, travelled and explored by one person in one lifetime. It was more than an 'imagined community'.[3] It was a country that could be (and has been) walked, run, rowed, swum, ridden, hunted, stalked, journeyed, camped and fought over, a comprehensible and remembered piece of the world in which the ensuing vision is something other than just 'imagined'. Imagining England is a central theme of this book. Imagining an English commonwealth was the perennial topic of the vernacular culture that becomes accessible to systematic, archives-based historiography in c.1300 with a ready-made common language. I trace the meanings of a

---

[1] Thomas Hobbes, *Behemoth: the History of the Causes of the Civil Wars of England*, ed. William Molesworth (London 1840), 58.

[2] David Lewis Williams, *The Mind in the Cave: Consciousness and the Origins of Art* (London 2002), 26.

[3] For Benedict Anderson, *Imagined Communities: Reflections on the Origins and Spread of Nationalism* (London 1983), the essential quality of modern nations and nationalisms.

commonwealth in some vernacular English classics: John of Salisbury's *Policraticus*, the *Vision* of Julian of Norwich, William Langland's *Piers Plowman*, Thomas Wimbledon's Paul's Cross sermon in 1387, Chaucer's *Canterbury Tales*, contemporary chroniclers and vernacular translators, fifteenth-century reactionaries, heretics and dissenters, Sir John Fortescue's constitutional musings, Tyndale's Bible, Sir Thomas Smith's pioneering social anatomies, the elder Richard Hakluyt's utilitarian plans for English overseas empire, Shakespeare's demolition of the body politic idea and, finally, Thomas Hobbes's *Behemoth* and *Leviathan*, those epic reactions to the long revolution that I call the 'English explosion'.

These landmarks of 'middle' and 'early modern' English relate to a greater vernacular revolution whose precept and keyword was 'commonweal'.[4] The term referred to an ideal that has been all but invisible in traditional constitutional history, with its emphasis on institutions of state and power elites. Rulers and institutions of state, I argue, must be located in an evolving constitutional culture that connected and encompassed all the communities and inhabitants of England. In a succession of crises from the fourteenth to seventeenth centuries, commonwealth ideology formed in opposition to existing government. At such times the state and senior ruling classes were forced, if only momentarily, not only to acknowledge but negotiate with and even bow to a higher authority: commonweal. All estates, including kings and their closest associates, were subordinate to it. At its most dramatic, in a series of large-scale regional rebellions from 1381 to 1649, commonweal's army rose in the form of a popular army with the capacity, momentarily, to defeat any band of knights the state could put into the field against it. Before the 1640s, the popular armies melted away as quickly as they had formed, but not without leaving memorable signs of their having been there, alongside an equally tenacious memory that, for a day or two, common rebels had the regime at their mercy. In the 1640s, in different circumstances, similar forces were articulated but the rebels did not melt away. They defeated and executed Charles I in terms which rebels against unjust kings and lords had been using since *Magna Carta* (1215): in the name of commonweal or (a common usage after the 1540s) common-wealth. In 1649, however, commonwealth replaced kingdom and became what it had been fighting for centuries, the state.

This movement was shaped and framed by a long collective ('social') revolution. Seeking to classify the great modern revolutions in France,

---

[4] Except where otherwise indicated, I use 'commonweal' to stand for the various spellings and usages prior to c.1520 and 'commonwealth' to refer to those in use after that date. As I argue below (e.g. Chapters 3.8, 5.3, 7.1), however, a shift of meaning, roughly from moral and spiritual to materialist values, is implied in the change.

Russia and China, Theda Skocpol defines 'social revolutions' as 'rapid, basic transformations of a society's state and class structures'. This book is a study of an historical precursor and exemplar of modern world revolutions. The 'English explosion' was, as Skocpol says of social revolutions in general, 'accompanied and in part carried through by class-based revolts from below'. Social revolutions are 'set apart from other sorts of conflicts and transformative processes above all by the combination of two coincidences: the coincidence of societal structural change with class upheaval; and the coincidence of political with social transformation'. Social revolutions are defined by 'basic changes in social structure and in political structure [which] occur together in a mutually reinforcing fashion'.[5] The English explosion differs from Skocpol's abstract in only one respect. Measured against the French, Russian and Chinese revolutions, it was not 'rapid'. Although it came to a head in the 1640s in dramatic, 'revolutionary' fashion, such that the events of that decade have sometimes been described as the first of the modern world revolutions, I argue that it was the outcome of a collective transformation – a *social* revolution – lasting several centuries.

That social revolution marks beginnings of a movement that Nietzsche (and, in his different way, Marx) saw as the 'commoning' of English and, more generally, European constitutional culture. It involved an accumulative shift from the constitutional forms described by Aristotle as 'Monarchy' (rule by One) and Aristocracy (rule by Few) to what he called 'Polity' (rule by Many). Nietzsche's hatred of populism and admiration for nobility differed from earlier expressions in that they implied the great discovery of the nineteenth century: that *homo sapiens* is an interconnected global species.[6] Marx admired Darwin and applied the evolutionist vision to the histories of human collectivities. Everything that has happened since has strengthened the global species context. In such a context, this book is a local study in the formation of an exclusive community: the type of community (in all its forms) that has dominated identity-formation throughout human history and right up to the present. The passionately exclusive nationalism that became lucid and imperial in the generations of the Hakluyts, Shakespeare, Bacon and Hobbes (c.1550–c.1650) was a decisive cause of the slow and still far from complete realization of the modern world that, as archaeologist Clive Gamble puts it, 'human beings are everywhere'. As both Marx and

---

[5] Theda Skocpol, *States and Social Revolutions: a Comparative Analysis of France, Russia and China*, (Cambridge 1979), 4–5.

[6] See, for example, F. Nietzsche, *Beyond Good and Evil: Prelude to a Philosophy of the Future*, trans R. J. Hollingdale, (Harmondsworth 1973), Sections 257, 268, pp. 173, 186–7.

Nietzsche recognized, this implied a global agenda for historiography that national historiographies have been slow to adopt.[7] For what it is worth, my view is that to the extent that 'commonweal' words usually referred to an exclusive community, they do not offer a good model for a country looking to constitute or reconstitute itself in the early twenty-first century. The word is another matter, for the meanings of words change.

The history of early modern England is 'local history' in the sense that on a world scale, the territory and the population was small and 'knowable' in the empirical sense. It was interconnected by highways, roads, tracks and trails. It had an accumulating repertoire of common stories, many of them concerned with courts and kings. As Alan Macfarlane showed nearly forty years ago, very few English people born since c.1300 escaped being recorded by one or another instrument of the state.[8] Since the 1970s, the resulting archives have presented demographic, economic and social historians with opportunities to 'reconstitute' localities, districts and regions by means of serial and spatial networking techniques. This now extensive demographic, economic and social historiography explores the worlds represented in cultural, literary, intellectual, linguistic, political and constitutional histories through previously unexplored (even uncatalogued) 'archives of everyday life'. The new social history of early modern England begins with the ambitious hope of naming, enumerating and getting to know everyone. It still aims to address high politics, religious thought and practice, art, literature, ideas, mentalities and so on; it just starts a little lower down the food-chain, with the vast majority, the 'commonalty'. Social revolutions as defined by Skocpol cannot be understood in the absence of history from below. Nor can we understand the first phase (or 'nucleus') of the long revolution of modernity without an effort to sketch what was revolutionized: what came before.

---

[7] Wolf, *Europe and the People Without History* remains the outstanding synthesis of world systems theory; for which see Immanuel Wallerstein, *The Modern World System: Capitalist Agriculture and the Origins of the European World-Economy in the Sixteenth Century* (New York 1974). Both Wolf and Wallerstein were heavily influenced by the structuralist/global/interdisciplinary scholarship of Fernand Braudel, in my view the great historian of the twentieth century: see his *The Mediterranean and the Mediterranean World in the Age of Philip II* (New York 1972); *Capitalism and Material Life 1400–1800* (New York 1973); *On History*, trans. Sarah Mathews (Chicago 1980); *Civilization and Capitalism 15th–18th Century*, 3 vols.: *The Structures of Everyday Life* (New York 1979); *The Wheels of Commerce* (New York 1979); *The Perspective of the World* (New York 1984). Greg Dening, 'Living In and With Deep Time', *Journal of Historical Sociology* 18:4 (December 2005), 269–81, raises issues of history and identity that are relevant to the concerns of this book.

[8] Alan Macfarlane in collaboration with Sarah Harrison and Charles Jardine, *Reconstructing Historical Communities* (Cambridge 1977), 31–2.

In Chapter 1, I locate early modern England in relation to the 'new *longue duree*' implied by recent work in genetic archaeology, a synthesis of genetics, climatology, landscape history and demography. The 'timescape' set out in the early sections provides the setting for John of Salisbury's political masterpiece, *Policraticus* (1159). John gave memorable form to ideals of community and ways of distinguishing good government ('common weal') from bad (tyranny): the simple yet ruthless distinction that became an ineradicable precept of English constitutional culture from the thirteenth to seventeenth centuries. The final section of Chapter 1 introduces another recurring and accumulating theme: 'social mapping', the 'realization' of the social body in relation to landscape that is picked up again in several later sections, especially the discussion of '*landschap*' in Chapter 3.7. Part I, comprising Chapters 1 and 2, introduces 'structures' (abiding elements and forms) that were ingrained in English society by 1327 and continued to influence its history thereafter. Chapter 2 focuses on the formative period of rapid change from c.1159–1327, roughly (collective movements can rarely be assigned exact dates) from the year John of Salisbury finished the *Policraticus* to the demise of Edward II. It deals, successively, with the demographic turnaround of c.1250–1315, the enduring (and perhaps decisive) theme of *trafike* ('commerce'), enterprise, families and households, monarchy and resistance theory, the emergence of public opinion and a 'middle' class or classes, and the arming of the commonalty. Chapter 2 concludes with a vignette of a decisive and never forgotten 'event', the deposition and reputed murder of Edward II.

Chapter 3 offers a populist explanation for the rise of 'middle' English (a massively consequential 'linguistic turn' if ever there was one) from c.1300 to the 1520s. English literature is shown emerging from popular, predominantly oral and aural, language uses: as the literary efflorescence of a fundamentally populist movement 'from below'. Sections 3–4 describe the emergence of a discourse about 'commune opinioun', how it was conceived and what some of its key ideas were. Sections 6–8 explore the emergence of a universalist, populist vernacular theology in *Piers Plowman* and the *Vision* of Julian of Norwich; Sections 9–10 describe the 'old regime's' tenacious efforts to stop the vernacular revolution dead in its tracks. Section 11 interprets the ferocious public 'dialogue' between Sir Thomas More and William Tyndale, on the eve of Henry VIII's state Reformation, as the coming to a head of a century of systematic repression of vernacular religion instituted by Langland's and Julian's younger contemporary, Henry IV's Lord Chancellor and Archbishop of Canterbury, Thomas Arundel. The vernacular language, literature and theology movements were facets or symptoms of a complex but unmistakeable long-term 'revolution of commonalty'.

Part II (Chapters 4 and 5) examines another aspect of that long revolution, the emergence and accumulation of a great tradition of popular resistance and rebellion that shaped and was shaped by the discourse of the commonweal. Chapter 4 is a chronological series of microstudies illustrating the accumulation of popular demands that came together and exploded in the Commons Rebellion of 1381. Each episode, and the cumulative process as a whole, is interpreted in relation to Ernesto Laclau's recent reformulations of populist theory. Chapter 5 describes the explosion and accumulation, from 1381 to the 1540s, of a tradition of common rebellion in the name of 'commonweal/th'. The tradition is best understood as a dimension of the greater populist movement – 'the revolution of commonalty' – explored in the earlier chapters. The point is not that the revolution of commonalty was the only movement affecting the emergence of modern English constitutional culture, only that it was a preeminent (but not sufficient) condition. It was a very significant condition, since whatever else it means, 'modernity' is (or, perhaps, was) an epoch dominated, not only by strong states, but also by the politics of popular sovereignty.

The study of 'early modern' England is the study of the meanings and roots of modernity. What I call the 'commoning' of England is essentially the same epochal movement which philosopher Charles Taylor calls 'the affirmation of ordinary life'. In Taylor's account it entailed the decline of medieval and classical aristocratic world-views. Aristocratic ways of life and seeing were challenged and eventually swamped by a new and all-consuming emphasis on 'those aspects of life concerned with production and reproduction, that is, labour, the making of things needed for life, and our life as sexual beings, including marriage and the family'.[9] For Taylor, affirmation of 'ordinary life' in this political-economic and biological sense is a defining precept of modernity. As David Hume wrote of the history of one element of 'ordinary life', 'Trade was never esteemed an affair of state until the (seventeenth) century... There is scarcely any ancient writer on politics who has made mention of it.'[10] In my account this 'ordinary-life affirming movement' has the same heirs (Bacon and

---

[9] Charles Taylor, *Sources of the Self: the Making of the Modern Identity*, (Cambridge, Mass. 1989), 211. Taylor writes (213–14) that 'The Baconian revolution involved a transvaluation of values, which is also the reversal of a previous hierarchy... an inherent bent towards social leveling is implicit in the affirmation of ordinary life.'

[10] David Hume, 'Of Commerce', in Stephen Copley and Andrew Edgar (ed.), *Selected Essays* (Oxford 1993), 119.

the Scottish enlightenment, the political economy outlook) but a longer, more exclusive, more introverted English genealogy.

The goal of the movement as Bacon defined it was (in Taylor's words) 'to relieve the condition of man'.[11] In my account the political economy outlook emerged in the late fifteenth and sixteenth centuries as a movement to improve the condition of England. It only aspired to universality as an afterthought. I show that it expropriated an older movement and tradition which begins with John of Salisbury's surprising asides about the virtues of armed peasants and workers and the autonomy of the Feet of the Body Politic (Chapter 1.5). From there I trace the affirmation of commonalty through the movement to limit monarchical power in the 1250s and '60s (Chapter 2.4–6), the arming of the commonalty (Chapter 2.7), the earliest English political songs (Chapter 2.8, 3.1–5), the deposition of Edward II (Chapter 2.9), an early labour agitator (Chapter 4.4), *Piers Plowman* (Chapter 3.6–7), the vision of Julian of Norwich (Chapter 3.8), vernacular theology, including the Lollards (Chapter 3.6, 3.8–11), the rebellions of Jack Straw, Jack Sharpe and Jack Cade (Chapter 4.8, 5.1–5), the constitutional writings of Sir John Fortescue (Chapters 5.3, 7.1), the reactions of Thomas Arundel (3.9), Sir Thomas Elyot (3.10) and Sir Thomas More (3.11), the 'heresy' of William Tyndale (3.11), the rebel 'common-wealths' of 1536 and 1549 (5.6), Sir Thomas Smith (Chapters 6.4, 7.1), the Hakluyts (Chapter 7.3–5) William Shakespeare (Chapter 8.1–3), and finally, from c.1600–49, in the constitutional anatomies of Thomas Wilson, certain parliamentarians, lawyers and writers, Levellers and, last but not least, that supreme enemy of the affirmation of commonalty, Thomas Hobbes (Chapter 9).

Each of these sources, I suggest, affirms (not always with approval) that the 'ordinary' and 'common' was overflowing or had overflowed its assigned place in traditional hierarchy. The movement of commonalty threatened to 'displace the locus of the good life' in traditional theocratic and aristocratic (including renaissance humanist[12]) ideals. Its goal was to place them, as Taylor puts it, 'within "life" itself'. This revolution was embedded in a narrowing and secularization of older conceptions and is signified by the linguistic transition from fourteenth-century *wele* to sixteenth- and seventeenth-century 'wealth'. Eighteenth-century writers like David Hume, Adam Ferguson and Adam Smith further narrowed the definitions, but the collective revolution they described had deep roots

---

[11] Taylor, *Sources of the Self*, 213.

[12] *Ibid.*, 212, writes that 'The citizen ethic was in some ways analogous to, and could at times even partially fuse with, the aristocratic ethic of honour, whose origins lay in the life of warrior castes (as indeed the ancient citizenship ideals did also).'

in the English past. The system only became 'universal' and 'natural' by various forms of persuasion, not all of them rhetorical.

Part III, 'The English Explosion', focuses on a theme of the fourteenth to seventeenth centuries that traditional constitutional narratives have largely ignored: manufacture or 'industry'. Leigh Shaw-Taylor and E.A. Wrigley recently concluded that 'overwhelming' evidence now supports the view that 'nationally there was more growth in the secondary sector between 1500 and 1750 than there was between 1750 and 1850'.[13] In her account of social revolutions, Skocpol observes that 'processes such as industrialization can transform social structures without necessarily bringing about, or resulting from, sudden political upheavals or basic political-structural changes. What is unique to social revolution is that basic changes in social structure and in political structure occur together in a mutually reinforcing fashion. And these changes occur through intense socio-political conflicts in which class struggles play a key role.'[14] Chapter 6 describes an accumulating dialectic of landscape-transforming process and collective consciousness: this is my general theme throughout. Observation and imagination made the difference. It was not just that certain 'material' or 'social' (ultimately landscape-transforming) conditions came into existence and continued, but that communities and individuals were determined to make sense of their relationships, identities, experiences and observations in the light of often simple but extraordinarily powerful concepts, words and ideas. In this seminal epoch of English history, ideas, the lives of minds, made the difference. Chapter 6 is an account of how and when 'industry' and 'economy' began to enter political discourse.

I am not the first to suggest that the seeds of the theories and disciplines that dominated global political consciousness in the nineteenth and twentieth century – 'political economy' – were planted, as Marx put it, 'in the generations of [Sir John] Fortescue and [Sir Thomas] More'. Industry as process and discourse, I suggest, was the final crucial element in the coming together, after c.1570, of a systematic argument for imperialism. In Chapter 7 I enter that momentous conjuncture of collective process, imagination and propaganda. What came to be called 'industry' had always been a solution to 'necessity', meaning 'poverty', the opposite of common prosperity and healthiness. Imperialism as

---

[13] Leigh Shaw-Taylor and E.A. Wrigley, 'The Occupational Structure of England, c.1750–1871: a preliminary Report', Cambridge Group for the History of Population and Social Structure, Department of Geography, University of Cambridge, 2006, 2008, 1.

[14] Skocpol, *States and Social Revolutions*, 2.

conceived and propagated by the Hakluyt circle was, and was intended to be, the solution to the intensifying 'ensemble of demands' – collectively, the *common* 'wele' – that had accumulated since the early fourteenth century. England did not acquire colonies or become 'imperial' absent-mindedly, as has sometimes been suggested. It was planned and had causes that were recognized at the time.

Chapter 8 describes the disintegration of the classic, noble vision of the body politic that had exercised such enormous influence in shaping the English explosion: the birth of modern politics as seen by that master of the early modern vernacular, William Shakespeare. Chapter 9 describes the collective articulation in the 1640s of the now familiar 'ensemble of demands and structures' that characterize the age of the commonweal. The book ends with the execution of Charles I and the institution of a new 'Commonwealth'. My final chapter resumes a central theme of the book, the crucial importance of 'common (public) opinion'. The experience of the late 1640s and the 1650s meant that never again could the word 'commonweal/th' encompass popular ideals and inspire popular resistance and rebellion.

This is an enquiry into the historical roots and meanings of community in early modern England. It pursues another Australian theme in its exploration of the contexts of plebeian and egalitarian ideas and movements. Arguably, Australia is the most 'common' of the English settler-societies. An Australian editor of the *New Statesman*, Bruce Page, was once asked what made Australia different from England (and, for that matter, the USA). His answer was that Australia is the kind of society the English working class would have created in England if they'd had the field to themselves. It is now nearly thirty years since Page expressed that opinion, decades of bewildering change in all parts of the world, not least in Britain, the USA and Australia. Traditionally, and to some extent still today, Australian constitutional culture is self-consciously plebeian, deeply sceptical about certain types of pomp and circumstance, a child of Diogenes rather than Plato.[15] In this sense, the formation of Australian constitutional culture is a later development of the populist influence traced in these chapters.

In Chapters 4 and 5 I show that populist influences emerged in the fourteenth century and that populist conceptions of commonwealth inspired every popular rebellion from 1381 to the civil wars of the 1640s, through a crescendo in the 1540s when rebels simply called themselves

---

[15] I don't say 'old Australian' values had no dark sides, just as I am not saying that its earlier English variant was not riddled with cross-cutting, exclusivist prejudices.

(and were called) 'common-wealths'.[16] Commonweal usages raised the spectre of a constitutional (and substantial) alternative to 'kingdom', and helped to make 'country' in the modern, national, sense thinkable. The linguistic history, in my account, offers important clues to the underlying movement, 'the revolution of commonalty'. This, very broadly, means the rise of the commons as a parliamentary class, the progressive constitutional encroachments of 'middle ranks', *and*, from 1381 to the 1640s, the riotous and rebellious propensities of a heterogeneous working class that Sir John Fortescue feared and Sir Thomas Smith, in 1583, called the *proletarii*.[17] The study of this amorphous 'rascability of the popular', as Smith also called it, takes us to the coal-face of contemporary English historiography: reconstituting the people as well as the state.

Today the word 'proletarian' is closely associated with Marx, but Marx only borrowed an analogy that came easily to anyone familiar with the annals of Republican and Imperial Rome, where it referred to the mobile majority, the wage (or hand-out)-dependent *plebs*.[18] The agency of the *proletarii* – at least a third of English people were threatened by its embrace by 1600 – is given greater prominence than in traditional accounts of English constitutional history. Ongoing work in the historiography of early modern England, notably the microhistorical studies of Keith Wrightson, David Levine, Andy Wood, Steve Hindle, Pamela Sharpe, John Walter and David Cressy, is recovering some of the voices,

---

[16] Andy Wood, *The 1549 Rebellions and the Making of Early Modern England* (Cambridge 2007), 52.

[17] See ch. 24 of *De Republica Anglorum* by Sir Thomas Smith, ed. Mary Dewar (Cambridge 1982), where Smith defined 'the fourth sort of men which doe not rule' as comprising those 'which the olde Romans called *capite censii proletarii* or *operae*, day labourers, poor husbandmen, yea marchantes or retailers which have no free land, copiholders, all artificers, as Taylors, Shoomakers, Carpenters, Brickemakers, Bricklayers, Masons, &c. These have no voice or authorities in our common wealth, and no account is made of them but onelie to be ruled, not to rule other, and yet they be not altogether neglected'.

[18] Paul Veyne, *Bread and Circuses: Historical Sociology and Political Pluralism*, trans. Brian Pearce, (Harmondsworth 1990), is a fascinating account of *euergetism*, the cultural system within which Roman attitudes to the *proletarii* were enacted. Typically, Marx turned a denigrating label upside down: 'Before Marx, *proletarian* (*proletaire*) was one of the signifiers of the passive spectacle of poverty. In England, Dr Johnson had defined *proletarian* in his *Dictionary* (1755) as "mean; wretched; vile; vulgar", and the word seems to have had a similar meaning in France in the early nineteenth century, where it was used virtually interchangeably with *nomade*.' Peter Stallybrass, 'Marx and Heterogeneity: Thinking the Lumpenproletariat', *Representations* no. 31 (Summer 1990), 84, quotation from Ernesto Laclau, *On Populist Reason* (London 2005), 143; it is worth noting that Smith's earlier treatment seems to have been struggling with the impulse to *include* the *proletarii* within the circle of the constitutional order; where agency is concerned, earlier English writers like Sir John Fortescue were far from convinced of its passivity vis-à-vis the political and constitutional order: see below, Chapter 4.1.

words and landscapes of the extremely heterogeneous class of people of early modern England who depended on wages.[19] They make it possible to view early English constitutional history 'from the bottom up', or, more specifically, through the reported opinions of people who would later be called the 'working class'. 'Aggregative' and 'reconstitutionalist' approaches mean that we can now begin, in the light of the records of government, to distinguish between how (by what agencies) 'England' was actually constituted, from time to time, and to compare such 'reconstitutions' with how, in the prevailing 'literary' views, it ought to have been. From this wider perspective it is perfectly valid to begin with 'reconstitutions' of the contexts of the *proletarii* (or 'fourth sort of men' as Smith defined them), understood as they were understood at the time, as the lower ranks of the commonalty. They were part of the brew – in the eyes of some of the great English constitutional writers, the decisive part.

As for the larger class or estate to which convention assigned Smith's *proletarii*, knowledge about the cultures of the *communes*, 'commonalty' or 'third estate' has also increased greatly since the 1970s. We shall see that from the thirteenth and fourteenth centuries to the eve of the revolution of 1640–2 it became a discursive convention to divide the commonalty or third estate into two or three sorts, of which wage workers and servants always constituted the lowest, allegedly most 'dependent' class. The idea of a greater class of 'commons', as distinct from 'nobles' and (later) 'gentlemen', I argue, is an abiding theme or (in the language of phenomenology) 'spectre'. In spite of all the obvious disparities of vocation, character, circumstance and status that existed among the commonalty, they all had in common that they were defined by an ancient convention (rooted in conquest): that there was a fundamental divide between common people and nobles. This idea still retained great power in the Civil Wars of the 1640s.

Above the '*proletarii*' but still 'common' was a class that first made its mark on English records in the late thirteenth century, when it was described as *mediocris populi*. Hierarchical metaphors always fail to describe

---

[19] For example, Keith Wrightson and David Levine, *Poverty and Piety in an English Village: Terling 1525–1700* (New York 1979); David Levine and Keith Wrightson, *The Making of an Industrial Society: Whickham 1560–1765* (Oxford 1991); Andy Wood, *The Politics of Social Conflict: the Peak Country 1520–1770* (Cambridge 1999); Steve Hindle, *The State and Social Change in Early Modern England, c.1550–1640* (Basingstoke 2000); Pamela Sharpe, *Population and Society in an East Devon Parish: Reproducing Colyton, 1540–1840* (Exeter 2002); John Walter, *Understanding Popular Violence in the English Revolution: the Colchester Plunderers* (Cambridge 1999); David Cressy, *Literacy and the Social Order: Reading and Writing in Tudor and Stuart England* (Cambridge 1980).

social structures because in the real world people are not arranged hierarchically but in the horizontal plane.[20] People move in landscapes, they do not 'rise' or 'fall'. Social mobility actually occurs in the geographical plane. It is about movements, possessions and dispossessions in landscapes. The earliest references to 'middle people' imply hierarchy, but they also imply pragmatic terms of reference. To be 'middle' meant to *mediate* between the rulers and the ruled. 'Middle' ranks were often represented as local and provincial in identity, and thus incapable of grasping the problems of governing a kingdom that included thousands of localities and dozens of provinces. Clerks' and scribes' usages suggest 'mediocrity' in its modern sense: of estate, talent, intelligence, honour and so on. 'Middles' were 'mediocre'; they lacked the qualities that real superiors possessed, and were therefore not entitled to a voice in constitutional and political affairs. In the discourse of courts, nobles and also, at times, the Church, the terminology of the middle usually carried a whiff of contempt and disdain. The role of the voting and juror class of the localities, in later terminology the 'yeomen' and 'cives' or 'citizens of towns', became prominent in the late thirteenth century and its relative status and power increased thereafter. As the power and status of 'yeomen' and 'citizens', the upper ranks of the commonalty, increased, it became conventional to abandon older, usually tripartite conceptions, in favour of an 'estate' encompassing two classes. Sir John Fortescue thought like this about the commonalty and two generations later Sir Thomas Smith defined the commonalty as comprising a 'third' and 'fourth sort of men'.

The early modern period as I conceive it is defined by the emergence of commonalty as a constitutional agency. Except where other meanings are explicitly discussed, 'commonalty' implies the rising power and political presence of the 'middle ranks' and the agency, after 1381, of that heterogeneous 'fourth sort' that Smith likened to the Roman '*proletarii*'. The intention of bottom-up history, conceived thus, is not to detract from the agency of kings, lords and gentlemen, or any of the other ranks, degrees, estates, classes, limbs and members of the body politic that were conceived and institutionalized by writers and legislators of the centuries that concern me. I see this as 'constitutional history', but not in the exclusive sense of the study of institutions. Rather, to simplify a little, constitutions are dynamic, complex and changing 'fields of force' that are 'constituted' by movement and social relations (cooperative and conflicted), and by language used within a distinctive, historically contingent landscape.

---

[20] Rollison, *The Local Origins of Modern Society: Gloucestershire 1500–1800* (London and New York 1992), 'Introduction' and ch. 5.

2   Meanings of commonwealth

[Enter (Costard the) Clown].
Boyet: 'Here comes a member of the commonwealth'.
Costard: 'God dig-you-den all. Pray you, which is the head lady?'
Princess: 'Thou shalt know her, fellow, by the rest that have no heads'.[21]

The 'commonweal/th' family of words entered the vocabulary of intellectual 'counsellors' after about 1450, was taken up by the Tudor state
and by many theological and constitutional writers in the generations of
William Tyndale and Sir Thomas Smith (roughly 1480–1580). Tyndale
may have been the first to use 'common-wealth' (as against older deriva-
tions of *common wele*) in print, in his dialogue with Sir Thomas More in
the late 1520s.[22]

The terms had many meanings. Printed usages increase exponentially
from the death of Sir Thomas Smith in 1583 to the civil wars of 1642–9,
but this may be an illusion created by the survival of sources. Much more
was printed and written down, especially from the 1520s to the 1640s.
The English archives generally increase in volume and detail, progressively: they contain the paperwork of the nation-state. It was not all the
paperwork of the state. Few of the pamphlets that poured from the presses
in the revolutionary 1640s, for example, failed to use a variant of 'commonwealth' to mean whatever community of communities it was that the
author swore allegiance to.[23] 'Commonwealth' was an important political
word because it meant good things to all people. Whatever you were –
Protestant or Catholic, Puritan or Arminian, Cavalier or Roundhead,
Possessioner, Digger or Quaker – you were for the commonwealth. It was

---

[21] William Shakespeare, *Love's Labour's Lost*, IV, i, 36–7.

[22] Richard Britnell, *The Closing of the Middle Ages, England 1471–1529* (Oxford 1997), 202,
observes that 'commonweal' became 'one of the most useful rhetorical expressions in
the repertoire of political propagandists for the crown, petitioners, and other special
pleaders from the mid-fifteenth century onwards' and that 'there is no exact equivalent
in current English'. For Tyndale and More, see Chapter 3.11.

[23] For some examples, see *Certain Considerations upon the Duties of Princes and People*,
Thomason Tracts BL E85, p. 13; *His Majesties Last Declaration* of 19 January 1642 BL
E85/26, p. 7; *A Discourse upon questions in debate between the King and Parliament* (1642),
BL E69/26, 2, 3, 6, 8, 9; *Speciall Messages* of January 10, 1643, BL E85/10, p. 88;
*Touching the Fundamentall Lawes or Politique Constitution of this Kingdome, The King's
Negative Voice, and the Power of Parliaments* (London, 6 February 1643), BL Thomason
E85/21, p. 3; *A Discourse upon Questions in Debate between the King and Parliament* (Lon-
don 1643) BL E69/26, pp. 2–3, 8, 9; *A Discourse Consisting of Motives for the Enlargement
and Freedom of Trade, Especially that of cloth and other woollen manufactures Engrossed at
Present contrary to the Law of Nature, the Law of Nations and the Lawes of the Kingdome
by a Company of Private Men who stile themselves Merchant Adventurers*, BL E260/2; *The
Charge of the Commons of England Against Charles Stuart* (20 January 1648)BL E540/5,
p. 8; *The Power of Kings Discussed* (1649) BL E540, p. 3; *A Discourse . . . For the Enlargement of Trade* (London, 8 April 1645) BL Thomason E260/2, p. 4.

the native ('middle' and 'early modern' English) word for 'the community interest'. A motive, action or institution was good if it could be shown to be useful for the commonwealth. One problem in the 1640s was that princes and nobles thought monarchy and nobility were for the common good, while republicans (and common rebels for centuries) believed that it was in the common good to get rid, if not of monarchy, then certainly, if possible, of those other constitutional middle-men, high churchmen and nobles. There were many positions in between, and a very few that saw beyond national boundaries, to a world of countries that were not just there to serve the interests of the English commonwealth.

The archives of the 1640s contain sketches and glimpses of many possible constitutions: how an English commonwealth should be organized, what was most important, how people and classes should relate to each other, in the name of what values and ideals and in pursuit of what common goals. On this interpretation, the 'discourse of commonweal' emerged across a long period (about two centuries, 1450–1650) during which the condition of England was very much in question and was discussed and debated in one way or another from top to bottom of society. Wherever they took place, the discussions and arguments had different locations, experiences, perspectives, analyses and evaluations of 'the condition of England'. There was endemic disagreement about the facts (what *is* the condition of England?) and also about the question of how things *ought* to be. This complacency of reflexive usages of the word 'commonweal(th)' in early English usages still prevails today. It means everything and nothing. Perhaps that is why Paul Keating thought it might be a good name for an Australian republic to continue to call itself.

On this evidence, 'commonweal/th' denoted a field of contention, but the conjoined syllables also referred to some notable commonalities. First, the commonweal words were English; they signal the remarkably rapid rise of the vernacular from language of conquered subjects to that of public life (see Chapter 3). Second, almost from the outset, its users assumed that however it was conceived, 'England' was an autonomous, even autarchic empire or commonwealth, quite different from other peoples. All the usages I came across (with the possible exception of Winstanley and the Quakers) were unthinkingly nationalist. Everyone took for granted that the 'commonweal' was England. A third commonality was that the word originally referred to a greater community of which the state and ruling classes were only a part. It was not originally a synonym for 'state'. The state was there to serve this greater community. If the state failed the commonwealth would continue in a thousand localities and eventually reconstitute itself in more appropriate ways.

Until the 1640s 'commonweal/th' never implied a 'republic' in the classical and modern senses. Here was a difference, or at least a qualification of Prime Minister Keating's associations. English monarchs were and are frequently unpopular. The English deposed (and murdered) individual kings long before the commonweal words were first written down in the first half of the fifteenth century.[24] Yet at no time before the late 1640s was the cause of abolishing monarchy proclaimed or even hinted at. Before then it was taken for granted by the vast majority of the population that the English commonwealth would always include a monarch. Many of its usages did have one thing in common with Australian traditions, however. Its substance and origin were essentially populist. As such they have something to teach us about the remarkable political revolution of modernity: the displacement (at least in terms of theoretical sovereignty) of monarchical/tyrannical and aristocratic/oligarchic by democratic/political constitutional forms.

The all-consuming problem in the centuries covered by this book was how to make one community out of many parts – 'to make the community one', as David Malouf puts it. The parts took many forms: geographical provinces and localities, neighbourhoods, parishes, manors, lordships, religious movements, 'estate' in its entire complex of meanings, class, ethnicity, vocation, occupation, household, family and self. These were common foci of interest and association throughout 'early modern' England. In its contexts each was a perfectly legitimate form of identity and loyalty, as most of them still are today. But in relation to each other and to greater communities like the kingdom and Christendom, they were 'several' interests: always potentially and often actually 'severed' or 'cut off' from each other and liable to come into conflict. Legitimate though these subordinate interests were, in their contexts, it was also taken for granted that there was a 'greater community' to which all other communities and associations were subordinate. Because this greater community was an ideal, and no part had the power to indoctrinate all the other parts, there was continuous discourse within and between the parts about definition. What was the 'whole' to which all the parts were subordinate? Although they constantly disagreed about what it meant, they created a distinctively English name for it. Variants of 'commonweal' and 'commonwealth' were keywords of English constitutional culture from the fourteenth to

---

[24] James Holstun, *Ehud's Dagger: Class Struggle in the English Revolution* (London and New York 2000), ix and *passim*, in which 'tyrannicidal theory and practice' was a continuous English tradition that surfaced again in the 1640s; for John of Salisbury on tyrannicide see below, Chapter 1.5.

mid-seventeenth centuries. The evidential basis of this book is this 'discourse of the commonweal'.

My subject is the emergence of a 'civilization'. Political scientist Conal Condren suggests that one of the marks of a distinctive civilization is that it has distinctive political ideas. 'An idea', he writes, 'may best be understood generically as an identifiable response in discourse brought about by a distinguishably conventional circumscribed problem'. For the purposes of identification and analysis, 'the political thought of distinctive civilizations . . . (can) be understood in terms of three classificatory headings: summation terms, idioms of argument, and ethical structures'.[25] Summation terms, in Condren's system, are 'expressions or terms that function as reflexive abridgements of society's sense of political, religious, and temporal identity'.

Since political activity is largely verbal, summation terms abridge the given society's established idioms of public discourse and its ethical structures; as political activity changes, so the varying usage of summation terms may act as barometers of changing political identity.

'Commonweal/th' was a keyword, or 'summation term'. As Condren predicts, its recorded usages, in a myriad of different contexts over many centuries, are always 'reflexive abridgements of [a] sense of political, religious, and temporal identity'. Note my alteration of Condren's phrase: as already noted, there was rarely if ever one 'correct' meaning ('society's'), but almost as many meanings as usages and contexts. Throughout the period, individuals and associations had many different things in mind when they used the 'community' and 'collectivity' words and some of them were fundamentally at odds. 'Commonweal' usages from the thirteenth to seventeenth centuries do, I suggest, 'act as barometers of changing political identity' but only if all the usages are taken as symptomatic of a great collective argument. My aim is to locate this argument or (as I call it) 'discourse of the commonweal' in relation to underlying 'structural levels' of history. The enquiry proceeds chronologically, with sections and chapters on five phases of collective change that are essential to an understanding of the social revolution that framed commonweal/th discourse: 1066–1159; 1159–1327; 1327–81; 1381–1549; 1549–1649. The 'English explosion' took place during the last phase; out of the earlier phases emerged the national field of force or nucleus of the explosion.

The word 'commonweal' appears to have been first recorded in 1446 but it is likely that the words *comun* and *wele* had been joined together

---

[25] Conal Condren, *The Status and Appraisal of Classic Texts: an Essay on Political Theory, Its Inheritance and the History of Ideas* (Princeton 1985), 81.

in spoken 'middle' English for at least two generations before that. To understand why and with what meanings we must consider the etymologies. Old French *comun* derived from Latin *communis*, child of the prefix *com* ('together') and *munis* ('obliging, ready to be of service'). A 'community' was constituted by individuals and associations motivated by the desire to be 'obliging' and 'ready to be of service' to a community of communities that took precedence over all lesser parts or (as in John of Salisbury's influential image of the body politic, the topic of Chapter 1.5) 'members'. It was always an ideal, a sign or other representation of a community aspired to but never quite achieved. The *comun* sound (in Latin, French and probably old English forms) is represented in the earliest 'middle' English sources; it became a keyword of written discourse in English during the thirteenth and fourteenth centuries. From then on it is difficult to find a page of writing in English that does not use or allude to it. The 'discourse of commonweal' refers to a unique collective effort to define and serve a community with precedence over all lesser communities.

'Middle' English *co[m]mun* also had Germanic roots preceding the Norman conquest. Its usage to mean 'the body of freemen (of a country, city, etc.), the common people, the citizenry; the third estate of a commonwealth (as distinct from the nobility and clergy)' is the central theme of an English song or poem celebrating the victory of Flemish 'communes' over the flower of French nobility at Courtrai in 1302.[26] The *OED* etymologist noted that Latin *com-moinis* was 'cognate with Old Teutonic *ga-maini-z* and Old High German *gemeini*'. Anglo-Saxon *imene* derived from German *gemaen* and probably survived in various forms in local dialects. Hybrids of *comun* and *gemaen* may go back to the late Roman occupation of Britain, when Germanic troops and Roman officers must often have needed a word for qualities or commodities 'belonging equally to more than one', 'belonging to more than one as a result or sign of co-operation, joint action or agreement', 'ordinary, prevalent, frequent', 'the community or commonalty' or 'the common people [or soldiers] as distinguished from those of rank or dignity'.

All these meanings are cited as in use before 1350, most of them in *Cursor Mundi*, written, the author explained, 'for the common folk to understand'. A 'pre-literate' merger between the French *comun*, in which the stress is on the first syllable, and *imene*, where the stress is on the second syllable, may be alluded to in verse usages from the fourteenth to sixteenth centuries. 'The accentuation comu'n is found as late as the sixteenth century in verse,' writes the *OED* etymologist, 'but before the

---

[26] See Chapter 2.8.

dates of our earliest quotes in the thirteenth century, the popular form had become co'mun, . . . whence the modern pronunciations.' The point is that English speaking common folk, French nobles and Latin clerics each had constant need for the *comun* or *gemaen* family of words and that syntheses and conflicts, as and when they occurred, were not just of sounds but also of meanings and traditions.[27]

The provenance of the early modern *comun* exemplifies an ancient English duality. For nearly a thousand years, England has been seen as a child of two parents. Stereotypically, grandfather Latin and father French, because of their associations with the two senior 'estates' of 'middle' or 'medieval' England (church and nobility), were imperial, hierarchical, literate, universal, absolutist. Grandmother Germania and mother Anglo-Saxon, because of their association, after 1066, with the third estate or 'commonalty', were communitarian, egalitarian, predominantly oral, empirical, freedom-loving and populist. The date of their early courtship is uncertain. Latin and German are both Indo-European languages. The words 'common' and 'gemaen' were different ways of writing down the same sounds with the same essential range of meanings, adapted to variable contexts.

Vernacular English politics adopted and assimilated ancient ideas that came to its nobles, clerics, learned men and commons along convoluted, now-invisible channels, many via Muslim Spain from classical Athens and Rome. After c.1300 ideas associated with Aristotle's *Politics* were ubiquitous, in direct or implied forms; this raises questions of transmission, not only across space, but also social frontiers. Put crudely, when the rebel commons of 1381 claimed to be speaking and acting for the commonweal, were they echoing Aristotle (or Cicero)? It is not difficult to explain why learned men (like the chronicler who recorded the rebels' self-proclaimed service to the *communem utilitatem*) and counsellors so often alluded to or implied Aristotelian and Ciceronian ideas. By the fourteenth century it was part of their basic training.

This book traces commonwealth ideas to populist roots. Learned people picked and chose what they remembered and what they forgot about one of the greatest of all the sages who, across the millennia, have studied human constitutions. Aristotle's six-note chord classification of states is beautifully simple in its essentials and quite easy to explain to a lay (or *lewd*) audience. Shakespeare gave his contemporaries a live representation of an eruption of polity (or of a *res plebeia*) in *Coriolanus*, as I show in 'The revolution of politics' (Chapter 8). The importance of weighing the relative force of each of the contending voices of early modern England, and noting changes over time in the constitutional force-field as a whole,

---

[27] All quotations from *OED* 'common'.

should not obscure the 'eccentric variety factor': the record of many contending interests, opinions and ideologies begins in the thirteenth century and builds to climaxes in the 1540s and again, a century later, the 1640s.[28] That not every eccentric opinion is visible in the archival record all the time, only when vocal resistance and violent rebellion generated documentation and comment, does not mean they were not always immanent. Their recurrence suggests they were.

Most importantly, the populist or 'bottom-up' question asks where learned men got their ideas about tyranny and the common good. This study is informed by the precept that the basic ideas are simple and refer to universal human experience. 'Behind' the learned traditions lay a proverbial wisdom about the nature and problems arising from the universal need of human beings for community. Aristotle's, Plato's, Augustine's, Cicero's, Plutarch's and John of Salisbury's view that all good government is conducted by people devoted to the collective good, and all bad forms are when rulers and subjects serve their own interests, is proverbial wisdom. It is part of the grammar of human life, always imminent, often cited but most often implied. This approach posits a popular transmission of ideas, critiques and orientations alongside (or 'below') the learned discourse about Aristotle, Cicero and other classical influences. This was the common idea around which the English people built a residual common identity: the nucleus of the 'empty signifier' of commonweal, into which, in times of crisis, the ensemble of local demands 'condensed'.[29]

The central distinction in commonwealth ideology was between community interest, on the one hand, and class, caste, party, factional and individual interests on the other. It may be intrinsic to our species. The distinction between the collectivity as a whole and the lesser interests of its constituent parts is likely to arise wherever people think about government and politics. Rather than say classical authors like Aristotle and Cicero gave people a way of thinking about politics, I begin with the hypothesis that the classics confirmed what people already thought, and gave it prestige. Viewed in this way, the sources and definitions that were recovered by scholars throughout the long rebirth of classical discourses, and that are usually characterized as having 'trickled down' into common,

---

[28] 'Plurality of numbers is natural in a state; and the further it moves away from plurality towards unity, the less a state it becomes... The state consists not merely of a plurality of men, but of different *kinds* of men; you cannot make a state out of men who are all alike...': Aristotle, *The Politics*, trans. T.A. Saunders (Harmondsworth 1962, 1981), 1261*a*10, 1261*a*22, 104; for insight into some uses of Aristotle in sixteenth-century social and economic discourse, cf. David Harris Sacks, 'The Greed of Judas: Avarice, Monopoly, and the Moral Economy, ca.1350-ca.1600', *Journal of Medieval and Early Modern Studies* 28:2 (Spring 1998), 263–308.

[29] The quote is a synthesis of Laclau, *On Populist Reason*, 93–100.

vernacular usage, met vernacular discourses about community and the common good 'trickling' *up*.

The term 'commonweal' embodied this coming together of ideal and real experiences of the selfish struggles of the world. Popular political culture easily assimilated the 'common' words from Latin and Norman-French, though not without giving them new meanings. *Utilitatem* and *profyte*, to which *commun* was annexed in vernacular English records of the fourteenth century, were eventually dropped and replaced by the conjuncture that, I argue,[30] was probably the slogan of John Ball's rebels in 1381. It re-entered constitutional life on the tongues of Cade's rebels during the July Days of 1450. Foreigners and scholars provided 'common', the vernacular-speaking commonalty asserted the *wele*. The word constituted the history.

I trace the *longue duree* of a vernacular political, religious and constitutional culture.[31] It was, notoriously, magpie-like, picking up keywords and ideas from the language of French lords, Latinate clerks and classics, and using them for their own special purposes. The Norman Conquest, *Magna Carta*, Simon de Montfort's 'common enterprise', the rise of a common language, the depositions of Edward II and Richard II and other collective crises of the formative fourteenth and fifteenth centuries (notably the emergence of public opinion and the tradition of popular resistance and rebellion), the English reformation, Elizabethan imperialism and the revolution of the 1640s were causal links and chains of collective memory in a larger, essentially populist, movement. The *longue duree* to which, in my interpretation, they must all be joined, is termed 'the age of the commonweal'. 'Early modern' England, in my usage, begins in c.1300. Most of the elements, I argue in Chapters 1 and 2, were in place by 1327.

Abiding themes (the structuring elements) of this 'early modern' constitutional culture emerged in the century before the Black Death. Most of them, above all 'the idea of a community as a linguistic unity', emerged before the great famine of 1315–22, as I show in Chapters 1–3.[32] In my

---

[30] Below, Chapter 5.3.

[31] John Hale, *The Civilization of Europe in the Renaissance* (London 1993), 323–4, wrote that the intellectual and artistic revolution that has come to be called the Renaissance was a product of 'the European transmission system [having] speeded up'. 'As with a chain of whispers', he wrote, 'the original messages of literary or artistic ideas acquired a different import as they were passed along. They traversed regions which distorted or drowned them. They became confused by being mingled with messages passed along other chains.' Hale saw its English variant as 'simply the achievement of a largely native peak of creative ebullience'. This book is an account of the historical processes that generated the 'peak'.

[32] Malcolm Vale, 'Language, Politics and Society: the Uses of the Vernacular in the Later Middle Ages', *English Historical Review* 120:485 (February 2005), 28; Vale concludes 'that unity was certainly apparent in England from the later thirteenth century

usage 'constitutional culture' unites a population occupying a distinctive, remembered, memorialized and 'imagined' landscape and timescape, common language and common (interconnected) social relations of production. It included institutions, but above all it was formed by the collective dialectics of 'realist' descriptions and criticisms of actually existing society (an enduring 'condition of England debate') and well known, deeply embedded and verbally articulate ethical and constitutional precepts. I also show that from 1381 to the 1640s these precepts were very often most strongly maintained by the poorest and least privileged members of society, and the 'commonalty' (in its 'third estate' sense). This is the history of an ever more threatening 'spectre of the commonalty' that was understood, not only as a synonym of all-embracing 'community', but as a class.[33]

3   Revolutions of politics: revolutions of commonalty

To advance their interest, Kings and Princes have politiques, and Principles of their own, and certain state-maxims, whereby they soare aloft, and walk in a distinct way of opposition to the Rights and Freedomes of the People; all of which you may see in Machiavil's Prince. Hence it is that Kings have been always jealous of the people, and

onwards'. One of 'a number of fundamental ideas which have only really emerged in the work of the last generation' is that 'the broad character of the English landscape was already formed by 1100 and of its urban system by 1300': C.P. Lewis, 'The New Middle Ages', review of Christopher Dyer, *An Age of Transition? Economy and Society in England in the Later Middle Ages* (Oxford 2005), *History Workshop Journal* 63 (2007), 305. This review affirms the singular importance of Dyer's research in this *fundamental* revision.

[33] Except where otherwise indicated, I follow the definitions of G.E.M. de Ste. Croix, *The Class Struggle in the Ancient Greek World from the Archaic Age to the Arab Conquests* (London 1981), 43–4: '*Class* (essentially a relationship) is the collective social expression of the fact of exploitation, the way in which exploitation is embodied in a social structure . . . A *class* is a group of persons in a community identified by their position in the whole system of social production . . . It is of the essence of *class society* that one or more of the smaller classes, in virtue of their control over the conditions of production (most commonly exercised through ownership of the means of production), will be able to exploit – that is, to appropriate a surplus at the expense of – the larger classes . . . I use the expression *class struggle* for the fundamental relationship between classes (and their respective individual members), involving essentially exploitation, or resistance to it. It does not necessarily involve collective action by a class as such, and it may not include activity on a political plane, although such political activity becomes increasingly probable when the tension of class struggle become acute . . . *Imperialism*, involving some kind of economic and/or political subjection to a power outside the community, is a special case, in which the exploitation effected by the imperial power (in the form of tribute, for instance), or by its individual members, need not necessarily involve direct control of the conditions of production . . . ' Ste. Croix's usage is fundamentally materialist, but is otherwise very flexible. He had 'no wish to pretend that class is the *only* category we need for the analysis of Greek and Roman Society' (emphasis added) just as I have no wish to make such a claim for early modern England.

have held forth their own interests, as a Mystery or Riddle, not to be pried into by ordinary understandings.[34]

In *Spectres of Comparison*, successor to *Imagined Communities*, his influential book on the sources of nationalism, Benedict Anderson compares ideas published in 1913 by the Javanese nationalist writer Soewardi Soerjaningrat, with those expressed in memoirs composed nearly a century earlier by Soerjaningrat's ancestor, Prince Diponegoro. Diponegoro's heroic leadership in the struggle against Dutch colonialism between 1825 and 1830 has made him Indonesia's great post-colonial hero. Anderson notes that Soerjaningrat's 'sarcastic rhetoric took nonchalantly for granted this anonymous series: Dutchmen.' A century (and another universe) earlier, the noble Diponegoro's account never mentioned 'the Dutch'. His successful enemies were recorded by personal name and rank. Diponegoro did not conceive his enemies as 'Dutchmen'. They and he belong to a class or rank of nobles that is to be found, he assumed, in all cultures and civilizations. The distinctive quality of men and women of this class is that they are unique individuals determined to test and defend their honour against all other people or peoples. He is not 'a' prince, or 'a' Javanese, he is *Diponegoro*. In men of his class is embodied all that is great and noble in their cultures and countries. Like the antihero of Shakespeare's *Coriolanus*, Diponegoro is a man of quality and blood rather than nation; it is fitting for him to be pitted only against other men of quality and blood. In that old world, nobles were nobles wherever they were born; nobility of this sort is more like an inherited ethnicity and vocation for war. Such men are *aristos*, 'the best'. Similarly, to be what the English have tended to call 'common' is to share inherent inferiority with common people all over the world. In this world there are two classes, nobles and commons.

Traditionally, accounts of the evolution of English vernacular politics – the 'Westminster system' and the constitutional culture associated with it – have resisted class interpretation. The movement cannot be reduced to a simple struggle between nobles and commons, but class distinction of this simple type was all-pervasive and clearly understood in England, Europe and the rest of the world in what Western Europeans regard as 'the late middle ages' and the 'early modern' phases of their collective historical development. My contention is that English constitutional culture was driven by an abiding and many-faceted undercurrent of aversion to feudal ideas of nobility, based on experience of what nobles

---

[34] BL E.541 (12): John Warr, *The Privileges of the People of England, or, Principles of Common Right and Freedom* . . . (London, February 1648), 1.

were, in practice, as opposed to the ways in which they liked to represent themselves.

The political historiography of England traditionally assumes that although its subject classes and communities may not have liked or particularly identified with the aristocratic world order and the theologies associated with it, they could not imagine an alternative. That being the case, individual and collective resistance and rebellion necessarily took reformist or 'restorationist' rather than revolutionary forms. They were efforts to restore a corrupt system to something more closely resembling what, according to the dominant paradigm, it ought to be. I suggest that there was never a community or a time in these centuries that lacked people able to conceive of a society that was not divided into church, princes, nobles and commons. In the absence of a realistic alternative, such people went along with the dominant world view and rhetoric, and exploited it whenever they could use it for their own advantage. The institutions of aristocracy changed across the centuries, but the extreme version that Shakespeare embodied in the character of Coriolanus (Chapter 8), while a declining force, was never absent from the range of possibilities immanent in the highly complex society that emerged in the late fourteenth century and 'exploded' between 1549 and 1649. Conceptions of warrior aristocracy survived episodically after 1649, but were never the same again.

Anderson notes that something else was missing from nineteenth-century Javanese minds. 'Anything that we could honestly translate as "politics"', he writes, is entirely 'absent from (Soerjaningrat's) reflections':

This absence is not in the least idiosyncratic. In almost all of Asia and Africa, neologisms have had to be coined for this concept during the past hundred years, and the birthdate is typically close to that of nationalism. For 'politics' to become thinkable, as a distinctly demarcated domain of life, two things had to happen. (1) Specialized institutions and social practices had to be visible, and of a kind that could not be heedlessly glossed in the old vocabularies of cosmologically and religiously sustained kingship . . . (2) The world had to be understood as one, so that no matter how many different social and political systems, languages, cultures, religions, and economies it contained, there was a common activity – 'politics' – that was self-evidently going on everywhere.[35]

Viewed historically and comparatively, 'politics' is a type of constitutional culture that is peculiar to classical city-states and modern nation-states. In Anderson's account politics did not exist in the rest of the world

---

[35] Benedict Anderson, *Spectres of Comparison: Nationalism, Southeast Asia, and the World* (London 1998), 31–2.

until Europeans took it there and imposed its priorities. Just as they imposed the formal necessity of nationalism and the nation-state, Europeans imposed politics. They assumed that their constitutional cultures, like their religions and languages, had attained a degree of superiority towards which all peoples of the world were struggling. Their ideas defined norms against which everything else was measured. If this interpretation is correct, the question arises, when did the Europeans invent or discover politics for themselves? When did what we understand by the word become the characteristic way for European societies to think and organize themselves constitutionally?

The idea that a 'revolution of politics' really did take place around the turn of the sixteenth and seventeenth centuries is not new. Maurizio Viroli gives an account of a great watershed in the history of constitutional culture around 1600.[36] 'Between the end of the 16th and the beginning of the 17th century', he writes,

the language of politics underwent a radical transformation which could be called 'the revolution of politics' . . . Like all serious revolutions, it was global in scope, and had a wide range of intellectual and moral implications. Not only did the meaning and the range of application of the concept of 'politics' change, but also the ranking of political science, the role of political education, and the value of political liberty. The revolution entailed a loss of prestige. Having enjoyed for three centuries the status of the noblest human science, politics emerged from the revolution as an ignoble, depraved and sordid activity: it was no longer the most powerful means of fighting corruption, but the art of conforming to, and perpetuating it.

What was lost or submerged, in Viroli's conception, was a great tradition in which politics was the study and practice of constitutional life.[37] Its heroes, Plato, Aristotle and Cicero were philosophers and practitioners of constitutional life. The idea was that the *virtu* of a constitution is contingent upon the *virtu* of its citizen body. In classical theory the world of politics never involved more than a minority, usually a very small

---

[36] Maurizio Viroli, *From Politics to Reason of State: the acquisition and transformation of the language of politics 1250–1600* (Cambridge 1992), 1; M. Foucault, 'Governmentality', in James D. Faubion (ed.), *Michel Foucault: Power, Essential Works of Foucault 1954–1984* (London 2002), 212–13 assumed, 'schematically', that 'in the late sixteenth and early seventeenth century, the art of government finds its first form of crystallization, organised around the theme of reason of state'.

[37] 'By the beginning of the fourteenth century, the word *politicus* . . . had been squarely pre-empted for the republican regime . . . ' Sir John Fortescue's application of the word to monarchical regimes 'opens a new chapter . . . '; Elizabethan interpretations of Machiavelli created the cynical meaning: Nicolai Rubinstein, 'The History of the Word Politicus in Early-Modern Europe', in Anthony Pagden (ed.), *The Languages of Political Theory in Early-Modern Europe* (Cambridge 1987), 45, 49, 54–6.

minority. Politics, therefore, referred to the rights and duties of elites. In Viroli's account the climate of opinion amongst the political elites of early modern Europe underwent a massive sea-change around 1600. Classical, self-denying ideals of citizen (or aristocratic) *virtu* gave way to a cynical understanding of politics, grounded in 'reason of state', that has survived until today. 'The story begins', for Viroli, 'in the 13th century, when a shared language of politics reappeared in Italy, and ends in the 17th century, when politics became a synonym for reason of state . . . All through the seventeenth century learned men continued to invoke the restoration of the idea of politics as the noble art of good government. Their efforts, however, did not succeed in fighting back reason of state, nor did they prevent the decline of the notion of politics as the art of good government.' The core of the old republicanism was the *virtu* of the individual citizen. The new was 'reason of state'.

This school of virtue places the highest value on formal learning, wisdom and moral philosophy. The direction of civil society is determined by rational discussion between citizens inspired by classical notions of learning, *virtu* and the common good. One interpretation has Machiavelli as its *bete noire*. Under his influence 'the republican language of politics knew a new floridness'.[38] Machiavelli and Tacitus, wrote one eighteenth-century commentator, had 'so firmly established their wicked doctrine of politics . . . that it is impossible to speak of governing men according to the principles of virtuous politics without being ridiculed as a chimerical and extravagant mind'. Viroli concludes that 'Civil philosophy never regained the intellectual hegemony that it enjoyed before the "revolution" that brought *reason of state* to power.' 'Since then', Viroli continues, renaissance republicanism 'has been surviving only as a language of nostalgia or utopia, words that served to remember republics that had been, or to dream about republics to come'. Reason of state became a veil for private interests. Like Diogenes, we do not expect noble, dispassionate and virtuous behaviour from the human animals who engage in continuing struggles for power. If this is the state at which we arrived, Viroli invites us 'to go from reason of state to somewhere, to rebuild a language of politics that may help to overcome the sense of powerlessness that the ideological triumph of reason of state spread over modern times'.[39] Viroli's turning point is 'the end of the sixteenth century' when 'the ideological victory of the theorists of state . . . was almost crushing'.[40]

---

[38] Viroli, *Politics to Reason of State*, 201; Rubinstein, 'The History of the Word Politicus', 52–3, for the idealistic *and* reason-of-state-cynical Machiavelli.
[39] Viroli, *Politics to Reason of State*, 279–80.   [40] Ibid., 285.

This book suggests that neither the chronology nor the substance of Viroli's account fits the English case. It argues that 'reason of commonweal' had, for centuries, posited values other than those of the state, and put into the equation a populist tradition that up to the 1640s was at least as strong a moral and physical force as reason of state. 'Politics' was a keyword of European learned culture as soon as Aristotle was rediscovered,[41] but it did not enter English vernacular discourse much before the late sixteenth century.[42] From John of Salisbury forward, the realm it denoted was perennially suspect. It pointed to the heart of a poisonous contest, fought for the highest stakes of wealth and power. In the early English case, the locus was a Monarch's court at Westminster, the symbolic centre of English 'politics' since the fourteenth century. 'Westminster' denoted many things, but in the popular mind it often meant a suspect region of dirty deeds and unsavoury ethics. If 'Westminster' has always sought to represent itself as embodiment of the common good, Iago lurks in its courts and corridors, and the public relations views have been continuously subject to a spirit of Diogenes (and the good soldier Schweik) abroad among the people. 'Politics' has many meanings: baseline popular scepticism and cynicism has been relatively neglected. We shall see that on any rational evaluation, the record (and reputation) of government by church, lords and kings in fourteenth to seventeenth-century England was not good. As much an instinctive orientation as a distinctive idea, the prejudice of the unpleasant otherness of prescribed government was passed on in the homes, work-places, streets, churches and pubs of late medieval and early modern communities. In English vernacular culture the word 'politics' gave a new name to an older conception and orientation born in everyday resistance to manifestly unjust, incompetent and double-minded government.

The broad definition of 'polity' and 'politics' employed in these pages is as follows. For Bernard Crick, a political society is one that has embraced 'the fact of the simultaneous existence of different groups, hence different interests and different traditions, within a territorial unit under a common rule'. He acknowledges that to a modern (or post-modern) mind 'it may sometimes seem odd . . . to say that there is no politics in totalitarian or tyrannical regimes. To some it would be clearer to assert that while there is plainly some politics in all systems of government, yet some systems of government are themselves political systems: they function by and for

---

[41] Rubinstein, 'The History of the Word Politicus,' *passim.*

[42] *OED*; the author of Bodleian Library, Rawlinson MS D/23, 'Treatises by an anonymous writer . . . relating to money and trade' (c.1579) offers *politycke counsell* with regard to the 'stylyard controversy' (f. 20).

politics. But usage does not destroy real distinctions. And this distinction has a great tradition behind it'.[43] As Crick acknowledges, it is essentially Aristotle's definition.

For Crick, a political system of government is analogous to the nucleus of an atom. It is a field of force which is not necessarily 'decentred', but in which the 'centre' will always change as a result of changes in the quantum of power enjoyed by existing parts, groups, interests and traditions, and by the arrival within the field of new agencies. Such a conception is as capable of explaining and encompassing a society of kings, nobles, knights, gentry, yeomen, merchants, artisans, peasants and labourers as, for example, the paradigm of three estates or the late medieval theory of infinite degrees.[44] Rather than think of the state as central, it may be more accurate and helpful to think of a system or nucleus formed by relativities of power and influence over the whole by the constituent groups, interests and traditions.[45] The value of this way of looking at the history of complex communities is that it implies the inherently changeable and always abstract character of both 'society' and 'the state' in any system of politics. Crick has a positive view of this system, which is basically Aristotle's 'polity' without an absolute conception of *virtu*. Complex societies are collectivities in which many conceptions of virtue are in contention.

The word politics was an import, slowly seeping into vernacular usage via Latin and Norman-French discussions of classical concepts, theories and standards of government learned by generations of students from classical texts and innumerable commentaries. Scholars easily identified with it. Christ and Augustine taught non-involvement, but pagan philosophical sources taught learned men that it was the highest virtue to seek positions at courts to put their learning in the service of rulers. The Renaissance changed nothing in this respect. From John of Salisbury to John Trevisa, Fortescue to Sir Thomas Smith, Francis Bacon and Thomas Hobbes to William Petty, it was the highest vocation of learned men to act as counsellors to lords and princes. This orientation is as old

---

[43] Bernard Crick, *In Defence of Politics* (Harmondsworth 1964), 18–19, 162ff.

[44] Below, Chapter 3.9.

[45] Writing of eighteenth-century crowd behaviour, E.P. Thompson, *Customs in Common* (Harmondsworth 1993), 73, 94–5, described 'a school experiment . . . in which an electrical current magnetized a plate covered with iron filings. The filings, which were evenly distributed, arranged themselves at one pole or the other, while in between those filings which remained in place aligned themselves sketchily as if directed towards opposing attractive poles'. While stating that 'the field of force metaphor' does not supply 'an instant analytical resource to unpick the meaning of every action', he posited, as a general perspective, 'the underlying polarity of power – the forces which pressed to enter upon and occupy any spaces which fell open when ruling groups came into conflict'.

as universities. It spans our medieval, early modern, modern and post-modern epochs and it has militated in favour of the narrow, state- and government-centred conception of politics that prevails today. This book chronicles and analyses the gradual emergence and frequent explosions of an expanding and intensifying political field of force (or 'constitutional culture') from the thirteenth to mid-seventeenth centuries.

As I argue in Chapter 8, Shakespeare's *Coriolanus* exploded the duality between what is politics and what is not, by acting out a context in which politics spread like an epidemic into every corner of society. The whole community is politicized whether its members like it or not. Every act of every individual, every emotion, is a contingency of politics. One of the consequences of the long revolution of commonalty was a steady growth in the number of class and sectional interests that had to be served and represented by the state and its officers. A solution to this problem was not discovered until the emergence of the political economy outlook in the century after 1549.

The ancestors of our word politics were bug-words from the start. *Politicus* and *politique* denoted officially (and perhaps sinisterly) secret worlds. The convenient fiction that affairs of state ought to be protected 'mysteries' had been an official commonplace for centuries. In 1530 More haughtily rebuked Tyndale for making 'a speciall shewe of hys hygh worldely wytte and that men should have sene therein that there were nothynge done among prynces, but that he was fully advertysed of all ye secretes and that so farre forth, that he knew the pryvy practyse made betwene the kynges hyghnes' and his counsellors.[46] At the end of the sixteenth century Sir Walter Raleigh wrote that 'mysteries or sophismes of State are certain secret practizes, either for the avoiding of danger; or averting such effects as tend to the preservation of the present State as it is set or founded.' The last clause tends to confirm the radical principle that 'mysteries' or secrets of state were about preserving 'the present state as it is set' against domestic critics, as well as against potential foreign enemies. Commonwealth-man John Warr identified *politiques* with the enemy, in 1649: 'To advance their *interest*, Kings and Princes have *politiques*, and *Principles* of their own, and certain state-maxims, whereby they soare aloft, and walk in a distinct way of opposition to the *Rights* and *Freedomes* of the *People*; all of which you may see in *Machiavil's* Prince. Hence it is', he continued, 'that *Kings* have been always jealous of the people, and

---

[46] *The confutatyon of Tyndales answere made by Sir Thomas More* (London 1530); see below, Chapter 3:10.

have held forth their own *interests*, as a *Mystery* or *Riddle*, not to be pried into by ordinary understandings.'[47]

In the pessimistic model, cynical 'politics' grounded in 'reason of state' rather than in the ethical virtue of Ciceronian, Platonic or Aristotelian *virtu*, replaces humanist-classical idealism. These opposed contexts, humanism *versus* reason of state, stress borrowings by intellectuals and the educated class from the traditions of classical and late medieval city-states and empires. These intellectual definitions are too narrow. The movement chronicled in these pages was an accumulative, collective, *vernacular* movement that, while not unique in every aspect and tendency, was both populist and indigenous to England.[48]

4   Timescapes: defining the early modern

The search for the origins of 'commonweal', and for the roots of the English explosion, necessarily dissolves conventional boundaries between the 'middle ages' and the 'early modern'. In this and in other areas, periodization is being revised. 'The idea that there was a historical watershed somewhere around 1500 AD was invented in the early sixteenth century,' writes Wendy Scase. 'Ever since then, the present has been defined in relation to the time before this divide. Each subsequent age has produced its own Middle Ages'. The hegemony of 'great divide' theory is sometimes traced to William Stubbs, who ended *The Constitutional History of England* (1897) with the accession of Henry Tudor in 1485.[49] Heiko Oberman believes great divide theory has inhibited understanding of the *longue duree* of 'Protestant' Reformation. His great biography of Martin Luther begins with the precept that 'we no longer assume a

---

[47] BL E.541 (12): John Warr, *The Privileges of the People of England, or, Principles of Common Right and Freedom* . . . (London, February 1648), 1.

[48] See, for example, Randolph C. Head, *Early Modern Democracy in the Grisons: Social Order and Political Language in a Swiss Mountain Canton*, 1470–1620 (Cambridge 1995).

[49] Wendy Scase, 'Visions of Piers Plowman: a Medieval Poem and the Production of the Present' (University of Birmingham 2001), 2; Stubbs, *The Constitutional History of England* (1897; repr. New York 1967); John L. Watts, 'Introduction: History, the Fifteenth Century and the Renaissance', in Watts (ed.), *The End of the Middle Ages: England in the Fifteenth and Sixteenth Centuries* (Stroud 1998), critically discusses the 'great divide'; cf. also Peter Raedts, 'When were the Middle Ages?', in Solvi Soegner (ed.), *Making Sense of Global History* (Oslo 2001), esp. 304–5. George Huppert, *After the Black Death, a Social History of Early Modern Europe* (Bloomington 1986), and David Nicholas, *The Transformation of Europe 1300–1600* (London 1999), cover roughly the time-scale of this book, which in many respects takes up a story begun by David Levine, *At the Dawn of Modernity: Biology, Culture, and Material Life in Europe After the year 1000* (London 2001).

tripartite view of history with its periodization of antiquity, Middle Ages and modern times'. Oberman suggests 'that we must also heighten our awareness of geographical and sociological variability in our understanding of these movements: i.e. while one region has barely entered the thirteenth, another is leaving the fifteenth century.'[50] Closer to home, John Watts notes 'the difficulties twentieth-century historians have had with finding a satisfactory analogue for the nineteenth-century sense of collective consciousness as a key element in the making of society'. Because of this, he writes,

we cannot use terms like 'the nation' or 'the medieval mind' with conviction; we cannot talk about 'the constitution' or the 'public' without being provocative, or at least needing to explain what we mean. Yet there can be few of us who doubt that there were some kinds of collectivity in the past we study, some shared manners and rules, some propensity for words and ideas to become grouped together and to play off one another, and some relationship between these groups and the lives of individuals. An approach which takes language to be . . . 'the most important of social institutions' provides a way forward. It blurs the line between the ideal and the real, presupposing – on grounds that can be justified – that there are links between what people say, what they think and what they do. It underpins the notion of a political culture and, since changes in both language and culture can to some extent be documented, it helps to resolve [many questions].[51]

'The formation of collective consciousness' – language, ideas, discourses relating to the community of communities of the English – was the central preoccupation of 'early modern England'. I suggest in the early chapters of this book that if there is a great divide between the English medieval and early modern periods, it should be located in the first three decades of the fourteenth century. The movement began in the second half of the thirteenth century, but this can only be seen clearly in relation to the antecedent 'structures' examined in Chapters 1 and 2.

---

[50] Heiko A. Oberman, *Luther: Man Between God and the Devil* (Yale 1989); Oberman, 'The Shape of Late Medieval Thought' in Heiko Augustinus Oberman, *The Dawn of the Reformation: Essays in Late Medieval and Early Reformation Thought* (Edinburgh 1986), 19–20.

[51] John L. Watts, 'Conclusion', in Watts (ed.), *The End of the Middle Ages*, 267.

Part I

The emergent commonalty

1   What came before: antecedent structures and emergent themes

1.1   A new *longue duree*

Archaeological remains discovered in the late twentieth century suggest that hominids made stone tools, hunted and gathered near what is now the south-eastern coast of England 500,000 years ago.[1] They fled or died out about 25,000 years ago as the weather worsened and ice-sheets rolled across the landscape. For the next 10–13,000 years the regions were uninhabitable. An epochal climatic event 'left a clean genetic sheet, a blank slate, until about 15,000 years ago, with no confusing genetic traces remaining from any hunter-gatherers who may have lived there before the ice.'[2] The 'new *longue duree*' of English population history begins roughly twelve thousand years ago.[3]

The entire human and most of the animal and vegetable genetic stock now found in Britain and Ireland arrived (and continues to arrive) over the last 12,000 years. That fact alone, it is suggested, offers a new *longue duree* (or 'timescape') for population history. Common genetic markers

---

[1] Michael Pitts and Mark Roberts, *Fairweather Eden* (New York 2000) is an accessible introduction to the crucial Boxgrove excavations and their theoretical contexts; see also Clive Gamble, 'Early Beginnings 500,000–35,000 Years Ago', in Paul Slack and Ryk Ward (ed.), *The Peopling of Britain: the Shaping of a Human Landscape* (Oxford 2002), 18–20.

[2] Stephen Oppenheimer, *The Origins of the British: a Genetic Detective Story* (London 2006), 3.

[3] Barry Cunliffe writes in *Europe Between the Oceans 9000BC–AD1000*, (New Haven 2008), viii, that 'European history of the second millennium AD is comparatively familiar . . . but of the formative ten thousand years before that there is surprisingly little to read by way of synthesis. Favoured subjects, like Romans and Greeks, are generously treated, as are the activities of the leading personalities of protohistory. But how these brief episodes fit together in the *longue duree* of European history is seldom considered.' For more provincial topics, see also Cunliffe, *Iron Age Britain* (London 1994) and *Wessex to AD 1000* (London and New York 1993); Oppenheimer, *Origins*, 411, suggests that 'we should take Cunliffe's gradualist concept of the *longue duree* of the Atlantic cultural network as a paradigm for the genetics'. This book suggests that it is even more important as an approach to the economic, social and 'constitutional' history. Slack and Ward (ed.), *The Peopling of Britain*, outlines the demographic/archaeological framework for the 'new *longue duree*'.

in contemporary British and Irish populations trace back to immigrants who arrived before 6–8,000 years ago. According to a recent synthesis of the findings of genetic archaeology, 'three quarters of British ancestors arrived long before the first farmers . . . 88 per cent of Irish, 81 per cent of Welsh, 79 per cent of Cornish, 70 per cent of the people of Scotland and 68 per cent of the English.'[4] The peopling of 'modern' Britain began after the Last Glacial Maximum (LGM), between 15,000 and 8,000 years ago. There was always movement in and movement out – trickles and periodic 'waves' in all directions – but the 'founder genes' continued. The genetic ancestors of Mesolithic immigrants have worked the landscape left by the LGM continuously, up to the present. Not alone, it must be said, but the modern data implies that they have always constituted the vast majority of people alive at any one time.

Until about five hundred years ago, we can be fairly certain that every community (bands, alliances, 'tribes', federations, kingdoms and mini-empires) in successive English landscapes shared a common strategic attitude. Defence of the territory was paramount; it was an obsessive shaping force in formal and informal constitutions. We shall see that defence of the territory was the precept of every surviving attempt to define and explain the English constitution from the mid-twelfth to the late sixteenth century. In the second half of the sixteenth century the orientation changed. In c.1500 about 2.5 million people carried the marker genes of those Mesolithic immigrants and shared a common language. It was in this language that William Shakespeare's generation began to follow new priorities, immortally encapsulated by the elder Richard Hakluyt in c.1570: 'conquer, convert, *trafike*'. As far as I know, no-one has tried to estimate how many people alive today share genetic markers that show them to be descendants of the mongrel code that shaped those Mesolithic migrants to 'Britain'; we do know there are approximately a billion English speakers in the world today and that numbers are increasing.

Ultimately the transition from agrarian to industrial-capitalist modes of production would have been unthinkable without the 'local' (i.e. national) process described in this book. Unless otherwise indicated, I use the word 'constitution' to mean an active and continuing *process* rather than a written or unwritten codification. The process was a long social revolution in which the first Commons Rebellion in 1381 and the execution, 268 years later, of Charles I are historically – causally – related events. This book argues a case for understanding English history as an accumulating movement with certain continuing and observable themes that amount, in the long run, to a definable *collective* agency. By

[4] Oppenheimer, *Origins*.

constitutional culture I mean a collective agency with consistent and frequently repeated goals and ideals. One of its notable characteristics, a
rich and varied 'sociological imagination', is given pride of place here.
This sociological imagination was expressed in an ongoing discourse, oral
and written, concerning the condition of England. I call it 'the discourse
of the commonweal'.

What made the English want to conquer the world and what made
them powerful enough to have a fair shot at doing it? What makes human
tribes go imperial? This book bears out the judgement of a great scholar
of early English imperialism, David Beers Quinn. 'The main reasons why
Europeans thought of settling in North America and did so,' he wrote,
'arose out of problems in their own European societies.'[5] Ultimately it
was less adventure and imitation than 'social and economic uncertainties
in their particular polities' that generated the new expansionism. This,
I show, was how immensely influential Tudor thinkers like Sir Thomas
Smith, John Dee, the younger and elder Hakluyts justified what must, I
think, be called *English* imperialism. It was, they argued, intrinsic to the
condition of the English commonwealth as they observed, categorized
and classified it. The 'how' depended, at least in part, on the depth
and quality of the vernacular English obsession, evident from the mid-
twelfth century, with visualizing the condition of England. That was the
consciously developed 'why?'

In terms of the authorized ideas and precepts of the English state
throughout this long gestation of national identity, the movement was a
revolution of 'commonalty'. To paraphrase what Nietzsche said of Shakespeare, the archives of early vernacular English, from Langland and John
Ball to Tyndale and Shakespeare and Bacon and Hobbes, are increasingly
pervaded by what Nietzsche, from his aristocratic point of view, summed
up as a whiff of 'the sewers'.[6] I chronicle and analyse the populist theme
and the bottom-up provenance of much that has hitherto been assumed
to have been the work of popes, kings and lords.

My subject is a long revolution that began in the last third of the
thirteenth century and came to a head in the decades between c.1580
and c.1660. The moment of 'critical mass', when linguistic, cybernetic,

---

[5] David Beers Quinn, 'Why they Came', in D.B. Quinn, *Explorers and Colonies: America,
1500–1625* (London 1990), 153.

[6] 'We enjoy (Shakespeare) as an artistic refinement reserved precisely for us and allow
ourselves to be as little disturbed by the repellant fumes and the proximity of the English
rabble in which Shakespeare's art and taste live as we do on the *Chiaja* of Naples, where
we go our way enchanted and willing with all our senses alert, however much the sewers
of the plebeian quarters may fill the air': Nietzsche, *Beyond Good and Evil*, trans. R.J.
Hollingdale (Harmondsworth 1973), 134–5.

ideological, conceptual, philosophical, demographic, economic, political and religious themes of the late middle ages came together and gave birth to a new collective orientation, came in the generations of the two Richard Hakluyts and those two classic writers of literature and philosophy in English, William Shakespeare and Thomas Hobbes. Many scholars have seen the age of 'Tudors and Stuarts' (the dynasties that ruled sixteenth- and seventeenth-century England) as especially formative in the history of the nation. I see them in relation to a long social revolution that swelled up in many forms and expressions from the lower ranks of the social hier-archy, the peripheries of the state and ruling classes, and became world-imperial. This long social revolution was marked by the rise and rise of medieval England's 'working class' – the 'communes' or 'commonalty' – as a collective agency in constitutional life and national politics.

1.2   War bands, indigenes and the causes of change[7]

After the Last Glacial Maximum, the first people to settle Britain were descendants of beachcombing and river-hugging migrants from two broad directions: the Basque-Celtic Coast traffic was one, the other was constituted by a wider front of migrants along the Danube, Rhone and Seine Basins from Ice Age 'refuges' in the Balkans and the Ukraine.[8] Sea levels rose slowly after the LGM. In the early stages of the move-ment Britain and Ireland were joined to each other by a wide land-bridge. Genetic markers still strongly represented in Eastern Britain were carried across archipelagos of dry land connecting Scotland with Scandinavia and England with Belgium, Holland and France before these 'bridges' were inundated. Generations of 'beach-combers' (as Oppenheimer calls them[9]) travelled north from the 'Basque Refuge' along what are now the west coasts of France, Brittany, Cornwall, Wales and Ireland.[10]

---

[7] In this context, 'indigenes' means the people found in possession of a territory by successive migrants and war bands. It follows from this definition that not all the people found in possession of 'England' at any one time, or some part thereof, by successive migrants and war bands would have been carriers of the Mesolithic descent-markers, since they were, or were the descendants of, relatively recent migrants.

[8] Oppenheimer, *Origins*, ch. 4 and figure 5.2, 182.

[9] *Ibid.*, 125–8; Oppenheimer, *Out of Eden: the Peopling of the World* (London 2003), 124–7, 156–9. For the global migration model, see Clive Gamble, *Timewalkers: the Prehistory of Global Colonization* (Harmondsworth 1995).

[10] Oppenheimer, *Origins*, 107–16, 123–4; Cunliffe, *Iron Age Britain*, 85–6, emphasizes regional differences. An 'elite class whose patronage extended to providing leadership, protection and a range of services' is evident in the centre-south by c.200–100 BC and in the south-east intensified contact with the continent probably caused 'the grad-ual amalgamation of the smaller chieftain-dominated groups into larger confederacies' before the Roman invasions.

The 'English' descent-markers easily survived the war band invasions of legend and history: the Belgic (before 100 BCE), Roman (first to fourth centuries CE), Anglo-Saxon (fourth to sixth centuries CE) and Viking (seventh to tenth centuries CE) invasions.[11] The flow of traffic constituted by migrants and invaders from the north and east was continuous but fluctuated according to a variety of stimuli including changing geography, climatic and ecological circumstances.

As for their mode of production, the first settlers were hunters and gatherers. The underlying historical landscape of most of the British Isles today is agrarian. Systems of settled agriculture (sometimes called the Neolithic Revolution) came late – five thousand years after their first appearance in what is now called the 'Fertile Triangle' of the Middle East. The origins of agriculture and settlement are disputed. Did existing populations develop their own forms of agriculture, adapted to particular landscapes, or was it imposed by immigrants and conquerors? Imperial or populist? It is a crucial question in historiographical debates about the long 'early modern' period. In a nutshell, are 'indigenes' (the people found in possession of a place, territory or country) always conservative and is change introduced from outside, by immigrants and conquerors? Intellectual historians often assume that language and ideas are invented by clerical elites and then 'trickle down'.[12] Here we are considering the origin and spread of agriculture. Did agriculture develop autonomously in many places in many different ways, or was there an original, one-off 'discovery' that was then radiated by conquest, migration and cultural diffusion from the original homelands? The sensible consensus today is that agriculture was a development of the arts of hunting and gathering that happened differently in different times and places.[13]

---

[11] With regard to the Anglo-Saxon invasions, Brian Ward-Perkins, 'Why Did the Anglo-Saxons Not Become More British?', *English Historical Review* 115:462 (June 2000), 522, sums up the pre-genetic consensus by saying that 'even brutal invasion is most likely to have left the vast majority of the native peasant population physically unharmed, if only in order to exploit them and their land more effectively'. Genetic continuity in no sense implies cultural and linguistic continuity, of course. As Ward-Perkins writes (426), 'the Britons *decision* to become Anglo-Saxon is easy to parallel elsewhere in Europe'.

[12] J.G.A. Pocock, 'The Concept of a Language and the *métier d'historien*: Some Considerations on Practice', in Anthony Pagden (ed.), *The Language of Political Theory in Early-Modern Europe* (Cambridge 1987), 19–40; Ben Suelzle, review of Jean Guilane and Jean Zammit, *The Origins of War: Violence in Prehistory* (Oxford 2005), accessed 20 December 2006 at http://arts.monash.edu.au/publications/eras/edition-7/, discusses 'general theories that explained the growing technological sophistication of human societies through the repeated invasion of different groups of people who were the bearers of steadily more socially, economically and politically advanced cultures'.

[13] '. . . in all these Western European regions, the transition to the Neolithic was a process of change and adaptation by the indigenous population rather than the work of incoming populations of farmers': 'Europe: the European Neolithic Period', *The Oxford*

Like the Renaissance and the Industrial Revolution, Agriculture did not have a single origin and form. The deceptively monolithic term 'agricultural revolution' stands for a bundle of possible long-term responses to population fluctuations and other factors on the part of nomadic hunters and gatherers. Human domestication of landscape, flora and fauna was not a one-off event but an adaptation to particular environments across many generations. The domestication of wild nature proceeded in innumerable different ways, depending on need and opportunity. One major reason is landscape: local habitats are more variable, spatially and temporally, than human intelligence and other capacities. The dialectics of population and landscape belong to the same nexus as the community instinct. It is part of the human condition to exist in a landscape from which the species must obtain its needs. How it does this depends on many variables.[14] The dialectics of landscape, population and imagination change through time; they were central to collective identity formation in early modern England, as we shall see.

Genes record some kind of direct, continuous descent. Oppenheimer suggests that judging by their success in reproducing themselves, the first people to re-settle 'Britain' (and other parts of the world) must have enjoyed an evolutionary 'advantage' (measured by continuous reproduction of marker genes) over 'late-comers'.[15] How are we to explain the extreme longevity of major genetic descent-lines in the contemporary

Companion to Archaeology (Oxford 1996), 216; see also 'Diffusion and Indigenism', *ibid.*, 176–7. Alasdair Whittle, 'The Coming of Agriculture', in Slack and Ward (ed.), *The Peopling of Britain*, 79, discusses the colonization/indigenous acculturation models, noting later that 'These kinds of explanation in favour of indigenous people are certainly in tune with the modern spirit of self determination, but they push archaeological interpretation to its limits.' He concludes that 'we may still have to do with an element of restricted or filtered colonization.' (87) I think the point about 'filtered colonization' is that unlike the more dramatic war band incursions they tend to be forgotten. Christopher Taylor, 'Introduction' to W.G. Hoskins, *The Making of the English Landscape* (London 1988), ch. 1: 'The Landscape Before the English Settlement', 16, wrote that the first of three 'revolutions in the English landscape' occurred 'quite suddenly'. 'Around 1600 BC the population of England seems to have exploded . . . to as many as a million people within a few centuries.' Marshall interpreted the development of hill-top sites and weapons as showing 'that warfare was becoming endemic'. This date appears to be seen as a watershed in *The Peopling of Britain*, between the contributions of Whittle, 'The Coming of Agriculture' and Barry Cunliffe, 'Tribes and Empires c.1500 BC–AD 500'. Cunliffe reports that invasionist theories of the 'La Tene' style have now been abandoned in favour of migrationist and diffusionist theories, but on my reading a combination of small-scale invasions and continuous interconnections also seems to account for the evidence.

[14] This issue is discussed and in my view settled on a world-historical scale in Jared Diamond, *Guns, Germs and Steel: a Short History of Everybody for the Last 13,000 Years* (London 1997).

[15] 'Once settled, a founding population is hard to dislodge': Oppenheimer, *Origins*, 104, 106–9.

populations of Britain? Oppenheimer concludes that 'Celts, Angles, Jutes, Saxons, Vikings, Normans and others . . . are all minorities compared with the first unnamed pioneers, who ventured into the empty, chilly lands so recently vacated by the great ice sheets.'[16] In the new narrative not even the coming of agriculture (the 'Neolithic revolution') was accompanied by wholesale change in the genetic stock. The hypothesis that a large majority of the inhabitants of Britain today are the direct descendants of people who settled thousands of years ago is not new, as we shall see. Broadly speaking it uses genetic analysis to confirm a hypothesis that began to take shape nearly a thousand years ago, and continued, in a variety of changing ways, to influence thinking about national and class identities throughout the early modern period.

1.3   The last conquest, 1066–c.1150

Up to the eleventh and twelfth centuries 'English' genetic markers had been continuously transmitted, unknown to their carriers, across the generations of some of the most frequently conquered people in world history. The 'advantage' enjoyed by the people in possession of the territory in 1066 was the same as it had been with respect to armed war bands for at least a thousand years: it was merely numerical. What made already occupied and settled countries attractive to male war bands was precisely that they were occupied and settled. They had a people to lead and rule, a population to do the work. Because the Normans and Angevins were only the last in a great line of earlier invasions and part-invasions, they found systems of tribute-payment in place. Long ago English monarchs (leaders and descendants of successful invading war bands) had established 'the right to levy a land-tax under the name of geld or danegeld', nominally for the collective defence of the territory against marauding Vikings. As soon as William the Conqueror (1028–1087, king of England by right of conquest 1066) was crowned 'he laid on men a geld exceeding stiff.' The next year 'he set (another) mickle geld' and 'in the winter of 1083–4 he raised a geld of 72 pence (6 Norman shillings) upon the hide.' William the Conqueror never took his eye off the main reason for the conquest. The English commonalty had very long experience of being in a tributary state and 'mode of production'.[17]

---

[16] *Ibid.*, 421.

[17] F.W. Maitland, *Domesday Book and Beyond: Three Essays in the Early History of England* (Cambridge 1897; see <http:socserv.mcmaster.ca/econ/ugcm/3113/maitland/domesday>), 'Essay One: Domesday Book' is the source for the quotations in this section. J.C. Holt, *Colonial England, 1066–1215* (London 1997), chs. 2–4, qualifies the supposition that *Domesday* was exclusively and primarily a geld book in important ways,

Domesday Book (1087) represents the 'gigantic effort' to collect 'enormously heavy' taxes from the indigenes. It shows that 'just twenty years after the conquest, a mere 8 per cent of land in England was owned by people with English names'.[18] For F.W. Maitland (1850–1906) the aptly-named *Domesday* was 'a rate book . . . , a tax book, a geld book' such as no regime in Western Europe had been able to execute since the fall of Rome. It only tells us 'of such facts, such rights, such legal relationships as bear on the actual or potential payment of geld'. As might be expected of a conquest regime in 'a barbarous age', 'the quest for geld is their one main object'. What a war band conquered it had to be able to defend. What it defended was the power to direct and exploit the subject population. As might be expected of people so frequently threatened by invasion in the past, the English were inured to – we might say designed for – the payment of regular tributes and taxes. 'Unless we are prepared to bring against the fathers of English history a charge of repeated, wanton and circumstantial lying', wrote Maitland, 'we shall think of the danegeld of Aethelred's (958–1016) reign and of Cnut's (c.995–1035) as of an impost so heavy that it was fully capable of transmuting a whole nation'. Seen from an indigenous perspective, a seemingly inevitable succession of conquering war bands had imposed tributary 'lines' that were already 'deep and permanent'.[19] The Normans exploited and perfected but did not invent these 'lines' (or 'social structures').

A 'settled synthesis' of historical systems designed to enable constitutional warriors to collect tribute from their subjects already existed by the eleventh century. That such a synthesis (sometimes called the early English state or kingdom) existed was one of the things that made it attractive to warriors like William of Normandy and Henry of Anjou. It was a simple matter for William's 'commissioners' to adapt the perennial precepts of conquest to an ingrained constitutional landscape.

but concludes (p. 66) that 'no-one is likely to dispute that Domesday is in some sense a geld-book'. William E. Kapelle, 'Domesday Book: F.W. Maitland and his Successors,' *Speculum*, 64:3 (July 1989), 620–40, is a useful review of interpretations since Maitland. Kapelle shows that in the past century many scholars have rejected Maitland's 'geld hypothesis' on evidential and logical grounds, but that the objections have only qualified and complicated, not invalidated it. Recent work suggests that 'William (of Normandy) may well have been interested in making a survey which was to be the basis for reviving the great gelds of the (Ango-Saxon) past.' (638) Maitland presumed that the systematic collection of 'tribute,' in whatever form, was *inevitably* in William's mind, whatever his other motives, because systematic tribute collection (in whatever form) is so obviously what ruling classes and states do. If nothing else, it demonstrated rulership to every level of the conquered society. For the tributary mode, see Eric R. Wolf, *Europe and the People Without History* (Berkeley and Los Angeles 1982), 79–88; John Haldon, *The State and the Tributary Mode of Production* (London 1993).

[18] Francis Pryor, *Britain in the Middle Ages: an Archaeological History* (London 2006), 230.
[19] Maitland, 'Domesday Book'.

'As a general rule,' Maitland observed, 'the political geography of England was already stereotyped.' 'The geographical basis of the survey' was that 'England is divided into counties, hundreds or wapentakes and vills.' Although 'the commissioners seem to have held but one moot for each shire', internal evidence showed 'that each hundred was represented by a separate set of jurors (6)' and that 'within each hundred the survey was made by vills. (7)' New villages appeared in ensuing centuries, but Maitland could not help observing that 'the place so named (in *Domesday Book*) will in after times be known as a vill and in our own day will be a civil parish'.[20]

Although the commissioners of *Domesday* were concerned with 'manorial and fiscal geography', that is to say with lordship and tribute, what Maitland called the 'physical and villar geography' (actual settlement patterns and distributions of community-oriented land usages) can be deduced from their work. The intention of the document was to facilitate and maximize the collection of tribute, but in doing this it reveals much else that was not intended. Villages and towns were 'tract[s] of land with some houses' that had long constituted units in a 'national system of police and finance'.[21] We shall return to the formation of the early modern landscape and its influence on general movements throughout this book. The landscape of tenth-century England is, today, all but buried by later accumulations. The two centuries after the Norman Conquest saw dramatic and, by earlier standards of geographical history, rapid developments that laid the foundations of English life until the eve of the Industrial Revolution. I will now offer a sketch of developments of the twelfth and thirteenth centuries: the preconditions for the populist, vernacular revolution of the fourteenth to seventeenth centuries.

1.4   The Norman yoke

Lords of Mannors . . . were William the Conqueror's colonels and Favourites, and he gave a large circuit of Land to everyone, called a Lord-ship.[22]

There has never been much doubt about 'the scale and nature of the violence and brutality involved' in the Norman Conquest. In the next three or four generations (roughly 1066–1150) England came to be divided

---

[20] Maitland, *Domesday Book*, 1. Plan of the survey; he noted that in Cambridgeshire 'about a hundred and ten vills that were vills in 1086 are vills or civil parishes at the present day, and in all probability they then had approximately the same boundaries that they have now'.

[21] Maitland, 'Domesday Book', 1. Plan of the survey.

[22] G.H. Sabine (ed.), *The Works of Gerrard Winstanley* (New York 1941), 359, cited in Andy Wood, *Riot, Rebellion and Popular Politics in Early Modern England* (Basingstoke 2002), 163.

into two great classes, one comprising what the great constitutional historian William Stubbs called the 'circles around the throne', the other consisting of the descendants of the defeated. The two classes of Norman England were distinguished by ethnicity, heredity, language, culture, way of life, self-esteem, wealth, power and by everyday relations with the other class. *Domesday Book* listed 'more than 25,000 *servi*, . . . 82,000 *bordari*, . . . nearly 7,000 *cotari* and *cotseti* and nearly 110,000 *villani*'. These numbers must be multiplied to allow for the families of the men they counted. The fine distinctions of servitude in *Domesday* slowly gave way to a single, sharp distinction. The tendency of Norman jurists was to reduce 'the minute distinctions of Anglo-Saxon dependence . . . into the *class* of *nativi*'.[23]

English people came with the land. For two or three generations, Normans and their companions saw the indigenous majority in class terms, defining it in terms of 'immunities from the warlike life' of the nobility and freemen, and regarding the *nativi* as 'despicable for ignorance and coarseness'. Stubbs thought it was possible for conquered natives to escape servitude by renouncing their holdings and taking refuge in towns, where they could become members of a guild. 'Unclaimed for a year and a day' they could 'obtain the full rights of free men'. It has also been suggested that many native serfs felt no need of such actions as 'under a fairly good lord . . . the villein enjoyed immunities and securities that might be envied by his superiors'.[24] This may have happened later, but 'in periods of relative labour scarcity, such as the late eleventh and early twelfth centuries and the later fourteenth century after the Black Death', writes David Levine, 'the primordial characteristics of enforced servitude came to the fore'.[25] As for the exact nature of those characteristics, 'We will never know how many serfs were mutilated, tortured, burned or simply (if one can put it that way) hanged':

Such atrocities cannot, as a general rule, be known except when they concerned individuals who did not belong to the perpetrator of the violence. Only then was there complaint, hence traces in the archives. In almost every other case, silence reigned. It is nevertheless not unreasonable to assume that the gibbets adjacent to fortresses were there for more than purely decorative purposes . . . The image

---

23 William Stubbs, *The Constitutional History of England* (1897; repr. New York 1987), 1:466. Heinrich Harke, 'Kings and Warriors: Population and Landscape from Post-Roman to Norman Britain' in Slack and Ward (ed.), *The Peopling of Britain*, 163, describes the effects of the conquest as 'one of socio-ethnic change: some 4,000 to 5,000 Anglo-Saxon aristocrats were completely replaced, within a mere twenty years, by 144 Norman barons'.

24 Stubbs, *Constitutional History*, 1: 462, 466.

25 David Levine, *At the Dawn of Modernity: Biology, Culture and Material Life in Europe after the Year 1000* (Berkeley and Los Angeles 2001), 220.

of the thrashed villain, indeed, permeates the whole of medieval literature, and should not be treated simply as a cliché lacking historical significance.[26]

In the eyes of the first generations of conquerors, *nativi* were a distinct class, even caste or genetic and ethnic group of indigenes who carried inferiority in the blood.

Norman England was 'a world in which people took ethnic difference, and the distinctions between French and English, for granted'. Hugh M. Thomas shows that conquerors and natives came to be distinguished by an array of attributes and alleged qualities: by place of origin and, in succeeding generations, by ancestry; political allegiance; language; differences of religious custom and practice; favourite saints and heroes; law; appearance ('most notably with hair and clothes'); 'military equipment, technology and technique' – 'though the Normans could and did fight dismounted, they would have preferred warriors who were experienced both as infantry and cavalry.' Prejudices took many forms. 'William of Malmesbury wrote that the English consumed all their income in small and worthless houses while the French and Normans spent frugally but built ample and fine edifices.' The French were said to be wine-drinkers while the English preferred beer. 'The interplay between ethnicity and political allegiance', writes Thomas, 'was at first the most important factor in ethnic relations. Yet another distinction, at least once the invaders had largely destroyed the existing elites, was that of class.' In effect, once their elites were removed, the English became an inferior *class* distinguished by variations on the distinctions listed above. Thomas notes that 'there was at least a limited tendency among continental and immigrant writers to view the English as somewhat backward, even as barbarians.'[27] By c.1150 the English constituted the inferior subject population, that part of the realm whose function was not to rule but to work.

Norman practice was to exclude English subjects from social, political and religious power at every level of society. The distinction between a ruling class of conquering 'lords' and Latinate churchmen and a servile native-speaking commonalty was an inescapable social fact by c.1150. Natives were excluded from government and treated with disdain. By the reign of Stephen immigrant warriors had 'almost obliterated the native aristocracy in most areas of the country' and old warlords were beginning to look over their shoulders at enterprising new warlords from

[26] Pierre Bonnassie, 'The Survival and Extinction of the Slave System in the Early Medieval West (4th–11th Centuries)', 19ff, quotation from Levine, *At the Dawn of Modernity*, 217–18.

[27] Hugh M. Thomas, *The English and the Normans: Ethnic Hostility, Assimilation and Identity 1066–c.1220* (Oxford 2002), quotations from 46, 47, 50, 52, 54.

the continent.[28] 'English' and 'third estate' were synonyms. Like many of their predecessors, the conquerors only required a working population: they provided their own lords. Norman exclusion of natives from positions of authority was more systematic than the hegemony their fellow conquerors exercised in Sicily. It took three generations – about a hundred years. As Thomas puts it, 'relations between English and Normans started off in the worst possible way, which only makes the speed of assimilation that much more surprising.'[29] One of the reasons for the decline of slavery *per se* in the twelfth century was that the whole third estate became, from the point of view of the conquerors, 'slaves in nature if not in law'. At this stage the new 'centaurs' did not want or need Aristotle to justify their superiority.

What Thomas calls 'assimilation' began, in his view, almost as soon as class prejudice between conquerors and conquered reached a peak. It fell apart very quickly and 'seems to have been complete' by the end of the twelfth century.[30] The dissolution of ethnic difference may explain why 'there is not a word in [*Magna Carta*, 1215] that recalls the distinctions of race and blood, or that maintains the differences of English and Norman Law,' as Stubbs put it.[31] In fact 'assimilation' is misleading and 'completely' overstates the case. As we shall see, there is abundant evidence that the Norman Conquest was continuously and habitually remembered by subsequent generations of English people. It was re-minded by a battery of routine usages. So common did the habit of looking back on the Norman Conquest become and remain that we can call it a 'structure' of English constitutional culture. When later *literati* like William Tyndale, the revolutionaries of the 1640s and, at the very beginning of the American Revolution, Thomas Paine, wrote of a system of oppression, still in place, instituted by 'the Norman Yoke', they were writing down a popular way of thinking about government that had been passed from generation to generation, in different forms and receptions, since the last, and hence most remembered, conquest. The yoke that most 'English' people had worn for at least a millennium thus became the *Norman* yoke.

At one extreme of the spectrum were the populists, for whom conquest meant abiding subjection. At the other were those like the sophisticated seventeenth-century antiquarian, John Aubrey. For Aubrey, English aborigines had learned nothing that had not been taught to them by a succession of invaders. Before the conquest the English had lived in 'a mist of ignorance' for 600 years since the Romans left. 'The Normans then came and taught them civility and building: which, though it was Gothique as

---

[28] *Ibid.*, 118.   [29] *Ibid.*, 61.   [30] *Ibid.*, 57.   [31] Stubbs, *Constitutional History*, 1: 571.

also their policy (*Feudalis Lex*) yet they were magnificent.'[32] That the Norman Conquest had been bloody was not the point: the invaders brought civilization that earlier invaders had not. The commons are 'slaves in nature if not in law' and will be led by whatever band of nobles and kings happens to be in command of them. They have neither minds nor ideas of their own. The nobles and gentlemen who ruled England, its provinces and localities from the thirteenth to the seventeenth centuries often thought about gentility as essentially a matter of race and inheritance – of being born to rule.

The 'assimilation' (or rather synthesis) of French ruling class and English commonalty took place, in Thomas's view, between c.1250 and c.1350. In later chapters it will be shown that the racial and ethnic prejudices of French conquerors did not so much fade away as become more sophisticated and flexible. They were applied to changing circumstances and conditions. The hegemony of formal and informal distinctions between nobility and commonalty easily survived the emergence, in the fourteenth century, of a common language based on native tongues. Against the current of vernacular revival, the idea that it was the duty of the noble and virtuous few to rule the 'slaves in nature' became institutionalized alongside a range of opinions qualifying and rejecting what might be termed the 'inherent inferiority hypothesis'.[33]

Class prejudice of this sort never went away; it was simply adapted to changing social structures and contexts. The hard-core dualism of elite ruling class and subject multitude unites the world-views of medieval chroniclers, leading Tudor antipopulists like Sir Thomas Elyot and Sir Thomas More (Chapters 3.9–11), the imperial ideologue Richard Hakluyt the younger (Chapter 7) and revolutionary puritans like John Corbet (Chapter 9.6). As we shall see in the next chapter, it virtually guaranteed the creation of 'middles' to mediate between the two essential classes. We

---

[32] Anthony Powell, *John Aubrey and his Friends* (London 1988), 2, discussed in Rollison, *The Local Origins of Modern Society: Gloucestershire 1500–1800* (London and New York 1992), 255–7.

[33] Michel Foucault, *Society Must Be Defended*, trans. David Macey (London 2003), 61, 65–86, argues that 'the discourse of race struggle . . . first appeared and began to function in the seventeenth century . . . [It functioned] as a principle of exclusion and segregation and, ultimately, as a way of normalizing society'. Keith Thomas, 'Inferior Humans', in his *Man and the Natural World: Changing Attitudes in England 1500–1800* (Harmondsworth 1983), 41–50, is more grounded in detailed evidence but remains compatible with Foucault's theory. More of the discourse on 'inferior humans' was written down in the seventeenth century and has survived. We tend to identify it with that particular conjuncture but it represented the application of an abiding system of discrimination to the 'new world' opening up at that time. As Thomas shows (43–6) the habit of using it to define and explain 'the [indigenous] poor' remained dominant.

shall see that 'middle' classes and ranks emerged in the twelfth century, attracted the attention of writers in the thirteenth, and were a constant, powerful presence, socially, institutionally and discursively, in the fourteenth century (Chapter 2.5–7). The great antipopulist fight back that found key expression in Archbishop Arundel's 'constitutions' of 1409 (Chapter 3.9–10) polarized discourse again in the fifteenth century. The discourse tripped out so lightly by John Aubrey in the decades after the execution of Charles I had been nourished, adapted and passed on by ten generations of antipopulist clerics, academics, professors, counsellors and courtiers. Simplistic though it was and is as a description of an increasingly complex field of social forces, binary division (conquerors and subjects, lords and people, warrior and worker, learned and *lewd*, fine gentlemen and 'the rascability of the popular') has been an abiding theme in discourse about the condition of England for many centuries.

Antipopulist discourse consisted of variations of the idea that the Norman Conquest brought civilization to a backward people. It may have been cruel, but it was God's will. Moreover, it eventually improved the condition of the people Aubrey called '*indigenes or aborigines*'. It became an article of faith of this vehemently antipopulist tradition that 'indigenes' and 'common people', rustic peasants, truculent artisans and stolid labourers, and most definitively *crowds* of such people, lacked the capacity to form ideas and memories with any degree of sophistication. Popular thought, culture, religion and ideas were contradictions in terms. It was a question of who put what in their thick heads. The 'assimilation' thesis modulates class-interpretation by concentrating on 'mediating' or 'middle' ranks of English society where, in the later twelfth and thirteenth centuries, the descendants of invaders intermarried and were neighbours with the English-speaking natives. Higher in the social hierarchy, in the 'circles around the throne', in the late twelfth and thirteenth centuries, older generations of warlords and their privileged associates (or new lords who wanted to imagine themselves as 'English') increasingly felt a need (however notional) for the more than passive support of lesser lords and the oldest English people of all, the free and servile commonalty. There were many reasons for this alliance, which is evident in many clauses of *Magna Carta* (1215) and came to a head with Simon de Montfort's 'Common Enterprise'.

In the reign of Henry II (1154–89), priorities began to change. By the time Henry won the throne division between foreign lords and native subjects was as sharp and complete as it would ever be. This second conquest produced the lasting masterpiece of political philosophy that is the subject of my next section. In its English context, John of Salisbury's

Policraticus (1159) marked a sharp change of direction. Even more than that other great masterpiece of English political thought, Thomas Hobbes's *Leviathan*, it had, at its core, a simple mnemonic image that could be conveyed (and memorized) in common language. Even more strikingly, John's dissection of the English 'body politic' displayed great sensitivity to members not previously thought to have been worth consideration in matters of estate. It assumed that the conquest was over, in the past. The task now was not to conquer but to defend and develop Henry's prize territory, England. To do this he must begin to draw on its native population.

1.5   Return of the repressed: tyranny and the commonweal in John of Salisbury's body politic

A commune welthe is lyke a body, and soo lyke, that it can be resembled to nothing so convenient, as unto that.[34]

How many kings (and those good men too) hath this one error, that a Tyrant King might lawfully be put to death, been the slaughter of? How many throats has this false position cut, that a prince for some causes may by some certain men be deposed? . . . How many rebellions has this opinion been the cause of, which teaches that the knowledge whether the commands of Kings be just or unjust, belongs to private men; and that before they yield obedience, they not only may, but ought to dispute them![35]

At the core of the *Policraticus* is an elegant and memorable tool of thought. In centuries to come England would develop a word for the spiritual and physical well-being of the body politic: 'commonweal'. The idea that the commonweal was first and foremost determined by a healthy, happy, well-armed and relatively autonomous commonalty, or 'third estate', is one that would explode into the streets many times in the next five centuries.[36] Thomas Hobbes, John of Salisbury's greatest successor in the art of imagining political bodies, was perfectly right to place what James Holstun calls 'tyrannicide theory and practice' at the very heart of English constitutional development up to the 1640s. By Hobbes's time (1588–1679) the definition and punishment of tyrants, and the popular legitimacy of regimes, had been enduring preoccupations of English political and ethical thought – its 'constitutional culture' – for

---

[34] Richard Morison, *A Remedy for Sedition*, (1536), quotation from Anthony Fletcher and Diarmaid MacCulloch, *Tudor Rebellions*, 5th ed. (Harlow 2005), 150.

[35] Thomas Hobbes, *De Cive*, Author's Preface <www.constitution.org/th/decive00.htm>.

[36] In the thirteenth century official records usually use the 'commune' words (e.g. *communaute*) to mean the whole community. By the mid-thirteenth century this 'community of the realm' included the hitherto excluded 'communes' in the third estate sense. This marked a fundamental change in constitutional culture, as discussed below, Chapter 2.

centuries. In this sense *Policraticus* represents the first dawning of the age of the commonweal.

John's theory of tyranny added an idea not present in the pagan classics. 'Unlike preceding classical and medieval authors, who conceived of tyranny purely in terms of the evil or destructive use of public authority,' writes Cary J. Nederman, 'John identifies the tyrant as any person who weds the ambitious desire to curtail the liberty of others with the power to accomplish this goal. As a result, his theory of tyranny is generic in the sense that it permits the tyrant to emerge in any walk of life.'[37] If a king who persists in tyranny can be killed, as John explicitly says he can, then it does not take too much of a leap to conclude that any tyrant in any walk of life may meet the same fate.[38] John's rule was the precept that guaranteed 'reciprocity'.[39] Governors are duty bound to serve

---

[37] Nederman, 'Editor's Introduction' to John of Salisbury, *Policraticus: Of the Frivolities of Courtiers and the Footprints of Philosophers*, ed. and trans. Cary J. Nederman (Cambridge 1990), xxiv. William Tyndale, *Answer to More* (1530), xxxv, is virtually a vernacular-proverbial synthesis of John's principle: '. . . if any subiecte thynke any otherwise of ye officer (though he be an emperoure) then that he is but a servaunte only/ to minister the office indifferently/ he dishonoureth the office and god that ordeyned it. So that all men/ whatsoever degree they be of are every man in his rowme/ servauntes to other/ as the hand serveth the foote and every member one another . . .' J.N. Figgis, *Studies of Political Though from Gerson to Grotius, 1414–1625* (1907, repr. Bristol 1998), 148, wrote that 'John of Salisbury's *Policraticus* [was] the earliest medieval apology for tyrannicide'.

[38] Richard H. Rouse and Mary A. Rouse, 'John of Salisbury and the Doctrine of Tyrannicide', *Speculum*, 42:4 (October 1967), 695, note that if the whole text is considered 'his statement of that principle was inconstant', but that it was 'pure theory with a practical purpose'. 'A tyrant as head corrupts all parts of the body; and the result is a "commonwealth of the ungodly" . . . with a sacrilegious priesthood as its soul, and "its heart of unrighteous counselors"; its "eyes, ears, tongue and unarmed hand are unjust judges, laws and officials; its armed hand consists of soldiers of violence whom Cicero calls brigands"; and its feet are rebellious and disloyal husbandmen.' (*ibid.*, 702, quotation from *Policraticus*, VIII, 17). Therefore 'A "sane head" is the *sine qua non* to the viability of John's concept of commonwealth as macrocosm.' (*Ibid.*, 703)

[39] Tilman Struve, 'The Importance of the Organism in the Political Theory of John of Salisbury,' in Michael Wilks (ed.), *The World of John of Salisbury* (Oxford 1984), 307, writes that in applying the organological idea to the organization of the body politic John asserted that 'all the ranks and parts of the state were interrelated in a mutual relationship of functions. Each member had to accomplish its special task at its special place and in doing so he was supported by the others . . . The conclusion, that even the strongest body politic needed feet in order to survive, an idea which derived from the relationship of the organs, however, had impact for the future. This conclusion explicitly mediated the insight into the necessity of all social ranks and all kinds of professions, including the lowest ones, for the common weal. John called attention to that class, which was the largest in numbers and only made possible the stability of the medieval feudal world through its labour. This was the class of the peasants and workmen. Giving the serving class of peasants and workmen their place in the functional relationship of the body politic certainly meant an improvement compared to the archaic division of the society into *oratores*, *bellatores* and *laboratores*.' John H. Arnold, *Belief and Unbelief in*

'those who erect, sustain and move forward the mass of the whole body [and who] are justly owed shelter and support'. The inferior vocations of the commonalty or third estate, for their part, were bound to serve the superior. The whole was greater than the parts.

Notions of an organic 'commonweal' were pivotal in the development of English constitutional culture from the thirteenth to seventeenth centuries. The test of strong, virtuous government was not the condition of its elites, institutions, literature, art, monuments of history and culture, architecture, landscape, wealth or even religion, although they all counted. The final, absolute test of the strength of a commonwealth is the material and spiritual condition of the commonalty. Poverty (in a broad sense encompassing spiritual and material impoverishment) is the shame of a commonwealth, its guilty secret. If any part of the commonwealth is corrupt, it corrupts the whole body. John believed it was the sacred duty of every subject to scrutinize exercises of power, judge them and, if practicable, resist injustice and corruption wherever it occurs. The precepts and image of John's communalist vision of commonweal echo through every succeeding generation of vernacular English culture up to the civil wars of the 1640s. He also provides us with our earliest systematic literary portrait of the condition of England.

John conceived the political community as a complex, unpredictably and dynamically interacting commonwealth, constituted by strategic 'limbs' or 'members' working together. As a remedy for endemic corruptions and diseases of the state he prescribed a way of thinking embodied in an easily remembered and developed metaphor. Princes and chancellors of state need mnemonic systems like the body politic because they were 'not inclined to survey their realms without delay'. Even a king as young and vigorous as Henry II, John's secular lord, would not find it 'easy to traverse the length and breadth of the provinces [of his empire] in a short period'.[40] In the absence of personal experience princes had to have a mental picture of what a country or 'republic' actually consisted of and how it ought to interconnect. Otherwise, John implied, they would not rule it for long.

Medieval Europe (London 2005), 125, observes that the version of the body politic used in a sermon of 1373 by the Bishop of Rochester, Thomas Brinton, 'is hierarchical. The king is at the top and the labourers are at the bottom. Other classes of people are arranged according to taste . . . It is also *reciprocal* . . . The body is clearly a very useful symbol, the epitome of what is "natural", but actually highly mutable in its meaning. It was also an image with many sacred resonances, because of the importance placed on Christ's body in the Eucharist . . . '.

[40] *Policraticus*, V, 'Prologue', 65.

The sections of *Policraticus* that expound the body politic idea are styled as a commentary and discussion of an idea that was not John's creation, but that of the ancient author, Plutarch, written in a letter to the Roman emperor, Trajan. The conceit gave his exercise prestige and legitimacy it would have lacked if he had said peasants, artisans and labourers thought with it. There is no evidence that Plutarch ever wrote such a letter; if he did, his contribution, like John's, was to reshape the idea and adapt it to new circumstances. The image was eminently memorable, capable of being carried in the head and applied to all sorts of occasions and circumstances.[41] The analogy between the human body and the political community is simple, flexible and productive of thought about how (of what vocations, classes, estates etc.) society was actually constituted, and how they ought to relate to and live with each other. John encouraged flexible reading. An author or reader 'who follows everything in the text syllable by syllable,' he wrote, 'is a servile interpreter who aims to express the appearance rather than the essence of an author'.[42] The task of the commentator, reader or listener is to discern and clarify the 'essence' of an author's meaning. John's treatise rubbed against the grain of contemporary realities and usages of power in many ways and he wanted his audience to read between the lines.

In an age of conflict between secular and ecclesiastical jurisdictions, John regarded it as axiomatic that the Church was 'the soul in the body of the republic' and 'ought to be esteemed and venerated like the soul in the body'.[43] The head was king, but in Christendom kings were not 'living gods.' Only 'gentiles' like Darius of Persia and Augustus of Rome believed in 'god-kings'. If kings and lords failed in their duty (as John showed they invariably did) it was the role of the Church to remind them what their duty was. The soul had authority over the head. The Head was 'a prince subject only to God *and to those who act in His place on*

---

[41] Nederman, 'Editor's Introduction', *Policraticus*, xxi, writes that 'scholars now usually conclude that the "Instruction of Trajan" was actually a convenient fiction fashioned by John as a cloak for that intellectual novelty so despised by the medieval cast of mind'.

[42] *Policraticus*, V, 2, 'According to Plutarch, what a republic is and what place is held in it by the soul of the members', 67; for a remarkable example of an English king 'reading between the lines' of the body politic idea in order to think about the constitution of the realm, see King Edward VI, 'Discourse on the Reform of Abuses in Church and State' (April? 1551), in *The Chronicle and Political Papers of King Edward VI*, ed. W.K. Jordan, (Ithaca, New York 1966), 160–2; it may be significant that Edward VI uses the model to analyse 'temporal regimen', having dealt with matters 'ecclesiastical' in a perfunctory earlier section.

[43] The greatest emperor twelfth-century kings and scholars could imagine, 'Augustus Caesar himself was constantly subject to the sacred pontiffs until the time when he created himself a Vestal pontiff and shortly thereafter was transformed into a living god, in order that he would be subject to no-one.' *Policraticus*, 67.

earth'. John's first precept was that 'the head is stimulated and ruled by the soul'.[44]

Princely power was further hedged in by the fact that a good prince 'rules by the laws'. In John's conception laws were precepts worked out and formulated in counsel between all the members of the body. The most virtuous counsel, in John's view, came from the heart, a 'Senate, from which proceeds the beginning of good and bad works'. Importantly, membership of the Senate was not a privilege of wealth, estate or military power. Men did not qualify by warrior status, riches, property or heredity. 'Elders' were proved by long, empirical association with their neighbours: wise elders could come from any class, estate, rank or community. What mattered was that they put the community before any lesser interest, especially their own. In the 1150s, this meant natives.

John was a gerontocrat. Other things being equal, old people made the best governors. No individual or member of the body is perfect, nor ever could be. 'Old age is neither venerable according to its days nor computed in numerical years,' he wrote (Proverbs 20:29). 'Grey hairs are a man's judgement; the advancement of age is an unblemished life.' If 'the granting of counsel must await one who has never committed a sin' there would be no counsellors at all. Princes and commonwealths should choose for a Senator 'one who is not glad to sin, who hates sin, who rejoices in virtue and yearns for it with great desire, a man of manifestly

---

[44] Cary J. Nederman and Catherine Campbell, 'Priests, Kings and Tyrants: Spiritual and Temporal Power in John of Salisbury's *Policraticus*', *Speculum*, 66:3 (July 1991), 572–90, show that John's 'Hierocracy' was characteristically ambivalent, even slippery: ideally the world is hierocratic but *in practice* relations between Church and State involved contradictions. Rouse and Rouse, 'Doctrine of Tyrannicide', 703, perceive, in the many apparent contradictions between theory and practice in *Policraticus*, a 'John the Academic, who "will not presume to state definitely what is true in each and every case"'. On the 'sect' of 'Academics', see *Policraticus*, IV, 3: 'Academics express doubt with a forbearance proportionate to the pains I find they have taken to avoid the pitfall of rashness. So true is this indeed that when writers in passages not ordinarily subject to doubt use words that express it such as "probably" or "perhaps" they are said to have used them with Academic moderation. The reason for this is that the Academics were more forbearing than other sects, for they shunned both the stigma of rash definition and the pitfall of falseness.' It cannot be said that John always avoided 'rash' statements (e.g. in his bald statements on the supremacy of the Church, or on the validity of tyrannicide), even though for every apparently dogmatically stated ideal in one part of the book it is usually possible to find qualifying or contradictory statements elsewhere. However, with regard to relations between kings and the Church, Rouse and Rouse, 'Doctrine of Tyrannicide', 705, write that 'John was definitely apprehensive concerning Henry II's future intentions toward the Church' when he wrote *Policraticus*. At times it seems that John's intention was to say everything that could be said or reported on a topic, probably to protect himself; what is most memorable about the *Policraticus* is the organological ideal and the theory of tyranny.

good will'.[45] Elders were men whose lives testified to a desire to live up to the most difficult of all precepts, to 'love God and thy neighbour'.[46] The task of the heart, as we shall see, was to connect the head with its most important ally, the feet. If the head expanded beyond the capacity of the feet to keep it standing it would fall with the rest of the body. Government was all about balance and reciprocity. Other things being equal, elders were thought to be more likely to love and pursue such ideals.

The head also had at its service the organs of seeing, hearing, smelling and tasting, the eyes, ears, nose and mouth. The king would be wise to keep them under careful scrutiny. These were 'judges and governors of provinces', men delegated to smell out and taste the mood and spirit of 'provincials'. Their job was to represent the king by doing as he would do if he could be everywhere in his kingdom at once. If the head was corrupt, these organs of intelligence would be too, and vice versa. Judges and governors of provinces were admonished not to 'sin against the multitude of people' but also not to 'lower [themselves] among the people'. Once again, 'a good will is no less necessary for a judge than is knowledge or power'. Just, fair government was not much in evidence in Henry's English realms, especially in relations between foreign rulers and native English. John stated unequivocally that 'the power which (the king's agents) have is exercised in the service of greediness, ostentation, or their own flesh and blood'. Everyone knew the name of a judge or governor of a district or province 'who markets his duty to his king and queen . . . like merchandise in a doorway'.[47]

John had no time for feudal warriors. It has been suggested that between 1000 and 1200 'a new type of aristocrat – the courtier-statesman' began to replace the older 'Centaur/warrior' nobility. Fighting skills 'were transmuted into the organizational skills of logistics and finance required

---

[45] 'Yet the senate, as the ancients concur, is the name of an office and has maturity of age as its distinguishing mark': *Policraticus*, V, 9, 81, 82–3.

[46] 'Character has its origins in these two sources: good, if one does for another what he would have another do for himself and refrains from imposing upon another what he would not wish another to impose upon himself; bad, if one harms another or does not help him when he has the power. Instances of both types are numerous. From the first originate love of liberty, of country and ultimately of those outside its bounds. For he who loves himself and his country cannot fail to love liberty, and in due course whosoever loves his neighbour will love him outside this circle since consistent charity demands it. From the second comes greed for dominion, for praise and for fame. So strong is this that it is counted with the virtues (by) those who pass judgement without due deliberation. Those of good judgement class it with the major vices, although the virtues, in the estimation of the inexperienced who, nonetheless are rated wise, seem to form its basis': *Policraticus* VII, 5.

[47] *Ibid.*, V, 11, 93–4.

to put a force of men into the field of battle when the ties of dependence were attenuated by sub infeudation and the corrosive effects of money'.[48] The 'flanks' of the social body corresponded to the king's court, in Henry II's case very much a military court consisting of 'centaur/warriors'. The flanks consisted of 'those who always assist the prince', the inner circle of 'the powerful'. This too was a corrupt member, in John's experience. He complained 'about the venality of everything among courtiers when those things which cost nothing, such as the lack of some act, are subject to sale . . . No deed and no word is free of charge, no one keeps still except for a price; and thus, silence is a thing for sale'.[49] No-one listened, obeyed or served except for pay. The corruption of courtiers would be another enduring theme – and pretext for rebellion – throughout the age of the commonweal.

Beyond the court, the prince had two 'hands,' one armed, the other unarmed and concerned mainly with the business of collecting money. John had a peasant view of the unarmed hand. 'All tax collectors only have time these days for extortion', he wrote. The situation was worst when 'princes are infidels and companions of thieves', but *all* tax collectors, like 'locusts,' 'devour fortunes'. As always obeying the precept that counsel must be ruthlessly honest, John stated another precept that others left unsaid: 'princes' usually were (or acted like) 'infidels' and 'thieves'. Subjects who resisted the excess 'fees' which corrupt tax assessors and collectors tried to skim in the course of collection were accused of 'subversion of the people' or 'the cancellation of the laws of our fathers'. This hand was supposed to be unarmed but if anyone 'resists the various injuries of these plunderers, he is judged worthy of any punishment', wrote John.

If they mess up your hair by dirtying and dishevelling it, if they pluck your beard, if they pull on your ears as though they were too short, if they give you a slap on the head or impiously hit you with a fist, if they pluck out one or another of your eyes, patiently tolerate it (unless you prefer to lose both of your eyes) because whatever they take they boast is done with the right hand of Caesar.

No prince should be under any illusion about 'tax officials'. 'While [they] are harmful pests to the provincials,' John concluded, 'no one can be more harmful to the prince'. If the tax collectors are corrupt the other members will conclude that it is the prince himself who 'has unjustly and almost fraudulently plundered and destroyed [the people] with his

[48] Levine, *At the Dawn of Modernity*, 125.   [49] *Policraticus*, V, 10, 86.

unarmed hand'.[50] They would not care if the kingdom changed hands once again, as it had done so many times before, time out of mind.

Sins of the stomach ('treasurers and record keepers') were for John as for all his classical forebears, the most likely cause of indigestion, flatulence and constipation in the body politic. The members of the stomach recorded receipts and looked after the king's bills. 'If they accumulate with great avidity and tenaciously preserve their accumulation', wrote John, 'their infection threatens to ruin the whole body'. Pope Adrian's version of the parable of the belly recorded that when this happened 'all the members of the whole body conspired against the stomach', but what the historical anecdote that provided its seminal context (in the mouth of the Roman senator Menenius in 493BCE) recorded was that the plebeians revolted. 'Treasurers and record keepers' were primary targets of the rebels of 1381. Taxation was an ingredient of popular murmuring and uprising from the Commons Rebellion to the Civil Wars (1381–1649). John's parable of the belly pointed infallibly at the greatest point of tension between ruling states and classes and the subject population. The message was that a fat belly is the sign of all signs of corruption of the whole body.

The soul, the heart, the armed hand and the feet formed the circuit that contributed most to the health of John's body politic. The members clustered around and emanating from the head – all the upper parts of the body except the heart – were eminently corruptible and, as John repeatedly showed, invariably corrupt in practice. They always tried to expand at the expense of the rest. The good juices – what preacher Thomas Wimbledon, in 1388, called 'kindly heat' – flowed upward from the feet to the armed hand and the heart. The principle of greedy upper members is best illustrated by the image of a fat belly. A fat belly takes in more than it gives out and makes the feet work harder. In an age when dearth and famine were routine experiences a fat belly was not a good sign. The head, shoulders, flanks and stomach must remember that without strong feet the body collapses.

If the unarmed hand is an enemy of the feet, the armed hand, an especially important member in John's model, was their child. The armed hand 'is occupied . . . with marching and the blood-letting of warfare' (*Policraticus*, VI, 2: 109). 'The use of the military order' was 'to protect the Church, to attack faithlessness, to venerate the priesthood, to avert injuries to the poor, to pacify provinces, to shed blood (as the formula of their oath instructs) *for their brothers*, and to give up their lives if necessary'. (VI, 8: 116) All soldiers must swear an unbreakable oath 'by God and His

---

[50] *Ibid.*, VI, 1, 107–8.

Christ and by the Holy Spirit and by the majesty of the prince' that 'they will perform with all their energy that which the prince has enjoined; they will never desert the army or refuse to die for the republic'. (VI, 7: 114) Who were these brave warriors? John's answer is highly significant. He peremptorily dismissed feudal knights. 'Someone who does not know how to fight except on a horse,' he wrote, 'is little suited to the army.'

The best soldiers were 'rural plebeians . . . raised under heavens and upon hard work, enduring the sun, indifferent to shade, unfamiliar with bathhouses, ignorant of luxury'. 'The farmer and the fighter are the same', he wrote. Men who used swords and shovels in their daily lives without anyone to tell them what to do made the best diggers, swordsmen, pikemen and bowmen. They were tough, intelligent and good with their hands, but what was most important was their motivation. Such people fought, not for glory, but for love of their native country. It is significant that John prefaced his chapters on 'the armed hand' with some autobiographical reflections on being a 'simple rustic' from Wiltshire.[51] Given his populist constitution of the armed hand, it is not clear which version of rustic simplicity he was invoking. He had a European reputation as a scholar and thinker, so any reference to the proverbial 'thick' peasant could only be ironical. One available implication was that peasants and workers knew things that princes did not. In the English repertoire as it developed in ensuing centuries thick peasants lived next door to *Piers Plowman* and both knew potential rebels for the commonweal. By 1381, most of them were armed.

The prince is their general but John quietly insists throughout his treatise that to avoid falling into tyranny princes must be receptacles of wisdom and counsel emanating from all the members of the political body. A king is distinguished from a tyrant by this precept of precepts: he takes counsel from all the members and creates a synthesis that serves them all. Tyrants – kings who refuse to listen to counsel and allow the commonweal to be used for selfish, factional purposes – can be killed. It was not necessary for John to spell out that a decision by a king to use the armed hand (or any other limb or organ) was legitimate only insofar as it too was deployed in accordance with the disinterested counsel of the whole social body.

---

[51] John described himself as 'a plebeian and uneducated . . . half-rustic man' in *Policraticus*, Book VI, 'Prologue', 103. Hardly: David Knowles, *The Evolution of Medieval Thought* (London 1962), 135, 137, 139, described him as 'the Erasmus, the Johnson of the twelfth century'; he was not, wrote Knowles, 'a professional philosopher or theologian' but could 'criticise his age . . . not as a preparation for acquiring wealth or place or as a niche for academic research, but for a full life of Christian humanism'.

John recommended defensive caution with regard to a prince's use of the armed hand. 'England was equal to applying itself to whatever it might desire' in the arts of war. (VI, 19: 122) Yet recent history suggested that while men of Henry's rank and their mounted knights were 'invincible while roaming abroad', they were 'assailed more readily . . . at [their] own residence'. In their necessarily aggressive early phases, warrior regimes were inclined to neglect the defence of conquered territories. Harold, the last Anglo-Saxon king, was not the best example of a king who knew how to defend his territory, but by the standards of William the Conqueror or Henry II he was still England's last 'native' king and as such could be used to illustrate native wisdom regarding the defence of the territory. Before his defeat at Hastings Harold had led a series of notable victories against Scandinavian invaders in the North-East, and against Welsh threatening from the West. These successes, John explained, involved Harold's use of 'unencumbered' soldiers, drawn from amongst the 'plebeians', to throw back invading 'Britons of Snowdon' (the future Welsh). They imposed the law that 'any Briton (i.e. Welshman) whomsoever, when found with a weapon beyond the boundary which was prescribed for his people, that is, Offa's Dyke, would have his hand cut off by royal officials.' (VI, 6: 114) In John's account of the body politic mnemonic, a king's best allies and friends would not come from the inner circles of the state and ruling classes, but from the subject commonalty. In effect, John was urging his Angevin king to think English, and to look to the English commonalty for the defence of his realm, especially against those arch-enemies the Welsh and Scots.

Patriotism, instinctive, habitual love of country, is the essential virtue. John taught (or tried to teach) Henry II ('the second of that name since the conquest') to think English. It is somewhat puzzling to a modern mind that John described Henry II's now eternally disgraced predecessor, King Stephen, as 'a foreign man', whereas Stephen's predecessors Cnut (who spoke Danish), William Rufus, 'the illustrious Henry [I]' and 'the best king of England', Stephen's vanquisher Henry II, (each of whom spoke a dialect of French) were not. When we consider where these kings were born, their closest followers, their culture and their language, it is not easy to understand why, from a native perspective, they should be considered other than 'foreign'. Yet the 'Duke of Normandy and Aquitaine, foremost as much in the extent of his possessions as in the splendour of his virtues, his vigour, his magnificence, his prudence and the modesty by which he has lived from his infancy', as John put it, was not 'foreign'.

John's favouring of the heart, the armed hand and the feet taught that England's strength was its native population. To *defend* his kingdom and empire, Henry could not rely on heavily armed and ambitious knights.

No-one knew the territory better than those who worked it. Since it was their birthright, no class, if treated with respect, would fight with more passion. John's counsel was essentially populist. If he wanted to keep his kingdom it was now necessary that Henry's victory over King Stephen and his acquisition of the English throne 'will not be ascribed to men of foreign birth'. 'Henry's army . . . principally relied on fellow country-men.' (VI, 18: 121) At a time when the king and his chancellor were preoccupied at the siege of Toulon (1159) it was important to remind them where, in John's populist precept, the kingdom's enduring strength lay. John regarded himself as a subject of Christendom but where the armed hand was concerned he was thinking of England. The alliance he recommended between king and commonalty would be another abiding theme.

The armed hand, in John's conception, was a populist force recruited from the commonalty, motivated by love of country and respect for a king who respected them in return. The ultimate test of the fitness of a body and its capacity to maintain and defend itself was the condition of its feet. It was all too easy for mounted lords to neglect them, but if the feet were neglected the body fell down. The feet were planted in the soil and landscape, tended it, loved it, fed, clothed, housed and generally waited on the upper members, had bred and brought up soldiers to defend the territory, worked in the fields, formed households and neighbourhoods, built the bridges, abbeys, castles, palaces, parish churches, carted and shipped the goods, carved the market crosses and hunted game with bows and arrows on hills and in forests for centuries even though they were forbidden to do so.

When he came to define them his first thought was that 'the feet coincide with peasants perpetually bound to the soil'. Later on he extends this definition: 'The peasants who always stick to the land, looking after the cultivated fields or plantings or pastures or flowers' – husbandmen and gardeners – remained foremost, but the feet also included another very large class of people with vocations other than (or in addition to) husbandry, including 'the many types of weaving and the mechanical arts, which pertain to wood, iron, bronze and the various metals'. As we see in the next chapter, John was writing at a time when the quickening of European commerce was only just beginning to impact on English society. The feet represented the part of the body that invading (mostly male) elites like (in the English case) Romans, Anglo-Saxons, Vikings and Normans had found in possession of the territory, and whose productive and reproductive power made that territory worth invading.

We have noted that when John was writing, a century after the Norman Conquest, the division between an overwhelmingly foreign ruling class and an overwhelmingly native commonalty was at its sharpest. The old English nobility was extinguished and men of foreign birth or parentage were appointed to every position of governance in state and church above the local level. Entry to positions of authority was more or less officially barred to English subjects for several generations. Baronial nativism arose when, for a variety of reasons, the warrior classes decided they needed the active and independent support of the English-speaking commonalty. For the time being, French ruled and English meant subject.

In that context, John's statement that the feet cannot in fact be governed, that they were, for practical reasons, independent and autonomous, is somewhat startling. The 'management' of the vocations of the feet, he wrote, 'does not pertain to the public authorities', even though the whole 'corporate community of the republic derives benefit' from them. In John's formula 'acquiring nourishment', 'the sustenance of life' and 'enlarging the dimensions of family possessions' – essentially what we would call 'economic life' – 'does not pertain to the public authorities'. If the government of the feet did not 'pertain to the public authorities', what did it pertain to? The answer given by the rebels of 1381, 1450, 1536, 1549 and the 1640s, as we shall see, was 'commonweal'. The problem for a twelfth-century formulator of precepts governing the commonalty was that there were 'so many . . . of these occupations that the number of the feet in the republic surpasses not only the eight-footed crab, but even the centipede'. Here, first, was an allusion to the legendary multitudinousness of the commonalty or third estate. They were too many to count. 'One cannot enumerate them on account of their large quantity', wrote John. This was 'not because they are infinitely numerous according to nature', however. They were of the same general species or class of people. The problem was that their vocations were of 'so many varied kinds that no compiler of duties ever produced special precepts for each individual type'. The multitude is a mass not because its members are all the same but because they appear that way to 'authorities' who, by definition, do not understand what they do or how they do it. John allowed for the probability that the feet included as many people of the highest virtue and quality as any other member – and hinted, in his definition of elders, that they may even be the most virtuous of all God's subjects.

The history of the modern state is the history of the development of precepts (laws, offices, modes of analysis) to fill this vacuum between the ruling members and the feet. In John's conception, government of the Feet entailed a formal 'compilation of duties' that did not (and, from John's perspective, it seems, could not) exist. Confronted with the multitude of vocations and occupations upon which his (and all) civilization rested, John gave voice to what, from a modern perspective, is an absence. What came to be called 'economy', the first priority of governments throughout the world in the early twenty-first century, was beyond their brief. This book is an attempt to describe the revolution of governmentality that John had an important part in founding.

Government as John knew it was incapable of monitoring, supervising and administering the literally innumerable households and vocations of the feet. 'Political economy' was an oxymoron. It was not their inherent inferiority, stolidity or stupidity, but a felt moral principle alone that kept 'each one and all' of the vocations of the feet in order. They were not to 'exceed the limits, namely, law, and are to concentrate on the public utility in all matters'. (John here implied the distinction between 'common utility' [*communis utilitas*] and 'common good' [*bonum commune*], in which the former was concerned with means only, the latter with ends, what society or 'the republic' was for.[52]) Rulers could rule by fear but they could only mobilize the human resources of their lordships by winning and sustaining their goodwill and confidence. John's body politic was held together by authority, which could only derive from the moral and emotional conviction of the subject, not the physical force of rulers and ruling classes.[53]

'Remove from the fittest body the aid of the feet', John concluded, and it 'either crawls shamefully, uselessly and offensively on its hands or else is moved with the assistance of brute animals'. It is the duty of the wealthy and powerful 'to put shoes . . . on its workers'. Nothing is more 'ignominious' than a 'barefoot republic'. An impoverished commonalty is 'proof and irrefutable demonstration of the prince's gout'. Only when 'each individual . . . believes [that] what is to his own advantage [is] to be determined by that which he recognises to be most useful for others'

---

[52] The distinction is discussed in M.S. Kempshall, *The Common Good in Late Medieval Thought* (Oxford 1999), 10; Kempshall later suggests that John of Salisbury's usage is 'recognizably Ciceronian', that is to say, expressive of 'the view that *communis utilitas* should be the goal of individual involvement in political society': *ibid.*, 14–16; my contention, of course, is that John tended to work things out for himself. He did his own reasoning and then covered himself by pretending to be merely explaining classical authorities.

[53] For the distinction between power and authority, see Richard Sennett, *Authority* (London 1980). Sennett writes that 'Without ties of loyalty, authority and fraternity, no society as a whole, and none of its institutions, could long function. Emotional bonds therefore have political consequences.' (3) Steve Hindle, *The State and Social Change in Early Modern England, 1550–1640* (Basingstoke 2000), 236, writes that 'More sophisticated analyses of the early modern state . . . recognize the importance of *authority* rather than *power* in securing the ends of governance.' Like Sennett, Hindle distinguishes between 'power', which 'can be maintained by *force*', and 'authority', which 'depends upon some degree of *reciprocity* in that it implies the acceptance by the governed of the legitimacy of their superiors' view.' (Emphases original)

can 'the health of the republic...be secure and splendid'.[54] John of Salisbury's simple, elegant, memorable and immensely powerful vision, and the enduring critique of bad government that follows from it, echoed on through the ensuing centuries.

1.6   Remembering landscape: a story-map of c.1190

The imagination has a history, as yet unwritten, and it has a geography, as yet only dimly seen. History and geography are inextricable disciplines. They have different shelves in the library, and different offices in the university, but they cannot get along for a minute without consulting the other.[55]

It remains to introduce the germ of another mnemonic that was also a common – and developing – theme in the formation of English national consciousness: stories set in a distinctive landscape. Some time around 1190, a monk of Winchester, Richard of Devizes, wrote down a story about 'a certain Jew', living in France, who 'engaged a Christian boy', trained him up in the mystery of shoemaking, and encouraged him to try his fortune in England. He offered the boy a verbal map illuminated and made memorable by colourful prejudices. At its centre was London. The 'commonalty of the Londoners', he suggested, was *tumor plebes, timor regni, tepor sacerdotii*, 'the pride of the commonalty, the dread of the kingdom, the ferment of the priesthood'.[56] 'I warn you', he said,

Whatever of evil or perversity there is in any, whatever in all parts of the world, you will find in that city alone. Go not to the dances of panders, nor mix yourself up with the herds of the stews; avoid the talus and the dice, the theatre and the tavern. You will find more braggadocios there than in all France, while the number of flatterers is infinite. Stage-players, buffoons, those that have no hair on their bodies, Goramites, pick-thanks, catamites, effeminate sodomites, lewd musical girls, druggists, lustful persons, fortune-tellers, extortioners, nightly strollers, magicians, common beggars, tatterdemalions, the whole crew has filled every house. So if you do not wish to live with the shameful, you will not dwell in London.[57]

Although Richard did not say so, Londoners killed local Jews in 1189, anticipating an even more atrocious pogrom in York a few months later. Richard's imagined map of England reverberated with contradictory ironies constructed out of savage popular stereotypes and prejudices.

[54] *Policraticus*, 67.

[55] Guy Davenport, *The Geography of the Imagination: Forty Essays* (London 1984), 4.

[56] Quoted by Stubbs, *Constitutional History*, 1:455; Richard of Devizes, *Chronicle*, trans. J.A. Giles (Cambridge Ontario 2000), 43.

[57] Richard of Devizes, *Chronicle*, 49.

Jews were, repeatedly, popular scapegoats throughout the twelfth century: that century produced the first recorded allegations that Jews tortured and sacrificed Christian children; Richard of Devizes himself is accorded the dubious honour of being the first to use the term 'holocaust' in relation to the 'Jewish problem'. Anti-Semitism, then, was probably a factor in the emergence of national consciousness: it was ground upon which French nobility, Latinate clergy and English populace could make common, if shallow and brutal, common cause: Christians united against others. In the light of contemporary events, Richard's rich French Jew cannot have been expected to have a very favourable view of the country. Accordingly, England's religious centre, Canterbury, was actually an 'assemblage of the vilest' who were cynically 'entirely devoted' to the notorious Archbishop Thomas Becket, 'who has been lately canonized'. The 'vilest' profited from pilgrims but did not share their profits with the commons, who 'die in open day in the streets for want of bread and employment'. Rochester and Chichester were 'mere villages' whose only qualification to the status of a *civitas* was being the seat of a bishopric. Oxford 'scarcely . . . sustains its clerks' and Exeter 'supports men and beasts with the same grain'. Bath 'is placed, or rather buried, in the lowest part of the valleys, in a very dense atmosphere and sulphury vapour, as it were at the gates of hell'. Immigrants would be well advised to avoid 'northern cities' like Worcester, Chester and Hereford 'on account of desperate Welshmen', and York, which 'abounds in Scots, vile and faithless men, or rather rascals'. Ely 'is always putrefied by the surrounding marshes'. Richard assumed that speaking French meant being cultured. 'You will never hear anyone who speaks French' in Durham, Norwich and Lincoln. On the Westside, at Bristol, 'there is nobody who is not, or has not been, a soapmaker'. It was hardly necessary to add that 'every Frenchman esteems soapmakers as he does night[-soil] men'.

Stereotypically, Jews travelled on business more than their Christian neighbours and got to know the greater landscape. Naturally they viewed it as outsiders. Beyond the cities 'every market, village or town, has but rude and rustic inhabitants'. Cornish people were accounted as the Flemish were in France: they failed on two counts, being both foreign and inherently plebeian miners, artisans. 'For the rest, the kingdom itself is generally most favored with the dew of heaven and the fatness of the earth; and in every place there are some good, but much fewer in these all than in Winchester alone.' Winchester was the centre of Richard's England because it was his city, but also perhaps because it was the ancient capital of Wessex. Otherwise he cannot have expected anyone to take his Jew's description of Winchester as 'the city of cities, the mother of all, the best above all' very seriously.

Like any text, Richard's vignette can be interpreted in many ways. The imaginary young man who heard his Jewish master's verbal map would remember that England was a country with plenty of habitual prejudices and sins, not to mention absurd occupations designed to steal an innocent's hard-earned wages. He might misremember which absurdities were associated with which places, but the place-names would provide a structure, a range of choices, and a way of 'remembering' the whole thing. Doubtless a traveller would encounter Welsh people in Hereford and Scots in York. As for Hereford and Worcester being 'northern cities', we must ask 'north in relation to what or whom?' Rome? Jerusalem? Winchester? Cities whose importance would increase – Leicester, Gloucester, Newcastle, Carlisle for example – are not included in this catalogue. Certainly it was useful to know in advance that Ely is essentially an island and that London is home to all the guile and sin of which human beings are capable and therefore likely to attract adventurous young people. I am not certain but I think Richard of Devizes knew he was playing with absurd prejudices.

2   The formation of a constitutional landscape, c.1159–1327

This chapter introduces and explores changes that emerged in the period from John of Salisbury's writing of *Policraticus* to the fall of Edward II. Section 2.1 shows that from c.1150–1250 population doubled, that growth halted in the second half of the thirteenth century and that the reign of Edward II (1307–27) marks the beginning of the long demographic depression of c.1300–c.1550. The argument of this chapter is that most of the themes and structures that shaped English history from the fourteenth to mid-seventeenth centuries were present by the end of 1327. Section 2.2 introduces a theme with strong claims to being the precondition for all the rest. '*Trafike*' was the early modern English word for 'traffic', 'trade' and 'commerce'. Section 2.2 traces the emergence of a commercial landscape grounded in market towns, provincial cities, highways, roads, streets and tracks – and the 'vehicles' (including people and ideas) that kept them functioning. Section 2.3 introduces two more grass roots institutions, one (enterprise and resourcefulness) a tenacious attitude, the other (household and family) the primary locus of reproduction, upbringing, learning and production. Each of the sections introduces an enduring theme or structure, the chapter as a whole stressing the variability and complexity of an aggregative, fluctuating yet accumulative, process.

Having examined the emergence and survival of a tenacious commercial landscape, Section 2.4 describes the emergence of a discourse about what kind of community England was, how the parts should relate to each other, aided by what institutions and in what language. The central theme of this section is the struggle to limit monarchy and the popularization of resistance theory premised on ideas of tyranny and commonweal. Sections 2.5 and 2.6 describe and analyse early indications, in the decades of Simon de Montfort's 'common enterprise' (the 1350s and 1360s), of constitutional debate involving a politically active 'middle' class. Section 2.7 describes the emergence of an armed commonalty and Section 2.8 looks at a political song of the early fourteenth century in which the 'armed hand' of the commons inflicts a humiliating defeat on their putative rulers, foreign 'centaur-warriors'. The idea that kings could be deposed, but only if the whole community agreed, had begun to form, piecemeal, during the 'common enterprise' of the 1250s. Section 2.9 describes the moment when the conjuncture described in earlier sections came together and the enduring public discourse – and tradition – that ensued from it.

2.1   Demographic depression: population trends, 1066–1650

Thinking about society as a human body was a commonplace of the vernacular culture that emerged in the centuries following John of Salisbury. So, too, was visualizing its members in real landscapes, living near real, named towns in real, named villages and hamlets. The body and landscape 'ways of seeing' are recurring themes, clues to developing collective consciousness. In this section we draw on recent work on the historical demography of late medieval and early modern England to answer questions of numbers. To what extent do serial population trends explain other changes that took place over the same period? How big was English 'society' in terms of numbers of individuals, males and females, age-groups, households, villages and towns? How many people made up the feet, hands, arms, shoulders, neck, head, heart and soul of the whole social body? How many kings, barons, knights, esquires, serfs, *liberi homines*, artisans, labourers, merchants and so on? This section uses modern population estimates and calculations to define the *longue durée* retrospectively, as it were. It shows that the English nation-state emerged during a period of extreme demographic depression.

The crisis of fourteenth-century England is one of the oldest documented demographic crises in world history. Between c.1300 and c.1550 CE the population of the world contracted. The causes and effects were variable yet global. The great contraction was not restricted to the well-documented and studied European, British, English and Atlantic branches of human history. What makes the crisis in England and other states of Europe different is that demographic contraction coincided with a slowly but surely evolving intellectual and governmental revolution that generated a progressively increasing body of written information about itself. Written sources make it possible to understand the broad outlines of population change in England since 1066. More work is needed on the conceptual and evidential basis of the various estimates, and new evidence will become available, especially in demography and landscape archaeology. Yet the picture of long-term trends is clearer than it used to be.

How informative are the sources? By the standards of the day, the conquest regimes of Norman-Angevin England were efficient surveyors, assessors and collectors of tribute, as Maitland noted. Even so, the archives of thirteenth to eighteenth-century England yield only more or less accurate estimates. Study of the thirteenth to fifteenth centuries relies heavily on enumerating occasional runs of records relating to especially well-documented manors and estates, and the application of multipliers to dubiously reliable national tax assessments. Parish registers are a crucial new source for measuring trends from 1539 to 1801, the year of the first national census. The key to all demographic studies of periods and places before the Industrial Revolution is analysis of as large a range of contemporary sources as possible. If the range of sources and deductions point to the same general conclusion, it is taken as the best estimate for the whole society. None of this satisfies the requirements of modern statistical assessment and calculation. On the plus side, however, the archives of fourteenth to seventeenth-century England are exceptionally rich compared with any earlier period. If nothing else, they offer a detailed local study of the global population decline of c.1300–c.1550.

It is likely that there were 'fewer [probably well fewer] than 3m people in the 13,278 places recorded in Domesday Book'.[1] Between 1066 and 1300 population doubled – perhaps tripled, if a probable ceiling of two million in 1066 is compared with a high but well argued and evidenced estimate of six million in c.1300. Shortly before 1300 a 'tipping point' was reached in a long-term process by which increasing numbers applied greater and greater pressure to resources, given existing levels of technology and social organization. The boom of the long twelfth century peaked in c.1250, and then, remarkably, held firm for about fifty years. The 'enterprise cycle' of c.1100–c.1250 was to have a shaping influence on subsequent events; from it emerged the landscape that shaped English historical development at least until the eve of the classic Industrial Revolution, and in some parts of England until well into the second half of the twentieth century.

The last fifty years of the Norman-Angevin boom are marked, in traditional narratives, by enduring constitutional arguments, linguistic and conceptual confusion, baronial wars, the colonial enterprises of Edward I and the falling apart of the Angevin state under Edward II. Marked 'signs of saturation'[2] are evident in the apparent shrinkage of local

---

[1] R.H. Britnell *The Commercialisation of English Society 1000–1500* (Cambridge 1993), 5; older estimates involving the application of a multiplier of 4–5 to the *Domesday* figures yielded estimates of 1–1.5 million; Britnell's estimate is on the high side; John Langdon and James Maschael, 'Commercial Activity and Population Growth in Medieval England', *Past and Present* 90 (February 2006), 58, summarize more recent estimates and suggest that 'the figure of 2 million has become something of an orthodoxy among historians in the past generation'.

[2] Langdon and Maschael, 'Commercial Activity and Population Growth', 74.

populations in the first and second decades of the fourteenth century, even earlier. The first dramatic crash came in 1315–22 when a sequence of brutally inclement weather, harvest failure and increased vulnerability of the human and animal population to endemic bacteria decimated England in the Roman sense of that word.[3] Some places show signs of recovery in the 1330s but many do not. The long-standing consensus is that the 'Black Death' of 1348–9 struck an already weakened ecology, stripping away from a third to a half of local populations all over England in a matter of months.

Edward Miller sums up as follows. 'The present state of discussion suggests that a pre-plague population somewhere in the region of 4.5–6 million had been reduced to 2.5–3 million (though some would put the figure as low as 2.2 m) and by the mid fifteenth century to 2–2.5 m (one estimate for c.1430 is only 2.1 m). Recovery, moreover, had not gone far by the 1520s, when the most elaborate calculation gives a result of 2.3 million, although it has been suggested that this figure may be on the low side and that a range of 2.5–2.75 might be preferable.' John Hatcher had not exaggerated when, in an earlier publication, he described the two centuries after 1300 as 'the longest period of declining and stagnant population in recorded English history'.[4] This did not mean that it was the *first* such contraction, viewed in relation to the demographic

---

[3] Many scholars (including the present writer) find Michael Postan's ecological explanation of the demographic collapse broadly convincing: for a summary account, see M.M. Postan, *The Medieval Economy and Society* (Harmondsworth 1978), chs. 1 and 2. Postan 'attracted attention . . . away from approaches that had a strong strain of linear and evolutionary thinking and which had been so characteristic of the late nineteenth century, towards a style of measuring changes in terms of the relationships between resources, population and income. Therefore, given the tendency, as Postan saw it, for population increase in the twelfth and thirteenth centuries to outstrip growth in resources available for the production of food, fuel and clothing, the net effect was an aggregate decline in living standards': Richard M. Smith 'A Periodic Market and its impact on a Manorial Community: Botesdale, Suffolk, and the Manor of Redgrave, 1280–1300' in Zvi Razi and Richard M. Smith (ed.), *Medieval Society and the Manor Court* (Oxford 1996), 450. This explains the dramatic 'pruning' of 1315–22 and 1348–9, but not what ensued. If the ecological crisis model is correct, the pruning of population should have made things better for those who survived. The profound shocks of 1315–22 and 1348–9 were more easily forgotten if life got better for those who remained. Labourers' wages rose rapidly in the 1350s and many rich serfs and *liberi homines* accumulated larger holdings, picking and choosing from the many left unoccupied by visitations of famine and plague. Christopher Dyer, *Making a Living in the Middle Ages: the People of Britain 850–1520* (London 2003), 228–33, is an excellent summary of the 'Great Famine and Agricultural Crisis of 1315–22', which he estimates left 'a half-million dead'. Miri Rubin, *The Hollow Crown: a History of Britain in the Late Middle Ages*, 'Famine', 17–22. Brian Fagan, *The Little Ice Age: How Climate Made History 1300–1850*, (New York 2000), Part I: 'Warmth and its Aftermath', explains the climatic circumstances of the great famine.

[4] John Hatcher, quoted from Edward Miller, 'Introduction: Land and People', in Miller (ed.), *The Agrarian History of England and Wales*, vol.3 1348–1500 (Cambridge 1991), 6.

longue duree. It was the first to be quite fully documented, and thus qualified to enter '*recorded* history'.

The current Director of the Cambridge Group for the History of Population and Social Structure, Richard Smith, is the leading advocate for a more dramatic conception of this decline, involving a higher peak at the beginning and a lower trough at the end of the late medieval slump. On the basis of studies available up to 1991, he concluded that 'a population total substantially higher than 5 millions in 1300 must seriously be entertained'. If the experiences of certain well-documented Essex manors represent the national experience, writes Smith, 'they strongly suggest that the English population total prior to 1310 is very unlikely to have been less than 5.0 million and most probably exceeded 6.0 million.[5] In 2002, Smith drew on a wider range of evidence and deductions to affirm a 'strong case' for 'a national population total significantly in excess of 6 million in 1300'.[6]

A hundred years later it had fallen to no more than 3 million. Losses were not nearly as dramatic through the fifteenth century, but the pattern of stagnation continued 'to a late medieval demographic low point in the 1520s', when a particularly well-documented tax assessment analysed by Roger Schofield and E.A. Wrigley led them to posit 'a population total of c.2.2 million in 1524–5'. On Smith's reckoning, in just over two centuries the population of England fell from just over six to just over two million. If numbers are a measure of quality and demographic decline meant demoralization and depression, England was three times worse off in 1520 than it had been in 1300. In fact it was a much more integrated and interconnected commonwealth that began to show signs of demographic growth in the middle decades of the sixteenth century. The archives of language, literature, religion, constitutional life and economy present a picture of long-term vigour, growth and resourcefulness that is in sharp contrast to the picture of decline and stagnation presented by

---

[5] Smith, 'Demographic developments in Rural England 1300–1348', in Bruce M.S. Campbell (ed.), *Before the Black Death: Studies in the Crisis of the Early Fourteenth Century* (Manchester 1991), 48.

[6] Richard Smith, 'Plagues and Peoples: the Long Demographic Cycle, 1250–1670', in Slack and Ward (ed.), *The Peopling of Britain*, 180–1. Smith continues: 'The (six million) conclusion seems particularly compelling when it is recalled that the national population in 1801 was 8.7 million. Allowance, of course, has to be made for London which by that date had reached 900,000, as well as the substantial urban growth in the industrializing counties of the north and midlands . . . If all the urban settlements exceeding 5,000 were subtracted from the English population in 1801 a population of 6.3 million would remain.' In the light of fragmentary sources, for a range of reasons and in spite of an absence of systematic national data, Smith uses a new application of 'backward projection' to strengthen the conclusion that 'it is unlikely that the total English population in 1300 would have fallen below the non-urban total of the later date.'

the demographers. The demographic 'trough' was also the infancy of the English nation.

The earliest signs of demographic recovery are to be observed in 'three sets of data [that] point towards demographic growth between the 1520s and 1540s'. It was very slow growth and 'was not sustained through the 1550s when at the conclusion of the decade very heavy mortality caused the momentum . . . to be temporarily lost'.

By the 1570s there are signs that population had at last reached, and was beginning to move above, the level of 3 million, at which it most likely stood two centuries earlier. The third quarter of the sixteenth century exhibits some of the fastest and most sustained demographic growth rates of any phase of the parish register era before the late eighteenth century. By 1600 national population totals had risen to 4 million and the following half century saw a further million added to the total number of persons living within the national borders. None the less, in the early seventeenth century growth rates were on the wane and by the 1650s population was stationary. Indeed negative growth rates appear to have characterized the 1650s, 1670s and 1680s, ensuring that the long population cycle had run its course by settling down at a population total that was smaller by at least a million than it had been in the early fourteenth century.[7]

On these estimates the c.1300 population was not reached again until the eve of the Industrial Revolution, around the mid-eighteenth century.[8] It is still unclear whether the tipping point was the famine of 1315–17 (as in Essex) or the first impact of plague in 1348–9 (everywhere). 'By the early fourteenth century a great and growing proportion of the population found itself living in seriously reduced circumstances and ever more prone to crises of subsistence.'[9] Estimates of Black Death mortality range

---

[7] Smith, 'Plagues and Peoples', 183. In 1991 Smith had written that the high estimate for 1300 implied 'a population total [that] would have been equal to and could well have exceeded that which was reached after the next period of sustained demographic growth in the late sixteenth and early-seventeenth centuries. The more refined and firmly based estimates for the later period suggest that an English population of 5.2 million was achieved in the 1650s and that it was not until the 1760s that the population exceeded 6 million. Are we to suppose that the 'equilibrium' level of the early fourteenth century was a million greater than in the mid-seventeenth century? This possibility has seriously to be entertained. At present we can only speculate on reasons for the probable higher equilibrium level population in 1300 compared with that of 1600 or 1650. One highly plausible contributory factor may be the much lower level of urbanization in the earlier period. Recent estimates show that the proportion of the population resident in towns above 10,000 more than tripled between c.1500 and c.1650 when national population approximately doubled. Much of this relative decline in the non-urban share of the population was a product of London's remarkable growth so that by 1650 (sic.) it approached 200,000 and by 1650 was close to 400,000 when the national populations were 4.1 and 5.2 million respectively . . .': Smith, 'Demographic Developments', 50–1.

[8] Smith, 'Demographic Developments', 50–1; Edward Miller, 'Introduction: Land and People', 7.

[9] Bruce M.S. Campbell, 'The Agrarian Problem in the Early Fourteenth Century', *Past and Present*, no. 188 (August 2005), 3–4.

from 35–45 per cent, and in some places it was undoubtedly higher.[10] Further epidemics in 1361–2, 1369, 1375 and 1390 reduced the total to less than 3 million by c.1400. The downward trend continued less dramatically in the fifteenth century, to as little as 2–2.5 million by 1450.[11] Recovery began between c.1530 and c.1560. After what may have been a considerable set-back in the 1540s, caused by a very severe and general epidemic of influenza, overall growth, somewhat reduced in its impact by colonization and migration during the seventeenth century, continued thereafter. Between c.1550 and c.1800 population tripled. Growth began again, yet the pre-plague total may not have been passed until the eighteenth century.

The nucleus of the English explosion came together in a period marked by *declining* population. The movement was not a function of size and secular population trends. The remaining sections of this chapter will show that what made the difference were complex and densely interconnected forms of conflict and collective organization.

2.2   Signs of life: *trafike*

In the two centuries after the conquest of 1066 England was reorganized from above. The lords of Norman-Angevin England created what was, in effect, a new landscape by developing existing patterns of settlement and communication and complementing them with new institutions that would make government and surplus-extraction more fruitful and efficient. They built into and emphasized already existing frameworks and strengthened traditional Anglo-Saxon solutions to the problems of governing (e.g. taxing and mustering) a dispersed agrarian population. This section emphasizes the long-term significance of the emergence, by the second half of the thirteenth century, of a national network of market towns. The meaning of the records of this movement is disputed. Were the conquerors the innovators, as the dates of charters marking the institutionalization of markets and boroughs suggest? Or did charters institutionalize popular places of meeting and exchange within the districts and provinces served by the markets and boroughs? What is clear is that the total population at least doubled between 1100 and c.1290 and that production and trade also intensified considerably. The new lords of England were able to cash in on and develop one of the most productive and interconnected realms of its size in Europe.

---

[10] Dyer, *Making a Living*, 233, writes that 'it would be reasonable to estimate the death rate in 1348–9 at about half the English population'.

[11] Miller, 'Land and People', 1–7.

The broad pattern of the landscape they remodelled was present before they came, but in the course of the twelfth and thirteenth centuries they marked it out in stone churches, minsters, cathedrals, castles, abbeys and a thousand other more or less monumental buildings.[12] Specialists in the colonization of under-exploited territory were brought in, founding or strengthening many powerful abbeys. Strategic provincial towns were clothed in stone, some granted borough status, others placed under the lordship of a regional magnate, usually an abbot. Such towns linked provinces into longer-distance lines of communication with regional capitals like York, Norwich, Southampton, Exeter, Bristol and Gloucester. The towers and spires of thousands of churches came to form a buzzing network connected by streams and rivers of *trafike* ("traffic" or "trade") and *comunycacon* ("communications") to the twin capitals on the Thames, London and Westminster. London and Westminster became two distinct places, both "capitals", one of the *regnum*, the other of the commonwealth.

In the long run England's demographic experience after the Black Death did not significantly erode 'structures' that existed by c.1300.[13] Labouring families died in greater numbers than any other class: the power of increasingly scarce *proletarii* was enhanced. The late medieval decline inevitably reduced the number of labourers and tenants drastically, resulting, by c.1400, in a 'wide-ranging revision in patterns of estate organisation which had dominated England during the previous centuries'.[14] Demand for labour exceeded supply for nearly two centuries. The first plague seems to have affected adults; those that followed had a disproportionate impact on infants and children.[15] Mortality was higher among the smallholding and landless classes than among richer villagers and the ruling classes.[16] The initial impact on age-groups responsible for child-rearing and local government must, in itself, have had a

---

[12] For an excellent summary account of this 'great rebuilding', cf. Langdon and Maschael, 'Commercial Activity and Population Growth', 50–3 and notes 53–63.

[13] By 'structures' I mean 'the socially-determinate results of past human actions repeated on a regular basis sufficient to determine certain behavioural forms and social practices'. Any 'understanding of human action must take human beings as possessing intentions, beliefs and desires . . .': John Haldon, *The State and the Tributary Mode of Production* (London 1993), 28. In my interpretation structures include antecedent ideas and language usages.

[14] Miller, 'Land and People', p.1.   [15] *Ibid.*, p. 7.

[16] Smith, 'Demographic Developments', pp. 60–1; Dyer, *Making a Living*, 230–1, writes that 'wage-earners were doubly hard hit' by the famine of 1315–22 and notes 'a shift in the attitudes of those in authority. As their incomes diminished, they felt threatened by the poor, reduced their charitable giving, and were not prepared to tolerate or condone misbehaviour by the lower orders'.

distressing effect everywhere, but life had to go on for those who survived. Miller notes a 'profound modification of village society' between 1350 and 1450. That was so in some places, but overall geographic structures, routine movements and habits of mind established in the twelfth and thirteenth centuries proved their strength in changed circumstances. Local studies suggest that underlying social structures remained after 1349 what they had been before.

While the master-classes were affected and village priests endured particularly heavy mortality, the survival chances of the relatively wealthy were better than those of the relatively poor. Labour intensive arable farming was largely abandoned on demesnes by 1400. The proportion of sheep to people increased; wool prices were low throughout the fifteenth century; more wool was produced than could be absorbed by export markets and native cloth production.[17] Tenants and labourers became progressively more truculent with regard to their lords; there was a 'new fluidity in landholding', and 'intensified mobility is very evident in the late fourteenth and throughout the fifteenth century'.[18] There was a continuing drift of poor, enterprising and ambitious people to some towns: Richard Smith estimates the proportion of people in 1300 living in towns with populations greater than 10,000 in 1300 as 3–5 per cent, rising to 6 per cent in 1600 and 10.8 per cent in 1650.[19]

The demographic collapse halted the *trafike* in the worst years and places, but the commercial framework established by 1250 continued to structure long-term development. One sign of life in the age of demographic depression was an unmistakeable 'growth in the quantity of trade'. In spite of the dramatic population decline people 'became *increasingly* dependent upon market transactions as a rising share of goods and services were supposedly purchased and sold for cash'.[20] 'By almost any interpretation the economy was more commercialised in 1300 than in 1000', writes R.H. Britnell. The speed and volume of *trafike* depends on the criteria we use, but the general movement is clear enough. 'The decades either side of 1300 were outstanding for the volume of commerce and the quantity of currency in circulation.' Yet by 1500 'the volume of

---

[17] Miller, 'Land and People', 13.   [18] *Ibid.*, 17.

[19] Smith, 'Demographic Developments', 61–2 notes that at the high point of medieval population an increasing number of people had difficulty in obtaining a tenancy, thus leading to a movement towards towns; that the poor represented by far the greatest number of people living in towns is suggested at Norwich, where, of a population of 16–25,000, only 418 persons contributed to the subsidy of 1332.

[20] James Maschael, 'The Multiplicity of Medieval Markets Reconsidered', *Journal of Historical Geography* 20 (1994), 452.

trade and currency *per capita* was *larger* than two centuries earlier and . . . a larger proportion of total output was produced for sale'.[21]

The capacity of the commonwealth to sustain and even expand production for the market in a period of dramatic population decline was a function of its ability to keep an antecedent system going with a much smaller population and adapt it to changing circumstances. Urbanization is a major index of commercialization. 'Urban populations were larger (in 1300) than at any other period of the Middle Ages', writes Britnell, 'and the number of markets and fairs was at its height'.[22] Yet measuring urbanization by the number of people resident in towns with populations in excess of 10,000, 5,000 or even 1,000 excludes the most pervasive institutions of grass-roots commerce. The founding (or revival), development and institutionalization of market towns would prove to be the decisive enterprise of the twelfth-century boom. Ways of life previously associated with geographically concentrated cities spread across the whole kingdom. The emergence of a national network of interconnected local market towns with resident populations much lower than conventional horizons of urban measurement helps to explain the explosion – and, above all, the depth – of national public opinion that will be the subject of Chapter 3 and a recurrent theme of subsequent chapters. The survival and, in many cases, the expansion of larger towns and cities was also critical, but the depth of commerce in commodities and ideas was premised on the emergence of local market towns. That said, what ensured the vigour and depth of the system was not merely the structure itself (for that existed in parts of France and the Low Countries) but the intensity and quality of routine sociability, mobility, meeting and exchange – and the emergence of a common language.

The commercial landscape that created and served England up to and beyond the Industrial Revolution was in place by the end of the thirteenth century. The topic is well researched. Between 1200 and 1349 the number of markets ratified by royal and baronial grants tripled. A survey of market references for a sample covering 55 per cent of England's surface shows that from 1200–1350 '329 documented early markets' tripled to 1002. Nationally, '600 markets in c.1200 had increased to 1800 or more'.[23] The implication is that very few people alive in or after 1300 did not live near and routinely travel to and from a market town. Living near a market town meant being connected into regional networks

---

[21] Britnell, *Commercialisation of English Society*, 228.
[22] Britnell, *Commercialisation of English Society*; Edward Miller and John Hatcher, *Medieval England: Towns, Commerce and Crafts 1086–1348* (London and New York 1995), 274–9.
[23] Maschael, 'Medieval Markets Reconsidered', 453.

which were routinely interconnected into national networks. It has been shown that markets established after c.1250 had less chance of surviving. The structural roots of a national system of *trafike* and exchange were in place by 1300.[24]

2.3   Elementary particles: enterprise and the resourceful family

When the twelfth-century boom began to lose momentum, the dynamic, articulated landscape within which the next phase of English historical development would take place had been created. Although John Langdon and James Maschael do not address the functioning of this landscape in the fourteenth and fifteenth centuries, their new 'theoretical formulation connecting commercialization and population' in the boom centuries before 1300 has implications for the ensuing two centuries of demographic depression. In their view we now know enough about geographical, economic and social development in twelfth- and thirteenth-century England to 'ask whether there might be a particular "DNA" for economic development, so that it will grow according to its own internal precepts despite myriad outside forces acting upon it'. The challenge for Crick and Watson was to constitute a structure capable of encompassing all that was known about microbiology.[25] Langdon and Maschael sketch out the 'internal precepts' of the twelfth-century boom and focus on two 'mechanisms, so far largely ignored' by historians that were 'of particular relevance to medieval commercialization'.[26]

The first is 'entrepreneurship'. In Joseph Schumpeter's famous model economic growth is generated by the 'recognition of sizeable profits to be made in a promising new set of technological and commercial endeavours'.[27] Earlier generations of economic historians – the great George Unwin especially – would not have been surprised to find entrepreneurs and the spirit of enterprise in thirteenth- and fourteenth-century England.[28] Langdon and Maschael affirm that 'although [enterprise theory] is . . . more often associated with modern economies . . . it

---

[24] *Ibid.*, 461–3.
[25] See James D. Watson, *The Double Helix: a Personal Account of the Discovery of the Structure of DNA* (New York 1968).
[26] Langdon and Maschael, 'Commercialization and Population Growth', 37.
[27] See Joseph Schumpeter, *The Theory of Economic Development* (1934; New Brunswick 2004).
[28] R.H. Tawney (ed.), *Studies in Economic History: the Collected Papers of George Unwin* (London 1927) is the best introduction to the grand sweep of Unwin's historical vision; for enterprising merchants, see George Unwin, 'The Estate of Merchants', in his *Finance and Trade under Edward III* (Manchester 1918).

also has relevance for the medieval period'.[29] The first great cycle of enterprise was exhausted by 1300, when the system shows many 'signs of saturation'.[30] The network of stone churches, market towns, mills, bridges, minsters, cathedrals, castles, settlements, provincial and county towns, regional cities like Bristol, Norwich, York and Exeter, the twin cities on the Thames, London and Westminster, and the tracks, highways and routines that interconnected them, had become, by then, the constitutive landscape of English life. My contention is that this landscape would prove to be not only extremely durable, but that it was the basis of the whole system and would remain so until the eve of the classic Industrial Revolution. The hypothesis will need qualification. There were further auspicious accumulations in the centuries from 1300 to 1750. In the forefront were precociously capitalist hot-spots like the innumerable centres of cloth making for export, the lead mining communities of the Derbyshire Peak, iron workers in the Forest of Dean and the Sussex Weald and coal miners in places like Kingswood Chase, near Bristol, and Whickham in Northumberland.[31] Yet a disproportionate amount of the energy that drove the *trafike* in commodities, services, government and ideas was generated in the nurturing environments of local marketing districts. The enterprise came out of the same milieu that created 'middle' English: the milieu premised on the ubiquitous market town. The most significant long-term adaptation of this constitutive landscape in the 'depressed' fourteenth and fifteenth centuries concerned the rise in certain towns and districts of dispersed 'rural' industry.[32]

Secondly, Langdon and Maschael stress the agency of family formations in the economic 'DNA' of thirteenth-century England. They ask 'how the reproductive site of society – that is, the family – reacted to

---

[29] 'The healthy revenues or profits realized by the first wave of entrepreneurs encourage others to join in, thus creating a period of economic boom. Eventually however the competitive edge provided to the first set of entrepreneurs by the new technical or commercial inputs is eroded, as more and more investors seek to share in the prosperity and as demand reaches a level of surfeit. Over time profit margins dwindle and the economic boom loses momentum as investment confidence declines or even collapses. Future economic development must wait until a new set of technological innovations or economic reformulations occur to fire the enthusiasm of a new generation of investors and trigger a new economic surge': Langdon and Maschael, 'Commercial Activity and Population Growth', 38–9.

[30] *Ibid.*, 74.

[31] For clothmaking, see Chapter 6; J.U. Nef, *The Rise of the British Coal Industry* (Oxford 1932); Cyril Hart, *The Free Miners of the Forest of Dean* (Gloucester 1953); David Levine and Keith Wrightson, *The Making of an Industrial Society: Whickham 1560–1765* (Oxford 1991); Andy Wood, *The Politics of Social Conflict: the Peak Country 1520–1770* (Cambridge 1999); Michael Zell, *Industry in the Countryside: Wealden Society in the Sixteenth Century* (Cambridge 1994).

[32] See below, Chapter 6.

commercialization'. On current data there is a contradiction in the thirteenth century between evidence of rising population and evidence of declining real wages. If the wages of individuals were falling, as existing data suggests they were, 'optimism about being able to make one's way in the world – or to support a family – should have been similarly falling'. Other things being equal, falling wages should have led to population decline a century earlier than in fact was the case. The solution to this paradox is 'that "real wages" – based on the daily wages of *individuals* – may not be the vital indicator that so much recent literature has taken them to be. Rather the yearly incomes of families . . . were probably much more critical in determining well-being and social inclinations concerning family formation.' Individual wages were relatively unimportant compared to a multi-income unit in which all the members contributed to a common pot. Whilst individual wages may have fallen in the thirteenth century, they argue, 'opportunities for family earnings rose, either through producing for the market or working for wages'.[33]

As the economic boom of the long twelfth century began to slow and population growth ceased, the employment market contracted and more individuals competed for progressively lower wages. Families who worked together for the common good were able to maintain a common standard of living higher than they could have achieved as individuals. As the economy began, slowly and unevenly, to contract, families and households closed ranks to improve the conditions and chances of their members. They worked for each other. In this model family solidarity, however pragmatic its reasons, was at least as important to wage-dependent members of the commonalty as it was to the less dependent (in the prevailing convention) husbandmen, yeomen and lords of various rank to whom they had to sell their labour. Langdon and Maschael argue that what we might term (following Pam Sharpe) the 'resourcefulness' of families predominantly dependent on wages held up their standard of living through half a century of declining personal wages – a resistance that only collapsed, possibly quite rapidly, after c.1300.[34]

Families and households were pivotal institutions of English life throughout the period examined in this book and beyond. Love and loyalty to kin (although not only to kin), or regret or despair at its absence, was a key emotion, a key to 'commonweal'. If things went well in families they went well elsewhere. The English family was a patriarchy that

---

[33] Langdon and Maschael,'Commercial Activity and Population Growth', 41–2.

[34] Pamela Sharpe, *Population and Society in an East Devon Parish: Reproducing Colyton, 1540–1840* (Exeter 2002), esp. Chapter 4, 'Resourcefulness: Farming a Wood-Pasture Economy'.

allowed for the fact that many families and households were actually headed by a woman. In William Tyndale's formulae, matriarchy was, theoretically, a subordinate form of patriarchy. Whatever their form, if families habitually fell apart in violent conflict and contention, it was the sign of signs of dissolution of the kingdom and commonweal. If families were stable and nurturing the commonweal was safe. It was a culture with strong and abiding ideas of love – the spirit in which God wanted people to relate to each other. The quality of family life is critical in the bringing up of children. Other contexts, notably the native emphasis on personality, conscience and individual vocation, played a central part in the formation of modern English constitutional culture, as we shall see. But we must never forget family as a central *affective* institution, not only of reproduction and socialization, but also, as Langdon and Maschael imply, of production.

Another reason for emphasizing the history of families and households, as Langdon and Maschael say, is that it 'puts human agency, whether in an entrepreneurial role or in working out family strategies for the well being of its members, much more to the forefront of the research agenda'.[35] The *quality* of family life has not received enough attention. The least that can be said in justification of this kind of family history is that it builds from a core of common sense. There are exceptions to every rule where human beings are concerned, but all other things being equal, individuals from strong, self-supporting, loyal families will succeed more easily (however 'success' is defined) than those without such support. We should not idealize too far: prejudice and nepotism are also passed on in families. I think that this can be taken to have been the case throughout the period explored in these pages. That said, it was also continuously true that family formation and maintenance of a household was a more difficult and chancy business for landless labourers than for their landed neighbours.

In one of the most rigorous studies produced by the new social history of early modern England, Pamela Sharpe teases out the *quality* that was common to all the households she studied, at all levels of local society: she calls it 'resourcefulness'. Establishing, maintaining and improving a household were lifelong enterprises. The desire to create, sustain and increase a household was the norm that underpinned the enterprise and resourcefulness its individual members expressed. At most levels and in most cases adult members had to contribute or leave. Doubtless 'family' sentiment often interfered with the operation of this precept in different cases, but it was the bottom line for the vast majority of English people throughout the period covered by this book. England was a culture of

---

[35] Langdon and Maschael, 'Commercial Activity and Population Growth', 81.

households in a landscape because the household was the unit of production, reproduction and socialization. It was also, for most people, its affective centre.

2.4   Circling the king: the birth of resistance theory

And then come the lords of the realm, with all their counsellors, unto [the king] and said to him of his misgovernance and extortion that he had done, made and ordained, to oppress all the common people, and also all the realm; wherefore all the common people of his realm would have him deposed of his kingdom; and so he was deposed.[36]

King, they thought, was but a title of the highest honour, which gentleman, knight, baron, earl, duke, were but steps to ascend to . . .[37]

The first three sections of this chapter have been concerned with some abiding structures of the commonweal: numbers, landscape, traffic, commerce, resourceful families and households, industrious villages, neighbourhoods, manufacturing and mining communities. This commonweal was a source of energies that the state could rarely control, as John of Salisbury had insisted. The 'feet' had a collective mind of their own. We must now consider another crucial aspect of the community-making process: traditional constitutional history, the history of the state and the power elites and their relations with the ruled. Historians of early modern England and the American colonies often assume that resistance theory – the idea that subject populations have a right and a duty to resist oppressive states and ruling classes – was born in the sixteenth century. This section will show that it is not a question of which of two versions of kingship (absolute and political) is correct, but of noting that by the thirteenth century different people and classes were continuously aware of the existence and power of both versions.[38]

In one of the most important contributions to the subject since Marc Bloch's *Feudal Society*, English medievalist Susan Reynolds describes the community-creating impulse in one region of the world a thousand years ago.[39] Reynolds's starting point marks an *evidential* watershed. It refers to a period and place when the modern states of France and England began to emerge as distinctive nations. After c.900 written records associated

---

[36] F.W.D. Brie (ed.), *The Brut or The Chronicles of England* (London 1906), 359.

[37] Thomas Hobbes, *Behemoth: the History of the Causes of the Civil Wars of England*, ed. William Molesworth (London 1840), 7.

[38] See Gerald Harriss, *Shaping the Nation: England 1360–1461*, (Oxford 2005), 1–6.

[39] Marc Bloch, *Feudal Society*, trans. L.A. Manyon, 2 vols. (London 1975); Susan Reynolds, *Kingdoms and Communities in Western Europe, 900–1300* (Oxford 1992), 257, suggests (citing Regino of Prum [c.900]) that people of the time thought in terms of 'different *peoples*' (my emphasis) that differed 'between themselves in descent, manners, language and laws'. All ideas of community were grounded in a vague but pervasive 'idea of a people as a community of custom, law and descent'.

with state-formation begin to offer more direct evidence of how people of the time saw and thought about the worlds they inhabited. Professor Reynolds deduces the types of communities created by the activities of the people who lived, worked and defended these territories: parishes, neighbourhoods, villages, towns, lordships, provinces and '*countreys*' and 'communities of the realm'. Reynolds's view is that as early as the tenth to thirteenth centuries 'it was the fact of being a kingdom (or some lesser, but effective, unit of government) and of sharing a single law and government which promoted a sense of solidarity among its subjects and made them describe themselves as a people'.[40] In this section I use the framework of William Stubbs's classic *Constitutional History of England* to introduce the theme of 'court- and kingdom-centred history' and its limits.

For Stubbs the impulse for constitutional (as against absolutist) forms of government 'show[ed] itself first in the lower ranges of society and [rose] by slow degrees and unequal impulses towards the higher'.[41] His view that English constitutionalism was ultimately Germanic ('Anglo-Saxon') rather than Roman or Celtic had been an axiom of English popular identity since the sixteenth century. Anglo-Saxon constitutionalism was not state-centred like Rome, or nobility-centred like the Celts, but dispersed, local, community-based. The 'constitutional' impulse from below survived the Norman Conquest and would re-emerge later; but for two centuries, as we have seen, the conquest regimes practised effective 'enslavement of the subject population'. The 'kingdom' and 'regnum' became centred, as in Reynolds's conception, not on the dispersed communities, but on the king's household. Modern English constitutional history thus became, in Stubbs's model, king- and court-centred. Kingship already had a long history in England, but the turning-point for Stubbs was 'the terrible discipline of anarchy, prolonged for twenty years' under Stephen (1135–54). Stubbs's vision is basically the one learned by schoolchildren in England and its settler-societies throughout the nineteenth and twentieth centuries. Stephen was defeated by a strong king, Henry II, whose reforms, symbolized in the 'constitutions of Clarendon', inaugurated a centralizing process in which English institutional life, and its political community, took shape in what Stubbs envisioned as 'circles around the king'.

'It is from the person, the household, the court and council of the king that all constitutional power radiates,' wrote Stubbs. Writing in the 1880s, Stubbs thought that 'in very many respects both the machinery

---

[40] Reynolds, *Kingdoms and Communities*, 253.
[41] William Stubbs, *The Constitutional History of England* (1897; repr. New York 1967), 1: 4, 6, 11, 91, 103, 366.

and the terminology of government bear, down to the present day, marks of their origin in the domestic service of the palace'.[42] Concerning the *limits* of monarchical sovereignty, Stubbs followed the great tradition that he associated with the fifteenth-century author, Sir John Fortescue. In this view English kings were 'elected', and had to take an 'oath of good government' at their coronations. Kingship in general 'combined all the powers of national sovereignty' but as Fortescue defined it, English kingship was *dominium politicum*, not *dominium regale*. It was at first more a matter of practice and practicality than principle. 'Perfunctory as . . . the forms of election and coronation were,' according to Stubbs, 'they did not lose . . . real importance.' They 'furnished an important acknowledgement of the rights of the nation, as well as recognition of the duties of the king.' King Stephen, for example, was replaced by the Empress Matilda 'by renunciation of homage, by absolution of the oath of allegiance, and by a declaration that the rights conferred by consecration had been forfeited'.

Some historians have doubted Stubbs's provenance of the idea that kings could be legitimately 'set aside'. In suggesting that the 'principle' was 'kept prominently before the eyes of the people' by 'competition for the throne' Stubbs seemed to qualify the idea that 'Germanic' constitutionalism was somehow inherent. What is at issue is the question of whether we are dealing with an abiding – in Stubbs's usage potentially racial – principle that was passed from generation to generation and would always and inevitably define and resist arbitrary kingship and lordship. Or was English constitutional culture the accidental, incremental outcome of contingent resistances? Two leading constitutional historians, H.G. Richardson and G.O. Sayles, once observed that Stubbs's vision of English constitutional development was 'haunted by two ghosts'. In their influential view, 'the ghost of a mythical Germanic past of free institutions', for Stubbs, conjured 'the ghost of an imaginary constitution which the king is required to respect'. These ghosts allegedly 'prevented (Stubbs) from considering the facts objectively and . . . from setting down a plain history of institutions such as they appeared in contemporary documents'.[43] English history had been haunted by 'Anglo-Saxon' populist-communitarianism myth long before Stubbs, and still is.[44] It is not necessarily racialist, however; such a principle, if such

---

[42] Stubbs, *Constitutional History*, 1:319, 363, 366.

[43] H.G. Richardson and G.O. Sayles, *The Governance of Medieval England from the Conquest to Magna Carta* (Edinburgh 1963, 22–3, cited in Robert Livingstone Schuyler, 'History and Historical Criticism: Recent Work of Richardson and Sayles', *Journal of British Studies* 3:2 (May 1964), 3.

[44] See below, Chapter 3.2.

it was, may have been the collective ideological outcome of a dispersed landscape of necessarily communalist villages or, as we saw in the previous sections, marketing districts.

The idea of a greater community of which kingship was only a part or member was central to John of Salisbury's vision. It emerged as a force in constitutional struggles in the thirteenth and fourteenth centuries, against the grain of 'Angevin confidence in a royal immunity of coercion without law'.[45] Subsequent generations of scholars disclosed an ever richer, more complex, picture without seriously weakening the authority of Stubbs's central assertion. No writer after John of Salisbury went as far as to say that kings adjudged to be tyrants should be violently resisted and even killed; yet most generations after c.1250 behaved as if it were so.

Stubbs thought the Normans (and their successors, the Angevins) conquered a nation shaped by traditions of communitarian populism; like the English language, they were brought to England by waves of Germanic invaders. This essentially 'bottom up' (or reciprocal) constitutionalism was superseded as an influence in the history of the English by top-down Angevin state-building. Although the contingencies of King Stephen's fall were 'meant to serve a temporary purpose', they remained 'on record as an important statement of principle'. England was, by ancient custom and usage, a kingdom, but the idea that kings who failed to rule competently and administer justice in a way that was satisfactory to the people could be disciplined and even perhaps deposed was, in Stubbs's view, established by precedent.[46] What emerged was a pattern in which the kingdom or state was habitually evaluated in relation to what would later be referred to as the *commonweal*. In the centuries that concern us here, the vague and general 'common good' became incorporated into the accumulating specificities of the English *commonweal*.

Medieval kingship has been seen as incorporating two 'bodies', one mortal and fallible, the other eternal and sacred.[47] This idea served many purposes and had many expressions. One of its potential implications was that while the institution of monarchy was indispensable, individual kings could be deposed. As the epigraph at the beginning of this section implies, the view that came to dominate baronial discourse in the thirteenth century, and was etched into collective memory by the events of 1327, was that rebellion against kings was justified if the whole community

[45] J.E.A. Jolliffe, *Angevin Kingship* (London 1953, repr. 1970), 116.
[46] Stubbs, *Constitutional History*, 1:366–7.
[47] Ernst H. Kantorowicz, *The King's Two Bodies: a Study in Mediaeval Political Theology* (Princeton 1957), is the classic account; Harriss, *Shaping the Nation*, 5.

agreed. The questions left hanging were (1) how it was to be established what the 'whole community' was, and (2) that it, or a majority of it, was agreed on a particular course of action. These would be central problematics of constitutional discourse in England from the thirteenth to seventeenth centuries.

Rebellions of the thirteenth to seventeenth centuries were directed against the misrule of particular kings, but they were never republican in the modern sense of a polity without a monarch. Not until the late 1640s was a republic without monarchy seriously imagined by a significant number of people, or widely advocated in public. Until sixteenth-century humanists appropriated it for their own purposes, and placed it in classical contexts, the English word 'commonweal' never meant anything like 'republic' in this modern sense. The popular rebels of 1381, 1450, 1536 and 1549 took for granted that the English *commonweal* was and should always remain a monarchy. The ranks between the monarch and the commonalty never had anything like the 'aura' or 'charisma' of the monarchy, and were routinely downright unpopular.

At the time of *Magna Carta* (1215), the first 'circle around the throne' was occupied by the great officers of the king's household, providing the Norman-Angevin kings 'with the first elements of a ministry of state'. The 'second circle' was 'the great court or council' formed, at first, by the *sapientes* – literate, Latinate clerics with special skills required in domestic and foreign affairs. The employment of clerics without personal estates was resented by secular lords, who demanded that they be assimilated into 'the symmetry of the baronage', forming an inner house of the 'second circle' comprising secular lords, bishops and abbots. This was Stubbs's explanation of the origins of what became the Counsel or House of Lords. The baronial movement from the mid-twelfth century until about 1327 was about defining the limits of the royal power unleashed by Henry II's institutional strengthening of Norman practices. Those reforms drew in and began the institutionalization of the middle ranks of the localities, the amorphous juror-class, establishing what seemed like a direct link between the commonalty and the king that threatened to by-pass intermediate authorities and jurisdictions. This deeply threatened the barons and the Church. During the thirteenth century the barons asserted themselves as leaders of the community of the realm in movements to rein in the ambitions of the Angevin kings. Under Edward III the peers of the realm became an institution. The alliance of king and commonalty became natural for kings and commoners alike. If only because kings were distant lords, the people would naturally have preferred to be without the lords in between. It would mean, in effect, less external governance.

For Stubbs, the fact that the conquerors now realized a mutual interest with the leaders of local communities did not give commoners very much constitutional or political influence. 'The number of persons who were really consulted on business, or to whom the show of such attention was paid, must have been always very limited', he wrote:

> As both earlier and later, only the highest class was called on to treat of the highest matters; the people, if they were called at all, would hear and obey. And thus the constituent parts of the assembly are reduced to the archbishops, bishops, abbots, earls, barons and knights.

Stubbs's view was that throughout English constitutional history up to the nineteenth and twentieth centuries, 'only the highest class was called'. Two points can be made in qualification. First, conceptions of 'the highest class' changed. They became more precise, but they also represented a long-term deepening and broadening of the 'officer' or 'ruling' class. Second, while only those persons defined by authority as being of that class were 'called', those who were not called also participated in government in the sense that they played significant roles in the streets and neighbourhoods of the scattered commonalty. Individuals from this class played leading roles in local politics, and were prominent in the leadership of major rebellions. As Stubbs wrote, they were not called; they came anyway. In this sense, the constitutional movement from above instituted by the Norman-Angevin hegemony entailed local responsibility and empowerment, even if that had not been its intention.

Stubbs drew a sharp line between the classes encompassed within the inner 'circles around the throne' and the 'extensive portion of the population' below, the *liberi homines* and *sokemanni*, whom he regarded as equivalent to the medieval and early modern freeholders.[48] They came with the land. For two or three generations, Normans and their continental allies saw the indigenous majority in class terms, defining it in terms of 'immunities from the warlike life' of the nobility and freemen, and regarding the *nativi* as 'despicable for ignorance and coarseness'.

---

[48] Stubbs believed that the role of the senior ranks of the commonalty was for the most part marginal to politics and policy making. Legally they were called by the will of the king and could be immediately dismissed by him. They could petition but not demand, or question command personnel. Persons below the senior ranks of the commonalty were by definition not involved in government. Because they were excluded from policy and government, they were inconsequential. As for numbers, *Domesday Book* attested the existence of 'more than 25,000 *servi*, . . . 82,000 *bordari*, . . . nearly 7,000 *cotari* and *cotseti* and nearly 110,000 *villani*'. These numbers must be multiplied to allow for the families of the men they counted. In the long term, the tendency of Norman jurists was to reduce 'the minute distinctions of Anglo-Saxon dependence . . . into the *class* of *nativi*'.

The symbolic turning-point was *Magna Carta*. 'The Great Charter is the first great public act of the nation, after it has realised its own identity...', he wrote. 'The whole of the constitutional history of England is little more than a commentary on Magna Carta.'[49] For Stubbs, the great charter signified that the 'common enterprise' was on its way. In response to the enduring idea that warring barons, churchmen and kings were utterly indifferent to any interests but their own, he asserted that 'the demands of the barons were no selfish exaction of privilege'. Section 61 explicitly obliged barons to redress any wrongs that might, at the time or in the future, be committed by kings, 'together with the community of the entire country'. In cases of corrupt government the whole community under the leadership of the lords was required to 'distress and injure (the king) in all ways possible – namely by capturing our castles, lands and possessions ... until they secure redress according to their own decision, saving our person and our queen and ... our children'. As long as we accept the seminal importance of *Magna Carta* (a magnificent if not unambiguous source of information relating to the condition of the kingdom of England in the early thirteenth century), we must conclude that it made it the duty of the barons to lead popular resistance against unjust or incompetent kings.

Magna Carta constituted a community greater than the kingdom. It was not legal to do physical injury to or incarcerate a king or his family; the question of deposition was left hanging. The clause cannot have been understood as other than a diminution of kingship. 'Resistance theory' (the assumption that a people or commonwealth has a right and duty to oppose tyrannous, corrupt kings and lords) is much older than the sixteenth century. The American Revolution inherited resistance theory from the text and social contexts of *Magna Carta*. In this sense, Stubbs was right. To paraphrase Keith Thomas's comment about Shakespeare, not every culture has a *Magna Carta*. It may have resistance but rarely codified its resistance as resoundingly as in this landmark 'constitution'.

The right or duty of subjects to define and resist corruption and tyranny was, of course, ignored or denied by generations of kings and lords and their followers. That they nearly always took the trouble to deny the right of resistance suggests, at least, that it was a common error. When forced to do so, real kings naturally took cover behind their sacred, institutional bodies. James Stuart's later assertion of a biblically ordained divine right of kings merely restated a position that most if not all English monarchs before him had asserted or (more often) implied at one time or

---

[49] Stubbs, *Constitutional History*, 1:573–4.

another.[50] He took the step from viewing kings as agencies of God's Will to seeing them as gods on Earth. This revision of an idea that is as old as the god-kings of Sumer, Egypt, the Indus Valley and ancient China ordained, like them, that resistance was utterly illegitimate and heretical. Subjects could, through specially ordained channels, petition and even offer counsel to the Monarch, but his body and authority was God-given, absolute. Resistance was not permitted, as the draconian punishments inflicted on individuals and groups who dared to express or enact insults or disobedience to kings demonstrated.

We should not be surprised to find evidence of kings asserting or implying that they were 'above human law and answerable only to God'. Persons seeking lucrative employment in the service of kings were bound to appeal to their vanities. The idea that kings could be addressed respectfully concerning matters of policy, but not disciplined or deposed was to be a commonplace of royalist discourse for centuries. Against that, through the prism of rebellion, Claire Valente recently affirmed that divine right theory was *never* the prevailing view in England. Chronicles of Edward II's reign echoed medieval authorities like Glanvill and Bracton, who had asserted that if the king's laws were insufficient 'the king and his prelates, earls and barons were bound to amend them "by common assent"'.[51] Thomas Aquinas argued that a tyrannical king was no king 'and therefore subject to deposition, tyrannicide and divine vengeance (the preferred option)'. Like his predecessors, Aquinas formulated a common view that was always dangerous to express.

2.5   Enter the middle people

Like all successful conquest regimes, the ruling classes of Norman-Angevin England slowly discovered that they, in turn, needed to defend the territory they (or their ancestors) had won by conquest. During the thirteenth century various factions of the ruling class discovered a need for the active support of the people. As a result, conceptions of community which included rulers and subjects begin to appear in the archives of the age. The thirteenth was a century of baronial wars that saw the birth of English populism.

---

[50] James VI (of Scotland, later James I of England), *The Trew Law of Free Monarchies, or The Reciprock and mutual duety betwixt a free King and his Subiects* (1598). I am indebted here to Andreas Pecar's discussion of James's biblical sources: 'Using the Bible...', 'The Bible in History' symposium, University of East Anglia, December 2003.
[51] Reynolds, *Kingdoms and Communities*, p. 270, n. 45; Claire Valente, *The Theory and Practice of Revolt in Medieval England* (Aldershot 2003), 12, 14, 19, 27.

'The Song of Lewes, celebrating the victory of [the barons] over Henry III in 1264, left listeners in no doubt as to God's intervention in repressing wicked kingship. . . . The [later] deposition of Edward II was attributed in part to divine will as manifested by the "voice of the people"', writes Claire Valente.[52] The terminological obscurity and ambiguities of the constitutional jargon of the thirteenth century, as noted by a whole series of authorities from the 1820 Committee on the Status of a Peer of the Realm and Bishop Stubbs up to Valente and Reynolds, relates to a weak-spot of traditional constitutional history. It is evidence of a process in which the entire kingdom debated, discussed and tried to define and agree about what it was, how it was constituted, what its parts and classes were, and what were their legitimate roles and functions in relation to each other.

After *Magna Carta*, versions of which were issued in Latin and Norman-French, the next great constitutional moment, traditionally, is enshrined in a cluster of documents issued by Henry III, in Latin, Norman-French and English, in response to pressure from rebellious barons led by Simon de Montfort. Given Section 61 of the great charter, and the circumstances which led to the formulation and issuing of the 1258 documents, the addition of an English version that was to be distributed to the Shire-reeves of every county for public proclamation has been taken as evidence for baronial desire to legitimate their struggles with the king in the eyes of the English-speaking commonalty. This could be taken to mean that at this time something resembling public opinion not only existed, but was taken seriously, even, possibly, as a last court of appeal in struggles within the ruling classes over the relative legitimacy of their positions. In practice, predominantly French-speaking lords, the descendants of conquerors, were appealing to the natives.

The precise significance of the politics of the thirteenth century in the grand constitutional narrative is still debated. A recent historian of the sociolinguistic context points out that from 1066 to 1189 only fifty-five royal documents in English survive. After Henry III's proclamations of 1258 there are no more in English until the reign of Henry IV. These isolated uses, it is suggested, 'do not delineate a place – much less an

---

[52] Valente, *Revolt in Medieval England*; G.W. Prothero, review of *The Song of Lewes*, ed. C.L. Kingsford (1890), *English Historical Review* 7:25 (January 1892), 144–6 wrote that the Latin *Carmen di Bello Lewensi* was probably written by a Franciscan Friar in Simon de Montfort's household. At the York–Norwich Medieval Studies Conference (2006), Christine Donlan described the piece as 'an excellent focal point for the study of popular thirteenth-century expectations of the English nobility, showing that nobility was not defined by character or descent, but also by duty, responsibility, and the justice of one's actions'.

expanding place – for English [the language of the commonalty] in the powerful and prestigious domains of the late medieval period'. If Henry III's proclamation of 1258 signalled the arrival of English as a language of politics, why was it another 150 years before the experiment was conducted again? Machan's view is that English texts from the conquest to the middle to late thirteenth century suggest only 'sporadic and isolated efforts at cultivation . . . rather than a coherent and well-defined functional role across all England'. The vernacular literature of the period, such as it is, 'expressed alienation and also located the "speaking subject in a landscape of displacement"'. Royal government's use of clerics guaranteed that Latin would be the language of the state until the barons were sufficiently well organized as a class to resist the encroachments of royal power, as became the case in the thirteenth century. By this time 'a linguistic gap had opened between this Latin used for official purposes and the French and English spoken and read by the nobility'.[53] This analysis leaves little room for signs of populist revival.

The implication is that anyone outside the circles and retinues of the leading actors, the people of (in the three languages of Henry III's propaganda) the Latin *communitas regni*, French *le commun* (or *commune* or *communance*) *d'Engleterre* (or *de la terre*), and English *thaet loandes folk on ure* (i.e. Henry's) *kuneriche* . . . , were never more than pawns in a game that was restricted to the Franco-Norman baronial elite and the king. As in 1259, when a group described by a chronicler as the *communitas bachelerie Anglie* received support from the future Edward I 'when they protested that "the barons" were doing nothing for the public good (*ad utilitatem reipuplice*)', Henry III and his barons were simply positioning themselves in a game restricted to the inner circles around the throne. It was really a war over whether the *communitas regni* was composed by the king alone, or the king and the powerful barons. In Machan's view, the politics of the 1250s and 1260s were largely determined by the priorities of the political elite.

If this interpretation is correct, the report of a contemporary chronicler that 'almost the whole commune of the middling people of England' (*fere omnis communa mediocris populi regni Anglie*) rejected Louis XI as an arbitrator,[54] really meant no more than that he was rejected by those who represented themselves as their representatives: the barons. *Mediocris populi* ('middle' or 'mediocre' people) referred only to a 'spectre' used to legitimate proceedings that in reality involved only the leading players. Was it just rhetoric or was this 'class', as the allusive reference to the

[53] Tim William Machan, *English in the Middle Ages* (Oxford 2003), 34–7.
[54] Reynolds, *Communities and Kingdoms*, 271–2.

public influence of the *mediocris populi* seems to imply, a force in public affairs nearly a century before it became more firmly anchored, institutionally, as the *communes* in Parliament? In Machan's sociolinguistic view, its first language, English, lacked 'any implications as a medium for social unrest' at the time of the constitutional crisis of 1258. At that time, such vernacular 'literature' as existed reveals only 'the dislocation of what might be called Anglo-Saxon identity, the lack of a discourse of protest in English, and the absence of topicalization of vernacular language as a public issue'.[55]

Another possibility is that the phrases *communitas bachelerie Anglie* and *omnis communa mediocris populi regni Anglie* referred, not to the commonalty, but to the yet to be institutionalized knights, esquires and gentlemen, that is to say, to the lower ranks of the hereditary (post-1066) ruling class. On this interpretation Simon de Montfort and the fellow barons who supported him took the side of discontented and mainly young knights who, for various reasons, were especially concerned that their status and inheritance was being challenged by immigrants promoted by the king. As with the 'baronial' conception it is still a movement within the ruling class; its centre of social gravity is just below the barons but still above the commonalty.

D.A. Carpenter's study of English peasants in politics, 1258–67, shows how the painstaking accumulation of individual cases eventually provides new insight into old controversies.[56] Carpenter writes that 'it has long been recognized that during this period of profound "shaking" the political community in England was far wider than that of the great barons'. The question is, how much wider? Controversy about how far down the social hierarchy political thoughts and practices went, and how, precisely, they were expressed and enacted, is an abiding theme of British historiography, and indeed of the Humanities and Social Sciences generally.

The question is this: when the nobles of *Magna Carta* or the followers of Simon de Montfort claimed to be speaking and acting (in whatever language) for *the community as a whole*, what did they mean? If, as I shall suggest, nearly all forms of resistance, and not only the major rebellions, were enacted in the name of the commonweal, or its linguistic equivalent, we must consider the possibility that rebellions were major eruptions of a constitutional culture that reached into all ranks of society, as far as Arlette Farge's (and Jurgen Habermas's) 'plebeian public sphere' that

[55] Machan, *English in the Middle Ages*, 65.
[56] D.A. Carpenter, 'English Peasants in Politics 1258–1267', *Past and Present*, no. 136 (August 1992), 3–42.

'was suppressed in the historical process'.[57] The traditional view, confirmed by Reynolds, Valente and Carpenter, but rejected by Machan on 'sociolinguistic' grounds, is that discussion of politics and the constitution did indeed reach deeply into society, that by 1258 barons and kings were expected to conform to generally accepted values and ideals. In their struggles it was not only tactical, as Machan supposes, but *necessary* to heed public opinion. Is it conceivable that the barons of thirteenth century England *and* their juniors, 'knights' and 'esquires', like those of the mid-fifteenth century, were actually pressured by lower-middle and lower ranks to resort to the threat or even the act of revolt in order to eradicate corrupt and unjust kingship that was not seen to be for the commonweal? We know that this was the case in the fifteenth century, and cannot, as traditional constitutional historiography has so often done, rule out the possibility that it was the case in the thirteenth century and earlier.

Carpenter 'demonstrates that ideas about the community of the realm had percolated down to the level of the village' but leaves questions of motivation unresolved. In practice, 'the peasantry belonged to the community of the realm of thirteenth-century England.' Carpenter's studies of peasant involvement reinforce contemporary elite rhetoric representing rebellion as a movement of 'the whole community'. 'The wide circle of those intended to take the 1258 oath explains its proclamation in letters issued in English as well as French and Latin.' In October 1258 'another proclamation issued in English as well as Latin and French' instructed sheriffs to deal impartially with rich and poor alike, according to law; three months later the Ordinance of Magnates 'promised that their officials would take nothing unjustly from anyone, "cleric or layman, freeman or villain, house of religion or vill"'. Carpenter's thesis that this was 'more than mere rhetoric' is unproven, but the promise to give justice 'to rich and poor, serf and free, stranger and relation' was a consistent theme of the rhetoric of the 'common enterprise'. Carpenter suggests that under the baronial party 'peasants gained protection chiefly from *royal* officials' – that the barons used popular resentment against the king and his foreign followers for their own purposes. The barons of the 'common enterprise' almost certainly believed that their common followers belonged to a class of inferior people; they shared class prejudice of this sort with their royal enemies. Once in control they did not hesitate to insult the king and his companions by supporting their inferiors: 'By 1263 constructive reform had given way to violent ravaging of royalist estates.'[58]

---

[57] Arlette Farge, *Subversive Words: Public Opinion in Eighteenth-Century France*, trans. Rosemary Morris, (Cambridge 1994), 1.

[58] Carpenter, 'English Peasants in Politics', 3, 4, 22–3, 23–7, 28, 30.

Sources compiled during or in the aftermath of the crisis, notably the detailed Hundred Rolls of 1279 for Buckinghamshire and Cambridgeshire, show 'widespread peasant involvement in the physical "fighting" side of politics'. Common and elite Londoners were prominent in de Montfort's army at the battle of Lewes.[59] Most of the combatants and casualties on both sides at Lewes were serfs and free peasants. 'The pattern of fighting... was one of heavily armoured knights on horseback killing lightly protected peasant footsoldiers.' Many serfs and freemen were later fined for having fought for the rebels and in some case travelling far from home to do so. Roger Blancpain, a villager of Madingley (near Cambridge) led pillagers of royalist estates. The army mustered by the barons in Kent in 1264 'had numerous peasant contingents raised on a communal basis'.

Why did they take part? As would be the case in every subsequent rebellion up to 1649, many men charged later with rebellion claimed they were 'driven... by threats of death and arson': it is another recurring theme. Some probably were coerced, others fought for pay. Comprehension of and enthusiasm for the 'common enterprise' was undoubtedly variable, but Carpenter also notes many cases where 'peasants' fought 'with enthusiasm' and at times did so in spite of their leaders. 'That peasants acting against the king were sometimes acting beyond the control of their lords was stated explicitly, and from personal knowledge... for [at the time of the battle of Lewes]', a chronicler claimed, 'it was not in the power of lords to restrain their men'.[60] It is certain that when soldiers of the 'common enterprise' came together as companies, they discussed what the fuss was about. At the very least the upheavals intensified the distribution, across England, of common stories. 'Common enterprise' is also a fine slogan.

Like the Norman Conquest and *Magna Carta*, the conjuncture of the 1250s has always seemed to historians to mark a turning-point. For the early nineteenth-century research assistants who looked into ancient documents concerning 'The Dignity of a Peer of the Realm' for a Committee of the House of Lords, questions of national definition began in the second half of the thirteenth century. At first it was a public discourse focused on an absence: a language to describe an ideal community of all the confused, conflicted communities of the real.

The main question here is not who introduced the commonalty or third estate into the constitutional field of forces. Viewed from above it was first mooted, perhaps, by Franciscans at baronial courts, and picked up by barons simply to legitimate what they intended to do anyway.

---

[59] *Ibid.*, 11, quotation from Oman, *The Art of War in the Middle Ages* (London 1898).
[60] Quotations from Carpenter, 'English Peasants in Politics', 4, 6–7, 10, 11, 12, 16.

Knights and esquires living at least part of their lives in the communities may, by c.1250, have become practical mediators between magnates and commonalty. Franciscan preachers and counsellors were active in all the courts involved in the struggle; their humbler brethren were active in the communities.[61] Public discourse concerning the real and the ideal nature and condition of the greater community of the English people begins in the 1250s and henceforth, up to the present, never ceases. How should we understand this movement?

It was a populist movement in the sense that the magnates resisted and imposed restrictions on the king in the name of the people, thus forcing the king to adopt the same rhetorical orientation. According to Ernest Laclau, there are 'two clear preconditions of populism: (1) the formation of an . . . antagonistic frontier separating the "people" from power; and (2) an equivalential articulation of demands making the emergence of the "people" possible'.[62] According to the traditional case, Angevin ambitions for the expansion of *dominium regale* produced resistance. Henry III's supposed or real affinity for the company of his Lusignan (i.e. foreign) half-brothers and their retainers was a pretext. It created the opening for longer-established French barons like Simon de Montfort (who may not have spoken more than a few words of English) to proclaim themselves as the natural leaders of the English commonalty. Henry's Lusignan followers seem to have behaved as if they were conquerors. Wherever they were granted liberties by the king's patronage, they 'behaved in an arrogant and lawless fashion'.[63] In doing so they created a multitude of local and provincial grievances. As Carpenter has shown elsewhere, 'demands', as Laclau puts it, could be and were maintained against barons, knights and manorial lords on all sides of the conflict. The key combination, in an overpopulated country, was anti-foreigner feeling and ineffective kingship. It seems that Henry III's weakness was not his failure to listen to counsel but to listen too much and fail to keep too many contradictory

---

[61] David Knowles, *The Religious Orders in England* (Cambridge 1950), 163–70, is a brilliant synopsis of the reception of the Franciscans in the communities, universities, baronial and royal courts from their first arrival in 1221–3 to their 'virtual monopoly' as royal confessors 'from the reign of Henry III to the fall of Richard II' (167). The primeval populism and egalitarianism of St Francis and his companions waned, but not before the movement had spread such ideas among all ranks of the people, by example, conversation and preaching. Popular notions of Jesus and his disciples as common people speaking the common tongue probably existed before they came; but the popular influence of Franciscans and others influenced by them, 1221–1399, is underestimated for lack of detailed histories of the travels and foundations of the inspired early 'missionaries'. Fourteenth-century England has many marks of a society in the permanent grip of religious revivalism.

[62] Ernesto Laclau, *On Populist Reason* (London 2005), 74.

[63] Discussed by Carpenter, 'English Peasants in Politics', 21–2.

promises to different affinities. In the context a multitude of 'demands' (or points of conflict) at all levels of society became 'equivalent' as a result of common scapegoats: foreigners and the king. What emerged was 'an internal antagonist frontier' between the king and the rest. The obsessive references to *comun* words during this period marked the need for a word or formula for a community in which kingship was only one institution or class among many.

What we glimpse in early usages of the *comun* family of words are the many communities of England (estates, ranks, villages, towns, districts, provinces, regions) trying to decide what they are and how they relate to each other. The first thing a people has to decide is what to call itself. The reason why *comun* words had so many competing meanings was that there was still extreme contention about what kind of a community England was and what it ought to be. There were contending visions. Even when they shared features of the same vision, they viewed them from different places and perspectives. The only thing that could ever stop them engaging in permanent uncivil war with each other was war against a hated enemy overseas. It was not a peaceful, law-abiding, settled society, but its warring communities and classes were beginning to want it to be.

2.6   Meanings of 'commonalty': Peatling Magna, 1265

'It was in support of the community of the realm that the villagers of Peatling Magna fought their own little war against a royalist force in 1265.'[64] The Peatling Magna incident has a place in the canonical constitutional literature because it documents (or purports to document) villagers' opinions about 'the community of the realm' at a time when common villagers are not supposed to have had political opinions. The period from 1258 to 1327 is of immense significance in English constitutional history. A new conception, language and discourse of politics emerged in these years. As always, the written record concentrates on the struggles of great men, but the chronicles, proclamations and statutes of this period also record the formation of an ideology.

Rebels against the tyrannies of kings, and the kings themselves, consciously defined and legitimated their causes in relation to a larger English community that included 'middle people' and 'bachelors', men who, for at least two centuries and probably much longer had not been regarded as part of the counsel of kings and lords: the senior ranks of the conquered English and the junior, more 'assimilated' ranks of the French ruling

---

[64] Reynolds, *Kingdoms and Communities*, 271–2.

class. To put it more boldly, it was during this Indian summer of the
medieval boom that the 'commonalty' stepped forward in the formations
that would lead, in the fourteenth century, to the rise of the commons
house of parliament. This broadly bottom-up movement was constantly
in advance of the institutional history. It created 'middle' English, which
became the language of English political life in the fourteenth century.
It expressed and asserted itself by creating the tradition of popular resistance and rebellion that provides the unifying theme of English constitutional history from 1381 to 1649. This is the 'movement from below',
the 'revolution of the commonalty' as I have provisionally termed it. It
is there, in the archives, a whisper becoming a cascade and torrent in
less than a century.

Was it merely a rhetorical construction? Was the wildly proliferating
discourse about 'community' and 'commonalty' – an increasingly vernacular discourse about the condition of England – simply a developing
rhetorical construct, put in place so that barons and kings could feel they
really were acting for the *commune*? As Andy Wood writes in his account
of the rebellions of 1549, the task of reconstructing early modern popular
minds and memories 'lies at the limits of feasible research'.[65] Were the
civil wars of the period squabbles within a tiny ruling class of magnates
and the king, or did they (as documents prepared by the barons' and
king's party implied) involve the community as a whole? How 'common'
was Simon de Montfort's 'common enterprise'? How far down the social
scale did knowing and caring about the politics of kingdom go?

The incident involved a group of men described as the *liberi homines*
of Peatling Magna, Leicestershire, and a contingent of royalist soldiers
under the command of Peter de Neville and Eudes la Zuche. As Neville
passed through the village after the battle of Evesham the inhabitants
'accused him and his men of treason'. He claimed the villagers taunted
him and his men with the accusation 'that they were going against the
welfare of the commonalty of the realm and against the barons (*contra
utilitatem communitatis regni et contra barones*)'. De Neville responded by
ordering his men to round up the villagers into the parish church, where
he demanded a fine for the 'trespass' in the form of an on the spot payment of twenty marks. When the now compliant *liberi homines* told him
the community could not pay such a heavy fine, de Neville 'requested'
the provosts of the village, 'together with the whole commonalty (*cum
tota communitate*)' assembled in church, to select and hand over five men
as hostages, pending the payment of the fine. The *liberi homines* offered
a different view of events in which de Neville and his men demanded

[65] Andy Wood, *1549 Rebellions*, 241.

money with menaces in the time-honoured fashion of marauding war bands; when the community could not pay, de Neville's men simply 'dragged five men of Peatling Magna out of the church and imprisoned them'. Whatever the precise causes and tenor of the exchange – and we can hardly doubt that violent threats and perhaps acts were involved – Thomas the Provost handed over the hostages 'on behalf of himself and the whole commonalty of the township (*se et tota communitate ville*)'. Neville insisted that he took the hostages for the offence *per eaudem communitatem illata* and that he had continued their imprisonment because 'the aforesaid commonalty (*communitatis*) made default'.[66]

The *dramatis personae* were two French knights and their retainers, the king (at whose court the case was heard), the rebel barons (whose cause the villagers were alleged to have espoused), the *liberi homines*, the provost and the villagers. It is not too far-fetched to see Neville and la Zuche as stereotypical *Lusignan* mercenaries, foreign knights in the service of a king who was unpopular, in part, because he was believed to favour foreigners over natives. The recently defeated *barones* were off-stage, but it was their cause that the community of Peatling Magna is alleged to have espoused. The Peatling Magna incident represented all the parties in the constitutional struggles of the age coming together in a context in which the most shadowy presence in the general documentation – the commonalty in all its senses – was central to the action. The commonalty exhibited a simple authority structure. The *liberi homines* spoke for the community when they said the *barones* represented the commonweal of England, not the king and certainly not a gang of foreign soldiers in the king's pay. One of them was a kind of 'mayor' – the provost. The rest of the village was included in the negotiations but did not speak on stage. The French knights' version of what was said and done implied a structured and politically articulate commonalty.

The documentation takes us to the heart of an enduring controversy relating to what John Watts calls the 'problematical convention of translating "communitas" or "cominalte" [as class] instead of community'.[67] Class or community? Let us examine what the documents say. *Communitatis regni* means the whole community of the realm, but all the other usages refer to the community (parish? manor? vill, village or township?) of Peatling Magna. *Communitatis regni* is top-down and inclusive, but all the other usages necessarily imply *both* 'the community' *and*

---

[66] This and the following paragraph are based on Curia Regis Roll no. 175 (Hilary 1266), in H.G. Richardson and G.O. Sayles (trans. and ed.), *Select Cases of Procedure Without Writ Under Henry III* (Selden Society: London 1941), 42–5.

[67] John Watts, 'Public or Plebs: the Changing Meaning of the Commons, 1381–1549', in Huw Pryce and John Watts (eds.), *Power and Identity in the Middle Ages: Essays in Memory of Rees Davies* (Oxford 2007), 245.

'commonalty' (in the third estate sense) of Peatling Magna. In this context they meant many things simultaneously. Watts concludes that the word 'commonalty' was not widely used to refer to an entire class or estate until the early sixteenth century.[68] The implication is that before c.1500 no-one ever saw the English commonalty as a 'working class' distinct from the praying and fighting (and ruling) classes. Yet that is precisely how John of Salisbury defined them, and precisely how conventional estate theory saw them throughout our period. The word 'commonalty' inevitably attached itself to the class of people who shared the condition of being 'common' as distinct from 'honourable'. Contemporaries knew perfectly well that this class of 'people of no name' was extremely heterogeneous in status, wealth and power, and that its principal operational context was not the *regnum* but the local community. The convention was to regard 'provosts', mayors, aldermen and *liberi homines* as the legal representatives of the communities of the commonalty. That is how they are represented in the Peatling Magna documents.

This need not entail that the 'commonalty' of all the communities of the third estate were united by common consciousness, information and aims. Whenever documentation offers any information on the subject, the new social historians of early modern England have shown that local movements of the commonalty used regional and national 'commotions' for their own purposes. Yet it is also clear that from the Peatling Magna episode to the revolution of the 1640s, their spokesmen spoke, not only for the local but for the whole community of the commonalty acting for the whole community of the realm.[69] The inhabitants of Peatling Magna dishonoured the French knights, whom they saw as enemies of the commonalty in all three senses: the commonalty as third estate, the community of Peatling Magna and the community of the realm. Debate about the meanings of the 'commune' words in the crucial period of political and constitutional conflict from 1258 to 1327 has a long history.[70] There is always uncertainty about precisely what abstract collective nouns

---

[68] Watts, 'Public or Plebs', 249 and *passim*. However, the concession that 'it does seem that clerical use of the term "common people" (and more occasionally "commons") to mean the third estate goes back to at least the early fourteenth century' raises the question of how clerical authors were able to seal off these class usages from the rest of society for two centuries.

[69] Michael Bush, 'The Risings of the Commons in England, 1381–1549', in J. Denton (ed.), *Orders and Hierarchies in Late Medieval and Renaissance Europe* (Basingstoke 1999), 109, 111, 112, 113–14.

[70] I first encountered it in a copy of *Reports from the Lords Committee Touching the Dignity of a Peer of the Realm* (25 May 1820), vol. 1: the first report (printed 18 May 1829), BL: e.g. 19, 103, 109, 141, 152, 171, 187, 229–30. Carpenter, 'English Peasants in Politics', 31, n. 97, is a useful summary of the provenance.

refer to, but we should not assume that class divisions that are obvious in retrospect were not also obvious at the time. The *commune* words meant different things in different contexts. The Peatling Magna episode brought different contexts together and it is no surprise to find the words meaning several things at once.

Who were the *liberi homines*? Were the freemen of Peatling Magna representative of a national class? If so, in what ways were they representative? Was it their opinion the barons claimed to represent in their struggles against the king? It will help to begin with some rough estimates of how many *liberi homines* there were in c.1300, at about the time when the first moves were made to give the freemen of England below the barons an institutional presence in state affairs, most obviously in the nascent House of Commons. It was a vague term but implied important privileges, the most valued of which was the right to be heard in the king's courts. It also implied a distinction between freedom and servility that ran through all the many communes of England. In theory a free man had one lord only, the king. Beyond that *liberi homines* constituted a dispersed multitude that, in theory, encompassed barons, knights and esquires, as well as the future yeomen, urban burgesses, smallholders, artisans and labourers. By c.1300 any one of these could be, technically, a freeman. The Peatling Magna incident seemed to suggest a class alliance in which all the *liberi homines* were united in resistance to monarchical tyranny.

Bruce M.S. Campbell's revision of the ratio of servile to free tenancies before the Black Death offers a quantitative point of departure, based on the systematic analysis of over 10,000 post mortem 'inquisitions' covering 1300–49. Campbell's source provides 'coverage at the rate of one manor per 25 miles for most of England south of the Trent and east of the Exe and at least one manor per five square miles where coverage is best, in a band of counties to the north of London'. Campbell's results 'supersede the more impressionistic national estimates of free and villein rents, land and tenants upon which historians have so far had to rely'. He finds that 'free rents would have accounted for at least 40 per cent by value of all rents and services' averaged across the territory of the kingdom. Free tenants were commonest on smaller manors like Peatling Magna. A much higher proportion of the income of the biggest corporations of their day, magnate estates, came from servile tenancies. Magnates (especially religious magnates) and serfs went together. Smaller manors (those of the future knights, esquires and gentlemen) had more freemen, although even they usually featured a (usually somewhat smaller) 'servile labour force'.[71]

[71] Bruce M.S. Campbell, 'The Agrarian Problem', 24–8.

Campbell's data records revenues and tenancies, not free men, families and households. How far did distinctions between tenancies translate into distinctions of class? Some historians have suggested that the distinction between freedom and servility was an instrument of legal but not social discrimination in late medieval communities. They point out that freedom and bondage did not translate into economic classes. Campbell's estimates show that the mean portion of land held by bondmen exceeded that of the average freeman; bondmen sometimes enjoyed local privileges and affinities that free men did not. The largest landholders on many manors were technically servile and labourers were often technically free. A successful serf might employ a free labourer to do his boon works for the lord. Microstudies sometimes show the free and the servile working side by side in the collective fields, sowing, weeding and harvesting, gossiping, drinking, celebrating and worshipping together, apparently oblivious to legal, tenurial and other 'class' distinctions. Local reputation grounded in daily association may have often counted for more than legal and tenurial status. Collective opinion was reluctant to draw attention to relative freedom or servility. Occasions and individuals were judged on merit and not by class. Age – the vigour of youth or status of an elder – mattered more than class distinction. Friendships easily crossed the line dividing the free and servile members of the commonalty. If all these qualifications applied everywhere at all times it suggests that freedom and servility did not matter much to the commonalty of late medieval England. Serfdom was not killed off by passionate resistance, political pressure and rebellion but simply died of old age.

Such arguments must be set alongside evidence that the distinction between freedom and servility did matter. Free men were often unwilling to rent unfree tenancies for fear that it would compromise their status. The abolition of serfdom was a primary aim of the Commons Rebellion of 1381. Martyrs who killed themselves rather than lose their free status were stock figures of vernacular English culture from 1381 to 1450. Very late in the day in terms of the traditional chronology of the decline of English serfdom, in c.1500, freedom mattered to several young women of Norwich who broke off their engagements when they discovered their boyfriends were from unfree families. They refused to marry unfree men because they wanted their children to be free like them.[72] 'Independency' – the status of a freeman of the English commonwealth – mattered all the way down the line; it was probably especially strong in the minds of smallholders and *proletarii*, where, according to prescribed

---

[72] Percy Mullins (ed.) *Norwich Consistory Court Depositions 1499–1530*, Norfolk Record Society 10 (Norwich 1938): deposition numbers 48, 95, 233, 308.

tradition, unfreedom was the most common condition. In short there are signs that common English people were sharply aware of the line between freedom/independency and servile dependency, and thought it mattered. It seems to have mattered at Peatling Magna in 1265, when the free men are represented as the natural and (because of their access to the king's courts) legal spokesmen for the community as a whole.

Campbell shows that *liberi homines* constituted at least a third and very likely more than half of the households of England in c.1300–49.[73] This was a very substantial legal class indeed, spread liberally across the English landscape. Campbell finds that 'villein rents and services usually equalled or exceeded the combined value of assize and free rents... within that broad swathe of country stretching from the Scottish border, through Yorkshire and across the midlands, as far south as the south coast from West Sussex to Cornwall'.

It was outside this 'midland' zone, to the west and east, that free rents and tenures were most prominent... Within both these western and eastern zones there were also many individual manors on which villein rents and services were either insignificant or non-existent. This was most unambiguously the case in eastern Essex and Kent, where enserfment had been successfully resisted during the century following the conquest.[74]

Free and servile tenants lived next door to each other (and may often have been indistinguishable to disinterested outsiders) all over England. The distinction between freedom and servility was to be encountered on most manors in all the regions identified by Campbell. That the distinction existed is not to say that local communities were always divided and structured by it, or were even especially conscious of it. An attribution of consciousness requires a different kind of evidence.

What undoubtedly did vary from region to region and manor to manor was the ratio of free to servile tenures. As a general rule serfs existed in greater numbers and did more servile labour on magnate estates. Class distinction based on free and servile status may also have taken rigid and turbulent forms on some manors of lesser lords – the future knights and esquires. A few manors were composed of autarchic *liberi homines* with no lord below the king and no servile tenants, but even they would have known neighbouring manors on which *villeins* predominated. While

---

[73] Campbell, 'Agrarian Problem', 36, states that 'it can be estimated that almost half of all tenanted land (that is, 48–50%) was probably held by free tenants and just over half (that is, 50–52%) was probably held by servile tenants... Given the smaller mean size of free holdings, the number of free tenants is likely to have equalled or even exceeded the number of servile tenants'.

[74] *Ibid.*, 29.

some servile households were wealthier than some free ones, servility was most commonly associated with poverty (indicating a lack of a range of qualities and conditions like estate, intelligence, morality, enterprise and honour) and direct dependency on men of higher caste. In this case 'servility' was almost the exact equivalent of the 'dependency' that, for most literary commonwealth men of the sixteenth and seventeenth centuries (including some of the Levellers), excluded a man from local office and the national franchise. Estates deeply committed to serfdom like those of abbeys like Westminster constituted one pole of the spectrum. Some lords are bound to have demanded more servility of tenancy and/or demeanour than others. Others saw their estates as little armies in waiting that could be called upon to defend the lordship and kingdom. That meant inspiring loyalty and encouraging a certain amount of independency in their followers and tenants. Eastern Essex and Kent were at the other pole. It seems unlikely to be a coincidence that the commons of Essex, Kent, parts of Hertfordshire and perhaps East Sussex, were the leaders of the movement to abolish distinctions between free and unfree in 1381 and 1450.

The next constitutional milestone after the baronial wars, traditionally, points to a charter of Edward I. Edward's relentless ambitions and excessive taxations eventually led him into 'a considerable struggle with his people'. The context was a kind of dual colonization process. Edward set out to expand and consolidate the borders of his *regnum* by conquering neighbouring nations. 'By 1300', writes R.R. Davies, 'English power was present in the furthest reaches of the British Isles'. This hegemony was 'not only in terms of political annexation, military control, and the instruments of English governmental rule',

But also in colonies of English settlers in town and country alike, complex economic and commercial networks, the universal circulation of English coinage, the ubiquitousness of English Law and judicial mechanics, and the dominance of English cultural and even social norms.[75]

What nearly brought him undone was not external, but internal colonialism. Military expansion meant militarization and higher taxation of the commonweal. Wars of conquest like those of Edward I and Edward III kept unruly warriors (barons, knights and esquires, the members of the Second Estate) occupied other than in rebellion or oppression at home, but it necessarily empowered the commonalty in a number of ways. When lords were away, government and administration devolved

---

[75] R. R. Davies, *The First English Empire: Power and Identities in the British Isles* (Oxford 2000), 191.

to the communities. Warrior kings needed more money to finance their foreign enterprise. The more they asked for the more it was likely to be resented in the communities. The House of Commons emerged in the late thirteenth and fourteenth centuries. The English commonweal was prepared to countenance external colonization by kings, but not internal expansion at the expense of the other 'Estates'. The community resisted Edward's efforts to expand the space occupied by monarchs within the constitution as it had resisted John's and Henry III's before him. Successfully.

And like John and Henry before, Edward was forced to proclaim 'to the archbishops, bishops, abbots, priors and other of the Holy Church, and to the earls and barons, *and all the commonalty* of the realm, that he would take no aids, impositions or prises from the kingdom except by the assent of the whole kingdom . . . except the ancient aids and prises due and accustomed'. This is as good a source as any to define the germ of the revolution of the commonalty. It refers unambiguously to the whole community of people of England *other than* kings, nobles and church-men. The great tradition of English constitutional history has concluded that thirteenth-century references of this sort were gestural: the ruling class claimed to be acting for the benefit of the *commonweal* knowing full well that the three million or so of their contemporaries who did not rule would simply follow their lead. It is possible, but evidence suggests a more complex field. The possibility that the inner circles were under pressure from the outer communities cannot be ignored. Kings and nobles have received enough attention; there has been important recent work on movement and institutionalization of the subordinate knights and their subalterns, the gentry; *yeomen* and *cives*, the 'middle ranks' of the fifteenth to seventeenth centuries; and last but not least, the 'multitude' or 'rascability'. As we shall see in Chapters 4 and 5, it was assumed throughout our period that 'seditions and troubles', movements from below that affected (and were imprinted upon the memory of) everyone, the whole collectivity, were sparked by the vocal and eventually violent unenfranchised multitude. They were not called, as Stubbs put it; they came anyway.

Edward I affirmed the rules written down in *Magna Carta* – no taxation without representation, and no increase in customarily accepted levels of taxation – not because it was to his advantage, or to the advantage of any other interest or community, but, he said, 'for the *communem utilitatem regni*'. In this and later formulations, the common good is inseparable from the realm. *Communem utilitatem* go with *regni*. This is the Royalist position. In the thirteenth century the political community is still Latin, *communitas regni*. *Communem utilitatem regni* survives in royalist and

official discourse, but another theme appears in the process of vernacularization: the *regni* gets dropped. *Commune profytt* is common usage for
much of the fourteenth century.[76] *Common Wele* becomes conventional
usage after 1381. The Tudors appropriated it to their 'imperial monarchy' but common usages survived and exploded on to the public stage
in the 1640s. After the events and exploits of Edward I, the new constitutional nexus came together remarkably swiftly. The reign of Edward
II was evidently a major turning-point, in the sense that it eventually
brought together and gave vernacular expression to all the key sensitive
points of English political culture as it had developed, and become more
or less institutionalized, to that point.

2.7   The armed hand

*He that is master of the militia, is master of the kingdom, and consequently is in
possession of a most absolute sovereignty.*[77]

Carpenter's analysis of the social composition of the rebel armies of the
'common enterprise' points to another essential 'structural' theme of
the fourteenth to seventeenth centuries: the militarization of the commonalty. We saw in Chapter 1 that as early as 1159 John of Salisbury
had summarily dismissed the value of mounted knights for the defence
of kingdoms and republics. 'Someone who does not know how to fight
except on a horse', he wrote, 'is little suited to the army'. John's armed
hand, like that of his humanist successor, Machiavelli, comprised 'rural
plebeians . . . raised under heavens and upon hard work, enduring the
sun, indifferent to shade, unfamiliar with bathhouses, ignorant of luxury'. For an independent republic, 'the farmer and the fighter are the
same'.[78] The English state began to institutionalize the commoning of

---

[76] For usages of 'commune profit', see Doris Rayner, 'The Forms and Machinery of the
"Commune Petition" in the Fourteenth Century, Part One', *English Historical Review*
vol. 56, no. 222 (April 1941), 208; John Trevisa, *Dialogus Inter Militem et Clericum . . .*,
ed. Aaron Jenkins Perry (London 1925), 33; Langland, *Piers Plowman: the Prologue and
Passus 1–VII of the B-Text as found in Bodleian MS Laud Misc. 581*, ed. J.A.W. Bennett
(Oxford 1972), 5, line 148; R.W. Chambers and Marjorie Daunt (ed.), *A Book of London
English 1384–1425* (Oxford 1931), 29.

[77] Hobbes, *Behemoth*, 123.

[78] John of Salisbury, see above, Chapter 1.5; Nicolo Machiavelli, *The Art of War*, in Machiavelli, *The Prince and the Art of War* (1521: Collectors Library Edition, London 2004),
221. Machiavelli's Tuscan landscape was smaller and more sharply divided into country
and city than early modern England. Yet for the defence of his beloved Florence he very
much favoured rural vocations and occupations, distinguishing independent country-
dwellers from their rich but decadent urban contemporaries. Nobles and gentlemen
could not be trusted. Foreign war bands and mercenaries would always fight for the

English armies in the late thirteenth century, when the Statute of Winchester (renewed in 1437 and 1442) felt safe enough to require that 'all men between . . . 16 and 60 below the rank of knight or esquire had not only to be armed according to their status but to be trained in those arms. Those next to the bottom of a descending scale were obliged to supply themselves with cutlasses, spears, knives, and other lesser weapons, and all men below that status were to have bows and arrows or bows and bolts . . . the whole realm was part of the war machine'.[79]

Early modern England is an illustrative case of the hypothesis that, historically, 'changes in who fights will lead more or less directly to corresponding changes in who rules'.[80] Historians have postulated that the seeds of just such a long and momentous 'military revolution' were planted, in north-western Europe, at precisely this time. 'The armies that dominated the battlefields of Europe from the mid-eleventh century through the early fourteenth were composed primarily of feudal warrior-aristocrats, who owed military service for lands held in fief', writes Clifford J. Rogers:

They served as heavily armoured cavalry, shock combatants, relying on the muscle power of man and steed, applied directly at the point of a lance or the edge of a sword. They fought more often to capture than to kill. The armies which

highest bidder. The class that mattered in the defence of the territory of a genuine *res publica* was the class of independent (middling) households. To be truly independent in that world meant to be like the Roman Cincinnatus, an independent freeholder whose labour and land could support a family, labourers, needy neighbours and, through his taxes, the commonwealth. Machiavelli's ideal citizen army would draw upon a very wide range of occupations, from 'fowlers, fishermen, cooks, bawdy-house keepers' to 'ploughmen, smiths, farriers, carpenters, butchers, hunters and such occupations'. After them, wrote Machiavelli, 'I would take smiths, carpenters, farriers, and stone cutters' as men 'who can turn their hands to more services than one'. The very best people for defence of state and territory, however, were 'husbandmen and men who have been accustomed to work in the fields'. Free peasants loved their country more than any other class. They were *independent*, able to 'live of their own' and thus not dependent on anyone or anything less than the commonweal itself.

[79] I.M.W. Harvey, 'Popular Politics' in R.H. Britnell and A.J. Pollard (ed.), *The McFarlane Legacy: Studies in Late Medieval Politics and Society* (Stroud 1995), 165; for an account of the raising of troops in the fifteenth century, see Harriss, *Shaping the Nation*, 645.

[80] Clifford Rogers, 'The Military Revolution in History and Historiography', in *The Military Revolution Debate: Readings on the Transformation of Early Modern Europe* (Boulder, Colorado 1995), 30. This section supports the view of John Stone, 'Technology, Society and the Infantry Revolution of the Fourteenth Century', *Journal of Military History* 68 (April 2004), 361–80, that social (and cultural) change was an intimate cause of the 'infantry revolution'. Rather than call it a revolution I suggest thinking of it as a recurrence of constitutional circumstances that had arisen before, by reputation in Republican Rome. England had the potential to be the kind of republic Machiavelli envisaged in the *Art of War* and *The Discourses on Titus Livy*. It is associated with transitions from Monarchy and Aristocracy to Polity.

conquered Europe's first global empires, on the other hand, differed from this description on *every single count*. They were drawn from the common population (albeit often led by aristocrats); they served for pay; they fought primarily on foot, in close-order linear formations which relied more on missile fire than shock action; and they fought to kill.[81]

Rogers argues that 'the tremendous military revolution in warfare represented by these changes was well under way by the middle of the Hundred Years War, and solidly in place by the end of that conflict'. The 'first glimmerings' of this revolution were evident at the battles of Courtrai (1302), Bannockburn (1314) and Mortgarten (1315).

Rogers explains the change as the result of 'punctuated equilibrium', in which 'evolution proceeded by short bursts of rapid change interspersed with long periods of near stasis rather than constant, slow alteration'.[82] For Rogers the evolution of the military revolution of the late middle ages involved 'short bursts of rapid change' caused by technology, as in the introduction of the longbow, cannon and new artillery fortifications.

Against Rogers's theory that the military revolution was caused by technological change, John Stone argues that 'the character of war was conditioned chiefly by social and political factors'.[83] He points out that 'much of technology's interest derives from the manner in which it crystallizes the attitudes and beliefs of the society which created and used it'. I offer a third hypothesis: the infantry revolution of the fourteenth century was the outcome of the *recurrence* in certain regions of western Europe of constitutional circumstances favourable to the use of well-organized infantry forces using pikes and bows to defeat bands of mounted knights. Infantry had defeated various types of cavalry many times before the fourteenth century. The success of relatively small gangs of mounted knights between the fall of the Roman empire and the fourteenth century was due to the relative scarcity of states and societies with the human resources, leadership and organizational power to train, muster and marshal bowmen and pikemen in sufficient numbers, and in good enough order, to resist and overcome gangs of mounted knights. When these circumstances reappeared the military and constitutional balance began to shift towards the commonalty and the 'middle ranks'.

---

[81] Rogers, 'Military Revolution', 243–4.   [82] *Ibid.*, 277.
[83] Stone, 'Technology, Society and the Infantry Revolution', 362. Carpenter, 'English Peasants in Politics', 13, writes that 'the obligation to bear arms was . . . virtually universal. By the assize of arms in 1241 all those with land worth less than 40s. a year were to have "scythes, halberds, knives and other small arms". All those who were able . . . living outside the forests were to have bows and arrows. These were the minimum requirements'.

The infantry revolution was not the result of new technology; it was the outcome of changes in social constitution, distribution of power and the emergent discourse of the commonweal. The 'military revolution' expressed increasing recognition by the English feudal ruling class that indigenous *communes* could defeat them (or their counterparts elsewhere) in battle. The infantry revolution was especially important in fourteenth-century England because no country in the world at the time conformed more closely to the classical dictum that armed free citizens are the backbone of an effective army.

More research is needed before we can assess the significance of the arming of the English commonalty. It is an important area of research, particular in the USA, where militia traditions and the right to bear arms have continued to this day. There is only space here to illustrate the potential of the militia tradition in early modern England with reference to some local data relating to the Forest of Dean, a country situated east of the Wye and west of the Severn, in the 'marches' of England and Wales. Its borders and jurisdictions, its complex of rights, practices, customs, were highly contentious in the thirteenth century, when all classes below the king and his household resisted and cut back attempts by the Angevin kings to take land by defining it as ancient royal forest. Suffice it to say that what gave this particular *countrey* a highly distinctive political history was that from the reigns of Edward I to Charles I, relations with the state were distant. The late Christopher Hill once included it as 'a dark corner of the land', but in other ways it was highly typical. Put simply, the Forest of Dean provided the kingdom with special commodities (timber, iron, mill-stones) and occasional but essential services (bowmen, sappers and pikemen) and in return was trusted to be more or less self-governing.[84] The following table shows the results of counting the men of the Hundred of St Briavell's (the heart of the Forest district) whose military and economic status was assessed in Cardinal Thomas Wolsey's Military Survey of Gloucestershire in 1522.[85] It gives a solid impression of the military strength of the class contemporaries generally referred to as the 'commons' or 'commonalty' at the end of the military ascendancy of the longbow.

---

[84] Albert E. Prince, 'The Army and Navy', in J.F. Willard and W.A. Morris (ed.), *The English Government at Work 1327–1336, vol. 1 Central and Prerogative Administration* (Cambridge, Mass., 1940), 343, writes that 'among the foot [soldiers of English armies, 1327–36] there were the engineers, artificers, and work-men of various kinds attached to the army. The miners proved extremely useful in siege operations; normally they were drawn from the Forest of Dean'.

[85] Analysis of 'St Briavels Hundred', in R.W. Hoyle, *The Military Survey of Gloucestershire, 1522*, Bristol and Gloucestershire Archaeological Society Series 6, (Bristol 1993).

Men and armour in the Forest of Dean in 1522

Settlement Name	Names	Armed	Bows	Able-bodied
English Bicknor	45	24	15	24
Micheldean and Abenhall	101	73	26	51
Newland and Coleford	79	53	31	38
Clearwell	58	26	10	19
St Briavells	39	23	4	14
Bream Tithing	12	4	3	5
Hewelsfield	22	15	5	9
Staunton	37	25	15	15
Churchend Beam (Newland)	56	34	21	25
Little Dean	55	37	17	16
Lea Bailey	21	16	12	10
Ruardean	64	48	24	41
Northwood	15	14	11	10
Flaxley	17	16	7	10
Total	**621**	**408**	**201**	**287**

The source shows that the district had the equipment (and in many cases the training) to realize John of Salisbury's vision of an armed and confidently independent commonalty. The weapons and armour presented by the Hundred included 112 swords, 121 daggers, 8 shields, 114 glaives, 31 sallets, 18 Forest Bills, 7 horse and harness, 13 horses only, 16 harness only, 4 almain rivets, 1 lance, 22 hauberks, 5 gorgets, 1 splint, 1 axe and 1 javelin. Of 621 men recorded in the returns, no fewer than 408 were in possession of a weapon and armour, including no fewer than 200 longbows. How many of the men who possessed longbows practised often and knew how to use them? The 'able-bodied' category included men who were fit for military service: we must assume that many older and less fit men were also capable of using their weapons at target practice and hunting – though the latter was illegal, poaching was undoubtedly common before the state began to clamp down on it in the seventeenth and eighteenth centuries.[86]

---

[86] Later in the sixteenth century William Camden explained its history of lawlessness in ecological terms. 'The part that lieth West beyond Severne (which the Silures in old times possessed) along the river Vaga or Wye that parteth England and Wales was wholy bespred with thicke tall woods: we call it at this day, Deane Forrest.' Camden's description evoked the district's reputation as a 'dark corner of the land'. Dean, he wrote, 'was a wonderfull thicke forrest, and in former ages so darke and terrible by reason of crooked and winding, as also the grisly shade therein, that it rendered the inhabitants barbarous and emboldened them to commit many outrages'. 'In the reign of Henry VI,' he added, 'they so annoyed the banks of the Severn with their robberies, that there was an Act of Parliament (8 Henry VI) made on purpose to restrain them.':

The social structure of the Forest of Dean was unusual because it was archetypical. Gentlemen and labourers, the two poles of the local social structure, were present in larger than usual numbers, both explained in large part by the wealth the district produced and the ways it was produced. It was one of England's most important producers of iron and steel, industries that required relatively large labour forces. No fewer than seventy gentlemen attended the muster of 1608 from the district bordered by the River Severn in the east, the town of Newent in the North, Monmouth in the West and Tidenham and the River Wye in the South. This made it easily the most 'gentrified' part of its region. Gentlemen, generically, were the junior officers of the state system in war and peace. It was in such districts that the logic of the social structure that emerged between the thirteenth and eighteenth centuries was at its most stark. Kings and nobles were distant figures, rarely encountered. Barons lived elsewhere. Knights and wealthy gentlemen abounded, as they did in every wealthy district in England. The most powerful class was Smith's 'third sort of men', the yeomen and the little burghers of the district's market towns. Just as it had more rich, so it had more poor than other districts: the 'rascability' was well represented in every village and town, and in hundreds of extralegal 'cabins' in the Forest.

2.8   Commons versus nobles: news from Courtrai (1302)

The 'common' language of Norman-Angevin England emerged as a language of public rhetoric (and entertainment) in the fourteenth century. 'News' was spread in a number of ways. We know next to nothing about the composers of early fourteenth-century English, the details of how ideas and stories spread, and who spread them. Some of it can be deduced from what we have seen to have been a highly commercial society. What we do have are the original written appearances of some classic English stories. In this section and the next, foreshadowing specific discussion of language and public opinion in the next sections, I focus on contemporary stories about two events of seminal significance in the *longue durée* of English constitutional culture: the Battle of Courtrai (1302) and the deposition of Edward II (1327). In the first of these examples an early fourteenth-century English 'Song of the Flemish Insurrection' tells the story of how a mighty prince and a noble army was defeated and destroyed by the citizen army of the Flemings at the Battle of Courtrai

William Camden, *Brittania, or a Chorographical Description of Great Britain and Ireland*, transactions and additions by Edmund Gibson (London 1722), vol. 1, p. 280.

in 1302.[87] We do not know who wrote, read or heard it recited. We can only ask what classes of people it describes and addresses and deduce how they might have received it from other things we know about their society.

Its anti-French colouring was, after the anti-foreigner mood of the reigns of Henry III and Edward I, conventional and constitutionally neutral, but it also told of the solidarity of the Flemish commonalty:

> *Lustneth, lordinges, bothe yonge ant olde,*
> *Of the Frensshe-men that were so proude ant bolde,*
> *Hou the Flemmysshe-men bohten hem ant solde*
> *Upon a Wednesday.*
> *Betere hem were at home in huere londe,*
> *Then for te seche Flemmyssche by the see stronde,*
> *Wharethourh moni Frenshe wyf wryngeth hire honde,*
> *Ant singeth wylaway!*
> *The Kyng of fraunce made stauz newe*
> *In the lond of Flaundres, among false ant trew,*
> *That the commun of Bruges ful sore con a-rewe,*
> *Ant seiden amonges hem,*
> *'Gedere we us togedere hardyliche at ene,*
> *Take we the bailiffs by tuenty ant by tene,*
> *Clappe we of the hevedes an oven o the grene,*
> *Ant cast we y the fen.*

The commons not only defeated the foreign lords, they humiliated them and disdainfully 'cast [them] in the Fen'. Scholars have often conjectured that the primary audience envisaged by vernacular writers of the fourteenth century was the class or rank from which most of them came: what would later be called the 'gentry', the lower ranks of the nobility or 'second estate'. John of Salisbury, William Langland, John Trevisa, Geoffrey Chaucer, John Gower, John Wyclif, Thomas Hoccleve, Sir Thomas More, William Tyndale, Sir Thomas Smith, Shakespeare, Bacon and Hobbes are just a few prominent examples of writers who came from the heterogeneous 'middle ranks' between the king and magnates and the 'rascability'.

Many historians see this 'middle rank' as a significant agency in the constitutional struggles of the 1250s, as we saw earlier. They held small estates (and smaller inheritances – many were younger brothers) that many of them worked for themselves. At a time when the ability to read documents in Latin and Norman-French was becoming more important to landholding households, they had a special interest in ensuring that their households included members with literary skills, sons in wealthier

---

[87] All quotations in this section from Thomas Wright, *Political Songs of England from the reign of John to that of Edward II* (Camden Society 1839, repr. Cambridge 1996), 187–95.

lords' retinues and others in the Church. When 'The Song of the Flemish Insurrection' was circulating, in the troubled reign of Edward II, the native language of this class, where the lowest ranks of the conquerors intermarried with their English neighbours, was a dialect of English. It looks very much as if the prestige of English rose very rapidly in the aftermath of the 'common enterprise', at the very time when literary French was becoming popular in the inner circles of kings and magnates. Class lines were being redrawn.

In keeping with convention, the song addressed a noble audience (*Lustneth, lordinges . . .*), but the formality would work equally well with irony if the song was sung and even enacted under a market cross to an audience of English *communes* from any district in England and many parts of Scotland and Wales. For an English lord, imbued with the anti-foreigner sentiments that had informed a generation of baronial struggles with the king, one implication of the song was that the flower of French nobility was so feeble as to have been defeated by an army of commoners. This appealed to the patriotic vanity of lords who, in spite of their continuing use of French as their language of caste and record, were beginning to see themselves as 'English', or, at least, as the natural leaders of the English *communes*. At the same time the song carried the unmistakeable message that an army of the *communes* was capable of defeating an army of lords. It would prove to be another of those enduring themes that came to a head in the 1640s. It is notable that the song is in English, and may be a hint that vernacular English was becoming fashionable at the courts of *lordinges*, but my impression is that it would be another fifty years or so before great magnates went so far as to patronize what was, after all, the *common* language. Thomas IV, lord Berkeley, Trevisa's patron, was a pioneer and he was not born until thirty years after the battle of Courtrai.

The choice to report in English had political resonance that makes the central ambivalence of the song even more subversive. At first sight it is the 'commune', or city, of Bruges that is active in the resistance. The word was often used to mean 'community' in a vague but definite all-embracing sense, but it is made clear in the next verse, and throughout the song, not only that the 'commune' is composed of what in England would be called 'the commons' or 'the commonalty', specifically, those arch-heretics and rebels, clothworkers, but also that they *elect* their king, in exactly the way that weavers clubs elected their leaders in times of riot and insurrection, from the fourteenth to the nineteenth centuries. This would only intensify the disdain a noble Englishman might be expected to feel towards his French counterparts, but it also carried the obvious message that an army of commoners was *capable* of defeating an army of hereditary warriors, Europe's equivalents to the Japanese Samurai. They were capable of organizing themselves and possessed with the valour to defeat their class enemies:

> *The webbes ant the fullaris assembled in hem alle,*
> *Ant makeden huere consail in huere commune halle;*
> *Token Peter Conyng huere kyng to calle,*
> *Ant beo huere chevynton.*
> *Hue nomen huere rouncyn out of the stalle,*
> *Ant closeden the toun withinne the walle;*
> *Sixti baylies ant ten hue maden a-doun falle,*
> *Ant moni another sweyn.*
> *Tho wolde the baylies, that were come from Fraunce...*
> *Y telle ou for sothe, for al huere bobaunce ('vaunting'?)*
> *Ne for the avowerie of the King oif Fraunce*
> *Tuenti score ant fyve haden their mischaunce*
> *By day ant eke by nyht...*

Imagining an audience of *lordings* yields one probable reading. In a courtly context the song could be heard as a hard-edged piece of honest counsel. Sung in a market place, especially that of a town with magnate troubles of one kind or another (like Abingdon, Bury St Edmunds or Norwich), or in London, where *every* variant of *commun* words was in use, what stands out is that the *commun* defeats the French *king, bailiffs, lordes, fortye barouns and seaven eorles, a thousent five hundred knyhtes proude, sixti thousent swyers*. A kingdom in arms is defeated by a *comun* that shows itself to be eminently capable of organizing itself without the aid of lords of any kind. It is not so much a nation as a regime that is defeated. After the defeat *thenne seith the Eorl of Artoiis 'Y yelde me to the, Peter Conyng by thi nome, yef thou art hende ant free* [gentle and free] *that y ne have no shame ne no vylkte* [disgrace] *that y ne be noud ded.'* But the citizens of Bruges will have none of this assertion of caste:

> *Thenne swor a bocher, 'By my leaute! (loyalty)*
> *Shalt thou ner more the Kyng of Fraunce se,*
> *Ne in the toun of Bruges in prison be,*
> *Thou woldest consume bred.'*

The nobles are humiliated, imprisoned and reduced to the diet of the commonalty (*bred*). There was a class element to this, as well as a nationalist one. The song could be read or heard in either or both of these ways. As a class statement it was the story of the commons defeating the feudal ruling class. The song was a potential lesson for an audience of English lords, and a potential inspiration for anti-noble feeling in England, of which there was no shortage in Edward II's reign.[88]

---

[88] E.g. 'A Song Against the Retinues of the Great People', Wright, *Political Songs*.

2.9   The deposing of kings: the afterlife of Edward II

Cultural historian Annabel Patterson refers to such stories as 'paradigmatic anecdotes'.[89] Attitudes towards the Flemish (as with all foreigners) were mercurially changeable, but the idea that the *communes* could put fear into and defeat an army of chivalry was to enjoy a long shelf-life.[90] We encounter many hints of the existence of *commune opinioun*, as early as the first or second decade of the fourteenth century, in the 'Song Against the King's Taxes', which asserts that 'A king should not go out of his kingdom to wage war/ Unless the commons (*la commune*) of his land will consent'. To consent, *la commune* must presumably be informed of what he intended to do. If he failed to consult the community, 'by treason many will perish/ The king should not leave his kingdom without counsel'. That it was written in Norman French suggests an aristocratic, possibly a courtly audience: an early form of the 'mirror for princes' genre. It announces a theme that would build up, over the fourteenth century, into an angry roar: 'Now goes it in England from year to year/ The fifteenth penny to do thus a common harm (*commune dampnum*)/ The people (*commune*) must sell cows, vessels and clothes . . .', and concludes that 'It does not please the people to pay the fifteenth to the last penny', as if what pleases the people is already a matter of moral, political and constitutional significance.[91]

---

[89]   'By "anecdote", I refer to a brief, independent narrative about human behaviour, short enough to be emblematic, independent enough of its surroundings to be portable, and with one or more colourful individuals at its centre. Sometimes these individuals are nameless, but their independence of spirit, their refusal to be absorbed into the unifying texture of a grand narrative, is evident nonetheless. The better anecdotes, therefore, contain snatches of conversation, whose verisimilitude is a key to their memorability, the cause of their having remained in cultural memory; and they tend to function as signs that something in the system is under stress, something in the official account is up for question.': Annabel Patterson, *Reading Holinshed's Chronicles* (Chicago 1994), 42.

[90]   The defeat of the French by the Flemings on 11 July 1302 seems to have caught the imagination of the English. Adam of Usk interpolates a blasphemous *passio mirabilis* into his account of the events of 1410, which he 'discovered in the chronicles of this monastery' when he was at Bruges, 'written to mock the French for the defeat'. Usk, 219–25.

[91]   Wright, *Political Songs*. In Norman-French:

> *Roy ne doit a feore de gere extra regnum ire,*
> *For si la commune de sa terre velint consentire:*
> *Par tresoun voit honme sovent quam plures perire;*
> *A quy en fier seurement nemo potest scire.*
> *Non eat ex regno rex sine consilio . . .*
> *Ore court en Engletere de anno in annum*
> *Le qunizyme dener, pur fere sic commune dampnum . . .*
> *E vendre fet commune gent vaccas, vas, et pannum.*
> *Non placet ad usummum quindenum sic dare nummum.*

The 'Song Against the King's Taxes' was a rather daring expression of populist themes in the language of the ruling class. Another 'Song of the Times' (c.1308) expressed what may be the earliest written English version of the corrupt officers theme. The idea that corrupt officers (the Flanks, unarmed Hand and Stomach in John of Salisbury's political body) were to blame for unjust government, and not the kings and barons themselves, was a tactic employed by all opposition movements from this time: *Thos kingis ministris beth I-schend* (corrupted) . . . *Of those thevis hi taketh mede* (bribes).[92] These sayings (or singings) have a proverbial ring to them: memorable ideas stated in a minimum of words.

Moral and proverbial sayings, songs and stories, circulated at the speed of commerce. Economic historians agree that the English economy was as intense in the late thirteenth and early fourteenth centuries as it had been since the height of the Roman Empire.[93] It has even been argued that England did not regain this pitch of competitive, avaricious enterprise, dynamism, nor attain similar population levels, until the eve of the Industrial Revolution, c.1760.[94] Domestic *trafike* interconnected an expanding and overwhelmingly *acoustic* kingdom. Household communed with household, forming neighbourhood and parish. Parish and village was not always the same thing: some parishes, especially in upland, pastoral and forest districts, contained many hamlets, villages or 'townships'. Village communed with village on market days, at hundred courts, and via innumerable daily and weekly journeys, visits and consultations. Market towns were connected by routine traffic with provincial capitals. Provincial capitals trafficked with London. One of the most obvious themes of the long early modern period is the short-circuiting of the provincial capitals. Increasingly, manufacturing districts trafficked directly with London. The most obvious case is the institutionalization of cloth traffic between the provinces and the London cloth market at Blackwell's Hall.

The time it took for stories to pass throughout the system varied considerably. Communications may have been especially rapid along a line running from Gloucester across the Cotswolds to Cirencester, and thence along the Thames Valley, through London into Essex, Suffolk and Norfolk. Mavis Mate shows that *commune opinioun* reached deep into Sussex in the aftermath of Cade's Rebellion, beyond Ashdown Forest, as far

[92] Wright, *Political Songs*, 195–205

[93] Katherine Reyerson 'Commerce and Communication', in David Abulafia (ed.), *New Cambridge Medieval History* (Cambridge 2000), stresses the mutual dependence and interchangeability of the two terms and contexts.

[94] See above, Section 2.1.

south as Eastbourne.[95] Kent was intensively traversed by travellers to Canterbury, Dover and from most villages to the capital. The roads from Hertford and St Albans were busy with traffic, supplying the 'wen' of London with its daily and weekly needs long before Cobbet's day. But the routinization of administrative and commercial links between all parts of England – the emergence of a vernacular market – is the overall tendency, process or 'progress'. Even if 99 per cent of what went on within this linguistic and commercial system is completely invisible in terms of direct evidence, it is assumed and reported to have existed in sources from the late thirteenth century forward. We can only guess how long it took for a particularly important and memorable story to spread through all the districts encompassed by a line running north from Liverpool to Carlisle, along Hadrian's Wall to Newcastle, down the east coast to Kings Lynn, Norwich, Ipswich, Gravesend, Dover, Southampton, Exeter, Plymouth, Lands End, Bristol, Monmouth and Chester.

To travel, last, and be revised in multiple forms and placed within different ideologies, messages had to be concise and simple, allude strongly to or be directly about what we call 'celebrities' or celebrity events (concerning names everyone knew, or thought they knew) and have a 'hook' that would carry them from mouth to ear to mind and to mouth again, in this case, among the English, for centuries. The medium (broadly, routine traffic and mobility) had to exist, but everything depended upon a common language and the quality of the message. Stories about kings were particularly important. More than any other institution, monarchy embodied and incorporated the states of medieval Europe. It did so by being imprinted and reproduced in the minds of subjects. Before attention began to turn towards the commonwealth, the whole body of the people, stories about kings were the stuff of the kingdom, what made it a community. More official channels like proclamations, statutes, taxes and other information deliberately communicated throughout the realm were also important constituents of national community. To villagers and townspeople all over England, they faded into (or stood out from) a much richer repertoire of sayings and stories concerning kings and their courts.

The deposition and subsequent fate of Edward II was a subject of controversy at the time and every subsequent generation has received, embellished, revised and passed it on in various versions, discussed it, and pondered on its meanings and morals. As Patterson says of all 'paradigmatic anecdotes', the stories of Edward II testify that 'something in

---

[95] Mavis Mate, 'The Economic and Social Roots of Medieval Popular Rebellion: Sussex in 1450–1451,' *Economic History Review*, new series, 45:4 (Nov. 1992), 661–2, 664.

the system is under stress, something in the official account is up for question'.[96]

John Trevisa translated an earlier Latin version of the causes and consequences of the events of 1327 at least thirty years after the events, for Thomas lord Berkeley, a great patron of translation. Thomas Fitzharding was 'the fourth lord [Berkeley] of that name since the conquest'. The events of 1327 touched his dynasty very intimately. A tenacious legend had arisen that Edward II endured his final imprisonment and was murdered in a stinking cell at Berkeley Castle, where his gaoler was Thomas IV's grandfather.[97] In addition to being Thomas IV's household intellectual and scholar, Trevisa was also his personal religious adviser. As priest to the town and parish of Berkeley, he was pastor to the core of a small but powerful barony. Thomas was already one of the few lords in England whose line (arguably) ran continuously in the male line 'since the conquest', a phrase that did not cease to be applied to lords and kings of England until they were too weak and too few to insist on it. Trevisa knew he would have Thomas's attention with regard to this story, for it would inevitably bring to mind memories and stories of his grandfather's involvement in the alleged regicide, and of the enduring legitimacy crisis that ensued from it.

Trevisa's Englishing of the demise of 'the secounde Edward after the conquest', was one that Thomas IV ('the magnificent' as the family's chronicler John Smyth of Nibley titled him) could live with. It simply traced the king's downfall to 'the thrydde day of Averel' in that fateful and troubled year of 1327, when 'the olde kynge was i-brought out of Kelynworthe to the castell of Berkeley'. During his imprisonment 'many men conspired for to helpe at his delyveraunce', but to no avail, for Edward died.[98] Trevisa said nothing about the exact place and manner of the death, and no hint of murder was used. Trevisa did not complete his translation of Ralph Higden's Latin *Polychronicon* until 1387, but may have been working on it since the Berkeleys first retained him, perhaps

---

[96] Annabel Patterson, *Reading Holinshed's Chronicles*, 42. W.M. Ormrod, 'Agenda for Legislation, 1322–c.1340', *English Historical Review* 105:414 (January 1990), 8, 15–16, 25–6 and *passim*, sums up one aspect of a multifaceted crisis: 'The barons had traditionally claimed to speak for the community of the realm' but at the time of the Parliaments of 1324 and 1325 'the Lords were evidently perceived as a rump of cowed rebels' and 'the knights and the burgesses rejected the Crown's requests for subsidies'. 'The last years of Edward II's reign witnessed the emergence of the Commons as an independent force in English politics with the potential to influence the business of Parliament and to change the course of government policy.'

[97] The legend is referred to in Vita Sackville West's account of 'the room where Edward II was imprisoned and eventually murdered': *Berkeley Castle* (English Life Publications 1978), 4–5.

[98] John Trevisa, *Ranulph Higden's Polychronicon*, vol. VIII, 323.

as early as 1357. This was thirty years after the event, and the case was officially closed. The new regime accepted the lord of Berkeley's oath that he was not at Berkeley Castle when Edward was killed, and left in abeyance any question of the part he might, hypothetically, have played in the *coup de grace*.

The story has fascinated antiquarians and historians ever since Edward II disappeared from public view. In the late sixteenth century John Smyth of Nibley reported unequivocal evidence that Thomas III was in residence at Berkeley Castle when Edward died.[99] Modern historians show not only that Smyth was right but that Edward's son, the future Edward III, knew it too, at the time.[100] Knowing what he knew of the temperament, wealth, eminence, estate administration and management, military and political power and pride of the fourteenth-century Berkeleys, Smyth found it unthinkable that so great, confident and proud a lord would have allowed anyone to command him against his will in his own country. The Berkeleys 'kept the peace' in a region encompassing Bristol, Cirencester and Tewkesbury. This was a powerful Norman-Angevin barony at the peak of its power and reputation. To Froissart, the Berkeleys represented what chivalry was supposed to be in an age of decay.[101] Only a Berkeley could keep order and lead in this region. Smyth assumed that the murder was revenge for Edward's imprisonment and, effectively, murder of Maurice Berkeley, Trevisa's lord's great-grandfather, who, during the civil wars of the early 1320s, had come to him at St Mary's Abbey, Cirencester, under a flag of truce. Smyth believed that no-one betrayed the honour and trust of a medieval Berkeley without consequence. The Berkeleys could raise a large, experienced, loyal and well-trained army of knights, squires, bowmen-yeomen, artisans and peasants in less than a day.[102] The barony of Berkeley, for Smyth, was a place where what would one day be called 'feudalism' once actually worked.

---

[99] *The Berkeley Manuscripts: the Lives of the Berkeleys*, vol. 1 (ed. Sir John Maclean), 291–5 (death of Edward II), and 296–7 (Thomas II's involvement).

[100] Claire Valente, 'The Deposition and Abdication of Edward II', *English Historical Review* 113:453 (September 1998), 852–82; Ian Mortimer argues that Edward II did not die at Berkeley Castle: see Mortimer, *The Greatest Traitor: the Life of Sir Roger Mortimer, Ruler of England 1327–1330* (London 2004), 173–85; Mortimer, 'The Death of Edward II in Berkeley Castle', *English Historical Review*, 140:489, 1175–1214; Mortimer, *The Perfect King: the Life of Edward III, Father of the English Nation* (London 2006), esp. 66 and appendices 2, 3: 'The Fake Death of Edward II' and 'A Note on the Later Life of Edward II'.

[101] Geoffrey Brereton (trans. and ed.), *Froissart Chronicles* (Harmondsworth 1978), 114.

[102] S.L. Waugh, 'The Profits of Violence: the Minor Gentry in the Rebellion of 1321 in Gloucestershire and Herefordshire', *Speculum* 52 (1977), 843–69, is a useful study of the regional context at the time of Edward II's betrayal of Maurice Berkeley.

For Smyth, Thomas's involvement embodied the law of the times: Edward II betrayed the laws of chivalry and honour. A few years later Thomas was presented with an opportunity to do to Edward what Edward had done to Thomas's grandfather. Like Maurice, lord Berkeley, Edward was killed slowly, with indignity and finally (according to the best known versions of the story) in agony, over a period of weeks. The magnates of England wanted rid of him, and there could never have been any doubt what would happen if he was handed over to Thomas Berkeley. It was important that Edward should appear to have died of natural causes, and in an effort to achieve this he was put in a cell filled with the fumes of rotting cattle placed below it. He had a strong constitution and did not die. A method of killing was finally employed that alluded, and was probably intended to allude, to Edward's alleged homosexuality, and also killed without leaving an outward mark on the body. When he considered the case three centuries later, Smyth seems to have concluded that no-one at the time really doubted lord Thomas's intimate involvement in the death of Edward II.[103] Smyth was almost certainly wrong, but he was not the last to be misled by the 'display of political theatre' woven by 'Mortimer and the leading bishops', by Edward III himself, and by the welter of subsequent stories and legends.[104]

Recent scholarship doubting the veracity of stories of Edward's murder is irrelevant to the crucial point that they did not have to be true to memorialize what *was* undoubtedly true: that an English king had, in fact, been deposed and, conceivably, murdered. Stories of ghastly murder assisted the mnemonic process. They did not have to be true. The medium – 'murmuring' – was created by the message, a story that more than any other gave a constitutional edge to all the woes of the age. Writing decades after the event, Trevisa was clearly anxious about its impact on public opinion. Of Edward's 'levyng and his dedes is yit among the peple stryf . . . whither he schulde be accounted amonge seyntes other no', he wrote. Edward's fate caught the popular imagination; very soon the 'likynge and wille that wyves have to wende aboute make tydynges springe and sprede hugeliche of suche worshippyng'.[105] The handsome Edward became a popular saint, a victim, like 'wyves' and other pilgrims, of over-mighty lords and evil counsellors surrounding the only one who *might* listen to the voices of the people, and *might* do justice: the king.

---

103 Harvey, 'The Berkeleys of Berkeley: a Study in the Lesser Nobility of Late Medieval England' St Andrews University Ph.D. thesis (nd) (Gloucestershire County Records Office), 202–23 suggests that about half the county gentry were members of the Berkeley affinity in the fourteenth century and recourse to violence was commonplace. Smyth, *Lives*, vol. 2, 5–7.
104 Mortimer, *The Perfect King*, 52.   105 Trevisa, *Chronicon*, vol. 8, 323.

In the words of another contemporary chronicler, Edward's deposition arose from 'the commune clamour of the Englisshe-men, of the myche diseses that were done in Engeland, and also for diverse wronges that were done amonges the commune peple, of which the Kyng bare the blame with wrong, for he nas but ful yonge and tendre of age'. Public opinion, he thought, had been wrongly informed and it was necessary to correct its 'slaundre of the kinges persone'.[106] In troubled times it was bruited that 'diverse wronges that were done amonges [to] the commune peple' were proof of Edward's tyranny. In the eyes of the 'communes, . . . the Kyng bare the blame.' In the view of this anonymous chronicler the king should have been excused because he was 'but ful yonge and tendre of age'. He was young and inexperienced, and lacked good counsel.

The king was not to blame. This interpretation has implications, for although it was common opinion that tyrants could, legitimately, be over-thrown, if Edward was not responsible for the troubles of his reign he was not a tyrant, and therefore could not legitimately be deposed. Nor did the chronicler point a finger at ambitious, warring nobles. The blame for terrible times, and God's displeasure, lay not with the king, but with a handful of ill-bred counsellors and a rapacious, licentious and avaricious scarlet woman who conspired in her husband's murder and profited by it. In the *Brut* chronicler's account, the *communes* insist she should give up lands obtained unjustly, and by a woman, from poorer, less powerful men. She defied immemorial laws of patriarchy. The real culprit was her shifty paramour, Sir Roger Mortimer, who the *communes* believed, 'shulde dwelle opponn his owen londes, for the whiche landes he hade holpen disherite miche peple, so that the commune peple were nought destroied through her takyng so wrongful'. The Scarlet Woman theme is another recurring theme of popular politics in the fourteenth and fifteenth centuries.[107] The culprits had not yet been punished for the shocking murder of a retrospectively beloved and handsome king. Whatever the retrospective views, the chroniclers seemed to suggest that everything that was bad about life came to be signified by the tomb of the king at Gloucester Cathedral.

In the chronicler's account, the *communes* saw and heard the common clamour for government to be taken in hand, and the *real* government

---

[106] In Edward's reign the distinction between Norman-French and English was still strong, so *commune clamour* and *Englisshe-men* may be an obscure early reference to *commune opinioun* as the opinion of the commonalty, the subject population.

[107] The 'scarlet woman' theme occurred next in 1376, when reference was made to the 'lewedness and evell counsell' of Edward III's lover, Alice Perrers: F.W.D. Brie (ed.), *The Brut or The Chronicles of England* (London 1906), 331; for the case of 'Dame Alianore Cobham', see *Brut Chronicle*, 477–82.

of the people (the *communes* in Parliament) moved out of the shadows to restore order. Proper constitutional procedures for calling upon the counsel of the community were followed. A parliament was called. The magnates, church and *communes* came together to consider what had to be done to end the troubles of the realm. The 'assent of the communite in plein parlement was that Kyng Edward, sometyme Kyng of Engeland' was to be placed 'vunder the warde and governaunce of Henry, Erl of Lancastre, his cosyn', pending education and the recovery of his powers. But somehow, in a maelstrom of confusing circumstances and occasions, custody of Edward's body slipped from the hands of the wise nobles and into those of his faithless wife and her paramour. Events took the matter further than the *communes* of England had agreed to. The 'assent of the community in plain parliament' was only to place the king under the wardship of his cousin. The *communes* never sanctioned close imprisonment, torture and murder. Against the will of the people, Edward 'was takyn out of the castle of Kenylworth . . . and through colour of the Quene Isabel and of the Mortimer, without consent of any parlement, thai toke and lade him ther that never after none of his Kynrede might with him speke ne see, and after traitorously toke and mordrede him, for whose deth a foule sclandre aroos through-out all Christendome, when hit was done'.[108] What happened at Berkeley Castle was a foul crime that would forever stain the souls of those who perpetrated it. As an event, it was powerful enough to raise the thousands of doubts that became an enduring legitimacy crisis at the heart of the Norman-Angevin system. This was the case Trevisa, Thomas Berkeley, and the noble class as a whole, had to answer.

Trevisa too recorded the eruption of stories and murmurings that followed the event, but the villain in his version of the 'comoun tale' was the king himself. *Communes* only ever knew myths, a lord like Thomas Berkeley knew the man himself. The interpretation that Trevisa Englished at Berkeley Castle was that Edward had been a vulgar man in a king's place. He had betrayed his caste. Throughout his life, Edward 'forsooke the companye of lordes'. For Thomas Berkeley, *lordes* was not only an Estate but a moral and constitutional category which Edward had failed to live up to. Edward was like a common man born into a king's body, a man of plebeian habits and sensibility. He 'drownk hym to harlottes, to syngers and to gestoures, to carters, to delveres and to dykers, to rowers, shipmen and bootmen, and to other craftesmen, and yaf hym to grete drynkynge'. He discussed secrets of state inappropriately. When drunk, he 'wolde lightliche telle oute prive counseille'. He was a bully. At court

---

[108] De Brie, *Brut Chronicle*; this part c.1400: 258–9.

or in the alehouse, he was arrogant, and would petulantly 'smyte men that were aboute hym for wel litel trespas'. He was frivolous in religion and 'avaunced to staates of holy chirche hem hat were unable and unworthy, that was afterward a stake in his thye, and a spere in his side'. He was weak, indecisive and easily led, doing 'more by menis counsel than his owne. Worst of all, Edward loved strongliche oon of his queresters, and dede him grete reveraunce, and worshipped and made him grete and riche.' This, we may assume, was Thomas Berkeley's view of the man.[109]

In this account everything came back to the character and person of the king. He is the cause of all that follows. The king's personal weaknesses of character and judgement bring evil consorts and counsellors to the fore. Out of weaknesses of character at the very heart of the monarchy, the pivotal institution of Norman-Angevin rule, 'fel vilenye . . . , yvel speche and back bitynge . . . , sclaundre to the peple (plebi scandalum), harme and dame to the reume (regno detrimentum)'. God saw and was displeased. Edward's reign seemed to have ushered in an age dominated by devastating and providential signs of doom: 'in his time was so grete derthe of whete, and continuel moreyn of bestes, that noon suche was I-sene tofore that tyme'.[110] In terrible times, tyrants must be overthrown. The aggression and land-hunger that Edward I directed at enemies abroad turned in on itself when Edward failed to continue his father's victories. The system was in crisis. Edward's death was the capping sign of all signs (and story of all stories) for the spirit of the age. England's troubles circled around the king. Thomas Berkeley did what he did for the Common Good.

Trevisa left a translation of the constitutional theory that underpinned the Berkeley spin on Edward II's demise and foreshadowed their rebellion against Richard II. He turned his pen to Giles of Rome's *De Regimine Principum* in c.1388–90, a time of baronial unrest concerning the propriety of Richard II's manner of ruling. As had happened in Edward II's reign, and as had not happened in 1376 and 1381, the chronicle of troubles was beginning to focus, again, on the person of the king. Trevisa's translation 'was probably undertaken during a critical period of the reign of Richard II', writes David Fowler. Giles's distinction between a king and a tyrant was highly relevant to Lancastrian resentment of Richard II's oppressions in the 1380s. Thomas lord Berkeley joined the vengeful

---

[109] Hilda Johnstone, 'The Eccentricities of Edward II', *English Historical Review* 48:190 (April 1933), 265, quotes 'contemporary conversation on the demerits of Edward II' suggesting, amongst other faults, 'mental derangement' (1315) and a capacity for 'idling and applying himself to making ditches and digging and other improper occupations'.

[110] De Brie, *Brut Chronicle*, 299–301.

'lords appellants' who imposed their will on the king in 1387. 'It would appear from Trevisa's choice of this Treatise that, during the decade preceding his involvement in Richard's deposition, Thomas was doing his homework', writes Fowler.[111] Given Trevisa's and Thomas Berkeley's natural interest in the earlier crisis of 1327, Trevisa's translation of a key passage in Giles's *De Regimine* connected the two contexts.[112] They were not 'isolated events', but were linked by constitutional principles – and, above all, by a common language.

---

[111] David C. Fowler, *The Life and Times of John Trevisa, Medieval Scholar* (Seattle and London 1995), 190.

[112] Fiona Somerset, *Clerical Discourse and Lay Audience in Late Medieval England* (Cambridge 1998), 77, observes that Trevisa is more than a translator and is keen to adapt his text to immediate context: in his painstaking account of the meaning and application of 'counsel' he alters Giles's account of tyranny by adding an 'emphasis that a select group of lords, no less than a king, can be tyrannical'.

3 The power of a common language

Let us consider the false appearances that are imposed upon us by words, which are framed and applied according to the conceit and capacities of the vulgar sort: and although we think we govern our words and prescribe their meanings, and prescribe it well loquendum ut vulgus, sentiendum ut sapientes[1]; *yet certain it is that words, as a Tartar's bow, do shoot back upon the understanding of the wisest, and mightily entangle and pervert the judgement. So as it is almost necessary in all controversies and disputations to imitate the wisdom of the mathematicians, in setting down in the very beginning the definitions of our words and terms, that others may know how we accept and understand them, and whether they concur with us or no.[2]*

Empires are, first and foremost, cultural entities; and it's language that does the job, not legions.[3]

3.1 Vernacular populism to c.1400

In Inglysch toung I sall you telle...
For that es oure kynde langage
That we have here maste of usage...
Som canne Frankes and na Latin
That have used courte and dwelled ther-in,
And som canne o Latyn a perty
That canne Frankes bot febely
And some understandes in Inglysce
That canne nother Latyn na Frankes...
Bot ler[n]ed and lewed, alde and yonnge
All understande Inglysche tonng. (c.1350)[4]

---

[1] 'Speak with the people, think with the wise'.

[2] Francis Bacon, *The Advancement of Learning* (ed. G.W. Kitchin, London 1915), 134.

[3] Joseph Brodsky, 'On September 1, 1939, by W.H. Auden', in Brodsky, *Less than One: Selected Essays* (Harmondsworth 1987), 309.

[4] William of Nassington, *Speculum Vitae*; quotation from Nicholas Watson, 'The Politics of Middle English Writing', in Jocelyn Wogan-Brown, Nicholas Watson, Andrew Taylor, Ruth Evans (ed.), *The Idea of the Vernacular: an Anthology of Middle English Literary Theory 1280–1520* (University Park, Pa. 1999), 336.

The linguistic conjuncture of the thirteenth and fourteenth centuries is different from anything earlier: the rise of 'Middle' English (c.1300–1526) is blessed with a growing abundance of textual sources. Scholars naturally tend to treat 'Middle English' as a literary language. It is in relation to this tradition that Jeremy Catto recently argued that 'far from being a natural development from early Middle English', as older generations of linguists and literary scholars from Wright and Stubbs on tended to assume, 'it was effectively the artificial construct of a single generation of writers', active between 1370 and 1400.[5] If 'Middle English' is regarded exclusively as a literary language then Jeremy Catto is surely right: it was during this period that the two great literary masterpieces of early English, *Piers Plowman* and *The Canterbury Tales* were completed, along with a large number of works like the *Brut* chronicles, the Lollard Bible, the *Vision* of Julian of Norwich and John Trevisa's historical and political translations. If, however, the 'triumph of English' as a written language is regarded as only a part and, as I suggest, ultimately only a consequence, of the larger history of English as an increasingly inevitable language of public culture and everyday life, different analysis and perhaps conclusions are required.[6] The influence of their generation accepted, it remains to explain why men of such different circumstances and intentions as Langland, Chaucer, Julian, Trevisa, and lesser literati like Thomas Usk decided to wager their different careers and fames (or in Julian's case, her soul) on the future of English.[7] Their circumstances and projects were different, but they were responding to the same social conjuncture. That conjuncture deserves the attention of constitutional historians because more than any other movement it constituted modern

[5] Jeremy Catto, 'Written English: the Making of the Language, 1370–1400', *Past and Present* (October 2003), 25.

[6] Catto, 'Written English', 24, dates 'the point at which it began to be learnt as a cultural acquisition by native speakers of other tongues... effectively, [to] between 1750 and 1820'; Tim William Machan, *English in the Middle Ages* (Oxford 2003), 64–5, contends that 'It is not until well into the seventeenth century (or even the eighteenth) that English can be said to have something like official status', by which he means 'indigenous in powerful domains of business and government, codified, and widespread as the vehicle and subject of education'.

[7] E.g. on Trevisa: David C. Fowler, *The Life and Times of John Trevisa, Medieval Scholar* (Seattle 1995); Ralph Hanna III, 'Sir Thomas Berkeley and His Patronage', *Speculum* 64 (1989), 878–96; Ronald Waldron, 'John Trevisa and the Use of English', *Proceedings of the British Academy* 74 (1988), 171–202; 'The Life of Thomas the Fourth', *The Berkeley Mss, vol. 2: The Lives of the Berkeleys*, ed. Sir John Maclean (Gloucester 1883); on Usk: Paul Strohm, *Hochon's Arrow: the Social Imagination of Fourteenth-Century Texts* (Princeton 1992), ch. 7; 'The Appeal of Thomas Usk against John Northampton', 'Proclamation of Nicholas Brembre' and 'A Petition of the Folk of Mercerye' in R.W. Chambers and Marjorie Daunt (ed.), *London English* (Oxford 1931).

England.[8] Henceforth it was the language of an enduring 'condition of England' debate.

Although 'much remains speculative about the beginnings' of the vernacular languages of Europe, decisive influences are clear enough in the case of English. The impact of the Norman Conquest was not that it led to French becoming the mother tongue, but that 'the displacement of Anglo-Saxon as the language of government caused written English to diversify into regional dialects and simplify its noun endings, much as the collapse of Roman power had accelerated the breakaway of the Romance languages from Latin'. When vernacularization became an assertive movement in the fourteenth century, 'colloquial English now affected the written language, because the old standard was no longer being maintained by a public authority'. By this time, in Michael Clanchy's view, English had become the first language of all sections of English society except the royal court, where French remained strong. It was not its colloquial use by the ruling class, but 'the advance of French as an international literary and cultural language, particularly in the thirteenth century, which caused its increased use as a written language for English records'.[9]

In 1300 five to six million people used a recognizable dialect of *Inglysch toung* as their first or second language. At that time, late in the reign of Edward I, the king and barons spoke French.[10] The king's and lords' clerks recorded their transactions in Norman-French or Latin, the 'sacral' language of religion, philosophy and high culture. For two centuries *Inglysch toung* 'had to struggle with French [and] Latin for its hold on the sermon and popular poem', and only 'one class . . . the *rustici* or *nativi*', that is to say the unfree, was, in linguistic terms, 'exclusively English'.[11]

---

[8] Christine Carpenter, 'Political and Constitutional History: Before and After McFarlane', in R.H. Britnell and A.J. Pollard (ed.), *The McFarlane Legacy: Studies in Late Medieval Politics and Society* (Stroud 1995), advocates a return to K.B. McFarlane's interests in 'aggregates and beliefs and . . . in "the complex organism" of "the English body politic"', suggesting that 'we can take this further. We must include the public dimension neglected by McFarlane.'

[9] M.T. Clanchy, *From Memory to Written Record: England 1066–1307*, (Oxford 1993), 212–13.

[10] William Stubbs, *The Constitutional History of England* (1897; repr. New York 1987), vol. 1, 379–80; Clanchy, *Memory to Written Record*, 214, cites 'the remark of Richard Fitz Neal that English and Normans were so intermarried by his time (c.1179) that they were indistinguishable, has often and rightly been cited . . . It was not primarily the Norman Conquest but the advance of French as an international literary and cultural language, particularly in the thirteenth century, which caused its increased use as a written language for English records.'

[11] Stubbs, *Constitutional History*, 1: 479, 587, 590; Catto, 'Written English', 33, writes that 'the vernacular, in the twelfth and thirteenth centuries, was a spoken language . . . no

During the ill-starred reign of Edward II, and increasingly during the middle and later fourteenth century, the *communes* in parliament and in the streets greatly increased their activism and efficacy in constitutional and political life – their membership of 'the political community' – and their language began to erode the political dominance and cultural superiority of Latin and Norman-French. By the end of the thirteenth century, local cultures (rural as well as urban), but not all households, were for practical purposes multilingual. By c. 1300 only the poorest, most oppressed, unfree sections of the community were monoglot, speaking and understanding English alone.[12] Early English history is a special case of a more general historical phenomenon, in which the vernacular languages of conquered people swallow the languages of the rulers.[13]

'Middle' English, therefore, was originally the language of the estate or class to which (as Thomas Wimbledon formulated it in 1387) 'it fallith to travayle bodily and with here sore swet geten out of the erthe bodily liflode for hem and for other parties'[14] – the 'feet', 'third estate' or 'commonalty'. For about four or five generations after the conquest of 1066, English was the definitive mark of subjection. Between c. 1150 and c. 1300, an age of population growth and commercial intensification, transactions between the commonalty and the ruling classes multiplied. By c. 1300 English was no longer merely the language of conquered *nativi*. The second, third and fourth generations of run-of-the-mill 'lords', men with small, localized estates, grew up speaking English. They formed part of the very first formation of the abiding, dynamic netherlands of English constitutional culture – the 'middles'. Chroniclers searched for words to describe this in-between class during the constitutional crises of the 1250s and 1260s, when political pressure was applied to the barons and king by a *communitas bacheleria*, a 'class' that encompassed the 'rash

---

trace of the use of written English as a first step in learning letters has survived in extant early Middle English books'. Tim William Machan, 'Language Contact in *Piers Plowman*', *Speculum* 69:2 (April 1994), 378–9, writes that English was 'the language associated with economically, educationally and socially disadvantaged speakers and domains . . . [It was] the language of an underclass'.

[12] Stubbs, *Constitutional History*, 1: 479, 587, 589–90; Catto, 'Written English', 33, 35, writes that twelfth- and thirteenth-century English 'was a spoken language . . . By the fourteenth century, Latin was available in virtually all English communities'.

[13] Robert Bartlett, *The Making of Europe: Conquest, Colonization and Cultural Change 950–1350* (London 1993), 198–204. If the interpretation of the history of the British Isles set out in Stephen Oppenheimer, *The Origins of the British: a Genetic Detective Story* (London 2006), is correct, it is likely that members of the Germanic language family came to England before, perhaps long before, the Roman conquest. This would mean that 'Anglo Saxon' had assimilated many other conquering tongues before the Norman Conquest of 1066.

[14] *Wimbledon's Sermon, Redde Rationem Villicationis Tue: A Middle English Sermon of the Fourteenth Century*, ed. Ione Kemp Knight (Pittsburgh, Pa. 1967) lines 38–46, p. 63.

young' sons of knights and 'the apprentices, the ribald and irresponsible multitude' that appeared in the streets of London in 1263.

In practice, the 'nativist' movement of the thirteenth century was also, necessarily, populist. As we saw, it began to emerge three or four generations after the conquest. John of Salisbury first raised the question of what constituted a native and a foreigner in his book of counsel for Henry II. A new definition found social expression a century later in Simon de Montfort's 'common enterprise'. The language was tentative and vague, in Latin, French and English, but the new idea was that anyone manifestly dedicated to the common good of England, above all else except God, was a native. Baronial nativism came to the fore when a regime or class felt threatened by newcomers. Seen through, it entailed not just alliance, but identity with the common, English-speaking people, Piers Plowman and his neighbours, effectively (in the English context) the subject class. It is not so difficult for us to see that this simple, populist ideal might appeal to 'rash (anti-authoritarian) young men' and 'middle people' (*mediocris populi*) like the frustrated *liberi homines* of Peatling Magna. In a contracting ecology, lords secular and religious, and the king, were tightening their systems of expropriation, cutting out middle men and living longer than their sons could comfortably abide. Henry II's sons and grandson did not heed John of Salisbury's warning that a king who failed to gain the support and consent of the heart, armed hand and feet was a weak king: his kingdom was bound to be prey to foreigners. Great lords felt the pinch but lesser lords felt it more acutely. The children of lesser lords ('knights', 'gentlemen', 'esquires', 'yeomen', 'burgesses') grew up closer to the working population and English became their natural tongue before the senior ranks of the ruling class. Given the number of children of this class who became the great pioneers of 'middle' English, it is likely that the 'middles' had embraced 'English tongue' by the decade of William Langland's birth, the 1320s.[15] English became a cause in the lifetimes of Langland (putative father a squire from the West Midlands)

---

[15] In September 1295 Edward I issued a writ of summons to the clergy claiming 'that the French had not only unjustly occupied the duchy of Aquitaine, but had prepared an invasion fleet against England, and were planning to "obliterate the English language from the land" (*linguam Anglicam . . . omnino de terra proponit*) . . . these claims may have been intended to appeal to popular sentiment. The presence in the assembly of 1295 of representatives of the parochial clergy . . . provided a means whereby the crown's "evident necessity" at a time of crisis might be preached – in their allegedly endangered vernacular language – to the people': Malcolm Vale, 'Language, Politics and Society: the Uses of the Vernacular in the Later Middle Ages', *EHR* 120 (485) (2005), 15–34.', 19–20, citing W. Stubbs, *Select Charters*, revised H.W. Davis (Oxford 1960), 480. Vale writes (28) that 'the idea of a community as a linguistic unity which was (at least in part) constituted by that unity was certainly apparent in England from the later thirteenth century onwards'.

and Julian of Norwich (probable father a well-off Norwich merchant). English became fashionable as well as functional in the castles of greater lords a generation or two later. John Trevisa's English translations of Giles of Rome on the definition and reforming of tyrants, done for his master, Thomas, lord Berkeley, in 1387, symbolizes the encroachment of native speech into magnate courts, a process that had greater social distance to cover and therefore took a little longer. Henry of Lancaster's choice of 'Englysshe tung' to make his formal claim to the English throne on 30 September 1399 marks the English conquest of the innermost circle of power, thus completing a process begun when Henry III first responded to the demands of the *bachelerie* and *mediocris populi* in 1258.

In the name of the father, of the Sone and the Holy Gost I Henry of Lancastre chalange this reme of Inglond... as that I am descendit be right line of the blod comyng fro the good lord kyng Henry thrid and thorowgh the right that God of his grace ath send me with the help of my kin and my frendes to recover it, the whych reme was in poynt to ben undoo for defaute of governance and undoying of the good lawes.[16]

The business of Henry IV's court and administration continued to be recorded in Norman French, letters to ecclesiastical notables and foreign courts were in Latin, but English was Henry's political language of choice. A letter from Henry to his chancellor, Thomas FitzAlan, dictated in 1407, is in Norman French, but it has a postscript in Henry's own hand, in English: 'I thonk the wryter of youre lettre, and byd God gyve him good lyff and long, Vostre HR.' Likewise another letter to the same correspondent in 1409 concludes with the PS, again in Henry's own hand, 'My dere worshypful and wel beloved cousyn, I thank you hertely of the grete busnesse that ye do for me and for my Reaume, and trust pleynly in youre good conduite, and hoping to God to speke to you hastely, and thank you with good helthe, Youre true Frend and chylde in God, HR.' This may mean that Henry's court wrote Norman French and, in perhaps deliberate contrast to that of the deposed Richard II, and possibly with self-conscious *avant-gardism*, spoke English.[17]

On the evidence of Henry's correspondence, Scots, Welsh, women, common soldiers, the king and his chancellor now spoke and wrote in English, ecclesiastics wrote in Latin, but clerks, the most old-fashioned, wrote in Norman French.[18] This was the greater context that produced

[16] G.O. Sayles, 'The Deposition of Richard II: Three Lancastrian Narratives', *Bulletin of the Institute of Historical Research* 54 (1981), 257–70.

[17] Cf. Russell A. Peck, 'Social Conscience and the Poets', in Francis X. Newman (ed.), *Social Unrest in the Late Middle Ages* (Binghamton 1986).

[18] *Royal and Historical Letters of the Reign of Henry the Fourth*, ed. F.C. Hingeston, 2 vols. (London 1860). Richard Kingeston, Dean of Windsor, to Hen IV re. Welsh revolt

two parallel efforts by intellectuals and clerks towards a standardized, authorized vernacular: Chaucer and the Chancery Clerks of Henry V.[19] English completed its transformation from language of the common people to language of the whole community in three or four generations. This movement was the linguistic form of a social revolution – the revolution of commonalty.

3.2   Native tongues

If language is an implicit social contract that binds members of the linguistic community to prescribed usages, without which communications and the production of meaning would be impossible, then any given language is necessarily a historically specific occurrence, for the investigation of which historicism would appear to hold out the best hope.[20]

As Clanchy's account of the fate of English after the conquest would predict, early 'middle' English texts show strong traces of the dialect of the regions in which they were written. The question addressed here is pretextual: what came before the literature? My hypothesis is that speakers and writers of 'middle' English used language as they found it. Dialect elements lingered on but what mattered to the experimental generations of the fourteenth century was to create language that was *common* in the sense of being understandable by everyone everywhere in England. They were not fixated on grammar and spelling in the way that subsequent scholars and scribes have been. Many of the great English sentences and sayings from Langland to Tyndale seem to have been heard and memorized by their authors before they wrote them down. The best sentences of Langland, Julian of Norwich, Chaucer, Margery Kempe, Lollards and William Tyndale sound as if they had long been shaped by 'the tongues of the common mouth'. The poets and visionaries aimed at language that any person, *lewd* or learned, would understand if spoken aloud by someone who wanted to be understood. At the beginning of this vernacular revolution, in c.1200, England was a seething world of local, district and provincial dialects of English governed by lords speaking French

in 1403 starts in NF, breaks into passionate English in the third last para., and the penultimate para. begins in English and ends in NF (1.155–9); Gray of Ruthin to H IV 1400 is English (1.35–8); Earl of March to Hen IV 1400 is English with a Scots accent; Margery Marten to the earl of Oxford (1.171) is a begging letter in English; Hen IV to FitzAlan (1407, 1.180); Hen to FitzAlan (1409 2.277); Soldiers of Calais to Henry IV re. wages (1405, 1.146–7); James of Douglas, Warden of the March, to Hen IV (1405, 1.733–6); David Fleming of Bygar to Hen IV (1.153).

[19] See 'An Anthology of Chancery English', Electronic Text Centre, University of Virginia.

[20] Gabrielle Spiegel, 'History, Historicism and the Social Logic of the Text in the Middle Ages', *Past and Present*, 131 (1991), repr. in Keith Jenkins (ed.), *The Postmodern History Reader* (London and New York 1997), 181, 185.

and priests speaking Latin. 'Because our only evidence comes via the medium of writing, we shall never know what the most colloquial varieties of English were.'[21] Languages leave no trace unless they are written down. Yet there may be a way of working our way into the grass roots condition of English as an exclusively oral language, from the bottom up. What can be deduced about the approximate condition of the language in c.1300 by 'backward projection' from modern observations of dialect?

Certain things are assumed about the dialectal condition of English in c.1300. At the grass roots, in the localities, heterogeneity was the rule. A great historian of the English language, David Crystal, writes that 'in the history of a language, there are always several trends taking place simultaneously. A richness of diversity exists everywhere, and always has'. Traditionally, historians of English language and literature have traced the history of standardization and, in various ways, marginalized non-standard versions. Crystal shows that 'Standard English . . . is only a small part of the kaleidoscopic diversity of dialects and styles which make up "the English language"'; there is not one but many 'stories of English'.[22] What follows is an illustrative 'story' of a type of non-standard English that has prevailed throughout its history: local dialect. It is taken from a study conducted in 1943, when its author, C.H. Lemmon, reviewed and analysed a century of studies of rural Gloucestershire speech and concluded that it was 'a dialect which has had a separate and parallel existence with the standard language for fifteen hundred years'. 'However crowded it may have become with standard words, influenced by standard pronunciation, or grammatically changed by the adoption of standard grammar', wrote Lemmon, studies of contemporary oral culture 'proved' the existence of 'a definite structure of historic origin'.[23] In Lemmon's opinion, it was essentially the language of Alfred's Wessex.

If this still standard interpretation of the provenance of the recorded rural dialects of the nineteenth and twentieth centuries is true, it has implications for historians of the early modern centuries. It implies an unbroken transmission. One failed generation would break the chain. Much changed, of course, but certain core elements of vocabulary, idiom and ways of speaking were transmitted. How did these 'little traditions' relate to the written English that became so powerful an agency in England during the early modern period? How did spoken dialects relate

---

[21] David Crystal, *The Stories of English* (London 2005), 175.   [22] *Ibid.*, 1, 5.
[23] C.H. Lemmon, 'The Native Speech of Gloucestershire', *Transactions of the Bristol and Gloucestershire Archaeological Society*, vol. 64 (1943), 164.

to the themes of 'middle' and 'early modern' English literature and other forms of writing, from the generation of William Langland to that of Samuel Johnson?

For Lemmon, Gloucestershire speech was 'the modern development of the Wessex or West Saxon tongue, formerly the literary language of England'. Its usage, he acknowledged, varied from place to place and even from household to household, but to the analyst and the outsider it had a common source: 'Wessex'. Lemmon thought an especially archaic strain had survived in Shakespeare's 'high, wild hills', the 'Cotteswolds'. It had no fixed spelling for it had not been a literary language for over a millennium. It included vocabulary not found elsewhere, but ultimately it seems to have been shaped less by any recognized principles of vocabulary and grammar than by the teaching and transmission by example, generation after generation, of ways of making sounds. Its transmission depended upon the training of the physiological organs of speech to shape twenty-two consonants, four semi-vowels and thirteen vowels in a distinctive dialectal way.[24] It was a variant of a language common to all people living south of the Trent and east of the Severn: 'southern English' as a twenty-first century northerner might think of it. Julian was a 'northerner' and seems to have spoken beautiful 'middle' English.

In common with all such studies, Lemmon focused on usages that were not standard or common. The word *stwun* was not the local pronunciation of 'stone' but a derivation of the West Saxon *stan*; likewise *ax* was not local for 'ask' but 'the unchanged stem of (teutonic-Wessex) *acsian*'. Rural Gloucestershire dialect, in Lemmon's view, was a variant of the regional dialect of Wessex that still existed in West Hampshire, Dorset, Wiltshire, North Somerset and Gloucestershire. He suggested that it left few marks of having been 'affected by Norman-French and contained stronger elements of Celtic and possibly pre-Celtic sources'. Wessex dialect retained more of the pronunciation, word order and construction of its historical source. Lemmon estimated that 61 per cent of its vocabulary derived from Anglo Saxon, as compared with 31 per cent in the standard language; 15 per cent was Celtic as against 4 per cent in standard. Gloucestershire borders Wales.

'Norman-French which together with Latin-through-French and Celtic-through-French forms thirty-eight per cent of standard language', he wrote, 'is represented by only thirteen per cent in pure dialect. Latin words, forming twenty-one per cent of Standard English are represented by a meager three per cent, and such as do exist appear to have sur-

---

[24] *Ibid.*, 164, 167, 171–8.

vived rather from the Roman occupation than from a later introduction by scholars. The proportion of Scandinavian words . . . is almost negligible. The balance of dialect words is made up of 3% of non-indigenous borrowed words and 2% which are non-Aryan and suggest an aboriginal source.'[25] We may question the exactitude of Lemmon's deductions without doubting that they represent a permanent tendency for local and regional communities to talk amongst themselves in language suspected outsiders would not be able to understand.

The vocabulary of 'pure' dialect comprised (1) words like *daddocky, hox and lizzen* not appearing to have entered standard language at all; (2) those like *winder, spurtle and ax* that have developed differently from cognates in standard; and (3) words dropped out of standard like *rath, frum* and *pargiter.* Added to 'pure' are (4) standard words pronounced in the local manner (*speek, purty and crud*) which 'naturally form the bulk of the whole vocabulary', and (5) 'malaprops' like *jommetry, zoopervossat* and *comical.* The 'Wessex' dialect often retained gender indicators and the Saxon plural 'en' was retained, as in *wenchen* and *primrosen.*[26] This was also the case with Gloucestershire words and sayings recorded by John Smyth of Nibley 300 years earlier, in 1639.

In this account, dialects are passed like genes along an unbroken line of generations. In practice the collection and definition of dialects always involves emphasis on the arcane and obscure; these *may* represent the core differences. Note Lemmon's assumption that Gloucestershire dialect was originally an elite language, that of the state of Wessex. Significantly, however, Lemmon's hypothesis entailed the idea that rural dialects also retained more elements from the pre-Saxon *Dubunni* and *Silures* than Standard English. Gloucestershire speech was the living descendant of the language spoken by the people in occupation of the territory in the sixth and seventh centuries, by the end of which time (if not before) Germanic influence was paramount.

The direct descent hypothesis postulates that the Gloucestershire synthesis then survived incursions of Vikings and watched the apocalypse of the Anglo-Saxon state and ruling class in 1066. Gloucestershire speech continued to be spoken by villagers under the dominion of a French-speaking state and a Latin-writing church in the twelfth and thirteenth centuries. In c.1300, not immune to innovation yet still itself, it was one of a patchwork of as yet unstandardized, largely unwritten regional and local dialects. A century later it was the dialect of John Trevisa's congregation at Berkeley parish church and was one of the ways of speaking

[25] *Ibid.*, 169.   [26] *Ibid.*, 180.

Chaucer feared would ruin his rhymes.[27] Many authorities believe it was
the dialect William Tyndale adapted as a medium for national speech
and writing in the 1520s.[28] John Smyth of Nibley recorded a selection of
its usages in 1639.[29] John Aubrey commented on local speech, customs,
physiognomy and relatedness to the soil of the native country later in
the seventeenth century.[30] Lemmon's article recorded the state of play
in 1943.

3.3   'Middle' English

Commyn lernyng of speche is by heryng.[31]

We need not accept the direct descent hypothesis to be persuaded that,
amongst themselves, the natives of thirteenth-century Gloucestershire
(and all other localities and provinces) spoke a language that was different from, and potentially opaque to, dialects spoken by their contemporaries elsewhere. It may or may not have included some of the usages
noted by Lemmon and the tradition of nineteenth- and twentieth-century
folklorists. Crystal's non-hierarchical vision of *many* Englishes suggests
that the written forms we call 'middle' English arose as the medium of
communication *between* the dialects. The implication is that most of the
people who used the archaic words and word-formations recorded by
nineteenth- and twentieth-century linguistic folklorists were also, when
occasion required, capable of speaking 'middle Englishes', that is to say,
to create and use *common* features of language for verbal transactions
between people with different dialects and accents.

---

[27] For Trevisa see Ronald Waldron, 'John Trevisa and the Use of English', *Proceedings of
the British Academy* 74 (1988), 171–202; Waldron, 'Trevisa, John (1342–1402) Translator', *DNB Archive* (Oxford 2004); David C. Fowler, *The Life and Times of John Trevisa,
Medieval Scholar* (Seattle 1995); Ralph Hanna III 'Sir Thomas Berkeley and his Patronage', *Speculum* 64 (1989), 878–916; Wogan-Brown *et al.*, *The Idea of the Vernacular*,
130–1; for Chaucer's fear, see *Troilus & Criseyde*, Book V, lines 1793–8, in Robinson
(ed.), *Complete Works*, 479

[28] Rollison, 'Tyndale and all his Sect', *The Local Origins of Modern Society: Gloucestershire
1500–1800* (London and New York 1992), 84–96; David Daniel, *William Tyndale: a
Biography* (New Haven 1994), Part 1; Peter Auksi, 'Borrowing from the Shepherds:
Tyndale's Use of Folk Wisdom', in John T. Day, Eric Lund and Anne M.O'Donnell
(ed.), *Word Church and State: Tyndale Quincentenary Essays* (Washington 1998), 115–27.

[29] Smyth, 'Phrases and Proverbs of Speech Proper to this Hundred', *Berkeley Mss., vol. 3:
Description of the Hundred of Berkeley*, 22–3; cited and discussed in Rollison, 'Proverbial
Culture', *Local Origins*, 68.

[30] 'In North Wiltshire and the Vale of Gloucestershire (a dirty claey country) they speak (I
mean the *Indiginae* or Aborigines only) drawning': Oliver Lawson Dick (ed.), *Aubrey's
Brief Lives* (London 1971), 46.

[31] Trevisa, *Dialogue*, 131.

Efforts to overcome dialectal heterogeneity responded to need and opportunity. They accumulated and multiplied during the demographic and commercial boom of the twelfth and thirteenth centuries, preceding and providing the conditions for the deliberate literary efforts by authors, translators and departments of state (as in the appearance of 'Chancery English' in the reign of Henry V) in the fourteenth and early fifteenth centuries. In the light of what we know about the history of commerce and other routine and exceptional forms of mobility in thirteenth- and fourteenth-century England, the necessary condition for the progress of English, and the reason why authors, translators and (eventually) Chancery took up the case (always for their own reasons) was this. People from all ranks and parts of the country except the courts and offices of Westminster were *already* communicating with each other and transacting the bulk of their collective business in a common language.[32]

Thus the situation of English in c.1300 was like its global state today. Worldwide there are many Englishes. Beyond strong domestic survivors today like Cornish, Scouse and Geordie English, American, South Asian, Australian, Canadian and African dialects are sometimes said to be evolving into different languages. Yet with a will and common business, it is possible to understand and be understood from Liverpool Eight to East London, New York, Chicago, Washington and Death Valley, Calcutta, the Nullarbor and Hay, New South Wales. In spite of its dialectal diversity, this was the practical condition of late medieval and early modern England. People had strong accents, but they could make themselves understood if they needed to. This created a medium in which common ideas and stories could circulate.

Writing was only the visible tip of the vernacular iceberg. The vernacularization of English culture was accomplished three centuries before Francis Bacon reflected on its constitutional implications, in the words of this chapter's epigraph. Vernacularization crept up on the elites. Its infiltration into politics began in the second half of the thirteenth century. Wright traced 'the first political song in English' to the civil wars of Henry III, yet cautioned that 'our finding no songs in English of an earlier date does not . . . prove that they did not exist'. English songs became 'much more frequent' *in the literary record* of the reign of Edward I, stimulated, Wright thought, by 'patriotic hatred of Frenchman and Scot'. Another 'Song against the King's Taxes' (there were many), composed towards

---

[32] Against Derrida, my interpretation assumes the primacy of social being over consciousness, voice over text: cf. Richard Kearney, 'Derrida', in *Modern Movements in European Philosophy* (Manchester 1994), esp. 120.

the end of the thirteenth century, is the earliest surviving specimen of a distinctive 'macaronic' genre in which each line began in one language and ended in another. There is at least one example of a song from the reign of Edward II that presented 'in alternate succession all the three languages which were then in use.' 'The wars of Edward III produced many songs, both in Latin and in English, as did the troubles which disturbed the reign of his successor.' Wright saw the ill-starred reign of Edward II as a watershed. After it 'we begin to lose sight of the Anglo-Norman language, which we shall not again meet with in these popular effusions'.[33]

The idea that there was one English, capable of reaching all dialectal communities, may be present in *Cursor Mundi* (c.1300–50), where the English language was represented as 'a single community, devoid of difference of dialect, social status or gender', and, tellingly, a century later, in Reginald Pecock's casual distinction between writing 'in Latin or in the common peplis langage'.[34] To comprehend the emergence of an English linguistic community, the development of learned and literary Englishes must first be set in a conceptual framework that neither assumes nor excludes collective, popular agency. English literature was an outgrowth (and very often an expression) of an *acoustic* commonwealth. The greatest 'middle' English literature was intended to make sense when spoken aloud.

Focus on dialectal differences leads scholars to exaggerate the opacity of dialectal communities.[35] The 'native speeches' of localities and self-conscious sub-groups can be and often are used to exclude outsiders. Chaucer was not the first to worry about the 'so gret diversite/ In Englissh', not only among speakers, but also 'in writyng of oure tonge'. Chaucer's were a poet's ironic fears, sending his verses into the world with a prayer: 'So prey I God that non miswrite the[e],/ Ne the[e] mysmetre for defaute of tonge. Red wherso thow be, or elles songe'; in the 'wrong' dialect or idiom, his rhymes would not rhyme nor his metres scan.[36] That was one – literary – motive for desiring uniform, standard or official English. In truth Chaucer wanted to be understood, regardless of poetic convention. Not one, but many quests for a 'middle' English sprang from the precept of the generation of Langland, Trevisa, Julian, Chaucer

[33] Wright, *Political Songs*, lxxii–v.

[34] Wogan-Brown *et al.*, *Idea of the Vernacular*, 335, 99; the quote also indicates that as late as the fifteenth century English was still instinctively thought of as the common people's 'contribution'.

[35] Including myself: 'The Bourgeois Soul of John Smyth of Nibley', *Social History* (1987); 'Proverbial Culture', *Local Origins*.

[36] *Troilus & Criseyde*, Book V, lines 1793–8, in Robinson (ed.), *Complete Works* (Oxford 1957), 479.

and Wyclif that *Inglisch toung* had arrived.[37] The motive was not necessarily to resolve the everyday dialects carried by generations of *trafike*
into the Cambridge-London-Oxford triangle into something they could
all acknowledge and share. That was happening anyway. State-inspired
standardization is also a process of exclusion. Many of the jargons Orwell
complained about sixty years ago are patently about *ex*clusion.[38] On the
other hand, the archaic-sounding language of John Ball's riddles and
broadsides in 1381 are not so different from Chaucer's; they use language in a way that can include anyone whose native tongue it is, in
whatever dialect. Preachers and other storytellers had to know this inclusive, accommodating *skyl*, adjusting what they said and how they said it
to particular local congregations.

Dialects did not hinder the spread of ideas and information. 'Middle'
English existed before writers began to use it with a purpose. The power
of London English to cut through dialects is implied in the observation
of a late fourteenth-century bishop that 'each Bishop of England has
subjects of parishioners in London, therefore, when he gives instructions there, it is as if he were preaching to his own people and to the
other churches of England'.[39] A few years later, John Whitelock's English
'proclamation' was affixed 'to the doors of the church of Westminster and
elsewhere in various places in London and at Bermondsey and in various
other places in the realm where people gathered together'. He and his
companions 'all went round the land of England and Wales, if not the
whole of it, then the greater part of it, everywhere announcing in public
and asserting as true that the late king Richard was alive in Scotland and
would return in a short while to the land of England'.[40] They intended
and expected to make themselves understood wherever they were.

Early 'middle' English (c.1066–1250) was a dynamic 'creole' tongue,
a locally and regionally variable pidgin generated by five or six generations of especially tense and loaded Latin, French and multiple English
interactions.[41] We need not think of this early phase of what turned out to

---

[37] Thus I would qualify Jeremy Catto's conclusion ('Writing in English', 38) that 'the
English of public business was adapted from a literary medium' with the words 'in part'
or 'sometimes'; John Ball's English was used for a different kind of public business than
that of, say, Hoccleve, or Chancery clerks.

[38] George Orwell, 'Politics and the English Language', in *The Collected Essays, Journalism
and Letters of George Orwell*, vol. 4, *In Front of Your Nose* (Harmondsworth 1968), 156–70.

[39] *Wimbledon's Sermon, Redde Rationem Villicationis Tue: a Middle English Sermon of the
Fourteenth Century*, ed. Ione Kemp Knight (Pittsburgh, Pa. 1967), 44, citing Owst,
Sermons, 208–9.

[40] G.O. Sayles (ed.), *Select Cases in the Court of King's Bench under Richard II, Henry IV and
Henry V* (London 1971), 213–14; includes a transcription of Whitelock's document.

[41] Crystal, 'A Trilingual Nation', *Stories of English*, Chapter 6.

be a remarkable vernacularization of the national culture as conscious or intended. It was a classic collective ('social') movement. The existence of a state unified under one monarch raised practical questions of how travellers around the kingdom could understand and be understood. As soon as the elite classes who made up the inner circles of the state decided that they wanted the indigenous commons to understand their instructions and carry them out willingly without the presence of armed men, they were bound, eventually, to encounter linguistic (and conceptual) barriers that had to be negotiated and overcome. English speakers learned they needed to understand the words of the conquerors in order to pursue their own vocations and interests. Latin and French users of the eleventh to thirteenth centuries were never more than a tiny minority of the population, albeit, during the twelfth century, they monopolized secular and religious lordship. In time the sheer numerical weight and necessity of vernacular usages simply overwhelmed French, and then more slowly, Latin. The origins of English as we know it – the absorbent *langue* – may have been as a statistical medium, the unintended consequence of a multitude of contingent interactions.

To sum up, English was not used extensively as a written language for nearly two centuries after 1066. During those two centuries English rural and urban communities everywhere had begun to assimilate useful words and sentences not already borrowed from earlier invaders and traders from the languages of the twin cadastral states, the kingdom and Christendom. In the two centuries of ruling class instability after the conquest of 1066 it slowly dawned upon the royal and baronial contestants that the willing and active support of their *countreys* could be advantageous. Each generation of immigrants from the continent produced a native-born generation. Whatever language they still spoke at home, they resented immigrants who came after them. This produced absurdities like Simon de Montfort criticizing Henry III for relying on foreign counsellors and retainers. As time passed there was natural slippage from the state of holding an English lordship to the state of being English. To men whose primary associations were with the villagers and townspeople, being English meant speaking and understanding vernacular English. That became the test.

As for the literary response, writers of the last third of the thirteenth century were thinking hard about reaching all three of the realm's linguistic spheres. Experimentation in literary synthesis began with virtuoso demonstrations of simultaneous lucidity and fluidity in Latin, French and English. The audience for this 'macaronic' literature was necessarily limited to clerks who were practised in the use of all three languages. In a culture where the dissemination of written works was still predominantly oral and aural, English could reach the largest audience. Norman-French began to fall into disuse everywhere except at the courts of lords and kings during the reign of Edward II. Edward III is said to have been the first English monarch who spoke English fluently.[42] Trevisa reported that English became the first language of primary and secondary education around the middle of the fourteenth century.[43] Richard II's court and some of his nobles resisted the fashion for English and paid the price. The adoption of Parisian French as his language of preference suggests that Richard may have been keen to distinguish the culture of government from that of his subjects, and in doing so reinforced the sense of alienation from the wider community that the usurping Henry IV was able to exploit.[44] In grounding his legitimacy in the support of the *communes*, Henry of Lancaster committed the state to using their language for domestic transactions.[45] Following Chaucer's complaints about the worrying 'diversity' of English, Henry V's Chancery clerks set about the first efforts to create standard bureaucratic usages.

The remarkably rapid emergence of literary English flowed from its dominance of aural and oral transactions. The rise of middle English was the linguistic expression of a sharp and sustained rise in the power, self-confidence and public influence of the classes of people whose everyday language it was – including, most influentially, the ubiquitous 'mediators' between secular and ecclesiastical lords and the working population. The social ranks associated with this constitutionally mediating role moved steadily down the social scale. By the late fourteenth century the core of the dangerous class had acquired a name (in various spellings, 'commonalty') and an ideology centred on a new coinage, the *commune wele*.[46]

---

[42] Bartlett, *Making of Europe*, 203.

[43] Trevisa, *Polychronicon*, vol. 1, ch. 59; Tim William Machan, *English in the Middle Ages* (Oxford 2003), 84–5, is sceptical.

[44] John Scattergood, *Reading the Past: Essays on Medieval and Renaissance Literature* (Dublin 1996), 121; for Richard's legitimacy problems, cf. Fowler, *Trevisa*, 190–9.

[45] Proclamation in G.O. Sayles, 'The Deposition of Richard II: Three Lancastrian Narratives', *Bulletin of the Institute of Historical Research* 54 (1981), 257–70; for Henry's use of English, see *Royal and Historical Letters of Henry the Fourth* ed. F.G. Hingeston, 2 vols. (London 1860), 1.35–8, 1.117–18, 1.146–7, 1.155–9, 1.180, 1.733, 2.277; for Henry's legitimacy problems, cf. Paul Strohm, *England's Empty Throne: Usurpation and the Language of Legitimation, 1399–1422* (Yale 1998).

[46] *William Gregory's Chronicle of London*, Camden Society 17 (London 1876–7), 191; earliest usage in *MED* by clerk of the Privy Council 1446, but *Knighton's Chronicle 1337–1396*, ed. and trans. G.H. Martin (Oxford 1995), 208–9 attributes *communis utilitatis* to the *plebs* of 1381; *wele* is from OE *wela*, *weola* . . . , whereas the invariable literary usage before 1450 is *profit*; a popular provenance is extremely likely. On the Cade conjuncture, I.M.W. Harvey, *Jack Cade's Rebellion of 1450* (Oxford 1991) and Montgomery Bohna, 'Armed Force and Civic Legitimacy in Jack Cade's Revolt', *English Historical Review* 118:477 (June 2003).

Like all classes, the late medieval and early modern commonalty was a mythical beast, a 'spectre' that nonetheless haunted English polity throughout our period, and sometimes, as in 1381, 1450, 1536 and 1549, sprang into existence as a force threatening the status quo. Like modern class language, such words had multiple meanings and involved variable distinctions. They were 'empty signs', ready to be filled with different meanings and emotions.[47]

Before the decay of serfdom, the commonalty was dividable into free and unfree, a division that ran through most communities in England. After the Rebellion of 1381 another distinction creeps into common usage in references to *the trewe comunes*,[48] implying that the commonalty was not singular, and that its other part was not *trewe*.[49] There were several versions of this dualism. In one version, the juror class of towns and villages, who ran local affairs and gave their voices at parliamentary elections, were the *trewe comunes*. Behind and surrounding them was a more spectral 'multitude'. In other usages, rebels were the *trewe comunes* and, later still, 'common-wealths'.

The constitutional culture of the fourteenth to seventeenth centuries was an enduring, if changing field of contentious forces. The vernacular movement is an unmistakeable clue to an intense, collective striving for a community based on consensus about more than the fundamental agreement that England was and should remain a monarchy. A quest for substantive unity necessarily translates into the symbolic order. One area stressed in recent studies, is the 'unity' created by intensifying circulation of information.[50]

---

[47] Words change their meanings 'in ways continually related to the contexts in which, about which, and by whom the terms are used': Alexandra Shepard and Phil Withington, 'Introduction: Communities in Early Modern England', in Shepard and Withington (ed.), *Communities in Early Modern England: Networks, Place, Rhetoric* (Manchester 2000), 1.

[48] 'A Petititon of the Folk of Mercerye', *London English*: '*the same Nicholl, ayeinst the said fredam and trew comunes, dyd crye openlich that no man shuld come to chese here Mair but such as we sompned*'; R.H. Robbins, *Historical Poems of the XIV & XV Centuries* (NY 1959), clii and Song 19, wrote that 'the claim of *laddes* to be *Anglorum corpora viua* shocked the commons in Parliament, who claimed they were *the fayrest flour, that evere god sette on erthely crown*'.

[49] On the meanings of *trewth*, cf. Richard Firth Green, *A Crisis of Truth: Literature and Law in Ricardian England* (Philadelphia 2002), Chapter 1 'From Troth to Truth' & *passim*.

[50] Most of the conclusions of C.A.J. Armstrong, 'Some Examples of the Distribution and Speed of News in England at the Time of the Wars of the Roses', in R.W. Hunt, W.A. Pantin and R.W. Southern (ed.), *Studies in Medieval History Presented to F.M. Powicke* (Oxford 1948), remain important and are applicable to earlier centuries, i.e. the means of communication remained the same; Janet Coleman, *English Literature in History 1350–1400, Medieval Readers and Writers* (London 1981), 60; Wendy Scase, 'Strange and Wonderful Bills. Bill Casting and Political Discourse in Late Medieval England', in Rita Copeland, David Lawton and Wendy Scase (ed.), *New Medieval Literatures*, vol. 2 (Oxford 1998).

3.4   Storytelling: public opinion before the invention of print

Men may not staunche a comoun noys,
Nother for love ne for awe.
After men lyve is comoun voys,
In wrongwys ded, or right lawe.
Who doth hem pyne, who doth hem pawe,
Eche on tell other, child and man.[51]

If that a prince useth hasardrye
In all governaunce and policye
He is, as by commune opinioun
Yholde the lasse in reputacioun.[52]

The idea that fourteenth-century England had something resembling 'public opinion' flies in the face of an orthodoxy that has prevailed in the West since the eighteenth century. This tradition sees the origins of the modern world in the enlightened rationalism of men like Voltaire and David Hume. Not until newspapers graced the breakfast tables of the citizens of the Atlantic world of the eighteenth and nineteenth centuries, did 'public opinion' and 'civic consciousness' become forces in political life. In this widely prevalent theory opinion-making, disseminating and 'spin' are peculiarly modern phenomena, associated with technologies (print) and ideas ('enlightenment rationalism') that were absent from the politics of earlier times, especially the 'middle' ages, that legendary epoch of disorder and superstition between the fall of Rome and the rise of Modernity. While it is quite true that fourteenth-century England was very much a foreign country whose signs have to be read in their own contexts and not ours, that it is, in its landscapes and furniture, mental and physical, very different from us, we shall see that, as far as such a thing can ever be said to exist, fourteenth-century England had a routinized and enduring public opinion, and a clear and frequently articulated 'civic consciousness'. From the moment it appears in the written archives, in the early thirteenth century, public opinion had certain enduring themes concerning government and constitutional legitimacy. Written reports of 'public' or 'commune' opinion as a vital element of constitutional life begin with John of Salisbury and are continuous from the thirteenth to seventeenth centuries.

Modern accounts of the history of 'civil society', 'civic consciousness' and 'public opinion' emphasize the role of media technology – especially

---

[51] J. Kail (ed.), *Twenty-six Political and Other Poems from the Oxford Mss. Digby 102 and Douce 322* (London 1904), verse 3, p. 15.
[52] Chaucer, 'The Pardoners Tale', *Canterbury Tales* ed. A.C. Cawley (London 1975), 352.

the birth and impact of print. Yet in his classic account of the 'structural transformation' that gave rise to the public spheres of modern states, Jurgen Habermas postulated 'a causal homology of culture and economic..., growing from "the traffic in commodities and news created by early capitalist long-distance trade"'.[53] In other words, the print revolution was premised on some important economic preconditions. First, public communication requires the routine movements that early modern English people called '*trafike*' and we call 'trade' and 'commerce'. Fluctuations in the quantity and quality of traffic are bound to impact on the size and intensity of information communities. Communications are signs, manuscripts, phrases, anecdotes, proverbs, stories and ideas travelling as medieval and early modern monarchs and artisans travelled, along the roads and highways, alongside packs of wool and herds of cattle.

Secondly and perhaps most in need of emphasis, however, is that in order to get some idea of the power of messages to travel through a broadly preliterate (or mixed) milieu, we must consider their quality and content. Messages spread because the communities into which they spread were connected to each other. There had to be lines of communication. To demonstrate that a society had 'public opinion' it is necessary to show that such lines of communication existed, *and* that contemporaries were aware of the wider information community that existed as a result of this '*trafike*'. '*Trafike*' must be routine for messages to be trafficked. But to understand the impact of these structures of communication on the political and constitutional development of English society it is crucial to pay attention to what was being said – the ideas. The rest of this chapter is concerned with some of the key ideas that circulated in the language we have been discussing.

To say that fourteenth-century England had something resembling 'public opinion', and that shared ideas, sayings and stories spread across its landscape to the vast majority of its inhabitants, is to revise and qualify the old myth that 'preindustrial' (and especially 'medieval') England was a world of more or less isolated and parochial neighbourhoods, districts and provinces worked by peasants with no idea what lay over yonder hill. Fourteenth-century messages took longer to cover the ground than would be the case in later centuries, but if the stories and sayings were

---

[53] Geoff Eley, 'Nations, Publics and Political Cultures: Placing Habermas in the Nineteenth Century', in Craig Calhoun (ed.), *Habermas and the Public Sphere* (Cambridge, Mass. 1996), 291. Eley also points out that in Habermas's account 'the public sphere was the manifest consequence of a much deeper and long-term process of societal transformation that Habermas locates between the late middle ages and the eighteenth century as a trade-driven transition from feudalism to capitalism in which the capital accumulation resulting from long-distance commerce plays the key role...'.

memorable enough, the lines of domestic commerce, migration, church and state were eminently capable of carrying them into every community and household in fourteenth-century England within weeks.[54] If the stories and information fitted existing repertoires, precepts, chronologies and narratives, and had what modern film-writers call a 'hook' to make them catch hearers' and readers' memories, they stuck and became part of the repertoire and world view of the people who heard and told them to each other. The structures of communication – a specific landscape increasingly centred on London and Westminster, interconnected by highways, roads, tracks and paths – existed before the coming of print. Indeed, the print revolution was premised on this network and the intensification of commerce and other forms of traffic within it. Printed works, when they became a significant force in the 1520s, circulated along antecedent lines of communication.

'Public opinion' is a two-way process. It implies a reasonably informed public, but it also implies feed-back into the political and constitutional process. This is to say more than that it simply existed: it had practical consequences. It affected constitutional development in that it was premised on critique of the state.[55] We shall look more closely in succeeding chapters at the ways in which public opinion fed back into the political-constitutional life of the state in the form of various kinds of resistance and rebellion. Here we are concerned with what a late fourteenth-century English person would have understood by Chaucer's term: *commune opinioun*.

It derived from *commune*, a very dynamic word that did service in documents of the last third of the fourteenth century as a verb, a noun, an adjective and an adverb. In all its many meanings it evoked the most fundamental activity of any community: 'to make common to others with oneself; to communicate, impart, share', hence 'to tell, declare, publish, report'.[56] Add other associations, and you get the variant of Thomas

---

54 Rollison, *Local Origins*, ch. 2: 'Trails of Progress: the Reorientation and Intensification of Traffic, 1600–1800' is an account of a later phase of this *longue durée* in one region of England, especially after the 1690s.

55 James Van Horn Melton, *The Rise of the Public in Enlightenment Europe* (Cambridge 1998), 5, writes that in Habermas's theory an essential premise of the appearance of public spheres 'was the rise of the modern nation state dating from the late middle ages, a process that went hand in hand with the emergence of society as a realm distinct from the state', but adds that 'The middle ages had known no such distinction, for the medieval "state" did not exercise anything like sovereignty in the modern sense.' The problem with this formula is the vague and sweeping use of 'middle ages', as if it was a homogeneous spatial and temporal period which saw no significant change.

56 *OED*, 'commune', obsolete senses; Stubbs, *Constitutional History of England*, 1: 171–80; Hans Kurath (ed.), *Middle English Dictionary* (Ann Arbor, Mich. 1959); Machan, *English in the Middle Ages*, 36–7; *Reports from the Lords Committee* I: 141; the first twenty-

More's age, in which *commune* evoked the (often seditious or heretical, always, in More's view, ignorant) whispering and gossiping of the
commonalty. 'Commune' (the activity) merged into vernacular English
alongside that which it created, a 'com(m)un(e)', meaning the community within which the communing goes on – usually a vill, township or
urban community of some kind – up to the 'communaute' of barons and
kings who claimed absolute rights to the community of all the communities, the *regni*. It was a word with application to activities and places that
everyone participated in all the time.

Commune words were linguistic fireworks, exploding in the crowded
streets, setting up a multitude of associations. The dangers of *commune*
were in Chaucer's mind when he wrote that kings should be attentive to *commune opinioun*. *Commune* meant 'to take a part in common
with others; to participate, partake, share with', and 'to have inter-
course . . . associate with' (including sexually). *Commune* was the root of,
and in certain respects a synonym for another word that was coming into
use to refer to the habit of words to spread from their point of departure,
beyond the intentions of those who spoke or wrote them: *communicaycon*,
our word for the media of *commune opinioun*, that which, collectively, is
produced by the activities of communing. This effort, by ordinary people, scholars, and finally by government, to grasp what might be termed
the cybernetic dimension of their lives, is part of the milieu of the written
sources from Trevisa's early recording of *communycacyon* to the last third
of the fifteenth century, when the usages of various members of the Cely
family signal that it was already common usage in the spoken, but not yet
written, vernacular. They never used the same spelling twice: at first, *com-
municacon* may have been a pretentious word for 'talk', but *comynycasyon*,
comenycacyon, and *commynnecaschon* clearly meant 'being talked about',
and *commyngaschon* is used to refer to 'news and information'.[57]

It was *commune opinioun* that a prince or lord who jeopardizes the
kingdom in pursuit of personal profit or glory is to be held in contempt.
Whilst Chaucer's rule stops well short of John of Salisbury's dictum
that if a prince is a tyrant he can be deposed and killed, it implies a
'commune' that is far from passive. The idea that the whole community

five of the 'interrogatories' written by Thomas Cromwell for the interrogation of the
leader of the Northern Rebellion, Robert Aske, in 1536 concerned 'brutes [that] were
spred abrode in those countreis . . . long afore the insurrection in Lincolnshire'. Item
21 asked 'whether eny [rebels] *comonid* with you' about the 'reformacian' of the king's
Reformation statutes, and Item 25 referred to 'any suche as comoned with you uppon
the said statutes': Mary Bateson, 'Aske's Examination', *English Historical Review* 5:19
(July 1890), 550–1.

57 Alison Hanham (ed.), *The Cely Letters 1472–1488* (Oxford 1975), 43, 106, 147, 207.

had to agree before a tyrant could be deposed was central to public discourse during the depositions of Edward II in 1327 and Richard II in 1399. For Chaucer's generation the right to resist unjust rule was a repressed commonplace. Its legitimacy was constantly questioned, not only by princes, but also by the vernacular tradition of social theologians from Langland and Wyclif to Tyndale. The latter has been aptly called the tradition of 'angry obedience'.[58] It was aware of tyranny theory, accepted that monarchical and aristocratic corruption and tyranny was the rule rather than the exception in the real world, but denied the right of subjects to resist or rebel against it. In this variant of the populist commonweal tradition bad government was God's punishment for tyrants and test for the faithful. In such circumstances the duty of a godly subject was to imitate the example of Jesus, strive for perfection in everyday life and leave God to deal with the big picture. The punishment of tyrants in the afterlife was particularly severe, in their view. They would be denied entry to the kingdom of heaven. Chaucer seems to have taken for granted that the idea that government should not be entrusted to people who would gamble with the *comon weal* was common enough for his readers to accept it as the 'opinioun' of the *commune*. *Commune opinioun* was part of the constitutional repertoire of fourteenth-century England.[59]

To approximate what it meant in Chaucer's contexts, we have to be aware of its multiple meanings. It referred to a specific, incorporated and in some way independent community, usually (but not always) a town or city. Florence was a commune, as were English cities like London and Bristol. From an aristocratic or monarchical perspective, the *hoi polloi* of such places was 'common' in another sense, meaning 'found everywhere, and really rather vulgar'. Chaucer's usage of 'commune' includes what we mean by 'community', but his meaning also encompassed the *activity* people engaged in to make their places ongoing *communities*, i.e. places within which communing of many sorts went on. It was then, as it is today, an amorphous and ubiquitous term, and could be used neutrally or with disdain, pride, exclusiveness, and universality. It represented the way people thought they ought to live with their neighbours (and rulers), though not necessarily how they actually lived. Community went on within and between these communities, and was not always sanctioned by official regulations or contained within existing institutions. *Commun*

---

[58] Donald Dean Smeeton, *Lollard Themes in the Reformation Theology of William Tyndale* (Kirksville, Mo. 1986).

[59] D.A. Carpenter, 'English Peasants in Politics 1258–1267', *Past and Present* 136 (August 1992), 30–1, n. 97, traces 'the earliest appearance in an English text of the French "commune" or "commonaute"' to a manuscript life of Thomas Becket dating to c.1290–1300.

was also a synonym for *commonalty* in all its variants. It was used in Chaucer's age to mean only the unfree, the subject population – not those who fought or those who prayed, but the other 80 per cent who worked. Using it this way was also potentially dangerous, since it suggested that the *commonalty* could become *one* many-headed monster. If this beast struck, as one, simultaneously, it would defeat the best army the master-class could put into the field. This did not happen until the 1640s, but the warning signs were present from 1381 forward.[60]

What Chaucer called *commune opinioun*, historians have illustrated with one of its most important media, bill-posting, a pre-print form of publication in which 'vernacular texts were very easily disseminated by public reading'. In 1327 Scots invaders pinned verses satirizing England to the doors of York Minster. The habit of nailing up important public statutes, songs, manifestoes and so on in vernacular English, in public places (usually the gates of towns and cities, cathedral and church doors) also emerges in the early fourteenth century, although it had almost certainly been going on for much longer.[61] Broadside bill-posting features in every crisis, major or minor, from the early fourteenth century. A letter demanding the arrest of the king's hated companion, Despenser, was nailed to the cross in Cheapside on 6 October 1323 'and copies of it were circulated', rousing 'the commonalty', who 'forced the mayor . . . to declare for the queen'.[62] Parchment was expensive. The revolt of 1381 may have been initiated by a systematic campaign of bill-sticking. Subsequent revolts definitely were.

With or without written bills or letters, once a movement had gathered word of mouth and was on the move, ideas, tactics and strategies were served by the invention and dissemination of rhythmic and

---

[60] The tendency to elide divisions within the commonalty is evident in Kurath (ed.), *Middle English Dictionary*, 'commune', second sense: 'The body of freemen (of a country, city, etc.), the common people, the citizenry; the third estate of a commonwealth (as distinct from the nobility and clergy) (2: 437). As we have seen, the body of freemen or citizens was not coextensive with the common people, many of whom, at the time of the first recorded usage in this sense (1325), were not citizens or *liberi homines*. For the interlocking and developing political contexts of the commons in the fourteenth and fifteenth centuries, see George Holmes, *The Good Parliament* (Oxford 1975); Linda Clark, 'Magnates and their Affinities in the Parliaments of 1386–1421', in Britnell and Pollard (ed.), *The McFarlane Legacy*, 127–54; R.B. Goheen, 'Peasant Politics? Village, Community and Crown in Fifteenth-Century England', *American Historical Review* 96:1 (February 1991), 42–62; Marjorie Keniston McIntosh, *Controlling Misbehaviour in England, 1370–1600* (Cambridge 1998); 'Commune' is used to mean community in William Langland, *Piers Plowman*, in *Fourteenth-Century Verse and Prose*, ed. Kenneth Sisam (Oxford 1967), 90, line 20.
[61] Wendy Scase, 'Strange and Wonderful Bills', 227, 239, 240, 247.
[62] May McKisack, 'London and the Succession to the Crown During the Middle Ages', in Hunt *et al.*, *Studies in Medieval History*, 81–2.

proverbial chunks of words. These literary squibs would be remembered by everyone who heard them, talked about and passed on. Such lines of communication were assumed by the chroniclers. Not every source went along with the myth that the reign of Edward III had been one of harmony. 'If you must know the absolute truth', wrote one of them, it was on the occasion of the Parliament of 1339, when Edward III 'asked the fifteenth part of all the movable goods of England, and the wools, and the every ninth sheath of corn', that 'the inner love of the people was turned into hate, and the common prayers into cursing, because the *commune peple* were strongly aggrieved'.[63] This was one of the earliest recorded usages of the phrase *commune peple* to mean the 'commonalty' or 'Third Estate'.

Chaucer, a Londoner, is bound to have associated *commune opinioun* with the whole body of the people of the Commune, and *communes*, of London, a dense and extended cluster of religious and secular jurisdictions within which 'communing' was sometimes structured yet always exceptionally rapid. Not much happened between Westminster and the Tower that was not soon *commune opinioun* in the courts, churches, guildhalls, streets, alehouses and households of the citizens and non-citizens of London. Londoners were active in every succession crisis from the eleventh to sixteenth centuries. In king Stephen's reign they even claimed the right to elect the king.[64] May McKisack stressed the need of a succession of 'ruthless and astute schemers' to receive popular acclamation. 'By reason of their numbers, their notorious susceptibility to propaganda, and the geographical position of their city, the Londoners are those most evidently fitted to give the genuine *collaudatio*.'[65]

Chaucer was sharply aware of women's networks. *Commune opinioun* meant names and stories on *everyone's* lips, news of the day gossiped, joked, and talked about earnestly in all the households within the walls, plus Southwark and the district of St George, passed on with variable additions and omissions to every traveller to and from the regions and provinces, daily, and spread round the kingdom. The story of the day, week or month (some lasted longer than others) could begin elsewhere than in London and Westminster, be packaged in hopefully memorable verbal form in the localities and sent to London for onward transmission. In ideal circumstances a good enough story could get from London to Bristol, Norwich, York, Abergavenny and Launceston, and back to London again in a few days. Speed of communication was less important,

[63] *The Brut or The Chronicles of England*, ed. F.W.D. Brie (London 1906), 293–4.
[64] McKisack, 'London and the Succession', 76–89.   [65] *Ibid.*, 89.

however, than the content and quality of the story. If it was a good one, like 'the Song of the Flemish Insurrection', the stories about Edward II, and *Piers Plowman*, parts and embroidered versions of it were never forgotten.

3.5   The common voice

Thus my Gode lorde, wyneth your peples voice;
For peples voice is goddes voys, men seyne . . . [66]

Bills and libels were nailed up in prominent public places all over the country as far back as vernacular records will take us. They are surviving signs of the early emergence of a 'public sphere' that was capable, in times of political crisis, of reaching deep into society, and that was premised on popular ideas of tyranny. Multiple references to something closely resembling public opinion in medieval England do not so much contradict Habermas's now classic 'formulation of the "emergence of the public sphere"' as Wendy Scase puts it, as alert us to historically repressed realms of 'civil (or uncivil) society'. For Habermas, 'medieval and early modern political culture knows no concept of the public domain that is differentiated from private individuals and their interests. The English king enjoyed "publicness" as a status attribute.'[67] As we have seen, 'publicness' is too tame for the functions that monarchy 'played' in the fourteenth century. Nor should we see late fourteenth-century public culture as something emanating from the centre, or from the courtly apex of a celestial pyramid of degrees and vocations. Kings and lords had their equivalents to what we call 'public relations', and they put different 'spins' on events and relations between the classes of constitutional life. They read the auspices differently, and operated within different practical and theoretical boundaries.

Barons like Thomas lord Berkeley almost certainly believed that it was the duty of men of his rank to discipline and if necessary depose and murder kings who proved to be tyrants.[68] If resistance was the duty of men of his own rank, he certainly did not believe that lesser ranks and the commonalty had the right to resist and overthrow barons who likewise proved tyrants. The rebels of 1381 disagreed. If Wyclif is to be believed, the idea that popular sovereignty was a practical reality did not

---

[66] Thomas Hoccleve, 'The Regement of Princes', in *Hoccleve's Works* ed. F.J. Furnivall (London 1897), l. 2885.

[67] Scase, 'Strange and Wonderful Bills'.

[68] Smyth, *Lives* II, on 'Thomas the Magnificent', esp. his usage of 'we'.

go away after they were dispersed. The story went that itinerant preachers continuously spread dangerous ideas. 'Summe men', wrote Wyclif, 'sclaunderen pore prestis with this errour, that servauntes or tenauntis may lawefully witholde rentis and servyce fro here lordis whanne lordis ben openly wickid in here lyvynge'. Such libels against 'pore prestis' were made 'to make lordis to hate them'. The problem with this widespread opinion, however, was that if 'sugetis [subjects] may leffully withdrawe tithes and offryngis fro civatis that openly lyven in lecherie or grete othere synnes & don not here office, than servantis and tenaunts may withdrawe here servyce and rentis fro here lordis that lyven opynly acursed lif'.[69] 'Lords who love themselves more than the community may be deposed' is an easily remembered 'conceit', well within the 'capacity' of common people, as Bacon would later remind his Elizabethan and Jacobean peers. As John of Salisbury had insisted, the commonweal test applied to authority at every level of society.

The body politic image is also easily remembered and infinitely adaptable. In simplistic versions policy was passed down from the head to the parts nearer the ground. In John of Salisbury's version the heart and soul were central, fed by the lower members and transmitting their wisdom to the higher. Other metaphors were in use. Once, in the past, 'an Englisch schip we had',

> Thorw al Christendam hit was drad
> Edward the Thridde was the roother (rudder) that steered the schip
>   and gouerned hit . . .
> Whyl schip and rother togeder was knit,
> Thei dredde nouther tempest, druyghte nor wete
> Nou be thei bothe in synder flit,
> That selden seyth is sone forgete

The king had kept the 'goode schip togeder', but only because he retained the support of

> This gode Comunes, bi the rode [cross]!
> I likne hem to the schipes mast,
> That with heore catel and heore goode
> Mayntened the werre both furst and last.

Now the ship is wrecked. 'Nou is deuoutnes out icast/ And mony gode dedes ben clen forgete.'[70] The mood of the ship had changed, the parts

---

[69] Cf. Margaret Aston, 'Lollardy and Sedition 1381–1431', *Past and Present* 17 (April 1960), 8–9.

[70] 'On the death of Edward III, A.D. 1377', *Bodleian MS. Vernon (c.1400)* f. 410b, in Kenneth Sisam (ed.), *Fourteenth Century Verse and Prose* (Oxford 1921, 1967), lines 17–19, 29, 74–80, pp. 157–9.

no longer worked together. According to this retrospective reading, the generations of the Black Death and its aftermath had enjoyed stability and glory under a wise and just king. It may have seemed so to the survivors.

The commons stepped onto the stage of English history in the last third of the fourteenth century. Dynastic crisis signified deeper social and, in the fullest sense of the word, 'constitutional' crisis. The spectre of popular rebellion came to the fore:

> Whan the comuynes began to ryse,
> Was non so gret lord, as I gesse,
> That thei in hert bigon to gryse,
> And leide heore jolite in presse.
> Wher was thenne heore worthinesse,
> Of aalle wyse men I take witnesse,
> This was a warnynge to be ware.

God decided 'that lordes schulde his lordschup feel/And of heore lordschipe make hem bare'. He would take away their power and privileges – and (by implication) distribute them amongst the 'comuynes'. A year later came another sign: an 'eorthe qwok' that left 'non so proud he nas agast/ And al his jolite forsoke'. That was immediately followed by a devastating plague. Wealth was no defence against these terrors:

> Of gold and selver their tok non hede,
> But out of ther houses ful sone thei past.
> Chaumbres, chymeneys, al to-barst,
> Chirches and castelles foule gone fare;
> Pinacles, steples, to grounde hit cast;

'This earth . . . That schulde be cuynde be ferme and satabele' was moved twice, 'as a verrey tokyn . . . that mennes hertes ben chaungabele/ And that to no falsed thei ben most abele'. The commons were bursting out of their ranks and vocations, creating disorder. Who was responsible and what should be done? The poet did not directly answer the question, but taken together, his poems present a coherent view of how things were contrasted with how they ought to be: John of Salisbury's approach.[71]

Written within a few years of Henry of Lancaster's *coup d'état*, the 'Digby poet', so-named after the seventeenth-century antiquarian who preserved and transmitted his writings, targeted people who injured the commons 'by flattering the king and the lords, and by misleading them, by their counsel, to bad actions'. The persistent theme is that, one way

---

[71] Kail (ed.), *Twenty-six Poems*, viii.

or another, truth will be told, and that its most likely medium is *commune opinioun*:

> Though men hide truth in earth
> On hall roofs it shows.
> Bottom of sea it will not bide,
> But show in markets, on the plain.
> And though truth be slain,
> And buried deep in clay,
> He will rise to live again,
> And all truth [*sothe*] will tell.[72]

Truth speaks through the people:

> The common voice won't be restrained,
> But love, or hate, as work is done.[73]

The 'comoun voys' is based on observation of how rulers behave, and with what results ('as werke is wrought'). If once *communes* begin to speak they *will* be heard. They are not only a moral pretext but a power:

> Men may not staunch a common noise,
> Neither for love nor awe.
> How men live is common voice,
> In evil deed or right law.
> Who does them pain
> Each one tells other, child and man.[74]

The common voice is historical agency as well as moral force, an 'is' as well as an 'ought'.

The imperative 'to stand with the commons in justice/ Is the highest form of love' was practical as well as moral.[75] To rule in the common good is certainly a religious duty. Over again the Digby poet insists that

> Those who have estate over people,
> In college or other degree
> Maintain no debate
> For personal profit or temporality.
> Your rule is grounded in love,
> As light of lantern to lead the way.
> To govern the people in love,
> God wills you make no single day's delay.[76]

---

[72] 'Lerne say wele, say litel, or say nought', verse 13, Kail (ed.), *Twenty-Six Poems*, 18.
[73] Kail (ed.), 'Lerne say wele', verse 20, p. 20.   [74] *Ibid.*, verse 3, p. 15.
[75] Kail (ed.), *Twenty-six Poems*, 'Dede is Working', 56.
[76] *Ibid.*, 'A good making of iour delaye', verse 8, p. 33.

By the end of the fourteenth century the idea that authority and the social order ought to be 'grounded in love', naïve though it may seem to the subjects of twenty-first century states, was taken very seriously indeed; it leapt into mind and voice in every crisis. The simplicity of the message was in direct proportion to its power to judge every relationship in which power was unequal. It generated active hatred of bad government.

The Digby poet made several attempts to formulate the glowing ideal. In another poem he or she formulated the earliest surviving Englishing of John of Salisbury's body politic, likening 'A kingdom in good order'

> To stalwart man in strong health.
> As long as none of his limbs offer hate,
> He is powerful and capable of defence.
> If his limbs argue with each other,
> He waxes sick, for flesh is frail.
> Dawn to dusk his enemies wait and watch,
> To steal upon him in his feebleness.[77]

He is an English giant rather than a classical abstraction, Hobbes's *Leviathan*'s first appearance in the realm of vernacular rhetoric. The head is king. The neck holds up the head and is a just judge, the pillar of justice. The breast fills the body with life-giving breath, allowing good spirits in and keeping bad spirits out, just like a good priest. Lords are shoulders and backbone; arms are knights. 'Yeomen' are fingers. They grasp and control the earth and the commonalty that works it. Lawyers are ribs to protect the heart, thighs are merchants 'that bear the body' and 'maintain boroughs and cities . . . and good households of great plenty'. Artisans are the legs, 'for all the body they bear, As a tree bears branches'. The feet are 'all honest [*trewe*] tillagers of lands [with] the plough and all that dig the earth; All the world stands on them'. The toes are faithful servants, without which the tillagers themselves 'may not stand'. Yet toes, feet and legs do not speak. As the anonymous Digby poet well knew, commonalty was now in every English person's mouth. The most momentous change of fourteenth-century England was that by its last third the dramas of court, diplomacy and battlefield were now enacted in the common tongue. Until the civil wars of the 1640s it would become a convention to describe the commonalty as speaking and murmuring tongues and mouths.

The vernacular movement reached a first peak in the aftermath of 1381. As Chapter 4 will show, 1381 was a decisive moment in the revolution of commonalty and the true birth of the age of the commonweal.

---

[77] Kail (ed.) *Twenty-six Poems*, 'The descrying of mannes membres', verse 16, p. 68.

In the decades when Langland, Julian of Norwich, Trevisa and Chaucer were at their most creative and confident, reactionaries were preparing to strike back. Led by the universities and higher levels of ecclesiastical government, they aimed to halt the march of the vernacular at the gates of religion. Their moment came in the years immediately following the Lancastrian coup of 1399. This will be the topic of Sections 3.9 and 3.10; Section 3.11 will focus on its partial defeat, by William Tyndale, in the 1520s. It was an impressive reaction, succeeding for a century in holding back the tide. First we must try to understand what the reaction was about.

3.6   Lollarene man: Piers Plowman's quest for truth

Lat peres the plowman my brother duelle at home and dyght us corne.[78]

William Langland has strong claims to have been England's first popular author. He was born after the famine of 1315–22 and before 1348–9, the years of the Black Death.[79] When he wrote his latest version of *Piers*, in the decades either side of 1381, he was living 'among lollares of London' leading 'lollarene lyf that lytel ys preysed'.[80] Much ink has been spilt explaining what Langland meant by this, and how he stood with regard to the theories of his contemporary, the theologian John Wyclif.[81] Early English 'protestants' like William Tyndale, Robert Crowley and John Foxe took for granted that the seeds of reformed vernacular religion in England were sown by Wyclif and passed on in the fifteenth century by people called 'Lollards'. The early English Protestants saw 'Reformation' as a long, historical movement of opposition to a manifestly corrupt Church. The movement to reform the English Church survived a century of the harshest repression because of the heroism of its early martyrs and because it was God's will.

---

[78] The letter of Jakke Carter (1381), in R.B. Dobson (ed.), *The Peasants' Revolt of 1381* (2nd edition, London 1983), 382.

[79] Miri Rubin, 'Famine and Deposition, 1307–1330', *The Hollow Crown: a History of Britain in the Late Middle Ages* (London 2006) is an excellent and moving synthesis of the 'Great Famine of 1315–22'.

[80] Anne Hudson, *The Premature Reformation: Wycliffite Texts and Lollard History* (Oxford 1998), 406.

[81] Hudson, *Premature Reformation*, 399–409. Hudson points out several parallels with the later Lollards. 'The issue on which *Piers Plowman* seems most closely in accord with Wycliffite thought', she writes, 'concerns the question of clerical temporalities and endowment' (405); for a brief survey of the interpretative traditions, from Langland the 'literary father of English dissent' to the more recent 'politically quietist Langland', see Larry Scanlon, 'King, Commons and Kind Wit: Langland's National Vision and the Rising of 1381', in Kathy Lavezzo (ed.), *Imagining a Medieval English Nation* (Minneapolis and London 2004), esp. 195–9.

Piers Plowman expressed the religious, literary, linguistic and social conflicts and contradictions of a period of intense and remarkable change.
The roots of those changes went back at least a century, as we have
seen. *Piers* embodies the major tension of English public discourse in
the decades either side of, and especially those following, 1381. Since
the late 1980s the view that 'there was very little popular demand for
Reformation' has dominated English Reformation historiography.[82] The
interpretation advanced in this and the following sections is that the 'top-
down' view of a Reformation led by intellectuals, lawyers, courtiers and
the monarch – in short, by 'minorities' within local, regional and national
society – is premised on radically foreshortened historical perspective.
The remainder of this chapter will suggest that the sixteenth-century
Reformations must be seen in relation to the vernacular revolution discussed in earlier sections. To some extent the degree to which 'vernacular'
means 'popular' in this context is a matter of definition. The contention
here is that the vernacular movement was popular in the sense that it was
a collective, aggregative and accumulative movement of the 'people' or
'commonalty' as against (though not always excluding) the court, nobility and ecclesiastical elite. It need not have been and almost certainly was
not always a completely conscious movement, although at times resistance to traditional hierarchy and established institutions certainly was
conscious and lucid, as we shall see in Chapter 4. But it was, unques-
tionably, a movement in which the people's language triumphed over all
alternatives. By the end of the fourteenth century the chief instrument
of the vernacular movement, 'middle' English, had become the principle medium of communication in all the households of the realm except
those of the Church.

In this and the next section I explain what William Langland meant
by his ironic identification with *lollares* and *lollarene lyf*. What did it mean
in the 1380s? Secondly, I ask how might a popular teacher and preacher
of his day have used *Piers Plowman*. I use an attested primary source to
ask a hypothetical question. What would such a person's eye and ear
have alighted on, committed to memory, starred, underlined and commented on for future reference? How could this epic vision of the
commonwealth and kingdom of England be used to teach and inspire
common people? What could a popular teacher or preacher take from
it that would catch and keep the attention of a mixed congregation of

---

[82] The quote is from Christopher Haigh, 'Conclusion', in Christopher Haigh (ed.), *The
English Reformation Revised* (Cambridge 1987), 209: a highly influential collection; see
also Eamon Duffy, *The Stripping of the Altars* (New Haven 1992) and Christopher Haigh,
English Reformations: Religion, Politics, and Society under the Tudors (Oxford 1993).

commoners – in church, in a tavern, under a market cross or (the pinnacle of national preaching) St Paul's Cross, London?

Langland supported himself, he says, by part-time clerical and priestly work, which was badly paid, insecure and held in low status.[83] He was married. Like Socrates's Xanthippe, Langland's Kit (she gets an acknowledgement in the "C"-text) may have been a strong-minded woman. As far as is known, they had no children. The various manuscripts of *Piers* that have come down leave no doubt that an entire life was spent conceiving, writing, reconceiving and rewriting his vision. If he had not died we might now have 'D' and 'E' texts to add to those which scholars have dubbed 'A', 'B' and 'C'. A definitive text, I suggest, is not necessary. The point about the writing is the populist vision and mnemonic that encompassed it. He could go on editing and adding to it, changing his mind about this or that idea or way of presenting it. He did not invent the *Piers* vision and it did not stop growing, incorporating and influencing new generations after he was dead. It was eminently suited to selection and abstraction. In other words, we should not imagine an audience of readers who started at page one and continued to the end. More common were preliterate listeners who heard and remembered bits and pieces. *Piers* was an epic that (probably like all epics) spread in fragments.

Nothing is certain about Langland, but it has been suggested that he was an illegitimate son of the gentry. We saw in the last chapter that the role and status of knights, esquires and lesser 'king's men', the later 'gentleman' and 'esquire' ranks below the great barons, were becoming institutionalized in Langland's lifetime. Infants born into (or under the patronage of) landholding households like that of Stacy de Rokayle, Langland's possible father, were more likely to survive to grow into children and adults, and to receive an education. The author of *Piers Plowman* gives the impression that he felt the fame of his poem had not made him any richer or socially regarded. When he was young, in the 1330s and 1340s, there were places to fill left by those who had not survived the lean years of 1316–22, but he was not one of those who had benefited, materially, by his survival of the catastrophes of his lifetime.[84] It seems likely that in the end it was a matter of choice. He must have been a driven man to have stuck to his single great work.

---

[83] J.J. Jusserand, *Piers Plowman: a Contribution to the History of English Mysticism* (London and New York 1894), 66–9; Eamon Duffy, 'Religious Belief', in Rosemary Horrox and W. Mark Ormrod (ed.), *A Social History of England* (Cambridge 2006), 322, writes that 'Langland was almost certainly a clerk in minor orders'.

[84] George Kane, 'Langland, William (c.1325–c.1390), poet', *Oxford DNB*, sums up what is known and concludes that Langland came from 'a family of substance'; but for a persuasive argument that he was low-born, see Jusserand, *Piers Plowman*, 59–73.

He was born not many years after that legendary landmark in the history of English constitutional culture: 1327. Through his lifetime England's constitution was a flux of young institutions, emergent ideologies expressed in a new and increasingly voracious vernacular, a field of force of shifting social coalitions that were, as yet, not clearly defined and interpreted. The monarch is as prominent in the constitutional landscape of *Piers Plowman* as he probably was in the imaginative worlds of the common people. He was a distant receptacle for ideals and hopes for justice. The poet says nothing to the detriment of kingship. If the king is a powerful figure in Langland's vision, he is set in a much larger and richer landscape than in any existing theory. The setting is a teeming commonweal that has practical and, at times, moral priority over every one of its constituent vocations, including kingship. Although the salvation theology of the poem aims 'to include all the estates among the saved', with the possible exception of corrupt clerics and merchants, *Piers Plowman* is a journey through a populist landscape.[85] It is teeming with idiosyncratic individuals and crowds moving across a landscape. Whoever appears, allegorical or naturalistic, has a vocation.[86]

The great nobles are almost as distant as the king. The poem is only indirectly informative about popular attitudes towards the great secular divide between nobility and commonalty, the second and third estates. Writers of Langland's generation were probably conscious of a class of 'middle' households, knights and lesser gentlemen, who were expected to mingle with, speak for, identify with and lead the commons of their *countreys*, and represented them in Parliament.[87] Again, the stereotype was forming, not formed. Many, perhaps most of the great writers and translators of his age – Trevisa, Chaucer and Gower for example – were

---

[85] For Langland's universalism, see Nicholas Watson, 'Visions of Inclusion: Universal Salvation and Vernacular Theology in Pre-Reformation England', *Journal of Medieval and Early Modern Studies* 27:2 (Spring 1997), 153–60; for the ambiguous status of merchants and money, see D. Vance Smith, '*Piers Plowman* and the National Noetic of Edward III', in Lavezzo (ed.), *Imagining a Nation*, 237.

[86] Hudson, *Premature Reformation*, 400, writes that the poem's 'subject is the relationship of the secular ruler to his advisers, the duty of the latter to tell the truth and not flattery to their superior, and the perversion of the contemporary world and particularly the legal system by the wiles of self-seeking schemers.' I suggest that it was also full of positive inspiration, especially for common people: above all, because it was in their language.

[87] 'The barons had traditionally claimed to speak for the community of the realm' but at the time of the Parliaments of 1324 and 1325 'the Lords were evidently perceived as a rump of cowed rebels' and 'the knights and the burgesses rejected the Crown's requests for subsidies'. 'The last years of Edward II's reign witnessed the emergence of the Commons as an independent force in English politics with the potential to influence the business of Parliament and to change the course of government policy.': W.M. Ormrod, 'Agenda for Legislation, 1322–c.1340', *English Historical Review*, 105:414 (January 1990), 8, 15–16, 25–6 and *passim*.

sons of what would later be regarded as minor 'gentry'. Two centuries later Sir Thomas Smith drew a sharper distinction between minor gentry, defining them as the 'second sort' as distinct from a commonalty comprising a 'third' and 'fourth' sort – the common 'middles' and, in Smith's unforgettable term, the 'rascability' or *proletarii*.

As might be expected, lower ranks of nobility were closer to the people than the higher. Langland assumed his audience would have no difficulty imagining knights and esquires as members of crowds largely composed of common people. A gentle knight (too gentle, events will prove) is at hand to discuss theology with Piers when he emerges from the crowd listening to the teachings of Reason and Repentance. Knights and gentlemen were more likely to be found in such congregations than barons and kings: an assumption that was also embodied in the social composition of Chaucer's pilgrims in *Canterbury Tales*, which has tales told by a knight, esquire and yeoman, but, of course, no 'baron's tale' or 'king's tale'.

The main class divides in Piers's mind are not between the commonalty and the secular ruling classes. The first recurring distinction is between the respectable common people, including those whom later writers would call the 'deserving' poor like hard-working widows and the 'blynde and broke-legged or bolted with yren', on the good side, and, on the bad or dangerous side, Smith's 'rascability'. When Piers asks for help to plow his strip, everyone agrees to help except Waster and his vagrant, wayfaring hangers-on: they bid Piers 'go pisse with his plow' (VIII: 152, 152). People like these are as great a danger to the commonweal as corrupt kings, barons and church magnates. Piers turns to secular authority (the knight) for support. The knight is full of promises, but Waster pushes him aside: a sign, perhaps, that the prestige of the knights of the shires was not as great as they liked to imagine. In spite of his desire to love *all* his neighbours, Piers is resignedly 'realistic'. He reluctantly admits that only one lord can provide the spur that will keep Waster and his 'werkemen to wedying and to mowing' (VIII: 185, 154). They will only work honestly, he says, for 'fere of syre Hunger'. This may be the earliest literary construction of the 'undeserving poor' in English literature.

The other divide is between the 'commune' and the Church. In *Passus XVII*, for example, the dreamer asks Free Will 'What is holy churche, chere frende?' Will's answer is identical to that of Tyndale 150 years later:

> Lief and louue and leutee in o byleue and lawe,
> A loue-knotte of leutee and of lele byleue,
> All kyne cristene cleuynge on o will,
> Withoute gyle and gabbing gyue and sulle and lene.[88]

[88] 'Happiness and love and loyalty in one belief and law,/ A love-knot of loyalty and of true faith,/ All natural Christians cleaving to one will,/ Without guile and lying, gifts, sales and lending.': XVII, 284–5: 125–30.

Further on the implication of this communitarian *and*, as we shall see, individualist definition is spelled out. 'If knighthood and sympathetic intelligence and the community and conscience together love honestly', wrote Langland, 'believe it bishops, the lordship of lands you shall lose forever'.[89] The popular view was that lords of the Church were, of all lords, supposed to prevent 'lordes and ladyes' from taking 'of here tenauntes more than treuthe wolde'. Equally commonplace was knowledge that many churchmen were masters of the arts of expanding their estate at the expense of others. This was the barely submerged rock upon which the medieval Church eventually foundered. 'Knighthood' represented an ideal leadership that strongly appealed to the vernacular writers of Langland's generation; it has enjoyed a long afterlife. The ideal knight lived among the people, listened carefully to the petitions and complaints of his *countrey*, organized and led them against their enemies, administered justice and fought for their interests in the courts and councils of Westminster.

The ideal knight and gentleman is difficult to reconcile with the men who accompanied the Black Prince in the ravaging of hundreds of towns and villages in France in the 1350s, or with the opportunistic bandits and bullies who returned and returned again from the devastation of the French commonweal to havoc their homelands throughout the fourteenth and into the fifteenth centuries.[90] The point is not that few of the junior ranks of the warrior nobility came near to practising the ideal, but that everyone thought that was how they *ought* to behave – at least at home. The reason for ideals is that they make oppressions and transgressions stand out, and provide a moral centre from which to judge them. It seems likely that the ideal English gentleman was invented by Langland's generation to replace the ideal baron and that he filled some of the emotional space vacated by the Church in its pursuit of wealth and power.

There has never been any serious doubt about where Langland stood on the subject of the actually existing Church; there is no mistaking his angry antipathy to all kinds of religious professionals, careerists and the corporations they manned. *Piers* is consistently scathing about the existing Church, as scathing, in his way, as Wyclif and, as we shall see,

---

[89] This is my translation of *Piers Plowman: the C-text*, ed. Derek Pearsall, *Passus XVII*, lines 17–19, p. 287: 'Yif knyghthoed and kynde wit and the commune and conscience/ Togederes louen lelyche, leueth hit, bisshopes,/ The lordschipe of londes lese ye for euer.'. For lords and ladies, tenants and truth, see *Passus XVII*, 45: 280.

[90] Jonathan Sumption, *Trial By Fire: the Hundred Years War II* (London 1999), *passim* and ch. 8, 'The Companies, 1357–1359'; Nigel Saul, *Knights and Esquires: the Gloucestershire Gentry in the Fourteenth Century* (Oxford 1981) contains many *vignettes* of returned knights and gentlemen getting away with murder.

Langland's later successor, William Tyndale. High churchmen did not like William Langland and he did not like them.

How did Langland conceive his audience? Langland did not write, or even pretend to write counsel for a prince, like John of Salisbury, or serve as confessor and clerk to a baron, like John Trevisa. He did not have a place in a monastery, a job with an abbot or bishop, a contract to collect customs, or even full-time work as a Chancery or court-clerk. He was not an academic or a member of a college and never had a sinecure, scholarship or bursary. He never attached himself to a trade, profession, university, monastery or parish church. He chose to write for the people in the people's tongue. This makes him the first English popular writer. As suggested above, it was not necessary to be literate to be touched by *Piers Plowman*; instinctively, Langland wrote to be read aloud and be adapted to different contexts and occasions. In this sense he is more like our screenwriters than writers of the eighteenth and nineteenth centuries, who mainly wrote for silent readers. There is no evidence that he made any serious money out of his performances and writing, or that he expected to. Without a patron, he made himself the poet of the commonweal. This was a radical choice, even though he may not have liked being thought of as a 'radical' and was eminently capable of formulating perfectly conservative views on a range of contemporary theological issues. What obsessed him all his writing life was the quest for *treuthe*. This he had in common with the 1381 rebels.

What did he mean by *lollarene lyf*? The etymology of 'lollard' is not as obscure as is sometimes supposed. The English word 'lollare' referred to a 'loller, idler, vagabond', a person who 'lolled' or, metaphorically if not physically, 'hung down loosely'.[91] As Derek Pearsall writes, 'during the 14th century the word is confused, perhaps deliberately, with a new borrowing, lollard (from Dutch *lollaert*, a pious layman who mutters his prayers, from *lollen*, "to mumble")'.[92] Many travellers with no obvious means of support were religious of one kind and degree, like Richard of Fulham (whom we meet in the next chapter). English 'loll' had no religious connotations at all. The addition of Dutch *lollaert* implied a causal connection between being lazy (and hence disobedient to the laws of God and the kingdom) and having (and expressing) independent religious thoughts. It must be remembered that our word 'work' has a universal sense that it lacked in the fourteenth century, when by

---

[91] *OED* 'Loll', meaning (1); the earliest usage of 'Loll' to mean 'to thrust out the tongue in a pendulous manner' is assigned to Shakespeare, but in view of the connotation of 'mumbling prayers' it may well have had this connotation for Langland's contemporaries two centuries earlier.

[92] Pearsall (ed.), *Piers Plowman*, 97: 3, and note 2.

conservative convention it meant assiduously to perform the tasks allotted to the particular vocation and estate to which a person was born, *and only those tasks*. To pursue a vocation was not only a matter of being industrious but of avoiding activities that were supposed to belong to other vocations and estates. It was not the vocation of laymen to utter or mutter prayers of their own, nor to meddle with religion and religious ideas. Like the fourteenth-century Dutch and their 'middle' English borrowers, Shakespeare associated lolling with activities and characteristics of the mouth: it was the condition of a tongue thrust out 'in a pendulous manner'. 'Lollarenes' poked out their tongues at religious authorities.[93]

The English and Dutch usages combined to create a loose stereotype that gained urgency from a fourth association, this time especially evident to the probable inventors of the Lollard stereotype, conservative university men. As Paul Strohm writes, the term 'Lollardi', first recorded in 1382, gained 'at least some of its anti-heretical force from its near-homology with the Latin term *lolium/lollium*, already well established in late-twelfth-century and subsequent orthodox discourse. A *Lolium*', writes Strohm, 'is a cockle or tare . . . the metaphorical corruption of good grain by tares provided an obvious, and highly suggestive, metaphorical vehicle for orthodox distress over invasive and unwelcome doctrines.'[94]

What do these reflections tell us about Langland's associations with 'loll' and 'lollarene' in the very decades in which the reactionary stereotype entered English usage, before it became the word for a sect of heretics? What information did he expect to convey to a reader by indicating his associations with *Lollarenes*? That he *was* a canting, mumbling, lounging, pretend-pious, loose-tongued vagabond, or that his enemies would inevitably use the bug-word 'lollarene' or 'lollard' to put him down? A great scholar, Walter Skeat, thought Latin-writing scholars like

---

[93] W.W. Skeat (ed.), *The Complete Works of Geoffrey Chaucer* (Oxford 1899), vol. 5: 'The Shipman's Prologue', note 1173: quotation from *Piers the Plowman*, C-text (ed. Skeat), X, 188–218, which adds another association – with physical lameness: '*now kyndeliche, by crist / beth suche callyd* lolleres, *As by englisch of oure elders / of olde menne techyng. He that lolleth is lame / other his leg out of ioynte.*' 'Loller' was 'a term of reproach, equivalent to a canting fellow', wrote Skeat. A 'reader will not clearly understand this word till he distinguishes between the Latin *Lollardus* and the English *loller*, two words of different origin which were *purposely* confounded in the time of Wiclif.' 'The Latin *Lollardus* had been in use before Wiclif . . . Kilian, in his Dictionary of Mid Dutch says "*Lollard*, missitur, mussitibundus", ie a mumbler of prayers. This gives two etymologies for *Lollardus*. Being thus in use as a term of reproach, it was applied to the followers of Wiclif, as we learn from Thomas Walsingham who says, under the year 1377 – "Hi uocabantur a vulgo *Lollardi*, incedentes midis pedibus"; and again – "Lollardi sequaces Joannis Wiclif." But the old English *loller* (from the verb to loll) meant simply a lounger, an idle vagabond, as is abundantly clear from a notable passage in *Piers the Plowman*.'

[94] Strohm, *England's Empty Throne*, 37.

Walsingham 'purposely' created the synthesis to describe men who were neither priests nor settled laymen, *lered* nor *lewd*, neither clerics nor manual workers, neither gentlemen nor commoners, yet assumed and combined characteristics of them all. A lollarene was a lazy, insubordinate, idle fellow who wandered aimlessly from place to place (and probably from tavern to tavern) mumbling and moaning about the many corruptions of mother Church.

That was what Langland and his persona 'Long Will' was, and what, in his poem, he demonstrated himself to be. *Lollers* not only mumbled prayers but spoke and wrote about theological issues in English. They were also idle and, worse still, not apparently ashamed, whilst *not* working, 'to lean idly, to recline or rest in a relaxed manner'.[95] They 'didn't have a regular job'. All the evidence suggests that, as Skeat implied, reactionary scholars from a conservative establishment invented 'Lollard' to demean vernacular religion as laid out in *Piers Plowman*. In practice the term was used to embrace a spectral multitude of quite different and often unconnected people and types. The common attribute, as we shall see, was insistence on a personal search for what Langland and John Ball called *treuthe*.[96] For the enemies of this quest, most obviously the

---

[95] Langland, *Piers Plowman*, B-text, xvi, 269 has '. . . lying thus euere lollynge in my lap'; Stubbes, *Anatomy of Abuses* (1583) has 'a shepherd and a dog lolling under a bush': *OED 'loll'*, meaning (4); for the implications of being an unemployed cleric, see Jusserand, *Piers Plowman*, 68–9.

[96] Stephen Justice, *Writing and Rebellion: England in 1381* (Berkeley 1994), 111, writes that 'Ball's meaning is outlandishly different from Langland's . . . His appropriations are willful, at least tangential to and mostly at odds with Langland's purposes.' Like Scanlon, 'King, Commons and Kind Wit', in Lavazzo (ed.), *Imagining a Nation*, 197–9, I doubt that Langland's purposes are easily pinned down. It is likely he was aware that his epic would be put to many uses. Like John of Salisbury before him, he tended to say everything that could be said or implied about a subject, making it difficult for reactionaries to pin him down. Justice, *Writing and Rebellion*, p.121, argues that the rebels 'invoke *Piers Plowman* among their own company, they treat him as having the malleability of a fictional creation, available for the creation and elaboration of other fictions, and indeed for his own recreation: their Piers is their own Piers . . . The letters in effect ally themselves with Truth against the poet; they enjoin Piers to stop being Langland's creation and become their own.' chss.montclair.edu/English/furr/sukonpp.html: Diana V. Suk, 'The Dichotomy in the Piers Plowman Character: Langland's intent versus rebel symbol', likewise presents Langland as defending established order and agrees with Justice that the rebels 'completely overturned and turned upside down . . . the writer's obvious intent'. I have two points of disagreement. First is the idea that Langland invented Piers Plowman. I am not the first to suspect that he developed an existing popular stereotype. If I am right it can be surmised that John Ball drew from the same popular repertoire as Langland but had no knowledge of the poem or its author. Second, the assumption that 'the writer's intent' is 'obvious': this is no truer of Langland than of Shakespeare, whose meanings, legendarily, are far from obvious, and for a good reason: it was imprudent to be unambiguous. The safest way was to represent all the available opinions, first in the interests of verisimilitude and, second, in the hope that the

Church, 'lollard' became a flexible and elastic term of abuse. Like later dissenters from the Lollards to the Levellers, Diggers, Ranters and Quakers, Langland's tactic was to embrace the insult with ironic pride. This tactic naturally infuriated the reactionaries, who got their own back with a vengeance a few years after Langland died, probably in the 1390s. No-one knows where his grave is but his stories echo on.

3.7   Individual souls in a communal landscape

Hit semeth that Criste gat his liflode sometime with travail and with his hond werk; for he was nought y-cleped oonlich a carpenters sone, but also he was cleped a carpenter. And for that he was cleped a carpenter openlich among the peple, hit semeth that for his liflode he used somtyme carpenters crafte with Joseph that was cleped his father.[97]

Thow shalt se Treuthe sitte in thy sulue herte.

As for the social distribution of vice and virtue, Langland expected them to be equally distributed (and equally rare) across all vocations, degrees, estates and classes of people. Yet the common concourse, *commune opinioun*, whilst academically and theologically simplistic in its thoughts and actions, possesses wisdom that is often lost or forgotten in the high and learned circles of courts, universities and kings. The idea that wisdom and formal learning are incompatible is a common axiom of most if not all populist ideologies and mentalities. The belief is that academics, learned men and politicians obscure *treuthe* in foreign words, jargon, abstruse comparisons and qualifications, thickets of sophistry and what Tyndale (turning one of their own words against them) called 'sotelty'. The first precept a popular story-teller would take from *Piers Plowman* was

different 'schools' would fasten onto the phrases and passages that were most congenial to them. Many scholars stress reactionary passages, but for a penetrating account of the affinities of *Piers Plowman* with Wyclif and the 'lollards' see Anne Hudson, *Premature Reformation*, 398–408. T. Torlac-Petre, Review of Wendy Scase, *Piers Plowman and the New Anticlericalism* (Cambridge 1989), in *Review of English Studies* 42 (November 1991), 562–3, traces the poem's 'antifraternal polemics' to the earlier Latin author, Archbishop FtizRalph, but notes that Langland took the arguments much further. In *Piers Plowman*, FitzRalph's arguments were reformulated as 'an attack on the clergy as a whole'. Second, Torlac-Petre draws attention to another crucial difference. 'To write anticlerically in Latin is inevitably to write as one member of the clerical establishment attacking another; to write in English is to question the authority of a whole section of society.' Torlac-Petre also discusses Scase's discussion of the tradition of the *gyrovague*, a 'wandering hermit, living in the city on alms, whose main occupation was to avoid work'. Langland's wholesale critique of the clergy was by no means unprecedented: J.I. Catto, 'A Radical Preacher's Handbook, 1383', *English Historical Review* 115:463 (September 2000), 897, writes that 'William of St Amour included the whole of the regular clergy . . . in his category of *pseudo predicators*.'

[97] Trevisa (trans.), *Defensio Curatorum*, in A.J. Perry (ed.), *Dialogus inter Militem et Clericum* 87.

that blunt wisdom and a naïve but pure love of holiness comes from the people, the commonalty not the elite. The collective voice of the people is the voice of God. A critic and perhaps (in certain moods) Langland himself would object that this was a gross simplification of what he intended. Why then, reactionaries asked, write about the deepest mysteries of religion in the language of the people? Why not do as learned men had done for centuries, write in Latin? If it was a theology for Christendom and not just for English *plebs*, why not use the language of Christendom? The Lollarene's reply was that common language was the carrier of wisdom. English is as sacred a language as Latin. The commonweal is greater than the state and its centre of gravity is much lower than in conventional notions and institutions of hierarchy. Common people are in the foreground, courts and castles are in the distance.

What else might an itinerant teacher and preachers like the leader of the 1381 Commons Rebellion, John Ball, have got from *Piers Plowman*?

'The dreamer looks eastward' from the western borders of England's hills, his vision encompassing 'a good half of the countryside over which London presides' and constituting 'a vision of the nation's center from its periphery'.[98] To understand the poem's landscape vision it is necessary to consider archaic meanings of 'landscape' that were lost in translation from Dutch into English, and need explaining. Like the rebel letters of 1381, *Piers* is set in a detailed landscape of fields, farms, neighbourhoods, hills, vales, mills, cottages, stocks and ponds, wicket-gates, alehouses, churches, hedges, ditches, woodlands and clearings, rivers, streams, fields and pastures, markets, castles, abbeys, bridges and fords, roads and highways, provincial capitals, castles, abbeys, palaces and the streets of London where Langland lived. From the opening lines a pervasive visual imagination frames and holds the vision together. The English word and concept of landscape was not recorded until two centuries after *Piers* was written. According to the *OED* and most accounts since, *landschap* was introduced into English by courtiers and learned men from 'a sixteenth-century Dutch term describing a type of painting'. In this usage, a *landschap* was 'a picture representing natural inland scenery, as distinguished from a seascape, portrait, etc.'.[99] Such 'pictures', like Christopher Saxton's sixteenth-century county maps, were made to hang on the walls of territorial princes, nobles and gentlemen. From this highly partial perspective the commonalty, the subject and working people, did

---

[98] Scanlon, 'King, Commons, and Kind Wit', in Lavazzo (ed.), *Imagining a Nation*, 200.

[99] Denise Lawrence-Zuniga, Review of Eric Hirsch and Michael O'Hanlon (ed.), *The Anthropology of Landscape: Perspectives on Place and Space* (Oxford 1995), *American Anthropologist*, new series 98:4 (December 1996), 915. *Oxford English Dictionary*, 'Landscape', meaning (1).

not view landscapes, they were part of them. It was not necessary to represent them because they were obviously there. They could be taken for granted unless troublemakers stirred them up.

The characters of Langland's spiritual epic – 'Long Will', the author's alter ego, Piers and the whole congregation of people – are in the landscape. Only in his dream does 'Long Will' see the 'fair field full of folk' from an external perspective. His imagination quickly takes him into the concourse. In his own halting journey, and when he falls asleep and dreams, the concourse includes kings, princesses, barons and burgesses, bondmen of 'thorpes' (villages), bakers, brewers, butchers, weavers, walkers (fullers), gamblers, tailors, tanners, tillers of the earth, ditch-diggers, gardeners, cut-purses, market women, wayfaring entertainers, learned men, preachers of God's word, tinkers, a *hackenayman*, church clerks, priests, immigrants like *Purnele of Flaundres*, haywards, hermits, hangmen, porters, pickpockets, tooth-drawers, garlic mongers and a host of more archaic vocations like *ribibours, redyngkynges, dissheres,* and *vphalderes*.[100] The scale of kings, lords, high counsellors, abbots and bishops, of palaces, castles, abbeys and cathedrals is reduced relative to a moving and extremely heterogeneous concourse. As with the German, Flemish and Dutch landscape painters of the fifteenth and sixteenth centuries, and with the later tradition of writers like Rabelais, Tyndale, Shakespeare, Winstanley, Defoe, Fielding, Dickens and Brecht, he envisages an extremely heterogeneous concourse of people moving through and engaging in a multitude of different activities in a landscape.[101] Piers Plowman emerges from the great acoustic congregation of such people.

To understand the horizontal, experiential constitution of landscape that shaped *Piers Plowman* it is necessary to strip away later definitions of the word. Before it acquired its earliest recorded English form, in the late sixteenth century, *landschap* was one of a large family of words common to Germanic and Scandinavian languages. Kenneth Olwig points out that landscape words were in wide and variable use in North-Western Europe before the artists, learned connoisseurs and princes of late sixteenth- and early seventeenth-century England began to paint and hang them on their walls. The implication is that the Dutch landscape tradition originally set out to represent, comment on, and interpret an already rich vernacular or popular tradition that took for granted that human community is a

---

[100] *Piers Plowman: the C-text* (ed. Derek Pearsall), *Prologue* 220–5, *Passus* VIII, l.42, p. 148; VII, l.283–5, p. 144; VII, 105: 133; VII, 88: 132; VI, 364–74: 125–6.

[101] Larry Silver, *Peasant Scenes and Landscapes: the Rise of Pictorial Genres in the Antwerp Art Market* (Philadelphia 2006), is an excellent introduction to the emergence of the common people and their contexts as a dominant genre of pictorial art from the late fifteenth century.

relationship with the face of the earth. Community and landscape were inseparable. This reciprocity was taken for granted – a way of seeing.[102]

The landscape painters of Germany and the Low Countries drew attention to an often ignored aspect of human constitutions, in which the relationship between a people and a 'land' or '*countrey*' was constitutive. *Landschap*, like *landskab*, its Danish equivalent, meant a constitutional state, not a scene or a backdrop: it was not a form of representation; it was the state or condition represented. A *landschap* was a region continuously invested with the presence, practices, customs, rituals, ceremonies and beliefs, in short, the everyday lives, works, journeys and imaginations of its people. It was seen and experienced from within. *Landskab*, Olwig explains, 'was a nexus of law and cultural identity'.[103] The nearest early modern English equivalent of this conception is not 'landscape' but 'countrey'.[104] In the sixteenth and seventeenth centuries a 'countrey' was 'a tract or district having more or less definite limits in relation to human occupation, e.g. owned by the same lord or proprietor, or inhabited by people of the same race, dialect, occupation etc.'. As the *OED* states, 'with political changes, what were originally distinct countries have become provinces or districts of one country... the modern tendency being to identify the term with the existing political condition'.

It would be misleading to think of these *landskaber* as entirely 'imagined' communities, like modern nations. 'Countrey' in the sense that I am using the word was first and foremost the experiential basis and point of departure for imaginings like those of Langland. Stories framed in this way made sense because they drew on the universal experience of being in and moving through physical landscapes. Life is a journey of the eternal soul through a landscape with people. *Piers*'s accessibility owed much to the *landschap*-vision that informed it. Unlike learned mnemonic systems, landscape vision, indifferent to prescribed hierarchies, ordered and located people and classes horizontally; it was teemingly populous, various and unpredictable. It had monasteries, great abbeys, and palaces and finely constructed and furnished castles, but they were only features of a much larger, more comprehensive, 'horizontal' vision of a commonweal. Langland committed this populist vision to writing more than a century

---

[102] Kenneth R. Olwig, 'Recovering the Substantive Nature of Landscape', *Annals of the Association of American Geographers* 86: 4 (1996), 630–53.

[103] Olwig, 'Substantive Landscape', 672.

[104] 'Ac Symonye and Syuile and sysores (jurors) of *contrees/* Were most pryue with Mede (bribery and corruption) of eny men, me thoghte.': Pearsall (ed.), *Piers Plowman*, II, 63: 58.

before German and Dutch painters began to place common people in the foreground of their canvases.[105]

All classes took for granted that spirits lurked behind and animated the *landschap*. Lucifer and other invisible agents (personifications of vices, virtues, sins and so on) could appear and, in human or other forms, speak, tempt, undermine and inspire the children of God as they passed, mingled, hailed, argued and conversed in the general concourse. In 1362 it was reported that 'the devil appeared bodily in man's likeness [and spoke] to many people as they went in divers places in the country'. In July 1441 'it was spoken amongst the people that there were some wicked fiends and spirits, reared out of hell by conjuration, to annoy the people of the realm and to put them to trouble, dissension and unrest'.[106] The devil and his fiends hid most of the time in places that were friendly to them. They were 'there' all the time but only showed themselves in times of crisis when God was so angry that He appeared to have abandoned His people. Lucifer showed himself in 1362 after a 'sudden tempest and lightning'; fiends stalked the streets of London in 1441 after another violent storm of hail, rain and lightning. The only variable was how far classes, communities and individuals took their sense of being constantly at the mercy of a *habitus* that was animated by invisible forces.

In sum, 'landscape' was the mnemonic of mnemonics, capable of encompassing the whole of life, and not just a part of it as in the memory palaces of contemporary scholars. Piers's directions to Truth constitute the moral and spiritual centre of the poem. Like the limbs and members of John of Salisbury's body politic, Piers's directions were memorable, in part, because they could be stated concisely.

When Piers emerges from the concourse in *Passus VII* the pilgrims automatically see him as authoritative and believe him when he tells them that he has served the lord of *treuthe* 'al this fourty wynter'. All this time he has 'yserved Treuthe sothly' (VII, 189–90: 139). In my populist interpretation, this passage is the heart of the epic.

Before we can understand the quest for truth, we need to consider what Langland meant by the keyword. '*Treuthe*' was another spelling of the 1381 rebels' '*trewth*'. It did not mean then what it came to mean later. It meant 'faithfulness' (to a lord, to God, to one's family and neighbours and, in a rather profound sense, to oneself) rather than 'in

---

[105] Larry Silver, *Peasant Scenes and Landscapes*, explains the development of *landschap* painting (though not by this name) in the work, amongst others, of Hieronymus Bosch, Pieter Bruegel the Elder, Pieter Aertsen and Joachim Beuckelaer. The religious pretext retreats into the background and the secular context becomes ever more dominant. *Piers Plowman* is of course pervaded by the supernatural, but the landscape is secular.
[106] *Brut Chronicles*, 313, 417.

accordance with the known facts', a definition that came to the fore later.[107] In the case of *Piers Plowman* and the 1381 rebel letters it meant fidelity to customary ideals of community and social relations as carried, primarily, by oral tradition. Such ideals are universal but in times of crisis – local, provincial, national – they came to focus on particular authority figures and institutions, whose character and behaviour was judged in relation to their concordance with the customary ideals. As writing was increasingly used to validate claims a potential was created for conflict between two kinds of testimony. By the mid-fourteenth century it had been established that spoken testimony was a less authoritative source of truth than authenticated writing. Written records emanated predominantly from the courts and offices of the higher estates; oral testimony was, for the most part, the medium of the subject population.

One of the claims or demands implicit in the 1381 rebels' burnings of records, discriminating though it often seems to have been, was that writing was partial to lords and oral testimony favoured the people.[108] The 'great rumour' of the 1370s was significant because of its new tactic of using lords' written records (*Domesday Book*) to prove a popular cause: usually that the inhabitants of this or that village or town once had liberties that later lords had illegitimately curtailed.[109] All this fed resentment between lords and their subjects. Every time a piece of parchment or paper with Latin writing was used to disprove oral testimony it questioned the faithfulness of a witness.[110] In some places – Cirencester, Abingdon, Bury St Edmunds, St Albans – use of written record to discredit social memory was undoubtedly relentless, often shameless and invariably concerned to increase the dominion and wealth of the lord at the expense of remembered liberties of the people. Allegations that convenient charters had been forged and inconvenient ones destroyed surfaced whenever trouble erupted in such places. The struggles of provincial centres are well documented. The first Commons Rebellion was at least in

---

[107] Richard Firth Green, *A Crisis of Truth: Literature and Law in Ricardian England* (Philadelphia 2002) is the definitive account of this epistemological shift.

[108] A central theme of Stephen Justice, *Writing and Rebellion*, that the rebels were literate enough to be able to discriminate between texts to burn and texts to save, is compatible with my interpretation. His further argument that the rebels were not antagonistic to literates and written records needs qualification. I suggest that it was a precept of popular culture throughout the fourteenth century that certain types of literates and their texts (clerks and lawyers especially) were constitutionally hostile to honest testimony spoken in the common tongue. As Justice argues, however, this did not mean the rebels were hostile to writing *per se*.

[109] For the 'great rumour' see Chapter 4.5, below.

[110] James Fentress and Chris Wickham, *Social Memory* (Oxford 1992), 10, write that 'To groups emerging from preliteracy written knowledge, substituted for community memory, can seem a frightening and alienating possibility'.

part an eruption of accumulated resentment of a constantly rehearsed implication: words spoken in English by respected elders of a community were less faithful to truth than documents written in Latin behind closed doors by monks, canons and clerks. In such contexts the transition from memory to written word often created systematic mistrust between lords and subjects. Other things being equal, lords and their faithful servants were always bound to exaggerate the subordination and dues of the people and the witnesses of the people necessarily reported the memory of the community, not the lord. Truth was a concept in crisis.

Piers describes 'the perversion of the contemporary world' relentlessly.[111] If truth – faithfulness to God and neighbour – is not to be found at the courts of kings, in parliaments, in law-courts and least of all in the many institutions of the Church – in short nowhere in Church or Estate – where is it to be found? The pilgrims naturally respond to Piers's claim to have followed Truth all his life by asking him where truth lives and how to get there. It has been established that the only justification for a pilgrimage is that it is a journey in search of truth. Piers offers directions. The pilgrims are to proceed through the nearby villages of 'Meekness' and 'Conscience', cross the dangerous ford of Patriarchal respect and proceed along the path to the shrine of Don't Take God's Name in Vain. Like every place, Don't Take God's Name in Vain (a market town, perhaps) offered temptations that had to be mastered before a pilgrim could continue on to the next place, the croft of Covet Not and those instruments of shame, the village stocks of Steal-Not and Kill-Not. Past them Bear No False Witness Hill came into view – a deceptively dangerous climb that must be completed without stopping in order to reach the place of Honest Speech. From the place of Honest Speech the Castle of Truth is in prospect. Visible in the distance the pilgrim will see its moat of Mercy and its walls of Intelligence, buttressed by impregnable battlements of Faith. Piers warns pilgrims not to be in too much of a hurry to cross the bridge to the great gates hung on 'hokes' of 'almes dedes', where Grace, the gatekeeper, will wish to see their credentials. Give what you still possess to the poor, Piers counsels, and only then proceed to the gate. There you will be questioned by Grace's assistant, Amend-You. The location of penitence so close to the end of the pilgrim's journey identifies Langland with another powerful religious movement of his age. Only if Amend-You is convinced that you have truly learned from your pilgrimage and are genuinely penitent for sins past, will Grace obtain the key to the gate from the Virgin Mary (who, as Jesus' mother, had redeemed it from Eve). You have reached the end. 'And yf Grace graunt

---

[111] Hudson, *Premature Reformation*, 400.

the to go in this wyse', says Piers, 'Thow shalt se Treuthe sitte in thy sulue herte.'[112]

This is the heart of the poem. If Grace allows pilgrims to complete their journeys, they will find Truth in their own hearts. For Langland truth meant fidelity to God and to a unique, individual vocation, fraught with endless temptation, that would not become fully clear until the journey was at an end. Only God knows Truth – but it matters to Him that, in following our vocations, we strive to move towards it. When he wrote his final drafts of the poem he must have been aware that Truth had been the shibboleth of the Commons Rebellion. He must have at least suspected that versions of parts of his poem actually inspired some of the rebels. The 1381 rebellion made truth a very dangerous word.

The idea that God dwelt in every individual's self and that truth came out of an irreducibly personal quest or journey was thoroughly subversive. 'I be so festened to him that thare be right nought that is made betwyxte my God and me,' wrote Langland's younger contemporary, the supposedly orthodox Julian of Norwich.[113] What would happen, not only to religious but also to secular authority, if everyone thought they could discover and pursue their own vision of truth? But if it was potentially antinomian with regard to the institutions of church and state, it was hardly compatible with subjection to the common will of crowds. What if, standing on Bear No False Witness Hill, within sight of the end, a pilgrim is subjected to inquisition by the authorities and instructed to recant? Having come so far, dare she recant for fear of punishment, like Peter at the time of Christ's trial? Christ forgave Peter. Mercy granted, pilgrims must then give away everything they own, show memory and penitence for every sin and failure. These rules applied to everyone from the king down to the humblest labourer. Each one had truth within.

Note that Honest Speech (presumably what Langland, distant ancestor of Orwell, most sought after) is not attained until well into the journey, but is still some way from the end. Honest Speech is just another stage. Humility, conscience, respect for elders, respect for God, testimony must all be passed through first. All can be undone at any time by covetousness. God speaks to and appears in, is indeed (as in Julian's vision) one with, the soul of every individual. The individual can choose not to listen or notice and many do so. In many cases the urgings of the Devil swamp souls and corrupt them. Two precepts in one proverbial phrase provide

---

[112] Pearsall (ed.), *Passus VII*, lines 183–255, pp. 138–42.

[113] 'A Vision Showed to a Devout Woman', in Nicholas Watson and Jacqueline Jenkins (ed.), *The Writings of Julian of Norwich* (University Park, Pa. 2006), Section 4, lines 17–18, p. 69.

guidance in difficult cases: 'love God and thy neighbour'. *Piers* applies the Christian communalism of the Epistle of James to a much larger and more complex community of Christians than Jesus or James ever imagined.[114] He probably did not realize that this was what he was doing. The populist tradition would always dress Jesus, the disciples and their reported contexts in its own clothes. They imagined Jesus's world as the same as their own. Jesus was one of them.

'Iesu Cryst of heuene / In a pore mannes apparaille pursueth vs euere' verbalized the all-pervasive populist religious outlook at the heart of *Piers Plowman*. As noted earlier, it is possible that the seeds of this gathering movement were planted by the first generation of Franciscan missionaries in the thirteenth century. We can be sure that it would have fallen on receptive ears. Popular Christianity has always been influenced, above all, by the story of Jesus, bracketed by the popular festivals of Christmas and Easter. The story is familiar and memorable: the baby Jesus, born in a stable, son of a simple carpenter, who grew into the learned little boy who spoke wisdom to scholars and, in the last phase of his life, became the uncompromising miracle worker who set about the merchants in the temple and was willing to die rather than renounce his vocation. He sprang from and spent his life among the labouring poor, insisted that his followers give away all they had, and was crucified by the bishops and archbishops of Judaism with the permission of a vacillating imperial state official. There are many Jesuses in the Christian sources, forming a spectrum from the illiterate peasant-artisan envisaged by Trevisa in the epigraph to this section to the imperial king of kings favoured by Constantine and succeeding religious establishments. It is this life of Jesus, not the theology of Paul, or the fine disputes of all the doctrinal acrobats who followed him, that captured the imagination of the millions of people Bob Scribner called 'the simple folk'.[115] This Jesus was manifestly born into the commonalty and spent his life amongst common people in the everyday contexts of villages, market towns, provincial capitals and the streets of a great city. This is the great paradox of Christianity. Why did God send his son to live amongst the common people, the subjects of states? His life was testimony to the populist precept that truth

---

114 And in Matthew 22, in which 'a doctor of law' asks Jesus 'which is the great commandment? Jesus said unto him: thou shalt love the Lord thy God with all thy heart, with all thy soul, and with all thy mind. This is the first and great commandment. And there is another like unto this. Thou shalt love thy neighbour as thyself.'

115 Of particular relevance here is Scribner's observation that artisans were the 'centre of gravity' of the 'popular' (as against 'the magistrates") reformation: R.W. Scribner, 'Religion, Society and Culture: Reorienting the Reformation', *History Workshop Journal* 14 (Autumn 1982), 2–22.

came first to the people, in the households, fields and streets of villages, market towns and cities and on the common wastelands beyond. This Jesus combined the life of a *lollarene* with the spiritual integrity of *Piers Plowman*.

The vernacular revolution was much more than simple translation of ideas from imperial languages like Latin and French into a language that lacked them. Early vernacular scribes, commentators and authors certainly saw *translatio studii et imperii*, the transmission of classical 'studies' (texts and procedures regarded as canonical) and precepts of empire (political theology) from Latin into the *lewd* (uneducated) language of the commonalty, as part of their task. The implication, controversial enough from the perspective of the hereditary ruling classes and a church that was deeply suspicious of popular religion, was that it was a good idea for the common working population to have access to the texts and hence the precepts of the common Christian culture.[116] That was revolutionary in itself, but Langland took it much further. It has been said that English writers of the fourteenth century 'often seem . . . more concerned with the projected *audience* of a text' which, in turn, involves ideas about 'the kind of *community* that writing can make or sustain.' 'The question of who should be able to read [and hear] what is pivotally important to the vernacular politics of late medieval England and is inseparable from contentious issues of gender, class, education and community.'[117] As we shall see in the next section, the question of who was allowed to read, speak and listen to what became an intense concern of church and state in the first decade of the fifteenth century. The repression of vernacular discourse followed the realization, premised above all on continuing evidence of class conflict after the social earthquake of 1381, that the rise of English had far-reaching social and constitutional implications. How to keep mysteries of state secret from subjects by suppressing vernacular discourse became a major preoccupation of three or four generations from the reactionaries of Langland's world to that of Sir Thomas More and Sir Thomas Elyot – and the greatest of all the proponents of English vernacular piety, William Tyndale – in the 1520s and 1530s. The vision of *Piers Plowman* had a lot to do with bringing that situation about: more than

---

[116] 'Holy writ in Latyn is bothe gode and fayre, and yet for to make a sermoun of holy writ al in Latyn to men that kunneth Englisshe and no Latyn were a lewde deed, for they bith never the wiser for the Latyn but it be told hem an Englisshe what hit is to mene', says the Lord in John Trevisa, 'Dialogue between a Lord and his Clerk' (1387), in *The Idea of the Vernacular*, 133; the cleric objects that 'holy doctours' are needed to explain them, to which the Lord replies, 'Hit is wonder that thou makest so feble arguments.' It is the lay figure, the Lord, who speaks for the vernacular and the cleric who objects.

[117] *The Idea of the Vernacular*, 322.

any other work of his age, it carried and reinforced a powerful populist image of a teemingly heterogeneous and implicitly heterodox community that common people could identify with.

3.8   Ubiquitous vernacular heterodoxy: the case of Julian of Norwich

One of the central points common to all Reformers was their rejection of mediation.[118]

Langland covered more ground, in every sense, yet without ever ceasing to be entirely unique and exceptional, no English writer better illuminates the vernacular piety (or as Eamon Duffy puts it, 'radical orthodoxy') that characterized Langland's generation, than Julian of Norwich (c.1342–c.1416). If Langland, Wyclif and the Lollards stand for an angry, rebellious response to a Church now characterized more by 'lawyers and administrators', rents and dues and courtly nepotism, than by the 'scholars and theologians' who were prominent in the episcopate of the previous century,[119] Julian represents the loam out of which they grew: a simpler vernacular piety grounded in an almost casual indifference to Church hierarchy and dogma. Recently described as being 'among the greatest mystical writers of all times and all places', Julian was one of 'fifty other hermits and anchorites [who are] known to have lived in medieval Norwich', then as now an unusual and distinctive city. On the grounds of her vocation alone she will not have appeared unusual in her lifetime. Hermits and anchorites were vernacular, popular institutions. A daughter of the merchant class, Julian seems to have been well known locally during her lifetime in her role as an anchoress, only achieving extensive fame as a theologian in the second half of the twentieth century.[120]

On the basis of a powerful vision experienced during a sickness between 8 and 13 May 1373, beautifully and intensely realized in the *Vision Showed to a Devout Woman*, Julian gave feminine testimony to the infinite depth of God's love. Her faith, as described in the *Vision*, derived directly from experience and not from any external intermediary or authority. As her text amply demonstrates, 'I be so festened to him that thare be right nought that is made betwyxte my God and me.'[121]

---

[118] Charles Taylor, *Sources of the Self: the Making of the Modern Identity* (Cambridge, Mass. 1989), 215.

[119] Duffy, 'Religious Belief', 322.

[120] Norman Tanner, 'Hermits and Anchorites', *The Church in Late Medieval Norwich 1370–1532*, (Toronto 1984), 58–9; Tanner, 'Religious Practice', Chapter 6 of Carole Rawcliffe and Richard Wilson (ed.), *Medieval Norwich* (London 2004), 138–9.

[121] 'A Vision Showed to a Devout Woman', *Writings of Julian*, ed. Watson and Jenkins, Section 4, lines 17–18, p. 69.

Although at the time of her vision she may have been 'illiterate' in the clerical sense of not knowing Latin, Julian claimed to be 'learned in the ghostly showing of our lord'.[122] Her vision, in terminology that is familiar to historians of radical religion in the 1640s, made her a spiritual 'sekere', convinced that 'God wille ever that we be sekere in luffe.' The faithful person moves amongst her *evenchristene* ('christian neighbours') in love, 'calm in character and graced with a determined mind, leading an outwardly undisturbed life while striving to reach her goal'.[123] Julian's thought is sublimely indifferent to the Church; the transparent, simple authenticity of her vision renders questions of mediating orthodoxy irrelevant. Many passages entirely short-circuited the Church's claims to be the exclusive mediator between God, humanity and the individual soul. Every soul is saved by 'His precious blood shedding'; women are especially beloved of God; the 'blessed godhead' is 'all mighty, all wisdom, all love'; He made 'alle thinge' and 'alle that is made is mekille and faire and large and good'; God made all things for love and His love 'ever shall be withouten ende'; and most characteristically, 'God is alle thinge that is goode. And the goodness that all things have is his'.[124]

Yet Julian is not other-worldly. The question that made her a 'seeker' in explosively troubled times was 'howe might alle be wele?' Each element of the holy trinity – father, son and holy ghost – is present and active, always and infinitely concerned with '*worldlye* wele'. In her vision Jesus tells her 'I may make alle thing wele, I can make alle thinge wele, and I shalle make alle thinge wele. And thow shalle see it thyself that alle thinge shalle be wele.' Seeing for oneself, without mediation, was her silent, central precept, as it would be, 150 years later, in Tyndale's much angrier and explicitly rebellious theology. Julian's statement that 'in mankind that shalle be safe is comprehende alle that is . . . For in manne is God, and so in man is alle' does not, on the face of it, leave much room for institutions of a Church; institutions are relentlessly absent from her thoughts. Her theology is indifferent to the Church and nothing is further from it than the imposition of orthodoxy by threat and cruelty. God, quite simply, is infinite, universal love and forgiveness.[125]

---

[122] Grace M. Jantzen, *Julian of Norwich, Mystic and Theologian* (London 1987), 25, suggests that she may have learned to write in English between the first, shorter version of her vision, which was dictated to a scribe, and the 1390s, when she wrote the longer commentary, *A Revelation of Love*; 'A Vision', 4:17–18, p. 69; 6:21–2, p. 73.

[123] 'And he that thus loves alle his evenchristene, he loves alle. And he that loves thus, he is safe': 'A Vision' 6:27–8, 75; Verena E. Neuburger, *Margery Kempe: a Study in Early English Feminism* (Frankfurt 1994), 15.

[124] 'A Vision', 5:5–21, 73.

[125] *Ibid.*, 4:40–1, 71; 15:2–4, 95; for Julian's universalism, see Watson, 'Visions of Inclusion: Universal Salvation and Vernacular Theology in Pre-Reformation England',

Julian's native city was notable in several respects. England's second largest city, Norwich grew from 10,000 to 25,000 souls between the Norman Conquest and the Black Death. Between the twelfth century and the 1340s, when Julian was born, it was served by no fewer than sixty parish churches, many of which, like St Julian, Conesford, a stone's throw from the busy Conesford docks on the River Wensum, housed a hermit or anchoress like 'Julian' (who took her official name from the church in whose grounds her anchorage was located). In addition to its ubiquitous solitaries, Norwich is the only city in medieval England known to have been home to communities of beguines, mature secular women who chose a religious life and lived in communities, unlike the solitary hermits and anchoresses.[126] One commentator has speculated that Julian may have been a beguine.[127] In the sense that solitaries and beguines were both popular institutions, formations of common, vernacular, religious sensibility, it was possible to be both.

Where open heresy is concerned, Norwich's records yield only two Lollards with addresses within the walls, in marked contrast to contemporary English towns like Coventry, Leicester, Colchester, London and Bristol. Tanner suggests that there were few Lollards because a certain amount of heterodoxy was permitted by the richness and diversity of the city's mix of religious institutions and traditions. Countervailing and chronically contentious institutions left room for people to 'seek', like Julian, for the kernel of truth at the heart of all the countervailing interests and opinions: the kernel of collective wisdom concerning the achievement of spiritual '*wele*'. The people of Norwich 'did not feel the need for, or the attraction of, Lollardy as they might have in a more spiritually barren landscape'.[128] Those complexities included enduring trade and cultural connections with Belgium and the Low Countries, the continuously occupied hermitages and anchorages, and, of course, the enigmatic beguines. They included a great late fourteenth-century reactionary, the aristocratic Henry Despenser, bishop of Norwich when Julian was at Conesford. Despenser's rule constantly irritated the local

---

Journal of Medieval and Modern Studies 27:2 (Spring 1997), 160–6; for the 1381 rebels' usage of *wele*, see Section 5.3, below.

[126] Tanner, *The Church in Late Medieval Norwich*, 64–6: 'Communities Resembling Beguinages'.

[127] Jantzen, *Julian of Norwich*, 25.

[128] Tanner, 'Religious Practice', 138–9, 150–2; the situation in Norwich almost certainly left political and social space for various forms of 'voluntary religion', for which see W.J. Sheils and D. Wood (ed.), *Voluntary Religion* (Oxford 1986), and Beat Kumin, 'Voluntary Religion and Reformation Change in Eight Urban Parishes', in Patrick Collinson and John Craig (ed.), *The Reformation in English Towns 1500–1640* (Basingstoke 1998), 175–189.

religious communities, the parishes, priors, abbots and aldermen of the borough. He scourged popular rebels in 1381, administering savage retribution when the world, turned upside down, was restored to proper order. Julian's anchorage was only a few hundred metres below that most bluntly forbidding symbol of the Norman yoke, Norwich castle, between the castle mound and Conesford's docks on the river Wensum. She would have known – literally heard – immediately when, in 1381, popular rebels took and held the castle, just as their counterparts in London reduced the government of the City of London: for a day or two they had the regime at their mercy.[129] 'Religion' in the fullest sense encompassed a very complex and heterogeneous field of force of contending interests and opinions, nowhere more than in late fourteenth-century Norwich. It is hard to imagine that heretical whisperings were never uttered, heard and passed on in the households, taverns and even the parish churches of Julian's city. Norwich had a more sophisticated range of opinions to which its inhabitants could retreat for another good reason. Julian's anchorage was within sight and smell of the place where heretics of the diocese were burned, about a quarter of a mile upstream along the Wensum.

There is no doubt about its diversity. Norwich was a cathedral city, the capital of East Anglia, and featured the full range of monastic foundations.[130] Carrow Priory, to which the parish church of St Julian was attached, 'was a centre of the Brigittine spirituality which so profoundly affected figures as diverse as King Henry V and the East Anglian mystic, Margery Kempe. The house's anchoresses, of whom Dame Julian of Norwich is now by far the most celebrated, played an important role in transmitting and explaining these ideas to the laity, who turned to them for guidance in times of emotional crisis.'[131] This is another reminder that hermits and anchoresses were in no sense isolated from their local communities; they were not encouraged to engage in rigorous forms of asceticism and isolation: it was a matter of choice. Grace Jantzen compares the anchoress to 'a modern psychotherapist or professional counsellor . . . able to listen effectively and sympathetically, without letting her own preoccupations get in the way'. Anchoresses counselled men as well as women, as long as they were discreetly hidden behind a curtain. Margery Kempe's pilgrimage to Julian's cell 'well illustrates the wider pastoral activities undertaken by such holy women'.[132]

[129] Charles Oman, *The Great Revolt of 1381* (Oxford 1969), 116–20, 133–7.
[130] Tanner, *The Church in Late Medieval Norwich*, 18–56.
[131] Christopher Harper-Bill and Carole Rawcliffe, 'The Religious Houses', *Medieval Norwich*, 99.
[132] Jantzen, *Julian of Norwich*, 34–5, 37; Harper-Bill and Rawcliffe, 'The Religious Houses'.

Anchoresses continuously occupied St Julian's until the Reformation. Hermits and anchoresses were not always merely indifferent to institutional orthodoxy. The hermit William Swinderby, at Leicester, and the anchoress Anna Palmer, at Northampton, were 'chief Lollard ringleaders' of their respective communities.[133] In the next chapter we meet a Hertfordshire hermit who condemned the Statute of Labourers as the heresy and blasphemy of a profoundly class-biased state. A century after Julian's death, 'Katherine Mann, an anchoress attached to the Norwich Blackfriars, was supplied by the heretic Thomas Bilney (d.1531) with illicit copies of William Tyndale's translation of the New Testament and his *Obedience of a Christian Man*.'[134] This does not make her a Lollard or a Protestant, but it does suggest access to many streams of local and national religion, and curiosity to learn more.

The tension between experience and institutional orthodoxy is implicit but unmistakeable in Julian's writings. It is well said that, as far as the Church was concerned, her 'faithfulness consisted partly in recalling it to its ideals.'[135] If so she failed – or was utterly mistaken in her estimate of what its 'ideals' were.

3.9   Reactionaries

. . . the free servaint of Christe ought not to be brought violently into captivitie under the bondage of the traditions of men.[136]

No empire or corporation, however pure its inspiration, is greater than the sum of mixed individuals who constitute it. Like 'heresy', 'corruption' is defined by predetermined rules and standards; the ideals of medieval Christendom were as high as ideals can be, impossibly so. Even the simplest Christian proverb – 'love God and thy neighbour' – makes demands that not even Jesus himself could live up to all the time. Simple precepts governed popular judgement of the Church. Although the Franciscans came to England when the common language movement was in its infancy, too early for systematic evidence to be available, they probably inspired something akin to a national revivalist movement. This movement was probably part of the assumed context of the 'common enterprise' of the 1250s and the vernacular movement of the fourteenth century. It revived populist conceptions of Jesus. One hundred and fifty years later this movement, now increasingly feared in the higher realms

[133] Duffy, 'Religious Belief', 326.
[134] Harper-Bill and Rawcliffe, 'The Religious Houses', 99.
[135] Jantzen, *Julian of Norwich*, 10.
[136] *An Answer Unto Sir Thomas More's Dialogue made by William Tyndale* (1530).

of the Church, merged with the equally powerful vernacular revival to produce its masterpieces, *Piers Plowman* and Julian's *Vision*.[137]

The Jesus of St Francis and *Piers* was not an emperor with a jewelled crown. He was the son of a carpenter, kin to peasants and artisans.[138] He was born in a stable, grew up and lived all his life among the people. He was egalitarian in his social relations, not 'respecting persons'. He did not discriminate between people on the basis of birth, rank, class, gender, degree or status. His disciples were working people. He was loved by and loved women and children. Above all, he died, as Julian insisted, to redeem *everyone*. Because the populist Jesus is inherent in the Gospels, and because the idea that Jesus was a common, all-forgiving, man is inherently subversive of secular hierarchies and systemic inequality, institutions that stand for authoritarian hierarchy must prevent popular access to the sacred texts. The most effective way to prevent diffusion is to restrict the scriptures to sacral languages. Such a system operated in all the great agrarian empires: Mandarin Chinese, Sanskrit, Arabic, Greek and Latin all restricted knowledge of the sacred precepts of civilization to specially educated elites. In this respect medieval Christendom was a local case of a phenomenon that can be observed in every Iron Age agrarian empire.

The march of 'middle' English into the realms of the sacred was halted by 'one of the most draconian pieces of censorship in English history'.[139] Traditionally, scholars have seen Archbishop Arundel's 'constitutions' of 1409 as instruments for the repression of Lollards. Lollards incautious enough to be defined as such in the records of church and state were a very small minority of English people. Therefore, it is argued, Lollards were a fringe group and the institutions set up to repress them were marginal

---

[137] Watson, 'Visions of Inclusion', 170, traces vernacular universalism back to the late thirteenth and early fourteenth centuries, when 'the vernacular itself . . . was conceived as a powerful, affective, natural bond linking all the English people'; he writes (*ibid.*, 167) that what made writers like Julian and Langland 'worrying for the likes of Hilton is that they cannot be reduced to a school, let alone a sect like the Lollards, but are symptomatic of a general tendency towards theological speculation in English'.

[138] As Trevisa noted, see above, epigraph to Section 3.7.

[139] Nicholas Watson, 'Censorship and Cultural Change in Late-Medieval England: Vernacular Theology, the Oxford Translation Debate, and Arundel's Constitutions of 1409', *Speculum* 70:4 (October, 1995), 826. Anne Hudson, 'Lollardy: the English Heresy', in Hudson, *Lollards and their Books* (London 1985), 145, writes that the movement associated with Arundel 'came to see that the vernacular lay at the root of the trouble'. It 'threw open to all the possibility of discussing the subtleties of the Eucharist, of clerical claims, of civil dominion and so on'. Eamon Duffy, 'Religious Belief', 331, has 'little doubt that official censorship had an impact on the ethos of fifteenth-century English religion'. This was anticipated, he thinks by the 'self-censorship' evident in the revisions of Langland and Julian of Norwich in the 1380s and 1390s. Yet 'It would be absurd to attribute what is arguably a generalised drop in cultural temperature to religious repression . . . Fifteenth-century England had no thought-police.'

to the mainstream of English historical development. 'Lollards' (effectively the English word for 'heretics') were 'extremists' distinguished from the supposed mainstream of ordinary sensible people who accepted the authority of those better educated, and therefore wiser, than they were. Everywhere in pre-Reformation England, it has been argued, 'traditional Catholic' practices and institutions went on regardless – because they were *popular*, 'of the people' and loved by the great majority. Where they could do so safely in the 1530s, 1540s and 1550s, a generation of revisionist historians have contended, a 'survivalist' majority of English people continued to practise 'traditional religion' in spite of the efforts of king, counsellors and intellectuals to impose new precepts. People continued to cherish icons, cross themselves, light candles and recite barely understood Latin incantations in traditional contexts like ploughing, birth and death.[140] The new orthodoxy is that the English Reformation took place in spite of the traditionalism of English popular religion.

If its predestinarian redemption theology made it less attractive and popular than Langland's and Julian's universalism, Lollardy was, by the 1390s, profoundly 'traditional' in one crucial way: its insistence on the vernacular. *Piers Plowman*, Wycliffite Bibles, the 'dangerous words' of fifteenth-century Lollards, the vision of Julian of Norwich and the strange, relentless late pilgrimages of the doughty Margery Kempe, each in its own way, signifies the march of the vernacular into the realms of religion. At their back was the many-stranded but ubiquitous, populist vernacular movement described in this chapter.[141] By c.1400 'Lollard' ideas and beliefs, their criticisms of clerics and friars, and above all their language, had moved into every corner of English society, governance

---

[140] Richard Rex, *The Lollards* (Basingstoke 2002), xiv–xv and *passim*, states the revisionist-Catholic case. His proposition that pre-Reformation 'Lollardy' did not denote a sect but is best understood as the English word for 'heretics' is generally accepted. Yet his claim that Lollardy 'was simply never as popular or as powerful as many nervous contemporaries feared and some recent historians have hoped' implies that it was a sect. 'Lollardy,' he writes, 'is of virtually no importance for the success of the English Reformation.' The question arising is 'Why, if the Lollards were neither numerically significant in their own time nor of great importance for the course of English history, they have attracted so much scholarly attention.' My answer is that they deserve such attention because they represented a vernacular movement that had already transformed English constitutional culture and would continue to do so in the realms of theology and ritual after the 1520s and 1530s, when the reactionaries lost support in the circles around the king.

[141] Duffy, 'Religious Belief', 329, dates the struggle with Lollardy 'almost exactly from the outbreak of the papal schism in 1378 until the settlement of the western Church in the pontificate of Martin V, which ended in 1431'. It was a momentous period which saw the writings of 'William Langland, Geoffrey Chaucer, the Gawain poet, John Gower... while the great religious texts of the period included the works of Walter Hilton and the *Cloud of Unknowing*, the *Shewings* of Julian of Norwich, the earliest York and Chester mystery drama cycles and, not least, the *Book* of Margery Kempe'. This, for Duffy, was the tip of the iceburg of what he calls 'vernacular piety'.

and religion. 'Lollard' ideas were every bit as 'traditional', 'popular' and 'mainstream' as the allegedly orthodox 'majority'. The 'sectarianization' (or isolation) of 'Lollards' was central to the strategy of a constitutionally reactionary Church and a disturbed, insecure and fearful secular state.

The vernacular tide was officially halted at the gates of religion – events would show, for over a century – in the early months of 1401. In the midst of a wildly burgeoning legitimacy crisis, at a time when the king was being bombarded with dire warnings of a world turned upside down, the key institutions of the English state – Parliament, Convocation and Court – were ordered to gather in London, Parliament meeting at Westminster, Convocation at St Paul's. The king and the Archbishop of Canterbury, Thomas Arundel, thus made the kingdom aware of a new statute (3 Henry IV) 'For the Burning of Heretics', designed to end the 'innovations and excesses' of 'a certain new sect' that currently threatened secular and sacred order.[142] The statute and its reasons thus explained, in case words and persuasive arguments were not enough, the assembled ranks and representatives of church and state were invited to Smithfield, to witness a demonstration of how the statute worked. How were the 'tares' that threatened established order to be removed? The answer was by fire. The first martyr of the 'new sect', William Sautre, was placed in a barrel and burnt at the stake.[143]

It was a carefully orchestrated gathering, calculated, as the statute put it, to 'inspire fear in the minds of others and prevent such nefarious doctrines and heretical and erroneous opinions . . . from being supported or in any way tolerated'. The lesson may have been learned, for there were no more burnings until the similarly theatrical execution, in 1410, of John Badby.[144] We can be sure that the message carried back to the provinces, towns and villages by the religious and secular leaders of the communities was that the statute meant what it said. Its larger aim was to halt the extraordinary populist vernacular movement that had swept up all sections of English society except the Church and universities in less than a hundred years. The English inquisition against heresy was born in the troubled reign of Henry IV. By naming the Lollards, reactionaries sought to isolate the movement's most determined spokespeople from a

---

[142] Carl Stephenson and Frederick George Marcham (ed. and trans.), *Sources of English Constitutional History: a Selection of Documents from A.D. 600 to the Present* (New York, Evanston, London 1937), 274 and n. 2.

[143] Paul Strohm, *England's Empty Throne*, 40–5, discusses the timing and the king's motivation: 'In burning Sautre by royal writ, [the king] moved ahead of his own carefully forged consensus, laying deliberate claim to the burning as a distinctive component of his personal political program.' (45)

[144] Peter McNiven, *Heresy and Politics in the Reign of Henry IV, the burning of John Badby* (Woodbridge, Suffolk 1987), 199–218.

presumably more politic majority. As the academic debate that intensified following the events of 1401 would show, and Archbishop Arundel's constitutions would roundly affirm, the aim of the reactionaries was to halt the populist tide.

After 1401 efforts were made to define what the reactionaries wanted to suppress.[145] 'For the Burning of Heretics' dictated that 'no one either openly or secretly shall preach, hold, teach, or impart anything, or compose or write any book, contrary to the catholic faith . . . or anywhere hold conventicles . . . or [anyone who] in any fashion teaches, instructs, or excites the people'. Vernacular religion was not yet proscribed *tout court*, but was banned from all the main forms of vernacular religion: preaching, proclaiming, teaching, imparting, composing and writing books, and holding discussion groups or 'conventicles'. The implications of 'For the Burning of Heretics' were then refined by academic scholars and theologians. The anti-vernacular precepts embodied in Arundel's constitutions were refined by conservative contributors to what has come to be called the 'Oxford Translation Debate'.

The reactionaries argued that English was not suited to higher learning and religious discourse. Suitable it may be for the writing of songs and stories for popular consumption, but never for higher thought and study. As a medium of translation of sacred scripture it was only capable of conveying simple messages; the deeper meanings are bound to be lost in translation. Understanding religion was a deep and complex matter. It required rigorous training, years of selfless dedication to problems of meaning and translation, and continuous caution in the difficult matter of applying the fruits of theology to the common good. The danger of making sacred texts available to uneducated readers (*illiterati*) was that misreading was inevitable. Consider the fact that certain passages of the Bible seemed to suggest that at certain moments in history, God favoured popular rebellion against states. When ignorant people heard these passages a few were bound to prick up their ears. Had they not been taught by the Church that rebellion was a cardinal sin? Their ignorance lay in not knowing all the other passages of the Bible that qualify and contradict the pro-rebellion passages. Similarly, the Bible also gave examples of kings-become-tyrants who got their comeuppance at the hands of their subjects. Scholars of the Latin Bible could show that these were merely

---

[145] Anne Hudson writes that 'in Oxford in 1401 it was still possible for men to urge the desirability of vernacular translations of the bible without being suspected as heretics', quoted from Alastair Minnis, 'Absent Glosses: a Crisis of Vernacular Commentary in Late Medieval England?', *Essays in Medieval Studies* 20 (2003), 5; Hudson, 'The Debate on Bible Translation, Oxford 1401', 3: 'the legitimacy of biblical translation [was not yet] a closed argument'.

exceptions that proved the rule that subjects must be passive with regard to established authority. It was the Church's function to communicate the deeper meaning of religion to the common people: in two words, unquestioning obedience.

Rebellion was an especially hot topic in the decades following 1381. Whatever John of Salisbury may have said (in Latin, thanks be to God) communities must never seek to overthrow an anointed king, however great a tyrant he is. The reactionary or anti-populist view was that vernacular theology is a contradiction in terms. 'Christians of a lower order' were unfitted to engage in discourse about points of religion. Because they lacked Latin (and therefore education and learning), 'the passive illumination given to Christians of a lower order should depend utterly on the wills of Christians of higher orders' (*Illuminatio passive viantium de ordine inferiori dependere debet complete a volitiva viantium in ordine superiori*). Aristotle and Genesis agreed that 'since the clouding of the human intellect at the fall, only the elite have had access to clear thinking'. It was axiomatic that 'the more people there are, the smaller and feebler are their minds'. To protect them from their ignorance, it was vital to prevent direct access by the 'populus vulgaris' to Scripture and to protect them from unscrupulous users of works like *Piers Plowman* – a misguided effort in itself, with so many passages (if not explained carefully and put in context) suggesting that *anyone* could understand Christian truth.

God and the pagan philosophers agreed that the multitude was many-headed and therefore incoherent. 'Only the elite have access to clear thinking', wrote one anti-vernacularist. Vernacular theology violated Matthew 7:6 ('do not throw bread to dogs or pearls before swine'). Popular education should be catechism, not dialogue. The commonalty should be taught to think only on 'things to avoid, that is, the seven deadly sins; things to fear, that is, the pains of hell; things to believe, found in the creed; things to do, the ten commandments; things to hope for, everlasting reward'. The conservative participants in the translation debate revealed 'the emotional foundations of the Constitutions' harshly repressive regulation of vernacular theology'.[146]

Arundel's constitutions were the crowning achievement of a reactionary movement of churchmen, university academics and assorted linguistic traditionalists, heirs of church institutions and traditions that long preceded the generation of William Langland and John Wyclif. Led by

---

[146] Quotations from Watson, 'Censorship and Cultural Change', 838, 841 and n. 51, 842, 843.

such men, the Church resisted the populist movement on all fronts.[147]
Religious foundations were reactionary in other ways: they generally held
out longest against the abolition of serfdom. Where other classes and
institutions vacillated or simply accepted, conservative elements in the
Church *reacted*. Monastic estates *held out* against another aspect of a great
populist movement that threatened established order, and were deeply
resented for it: serfdom.[148] Bondage was a mark of shame. The shame
intensified as the number of unfree people shrank. Too many monasteries, especially in the English heartlands – roughly East Anglia, Wessex
from Dover to Exeter, and the southern parts of Mercia – were essentially corrupt. Too many religious institutions were manifestly concerned
above all with their worldly estate. The new Reformation historians simply ignore the hundreds of English communities and districts with histories of resistance that went back to the Norman Conquest and sometimes
long before it. Some monastic houses did live up to their duties of *caritas*
and *communitas* from time to time. As a rule those that did were furthest
from London and Westminster. The common expectation of churchmen
was that they should love God and the community more than they loved
themselves; they should live the spirit of their religious vocation.

The vernacular movement was the sign of signs of a subversive 'commoning' of English literary, political and constitutional culture. A new
populist vision emerged and found expression with remarkable speed
in the last third of the fourteenth century. *Piers Plowman* was the great
work of a populist theology that, in practice and probably in intention,
encroached upon ground that the more conservative acolytes of the imperial Church were bound to resent.

The Church as commonly conceived was unnecessary. Some barons,
knights and gentlemen thought they could live with a little harmless vernacular populism; many of them genuinely felt more affinity for the commonalties of their estates and countries than they did with the court and

---

[147] Alastair Minnis, 'Absent Glosses', 7, writes, for example, that 'late medieval vernacular
culture was, particularly after Arundel, in no position to nurture a Middle English
commentary tradition' comparable to those that had already existed for some time in
Italy and France.

[148] 'In the traditional societies of the kind that peopled medieval England, a special importance and significance attaches to the truly great landowner. He epitomizes the values
of those societies – their acceptance of extremes of wealth and poverty, their capacity
for waste, their cult of hierarchy . . . he can do much more than other human agencies
to ensure the continuance of the *status quo*.' More specifically, in the second half of
the fourteenth century, 'though land was abundant [the monks of Westminster Abbey]
refused to allow it to be cheap, thus denying to their tenants for several decades the full
benefits, and, in some cases, any of the benefits, of the new balance between land and
people'. Barbara Harvey, *Westminster Abbey and its Estates in the Middle Ages*, (Oxford
1977), 2, 7.

crown, lordly abbots and archbishops. They were not averse to clerks who glorified their paternal populism. The Church was in danger of becoming isolated and irrelevant. English chronicles, poems, stories, proverbs and sayings were all the rage amongst the *literati* and their audiences, at the expense of Latin. The victory of English in every realm of life seemed inevitable, taken for granted. Did it matter? Enlightened magnates like Trevisa's patron, Thomas IV, lord Berkeley, were comfortable with a certain amount of paternalistic populism and social mobility. As the baronial movement against Richard II gathered force, the rule that tyrants could be deposed only if the whole *commune* was agreed gave additional force to the rise of English as a language of politics. Just when it seemed that English was poised to sweep Latinate religion aside, the reactionaries struck. The opportunity came when the Lancastrian usurper, Henry IV, lost faith with his erstwhile ally, the commonalty, whose support had been essential to his 'revolution', and in whose language he had declared his coronation oath.

Against the tide, the reactionaries refused to abandon a prejudice that is common in all hierarchical corporations. In the first decade of the fifteenth century they responded to what they considered to be a threat to everything they stood for. If English became the language of religion, what would become of higher learning? English, they argued, was the language of inferiors and subjects, not suited to finer thought and expression about truth, religion and government. In their view, 1381 and the decades of class and constitutional struggle that ensued from the Commons Rebellion were the results of teaching, preaching and telling stories in English. Hearing tell of sacred precepts of religion and government in their own language, the common people of England got ideas above their station. Although gentlemen and nobles initially flirted with it (as Simon de Montfort had flirted with the *mediocris populi* a century earlier), Lollardy was essentially a heresy of the commonalty. It is likely that most of the ideas later associated with Lollardy circulated in England for decades before Langland and Wyclif, in their different contexts, brought together ideas and perspectives that had been developing for over a century. Stories and images from *Piers Plowman* were more potent exemplars of vernacular religion than anything written by Wyclif.

One way or another it boiled down to language. The view of the reactionaries was that as long as dangerous ideas were restricted to Latin they were tolerable.[149] Like young people then and now, university

---

[149] 'It is a dangerous thing to translate the text of the Holy Scripture out of one tongue into another; for in the translation the same sense is not easily kept': the relevant article of Arundel's constitutions puts the pretext in academic terms: McNiven, *Heresy and Politics*, 116.

students were especially susceptible to dangerous ideas that more mature minds saw the folly of. Universities were trusted institutions of state, arms of government. They often tolerated, even encouraged, an open and critical approach to ideas. This admirable tolerance of voraciously curious and occasionally rebellious adolescents has been a tendency of higher education since Plato's academy.[150] In corporations the less tolerant usually outnumbered their permissive colleagues. Hierarchy usually wins over lateral thinking when careers are at stake. As long as the authorities appointed wise men to govern them, universities could be counted on to marginalize dangerous ideas in a variety of ways. Usually they could be counted on to exclude or marginalize stubborn mavericks and rebels. They had careers to think about. The basic premise of the reactionaries was that ideas were only dangerous when they were expressed in English, in the presence of uneducated common people. Teachers and undergraduates were allowed, perhaps encouraged to learn and play with dangerous ideas in Latin. Ideas in themselves were not dangerous, except when ignorant people got hold of them and translated them into their own language and experience. Opening the holy books to a *lewd* popular audience was the heresy of heresies in the eyes of the reactionary party whose victory came in the first decade of the fifteenth century.[151]

Beyond capital punishment of the more extreme 'Lollards' who refused to recant, the reactionaries aimed to install and police rigid limits to 'the laity's too eager pursuit of knowledge' in general. The policing of vernacular religion never targeted the whole of the 'laity', only the commonalty. 'The Constitutions would not be used to target aristocratic book owners', writes Nicholas Watson. 'There was plenty of vernacular theological writing available in the fifteenth century for professional religious and

---

[150] K.B. McFarlane, *The Origins of Religious Dissent in England* (New York 1966), pp. 25, 27–9, described the transcendent continuities of the higher education system of fourteenth, fifteenth and sixteenth-century England as follows: pupils were encouraged to engage in disputations, which consisted of 'declamations' in which the master raised 'a controversial question' and invited one pupil to speak for, and another against it. The rules were 'learn Latin, learn the rules of disputation, dispute . . . Considered as an education for public life rather than as a scholar's apprenticeship', wrote McFarlane, 'this curriculum had much to be said for it.' In the larger context of vernacularization, neither the Reformation nor Renaissance Humanism changed the basic system. McFarlane also noted that 'minds thus sharpened could not but be enquiring. The more one reads about medieval universities the less one can believe in that sedulous regard for authority which is often denounced as their gravest defect. On the contrary, it is only too clear that the anxious interference of papal and Episcopal superiors, intermittent as it was bound to be, was quite ineffective as a check upon the speculative license permitted in the schools'.

[151] McNiven, *Heresy and Politics*, 114–17, argues that Arundel's constitutions aimed to reform heterodox Oxford first, then the Church more generally; he had to do this in order to strengthen them as instruments of suppression of vernacular-populist 'heresy'.

laypeople of rank.' In short, the 'constitutions' were naked class legislation. They were 'repeatedly used to identify lower-class owners and
readers of non-Lollard works as heretics'. In practice not only 'Lollards'
but all the ranks and members of the commonalty were barred from using
their language in ways that had long since become second nature. The
constitutions were used to make common people afraid to speak or even
listen to religious talk in English. 'It remained dangerous throughout the
(fifteenth) century for those beneath the ranks of the gentry and the urban
elite to be known as readers of texts as diverse as *The Canterbury Tales,
The Prick of Conscience, Dives and Pauper,* and *The Mirror of Sinners.*'[152]
It was forbidden for groups of common people to gather together to pray
and talk about religion in English. For that, they could be burned at the
stake. In fact only obdurate and explicit heretics were burned, but the
burnings were symbolic of an unprecedented and long-lasting repressive
machinery of fear.

The reactionaries were anti-populist and anti-women. Hoccleve
summed up their fear of women: 'Some women eeke, thogh hir wit be
thynne,/ Wole arguments make in holy writ!', he wrote, the exclamation
mark indicating the horror he knew his hoped-for audience instinctively
felt towards women with opinions like Julian of Norwich. The 'horizontal mode of address' that Watson perceives in much of the vernacular
theology written in the two decades before the constitutions, was in
fact characteristic of the whole vernacular movement. It 'seems precisely
designed to displace existing notions of religious (and, in some cases,
secular) hierarchy by implying that common humanity and desire for
truth make writer and reader fully equal, whatever their worldly status
may be'. Julian's *Vision* 'provides the most striking confirmation of the
worst fears' of the reactionaries. She was a 'simple creature that cowed
no letter'. The persona she projected was representative of all Christians
and, as her editor observes, she effectively 'dissolv[ed] the hierarchic
distinction between cleric and non-cleric' on which the Oxford debate
was based. The only distinction that mattered, spiritually, was 'between
God and humankind in general'. Julian and her contemporaries, writes
Watson, 'must have been aware on some level of working in controversial
cultural space'. We shall see in Part III that 'controversial cultural space'
is too tame to describe the condition of England from the Commons
Rebellion of 1381 to the constitutional crisis of 1450. 'Class-struggle' is
simplistic, but conveys the constant threat of anger and violence in all
social relations at this time.[153]

---

[152] Quotations from Watson, 'Censorship and Cultural Change', 828, 857, 835, 831.
[153] *Ibid.*, 848, 849, 850, 851, 852.

Watson concludes his study with a quotation from the *Sermon of Dead Men*, a fifteenth-century text 'which directs attention . . . at the less privileged parts of late-medieval English society: the society that, in Eamon Duffy's . . . *The Stripping of the Altars*, seems so idyllically preoccupied with the round of "traditional" devotion, so unconcerned with hard religious questions or the desire for theological knowledge'. 'The passage can stand as a reminder of the extent to which Duffy's "traditional religion" . . . was itself the creation of a movement that was equally imposed on English society from above, equally held in place by decades of religious repression.'[154] 'Traditional religion' in this sense was what common people were supposed to believe and do, according to Arundel's constitutions.

3.10   Obedience and authority: the great chain of meaning

The march of the vernacular was restricted for over a century by boundaries of repression policed by a reactionary Church. The issue, as we have seen, was authority and obedience. It was the task of selected, educated, church- and state-licensed men to impose meanings. Their first instinct was to nullify the problem by restricting discourse to Latin. By the second and third decades of the sixteenth century it had become obvious that the march of English could not be halted. This being the case, it was the corporate duty of the state to police translation of sacred discourses by providing authorized English meanings for Latin (and, increasingly, Greek and Hebrew) words. Sir Thomas Elyot's *Dictionary* of 1538, licensed by Chancellor Thomas Cromwell, was 'the first Latin-English lexicon'.[155] But it was in an equally influential earlier work, *The Book of the Governor*, that Elyot defined his 'great chain of meaning'.

Elyot set out to prove 'of what estimation ordre is, nat onely amonge men, but also with god' by scholarship and experience ('those thynges that be within the compasse of mannes knowledge'). Order, in his estimation, was a hierarchy composed of as many 'degrees' as there are individual human beings. In this sense, Elyot rearranged the horizontal distribution of unique vocations into a cosmic hierarchy. God arranged Creation 'in divers degrees, called hierarches'. Mankind, for example, is constituted by four elements: fire, 'the most pure element'; air, 'whiche next to the fyre is most pure'; water, which 'approcheth to corruption'; and 'the erthe whiche is of substance grosse and ponderous . . . set of all

---

[154] *Ibid.*, 859.
[155] Stephen Merriam Foley, 'Coming to Terms: Thomas Elyot's Definitions and the Particularities of Human Letters', *English Literary History* 61:2 (Summer 1994), 211.

elementes most lowest'. Likewise, the creatures of the earth constitute a hierarchy 'begynnyng at the moste inferiour or base, and assendyinge upward'. God made 'trees of a more eminent stature than herbes':

So that every kynde of trees, herbes, birdes, beastis, and fisshes, besyde theyr diversitie of fourmes, have a peculier disposition appropered to them by god theyr creatour: so that in everything is ordre: and without ordre may be nothing stable or permanent: And it may nat be called ordre, excepte it do contayne in it degrees, high and base, accordynge to the merite or estimation of the thynge that is ordred.

Order is an ascending chain of being in which position is allocated according to 'gyfts of grace, or of nature'. The key variable is what we call 'intelligence'. God did not distribute gifts of grace or nature equally, 'but to some more, some less'. In keeping with the universal theory of vocations, if everyone stuck to the vocation endowed upon them by God all would be well. Elyot knew an alternative theory and rejected it out of hand. Material and spiritual gifts 'ne be they nat in commune', Elyot growled, 'as fantasticall foles wolde have all thyngs'.[156] The definitive 'gift' that distinguished mankind was 'Understandyng', which, for him, meant formally licenced men of learning, who 'approche most nyghe unto the similitude of god' and were therefore of the highest degree. 'Understanding', wrote Elyot, is 'the principall parte of the soule'. It therefore follows 'that as one excelleth an other, in that influence, as therby being nexte to the similitude of his maker, so shulde the astate of his persone be *advanced* in degree, or place, where understandynge may profit: whiche is also distributed in to sondry uses, faculties, and offices necessary for the lyvyng and governance of mankynde'.[157] Who, or what, was to 'advance' such men? It was the role of church and state to ensure that the great chain of meaning was imposed on secular society.

The whole universe was hierarchical. Just as fire, the most pure element, 'clarifieth the other inferiour elementes', and is therefore assigned the highest place, so those who exceed others in their understanding 'imploye it to the detaynyng of other within the boundes of reason, and shewe them howe to provyde for theyr necessarye lyvynge'. Educated men were set above others. 'By the beames of theyr excellent witte,

---

[156] This passage echoes Walter Hilton's condemnation of doctrines of universal salvation in *Scale of Perfection* (c.1390), which Nicholas Watson, 'Visions of Inclusion', 247, describes as 'a quasi-official statement of what [the Church] deemed appropriate for laypeople to believe': 'If thou trow that the passioun of oure Lord is so precious and his mercy is so mikel that ther schal no soule be dampned – and namly no cristen man, do he never so hille – as summe foles wenen, sothly thou erres gretly'.

[157] Elyot, *The boke, named the Governour, devised by Thomas Elyot Knight* (London 1531), A3v–A4r.

shewed throughe the glasse of auctoritie,' Elyot wrote, 'other of inferiour understandynge, may be *directed* to the way of virtue and commodious livynge'. Such men 'by verie equite' should be honoured and assigned degree, and should 'by other mennes labours . . . be mainteined, according to theyr merites'. It was for the public good that 'saide persones excelling in knowledge, wherby other be governed, be ministers for the only profite and commoditie of them, whiche have not equall understanding'. Persons and classes 'whiche do exercise artificiall science, or corporall labour', that is to say, artisans, peasants and labourers, ordered and allocated vocations by their learned betters, 'do not travayle for theyr superiours onely, but also for theyr owne necessitie'. Husbandmen fed themselves 'and the clothe maker', for example. 'The clothe maker apparayleth hym selfe and the husbande: they both socour other artificers: other artificers them: they and other artificers [work for] them that be governours.'[158] The commonalty was to provide sustenance to learned men so that they could, in return, be taught the true meaning of everything that happened, and what words to use when they spoke of them.

Elyot clearly felt it was necessary to counter the populist suspicion that learned men gained place and profit for themselves 'by the sayde influence of knowledge'. Such men were by definition virtuous. They were unconcerned 'for theyr owne necessities, but do imploye all the powers of theyr wittes and theyr diligence, to the only preservation of other theyr inferiours'. And because they were so self-denying as to have devoted themselves to learning, they 'shulde be esteemed' and receive 'an augmentation of honour and substance'. Honour and substance were not pursued for personal glory, but only because they 'impresseth a reverence wherof procedeth due obedience amonge subiectes'. The problem was that simple minded or corrupt 'inferiours' failed to see that learning was an end in itself. They saw only the material rewards that 'inflameth men naturally inclined to idelnes, or sensuall appetite, to coveyt lyke fortune: and for that cause, to dispose them to studie or occupation'.[159]

Elyot clearly does not have in mind anything as simple-minded as the three part hierarchy of estates that George Duby saw as the essence of French feudalism. His hierarchy is a great chain of meaning with many more 'steps' or 'ranks' than that. It was subversive of feudalism in its elevation of 'understanding' and 'studie' over the military traditions of knighthood. His book of counsel is indeed a mark of respect, humble advice on how kings and nobles should educate their children. The necessary condition for its publication was that his king, Henry VIII, in

---

[158] *Ibid.*, A4v–A5r.   [159] *Ibid.*, A5r.

practice a self-centred tyrant, was intellectually vain. He liked to think of himself as a learned man and was naturally encouraged to do so by his closest counsellors, including Elyot. In education as in the rest of the universe, there is a centre. Henry could assume that he was the centre of the universe. What remains is the proposition that the scholar's vocation is the highest. Just as a learned king is far above an ordinary counsellor like Elyot, so is even an ordinary scholar high above the multitude of unlearned folk. 'Degree' must also be strictly maintained within the commonalty, among whom it 'also behoveth to be a disposition and ordre accordynge to reason: that is to saye, that the slouthfull or idell persone, do nat participate with hym that is industrious, and taketh payne: whereby the frutes of his labours shulde be diminisshed'. Even among the commonalty such mixing of degrees of people should be discouraged at all costs, for from it 'shulde procede discourage (i.e. demoralization), and finally disolution for lacke of provision'.[160]

Elyot's great chain of meaning formulated the precept of Arundel's constitutions: meaning is to be determined by licensed scholars and imposed by authority. The rightness of a proposition is determined by the rank and degree of the proposer. How a Latin word like 'Republic', or Greek words like 'Ecclesia' or 'Presbyteros', should be expressed in English, or what the eucharist signified, was to be discussed in Latin by discreet university men, decided by scholars, submitted to bishops, archbishops and counsellors of the king, and only then proclaimed as the official meaning. Once that procedure had been carried out, official meaning was then passed down the line to the *lewd* multitude.

3.11   Two ideas of politics in the disputation between William Tyndale and Sir Thomas More

Quentin Skinner writes that to understand the meanings of words we must 'recognise the implications of the fact that a term . . . gains its meaning from the place it occupies within an entire conceptual scheme'. Dispute can and does arise 'about whether a given set of circumstances can be claimed to yield the criteria in virtue of which the term is normally applied'. Such differences are not merely linguistic, but 'will certainly be . . . substantive social one[s] . . . For what is being contended in effect is that a refusal to apply the term in a certain situation may constitute an act of social insensitivity or a failure of social awareness'. Skinner illustrates his point by suggesting that there have always been two distinct ideas of 'politics'. The conventions of everyday usage tend to limit

---

[160] *Ibid.*, A5r.

'politics' to the institutions of the state. Other theorists (especially Marxists) argue that politics go on in every human context, wherever power operates. The conventional and the 'Marxist' views thus involve two very different conceptions of politics. The narrow view concentrates on the inner circles of the state; the broad view sees power (and thus 'politics') operating in all human contexts, including families, households and the institutions and communities of everyday life. These divergent meanings of politics present us, Skinner observes, with a case of 'rival social theories and their attendant methods of classifying social reality'. Which is 'correct'? When we have understood more than one 'rival social theory' how do we decide which one is right, or appropriate? The historians' answer is that it is not necessary to address the question of correctness. All we have to do is to describe the ideas of an age in their (not our) contexts. If there are contending theories, this too should be noted.[161]

In wide conceptions, 'politics' means little more than 'power relations'. Politics describe intrigues and manoeuvrings for place and goods in all areas of life, including the family, the work-place, the streets and all forms of social interaction. Power is always present, in this conception, and so, therefore, are 'politics'. Politics is the study and practice of power. Popular usages of 'politics' today, however, tend to focus on formal institutions of government and their personnel. These kinds of 'politics' happen in places like Westminster, Canberra or Washington, the archetypal places of 'politics' for most people in Britain, Australia and the United States. 'Politics' is a special sector or theatre conducted by 'politicians'. Thus Professor Skinner's restriction of the term is grounded not only in classical philology but also in contemporary popular opinion. For most people, then and now, 'government', and therefore 'politics', is 'them'. 'We the people' are not part of 'their' world. 'They' run the place, form policy, and are supposed to take the flak when it all goes wrong. Skinner suggests that this being the conventional view, if we have an alternative to the narrow conception of politics, it is our responsibility to explain what it is and, if we can, persuade learned authority and public opinion that it is better than the old one.

Debate about the two meanings of 'politics', narrow and wide, has a history. In the late 1520s it formed the context of one of the most momentous 'disputations' in English history: the 'dialogue' between William Tyndale and Thomas More. Arguably, this was the seminal debate of the English Reformation: two great minds locked in lucid dispute over two clashing world views. The opening act was the publication, in 1526, of

---

[161] Quentin Skinner, 'Language and Social Change', in James Tully, *Meaning and Context: Quentin Skinner and His Critics* (Oxford 1988), 123–5.

Tyndale's New Testament in English. This threw down the gauntlet to what would subsequently turn out to be the tail-end of a repressive and intolerant regime that had been struggling to ban and suppress the march of the vernacular since Arundel's landmark 'constitutions'.

By the time copies of Tyndale's New Testament began to show up in England, More had already established himself as the scourge of Lutherans. In his polemics against Tyndale, More called him 'Luther's dog'.[162] The idea that Tyndale – and the English Reformation generally – got his ideas from abroad (German Luther, French Calvin, Swiss Zwingli) has been a tenacious precept of conservative historical studies ever since. Tyndale registered More's put-down and answered it. He was inspired by Luther's populist style of translation and centre of social gravity (and shared them) but it is unlikely that many contemporaries of Tyndale and More would have believed the implication that Tyndale's roots were German. Tyndale's 'reformation' was grounded in traditional English movements and precepts. It was convenient to impute passivity to the English commonalty, but as we shall see in Chapters 4 and 5, it went against history to do so. Several centuries of vernacular Christianity came together and found expression through Tyndale's pen. Arundel's articles of repression had been formulated 120 years earlier to root out men and women who not only translated but colloquialized Christian scripture and populist theology. Had it not been for the reactionaries of Arundel's generation there might well have been an English bible, or parts of English bibles, in most English homes by the end of the fifteenth century. Tyndale marks the realization of a long movement to have religion expressed, taught and discussed in the people's tongue.

More refused to believe that heresy was vernacular at all. Heresy was foreign, unnatural to the stolid English peasant, for whom obedience and deference came naturally. Just as reactionary intellectuals of Wyclif's generation blamed the Low Countries for originating 'mumbling', More called Tyndale German Luther's 'dog'.

---

[162] *A Dyaloge of Syr Thomas More knyghte: one of the counsayll of our soveraoyne lorde the kyng and chanselloure of hys duchy of Lancaster. Wheryn be treatyd dyvers maters/ as of the veneracyon & worshyp of ymagys & relyques/ prayng to sayntis/ & goyng on pylgrymage. Wyth many other thyngys touchyng the pestylent secte of Luther & Tyndale/ by the tone bygone in Saxony/ & by the tother laborys to be brought in to England Newly oversene by the sayd Thomas More chauncellour of England, 1530*, 'The Thyrde Boke', ch. 8, began by declaring 'that at the tyme of this translacyon Hychens was with Luther in Wyttenberg'. Tyndale, *An Answer Unto Sir Thomas More's Dialoge mad by William Tyndale*, xcii: 'And when he sayth Tyndale was confederate with Luther [in Book III, Part viii] that is not trueth.' For the context of the 'dialogue' in relation to More's career, see David Daniel, *William Tyndale: a Biography* (Yale 1994), ch. 10; Richard Marius, *Thomas More* (London 1999), ch. 21 and *passim*.

The drama was played out, in print, to an audience potentially including the whole commonweal. The two men's words and ideas would be read in London, explained or overheard, and transmitted to most districts of England, in book form or gossip, by long-distance carters, clothiers and travelling trades- and journeymen in workshops, churches and ale-houses all over the kingdom.

Much of this is impossible to trace. We don't know how many people actually read what More and Tyndale wrote and committed to print, or heard it recited, paraphrased and simplified. Tyndale's works were banned and burned, but heretical sayings and writings litter the archives of the fifteenth century, as Anne Hudson shows in *The Premature Reformation*. Clandestine 'Lollard' networks followed the trails of intensifying *trafike* through a kingdom that was always integrated by routine commerce. This fluctuating process of intensification had been going on for centuries, and its structures were not much affected by the Black Death and the population downturn of the fourteenth and fifteenth centuries. Good stories and arguments spread. When More took up his pen, public opinion was that corrupt and obscurantist church authorities had banned and burned Tyndale's works because he told the truth, and wanted to make the truth accessible to all men everywhere.[163] For this reason the Church was afraid of him. How many of the messages would present the arguments impartially? How many recipients in village and provincial England would have understood the issues? What stood out, of course, was that Tyndale wanted religion to be in English, the

---

[163] Thomas More's pretext for writing *A Dyalogue* was that he had received a letter from a well-meaning man who sought advice about rumours 'spoken/ but also thyder wrytten by dyvers honest preestes out of london' that a certain man 'was . . . borne wrong in hande/ and . . . so sore handeled/ that he was forced to forswere and abiure certayn heresyes/ and openlye put to penaunce therfore/ where he never helde any suche. And all this was done for malyce and envye/ partely of some freres (agaynst whose abusyons he preched) partely for that he preched boldely agaynst the pompe & pryde and other inordynate lyvynge (that mo men speke of than preche of) used in the clargye. And they take for a great token/ that he sholde not meane evyll/ the profe and experyence which men have had of hym/ that he spyed well/ and was a good honest vertuous man/ far from ambycyon and deyre of worldely worshypp/ chast/ humble/ and charytable/ free and liberall in almouse dede/ and a very goodlye prechoure/ in whose devoute sermons the peoplee were greatly edyfyed. And therefore the people saye that all this gere is done but onely to stoppe menes mouthes/ and to put every man in sylence that wolde any thynge speke of the fautes of the clargye. And they thynke that for none other cause was also burned at Saynte Poules crosse the newe testament late translated in englysshe by mayster Wyllyam Huchyn/ otherwyse called mayster Tyndall/ who was (as men saye) well knowen or he wente over the see/ in dyvers places in England was very well lyked & dyd gret good with prechyng. And men mutter amonge them selfe that the boke was not onely fautles/ but also very well translated . . . ': 'The furst chapyter: 'The declaracyon of the credence by the mouth of the messenger wheruppon the matter of all the hole worke dependeth,' v.

language of the people. This naturally brought him to the attention of a reactionary church and state. More stood for a deeply anti-populist tradition and a repressive state, and had authority on his side. Tyndale and More differed on every subject of contemporary controversy except the king's divorce. (Both were against it.[164]) The debate between Tyndale and More involved rival conceptions of state, people and commonwealth, one broad and encompassing, and the other narrow, institutional: essentially the parallel contexts to which Professor Skinner draws our attention.

In 1526 copies of Tyndale's translation of the New Testament were circulating in various parts of England. As David Daniel points out, this was when More, the great English scourge of Lutheranism, Lord Chancellor of England and one of the king's closest counsellors, entered the scene. He entered, as Daniel puts it, as 'a trained and experienced assassin'.[165] This way of describing his relations with Tyndale dramatizes what More would have seen simply as his duty as a properly qualified scholar, counsellor and state official. Tyndale's writings were becoming too well known. More chose to publish his responses in English. We must assume he wanted to reach a wider audience than a Latin denunciation would have obtained. Thus he fought on Tyndale's (and the Lollards') ground.

More's position was that Tyndale had no authority to translate the Bible or to pronounce on ecclesiastical or state policy. As a man who within weeks would become Lord Chancellor of England, as an esteemed lawyer and judge, and as a university professor, More did have such authority. Maintaining what he regarded as established conventions in religion and in secular government was fundamental to his position. His authority included the right and duty to pronounce on the meanings of words, particularly words with social implications. In his polemical writings Tyndale broke with More's conventions in two ways. First, as a writer, he appeared to address the king directly and without deferential ceremony. Second, in his polemics, Tyndale openly addressed all English people. As I have argued elsewhere, Tyndale had a traditional populist or, more precisely, 'middle rank' view of the English constitution, one that was instinctively sceptical about all the ranks, degrees and institutions between free individuals (men and, more equivocally, women) and the king.[166] His ideal England was a *regnum* composed of all its local and regional communities.

---

[164] Wilyam Tyndale, *The Practice of Prelates, Whether the Kinges grace maye be separated from hys quene/ because she was his brothers wyfe.* Marborch MCCCCC & XXX (1530), 'Of the devoircement', Hvi.

[165] Daniel, *Tyndale*, 262.

[166] In Rollison, *Local Origins*, ch. 4.

Men like Tyndale's father and brothers ran these local communities.[167]
They were also, as Fortescue pointed out to the generation before Tyndale and More, the bowmen who struck fear into England's enemies.
They organized their parishes and manors, as coalitions and cabals of
their own yeoman estates. In association with their communities they
conducted tax assessments and collections, mustered troops, kept order,
employed the labouring poor, sat on juries, increasingly sent their sons
to school and university, and played a part in electing members of parliament. In their view, gentlemen, knights, barons, dukes, abbots, bishops,
cardinals and popes were unnecessary, parasitic classes, necessarily committed to obscurantism to cover their essential lack of legitimacy. The
world would continue perfectly well if they disappeared tomorrow.

More regarded these ranks as mediating institutions and considered
the chain of command they were supposed to form as the very essence of
governance. The cybernetics or *communicacyon* implied by this universe
of degree was that information, governance and policy must pass up
and down the chain of command without missing any degree out. Each
degree or link would decide whether the message needed to be passed up
or down to the next link. More's position, like Elyot's, was that when the
monarch or any of his duly appointed counsellors addressed the public
they were not consulting but instructing. No-one had the right to address
or instruct the people without licence. Tyndale's crime (and More was
quite right to say that under Arundel's rules it was a crime) was that
he had not followed proper channels of authority. He was not licensed
to publish, teach or preach. In matters of state, licence was granted by
'kynges', the summit of 'highness', who were to act with 'the consayle and
advyce not of his nobles onely, wyth hys other counsaylours attendynge
uppon his gracys person/ but also of the ryght virtuouse and specyall well
lerned men of eyther unyversyte & other partys of the realme specyally
called thereto'.[168] This meant men like Elyot and More. Government,
'politics' in the narrow sense, was not a matter for all, but only those
who are qualified by birth, by being 'specyall well lerned', or by being
'specyally called thereto'.

More's was a classic top-down epistemology in which matters of government are narrowly circumscribed and restricted to a minority of people who are 'specyall', that is to say, not common or found everywhere.
The way he described himself on the title page – as 'knyght and chancellor of England' – was a sign to readers telling them how to receive what

[167] Rollison, *Local Origins*, ch. 4; Daniel, *Tyndale*, 9–21.
[168] *The Confutation of Tyndale's Answere made by Sir Thomas More knyghte lorde chancellor of Englonde* (London 1532), cxxix.

followed. More was *authorized* by his status as a knight to speak for the people, and by his position as Chancellor to instruct them as to correct and incorrect meanings. He was not in the business of 'persuasion'; what he wrote was not polemic or propaganda. It was instruction from one who knew and was licensed to know. He was a properly authorized counsellor of state. He belonged to the world of policy and was thus duty-bound to pronounce upon it.[169] He belonged to the world Tyndale's theology aimed to dissolve.

In More's view, it was both lawful and necessary to confine politics, to restrict them to the inner circles around the throne: lords and learned men constituted the first circle of authority, gentry and lesser freemen were there to be consulted whenever it was absolutely necessary. His opponent went beyond this 'political' community and spread 'thenfeccion of his contagious heresyes' amongst the people.[170] More assumed that affairs of state were and ought to be protected 'mysteries'. He accused Tyndale of making 'a speciall shewe of hys hygh worldely wytte and that men should have sene therein that there were nothynge done among prynces, but that he was fully advertysed of all ye secretes and that so farre forth, that he knew the pryvy practyse made betwene the kynges hyghnes' and his chief counsellors.[171] Tyndale not only lacked licence, it would never have been granted to a man whose status and distance from the king made understanding of policy impossible. It was a variant of the argument against translating scripture: if affairs of state (and church) were put before the people in their own tongue they were bound to misread and misunderstand the reasons and motives of the king's most important counsellors.

In some ways the essential difference between the two men's conceptions, respectively, of the 'common-wealth' (Tyndale) and 'publike weal' (Elyot and More) centred on their definitions of the Church.[172] For Tyndale *ecclesia* should be translated as *congregaycon*. This was the most internationalist aspect of Tyndale's world view. Ultimately, *ecclesia* meant what it had meant to Julian of Norwich: every Christian person everywhere, without exception. Depending on context it could also mean all the people of a neighbourhood, a town, a city or a common-wealth, but it always meant all the Christian people. The framework was obviously contentious, but it does seem at first sight a plausible way

---

[169] *The confutatyon of Tyndales answere made by Sir Thomas More knyght lorde chancellor of Englonde: The seconde boke whych confuteth the defence of Tyndale's boke, why he translateth the worde chyrche in to this worde congregacyon* (London 1530), cxxxv.

[170] More, *Confutacyon*, cxxxv.

[171] *Ibid.*, xciii.

[172] Elyot's distinction between 'commonweal' and 'publike weal' is explained in ch. 5.1.

of comprehending social phenomena. Tyndale's world was the world as experienced from within: an interconnected landscape of tracks and roads connecting parish churches, market crosses, and provincial capitals with the twin capitals on the Thames, London and Westminster. Eventually, for Tyndale, this constitutional landscape stretched from Gloucestershire to Wittenberg, Antwerp and Vilvorden, where he was publicly strangled and burned in 1536. What is the nature of the world we inhabit? For Tyndale the answer was, see for yourself, work it out on the experience of the senses God gave you. For More, it was the function of language, of words, to *instruct* people in how to 'read' the world they lived in. It was the job of government-licensed learned men, in consultation with their lords, the king, and the pope, to determine what words meant. More's vocation, as lawyer, judge, university scholar and chancellor, was to decide and pronounce upon correct meaning. Hearing and reading, from his perspective, serve the function of shaping perception. For Tyndale, meaning welled up from the people; for Elyot and More it was imposed by authority.

In Tyndale's theology, personal observation takes precedence over words. 'In all ceremonyes and sacramentes [More] searcheth the significations and will not serve the visible things', he wrote. Where More pointed to words, he pointed to what we would call 'social reality', 'the material world', the as it were uninterpreted reality that enters by the senses. For Tyndale, experience is primary. More belongs, for Tyndale, to a class of men who use words to mystify reality by claiming that words are all it is about. 'Ayenst the mist of their sophistries', he urged his readers to rely on examples from the Old Testament and, above all, 'present practice which thou seist before thine eyes'. Tyndale believed that scripture and experience were the keys to what he called 'felyng fayth'.

Tyndale encouraged people to inform and teach themselves as he had taught himself, by means of scripture, chronicles ('autentyke storyes') and experience. Bible, chronicles and histories were to be read, not in the light of authorized tradition, but in the light of 'present practice which thou seist before thine eyes'. First-hand observation of 'present practice' was the bottom line. The 'sophistries' and 'sotylties' of More's rhetoric are to be tested against personal observation. Watch what they do before you judge what they say and write. Tyndale's congregation watched More's inner circles of government from outside. 'It is time to awake and to se everye man with his owne yies', he wrote.[173] More's state

---

[173] *An Answer Unto Sir Thomas More's Dialoge made by William Tyndale*, f. iii; on 'historicall faith' versus 'felyng fayth', xxx.

issued directives, Tyndale's 'common-wealth' watched, received, thought about it and then continued to go about the business of everyday life according to what common sense dictated – if they were not prevented from doing so by the corrupt or incompetent intrusions of the kingdom. If government became too insensitive, absurd, corrupt or incompetent, the outer circles put pressure on the inner to reform themselves before it was too late. If that failed, grass-roots resistance intensified, little risings took place, and something like the miracle of Corpus Christi, the symbol of symbols of suffering humanity, galvanized the little resistances into a multitude marching to Blackheath, London and Westminster to execute evil counsellors and warn that negotiation was over. Tyndale did not favour resistance and rebellion, but he knew it happened and probably would always happen in a congregation that was not governed by the 'felyng fayth' of its members.

This spectre haunted English constitutional life from the fourteenth to seventeenth centuries. More feared that Tyndale's Bible, by encouraging discussions about matters that *lewd* (unlearned) men, women and children could not possibly understand, would release the collective energies that had erupted so often since 1381. He feared that if policy was allowed to escape the inner circles, the fragile world he represented was bound to be misunderstood. Read in the light of his commentaries and polemics, Tyndale's New Testament dissolved boundaries between his common-wealth and More's state. Legitimacy flooded out of traditional institutions into the neighbourhoods and households of Tyndale's dispersed *congregacyon*. More defended a narrow conception of politics that was absolutely and utterly central to his entire philosophy. Birth and learning were the only qualifications for entry. Anyone not included by will of the monarch, heredity or a degree in the highest learning at Oxford, Cambridge and (increasingly) other ratified European institutions of their sort, belonged outside these inner circles. It is in the same category of ideas as the monarchical absolutism that we often find being expressed at royal courts throughout the age of the commonweal; more specifically, More was a child of Arundel's constitutions and the regime of repression that ensued from it.

With regard to the keyword *ecclesia*, More's criticism was that *connynge as Tyndale wold seme*, he had not understood either the usages of the Greeks or, indeed, of his own English contemporaries. 'This worde ecclesia in the Greke tongue', he wrote,

Dyd not signifie every manner company or congregacyon, nor synyifyed not all the cytesayns of any cytye, wyth that respecte that they were cytesayns of that cyty, or that they were gathered for pleyeng or fyghtynge or any such other cause: but

onely these congregacyons that were gathered together to commen upon matters
of judgement or polycye, ... aboute the comen affayres of the towne.[174]

Government, 'politics', referred 'only to those congregations that were
gathered together to commune upon matters of judgement and policy... about the common affairs'. Christendom, a kingdom, a parish or
a manor is not constituted by the people as a whole, all the people; it is
constituted by those who are called upon by higher powers to participate
in the institutions of learning and judgement that tradition had ordained,
to govern them and intercede for them with God. The people had no
right to resist or rebel against those who had been born, trained and
educated in the mysteries of religion, government and policy.

Tyndale was a monarchist, but of a peculiar and perhaps tactical kind.
His vision was grounded in a popular landscape and language. He accepts
that certain types of lordship will continue after the change. His social
vision is orthodox; his social ideal is entirely traditional and he is firmly
against *violent* resistance to tyrants.[175] The world God sends our souls
into has many forms of hierarchy and inequality, which God is also
responsible for. Who, where and what you are born is ordained by God.
No-one should aspire to leave the class, rank or vocation to which they
were born. We are born to a particular family, place and time. Each
individual has a unique 'vocation', a path God wants us to follow through
the vagaries and variations of life. The rules are the same for everyone.
If we pursue our vocation as ably as we can, we acquire memory and
experience to be passed on to the next generations. This memory and
experience, and our reputation with our neighbours, gives us authority
as 'elders'. It also gives us the right to speak as an equal to any other
elder, whatever their rank in the secular hierarchy, for we are also bidden
by God to be honest and plain-speaking. He will be waiting for us on the
other side of the gates of death, and will have a final reckoning.

Very few followed a presumed vocation into practice as Tyndale did;
if liberal social mobility and the career open to talents is a condition
of bourgeois ideology, Tyndale was no bourgeois. He shares with every
political and constitutional thinker of his age the idea that strict 'vocationalism' is the *sine qua non* of a harmonious commonwealth. However,

---

[174] More, *Confutation*, cxxii.

[175] 'Obedience unto father, mother/ master/ husbande/ emperoure/ kinge/ lordes and rulers
requireth God of all nacyons ... Nether maye the inferior person avenge himselfe upon
the superior or violently resiste him for what so ever wronge it may be ... The kinge
must be referred unto the vengeance of God ... It is not lawfull for christen subjects to
resiste his prince though he be an heathen man': Tyndale, *The Obedience of a Christen
man and how Thrifte rulers ought to governe*... (Marlborow Hesse, October 2 1528), BL
C.53.6.1, xxxi–xxxiii.

the moral worth of every vocation lies in the purposes to which it is dedicated. It must not be for oneself but for one's neighbours and for the common weal. This cast of mind has often been described as 'corporate', as against sectional, factional, or individualist, but the word has a false ring in relation to its usages today. The question with regard to Tyndale is not whether he was 'corporatist', but what kind of 'corporation' or 'body politic' he had in mind. How did his corporatism compare with those of John of Salisbury, the rebels of 1381, 1450, 1536 and 1549, the Digby poet, Fortescue, More, his friend Sir Thomas Elyot or Sir Thomas Smith? The point is that, yes, the medieval world view was corporatist. Maybe it is time the word 'communist' was clawed back from the Marxist monopoly. The point is that there were many competing variations on the corporate theme.[176]

Tyndale's 'common-wealth' was a population of patriarchal households dispersed across and interacting within a landscape that, if not corrupted by false religion and granted routine access to a vernacular Bible, would effectively govern itself. His patriarchy was qualified by his observation that in practice many households were quite capably headed by a woman, and his insistence that in the absence of a suitably qualified male, women could administer last rites. In Tyndale, 'common-wealth' emerged from *landschap*, which, as we saw in discussing *Piers Plowman*, referred to people and offices dedicated to each other and to preserving and maintaining their 'commodities' in Fortescue's sense: all was framed, in this conception, by what came to be called 'landscape'.[177] As for the organization of duties, Tyndale, like all his predecessors from

---

[176] F.W. Maitland, 'The Corporation Sole', *Law Quarterly Review* 16 (1900), 335–54, wrote that 'the essence of corporations', according to a legal thinker of the early sixteenth century, was 'the permanent existence of the organized group, the "body" of "members", which remains the same body though its particles change'.

[177] *Answer to More*, xviii, '. . . the building of [steeples] and soch like/ thorow the false faith that we have in them/ is the decaye of all the havens in Englande and of all the cities/townes/hiewayes and shortly of the whole comen wealth'; 'And as for the dedes/that perteyne unto oure neyboures and un to the comen wealth/ we have not regarded at all'; 'Yet Goodwin-sandes ner any other cause alleged was the decaye of Sandwiche haven/soe much as that the people had no lust to mayneteyne the comen wealth/for blynde devocion which they have to popeholy workes.' Tyndale, *The Parable of the Wicked Mammon* (Printed at Marlborowe in the londe of Hesse the viii day of May Anno M.D.xxviii.) BL C.37.a.23: 'As thou seyst [1536 seest] in ye world how the lordes & offycers minister peace in ye commune wealth [1536 wealthe] / punnysh murderers / theyves & evyll doers / & to maynetene there ordre & estate doo the comunes minister to them againe rent tribute / tolle & custome . . . and even so ought ye other officers which are necessarily required in ye comune wealth of Chryst; *Practice of Prelates*, Fiv–vi: 'the cronycles testifye that [Humphrey of Gloucester] was a vertuous man/ a godly and good to the comen welth'; 'For to be good to the comen welthe is to be hurtefull to the spiritualtye/ seynge the one is the others praye as the lambe is the wolves.'

John of Salisbury to Langland, Wimbledon and the Lollards, was a strict 'vocationalist'. 'Let every man of whatsoever craft or occupacion he be of', he wrote, 'whether bruer baker tailer vitailer marchant or husbande-man refer his craft & occupacion unto the commune wealth/ & serve his bretherne as he wold do Christ him selfe.'

Lett him bye and sell truly and not set dice on his bretherne/ and so showeth him merci/ and his occupacion pleaseth God. And when thou receaveth money for thi laboure or ware thou receaveth thi dutie. For wherin so ever thou minister to thi bretherne/ thi brether are dettours to give that where with the[e] maintene thi selfe and thi houshold. And let you[r] superfluites succoure the pore/ of which sort shall ever be some in all townes cityes and villages, and that I suppose the greateste nowmbre. Remember that we ar membres of one bodie and ought to minister one to an other mercifully. And remember that whatsoever we have/ it is gyve us of God to bestowe it on our bretherne.[178]

For Tyndale 'mammon' was virtually synonymous with 'comen wealth': it meant all the people *except* 'the spiritualte': 'For to be good to the comen welthe', he wrote, 'is to be hurteful to the spiritualte', which was dedicated to 'popeholy workes'.[179]

Against More, the 'spiritualte' that he served and the secular state that, in Tyndale's understanding of history, had been repeatedly fooled into supporting it, Tyndale posited a third entity, the 'comen wealth' that had to be saved from the corruptions of church and secular state alike. The court-centred state, though not strictly necessary, had useful functions to perform and could be saved, he thought, but More's church (*wicked* mammon) could not. Tyndale's 'third entity' was what later generations would think of as the nation, but Tyndale imagined it in relation to what was plainly visible to the senses: a working population, villages and towns, churches and steeples, a coastline with 'havens', London and St Pauls, Westminster, the king's palace and the parliament, households and settlements in a landscape that could actually be observed from vantage-points like his native Cotswold Edge. This 'comen wealth', not the state and definitely not the 'popeholy' Church, was God's gift for people (Julian's 'evenchristen') to nurture and work communally. To obscure

---

[178] *Wicked Mammon*, xliv.
[179] 'Mammon ys an Ebrewe worde and signifyeth riches or temporall goodes and namelye all superfluyte and all that ys above necessyte and *that which is requyred unto oure necessarie uses wherewyth a man maye helpe an other with oute undoinge or hurtiinge him selfe*. For mamon in the Ebrewe speech signifieth a multytude or abundaunce or many . . . Secondaryly/ it is called unrighteous mammon/ not because it ys gotten unrighteously or with usury. For of unrighteous goten goodes can no man doo good workes/ but ought to restore them whom agayne,' *Wicked Mammon*, xix (emphasis added).

the manifest, physical, sensual character of the world of experience, the 'traditional' Church had conjured 'a thinge of . . . ymaginacion . . . a foolish dreme and a false vision' to conceal the truth from 'many hundred thousandes' that 'trust in a bald ceremonye or in a lowlie freris corte and merites or in the praiers of them that devoure widowes howses and eateth the pore oute of house and herboure . . . All these are faythlesse/ for thei folowe ther owne righteousness.'[180] Tyndale invented a word for it: their *storifaith* was 'a feigned faith of their own makinge'.[181]

The decisive perspective is his second nature identity as a member, first and foremost, of the commonwealth, not the state. From this perspective, his view of Sir Thomas More comes into focus. Tyndale represented men like More as the contemporary exemplars of generations and centuries of cynical careerists, 'Judases' who lived in the service of a church that exploited and abused the commonwealth in the name of a corrupt, foreign empire. More represented a class of men recognized by their skilful *jugling* of ideas and rhetoric and their *sotell counsell*. In Tyndale's mind, juggling with ideas is always a sign of fantasy-conjuring double-mindedness intended to blind people to what is before their eyes; to be *sotell* means to deceive. For 800 years, he wrote, the commonwealth of England was in captivity to generations of advisers and experts, counsellors and consultants, grouped around the king, but in reality serving the sworn enemy of the commonwealth.[182] He spelled out the strategy that had maintained their 'evil empire' for so many centuries. What followed was a sketch of corporate politics that has lost none of its edge in the intervening centuries. The servants of Antichrist begin with a carefully hidden agenda, inspired by loyalties and interests that are plainly not those of the commonwealth. Two or three 'wily foxes' work their way into the trust of king and court. They 'conceave in their own braynes' a plan that will serve their own careers and satisfy their secular masters by beguiling and bringing the state and commonwealth into their power. It may take them a year or twenty years of 'castyng canvesynge and computyng'. Here and there, they open the matter privately and little by little to men who look as if they can be trusted ('certayn secretaries'). The task of these trusted men is to be always on the lookout for 'men of activite

---

180 *Wicked Mammon*, lx.   181 *Answer to More*, xliii.
182 'What soever other cause duke Wylliam had agenst Kynge Herold/ thou mayest be sure that the pope wold not have medled yf Herold had not troubled his kyngdome: nether shuld duke Willyam have bene able to conquer the londe att that tyjme excepte the spiritualtie had wrought on his syde. What bloude did that conquest cost Englond/ thorow which all most all the lordes of the english bloud were slayne/ and the Normandes became rulars/ and all the lawes were chaunged into french . . . ' *Practice of Prelates*, fiii and *passim*.

and of corage/ prepared to sel soul and body for promocion'. They want men who will obey any order, conform to any line, as long as they are rewarded with promotion.[183]

They operate secretly. They are double-minded, saying one thing in public and the opposite in private, among themselves. Sometimes, like More, they publish their words out loud and clearly like honest people, but they always have a hidden agenda and hide what they mean in rhetoric and double-minded 'subtlety'. They identify and recruit members to their secret society. Those few innocent hearts who have seen the danger from the start, and watched the enemy's strength grow, gradually at first, but then so rapidly that it is too late to stop them, are finally branded as the heretics, outsiders, 'stand-alones' who, it is said, care more for their own opinions than for those of the righteous majority. As More put it, Tyndale's 'chyrche is a secrete congregacyon of unknowen chosen heretykes, scattered abrode in corners, and studyenge to destroye the chyrche'.[184] Tyndale stood this on its head, and set out to demonstrate that More's class were the conspirators to end all conspirators, against a *congregacyon* that, in Tyndale's powerful conception, was national and international. Tyndale contends that in those rare corners of *commune opinioun* where More's ideas are accepted, the 'righteous majority' has been beguiled and blinded by a thousand *sotell* stratagems, bamboozled by a million *sotyltes*, and had the wool pulled over its collective eyes with regard to what *ecclesia* and *congregacyon* truly mean. Tyndale detests the *sotylte* of these *juglers* who spin and control what is taught in the churches, schools and universities as propaganda for their ungodly lord, Antichrist. In slavish obedience to the masters who can best serve their own ambitions, they control and manipulate ideas, theology, logic, religion, law, pull the strings of the official media. Those, finally, who can be converted to the cause by *sylver sylogismoses*, have been. Those who can't have been beguiled, bullied or bribed in some other way. Those still standing are

---

[183] 'And loke in what captivity the parlements be under the privatt counsels of kynges/ so are ye generall counsells under the pope and his cardinales. And this is the manere of both. Some one two or three wilie foxes that have all other in subiection/ as ye have sene in my lorde cardenale/ imagen/ not what ought to be/ but what they lust to have and conceave in their own braynes and goo with childe/ some tyme a yeare, ii, iii, iiii, v, or vii and some tyme xx and above/ castyng/ canvesynge and computyng for the birth agenst opportunities: opening the mater privately under an oth a little and a little unto certayn secretaries whose parte is therein/ as they finde men of activite and of corage/ prepared to sel soul and body for promocion.' (*Answer to More*, xcix). See also *Practice of Prelates*, Hvi, 'their old cast and sotyltye/ [is] to pretend a contrarye thinge and to cast a mist before the eyes of the people to hyde their iugglinge: 'All that be shaven are sworne to gether. And all that be promoted by them must playe the Judases with them.'

[184] More, *Confutation*, Book 2, f.lxvii.

the heretics.[185] Yes, replies Tyndale, we are scattered now, but there are more of us than you think. Tyndale was perfectly serious in his belief that More and all *his* 'sect' were that simple: careerists who would serve any master for 'promotion'. In the 'popeholy' Church, as Tyndale conceived it, ambitious careerists had always found the perfect master.

In Tyndale's eyes only the 'heretics' now stood in the way of the dominion of Arundel's children.[186] Burn the heretics, say the reactionaries.

---

[185] 'And the matter in the mean tyme is turmoyled and tossed among themselves: and persuasions and sotle reasons ar forged to blinde the right waye and to begyle mens wittes. And whom they feare to have adversaries able to resiste them/ for soch meanes are sought/ to brynge them in unto their partie or to convey them out of the waye. And when opportunite is come/ they call a counsel or parlement under a contrary pretence. And a masse of the holy gost/ whom they desyre awaye as were possible/ is songe and a goodly sermon is made/ to blere mens eyes with all. And then sodenly other men unprovided/ the mater is opened/ after the most sotel manere. And many are begyled with sotle arguments and craftie persuasions. And they that hold hard agenst them ar called asyde and resoned with aparte and handelled after a facion/ an so some are overcome with sylver sylogismoses and other for feare of threatenynges are dreven unto silence/ And if any are found at the last/ that wyll not obeye their falsed and tyranny/ they rayle on him and iest him out of countenance and call him opinatve, selfemynded and obstinate/ and bere him in hand that the devell is in him that he so cleaveth un to his owne witte/ though he speak no sillable then Gods worde/ and is axed whether he wilbe wiser then other men. And in the spiritualte they excommunicate him & make a heretike of him': Tyndale, *Answer to More*, c.

[186] Tyndale's account of Arundel's role is in *Practice of Prelates*, iv–vi: 'in kinge Richardes dayes ye seconde/ Thomas Arundell archbisshope of canterbury & chauncelare was exiled with ye erle of Darbye. The outwarde pretence of ye varyaunce betwene the kinge and his lordes was for the deliveraunce of the towne of Braste in Britayne. But oure prelates had a nother secrete mistereye a bruynge. They coud not at their owne lust slee the poore wretches which at that tyme were converted unto repentaunce & to the true fayth/ to put their trust in christes deeth & bloudshedynge for the remission of theire sines by the preaching of Jhon Wyclefe. As sone as . . . kynge Richard was gone to Yrelond to subdue these rebellyons/ the bishope (Arundel) cam in agayne and prevented the kynge and rose up his power agenst him and toke him presoner and put him doune and to deeth most cruelly/ and crouned the erle of darbye kinge. O mercyfull Christ what bloude hath that coronacyon cost Englonde: but what care they – their causes must be avenged. He is not worthy to be kinge that will not avenge their quarels. For do not the kinges receave their kyngdome of the beest and swere to worshuppe him and mayntene his throne: And then when the erle of Darbye which is kinge Harrye the fourth/ was crouned/ the prelates toke his swerde and his sonnes Harry the fifte after him (as all kynges swerdes sence) and abused them to shede christen bloude at their pleasure. And they coupled their cause unto the kinges cause (as now) & made it treason to beleve in Christ as ye scripture teacheth & to resist the byshoppes (as now) and thrust them in the kynges presons (as now) so that it is no new inuencyon that they now do/ but even an old practyse/ though they have done their busye cure to hyde their science/ that their conucyaunce (sic) shuld not be espied . . . And in kinge harry the vi dayes how raged they as firce lyons agenst good duke Humfre of Glocetter the kinges uncle and protectoure of the royalme in ye kinges youthe and childod/ because that for him they might not slee whom they wolde and make what chevysaunce they lusted. Wold nolt the bisshope of Winchestre have faullen upon him and oppressed him openlye with might and power in the cityre of london/ had not the cityzens come to his helpe?' For Winchester, see below, Chapter 5.

More never attempts to come to grips with Tyndale's brilliant sketch of a class of men for whom popular opinion and rebellion had always reserved their most burning contempt: ambitious, double-minded politicians and counsellors who claimed to speak God's will. Ambitious careerists always gravitate towards the powerful and prestigious, just as, in the mirror-image of this prejudice, people who have been rejected for promotion always resent those who climbed corporate ladders successfully.

More evaded Tyndale's claim that the Church burned men whose arguments they could not refute. Constitutionally and legally, he wrote, bishops did not burn anyone. The task of the Church, he explained, as if to a child, was to define heresy, and to conduct the enquiries into particular cases; it did not determine or execute the punishment. Heretics were burned under a statute of Henry V. Burning was monarch's business – was Tyndale setting himself up against the king's authority, while representing himself as the king's loyal subject? If the king decided to let heretics go, go heretics would. The clergy did not burn heretics, the state did. They might be led to the stake by the bishops, but they were handed over to the king's officers before they were burned. Who *was* this upstart ploughboy ('*Huchyns*') to think he could discuss matters of law and constitution with the great lawyer, chancellor of England, and professor of rhetoric at Oxford University? Who was William Tyndale *als* Hochyns/ Hychyns, but an upstart farmer's boy who didn't seem to be sure what his name was? Who was he to argue matters of state? Wasn't it clear that he was motivated not only by malice to the holy mother Church, but also to God's anointed King?

Tyndale turned not to statutory authority but to history. For all their pretensions, a succession of English kings since Henry IV had never been fully in control of their kingdoms. As though 'the pope had not first found the law,' he answered, and as though 'al his preachers babbled not in every sermon/ burne these heretikes/ burn them for we have no nother argument to convince them and as though they compelled not bothe kinge and emproure to swere that they shall so do'. To justify burnings More 'bringeth in provisions of kynge Henrye the V'. In fact the great Harry (and his usurping father) had been no more than the dupe of Rome's English agents. 'Lest he shulde have had leyfer to herken unto the trouthe', wrote Tyndale, 'the prelettes . . . sent [him] into Fraunce/ to occupie hys mynde in warre/ and led him at their wil.' Henry the legend of Agincourt, *the fifth of that name since the conquest*, was led by the nose, against the common interest, by the *bisshopes*. There was more: 'And I ax [More] whether [Henry V's] father slew not his lege kinge and true enheretoure unto the crowne and was therfore sett upp of the bisshopps a false kinge to mayneteyne theyr falsehed? And I axe after that weked dede/folowed not the destruccion of the comenaltie and quenching of all the noble bloud?'[187] So much for the hereditary claims of the Tudors. For Tyndale, men ruled as kings for no other reason than that God put them there to rule; that was their only source of legitimacy. That the English king was where he was out of legitimate and hereditary descent was a proposition that a mere perusal of dynastic history would instantly refute.

Tyndale's hatred of double-minded clerics and counsellors who would serve any god for *promocion* was vitriolic: they were for him, as they had been for *commune opinioun* as far back as vernacular sources will take us, the archetypal corrupt counsellors, from foreign popes and cardinals down to the apologetic sophistry of academics and the superstitious maunderings of parish priests. This strand of popular opinion had always been suspicious of worldly, ambitious churchmen, from property-grubbing abbots to great clerical statesmen like Arundel and More's predecessor, 'Wolfsea'. Before his son was corrupted by the bishops, and he agreed to burn their heretics for them, Henry IV had deposed and murdered the legitimate king, Richard II. We get the impression that had the opportunity ever arisen, Tyndale would have spoken exactly these words to Henry VIII, but left him to decide for himself whether he and his father were not exactly those kinds of tyrant. No king who ever lived could feel comfortable with a phrase like *a false kinge to mayneteyne theyr falsehed*.

If the textual record tells us that a 'society' had rival social theories, we can regard the duality or multiplicity of meanings of politics as one of the characteristics of that 'society'. Historians are required to pay every rival philosophy or world view the respect of trying to understand it. The past is a foreign culture: it is not our business to judge, only to describe and understand. In Collingwood's idea of History, historians are supposed to think their way 'through' the evidence, to see how the world might have looked from inside the minds and practices that made it. Historians of the future, looking back on the nineteenth and twentieth centuries, will try to understand our conceptual systems equally well, as we understood and were motivated by them. They will note that, as Skinner suggests, we had more than one way of understanding what we call 'politics'.

Having made the effort to understand the differences within and between texts and their contexts, however, we can go one step further. What do these rival social theories have in common, what ideas and references do they share? If the contending voices agree about something, however trivial, we can set about reconstructing the world implied by the points they seem to agree about. Thus in sixteenth-century England

[187] *Answer to More*, cxxxii.

many of the rival theories assumed that the argument was about *common-weal*. We cannot rule out the possibility that all the rival social theories got it wrong in some decisively significant way. We are still in the world of ideas. However, out of their commonalities of usage emerges a residual pool of agreed meanings that tells us exactly what they all thought they were struggling for. This, it seems to me, takes us through the contending voices of the age to the *grande designe* that was hidden from contemporaries because they were too prone to becoming trapped in their own personal and party theories and their differences with everyone else. One of the things they all came to agree about after the Reformation was that they were all struggling for England. The *Commonweal* that concerned them all was England. Everything else was contingent and variable. Commonalities enable us to posit the existence of a more general level of culture, a larger social theory containing all the smaller, contending ones.

Part II

Accumulating a tradition: popular resistance
and rebellion, 1327–1549

4 Discords, quarrels and factions of the commonalty: an ensemble of popular demands, 1328–1381

When discords, and quarrels, and factions are carried openly and audaciously, it is a sign the reverence of government is lost[1]

4.1 Populism as a way of understanding the history of politics

Bacon was wrong about this, at least in one sense. Political discords, quarrels and factions, conducted 'openly and audaciously', constituted a – arguably *the* – dominant, and certainly the most novel, theme of English constitutional culture from the fourteenth to seventeenth centuries.[2] The tradition of resistance and rebellion was a sign that significant numbers of people routinely lost faith – or never had any – in actually existing government. Yet in an important sense that tradition was underpinned by 'reverence for government' – as common opinion thought it ought to be constituted.

Ernesto Laclau argues that 'populism' is not a particular type of political movement like, for example, liberalism or socialism; it is a way of thinking about politics and political processes that applies to all the political movements of modernity.[3] Part of its usefulness is that it frees us from the 'top down' or 'bottom up' alternatives that have tended to dominate historiographical thought and practice. Laclau's populist perspective posits a changing ensemble or constellation of differences. The

---

[1] Bacon, 'Of Seditions and Troubles . . . ', *Essays Civil and Moral* (New York and Melbourne 1892), 20.

[2] The articulation of the tradition in the 1640s is the subject of Chapter 9.

[3] Ernesto Laclau, *On Populist Reason* (London 2005), xi, 13–14, writes that his aim is not 'to find the *true* referent of populism, but to do the opposite: to show that populism has no referential unity because it is ascribed not to a delimitable phenomenon but to a social logic whose effects cut across many phenomena. Populism is, quite simply, a way of constructing the political.' Instead of seeing populism in terms of its 'vagueness, its ideological emptiness, its anti-intellectualism, its transitory character . . . populism appears as a distinctive and always present possibility of structuration of political life.' Populism is not 'a *type* of organization or ideology to be compared with other types such as liberalism, conservatism, communism or socialism, but . . . a dimension of political culture'.

top-down/bottom-up perspectives are residues of outmoded hierarchical perspectives. Instead of viewing constitutional history from the points of view of states, ruling classes and dominant ideologies, it is approached as movements within a collectivity in the process of constituting and providing legitimacy for itself. Instead of ranking the parts before analysis begins, every part (episode, event, movement, community, class, faction, party, etc.) is viewed as equivalent. The importance of the 'play of difference' perspective (e.g. between the motives, ideas and actions of kings, courts, barons, gentry, 'middle' ranks or the communes in rebellion or parliament) is that it does not privilege any part of society over any other.[4] The task is to 'reconstitute' an 'ensemble of differences' part by part, class by class, community by community. What makes complex societies complex is that they encompass many differences. The play of difference approach also allows for the possibility that while intentions are always present and historical changes are always intended, motivated or caused, the changes that actually occur are rarely fully predicted or intended. The next two chapters deal with the hard political edge of the constitutional culture of fourteenth to seventeenth-century England: the tradition of popular rebellion.

The 'play of differences' approach acknowledges that at any given time and place some 'differences' are more hegemonic than others. Differences that are at one time not powerful and not manifested by any considerable number of people may, in time, combine with other differences and become the dominant order – even if none of them actually intend this to happen and do not recognize it when it does. Laclau suggests that resistance turns to riot and riot merges into rebellion and revolution when a multitude of 'heterogeneous' local demands become 'equivalent'. Resistance escalates to the extent that different communities, associations and classes are aware of each other's 'demands' and realize that, in spite of their differences, they have commonalities or, most often, a common enemy. 'Think of a large mass of agrarian migrants who settle in the shantytowns on the outskirts of a developing industrial city', writes Laclau.

Problems of housing arise, and the group of people affected by them request some kind of solution from the local authorities. Here we have a demand which initially is perhaps a request. If the demand is satisfied, that is the end of the matter; but if it is not, people can start to perceive that their neighbours have other, equally unsatisfied demands – problems with water, health, schooling, and so on. If the situation remains unchanged for some time, there is an accumulation of unfilled

---

[4] *Ibid.*, 69: 'Whatever centrality an element acquires, it has to be explained by the play of differences as such.'

demands and an increasing inability of the institutional system to absorb them in a differential way (each in isolation from the others), and an equivalential relation is established between them. The result could easily be, if it is not circumvented by external factors, a widening chasm separating the institutional system from the people. *Ibid.*, 73–4

Laclau implies a historiography of collective imagination to set alongside and compare with 'structuralist' reconstitutions of the *longue duree*, in which thoughts and ideas often receive short shrift. Immemorial monarchy- and aristocracy-centred models of sovereignty began to be systematically challenged by popular and populist movements in the long period that is the subject of this book: these were seeds of the revolutionary fervour that began to grip Western Europe in the seventeenth to nineteenth centuries, utterly transforming the states and constitutional cultures ('*ancien regimes*') that had preceded them. To avoid misunderstanding let me say that I do not presume that populist polities are superior to aristocracies and monarchies, the official forms of most medieval and early modern states. This is not a positivist interpretation, nor is it 'negativist'. Laclau's populist perspective is useful to the extent that it helps us to think about and analyse the historical constitution of complex collectivities like modern nations.

Laclau draws on nineteenth-century discourse about crowd psychology and the emergence, from it, of a discourse about publics. If we add the landscape dimension, this may be a more tangible way of thinking about collectivities than the more abstract word 'society'. Simplistically, complex (early) modern 'societies' are more or less organized crowds operating in a larger theatre than the cities and regions that formed their contexts in earlier historical times. Nation-states are crowds unified by common identities and demands. Benedict Anderson described nations as 'imagined communities'. Sigmund Freud might have been thinking about the historical emergence of imagined communities when he wrote that not all crowds crystallize around charismatic leaders, as earlier theorists had supposed. Freud asked himself 'whether groups with leaders may not be the more primitive and complete, whether in the others an idea, an abstraction, may not take the place of the leader (a state of things to which religious groups, with their invisible head, form a transitional stage), and whether a common tendency, a wish in which a number of people can have a share, may not in the same way serve as a substitute'.[5] Primitive crowds have charismatic leaders. Lasting movements are animated by ideas. The ideas make the primitive crowds and their leaders

---

[5] Quotation from Laclau, *ibid.*, 61.

'equivalential' by subordinating them all, if only momentarily, to easily grasped and communicated ideals.

A tradition of popular rebellion emerged in the fourteenth century and became, from 1381 to 1549, and to an important extent until 1649, the most novel and forceful element in the emergent constitutional culture. Chapter 4 examines the dispersed ('heterogeneous') local roots of the tradition of rebellion by means of a series of exemplary episodes, from the 1320s to 1381, in which common people drew attention to and left records of their particular discontentments, discords and quarrels. I will not be suggesting that they were conscious of each other, although I present them chronologically in order to include the possibility that the participants in later episodes had general notions of the kinds of issues raised by the earlier ones. I want to sort out a question that always hovers around studies of particular episodes: how exceptional and how typical were they? In what ways were they different and in what ways, as Laclau puts it, were they 'equivalential'? This takes us through and beyond 1381 and leads into Chapter 5, in which I argue that every great rebellion from 1381 to 1649 was fought in the name of the commonweal and evoked 'the spectre of commonalty'.

In Chapter 5 I suggest that two galvanizing ideas or abstractions (Laclau's 'empty signifiers'), 'commonweal' and 'commonalty', first came together in 1381. In times of crisis 'commonweal' was capable of meaning an ideal community encompassing every English child, woman and man, regardless of estate, quality, degree, rank, class or sort. It stood for what ought to be the case. Its enemy, in times of crisis, was the actually existing state. At certain key moments large numbers of people living in localities and provinces of England were gripped by the conviction that, at that moment, the existing state was not ruling in their interests, but in direct opposition to them. The state was ignoring, excluding, treating them with disdain. Beginning with the rebels of 1381, this diffuse popular movement conjoined the words 'common' and '*wele*' (a word with great spiritual as well as material weight, as we saw with the usages of Julian of Norwich) to signify the greater community that the state was supposed to serve. In Laclau's terminology, 'commonweal' was capable, in times of crisis, of making heterogeneous complaints, most of them complaints against existing government, ecclesiastical and secular, 'equivalential'.

Finally, let me reiterate a theme that has been touched on many times in the preceding chapters. Laclau's framework has what Adam T. Smith identifies as *the* pervasive weakness of modern social, historical, political and constitutional analysis: 'its representation of politics [is] entirely removed from space and place'.[6] It cannot be repeated often enough that all historical episodes are first and foremost movements in space, animating and transforming constitutive landscapes. The challenge is to reconstitute the constitutional landscape that emerged from three centuries of popular actions.

4.2   Peasant resistance: Thornbury, 1328–52

In order to understand the causes of the revolts we must learn much more about the malfunctioning of local government and justice... [7]

Class distinctions within the commonalty varied markedly in time and place. Recent theoretical writing, writes Peter Franklin, 'has seen a dichotomy in peasant politics between rebellion, which is rare, highly organised and open, and passive resistance, which is very common and involves many acts carried out in secret'. The movement he documents on the Gloucestershire manor of Thornbury, ten thousand acres of more or less boggy Severn floodplain between Berkeley and Bristol, in the early years of the reign of Edward III, was somewhere in between. On the one hand it routinely involved 'acts of open defiance'; on the other, it 'stopped far short of rebellion'.[8]

Analysis of a series of 216 Thornbury court rolls (1328–52) enabled Franklin to identify no fewer than 759 cases of tenants not performing labour services, or deliberately doing them badly. He describes a consistent tendency on the part of the commons of a single manor to refuse and resist manorial instructions and oppressions. All the offenders were unfree in the sense that they were required to perform regular labour services for their lord, but the movement – if that is what it was – involved all sorts of offenders. Of the 138 identified villein men and women who took part in labour-service offences, 127 were direct tenants of the lord, 53 were rich peasants (38 per cent – 4.1 offences each), 41 were middle peasants (30 per cent – 2.9 offences each), and 25 were poor peasants

---

[6] Adam T. Smith, *The Political Landscape: Constellations of Authority in Early Complex Polities* (Berkeley and Los Angeles 2003), 79; Rollison, 'Exploding England: the dialectics of mobility and settlement in early modern England', *Social History* 24:1, 1–17 offers a model in which historical time is reduced to movements in space.

[7] E.B. Fryde, Introduction to Charles Oman, *The Great Revolt of 1381* (Oxford 1969), xxix.

[8] Peter Franklin, 'Politics in Manorial Court Rolls: the Tactics, Social Composition, and Aims of a Pre-1381 Peasant Movement', in Zvi Razi and Richard M.Smith (ed.), *Medieval Society and the Manor Court* (Oxford 1996), 173.

(18 per cent – 2.4 offences each).[9] They were united by a common oppressor. The manorial records lump together an unequal class or estate with a common enemy.

Measured by wealth and landholding, the wealthiest offenders had more in common with the *liberi homines*, 'king's men', the esquires, gentlemen and yeomen of a later age, than they did with their poorer neighbours. Judging by average numbers of offences, they were the most persistent offenders and may have been 'leaders': the details of their social relations and organization are hidden. The organization and dynamics of the movement, even the degree to which they represent a consistent and constant *movement*, as against a mere series of unrelated events, remain unclear. Franklin sees the individual offences as tactical moves in a larger movement of *communitas*, the commonalty as resistance *movement*, with contingent aims. As with the Peatling Magna episode, this movement of 'community' was also a movement of 'commonalty' in the 'third estate' sense. One year the aim was to get rid of an unpopular bailiff, other years saw demands to recover demesne parcels seized by unscrupulous stewards, to appoint their representatives as manorial surveyors, and for the deregulation, or at least simplification, of the land market. The latter would clearly interest the richer commoners.

The free and servile commons of Thornbury sustained a campaign of collective resistance across two decades. They had their own ideas about what the lord was entitled to in respect of labour services. Franklin also shows that incidents did not multiply in economically hard years, but at 'times . . . at which national opposition to the government was at its height'. 'Economic distress did not, at first, play a significant part in Thornbury', he writes. The movement had local causes and was restricted to one estate in South Gloucestershire, but it may also have been fuelled by rumours circulating the kingdom about their disgraced lord. 'Audley had probably risen to favour through a homosexual relationship with Edward II, and his wife was Edward III's first cousin . . . ', writes Franklin. He concludes that 'these records may thus relate more directly to national discontent than would at first appear'.[10] This conjuncture of local issues and the affairs of the kingdom is not often glimpsed in the records of the first half of the fourteenth century, but there is enough for us to suspect that local communities knew more about what was going on in the affairs of the kingdom than traditional conceptions of a 'cellular' landscape of autarchic, isolated villages and districts have allowed for.

---

[9] Franklin, 'Politics in Manorial Court Rolls', 192, and table 6.1 'Labour Service Offences at Thornbury, 1328–52'.

[10] Franklin, 'Politics in Manorial Court Rolls', 172–3.

This is a common feature of all the incidents related in this chapter. Franklin's conjecture that local movements were aware of and influenced by the politics of the kingdom defines a recurring pattern.

The chance survival of records relating to other magnate estates elsewhere reveal a similar pattern of resistance on the part of predominantly servile workers (256 cases in 29 years on the abbot of Ramsay's manor of Broughton, Hunts, and 271 in the same abbot's Holywell-cum-Needworthy), suggests 'a rural society seething with discontent'. To evoke one of the underlying passions behind such movements, he tells the story of 'the Worcestershire man who drowned himself in the Severn in 1293 rather than take up villein land of the earl of Gloucester and run the risk of becoming the earl's villein'. This may have been a factor at Thornbury, where some families were constantly 'in danger of losing their status as the lord's men tried to raise heriot'.[11] Studies like this, unrecorded by the chroniclers not because they were so rare, but because they were so many, take us into the infrapolitics of late medieval England, the very rich and deep soil that Jack Straw, Jack Sharpe and Jack Cade husbanded for larger purposes. They suggest that the *communes* of fourteenth-century England were perfectly capable of recognizing what their interests were, and knowing how and when to organize and act.

4.3   Mocking the king's justice: Ipswich, 1344

In 1344, the king's chief justice, William Shareshill, was sent to Ipswich to investigate a murder.[12] We are not told how the news reached him, but he had heard that 'many evildoers' had participated in 'the death of John Holtby', who had been 'feloniously slain for the reason that he busied himself about the king's business'. Holtby had risen to power at Ipswich by cultivating the patronage of Edward II. He did not fall with his master and was finally so hated that one day a large crowd, *tam de maioribus quam de mediocribus et minoribus*, 'from among the greater as well as the middle and the lesser folk', dragged him into the street and killed him. The community came together to depose and murder a tyrant.

The source reminds us that local tax assessors of the time reflexively put taxpayers into three clear-cut categories, leaving an 'invisible' fourth category of households and individuals who possessed nothing and were

---

[11] *Ibid.*, 166, 170–1.

[12] G.O. Sayles, *Select Cases in the Court of King's Bench under Edward III*, vol. VI (1340–77), Selden Society vol. 82 (London 1965), Michaelmas 1344, no. 19, 37–8. With regard to this case and others, Sayles comments that 'the rule of law had begun to collapse long before the fifteenth century', xxvii.

therefore not charged. Likewise the court scribe assumed a division between 'great', 'middle' or 'mediocre', and the 'small' people. 'The lesser folk' included people who were exempt from all except poll taxes from the early fourteenth to the mid-seventeenth centuries.

Judge Shareshill and his retainers arrived to find that the killers had taken sanctuary in the church. He watched a mocking procession of townspeople queuing up at the church door to give the murderers 'presents such as food and drink and gold and silver'. They 'sang so many songs of rejoicing in their honour', Shareshill reported, 'that it was as if God had come down from Heaven (*sicut Deus de celo descendisset*)'. They were celebrating the public assassination of the leader of an armed gang of bullies who had held the town to ransom for decades.

Unable to arrest the malefactors, the judge returned to London to consult the king. Witnesses later testified that as soon as he left town, the assassins, heroes, terrorists, respectable leaders of public opinion – whatever they were, they emerged from the church in triumph, and with 'many other accomplices . . . came to the hall of pleas', laughing and singing as if in celebration. They all sat down 'on the steps of the said hall' where, facing the crowd and 'in mockery of the king's justices and ministers in his service' ordered it to be proclaimed 'that William Shareshill was to appear before them under penalty of a hundred pounds and William Notton and likewise many others who supported the king'.

The town bailiffs, John Hirp and John Preston, were summoned to appear at Westminster 'in person and before the king' to explain how, 'in view of the fact that such unseemly and wicked things had been done in the town, they themselves, who were in the town at that time', had not arrested and detained 'the evildoers or those who in any way supported them'. The king's first questions addressed their authority. How were they elected? They replied that they 'were chosen as bailiffs . . . by the whole community of the town (*per totam communitatem eiusdem ville*)'. Did not such election mean that they had a mandate to arrest evildoers and disturbers of the king's peace? They replied that it did. Did not those who had elected them expect them so to arrest malefactors, and to support their elected leaders in so doing? They 'could not deny but that they were in the town at that time when the felonies were committed'. By the town's charter they were indeed responsible to the king for the peace and harmony of Ipswich. They had not arrested anyone. If they were unable to arrest the murderers why did they not 'cause to be arrested those who brought them presents such as food and drink and other necessities and provided them with things of solace and comfort'? 'They *say*', recorded the clerk, clearly disgusted by the stupidity of these *Suthfolk* yokels, 'that there was so great a crowd of those who were then in the town and who were rejoicing so much together at the aforesaid death that they could not have resisted or attached them by reason of their own feebleness of body, because they are now old men.'

The king's lawyer remained patient. 'Why, inasmuch as you are old men and were chosen as bailiffs by the community of the whole town, did you not take the community of the said town with you in order to attach the evildoers and their supporters?'

'The most substantial, powerful, strong and wealthy men of the whole community were among the relatives of the evildoers, my lord. We dared not.'

'If the evildoers and others who sympathised with them and who have now gone into hiding were to come back into the town, would you then dare to arrest them and attach them to stand trial?'

'We dare not of ourselves take such things upon ourselves unless twelve or six of the most substantial men of the town previously show their willingness to undertake these matters with us.'

They could not find twelve or even six 'substantial men of the town' willing to help them arrest the murderers. It was a rare case of unity within and between the greater, middling and lesser classes of townspeople. The cause transcended everyday differences and resentments. Holtby's unpopularity reflected unfavourably on the Crown. He came to power at Ipswich as a client of a deeply unpopular king, Edward II, led a *coup* in 1322 against the *cabal* that had governed the city for nearly thirty years, and sustained it with violence for the first seventeen years of Edward III's reign, until his murder in 1344. Both kings had shown themselves willing to pardon (or go easy on) his crimes (ranging from intimidation and outright attacks on households in and around the city, to kidnapping and extortion) against less well-connected local households.[13] There is no reason to doubt that he was killed at the will of the community, with its tripartite class-structure, *maioribus... mediocribus et minoribus*, who fully supported his murderer, William Malyn junior. Malyn, 'probably the wealthiest Ipswich man of his generation, was convicted of detention of the king's wool and money, wool-smuggling, and trading with the king's enemies'.[14] Neither he nor the town come across as lovers of monarchy.

Elite theory prescribed that the commonalty should only offer the king counsel (which could include disagreeing with him) if invited to be consulted. Otherwise, its members should be seen but not heard, governed but not participating in government. That was the theory. Not

---

[13] For Holtby (or de Halteby), see http://www.trytel.com/~tristan/towns/m6_pt5: Stephen Alsford, *The Men Behind the Masque: Office Holding in East Anglian Boroughs*, Chapter 6, Part V: 'The Practice: Crimes of Violence', n. 102–7, and Chapter 7.4, 'Discords and Disputes: Ipswich'.

[14] For the involvement of Malyn, 'probably the wealthiest Ipswich man of his generation', see Alsford, *Men Behind the Masque*, ch. 6.4, n. 83–5.

until the generations of Fortescue, Tyndale and Sir Thomas Smith do we begin to find vernacular constitutional literature raising querulous objections to this deeply mistaken and profoundly unhistorical myth of the passivity of the people. In 1344 towns were not permitted to enact disagreements with the laws and government of kings. What was the king to do, kill them all, hang their bodies in quarters and chains in London and all other towns vaguely like Ipswich? In 1344 this was a little tester on the front line of constitutional history, a probe from below. It is impossible to disagree with the court's decision that 'the king's peace in the town was improperly kept'. Ipswich was truly 'desolate so far as the maintainance of good peace was concerned'. What this meant was that the community at Ipswich had been able to maintain solidarity. It began with the deposition and murder of a man the whole community saw as a tyrant and traitor.

How public the decision to kill Holtby actually was, how many people were involved in the 'debate', and how long it had been going on, is not known. The events at Ipswich had two simple precepts in common with public discourse concerning the deposition of Edward II a few years earlier. Tyrants could and should be overthrown, but only if the whole community agreed. All parties stress the public and communal nature of the event. All parties and classes were agreed that Holtby must be not only deposed but killed.

Words spread. A cause capable of uniting many communities, even provinces, as hatred of a tyrant had momentarily united the classes of Ipswich. The solidarity of Ipswich might become an example to others. In view of the seriousness of the case, martial law was declared. The king took back the custody of the town into his own hands, ordering that 'someone else on the king's behalf, who dares to maintain the king's peace, is to be installed in the town to keep the king's peace . . . until the king shall decree otherwise . . . the bailiffs gave up their wands and it was handed over to John Haward, the sheriff, who was sworn to look after the town well and faithfully to the king's profit'. The malcontents at Ipswich had acted for the 'profit' or 'wele' of the *community*.

4.4   The heretical hermit of Hertfordshire: Richard of Fulham against the Statute of Labourers, 1357

There is no statute that would restrict labourers, artisans and servants from taking from their labours and services as much as they are pleased to take and from obtaining what they desire. If it was ordained or decreed otherwise, the said statute and ordinance were falsely and wickedly made.[15]

---

[15] Attributed to Richard of Fulham, 1357.

The Ipswich case belongs with an extensive series. The archives contain references to dozens of episodes of resistance on the part of individuals, households, kin-groups, accidental groups, parishes, crafts, 'covens', districts, risings and revolts of the commonalty, within the commonalty itself and against their appointed and prescribed lords. The most chronic local movements were in towns with monastic lords, but there are also well-documented examples of impressive local (and in the case of John of Gaunt in 1376 and 1381, national) campaigns against secular lords too.

The episodes we are considering took place against a background of endemic violence, lawlessness, and a common sense of the arbitrary nature of the king's justice. A man of Waltham Holy Cross named Roger Byndethef confessed he was a thief. After his trial he was condemned to 'abjure the realm of England... and a cross was handed to him and a road assigned him' from Waltham to Dover. Two men (a French knight and his esquire by the sound of their names), William de Camville and William Ferour, palfrey-man, were waiting for him on the borders of Essex and Hertford, and on 28 January 1343, 'while the said Roger was under the banner of Holy Church', Camville took out his sword and gave it to Ferour, who 'cut off the said Roger's head'. Someone accused Camville of murder, but he was granted a pardon for service with the king 'in the French wars'.[16]

The 'French wars' were at issue in another popular uprising that unfolded on the banks of the River Severn in the summer of 1348. In that year 'a very great assembly of most riotous and rebellious persons of Gloucestershire, Somerset and Bristol', took 'upon them regall power and chose a Captaine in the nature of a king to govern them'. They issued 'proclamations' and 'entered upon divers ships laden with corne and other provisions, readye to goe by the king's command into Gascoigne', beat up and 'wounded divers of the marriners' who tried to stop their confiscations. They gave Thomas lord Berkeley 'no maner of rest' when he and his retainers tried to stop them.[17]

In Surrey a very different gang of conspirators fooled and bribed the king into lending his name to a reign of terror that held the respectable folk of Surrey to ransom in the years after the Black Death. In 1354 jurors complained about a series of offences involving John Brocas, knight and lord of the manor of Guildford, Oliver his son and thirty-one other men including the vicar of Woking, the parson of Peper Harrow and 'master Robert of Perncote, notary'. Brocas and his men had made 'a confederacy by covenant in the chapel of the Friars preachers of Guilford... to

---

maintain the other in all plaints, lawful or unlawful, and to conceal felonies and wrongdoings committed in the parts of Surrey by them or by any one of them'. They swore 'to destroy John of Rowley because he refused to agree to the confederacy'. Eleven of Brocas's gang then dressed themselves 'in the vestments of canons, some as black monks, some as canons, some in the vestments of grey monks, and some of them in robes with fur-lined hoods – which they had borrowed – as though they were local officials of high rank.' In this guise they went to the king and persuaded him that 'there were no keepers of the peace or justices to make investigations in those parts' and nominated their own candidates. The king 'granted their request' and they used his commission to do 'great harm and great ruin to various people and made little profit for the king but only profit for themselves by putting the poor men of the district (*pauperes homines*) under their subjection'. The jurors complained that 'they were utter liars because they did nothing except destroy loyalty and justice and maintain thieves, murderers and malefactors'.[18]

A more general impact of the Black Death was that it didn't leave enough people to do the work. As soon as localities began to get over the initial shock of the great dying, labour shortages translated into demands by labourers for higher wages. Hertfordshire, like the Home Counties, Essex, the Thames Valley and the cloth making districts of the West of England, was part of London's hinterlands, and it was among the first counties to register a dissenting voice with regard to the Statute of Labourers. This Hertfordshire legend concerns the labour agitations of Richard of Fulham, a Hermit (*Eremitica*) and his comrade, Robert Gerrard, the vicar of the village of Aldbury.

On Tuesday 19 April 1356, 'John Atte Lee and his Fellows, the King's Justices for the ordinance and statute of labourers' gathered at the Hertfordshire market town of Ware, to hear the sworn testimony of twelve jurors of the shire. The role of the jury was to inform the justices of the King's Bench as to the peace (or otherwise) of the county, but it soon became clear that John Atte Lee and his retainers had made the acquaintanceship of Richard and Robert a day or two earlier.[19]

The jurors' spokesman declared Richard of Fulham, a man who was supposed to have renounced the world altogether, 'a common malefactor'. A sense of righteous outrage colours his testimony. Richard had been

---

[18] Coram Rege Roll no. 374 (Hilary 1354) m.35, Sayles, *Select Cases... under Edward III*, 94–7.

[19] 'Hertfordshire Michaelmas 1356, An Inquisition taken at Ware before John Atte Lee and his Fellows, the King's Justices for the ordinance and statute of labourers etc on Tuesday 19 April 1356 by the oath of 12 Jurors of Hertfordshire': Sayles, *Select Cases... under Edward III*, 110–11.

'wandering about with Robert, vicar of Aldbury church, night and day, at various times and places', in disguise, dressing 'in various changes of garments of various kinds' which he 'changed every day', eluding capture by the sheriff's men for what must have been months, possibly even a year or two. He 'wanders about, goes into hiding and dodges here and there on the king's highways as well as in other places, public and private'. Every so often, he leaps out of the forest 'carrying a long, thick stick', most recently 'waylaying the king's justices assigned to administer the statute of labourers in the county of Hertford'.

Images of Richard the hermit and Robert the priest 'horribly and savagely threatening' the justices and 'even [the jurors] themselves with death and mutilation and arson and other hideous and unspeakable evils', must be left to the imagination. He caught the imaginations of his contemporaries: a hermit, a man who was supposed to have turned his back on society, surreptitiously and invisibly wandering among the hamlets, villages and little markets of Hertfordshire, suddenly appearing and preaching his message, moving on leaving behind him knots of men and women discussing what he said, electing delegates to inform employers that higher wages would have to be paid or the work would not be done.

Whirling his stave, fearless of sheriff's men and justices, pouncing on knots of employers and frightening them almost to death, he 'scorned and poured contempt day after day on the king's statute and ordinance of labourers artisans and servants, made by the said king and his council for the common utility of the realm (*pro communi utilitate regni Anglie*)'. He and Robert went around 'publicly preaching and proclaiming that all who made the statute of labourers, supported, agreed to, executed or maintained them, or indicted such labourers (*operariorum, artificum et servitorum*), or punished those indicted, or prevented them in any way from exercising their absolute right to obtain whatever wages they could command... even abnormal wages, as they wish... are excommunicate'. Imagine their horror at a hermit excommunicating all the respectable peasant employers, nobles and even the king – in the name of the labourers. If he had not existed it would have been necessary to invent him.

Hermits and anchorites were the proletarians of the medieval Church. For two centuries after the generation of English monastics alive at the time of the Norman Conquest died out, it became very difficult for an English youth to achieve any seniority in a religious order, and legally impossible for a youth of the (largely English) commonalty even to join. This left a legacy of estrangement that weakened in the fifteenth century, but that was always to be a potentially explosive strand of English popular opinion with regard to the institutional Church. One effect of this exclusion was to enhance the popular prestige of people who adopted the life of a hermit or anchorite, in effect the only option for an independent, adult man or woman of the commonalty with a religious vocation.

Hermits and anchorites made an independent, personal contract, and communion, with God. In the centuries after the conquest they were more likely to be English than French. In his survey of the impact of the Norman Conquest on ethnic relations in England, Hugh M. Thomas stresses the vernacular character of hermits and anchorites. 'It would be a challenge to find one who was clearly of Norman descent', he writes. 'There were no legal bars to any free person becoming a hermit or anchorite.'[20] What is insufficiently stressed is the public roles of hermits and anchorites in the local and district communities whose parish churches they made their homes. Julian of Norwich, whom we met in the last chapter, is a well-known example. Richard of Fulham had made his home in a parish and district with large numbers of labourers. He may have been a labourer himself before becoming a hermit. We do not know why he made the change, but it is recorded that in the months or years before the Spring of 1356, he was responsible for delivering incendiary sermons on a text that was not from the bible.

His text or theme was that 'There is no statute that would restrict labourers, artisans and servants from taking from their labours and services as much as they are pleased to take and from obtaining what they desire. If it was ordained or decreed otherwise, the said statute and ordinance were falsely and wickedly made.' As far as he was concerned 'the aforesaid ordinances and statutes are abolished.' Richard the Hermit and Robert the Priest went around 'publicly and openly propound[ing] these wicked things'. They inspired labourers, 'setting a dangerous example, comforting and emboldening them' and 'nurturing their wrongdoings to the impairment of the statute'. As a result 'the labourers, artisans and servants of [Hertfordshire] were until now and still are more rebellious and bolder in their outrages and trespasses in disobeying court processes and judgements'.

The jurors had reason to exaggerate. It was as much an offence for a 'tenant' to pay as for a labourer to ask for higher wages than the statute permitted. The jurors claimed to represent the experience and opinion of all the 'tenants of land in the said county'. They spoke for a larger class of people who, like themselves, needed extra labour to sow, weed or harvest their fields at critical times of the year. Like the barons before them they claimed to represent lesser neighbours. It was not the fault of 'tenants

---

[20] Hugh M. Thomas, *The English and the Normans: Ethnic Hostility, Assimilation and Identity 1066–c.1220* (Oxford 2002), 208–9.

of the land' that they had to pay higher wages than the statutes allowed. They were intimidated and oppressed by a wicked hermit preaching discontentment to disobedient and disrespectful labourers.

'Noticing the preachings of the vicar and the hermit, [they] were all the more afraid and are still afraid to carry out the executions arising out of the . . . ordinance and statute.' After the Black Death the king, abbots, bishops, dukes, lesser barons, *liberi homines* and rich serfs had to compete for a drastically reduced pool of labourers. Richard the Hermit raised the possibility – even the likelihood – that God had sent the holocaust of 1348–9. Was it possible that God wanted the privileged and more comfortably-off 'tenants' to meet their labourers' irresistible demands? On this perfectly conventional (supernaturalist and possibly millenarian) reasoning the Statute of Labourers was blasphemy, in that it set out to prevent a consequence that God had intended.[21] God was on the side of the labouring poor and any act against them was 'falsely and wickedly made'. Richard of Fulham addressed the whole class of people who depended upon wages, working on the small and larger landholdings of richer peasants, yeomen, squire's or knight's manor and magnate's demesne. Local lords and contexts varied, but labourers were labourers everywhere.

Richard and Robert were caught and brought before the king at Westminster, where, on 14 November 1356, they pleaded not guilty and were committed to prison to await a full jury trial 'at a fortnight'. At the trial they were found guilty of denouncing the statutes and trespassing round the countryside, but nothing else. The judge treated them leniently. Parson Robert secured their release on good behaviour with a heavy fine. Richard returned to his preaching, and was outlawed again in the Michaelmas term of 1361.

4.5   The great rumour of the 1370s

The case of Richard of Fulham suggests one way that word could spread across regions. He could not be everywhere at once, but he could move through the rolling woody terrain of west Hertfordshire like a native, visit most of its towns and villages, and find a barn to sleep in, consecutively, leaving the country talking about the same thing. The movement at Thornbury drew attention to local leadership, and the extensive use

---

[21] The Ordinance of Labourers was issued on 18 June 1349 and 'a number of supplementary statutes [were] enacted between 1351 and 1378'; it was reenacted as a parliamentary statute in November 1378: E.B. Fryde, *Peasants and Landlords in Later Medieval England* (Stroud 1996), 33.

made of manorial organization, by peasant officials, for their own purposes. The situation in Hertfordshire, a county in routine daily connection with London, was different, as it was in neighbouring districts of
Essex. The Black Death is bound to have brought millenarian expectations to the fore at all levels of discourse, sharpening immanent structural
tensions of the pre-plague years. We still know too little about how leaders were 'elected', how communities decided who would put their case,
what case to put, and in what court or forum. Franklin notes that beadles
and tithing men have been 'neglected figure(s) in recent studies' because
of a historiographical perception that their 'importance was declining at
this time. Hampshire tithing men, however, played a part in resistance
to the abbot of Titchfield and it has been suggested that the 1370s idea
of getting exemplifications from Domesday Book in support of peasant claims may have spread through tithing men meeting at Hundred
courts.'[22]

The reference is to the 'great rumour' of 1377. One of many such
rumours, great and small, that circulated from time to time in a kingdom
that always seethed with *murmuring*, this one affected 'the villeins and
tenants of land in villeinage' of 'at least forty villages in Wiltshire, Hampshire, Surrey, Sussex and Devon'. We saw in an earlier section that this
was not a notably peaceful region. In 1358 Reginald Scot was robbed at
Guildford of a little bag containing eighty-four gold florins called 'Johns'
and fifty gold florins called 'Florence Mailles' and nineteen gold florins
called 'Phillips' to the value of 25.10s. The court determined that the
case should be decided by battle. John (the robber) defeated Reginald,
went free, and Reginald was imprisoned. Reginald escaped from prison
before paying his fine and John came before the king to ask that damages
be awarded to him. 'It [was] awarded that John is to recover his damages
from Reginald.'[23] In 1375, Nicholas Huntercombe with half a dozen
local men including servants and other menial occupations from Ipsden
and 'other strangers and unknown men, that is, some from the parts of
Scotland, up to the number of forty men, armed with habergeons, body
armour bassinets, lances, shields, bows, arrows, crossbows *and guns*',
attacked and occupied an Oxfordshire manor belonging to the abbot of
Dorchester. They turned the manor into a fortress, surrounding it with
'dykes, hedges, palisades and platforms', threatened to kill the abbot if
he tried to recover it and later refused entry to the ministers of the king
when they arrived after an enquiry at Reading.[24]

---

[22] Franklin, 'Politics in Manorial Court Rolls', 182–3.
[23] Coram rege Roll 391 Easter 1358, Sayles, *Select Cases . . . under Edward III*, 120.
[24] Sayles, *Select Cases*, 176.

Contemporaries saw the great rumour as a single movement that swept through a wide scattering of manors south-west of London in the decade before the Commons Rebellion of 1381. What seemed to unite them was the common idea that *Domesday Boke* recorded rights that 'completely discharged [them] of all manner of . . . customs and services due to their lords'. The idea that villeins and peasants could have thought up and enacted such a movement out of their own heads and wills was as unthinkable for contemporary parliamentarians, who put it down to 'the malicious interpretation' of 'counsellors, procurors, maintainers and abettors', as it has been for generations of chroniclers and historians ever since. Because the idea of autonomous plebeian action was so subversive, it was assumed that they *must have been* inspired by 'certain persons' (unnamed) who were *not* servile peasants.

Rosamund Faith draws attention to evidence of extraordinarily tenacious collective memory. They believed their ancestors were freemen under the king and only later (they claimed illegally) converted into the unfree tenants of a lesser lord. The 'charisma' of *Domesday* alone led them astray, at least in the question of whether their ancestors had been free king's men. On looking into facts not known at the time, Faith concludes that only three of the affected manors were ancient demesne in 1066 or 1086, but 'it is a striking fact that very many of the places involved had been royal property *before* the conquest, in some cases long before'. Faith cites the case of several generations of tenants of Crondall who made appeal to Edward I and later, in 1364, Edward III, that they were 'ancient demesne'. Faith shows (a) that they were ancient demesne before being granted to prior and convent of St Swithun by king Edgar in 972, and (b) that Edward III accepted their claim. 'An equally impressive feat of memory' applies to the tenants of the abbey of Chertsey at Thorpe, Egham, Chobham and Cobham in 1410, which had been granted to the abbey by Frithuwold, sub-king of Surrey, in 672–5.[25] But the most difficult thing to explain is how and why it was that forty villages scattered across five counties were involved in what appears to have been one 'rumour'.

Franklin's conclusions on the social dynamics of the Thornbury peasant movement stress the conditions required to overcome divisions within the commonalty. These divisions expressed themselves differently in different times and places, and the records depended upon who was speaking or writing. Although it is close to Bristol, the hamlets of Thornbury manor, even the little township itself belonged to a highly distinctive

---

[25] Rosamund Faith, 'The Great Rumour of 1377 and Peasant Ideology', in R.H. Hilton and T.S. Aston (ed.) *The English Rising of 1381*, 46, 54 (& n. 23), 56–7.

'country'. Land reclamation was a constant, focusing everyone's minds on the one type of work that had to be done for everyone's sake. It was clearly for the common good that ditches and dykes be maintained. Beyond that, under the lords, we encounter the familiar tripartite division: 'though rich, middle and poor peasants could work together', writes Franklin, 'villeins got little support from their neighbours'.

This seems to have been a widespread problem, and if the campaign for freedom was particularly active (in the 1330s) it may have driven a wedge between villeins and freemen, and between peasants and burgesses. In 1381 it was possible to make the abolition of serfdom a leading popular demand but in the 1330s it threatened real privileges, especially those of rich free peasants who were anxious to turn their holdings into little manors . . . What was needed to turn the separate local campaigns into an effective national movement was a single overwhelming grievance which affected both villeins and freemen, burgesses and peasants of all economic groups. The taxation and purveyance of the 1330s and early 1340s were never quite severe enough.[26]

The existence of 'ranks' or 'sorts of people', divisions within the commonalty, is very familiar in early modern historiography. The generally accepted view seems to be that before about the middle of the fifteenth century, perhaps even later, the division between free and unfree tenants and persons was a critical division, one that obviates any conception of the commonalty as a uniform movement. The division between free and unfree probably divided most communities in England, but it did not prevent them from forming alliances against common enemies. This began to happen in 1376.

4.6   Westminster: the Good Parliament of 1376

The rebels of 1381 took up again in a more extreme form the cry that the king was surrounded by traitors.[27]

The subsequently named 'Good Parliament' is a candidate for the first national mobilization of the plebeian public sphere. In 1376, the king 'asked the commonalty (*communaltee*) of the realm as he had done before, [for] a great subsidy. But the commons (*communes*) answered that "they were so often, day by day, aggrieved and charged with so many tallages and subsidies" that they might no longer suffer such burdens and charges; and that they knew well that the king had enough for saving of them and of his realm, if the realm be well and truly governed, but that it had been long evil governed by evil officers, that the realm might neither be

---

[26] Franklin, 'Politics in Manorial Court Rolls', 198.
[27] Fryde, in Oman, *The Great Revolt*, xxvii.

plenteous with cheap merchandise, not also with riches.' Government was not pursuing the interests of the common weal. Worse, it was acting to its detriment. No good government, no tax. The Chronicler continued:

And after this there were published and showed in the parliament many complaints and defaults of officers of the realm and namely of the Lord Latimer, the King's chamberlain; and at the last also there was treated and spoken of Dame Alice Perrers, for the great wrongs and evil governance that was done by her and by her counsel in the realm; the which Alice Perrers the king had held for some time his beloved. Wherefore hit was the lesse wonder thogh thrugh the freelte of the wommanys exciting and her streyng, [the king] consentid to her lewedness & evell counsel . . . [28]

The parliament of 1376 is a traditional landmark of constitutional history. It was not the first time 'the commonalty' had resisted the king's wish for a tax. But as long as he could persuade the people that their money was for the glory of England and the diminution of its enemies, the French and Scots, show that he respected their opinion, and above all win battles, he more or less got what he wanted. He always had to negotiate. The parliament of 1376 came together when the king was old and losing control of his faculties. Everything that went wrong came to be attributed, to some extent rightly, to his corrupt court. As the fate of his father had demonstrated fifty years earlier, England could only be ruled by the strongest and most saintly monarch.

The Angevin framework had arrived at its apogee. As usual, propaganda refused to blame the king. It was left unsaid that he was too senile to see through the corrupt machinations of a woman who had seduced him to slavery with her charms, to the sole benefit of herself and her 'peculating clique' of friends, corrupters of the king and caterpillars of the commonwealth.[29] Alice Perrers and the evil advisers were scapegoats for the system in collapse. The sense of the sources is that the 1376 parliament represented English public opinion. The old interpretation was that members of the commons were clients of the lords. In 1376 the lords sat in Westminster Hall, the commons across the road in the chapter house of the abbey. Their elected tribunes had to cross the road to appear before the throne.

The Parliament that assembled at Westminster on 28 April 1376 was 'a large and heterogeneous gathering' including nineteen archbishops and bishops, twenty-five abbots and priors, a selection of lay lords like John of Gaunt, duke of Lancaster, seven earls, and forty barons. More

---

[28] F.W.D. Brie (ed.), *The Brut or The Chronicles of England* (London 1906), 331.
[29] Oman, *The Great Revolt*, p. 4.

significantly, in terms of public opinion, the 240 members of the Commons included 160 representatives from the boroughs: all in all, a 'very diverse collection . . . ranging in status and influence from royal earls to the burgesses of small market towns'.[30] On 29 April the Chancellor Sir John Knyvet declared in the king's presence that the task was to make ordinances for the peace of the realm, arrange for the defence of the realm (there were rumours of invasion by the Castilian fleet), and to finance the king's quarrel with France by voting a tax. On 30 April the two houses separated, the lords assembling in the palace while the Commons met in the abbey chapter house, where they began with the swearing of an oath of 'loyalty and openness in their dealings with each other'.

Debate in the chapter house immediately focused on Alice Perrers and the peculating clique. The wars in France had been mismanaged. The clique had failed to supply the armies which had been left no choice but to 'oppressively plunder . . . the people of Brittany'.[31] Taxes had been pocketed by middle-men, and the army had been ordered to 'take by night as well as day from various people beef, cattle, cows, sheep, corn, hay, oats, and other victuals, for which they paid nothing'.[32] The communes sympathized more with their plundered French equivalents than they did with the seedy ambitions of a corrupt court. Complaints were made about toadying deference to the pope. Merchants and woolmen complained against court-licensed evasions of the wool Staple at Calais, and against Alice Perrers's clique's connections with Florentine financiers in Lombard Street. The spirit of the petition is not anti-foreigner, but anti-rich, powerful and selfish. What use were the rich and powerful if they didn't tend the commonwealth, couldn't govern or keep the peace in their own realm? *Commune opinioun* probably was against Florentines and other foreigners, but it was also against bankers, merchants and seedy politicians.

The assembly was of one voice, confident that it represented *commune opinioun*. Chroniclers later represented what happened next as 'a conflict between two contrasting antagonists, the traitorous courtiers and the surprisingly audacious knights of the shire who called them to account'.[33] Beside Alice Perrers and the evil advisers stood the other great object of popular vitriol, the duke of Lancaster, before whose throne the tribunes of the communes were forced to petition.

Holmes sees the nomination by the communes of Peter de la Mare as reflexive deference to rank. 'Socially the distinction between knights

---

[30] *Ibid.*, 108.   [31] George Holmes, *The Good Parliament* (Oxford 1975), 5.
[32] *Ibid.*, 40.   [33] *Ibid.*, 6.

and burgesses was much more significant than that between knights and lords.' It made political sense for the Commons to elect a knight, to put their case to Lancaster. De la Mare was admitted to the duke's presence, but refused to speak until all the Commons were admitted with him. He insisted that he was not empowered to negotiate, only to present their 'petition' that they be all admitted to Westminster Palace. After consultation, he finally agreed to the suggestion that a small committee of the lords and bishops be delegated to meet with and advise the Commons.[34]

Gaunt reacted furiously at the impudent insistence of the tribunes (or 'speakers') that they were only empowered by the communes to deliver a message, not discuss it. The implication that a man of his exalted rank had any obligation to discuss the steering of the ship of state with his inferiors offended his honour as the greatest noble in the land. The communes were there to be consulted, not to make policy and suggest the removal of government officials and courtiers. A counsellor cautioned Gaunt that they were not confronted with a mere rabble of the *commonalty*, waiting to be dismissed by men of blood. In language he knew Gaunt would understand, he pointed out that their leaders and spokesmen were 'knights, not plebs as you assert but men powerful in arms and active'.[35] Behind them were the non commissioned officers of town and country. In the street that separated the two halls of *commune* were crowds of Londoners with their own grievances. It was a moment when prudence had to be put before blood and honour.

The chroniclers assumed (by convention?) that it was the knights who took the lead, not the lords or the burgesses. Holmes accepts this: the knights 'evidently came to Westminster in a militant mood and were glad to make use of the commercial grievances as weapons of attack'; they 'were prepared to act to get rid of Alice Perrers' but the chronicles do not tell us why. Holmes concludes that 'in their attack on the court in which they had lost confidence, the grievances which (the knights) presented were mainly not their own, but the merchants' and that the political framework favourable to their attack was created chiefly by the bishops and the lords'.[36] This is in keeping with the convention of medieval historiography that the Commons was a largely deferential body, dominated, for reasons of birth and status, by the knights of the shire, who in turn were the clients of the magnates across the road in the king's hall.

The relationship between the tribune-knights, the communes at Westminster, and the commonalty at large was not as clear as this suggests. 'Of the 2,244 parliamentary burgesses sitting between 1386 and 1421',

---

[34] *Ibid.*, 5.   [35] *Ibid.*, 135.   [36] *Ibid.*, 138–9.

writes Linda Clark, 'only ninety-five are known to have had close links with magnates ... Even in the small towns there are few indications of the "pocket boroughs" to come.' Contemporary or near-contemporary poems like *Richard the Redeless* satirized 'hired men' who 'would not take any step for fear of their masters, and qualify the idea 'that parliament was usually guided by a very few highly articulate individuals'. John of Gaunt paid fees, annuities and gifts to his shire knights in Lancashire and Derbyshire, which may well have been one of the reasons for his unpopularity in 1376. He was corrupting the spirit of the communes, which was that it represented and spoke for public, not sectional, opinion in the communities. Clientage undermined the purpose of the Commons, which was the greatest jury in the land, reporting honestly to the executive on the condition, needs, and state of mind of the commonalty at large. 'The links between lords and knights made working together easier, but there were still difficulties in controlling the lower house. This, no doubt, was because the boroughs also fielded able spokesmen, among them many experienced lawyers, and merchants with a strong financial base, who could provide a powerful lobby.'[37]

It is around this time that we begin to encounter a sharpening of class distinctions within the commonalty, most obviously between prudent, respectable members of parliament and their more volatile and unpredictable constituencies. Magnate attitudes did not, as yet, leave much room for fine distinctions. Commons were common, be they great merchants or labourers. They were the subject population. Senior members might be granted the status and respect of non commissioned officers, but orders were orders and descended from above. It was not permitted for commoners to organize and lead other commoners *for their own purposes*. It was politic of the Good Parliament of 1376 to elect a knight as its spokesman, but the spokesman refused to negotiate until the whole body of the commons was allowed entry to the hall to listen to and observe the proceedings.

In 1450, when monarchy failed, the people stepped in. So it was in 1376–81. It was the as yet unwritten law:

And in the same year [1376] the man and the earles tenants of Warwick arose maliciously against the abat and the convent of Evesham and her tenants, and destroyed fircely the abbot and the town and wounded and beat her men, and slew of them many a one, and went to her manors and places and burnt and slew her wild beasts and chased them, breaking her fishpond heads, and let the water

---

[37] Linda Clark, 'Magnates and their Affinities in the Parliaments of 1386–1421', in R.H. Britnell and A.J. Pollard (ed.), *The McFarlane Legacy: Studies in Late Medieval Politics and Society* (Stroud 1995), 136–8 and 147.

out of her ponds, stews and rivers, runne out; and took the fish and bore eit with them and did them all the harm that they might. In so forferth, that forsooth they had destroyed perpetually that abbey, with all her appurtenances and members, but if the king the sooner had helpen hit and taken heed thereto. And therefore the king sent his letters to the Earl of Warwick charging and commanding him that he should stint, redress and amend the evil doers and breakers of his peace . . . '[38]

Common crowds marched through London carrying placards showing John of Gaunt's arms reversed, flaunting the legend of his illegitimate birth. After the parliamentarians had gone home and he had marshalled his retinues, Gaunt exacted a humiliating revenge. He forced the city leaders to parade to St Paul's carrying a candle marked with his arms correctly displayed. The city notables had much to lose, but the commonalty remained implacably hostile and was 'unwilling to bow to him'.[39] This is very much part of the background to many incidents directed against Lancaster in 1381, not least the burning of the Savoy, which seems to have been the most enthusiastic of all the rebels' acts of iconoclasm.

A sermon preached by Thomas Brinton, the bishop of Rochester, at the end of the third week of the parliament (18 May) 'was unusually sharp in its pointed references to the court'. He gave full representation to what had become the common view, that the king's wife or concubine, Alice Perrers, was the root of the problem. It is not difficult to imagine what people were thinking: an old king in his dotage, run by a scheming young woman and her allies, was putting the country at risk. Later in the month, perhaps as more information became available regarding the state of affairs in France, further charges were laid against seven named members of the court or their retainers, including Alice Perrers. The Black Prince died on 8 June. On 25 June the Commons assembled and 'prayed with one voice' that the Black Prince's son, Richard, be made Prince of Wales like his father.[40] This was almost certainly a response to rumours that Charles V had agreed to help Lancaster secure the succession to the throne of England after the death of Edward III by persuading the pope to declare Richard II illegitimate.[41]

4.7   Collecting the poll tax: Nottingham, 1377

All the causes of the great insurrection save the Poll-tax which precipitated it, had been operating for a long time.[42]

Poll taxes are offensive because they are unfair. The rich pay the same as the poor. The following episode shows that they also offended and

---

[38] *Brut Chronicle*, 331.   [39] Holmes, *Good Parliament*, 103–5, 192–3.
[40] *Ibid.*, 107.   [41] *Ibid.*, 5, 103–5.   [42] Oman, *The Great Revolt*, 2.

divided English communities of the late 1370s by disempowering them, removing local negotiations and politics from the business of assessment and collection. The poll tax removed the individual tax-payer's assent and word from the transaction. Custom and practice was that the state agreed a sum with every shire and community. Communities then worked out who would pay what proportion of the assessment, collecting the agreed sums themselves in a way that was conducive to the common peace. The old system taxed communities rather than individuals, individual payments being left to the community to assess and collect. The power to determine that local assessments were fair rested with the people of the community, i.e. those who were most qualified by observation and association to know if they were honest and fair. This meant that whenever a tax was imposed, communities all over England were awakened to the affairs of the kingdom, and mobilized amongst themselves. Power arrangements varied enormously within and between English localities and provinces, but taxation affected them all.

In 1377, Roger of Holme, John of Crowshaw and John of Plumtree were appointed by the king 'to levy and collect in Nottingham..., fourpence from every man and woman over fourteen years residing in the liberty'.[43] In evidence given later before the King's Bench at Westminster, Roger of Holme testified that because it was a new kind of tax, new methods of collection had proven necessary. 'In the past,' he said, 'whenever a fifteenth for the king or a loan or any taxation whatever was incurred, the mayor and the men of the town always used to take the said fifteenth taxes or loans from a common chest, in which the towns treasure always was and still is placed for the benefit and profit of the town and especially to aid the ... poor people.' Custom and practice was that assessment and collection of national taxation was sensitive to local opinion and subsumed by ongoing local government institutions and leaders. If there was to be any popular *murmuring*, this was where it began. If the distribution seemed unfair, it would register first in the localities. In the old system, the most important thing was somehow to persuade the leaders of the commonalty gathered in Parliament (at Westminster if London was quiescent or pro-government, in the provinces if not) that the payment of a tax would serve the common weal (i.e. was in their interests as well as those of the ruling class).

---

[43] Source and quotes throughout, G.O. Sayles's translation of Coram Rege Roll 465 Easter 1377, in Sayles, *Select Cases ... under Edward* III, vol. VI, 176–81. For the poll taxes, see R.B. Dobson, *The Peasants' Revolt of 1381* (London 1979), 54–7, 103–123. For an account of the opening of 'a period of experimentation which was to culminate in the three poll taxes of 1377, 1379 and 1380' see W.M. Ormrod, 'An Experiment in Taxation: the English Parish Subsidy of 1371', *Speculum* 63:1 (January 1988), 58–82.

Anticipating trouble, the mayor and his two assistant collectors held a meeting 'in the Guildhall of the said town concerning how the money could be levied to ease the community of the town [*communitatis ville*]'. Roger of Holme's party insisted the new tax should be assessed and collected in such a way as to 'help the many poor people of the town without arousing or causing murmuring and quarrelling among the community'. This was not simply a moralistic afterthought, a gesture to Christian charity, although it was certainly that too. Subsequent events would show that it deeply offended the sense of justice of at least some of those who attended the meeting and in the neighbourhoods they represented.

Two men named Richard Hanneson and John Cropwell suggested that 'in order to uphold and maintain peace and calm among their neighbours, it would be good to take the taxation of fourpence from the chest to ease the community and help the poor people', in the traditional manner. The door-to-door collection and census implied by the king's commission was bound to provide ongoing occasions for offence; every plea at every door would be in the eyes and ears of the streets and neighbourhoods. It was a recipe for disturbing the peace. Others agreed but the mayor and his officials, 'together with other their neighbours, were of the opposite opinion'. The mayor determined to follow the letter of the law, personally – and in a spirit, it seems, of righteous defiance. He led his fellow collectors with their clerks, servants and retainers along the streets of the town, knocking at every door, if necessary searching premises and demanding evidence of the ages of the older children and apprentices. To complete the tax return would require a household census anyway. The mayor and his collectors went forward house to house levying 'fifty shillings and more for the king's use from various persons in the street of lorimers and elsewhere without hindrance'. We may assume that the atmosphere was tense, but the collection went without a hitch for several hours, until the collectors and their servants arrived at the house of a master-craftsman named John Fletcher.

Every episode had a nucleus. The nucleus on this occasion was when the collectors 'asked for four pence from a lad called John Robynet, and he refused to pay on the ground that he had no money'. 'So he said', added the mayor's witness, suggesting there may have been something more to it, that Robynet's refusal was a prearranged sign for resisters to gather and offer something more than arguments. The collectors arrested him, 'whereupon John Fletcher, his master, immediately paid the four pence on John's behalf'. Robynet was not refusing payment for himself alone, however; he urged Fletcher not to pay and said to the collectors and a gathering crowd that 'it would be unjust and unreasonable for him to give as much to the aforesaid tax as a richer man ought to give to it'.

Whereupon two of the mayor's men 'harrassed John Robynet with insulting words and (one of them) drew his knife to strike him'. At this point Roger of Holme stepped in front of the mayor's men 'interfered with the said Robert of Howden, and Robert with malice aforethought and like a madman attacked Roger for this reason while he held the king's commission, and he would have struck him with the knife'. The mayor and Robert, his chief collector, had the king's authority. Roger then drew his knife for the common good, but only, he said, 'to curb [Robert's] malice and his boiling anger, without his doing any ill or harm against the peace'. Momentarily distracted from the recalcitrance of Robynet, the mayor ordered his men to arrest Roger of Holme and Robert of Howden and take them to the Guildhall cells. 'And thereupon Richard Hanneson, John Ewer, John Robinet, William of Sawley, Robert Massy, Hugh Goldsmith, John Fenell, Thomas Peyntour and John Thory' came 'with many other men of their way of thinking to the Guildhall with force of arms, and they rescued Roger and, with Roger, they laid hands on the mayor in the Guildhall, and proposed killing him with their drawn knives, and they threw him on the ground and would have slain him there if he had not been saved by some of those near him, and thus he hardly escaped from the Guildhall alive':

So Roger and those who had rescued him fled away and escaped. And similarly Richard Hanneson escaped to his house, to which the mayor, strengthened and helped by some of his neighbours, pursued him. And he attached and arrested Richard armed with a habergeon as well as John of Cropwell who was assisting Richard and preventing with force of arms for a long time his attachment and arrest. He then brought them to the Guildhall.

Richard Hanneson denied that he belonged to a conspiratorial coven which had been going from house to house in the street of the lorimers arousing the people against the new form of tax collection upon which the mayor was insisting. He claimed to have 'heard in his house from his neighbours how insults were flying between Roger of Holme and Robert of Howden'. He came to the street outside his house with the intention of restoring peace and getting his neighbours to agree to stop the insults [*verbis contumeliosis*] flying between them, but added that 'it would have been better if the money had been levied from the common chest to ease the city and to the great assistance of the poor people of the town . . . rather than that there should be such a dispute among his neighbours over the collection and payment'. This identification inflamed the mayor's bodyguards; Richard 'dared not say any more' and retreated into his house. He did not explain his involvement in the subsequent rescue of his neighbour from the Guildhall. The mayor was convinced these potentially seditious events were not accidental, but planned and 'by conspiracy hatched between them to nullify the said subsidy so far as it lay in their power and not to pay according to the terms of the commission'.

The town had divided into two parties, the mayor's, backed by 'the king's commission', and Roger of Holme's, united by custom and practice and the conviction that the commune should pay for its poorer neighbours. Witnesses took for granted that every household was armed. Following the liberation of Roger of Holme and the murderous attack upon him, the mayor gathered his forces and stormed the street of the lorimers, breaking 'down with violence the door of Richard [Hanneson]'s hall in order to arrest Richard and so to harass him'. Inside, Richard retreated to his chamber 'and put on his hauberk'. At that moment his father-in-law, John of Cropwell, arrived to mediate. He had been in church when 'rumour' [*magna murmuracione*] reached him concerning the 'great murmuring and about how the mayor and the community . . . had gone, with great malice aforethought on the part of the mayor, to the house of Richard Hanneson, who was his kinsman and the husband of Mary, the mother of John's wife, to seize and arrest him'. He arrived in time to mediate with the mayor's men confronting Richard in his parlour, persuading them to leave by swearing 'on pain of forfeiting all his tenements and goods within the said town that he would bring Richard Hanneson before the mayor to stand trial and submit to the king's law if anyone should wish to sue against him'.

Faced with serious injury, even death, Richard agreed to surrender 'to stand trial by the king's law', but only after receiving assurances 'that he should have no loss or bodily harm inflicted upon him by the mayor or the community of the town without reasonable cause'. The mayor handed him over to the bailiffs, who held him until he could be handed over to the king's Marshall. Then the mayor arrested John of Cropwell and handed *him* over to the bailiffs.

The court decided that the mayor had been acting in accordance with the king's intentions when he inaugurated his house-to-house collection. Roger of Holme and Richard Hanneson were convicted of having violently interfered with this innovation, in the name of community opinion and custom. Old, senile Edward III died during the proceedings. As the Good Parliament had insisted a year earlier, there was already a widespread sense that the country was being ruled by 'evil advisers' and unscrupulous middle men seeking to take advantage of lack of mature direction from the top. Edward's replacement by a boy-king, Richard II, an unknown quantity but the son of the popular Black Prince, left evil advisers and local opportunists in control. For this reason it is unlikely that popular resentment would attach itself to the king.

4.8   Reactionary fear and loathing: the Church and common rebels

It is reasonable to assume that local movements against poll taxes became more intent and angry as subsequent levies confirmed the government's indifference to common opinion. Poll taxes sparked uprisings in the townships of Brentwood and Fobbing, two nuclei of the 1381 rebellion in Essex.[44] They are bound to have stirred trouble in many places: the Brentwood and Fobbing incidents are documented. National poll taxes made many local 'demands', as Laclau puts it, 'equivalential'. Fires were lit in communities all over England. In many districts of Kent and Essex men (women do not seem to have been conscripted in 1381) moved off along paths, roads and highways connecting villages with market and provincial towns. How did they know Blackheath was the place to head for? It was the place where the spectre of the commonalty was realized and all the discontentments acquired a single explanation – misrule, evil government by evil governors – and a cause, the commonweal.

The horror inspired by the 1381 rebellion is evident in the torrent of emotional phrases that came into elite chroniclers' minds when they tried to name the collective beast that had spilled into the streets of towns, mustered on village greens, gathered into companies and converged on London from Kent and East Anglia in the summer of 1381. The chronicler of Westminster abbey began his account with *maxima multitudo ruralium Essexie pariter et cancei* ('very large numbers of peasants of Essex and Kent'), but his account then becomes a veritable riot of terminology: the rebels are *societas totum* ('peasants'), *rustica manus* ('yokels'), *turbulenta et tumultuosa turba ruralium* ('riotous and disorderly mob of peasants'), *villanis* (serfs), *rusticorum aggressionibus* (peasant mob), *communes* (London's lower orders), *civium equitatu* ('citizens'). In one incident a man is *duce villane turbe* ('leader of the servile mob') but *Waltero Tegulatore duce prefate multitudines [est]* ('Wat Tyler [is] the leader of the crowd'). The whole lot are *rebelles* ('insurgents'), John Ball is guilty of preaching to the *vulgum* ('masses'), and *plebum* ('populace'), and the whole is in pursuit of

[44] Dobson, *Peasants' Revolt*, 123–4.

what was all but inconceivable to the chronicler of a wealthy abbey that was already notorious for its refusal to acknowledge that demographic and economic conditions on its manors had changed: *rusticorum libertate* ('peasants' freedom'). When Tyler was struck down, *horruit vulgus videre* ('the populace shuddered at the spectacle').[45] The chroniclers of 1381 had a vocabulary for discoursing on the role of the many-headed monster of public opinion in the constitutional field of force but it was in the wrong language. Within fifty years it would be replaced by the discourse of the common weal, the vernacular political tradition. First Norman French, then, more slowly, Latin began to retreat. The discourse and rhetoric of 'the hysterical sublime', James Holstun's phrase for an institutionalized reactionary class rhetoric combining fear, contempt and horror at demonstrations of mass, populist power, was acquiring a new urgency.[46]

Another monk, Henry Knighton, named the rebel pretext – the common weal (*communis utilitatis*) – but left it clear that such a noble ideal could not be served by the *plebs ista nephanda* ('wicked commons'), *populares* ('commons'), *communes* (twice), *nephanda plebe* ('wicked commons'), *servi diaboli* ('servants of Satan'), *stulte multitudini* ('foolish multitude'). *In Essex, Southfolc, and Northfolk similiter surrexerunt communes in quibusdam locis* ('In Essex, Suffolk and Norfolk likewise the commons rose in many places'). At Peterborough the abbey was attacked by *compatriote et tenantes abbates* ('the abbot's neighbours and tenants'). At Julian's Norwich the rebellious commonalty were *malefactores* ('evil doers'), and, more neutrally, *apud Sancta Albanus communes de villa et multa a finibus* ('commons of the town and many from the neighbourhood'). Knighton's account disclosed another common 'discontentment', hatred for John of Gaunt, suspected of having ambitions for the throne. As the insurrection gathered, Lancaster was told that London was threatened by *due turme nephandorum luporum*, 'two packs of wicked wolves [of ten thousand men], one on the east and one on the west of the kingdom'. They burned down his palace on the Strand. Finally came the moral lesson of the whole horrible episode: *asperium nichil humili cum surgit in altum*: 'none is harsher than the lowly man when he is raised'.[47] The 'many-headed monster' orthodoxy was easier for monks than acknowledging the

---

[45] The Westminster Chronicle 1381–1394, trans. and ed. L.C. Hector and Barbara F. Harvey (Oxford 1982), 3, 4–5, 6–7, 7–8, 10–11, 12–13.

[46] James Holstun, 'Utopia Pre-Empted: Kett's Rebellion, Commoning and the Hysterical Sublime', *Historical Materialism* 16 (2008), 3–53.

[47] *Knighton's Chronicle 1337–1396* ed. and trans. G.H. Martin (Oxford 1995), 208–9, 210–11, 212–13, 214–15, 221–2, 224–5, 226–7, 230–1, 232–3.

universal themes, among which was hatred of rich abbeys, and monks who were thought to put their skills at the service of the exploitation, not the betterment, of the people.

Precise anatomy of the popular army has remained elusive. Thanks most recently to the efforts of Andrew Prescott, scholars are now aware of a still virtually unexplored archive of cases and traces arising from the repression that followed when all the rebels not dead or in prison went home to their villages and towns.[48] L.R. Poos's exemplary reconstitution of one of the epicentres in Essex (not far from Richard of Fulham's operational context in Hertfordshire), considerably 'thickens' our pictures of the social roots of rebellion. There is more to be learned, more research to be done. One lesson to be learned from social historians of sixteenth to eighteenth-century England is that local, district and provincial studies tend to complicate rather than simplify older generalities and theories. They leave unanswered the oldest question of all concerning the Commons Rebellion of 1381, the question that vexed the monastic chroniclers and that would fascinate and horrify the ruling classes of England from 1381 to the 1640s. Everyone knew by 1381 that somewhere in England a crowd was forming to discuss the latest tax, wages, rents, greedy abbots and bishops, the price of provisions, stories of corruption in high places, rumours that the king was dead or under the dominion of evil counsellors. We have seen how easily and how often links were made between local and national corruptions. Those responsible, locally and nationally, were working for selfish, profane profit, not for the *commune wele*. To explain how all the local causes, demands and mixes of motives came together, as rebellions of entire provinces threatened to link up into a massive national army, and to overthrow all distinctions of rank and class between the people and the king: how they came together, that was the question then and it remains so today. The unexplained miracle was how, in the dispersed landscape of agrarian England, common people mobilized as armies converging on London and Westminster. The commonalty was not supposed to be capable of articulating itself without officers executing orders issuing from the king and his counsellors. What made all the different demands equivalent was

---

[48] Andrew Prescott, 'Writing about Rebellion: Using the Records of the Peasants' Revolt of 1381', *History Workshop Journal* 45 (Spring 1998), 1–28; while working as an archivist at the Public Records Office, Dr Prescott undertook a 'comprehensive review of judicial records relating to the rising, and quickly found that the material already in print represented no more than the tip of the iceberg'. In this and subsequent work on the judicial records, Prescott has shown that the judicial records are susceptible to the same intense treatment as scholars like Stephen Justice apply to the literary source.

a common enemy – a corrupt state – and, above all, a common cause: the *commune wele*, the 'wellness' of the whole community, especially its poorest members. After 1381 'commonweal' became the slogan and the cause of popular rebellions: so much so that by 1549 popular rebels were called 'commonwealths'. How that came to be the case is the subject of Chapter 5.

5   The spectre of commonalty: popular rebellion and the commonweal, 1381–1549

Whan the comuynes began to ryse,
Was non so gret lord, as I gesse,
That thei in hert bigon to gryse,
And leide heore jolite in presse,
Wher was thenne heore worthinesse,
Of alle wyse men I take witnesse,
This was a warnynge to be ware.
            ('On the Earthquake of 1382',
            anon., c.1400)

It is a purpos'd thing, and grows by plot,
To curb the will of the nobility.
            (Shakespeare, *Coriolanus* III, i)

Haunting belongs to the structure of every hegemony.
            (*Jacques Derrida*[1])

5.1   *Res plebeia*

Debate on the meaning and significance of commonweal/th jargon has focused on the coming into existence of a literature that burst onto the public stage from the third to the fifth decades of the sixteenth century. It took the form of a body of texts which discussed and expanded upon the idea, and partook to some degree of the populist program of Protector Somerset.[2] An elitist, classical-humanist ('Renaissance') provenance has usually been assumed. Steve Hindle describes 'commonwealth' as 'a

---

[1] Jacques Derrida, *Specters of Marx*, trans. Peggy Kamuf (New York and London 1994), 37.
[2] Whitney R.D. Jones, *The Tudor Commonwealth 1529–1559: a Study of the Impact of the Social and Economic Developments of Mid-Tudor England upon Contemporary Concepts of the Nature and Duties of the Commonwealth* (London 1970); Ethan Shagen, 'Protector Somerset and the 1549 Rebellions: New Sources and New Perspectives', *English Historical Review* 144 (1999), 34–63; Diarmaid MacCulloch, *Tudor Church Militant: Edward VI and the Protestant Reformation* (London 1999), 44–5.

236

term derived from classical republicanism and mediated through Christian humanism'.[3] Diarmaid MacCulloch writes that 'talk of commonwealth had been pioneered by Thomas Cromwell's circle in the 1530s and not until Edward VI's reign' do we find 'it had spread down the social scale, and had become the property of humble people who were excited by it and yearned for justice and fairness in society'.[4] This chapter argues that the top-down or 'clerical authority' provenance of 'commonweal' is wrong.[5] The vernacular commonweal tradition outlined here was popular, populist and vernacular. English humanists like More, Elyot, Tyndale, Thomas Starkey and Sir Thomas Smith belong, I suggest, to a *second* and quite distinctive phase of a public discourse centred on the word 'commonweal'. That second phase only makes full sense in the light of what it had meant before state officials, humanists and printers got hold of it. For over a century before the concept was taken up by the remarkable generation of vernacular intellectuals active between 1520 and 1580, 'commonweal' was intimately associated with commons rebellions.

This chapter will show that in the absence of the tradition of popular rebellion inaugurated in 1381, and the accumulating populist associations of the 'commonweal' words, the populist strategy of Protector Somerset in the 1540s, and the Revolution of the 1640s, would have been inconceivable.[6] The structural condition for alliances between elite statesmen and populist 'commonwealths', a growing theme of fifteenth- and sixteenth-century English politics, was born in 1381. This was a more positive response than the horrified observation of the potency (and imputed irrationality) of popular rebellion registered by establishment chroniclers of 1381. They and their successors expressed equally dire warnings against Henry of Lancaster's populism during the coup of 1399–1400; the strategy and the fears surfaced again in the wake of Cade's rebellion, in the 1450s. Arguably, the ideological condition for the strategy originated in the 'convention' that had emerged, willy-nilly, in the months after the deposition of Edward II in 1327: namely, that for the removal of an anointed king to be legitimate, the whole community *including the commons*, had to agree that he was a tyrant. That

---

[3] Steve Hindle, *The State and Social Conflict in Early Modern England* (Basingstoke 2000), 55.

[4] Diarmaid MacCulloch, *Thomas Cranmer: a Life* (New Haven 1996), 432; however, in *Reformation: Europe's House Divided 1490–1700* (London 2004), 43–52, MacCulloch uses the term to denote the agency of vernacular, secular communities, against unpopular representatives of the universal Church.

[5] For the 'clerical authority model', see J.G.A. Pocock, 'The Concept of a Language and the *métier d'historien*: Some Considerations on Practice', in Anthony Pagden (ed.), *The Language of Political Theory in Early-Modern Europe* (Cambridge 1987), 19–40.

[6] For discussion and references to Somerset's 'strategy', see below, 283.

'convention' would have gone nowhere if it had not been ingrained by repeated conjunctures of popular resistance and rebellion and crises of state. Leaving aside rebels' motives and intentions (which raise other issues), the repeated *fact* of popular rebellion decisively affected the field of force of national politics between 1381 and 1549. The implication is that popular rebels must be given a prominent place as agents of a collective *longue duree* with accumulating consequences for English polity and constitutional culture. From 1381 to 1549 popular rebels acted, elite statesmen and counsellors reacted.

The provenance of 'commonweal' usages set out in this chapter also argues against the theory – it is virtually a precept of intellectual history – that political languages, ideas and discourses always begin in circles of the learned and, more generally, with the formally educated classes. It will be shown that 'commonweal' was the reflexive slogan of every popular rebellion from 1381 to the 1640s. The old idea that it was not until the 1530s that the use of commonweal discourse was pioneered in elite circles has been revised.[7] The word commonweal had been part of elite political thought since at least 1450, when it was attributed to Cade's rebels. I will suggest that Cade's men consciously used the slogan or keyword introduced into political discourse by the rebels of 1381. Far from trickling down from the usages of the learned, the great fear of some of the more profound conservative writers of the age was that plebeian usages were defying hierarchical gravity and trickling *up* from the usages of 'humble people'.

---

[7] J.G. Nichols (ed.), *The Boke of Noblesse Addressed to King Edward the Fourth . . . in 1475* (New York 1975), uses 'common profit' three times, 'comon wele' twice, and cites Cicero to the effect that *Res Publica est res populi, res patriae, res communis*; Paul Slack, *From Reformation to Improvement: Public Welfare in Early Modern England* (Oxford 1999), 6–7, notes that 'commonwealth' usages occur 'in Tudor legislation, notably on enclosure in 1489, and in proclamations from 1490, including a clutch of six, between 1514 and 1516'; *State Papers Domestic*, 10 September 1549 records that the country 'is apprehensive of the new party called commonwealths men' (popular rebels) thought to be favoured by Protector Somerset; G.R. Elton, 'Reform and the "Commonwealth-Men" of Edward VI's Reign', in P. Clark, A.G.R. Smith and Nicholas Tyacke (ed.), *The English Commonwealth 1547–1640: Essays Presented to Joel Hurstfield* (Leicester 1979), 23–38, rejected the idea that this literature represented a Party, 'the Commonwealth-Men'; J.A. Guy, 'The Tudor Commonwealth: Revising Thomas Cromwell', *The Historical Journal* 23: 3 (1980), 681–7; David Starkey, 'Which Age of Reform?', in C. Coleman and David Starkey (ed.), *Revolution Reassessed: Revisions in the History of Tudor Government and Administration* (Oxford 1986), traces the idea back to the crisis of 1459; Whitney R.D. Jones, *The Tudor Commonwealth*, is the best general account; for contrasting uses of the learned and literary discourse of the Common Weal; cf. Thomas Starkey, *A Dialogue between Pole and Lupset* (c.1530), ed. T.F. Mayer (London 1989); Robert Crowley, *An Information Against the Oppressors of the Poor Commons* (London 1548, facs. ed. Amsterdam 1979); John Cheke, *The Hurt of Sedicion howe greveous it is to a Commune welthe* (1549, facs. ed. Menston 1971).

Thomas Elyot made the meaning of 'common-weale' the first, urgent, topic of his highly influential *Book of the Governor*, published in 1531. Elyot was in no doubt that 'common weale' was popular in origin and potentially subversive of conventional hierarchy. Learned English counsellors, he wrote, 'have been long abused in calling *Rempublica* a common weale'.[8] A careful linguist, Elyot did not write 'are becoming abused', but that the English 'have been *long* abused.' He had no objection to *weale*, regarding it as an accurate translation of *Res*, which 'signifieth estate, condition, substance and profit'. Elyot was too specific about the popular associations of 'weal', but he saw no problem here, for 'in our old vulgar, profit is called weale'. Elyot was right about this. 'Weale' was the popular word; 'profit' was the word used by fourteenth-century poets, translators and scribes; 'common *weal*' only began to succeed 'common *profit*' between 1381 and 1450. Elyot was more worried about the translation of *publica*. '*Publike* took his beginning of people', he wrote: 'which in Latin is *populus*: in which word is contained all the inhabitants of a realme or city, of which estate or condition so ever they be'. *Publike* allowed for degrees of people, so the correct translation of *Respublica* was '*publike weale*'.

In Elyot's strict derivation, 'public' had the neutrality of the modern word 'population'. It meant the whole body of the people and was thus capable of incorporating the infinite hierarchy of degrees. 'Common' had no such neutrality, Elyot warned. In Latin it referred to the 'commune', the whole body of the people whatever constitutional form it took. This, however, was not the case in England, where 'common' had come to mean that class of people the Romans had called the *plebs*, which is, 'the base and vulgar inhabitants, not advanced to any honour or dignity'. Elyot 'prove[d] that Plebs in Latin is in English *commonaltie*' with references to usage. In London and other English boroughs 'they that be none aldermen, or sheriffs, be called communers: and in the country at a session, or other assembly, if no gentlemen be there, the saying is, that there was none but the commonalty'. *Common weal* meant either 'the commoners only must be wealthy, and the gentlemen and nobles needy, or else excluding gentility, all men must be of one degree and sort, and a new name provided'. What was that new name? *Common weal* was now so

---

[8] The quotations in this paragraph are from *Thomas Elyot's "The Governor": electronic edition*, pp. A1r, A1v, A2r. C.S. Lewis, *English Literature in the Sixteenth Century* (Oxford 1954), 274, wrote that Elyot 'borrows from Patricius the point that *res publica* means not "common" but "public" weal. But in Patricius this had been not much more than a philological note; in Elyot *it is the starting point for a refutation of egalitarianism and a glowing eulogy of degree* which anticipates, as so many authors have done, the speech of Shakespeare's Ulysses' (emphasis added).

common in statutes and the discourse of state as to be becoming something of a cliché. It actually meant *Res Plebeia*.[9]

We have seen that the vernacularization of political discourse feared by Elyot had taken place and that the process was not neutral.[10] Vernacular English carried ideas and connotations that 'the wisest', learned men steeped in the great writings and debates in Latin, Greek and even Hebrew, were unaware of, or thought they had refuted. Elyot may not have exaggerated the role of 'commune-ist' ideas. He would have read the most notorious vernacular radical of his generation, William Tyndale, with deep disapproval. 'Felyng fayth', the core of Tyndale's theology, suffused the faithful with love. 'Among Christian men, love maketh all things common', Tyndale affirmed. 'Every man is other's debtor, and every man is bound to minister to his neighbour, and to supply his neighbour's lack of that wherewith God hath endued him.' Tyndale's 'commonwealth of Christ' was communist. 'Commonweal', or as Tyndale was perhaps the first to spell it, 'common-wealth', was for Elyot and before him, as we shall see, for the seminal English constitutional writer, Sir John Fortescue, potentially the most subversive word around.[11]

5.2   The spectre of the commonalty

Usages of 'commons' and 'commonalty' to denote the 'third estate', *laboriaris*, 'those who work', were central to political and constitutional discourse in England from the Commons Rebellion of 1381 to the Civil Wars of the 1640s. Their emergence was part of a discourse of the commonweal that gave prominence to the constitutional and (after 1549) economic roles of the commonalty. The new social history of politics places popular voices and words above, or alongside, educated and classical ('Renaissance', 'classical humanist') accounts of the formation of the constitutional cultures of early modern England and suggests the existence of accumulative causal links between actual social struggles and the development of languages of politics. Studies of popular politics in late medieval and early modern Europe see dramatic episodes of resistance and rebellion as expressions of deep-seated political cultures and attitudes that otherwise left few traces in the archives. 'Without 1381

---

[9] 'And consequently there may appere lyke diversitie to be englisshe, between a publike weale and a commune weale, as shulde be in Latin betwene Res publica and Res plebeia.' *Ibid.*; Elyot also defines *publike weale* in *The Bankette of Sapience* (1534), Lillian Gottesman (ed.), *Four Political Treatises by Sir Thomas Elyot* (Gainesville, Fla. 1967), 186–7.

[10] Francis Bacon, *The Advancement of Learning*, ed. G.W. Kitchin, (London 1915), 134.

[11] Tyndale, *Parable of Wicked Mammon* (1528), BL.

and 1549 in England, or 1525 in Germany,' writes Patrick Collinson, 'we might never have suspected that there was a political culture at relatively submerged levels, well below the apexes of lordship and monarchy.' In truth, traditional historians overlooked popular politics because convention regarded them as a contradiction in terms. Social historians have shown that the search for popular politics does not rely on the analysis of large-scale rebellions. As we have seen, there is no need to privilege especially dramatic moments when the politics of the people broke into the elite chronicles. Popular politics become visible when historians ask new questions of previously neglected or narrowly read sources.[12]

Commonalty, a member of the family of English words that developed as a synthesis of Germanic *gemaen* and Latin-French *commune*, requires us to reconstitute these submerged levels, or 'outer circles' of late medieval and early modern governance. Popular movements must always be seen in relation to the more comprehensively studied levels described by Stubbs as the inner 'circles around the throne'. Classes and groups are always defined in relation to other classes and groups. During the fourteenth century, commonalty usages increasingly connoted the class of households that were not incorporated in the governing ranks. The increasing confidence of the House of Commons in affairs of state was an institutional symptom of a larger vernacular movement. It was a movement that reached more deeply into the lower ranks than the prejudices of the ruling classes bargained for. Another obvious symptom or effect of the rise of the commonalty in this third estate sense

---

[12] Patrick Collinson, *De Republica Anglorum; Or, History with the Politics Put Back* (Cambridge 1990), 15–16; William Stubbs, *The Constitutional History of England* (1897; repr. New York 1967), 1: 371; most of the new work has focused on the period after 1550: for a selection, see K.E. Wrightson, 'The Politics of the Parish in Early Modern England,' in P. Griffiths, A. Fox and S. Hindle (ed.), *The Experience of Authority in Early Modern England* (Basingstoke 1996), 10–46; all the essays in Tim Harris (ed.), *The Politics of the Excluded, c.1500–1850* (Basingstoke 2001); Andy Wood, *Riot, Rebellion and Popular Politics in Early Modern England* (Basingstoke 2002); Wood, *The 1549 Rebellions and the Making of Early Modern England* (Cambridge 2007); Wood, 'Subordination, Solidarity and the Limits of Popular Agency in a Yorkshire Valley c.1596–1615', *Past and Present* 193 (November 2006), 41–72; Wood, 'Fear, Hatred and the Hidden Injuries of Class in Early Modern England', *Journal of Social History* 39:3 (Spring 2006), 803–26; Steve Hindle, 'The Shaming of Margaret Knowsley: Gossip, Gender and the Experience of Authority in Early Modern England', *Continuity and Change* 9 (1994), 391–419; Hindle, *On the Parish? The Micro-Politics of Poor Relief in Rural England, c.1550–1750* (Oxford 2004); M.J. Braddick and J. Walter (ed.), *Negotiating Power in Early Modern Society: Order, Hierarchy and Subordination in Britain and Ireland* (Cambridge 2001); Adam Fox, *Oral and Literate Culture in England, 1500–1700* (Oxford 2000); John Walter, *Understanding Popular Violence in the English Revolution: the Colchester Plunderers* (Cambridge 1999).

was a corresponding increase in the prestige and literary use of vernacular English, the language of the subject population of Norman-Angevin England, as the language of public opinion.

The institutionalization, in the fourteenth century, of Sir Thomas Smith's first and second 'sorts of men', the peers and knights, was a factor in raising the question of what to call the rest. Knights and gentlemen sat at Westminster with the Commons, not the Lords, but were acknowledged members of the ruling class. The Commons Rebellion of 1381 revived abiding questions about the constitutional functions of the 'third sort', the '*yemani*' and '*cives*'. Between the twelfth and fifteenth centuries English social thought acquired a more graduated and complex model of the lower ranks. The rise of the House of Commons had, by 1376, expanded and formalized the ranks of the citizens to encompass the burgesses of every English borough. Urban citizens were joined, from 1381 to 1450, by a more formal conception of the legendary yeoman. This rural equivalent of the urban citizen was not at first seen primarily in terms of his role as a freeholding voter in shire and borough juries or parliamentary elections. Fifteenth-century writers were much more likely to envisage the yeoman in military terms. The best representation of him is a larger than life image, with stave and longbow, carved on a tomb in Newland parish church in Gloucestershire.[13] Like Smith's third sort, the fifteenth-century yeoman straddled 'the social boundary between gentleman and commoner'.[14]

Absent from John of Salisbury's anatomy, the yeoman makes an early appearance in vernacular literature in 'The Descryuying of Mannes

---

[13] Personal observation; for another impressive yeoman memorial, see the tombs of the two William Jervises (d.1597 and 1614) at All Saints Church, Peatling Magna, Leics. For Peatling Magna, see above, Chapter 2.6.

[14] On institutionalization of the first and second sorts, see P.R. Coss, 'The Formation of the English Gentry', *Past and Present* 147 (May 1995), 38–64; Coss, *The Origins of the English Gentry* (Cambridge 2003), which show that the basic categories and patterns were in place by the mid- to late fourteenth century, though, as Nigel Saul shows, the minor gentry of some regions were still intensely insecure and often pursued the good of their own households, families and retainers with violence – and got away with it: Saul, *Knights and Esquires: the Gloucestershire Gentry in the Fourteenth Century* (Oxford 1981), esp. 170–7. For knights, see above, Chapters 1–2 and Kemp Knight (ed.), *Wimbledon's Sermon*, 63; George Holmes, *The Good Parliament* (Oxford 1975). The institutionalization of 'all English free men', including knights, is described in Ralph V. Turner, *Magna Carta Through the Ages* (London 2003), 75. For the *yemani* and *cives* usages, see Thomas Wilson, *The State of England Anno Domini 1600*, ed. F.J. Fisher (London 1936), 17–21. Wilson makes a distinction between 'our great yeomen' of old and 'yeoman of meaner ability', locating the latter as part of the 'Cominalty' (19). For the emergence of the yeoman, see Richard Almond and A.J. Pollard, 'The Yeomanry of Robin Hood and Social Terminology in Fifteenth-Century England', *Past and Present* 170 (February 2001), 75.

Membres', a remarkable poem composed around 1400. Here the 'Yemen that byfore gon / with bent bowes and bryt brondes (swords)' constituted the 'fyngres' of the body politic. The yeoman was a synthesis of the soldier and the secular official – the definitive member of John of Salisbury's 'armed hand' – and is counted a member of the upper, not the lower part of the body. The economic basis of his status – freehold land and/or capital in the form of farming skills and equipment – was not yet prominent, as it would be in the more economically minded sixteenth to eighteenth centuries. The aspects of his estate that defined him as common, his working life and economic base, were suppressed in favour of the sides that defined him as a leader. In 'Mannes Membres' he was connected to the hands (squires), the arms (knights), and the shoulders and backbone (lords of the realm). The yeoman was thus first conceived as the hands-on member of the second estate, shaping, ordering and organizing the lower part or 'fourth sort'. When sixteenth-century writers like William Harrison, Thomas Wilson and John Smyth of Nibley observed that the yeomen and citizens had betrayed their prescribed constitutional role, they meant that yeomen were no longer unquestioningly loyal and deferential to the part of the body politic to which, as the fingers, they had once been firmly connected.[15]

If the economic side of the yet to be named yeoman was anywhere in John of Salisbury's version it was as a component of the feet, which encompassed 'the peasants who always stick to the land . . . [and perform] many types of weaving and the mechanical arts . . . and also the servile forms of obedience'. Between the Commons Rebellion of 1381 and Jack Cade's Rebellion in 1450, an effort was made to incorporate the leaders of the localities as the most junior members of the second estate and as tools and instruments of the magnates, lesser barons, knights and gentlemen. They were accorded 'privileged access to the otherwise exclusive gentle code of honesty, and entitled to wear and provide the array of the aristocratic hunter'.[16] They were also armed and proud of their

---

[15] 'The Descryuing of Mannes Membres', in J. Kail (ed.), *Twenty-Six Political Poems from the Oxford Mss Digby 102 and Douce 322* (London 1904), 64–8. 'Many [yeomen] are able and do buy the lands of unthrifty gentlemen': William Harrison, *The Description of England*, ed. George Edelen (New York 1968), 64–8; the rising status, wealth and influence of the yeomen and citizens 'was no matter invented and sett downe by authority for the bettering of that state of the people, but rather by the subtlety of them and the simplicity of gentlemen': Wilson, *State of England*, 38–9; for John Smyth of Nibley's invaluable anatomy of the historical provenance and power of the yeomanry of the Vale of Berkeley, see John McLean (ed.), *The Berkeley Mss* 2: 36–7 and the entirety of Vol. 3: discussed in Rollison, *The Local Origins of Modern Society: Gloucestershire 1500–1800* (London and New York 1992), 258–60.

[16] John of Salisbury, *Policraticus*, 125–6; in John's version, of course, the hands were 'officials and soldiers'; Almond and Pollard, 'The Yeomanry of Robin Hood', 75.

independence. The problematical loyalty of yeomen and citizens, and their relations with the lower, broadly landless majority of the commonalty, was to be an intensifying area of interest to writers on the constitution of England from 1381 until the Putney Debates and beyond.

In the post-1381 model vocations hitherto considered common had colonized the whole of the lower part of the body. The thighs were merchants and the legs were 'all craftes that worche with handes'.[17] The commonalty had come to encompass a much larger part of the body politic than in John of Salisbury's model; the rank that was officially responsible for governing it came to be defined and institutionalized as the yeoman. As in Jeffersonian models of revolutionary America, the local and military contexts were crucial. Yeomen, stereotypically and often actually, were trained soldiers, responsible for keeping the peace, guarding and accounting for the community treasuries, assessing and collecting local and national taxes and rents, governing the parish and manor, organizing musters, and serving on local, hundred and even shire juries. In view of the military priority of constitutional thought, the closest modern analogy is to a non-commissioned officer whose brief covered economy, law, policing, religious administration and, in fact, every imaginable dimension of local and district life.

It is helpful to visualize the emerging constitutional culture to which these changes contributed as a variable 'field of force'. Viewing local politics from within and below, Andy Wood suggests that 'middling sort', with its connotations of property holding and localized wealth, is too narrow to encompass a class that tended to run the affairs of every English locality. In the Derbyshire Peak Country, he points out, the leaders of the commonalty were 'adult, male, settled, skilled and independent' but not necessarily property-owners or 'yeomen' and not necessarily conscious of being a third sort as distinct from the fourth sort of mining households that formed the greater part of the district's population. Wood's definition is less exclusive than freeman, freeholder, yeoman or citizen, more specific than middle rank or sort and acknowledges the profoundly patriarchal prejudice of the culture. Independency was a much admired quality throughout the long early modern period, as was another theme: the repeated tendency of localities to use national political crises for their own purposes. The military dimension is unmistakeable. Sir John Fortescue's observation that every military success enjoyed by English armies in the fourteenth and fifteenth centuries rested, proverbially, on its bowmen, who 'be no ryche men', was the first explicit statement that the

---

[17] Kail (ed.), 'Descryuing of Mannes Membres', 65.

centre of gravity of English constitutional culture was shifting towards this extremely heterogeneous middle rank.[18]

Wealth and property were common but not necessary qualifications for local leadership. Local leaders were settled, skilled in weapons of peace and war and brought up their sons to be the same; most importantly, they were trusted by their communities (or not, as the case might be) on the basis of association and experience. Property was not necessary if the community or district regarded them as worthy men. Wood's definition emphasizes agency and leadership in localities. He also tries to see the field of force through the eyes of the fourth sort, Smith's *proletarii*. From this perspective possession of property and voting rights in parliamentary elections were useful but not necessary conditions for leadership. Lack of such rights would technically exclude the leaders of proto-industrial districts that, as we shall see in the next chapter, were very prominent in the tradition of resistance and rebellion. As 'fourth sort' it would leave them out of the constitutional field of force. Yet even Smith hesitated to exclude them. Were men of the fourth sort not routinely involved in com-munity management – as constables and tithingmen? We shall encounter another form of agency practised by the fourth sort: it came to be the conventional wisdom that the great popular rebellions of the fourteenth to seventeenth centuries fomented, not among local oligarchies of the third sort, but among the assorted *proletarii*. Rebellion literally reversed the prescribed order of things.

The growing agency and independency of a complex commonalty that could be divided into two sorts became a prominent theme of sixteenth-century condition of England literature. The commonalty was scattered across all English localities, densely interconnected by *trafike*, conscious of its role in local and national government and potentially capable of autonomous military organization. With the Armada scare of 1588 still prominent in his mind, Thomas Wilson emphasized that the strategic function of the *yemani* and *cives* was to stay at home to defend the ter-ritory should the conventional aggressive strategy (foreign wars) fail.[19] The best line of defence, as in Fortescue's influential evaluation, was the last. Militarily and in other ways, the constitutional orientation of local communities was defensive. 'The fourth sort of men which doe not rule'

---

[18] E.P. Thompson, 'The Patricians and the Plebs', in *Customs in Common* (London 1993), 73; Andy Wood, *The Politics of Social Conflict: the Peak Country 1520–1770* (Cambridge 1999), 260; John Fortescue, *The Governance of England: Otherwise called the difference between an Absolute and Limited Monarchy*, ed. Charles Plummer (1885; repr. London 1926), Chapter 12, 137.

[19] Wilson's anatomy of the English body politic is the subject of Chapter 9.1.

were mustered and nominated to fight, whereas the third sort ran the country and kept their bows and staves at hand should it ever be necessary to defend it. That was Wilson's ideal, but in truth, he wrote, the *yemani* and *cives* were too independent and had assumed constitutional functions that were neither for the common good (which also encompassed the formal ruling classes and the court) nor prescribed by formal tradition. They were still the leaders and organisers of their communities, yet they no longer followed their supposed masters, the nobles and gentry. This myth of a middle rank with constitutional teeth emerged in the fourteenth century, perhaps earlier if the distinction between *liberi homines* and the unfree is regarded as equivalent. It was an abiding feature of constitutional discourse from Fortescue to the Civil Wars, when John Corbet formulated his justly famous analysis of the class dynamics of the English Revolution.[20]

'Commonalty' was being used to describe the working classes of England by the second half of the fourteenth century. Jacques Derrida's representation of class as a spectre captures how class language works most of the time, and how it worked in late medieval and early modern England. It refers to a variable *imaginaire* that draws a multitude of differences and places into a homogeneous body. As is the case with modern nations, the people of early modern England never saw all the commons gathered from all the communities into one crowd in a single, visibly encompassed landscape, 'a feir feld ful of folk', as Langland pictured it.[21] They never saw all the gentry or all the barons and earls together, just as they never encompassed in one experience the whole of what was denoted and connoted by the word 'Church'. Only rarely, but decisively, did the commonalty (or *comuynes*), like the barons at Runnymede in the thirteenth century, manifest itself in a way that could be directly observed and experienced. To recapture the constitutional culture and the agency within it of the plebeian public sphere, one must imagine the *comuynes* as they appeared in the greatest rebellions, as the young Richard II saw them at Blackheath in 1381, as Henry VI heard them described in the summer of 1450, as Robert Aske encountered them in Lincolnshire in 1536, or as the earl of Warwick saw them arrayed on Mousehold Heath and at Norwich in 1549: as an army of redressers acting autonomously,

---

[20] John Corbet, *An Historicall Relation of the Military Government of Gloucester* (London 1645); Brian Manning, *The English People and the Revolution, 1640–1649* (London 1976); Rollison, *Local Origins*, Chapter 6; below, Chapter 9.6.

[21] Derrida, *Specters of Marx*. The full quotation from Langland is: 'A Feir feld ful of folk fond I ther bi-twene,/ of alle maner of men the mene and the riche,/ Worchinge and wondringe as the world asketh': *The Vision of William Concerning Piers Plowman* (1867; repr. Cambridge 1992), 2, lines 17–19.

without noble officers or a kingly general. Among them could be observed not only a multitude of men arrayed in platoons with staves and pitchforks, but also a bristling of bowmen, yeomen sergeants-major, some on horseback, a liberal sprinkling of non-commissioned officers, and even a gentleman or two. Like all enduring legends and collective memories, the spectre of the commonalty had its roots in remembered and reported, or misremembered and misreported, discourse-defying events.

5.3 'If the end be wele than all is wele': birth of a common keyword

Whan any Rysyng hath byn made in this Land, before these days, the porest Men thereof hath byn the grettest Causers and Doars thereyn. (Sir John Fortescue)

'Common weal' displaced the Norman-French borrowing 'common profit' as a keyword of English vernacular politics in the fifteenth century, as Sir Thomas Elyot implied.[22] The question arising is whether this linguistic change had the substantive meaning Elyot saw in it. The general answer is that it was associated with the most obvious novelty of the constitutional field of force of fourteenth- and fifteenth-century England: a turbulent, insurgent commonalty. Elyot assumed that the 'commune' words were, by the third decade of the sixteenth century, exclusively associated with the third estate. It will now be suggested that as well as being a cause, the linguistic process described by Elyot was also an accumulative effect of the fact that every rebellion from 1381 onwards that could remotely be called 'popular' (and, indeed, every other rebellion) had risen in the name of the common weal. The word is a clue to a very real social movement.

As a rule, as the predominant usages imply, what we call politics were communal, restricted to communities defined by routine association and sharing of information. Government was only noticed when it affected the communities directly and intrusively – or negatively, in its failure, say, to defend the coast against raiders. This pattern was built into English constitutional culture in the fourteenth century and was passed on to English plantations of the seventeenth. In England in the 1630s, in Virginia in 1676, the thirteen colonies a century later, and in the sixteen states two decades after that, taxes always stirred popular feelings against governments in general, and, most dangerous of all, against the government

---

[22] French 'commune profit' is the written formula throughout the fourteenth century: see above, Chapter 2, n. 76; 'commun(e) wele' is not recorded until 1446: Kurath (ed.), *Middle English Dictionary* (Ann Arbor, Mich. 1959).

of the day.[23] Especially intense was the tradition of hostility to poll-taxes like those of colonial Virginia. This is a constant of vernacular English politics from the clumsy efforts that sharpened the teeth of the rebellion of 1381 to the mass protests against Margaret Thatcher's local poll tax. Also paradigmatic, except in the later 1640s, was an aversion to blaming the king.[24]

1327 and 1376 had shown that queens were always susceptible, especially if they were foreign. But the fiercest resentment was always against 'evil counsellors', represented as sticky-fingered opportunists (sometimes, as in the aftermath of 1327 and in 1376, a 'scarlet woman') taking advantage of a king who was, for a variety of reasons, too weak (or in the Virginian case, too far away) to insist on the highest standards of probity and justice. Bacon the Virginian rebel followed ancient precedents in positing the existence of a circle of 'wicked and pernicious counsellors' exploiting the commonalty for their own selfish ends and deceiving the occupant of the distant, charismatic throne. The legend of 'private favourites' with 'sinister ends' was a routine trope of popular political movements from the songs and chronicles of the fourteenth century to the civil wars of the 1640s. English politics circle around the throne. What James Holstun calls 'monarcho-populism', a central strand of Lancastrian and Tudor propaganda, persisted in the American colonies up to 1776.[25] Arguably, the American presidency is the closest a republic conceived in anti-monarchism can get to monarchy.[26]

As for the provenance of the 'commonwealth' idea, we have seen that *Magna Carta* (1215) made it the duty of the senior nobles to discipline kings who ruled in their own interests and not those of the *communem utilitatem regni*.[27] It assigned them a collective duty to attack and occupy the estates and castles of a king who failed to listen to the right counsel: they were enjoined to every action short of harming the king or his family. This did not stop them in 1327 or 1399, by which time they

---

[23] I am grateful to Wythe Holt for reminding me of these continuities. Samuel K. Cohn, *Popular Protest in Late Medieval Europe* (Manchester 2004), 264, writes that 'the two principal revolts of the opening years of the 1380s were the tax revolts and theatres of disrespect directed against the king and his officers [in Rouen and Paris]'. He also notes (263) that 'the chronicles show the interconnectedness and networks of communication among insurgents across vast areas of northern France and Flanders'.

[24] But see Mavis Mate, 'The Economic and Social Roots of Medieval Popular Rebellion: Sussex in 1450–51', *Economic History Review*, new series, 46:2 (May 1993), 663–4.

[25] James Holstun, 'The Spider, the Fly, and the Commonwealth: Merrie John Heywood and Agrarian Class Struggle', *English Literary History* 71:1 (2004), 53–88.

[26] Written June 2004, during the days of mourning for former-president Ronald Reagan.

[27] *Magna Carta*, ed. Claire Breay (British Library online edn.), section 61, para. 3.

had acquired a more sophisticated grasp of logical distinctions between tyrants and kings. The institutionalization of the Peers raised the problem of naming that which the Barons acted in the name of, what they were not.[28] The intermediate ranks achieved some institutionalization as knights and gentlemen. Actions against kings were conducted in the name of the commonalty in both its senses, i.e. the community at large, and that part of the community that was not a lord of any kind. The commonalty was defined with reference to what its members were not ('gentle', 'men of blood'), and the fact that the whole class appeared to be capable, in times of extreme urgency, of rising as one. Baronial rebellions never involved all, or even a majority of the barons, but styled themselves as a class, capable of acting, with violence if necessary, in defence of its collective 'liberties' – and, of course, for the *communem utilitatem regni*.

Between the murder of Edward II in 1327 and Jack Cade's Rebellion in 1450, it became possible to imagine the commonalty acting together in this way. Out of this context there emerged a tenacious theory of the causes of popular rebellion. Sir John Fortescue's paradigm, in which the normal top-down structure of authority, agency and causation was reversed, became its seminal formulation. 'Whan any Rysyng hath byn made in this Land, before these days,' Fortescue wrote, 'the porest Men thereof hath byn the grettest Causers and Doars thereyn.' Out in the suffering, angry communities, the bowmen (or third sort) tried to keep aloof from the murmuring discontentments of their poorer neighbours. Their assigned role, after all, was to keep the fourth sort in order. But 'thryfty Men hath byn loth ... for Dred of losyng of their Goods', wrote Fortescue. 'Often tymes they have gone with [rebels] through Manasys, or els the same poer Men would have takyn their Goods.' The conclusion was inescapable. 'It semyth that Povertye, hath byn the hole and cheffe Cause of al such Rysyng. The poer Man hath ben styryd therto, by occasion of his Povertye for to get Good; and the riche Men have gone with them, because they wold not be poer, by lesyng their Goods.' At such times, Fortescue suggested, worthy men (that is, men who were worth something, paid the highest taxes, etc.) joined the multitude against their will, sometimes, as in 1450, 1536 and 1549, organizing and leading them into action. Fortescue then expressed the fear of fears evoked by the spectre of the commonalty, driven by poverty and led by the middle ranks. 'What then would fal, if al the Comons were poer', he asked. 'Truly it is like that ... Land ... wher the Comons for Povertye rose upon the

---

[28] Claire Valente, *The Theory and Practice of Revolt in Medieval England* (Aldershot 2003), 163–6, 170, 242.

Nobles, and made al their Goods to be comon.'[29] Fortescue's theory took account of the experience of the generations since 1381.

For the poet who wrote the first epigraph to this chapter, 1381 was not a rising of 'peasants' but of *comuynes*. 'Commons rebellion' allows for the occupational heterogeneity of the movement and is closer to the way the rebels saw themselves.[30] The famous rebel letters assured the men delegated to fight that they had the support of their neighbours.[31] Jack Miller, Jack Carter, Piers Plowman, John Trewman and John Ball fit Wood's definition of community leaders: they were 'adult, male, settled [excepting Ball], skilled and independent', and they did not place themselves above the rank and file. Jack Miller's letter evoked communal habits, asking for help to put his collapsing mill (a metaphor for the kingdom) *aright*; it urged the rebels to 'lat myght helpe ryght'. Jack Carter urged them to 'make a gode ende of that ye have begunnen'. They were assured that 'Piers Plowman' would stay at home to tend the fields, and that he, Jack Carter, would travel to and fro with victuals to sustain the 'pilgrims' as they travelled abroad in their search for *trewth*.[32] Jack Trewman was sick of the lies and corruption of the ruling classes – those whose place was to *serve* the commonweal, not exploit it for selfish gain – and he urged the rebels 'now is time'. Kings' counsellors, barons and parliaments had failed to put the mill of the commonwealth *aright*. When lords misruled and hunger stalked the land it was time for the commons to rise.[33] The third sort stayed at home while the fourth sort went off to fight. The *comuynes* of 1381 were the first to raise the banner of popular sovereignty. It would prove a tenacious cause.

The rebel letters described a unified commonalty: there were no third or fourth sorts, labourers, artisans or peasants, only *comuynes*. The paradox of popular rebellion consisted in the coming together of the otherwise divided households and neighbourhoods of core districts. In practice

---

[29] John Fortescue, *The Difference betwene Dominus Regale and Dominium Politicum et Regale, made in the time of Edward IV*, n.d., Bodleian Library Rawlinson MS D69, ch.11, f. 11; John Fortescue-Aland (ed.), *The Difference between Absolute and Limited Monarchy. . . being a treatise written by Sir John Fortescue* (London 1714), 19–21.

[30] Jane Whittle and S.H. Rigby, 'England: Popular Politics and Social Conflict', in S.H. Rigby (ed.), *A Companion to Britain in the Late Middle Ages* (Oxford 2003), 72.

[31] For the rebel letters, see R.B. Dobson, *The Peasants Revolt of 1381* (London 1983), 372–8: 'The Literature of Protest'; Stephen Justice, *Writing and Rebellion: England in 1381* (Berkeley 1994), 13–14, transcribes the letters from BL MS Cotton Tiberius C.viii, fol. 174a.

[32] 'Jack Carter prays you all . . . Let Piers the plowman my brother dwell at home and make us corn. I will go with you and help that I may bring your meat and your drink.' (my trans. of Stephen Justice, *Writing and Rebellion*, 13); 'Als longe as I lyue, I shall thee maintain', *Piers Plowman*, in Sisam, p. 80, line 37.

[33] *Ibid.*

'more than one distinct if overlapping factor or motive impelled different sectors of rural society to coalesce temporarily into common action',
writes L.R. Poos. 'Each episode managed, if only inadvertently, to tap
into an underlying stream of more diffused anti-authoritarian unrest
among ordinary rural people.'[34] Poos shows that the 'core' of resistance
and rebellion from the fourteenth to sixteenth centuries, 'drawn from a
variety of evidence of widely differing natures', consisted of 'a middling
band of agriculturalists, craftsmen and retailers with a smaller sprinkling
of the most well-off villagers and some labourers'. The closer we look at
early modern communities, the more 'sorts of people' we find. Organization depended upon 'that network of village notables and petty officialdom prominent in local organisation from the outset of the period'.
Revolt happened when this 'middle band' and the 'smaller sprinkling' of
richer sort could no longer hold back the murmuring or resist the pressure from below. Below the middle we encounter, once again, the spectre
of the multitude, the source of an anti-authoritarian culture with a whole
repertoire of reasons to revolt. 'A shifting calculus of grievances fuelled
revolts', writes Poos. 'Groups whose discernible or imputable motivations
differed . . . joined a common cause under a unifying rubric . . . As purely
anti-seigneurial concerns waned, economic and social factors of different
sorts, legal and political volatility (which the proximity of London doubtless helped stoke), and even religious nonconformity conspired to unite,
albeit briefly, a disparate rural society.'[35] This is a more complex description of the structure of popular rebellions than that of Fortescue, but the
common assumption is that in moments of rebellion the *comuynes* became
a class, and everyday class-struggle turned, momentarily, into class war.

As for their 'unifying rubric', Knighton reported that the rebels of
1381 fought in the name of the *communis utilitatis*, but it is not certain
what English word(s) he had in mind.[36] The rebel letters use 'wele' six
times and 'wel' twice. *Wele* was Anglo-Saxon for the condition, 'welfare,
well-being, happiness', for which 'wealth, riches and possessions' were
merely instruments.[37] It was 'applied to a person as a source of felicity,

---

[34] L.R. Poos, *A Rural Society after the Black Death: Essex 1350–1525* (Cambridge 1991),
229, 231, 233; see also Paul Strohm, *Hochon's Arrow: the Social Imagination of 14th
Century Texts* (Princeton 1992), 51–3; Mavis Mate, 'Economic and Social Roots', *passim*.

[35] Poos, *A Rural Society*, 261–1, 264, 266.

[36] *Knighton's Chronicle 1337–1396*, ed. and trans. G. H. Martin (Oxford 1995), 208–9.

[37] For the range of *wel* and *wele*, see Kurath (ed.), *MED* 2: 244–72. My reading of the *wel*
and *wele* usages is that ease of semantic slippage, from spiritual and material 'happiness'
to 'wealth', is present in the earliest references. For example, 'lutel weole to muchel
wele' and 'alle worldes wele' (both c.1225) can be read both or all ways. The tension
is ultimately substantive rather than linguistic; that is, it is inherent in the human tendency to assume that wealth and possessions lead to happiness. The abiding 'alternative'

or an object of delight', and is much broader in application than 'profit'. Julian of Norwich's repetition of the word in Christ's promise – 'I may make alle thinge wele, I can make all thinge wele, and I shalle make alle thinge wele. An thow shalle see it thyself that alle thinge shalle be wele' – suggests that the word carried much more freight and prestige than might be expected from the modern usage 'well': prosperity, wealth, health, harmony, happiness and collective well-being are all implied in her usage.[38] Julian's fictional (or stereotypical) contemporary, Jack Carter, advised the rebels of 1381 that 'if the end be *wele* than all is *wele*' and John Ball 'greeteth *wele* all manner men' and bid them 'do *wel* and bettre'. Its usages in the rebel letters suggests that in 1381 *wele* was a word of carters, plowmen and popular preachers as well as anchoresses and mystics, at a time when formally educated writers without exception used variants of *comun profit*.[39] The casual uses of *wele* in the rebel letters indicate that the rebel usage may have been *comun* or *comyn wele*. If so, it would be the earliest attribution, preceding a Chancery usage of 1446, and its unambiguous arrival on the political stage as the cause of Cade's rebels during the July Days of 1450. Yoked to *commun*, *wele* came to refer to 'the welfare and delight of a country or community', as when the governing class of Shrewsbury struck a bargain with 'the commonalty of the town . . . for the *weal* of peace, tranquility and good governance', in 1444.[40] The letters assured the rebels of 1381 that it was their duty to rise for the collective *wele*.

5.4   Unnatural heat: the crisis of 1381–1450

a body is sik whan his kyndely heet is to lytle or whan his unkyndely heet is to moche.[41]

Commons rebellion became a force in English constitutional life in the decades from 1381 to 1450. Writing a decade or more after the event, the composer of 'On the Earthquake of 1382' lived through the rebellion and its aftermath and feared it was a beginning, not an end: 'a warnyng to be ware'. In the late summer of 1382 murmurings of rebellion were circulating again in Norfolk. Men who fit Fortescue's and Poos' accounts

---

Christian theology sanctifying poverty as a condition for harmony and happiness obviously militates against people being comfortable with the idea that 'wellness' follows from 'wealth' in the narrowly materialistic sense and that, therefore, it is rulers' duty to promote what came to be called 'economy'. As I show below, Chapters 6–7, it was no accident that 'common-wealth' begins to displace 'common weal' at around the time that thinkers like Fortescue and Smith were beginning to formulate principles of political economy as we know it.

[38] Julian of Norwich, *Vision*, 15.2–4, 95.   [39] See above, n. 22.
[40] Kurath (ed.), *MED*, 436, 446.   [41] Thomas Wimbledon (1387).

of the provenance of rebellion travelled from villages around Norwich and attempted to raise a rebellion targeting the heroically antipopulist Bishop Despenser. The authorities reacted savagely: ten men were rounded up and executed.[42] Class-struggle haunts descriptions of London politics in the aftermath of 1381. The leader of a faction of guilds defied oligarchic traditions and 'drew to him the *comun people* for to stand by their purposes to live and die'. These were not corporate city politics as they were supposed to be, but class-struggle. It 'was evermore an excitation to the poor people to make them be the more fervent and rebel against the great men of the town'. It was poor against rich, not craft against craft, rank against rank or estate against estate. The popular party asserted 'that always the great men would have the people by oppression in low degree'. These were not just struggles between factions at city hall, but encompassed people who were 'common, small and poor'. Class-feeling, 'dissension... between the worthy persons and the small people of the town', polarized the city. Politics spread into 'many crafts and much small people that know not the skill of governance nor of good counsel'. It was all carefully planned by 'confederacy, congregation and *covyne*, purposed and intended to maintain by might their false and wicked meaning, under colour of words of *comun profit*'.[43]

The principle of the common good was in the air. At precisely this time, John Trevisa was translating Giles of Rome on kings and tyrants for his master, Thomas IV, lord Berkeley, at Berkeley Castle.[44] If a king was agreed among his subjects to be a tyrant, it was the duty of magnates of the realm to discipline and chastise him. So too, it must be the duty of the commonalty to chastise their own leaders if they, in their turn, proved tyrants. The principle of *comun profit* was loose. In the common tongue, I have suggested, it was already called the *commune wele*. As had been the case at Peatling Magna in 1264, 'commune' meant 'the community' and the 'commons' in the sense of third estate.

The rebellion of 1381 was a symptom and, as memory, a lasting cause. An episode in 1397 illustrated the tendency for local people to take the law into their own hands – indeed, to see themselves as executors of the law. The jurors of various wapentakes in Lincolnshire accused six men

---

[42] Herbert Eiden, 'Norfolk 1382: a Sequel to the Peasants Revolt', *English Historical Review*, 114:456 (April 1999), 370–7.

[43] *Book of London English*, 29. I.S. Leadam and J.F. Baldwin (ed.), *Select Cases Before the King's Council* (Cambridge 1918), xcvii–xcviii, suggest that it was a conflict between the victualling and non-victualling trades and that Brembre 'was a politician with a mailed fist'; on pp. 74–6 is a complaint by the Taylors and Linen Armourers' Company (Merchant Taylors) that Brembre had burned their charter.

[44] David C. Fowler, *Life and Times of John Trevisa, Medieval Scholar* (Seattle and London 1995), 190, 196–7.

of Spalding for beheading one Simon Geldere at 'a certain place called Pleyingplace in the said township' on 27 August 1391. Geldere 'had been indicted and outlawed for felony' and his executioners thought 'it was permissible in law to behead and slay anyone outlawed of felony'. They were arrested, but the Sheriff chose to see it as for the common good and pardoned them.[45]

Chroniclers of the Lancastrian coup of 1399–1400 were in no doubt that troubles at the top drew upon and stimulated intense class-feelings among the populace at large. In these uncertain months new signs of plebeian unrest began to appear. Two earls were captured and beheaded by the 'plebs' at Cirencester.[46] In the wake of the failure of a plot to kill Henry of Lancaster and restore Richard II, the earls of Kent and Salisbury, accompanied by Sir Ralph Lumley, Sir Thomas Blount, Sir Benedict Sely and thirty other esquires, made their escape up the Thames Valley, arriving at Cirencester after dark on 8 January 1400. They took over the Ram Inn, abutting the market place, where the landlord was William Tanner. None of the chroniclers tell us how the movement began, only that the lords and their retainers were soon besieged by 'an armed crowd of local villeins all armed with bows and sticks', led by John Cosyn, the bailiff, and some local merchants, including Reginald (or 'Reynold') Spicer, a wealthy wool monger whose memorial brass, dated 1442, describes him as 'a merchant of this town' and displays him with his four wives.[47]

A chronicler wrote that the inhabitants were suspicious 'of [the earls'] display of arms' and, after making enquiries, were convinced 'that they were not telling the truth'. Seeing 'that every way out was blocked with beams and other great pieces of wood', the earls and their retainers attempted to break out, attacking the townspeople 'with lances and arrows'. The locals forced them back and 'began to shoot arrows at the lodging – some through the windows, some at the doors and gates – with the result that no place was safe for them, and not only were they unable to get out, they were not even able to look out'.[48]

This fight lasted from the middle of the night until three o'clock the next day, when the earls eventually gave up, handed themselves over to the townspeople, begging not to be put to death before they had had an opportunity to speak to the

[45] Coram Rege Roll no. 544 Easter 1397: G.O. Sayles (ed.), *Select Cases in the Court of King's Bench under Richard II, Henry IV and Henry V* (London 1971), 91–2.

[46] *The Chronicle of Adam of Usk*, ed. and trans. C. Given Wilson (Oxford 1991), 88–9.

[47] The incident is described in W. St. C. Baddeley, *A History of Cirencester* (Cirencester 1924), 186–7. Spicer's brass, referred to in Baddeley, 188, n. 10, can still be seen on the walls of Cirencester Parish Church.

[48] *The Chronicle of Adam of Usk*, ed. Given Wilson, 226–8.

king. They were accordingly led to the abbey, where they heard mass and were given breakfast for the day. During the afternoon, however, at about the hour of Vespers, a certain priest who was one of their followers started a fire in some houses in one of the streets of the town, in the hope that while the townspeople were trying to put them out the earls could sieze the chance to escape. It was vain, however, for the townspeople anticipated such a ruse, abandoned the houses to the flames and rushed instead to the abbey to make sure that those whom they had spent so much effort in capturing should not be allowed to get away. By this time Thomas lord Berkeley had arrived and was preparing to take them to the king, which he would undoubtedly have done had the fire not been started in the town, but this wanton act so infuriated the townspeople, and indeed others who had begun to arrive from various parts of Gloucestershire and elsewhere, that no words could dissuade them from their determination to see the earls put to death. They even threatened Lord Berkeley with death if he did not hand those traitors to the king over to them.

The Lancastrian Thomas, lord Berkeley (Trevisa's master) was content, in the circumstances, to delegate justice to the townspeople. Walsingham added for good measure that the rebel lords were Lollard sympathisers and 'despisers of holy images'. A vernacular chronicler recorded that after the execution the townspeople stuck the heads on poles, 'and . . . carried them from Cirencester to Oxford, where they found king Henry lodging in the abbey of the Carmelites'.[49] He was less inclined to take sides: the dukes and their men had 'faught manly; but at the laste they were overcome and take; and there thei smote of the Dukes hed of Surrey, and the Erles hed of Salusberye, & mony other moo; and there thay putte the quarters in sackys, and ther hedes on poles, born on hy, and so thei were brought through the cite of London vnto London brygge; and ther her heddes were sette vp an hy, & her quarters were sent to other gode tounes and cites, and set vp there'.[50]

A large, very determined and well organized assembly is implied by this defeat of armed feudal warriors trained and hardened in the arts of war. No reference is made to any outside assistance or encouragement, but a contemporary chronicler, Adam of Usk, reports that the lords were led into the market-place by John Cosyn, Reginald Spicer, John Colman, Roger Carvill and Richard Small, all local notables, where their heads were cut off to the acclamation of the crowd. All accounts stressed the independent and spontaneous agency of the townspeople. Alone in the euphoric assumption of popular support for Henry of Lancaster, Adam of Usk spotted a constitutionally dangerous precedent – a sign of change that might, if not stamped out immediately, destroy the existing state

[49] *The Chronicle of Adam of Usk*, ed. Given Wilson, 233–4.
[50] F.W.D. Brie (ed.), *The Brut or The Chronicles of England* (London 1906), 361.

altogether. He was in no doubt that the citizens of Cirencester had an agenda of their own.[51] A few days later another Ricardian 'rebel', lord Despenser, was 'most despicably beheaded by workmen at Bristol'.[52] *Sed, quia omnia ista plebeiorum sola ferocitate exiterunt perpetrata, timeo quod gladii possessionem,* wrote Usk, *eis iam tolleratum contra ordinis rationem, in dominos magis in futurum vibrare causabunt.* 'And yet, seeing that all these acts were perpetrated solely by the violence of the common people, I fear that possession of the sword, which, although contrary to the natural order ... might at some future time embolden them to rise up in arms against the lords.'[53]

The convention that popular support was necessary for the legitimate removal of a tyrant undermined prescribed social hierarchy. Henry of Lancaster had summoned the *comuynes* to defeat great nobles who fought

---

[51] He was right. The earls had been carrying a fortune in cash and jewels. *CCR Hen iv, i* 22 February 1402, *CPR Hen iv, ii* 24 November 1402, *CPR Hen iv, ii* 10 January 1403, *CCR Hen iv, ii* 8 March 1403, *CPR Hen iv, ii* 13 June 1403 record the king's efforts to recover it and the town's continuing failure to comply. But the real motive for the townspeoples' intervention was realized in *CPR Hen iv, iii*, 14 July 1403: 'Charter to the men of the town of Cirencester granting ... a Gild merchant with all liberties, privileges and customs. ... And each year on the morrow of Epiphany may meet to appoint a Master and other governors, officers and ministers of the Gild.' This marked a major victory in a struggle of the townspeople against their lord, the Abbot of St John, Cirencester, that had been erupting with monotonous regularity since 1117. *CPR Hen iv, iii* 3 December 1403 records a Pardon to the men of Cirencester in council of their good service for all treasons ... grant of all gold and silver and gilt and jewels taken from the rebels. The fate of Cirencester reflects Henry IV's gradual retreat from his populist origins. The Beginning of Restoration of Abbey's rights is recorded in *CPR Hen iv, iii* November 28 1408 at Gloucester. Inspeximus and Confirmatio to Abbot and Convent of C of (1) Charter dated 20 September 17 Edward III (Charter Roll 17 Edward III no.13); (2) Charter dated 2 May 14 Richard II no. 9 exemplifying a charter dated at Westminster 12 November 1 Richd I; (3) Confirmation to abbot of charters of 17 Edward iii, 14 Richard ii, 42 Edward iii exemplifying 12 November 1 Richard I for 10 marks, 380. *CPR Hen iv, iv* 11 July 1412 reported that the earl of Kent's wife allowed to remove his bones and bury them at his own abbey. *CPR Hen iv, iv* 12 March 1412 is a Commission to arrest William Nottyngham, John Coston, Thomas Gage, John Lecke, John Greynden 'webbe', Richard Staines, William Kyng, William Bristowe alias Glovere and Henry Northcote all of C and bring them immediately before the king and council in Chancery. *Cal Pat Rolls Hen v, i* 1413–16 and *CPR Hen v, i* 5 June 1413 Exempl. Of 10 November 43 Edward III to Abbot. *CPR Hen V* 1.38 12 June 1413 records the new king's swift response to resistance on the part of the town: it is a Commission of oyer and terminer to Thomas of Berkeley and others touching the bondmen and tenants in bondage of the abbot of C ... who have leagued together to refuse their due customs and services. Anger exploded and the townspeople put the abbey under siege. Will lord Berkeley and his soldiers arrive in time? Would this be the spark of a new conflagration? In the event, no. *CPR* 1.168 15 Feb 1414–15 is a list of 104 men fined and 'pardoned' for rioting against the abbey when it tried to reassert its restored control of the borough and market.

[52] 'Plebeiorum pagensium tumultu decapitai fuerunt', *The Chronicle of Adam of Usk*, ed. Given Wilson, 89–90.

[53] *Ibid.*, 90–1.

for the restoration of an anointed and legitimate king. He encouraged common people to kill nobles. At Cirencester the commons executed nobles in the cause of one king, Henry IV, who had just deposed another king, Richard II. Whatever their intentions, such events raised the possibility that the hierarchy and constitution of England was contingent, not necessary. Henry's ambiguous appeal to the commonalty 'might at some future time embolden [the commons] to rise up' against every kind of lordship. Usk's fear that the commonalty hated *all* lords was shared by some members of the new government.[54] During Lent 1400 the apprentice boys of London constantly banded together in their thousands to choose their 'kings'.[55] On 12 May 1401, the tenants of lord Beauchamp rose up and freed three convicted thieves from the gallows, 'killing with their arrows Sir William Lucy, who had been given the task of executing them'.[56] This was the brew that would be finally co-ordinated in the 1640s, when the populist discourse of the commonweal finally achieved the ascendency in public discourse it had been threatening for nearly three centuries.

There is more than a whiff of class hatred in the literature of 1381–1520. E.B. Fryde's book on relations between landlords and peasants between the late fourteenth and early sixteenth centuries adds hundreds of little episodes from the records of manors and estates, lay and ecclesiastical, all over the country, which add up to a picture of tremendous pressure from below.[57] His canvass of hundreds of communities grinding away at the remnants of feudal unfreedom helps to explain the sense of panic that never seems far from the surface of elite politics in the next century and a half.

The complaint was that everyone, every estate, class, faction and institution was in it for themselves. Cynical self-interest, greed and corruption were, the complaint literature insisted, all-pervasive. Only a few years after the Commons Rebellion, in 1387, Thomas Wimbledon delivered one of the most powerful vernacular sermons ever preached at St Paul's Cross, prophesying that Antichrist would arrive in thirteen years' time.[58] St Paul's Cross was fourteenth-century England's closest

---

[54] *Ibid.*, 90–1, and n. 5; 'The problem, especially between 1380 and 1450, was seen by contemporaries as a general upward move by the whole of the lower class': R.H. Hilton, 'Ideology and Social Order in Late Medieval England', in Hilton, *Class Conflict and the Crisis of Feudalism* (London 1985).

[55] *The Chronicle of Adam of Usk*, ed. Given Wilson, 92–3.   [56] *Ibid.*, 131.

[57] Fryde, *Peasants and Landlords in Later Medieval England* (Stroud 1996).

[58] G.R. Owst, *Preaching in Medieval England: an Introduction to Sermon Manuscripts of the Period c.1350–1450* (New York 1965), 'Appendix V, A Note on Thomas (or Richard) Wimbledon and his Sermon at Pauls Cross in 1388', 361, observed that although his sermon was not exactly heterodox, Wimbledon 'was crying from the house-tops

equivalent to a transmitter of national broadcasts. At London, wrote Bishop Thomas Brinton, 'there is a greater devotion and a more intelligent people . . . Because each Bishop of England has subjects or parishioners in London, therefore, when he gives instructions there, it is as though he were preaching to his own people and to the other churches of England.'[59] A sermon preached in English at St Paul's Cross had a chance of reaching every member of the English body politic.

Wimbledon addressed one of the most controversial and socially-divisive topics of the century after the Black Death: wage labour. He likened the kingdom of heaven to 'an housholdynge man that wente out first on the morwe to hire werkemen into his vine. Also, about the thridde, sixte, nyenthe, and elevene houris he wente oute and found men stondynge ydel and sey to hem: Go ye into my vyne and that right is I wole yeve yow whanne the day was ago, he clepyid his styward and heet to yeve eche man a peny.' How could it be just to pay a labourer who worked only one hour the same as one who had worked all day? Yet the story was told with approval by the living God. Wimbledon's task was to explain the precept underlying the parable in spoken words everyone could understand.

All vocations, he explained, 'ben [equally] necessary'. If one set of labourers performed its task badly the whole community was threatened. What counted was not how long a person worked for, but that he or she contributed what he or she could to the communal process, and that his or her needs were satisfied at the end of the day. People should be paid according to need, which is the same for all: this is the spirit of the rebel letters. In the eyes of God every soul is equal, regardless of vocation. The world, however, requires a division of labour. 'As ye seeth that in tilienge of the material vine there beeth divers laboreris: for summe kuttyn awey the voyde braunchis; summe maken forkes and rayles to beren up the veyne; and summe diggen awey the olde erthe fro the rote and layn here fattere.' The world God made needed 'divers laboreris'. Some tasks take longer than others, but the need of every individual is the same. As long as every man, woman and child has everything needed

what others less exalted than (Thomas) Brunton (Bishop of Rochester) whispered to nobility and clergy in inner chambers.' The sermon is extant in thirteen English and two Latin manuscripts of the fourteenth and fifteenth centuries; there were eighteen printed editions in the sixteenth and seventeenth centuries, including a version in Fox. The quotations here are from *Wimbledon's Sermon, Redde Rationem Villicationis Tue: a Middle English Sermon of the Fourteenth Century*, ed. Ione Kemp Knight (Pittsburgh Pa. 1967), 1.

[59] Owst, *Preaching in Medieval England*, 208.

for sustenance and the maintenance of the vocation allocated to them by God, there should be no complaints. A person's value was not determined by supply and demand, but by circumstances determined by God alone.

Wimbledon assumed his audience would be familiar with the idea that humanity is divided into those who pray (the First Estate), those who fight (Second) and those who worked (the Third). He reiterated the idea proverbially, in concepts and phrases that were easy to remember and repeat. Christian societies, he preached, 'beeth nedeful these thre offices'. To 'prestes, it fallith to knitte awey the void braunchis of synnis with the swerd of here tonge'. 'Knytis', were responsible for the administration of justice, 'to lette wrongis and theftis to be do, and to maytene goddis law and hem that be techeris ther of'. The vocations of war came second to keeping the peace at home in that their functions were also 'to kepe the lond fro enemyes of other londes'. Wimbledon's dual definition of the second estate marks a long-term shift in perceptions of the relative importance of the military, civil and religious functions of the knightly class that is evident in many sources of the fourteenth century. To the Third Estate ('laboriaris') 'it fallith to travayle bodily and with here sore swet geten out of the erthe bodily liflode for hem and for other parties'.[60] This was a concise statement of three-estates theory.

Yet the governing principle was not hierarchy but reciprocity. All bodies are constituted by parts: the arts of community are to persuade different members to work together for the common good. Wimbledon explained that 'al mankynde is oo[ne] body' held together by 'kyndely (natural) heete'. It was possible to say very clearly and simply in what that 'kindly heat' consisted: 'charity... that is love to oure God and to oure neyghbore'. This rule applied to everyone, of whatever rank, vocation or estate. What tore society apart was 'unkyndely heet', which, again, could be stated simply. 'Unnatural heat' (heat that militated against the natural unity of God's creatures) was generated by 'lustful love to othre creatures'.[61] It manifested as people, groups and classes seeking to satisfy their 'lusts' at the expense of others. Wimbledon clearly anticipated that his congregation would include men who were active in the public lives of their communities, and showed how the precept applied to them. 'Yif [he that kepyng hath of eny comunyte] take... offys more for thyne owne worldly profyt than for helpe of the comunyte... thou art a tiraunt.'[62] Wimbledon reiterated John of Salisbury's precept. Tyranny was a disease that could break out in any member, estate, vocation, community

---

[60] *Wimbledon's Sermon*, lines 38–46, p. 63.   [61] *Ibid.*, pp. 110–11.   [62] *Ibid.*, p. 81.

or association. Anyone who had power – patriarchs over their families and servants, parents over children, lords over their tenants or kings over their subjects – could become a tyrant if he or she was driven by 'unkindly heat': literally, 'heat' that was incompatible with the 'kin' or 'kind', the unity of community. Like the organological model itself, Wimbledon's precept of 'kindly' and 'unkindly heat' was easy to think with.

Kings and treasurers in particular should take great care to avoid slipping into tyranny. Solomon's son, Reheboam, had demanded more of his people than they could pay, so 'the puple of Israel comen to hym and seyden':

Thy fadre in his laaste dayes putte upon us a gret charge. We prayeth that thou wole sumwhat make it lighttere, and we wole serve thee. And the king tok consel of the old wise men, and they conseiden hym to answere he fayre, and that shulde be for the best. But he left this olde wise mennis conseyl, and did aftir the conseyl of children that weren his pleiserin, and seyde to the peple whan they comen ayen: my lest fingere is grettere than my faadres rygge; my fadir greved yow sumwhat, but y wole eken more. And the peple herden this, and rebelledyn to hym, and toke hem another kyng. And sith come nevere the kyngdom ayeen hool.[63]

The anecdote defined a tyrant. Kings and princes more than anyone had the power to release kindly or unkindly heat into the community as a whole, binding it more closely together or driving its members apart. Reheboam's greed led to one of the most terrifying symptoms of the ascendency of unnatural heat in the body politic: rebellion. A careless listener could easily take this anecdote as impressive – biblical – evidence as to the legitimacy of rebellion against kings and their deposition. Wimbledon seemed to acknowledge that they (perhaps even some of the rebels of 1381) were 'lowere [lovers] of communytes'. They should beware of leaders who claimed to have their best interests at heart but were, in reality, their enemies. The people should take care 'that they be not lad be foolis . . . that ne have an eye of love to the comynite'. Again, a careless listener might draw the conclusion that rebellion was legitimate if it was led by wise men who *did* have 'an eye of love for the community'. If the powerful could not be motivated by humility before God and love of the community they should recall that the call of *deth* came to all people. 'For wyte he wel, be he nevere so high, that he shal come byfore his heiere to yelde the rekenynge of his bayle.' Every vocation including that of kings had a *bayle*, or set of duties. Death, 'the Third Summoner' in Wimbledon's sketch of the cosmos, was waiting in the wings.

---

[63] *Ibid.*, pp. 81–3.

Wimbledon's solution was very different from John Ball's, but the mood of his sermon was the same: 'for nowe is time'.[64]

Everyone will have a 'rekenynge' with God. God will judge the acts and thoughts of every individual at the moment of death. But if the world became too corrupt, He would inflict collective punishments, including 'mischiefs, losses and detriments by fire . . . dearths, famines and extreme want of corn and grain . . . , sickness and pestilence . . . and mortality of people'. The more extreme the sign, the more extreme God's anger at the corruption of the world by base, selfish motives. A mere forty years before Wimbledon's sermon, a third of Europe's population had been wiped out by plague in just over a year. Seditions, rebellions, conspiracies, insurrections and tumults were also acts of God. The Commons Rebellion of 1381 had been a sign of all signs that unkindly heat was threatening to burn up the community. The present world lived on the verge of the last days prophesied in Revelation, foretelling a second coming preceded by unbearable chaos and corruption under the rule of Antichrist. Wimbledon prophesied 'that the grete Anticrist schulde come in the fourteenthe hundred yeer fro the birthe of Criste, the which noumbre of yeeris is now fulfillid not fully twelve yeer and a half lackying'. Antichrist would take power in AD 1400. It was a strangely precise prophecy.

Thirteen years in the future, the accumulated sins and corruptions of the times did come to a head. Could nothing be done to avert the coming of Antichrist? The solution was concise and memorable:

Clerkes that treteth of kyndis seith that a body is sik when his kyndely heet is to lytle or whan his unkyndely heet is to moche. Whan therfore thou seest that the love of men to Godward and to here neighbores is litle and feynt and the love to worldly thyngis and to lustes of the flesch is gret and fervent, than wite thou wel . . . that unkyndely hete is to gret and kyndely heete is to lytle.[65]

---

[64] R.H. Robbins (ed.), *Historical Poems of the 14th and 15th Centuries* (New York 1959), xlii, contrasts John Ball's message with another contemporary song:

now raygneth pride in price	Now pride ys yn pris
couetise is holden wise	Now coetise ys wise
lechery without shame	Now lechery is schameles,
gluttony without blame	Now gloteny is lawles,
enuie raygneth with reason	Now slewthe ys yn seson,
and sloth is taken in great season	In enuie & wrethe is treson;
God doe bote for nowe is time	Now hath god enchesyn
Amen	to dystrie thys worle by reson.

'When does criticism become treason?' asks Robbins. 'In these two poems the distinction consists of a single line at the end of Ball's song . . . Previously many had regretted evils; Ball wanted to remove them.

[65] *Wimbledon's Sermon*, pp. 110–11.

Everyone of whatever Estate or vocation who is motivated by love of God and neighbour will be 'cured'. In proportion to the number of its subjects inspired by *felyng fayth*, the *comunyte* or, as Berthelet would translate Wimbledon's word in the 1530s, the *common wealth*,[66] will be cured too.

As Wimbledon implied, 'kindly heat' was absent during these ferocious decades. The deposition of Richard II by Henry of Lancaster was an obvious candidate for the coming of Antichrist.[67] 'Never since the time of my youth do I remember hearing such foreboding in the hearts of the wise, because of the disorder and unrest which they fear will shortly befall this kingdom', wrote a statesman of the age. 'Law and justice are exiles.' Was this why the Lancastrians had overthrown and murdered a tyrant, to create a world in which 'robbery, homicide, persecution of the poor, injury, injustice and outrages of all kinds abound, instead of the rule of the law'? Surely this war of each against all was God's punishment. There was a proverb for this occasion too: 'every kingdom divided against itself is brought to desolation', intoned Philip Repingdon. 'It is crimes, outrages and betrayals of all kinds which lead to the kingdom being transferred from one people to another.' Divided kingdoms fall to foreign invaders. Henry of Lancaster's coup was supposed to have led 'to the redemption of Israel, in other words to the correction of all these evils . . . but now it is the wise who weep and the depraved'. Most fearful of all was the challenge from below. 'The people . . . like wild beasts, without rule or reason, take justice into their own hands. Against nature they seize the reins of government from their betters, and rage savagely against all classes alike.' 'Insubordination of the people' was the spirit of the age. The consequence of *rebelione populi* would be that 'twenty thousand of [Henry's] subjects might fall by the sword;' the consequences for church, monarchy and nobility were impossible to predict.[68]

The divisions and struggles of the decades between 1381 and 1450 had many causes and innumerable contexts.[69] The outcome was that the English *comuynes* – the whole third estate in all its manifestations, the 'spectre' – became a taken-for-granted agency in the constitutional field of force. The idea that the *comuynes* – not just the middle ranks, but

---

[66] Thomas Wimbledon, *A sermon no less fruitfull then famous made in the year of our Lord God MCCClxxviii and found out hyd in a wall . . . imprinted at London by John Awdeley 1573.*

[67] Paul Strohm, *England's Empty Throne: Usurpation and the Language of Legitimation 1399–1422* (New Haven 1998).

[68] Repingdon's letter is in *The Chronicle of Adam of Usk*, ed. Given Wilson, 137–43.

[69] Michael Bush, 'The Risings of the Commons in England, 1381–1549', describes the 'tradition of revolt' in J. Denton (ed.), *Orders and Hierarchies in Late Medieval and Renaissance Europe* (Basingstoke 1999), pp. 109–125.

the rank and file, all the people who worked and they alone – were the commonweal was old when Fortescue and Smith developed its constitutional and economic implications. It is what the commons of 1381 had asserted: the *wele* of the commune is to be measured by the condition of its poorest, least prestigious members. If all the institutionalized layers of the ruling classes failed in their duty to serve the *wele* of the community, it was the duty of the *comuynes* to rise to its defence.[70] Since *Magna Carta* all the ranks successively had claimed to represent the common working multitude: kings, barons, knights and parliamentarian *liberi homines* had, successively, stood up for the common good, as, successively, the higher classes forgot or betrayed their claim to represent it. Between 1381 and 1450 a whole catalogue of grievances fuelled popular discontentment: the dubious legitimacy of the Lancastrians was only the most spectacular illustration of a legitimacy crisis that left no kind of lordship, religious or secular, unchallenged and unchallengeable.

Modern scholars read jeremiads like those of Wimbledon, Usk and Repingdon as 'formulaic', 'signs of the times', literary dirges drawing upon a routinized trope that exaggerated how awful everything really was.[71] For such scholars 'complaint literature' arose not in response to contingent corruptions of the day but from the pessimistic precept that the world is, by definition, a Vale of Tears. John Ball transformed one contemporary jeremiad into an urgent call to action, and even a cursory survey of published sources shows that this was not a peaceable, law-abiding society with a consensual sense of constitutional propriety. It was constantly being hit by violence, devastating plagues, bad weather and miserable dearths, not to mention stoppages of trade and exports of much-needed provisions whenever the nobles and monarchs resumed their wars. The utter callousness of state executions, the way the head and the four quarters were despatched to regional capitals for the encouragement of the others, are constants in the vernacular chronicles of the fourteenth and fifteenth centuries.[72] Ritual humiliation, formal and informal, was ordained and carried out in streets and market places everywhere, for lesser transgressors of law, religion and popular custom. Lords and even kings were regarded with greater suspicion, and were, however secretly,

---

[70] Bush, 'The Risings of the Commons', 113, argues that 'a principle of answerability to the commons' was assumed in all late medieval popular rebellions.

[71] John Scattergood, 'Social and Political Issues in Chaucer', in *Reading the Past: Essays on Medieval and Renaissance Literature*, 194, writes that 'poems of the "evils of the age" type are essentially generalized complaints, and nothing very particular can be deduced from them.'

[72] For the repression following the 1549 rebellions, see Andy Wood, *The 1549 Rebellions*, 70–88.

judged by the test of the common good. Was their lordship for the common good, or was it for their own selfish interests and ambitions? Henry IV was never as secure in his throne as he wanted to be.[73] The gentry were still lawless, the natives were still restless and at conflict with each other. An honest view from above would see exactly what Repingdon described. The sum of all the secret judgements, the unspoken rebellion, added up to what was known, from the time of Chaucer to that of Shakespeare, as 'murmuring'. The legitimacy of the Lancastrian claim to the English throne was never unchallenged by *commune opinioun*. The legitimacy crisis, that was born in 1327, that erupted ephemerally for many causes in many localities and districts for the next fifty years, and that had been brought to another head by the dotage of Edward III in 1376, entered a new and prolonged phase of intensity in 1381.

The collective nature of the rebellion of 1381, which involved many communities in *communicaycon* with each other, acting under common banners and slogans, expressed in the common tongue, may be the point at which, in the popular mind, *commun(itas)*, which customarily designated a specific, local community, began to be extended, in concept and word, to *common weal*, designating (if only tacitly) the entire national community under the authority of a single ruler, an 'imperial monarchy', as Tudor intellectuals would define it. The uprisings of the late fourteenth and throughout the fifteenth and sixteenth centuries were no longer restricted to single towns, manors or districts, but often became much more widespread. Fryde suggests that the fourteenth to sixteenth centuries mark an age of regional revolts. If so, the national and nationalist revolution of the seventeenth century served its apprenticeship in these revolts. We can only say that even if this or that specific case of resistance remained restricted in locale, 1381 had demonstrated that it could spread, and later events had shown in equally bleak manner that the anger would not necessarily be directed exclusively at certain specific fractions of the ruling class (this or that lord, abbot, bishop), but at any lord conceived as being guilty of injustice who it might, in the current political climate, be permissible to kill. Many English lords were guilty of injustice in the eyes of servile peasants like 'an elderly bondsman of the Abbot of Malmesbury in the 1430s. He wished to be free before he died, and his heirs and blood after him, "and if he might bringe that aboute, it would be more joiful to him than all worlelie goode"'.[74] Seditious conversation and rumour, fuelled by sentiments like these, and by the contempt and condescension that pervades the chronicles and most of the other records and literature of the age, were 'part of the

---

[73] See Strohm, *England's Empty Throne*.   [74] Fryde, *Peasants and Landlords*, p. 134.

"infrapolitics" of late medieval England', writes Simon Walker, referring to 'a broad area of discussion, complaint and dissent that fell somewhere between wholehearted consent and open rebellion'.[75]

The year 1381 belongs to a wider movement that comes into focus in the light of the events of the preceding century. This is the century when vernacular English steps tentatively at first, then ever more confidently onto the stage. The exact dynamics of national 'murmuring' usually escape us, but it is clear that words could spread very fast, especially if they were first formulated in a proverb, a song or a story that would be remembered and passed on quickly. At times it was a good deal more deliberate than that. Jack Straw's place in English constitutional life had been prepared before the rebels of 1381 took it. In the fullest sense, the 'Peasants' revolt stands for the moment when the commonalty at large demonstrated for the first time that the Commons House had an army too, even if its respectable citizens were always quick to disown it after the event. Even if the normally conservative knights and burghers of the Commons House invariably disowned and led resistance to its 'army', the potential existed long before the 1640s. Neither burghers nor knights had any truck with rebellion from below, but the fact that it happened gave them a weapon to use against their lords and masters across the road in the palace of Westminster.

There was not a decade, probably not even a year in the centuries separating Edward II and Charles I, which has not left us some evidence of dissidence, resistance or rebellion. How it was expressed and who expressed it varied according to opportunities and circumstances. Not even in Henry V's glory years was dissidence entirely crushed by nationalist fervour, although there has been a tendency to sideline 'Lollardy' on the grounds that it was religious, not political. There were a number of episodes in the 1420s that could have but did not spark wider rebellion. A chronicler described a Parliament that met first at St Albans and then moved to Northampton and Leicester, where it sat from 25 March until 'the first day of June'. This was the traditional season of rebellion. Such was the fear of violence at Leicester that 'every man was warned and cryed through the toune that they shulde leve here wepen in here Innes that is to say swerds and bokellers bowe and arowes'. 'The peple' adhered to the letter of the proclamation, but not its spirit. They deposited their swords, daggers, bows and arrows, but 'toke grete battes in here nekkes'. The next day they were told that they 'shulde leve here battes at here Inne', so 'they toke grete stones in here bosom and in here sleeves . . . and so they

---

[75] Simon Walker, 'Rumour, Sedition and Popular Protest in the Reign of Henry IV', *Past and Present* 106 (February 2000).

wente to the parlement with here lordes'. It was a disciplined and self-conscious movement intended to remind the bishop of Winchester that the common good was more important than his scandalous squabbling over precedence with the duke of Gloucester. The populace had done as they were told, but *only* what they were told, thus illustrating the point that ultimately government could only be effective if it had the assent of the people. 'And this sommen called the parlement of battes Atte the which parliament was made a good unite and accord betwixte the Duke of Gloucestre and the Bishop of Winchester.'[76] The class-constitution of the episode of the 'Parliament of Bats' is not clear, but there is no reason to doubt that it involved men, and possibly women, of every rank up to gentlemen and knights.

The lords and *communes* were summoned to Northampton because London was restive. Winchester complained that during the 'parliament of battes':

diverse persones of lowe astate of the Cite of london in grete nombre assembled on a day on the wharf atte the Crane in the Vynetrie wysshed and desired that they hadde there the persone of my lord of Wynchestre Seying that they wold throwe hym in Thamyse to teach hym to swymme with wynges For with billes and langage of sclaundre and manasse caste and spoken the said Cite be my said lord the Chauncellor caused hym to suppose that they that so said and dydde willed and desired his destruccion howe were hit that they had no cause.[77]

The bishop was unpopular with the city workers because of his support of 'certayn ordinances made by the Maire and Aldermen of london ayenst the excesife taking of Masons, Carpenters, Tylers, Dawbers and other labourers for here dayly journeyes and approvyd by the kynges advys of his conseill'. Following an attempt to control wages, 'there were caste mony hevynesses and cedicious billes under the names of suche labourers Thretyng Rysing with many thousandes and manasyng of astates of the lande and semble wyse cedicious and evill langage shewen and contynewed and lykly hadde shewed of purpos and entente of disobeissaunce and rebellion'. In a letter to the duke of Bedford in France, requesting his immediate return, Winchester complained that 'it semyd to my said lord the Chaunceller that my said lord of Gloucestre dydde not the devoir and diligence that he myght have shewed, of lak of which diligence they that were diposed to do dysobeyssaunce weren encoraged and emboldysshed'.[78] Divisions at court united disobedient commoners.

---

[76] *The Great Chronicle of London*, ed. A.H. Thomas and I.D. Thornley (London 1938), 138.
[77] *Chronicle of London*, 141.   [78] *Ibid.*, 143.

5.5 Good old cause or 'premature reformation': Jack Sharpe's rebellion

alle comyns of the reme, desyryng to wurschyp Godde, preyen that alle the temporaltes of chyrches thus appropred ayens Crystes lore be turned to Godde, and to the prosperyte of the reme.[79]

The insurrection that erupted in the Oxford-Abingdon district in 1431 has been defined as Lollard, but closer examination suggests that it also belongs to the larger category of local movements and risings against unjust and oppressive lordship. One contemporary source gave the events religious colouring. In 1431,

betwene Ester and Whitsonetyde the Duke of Gloucestre hadde wyting that ther was gadered a meyne of Rysers atte Abyngdon a yenst men of holy chirche For they say they wolde have three prestes hedes for a peny And the name of here Cheveteyn was Jakke Sharpe. And thanne anone in all haste the Duke of Gloucestre and his meyn ryden to Abyndone And there Jakke Sharpe was take and other moo The which were founde defectyfe And therefore they were put to the deeth And on the fryday in Whitsoneweke the heed of Jakke Sharpe was broughte to London And it was sette on London Brigge And alle the Remenaunt of his felashyp that myght be taken were putte to dethe at Abyndon.[80]

Another chronicler saw only 'distourbers of the kinges peple':

And in this same yere vpon the Whitsonday, a man of the towne of Abyngdon that is in Oxenfordshire, that called hym-self Iak Sharp, was take, with other mo of his company, for risers and distourbers of the kinges peple, and for his false ymaginacion and treson that he began to make and worke in that Cuntre aboute; and perfore he was drawe, and hanged and quartered at Abyngdon, and his hede smyten of, and set upon London Brigge, by the comaundement of the Duke of Gloucestre, Lieutenant of England, and by all the good and worthy lordes of the Kinges Consayle being that tyme in the Reame.[81]

They agree that Sharpe and his companions were condemned for treason, not heresy. They did not challenge the Church's spiritual authority, they challenged its secular estate. This was always the weak spot of its legitimacy as an institution. How could its wealth and secular power be justified in the name of Jesus?

Support for Jack Sharpe's rising, which affected the districts around Oxford and Abingdon, 'came in significant proportion from workers in the cloth industry . . . The leader and probable instigator was a weaver from Abingdon . . . named William Mandeville, who called himself Jack Sharp of Wigmoreland.'[82] The meaning of his adopted name has yet

---

[79] Jack Sharpe's Petition (1431).   [80] *Chronicle of London*, 155–6.
[81] Brie (ed.), *The Brut*, 457.   [82] *Ibid.*, 26.

to be unravelled, but that he adopted it means it must have had symbolic significance to his companions from the villages between Oxford and Abingdon. Another source describes Mandeville as 'the bailiff of the town' of Abingdon.[83] This would mean he was appointed by the abbot, which is possible but seems unlikely. Why would the abbot appoint a weaver to be bailiff? Harvey tells us that Sharpe and the other organisers each had 'a scribe or secretary and a messenger service'. The rising was 'built upon a wide-reaching campaign of bill-sticking through the southern Midlands and the West Country'.[84] One of the bills has survived, and begins as follows:[85]

The most excellent and dowty lord, oure lege Lord the Kyng, and to alle the Lordys of the reme of this present Parlement, we besechen mekely alle the comuns to ben herd of hem, mevyng that thei may have of the temporaltes as be Bysshoppys, Abbotys, and Priours, occupyud and wasted yvel wyth ynne the reme, fifteen Erledoms, fifteen hundred Knyghts, six thousand and two hundred Squyers, and one hundred houses of almes, mo than there ben atte thys tyme.

It proceeds to a detailed account of the annual value of all the leading religious houses in England, amounting to a sum of three hundred and thirty-two thousand marks, 'that wolde fynde fifteen Erles, fifteen hundred Knytes, six thousand Squyers, and a hundred howses of almesse, as ys above sayd; and yet twenty thousand pownde to the Kyng be yere, and no thyng harme to the reme'. If the government would then abolish lesser houses that were also 'wasted among worldly clerkys and religyous . . . they may getene a hundred and ten thousand pounde of mo temporaltes'. 'Jack Sharpe' claimed to speak for

alle comyns of the reme, desyryng to wurschyp Godde, preyen that alle the temporaltes of chyrches thus appropred ayens Crystes lore be turned to Godde, and to the prosperyte of the reme. For alle the worldly relygyous do nat the office of an hundred curates, ne of a secular lord, ne of a trewe laborer, ne lyve thereafter in penaunce ne in bodeley trawayle, as religyous shuld do, be here profectyon, but taken of astate a lust, and putten a way travayle, and take away the profyte that shuld come to the trewe men.

The assumption that Jack Sharpe's Rising was 'Lollard' derives from the anti-clerical substance of its manifesto. It urged confiscation of church estates, a view which the Church naturally defined as heretical ('Lollard'). Other issues also need consideration. First, the background includes a

---

[83] *VCH Berks*, vol. 4, p. 438.
[84] I.M.W. Harvey, *Jack Cade's Rebellion of Fourteen-Fifty* (Oxford 1991), 75, 77.
[85] Jack Sharpe's handbill, BL; repr. in Rolls Series vol. 28 (1857), *Annales Monasterii S.Albani* vol. 1 (1857), Appendix F, pp. 452–6.

general movement that Barbara Harvey has called 'a revolution in concepts of status', that is to say, a movement of the late fourteenth and first half of the fifteenth century against lords who resisted the desire of tenants to cast off feudal bonds, in imitation of innumerable contemporary examples of local movements which had succeeded in doing so.[86] The cloth industries of Oxford and Abingdon were under pressure, in these years, from the spread of clothmaking beyond their city limits and thus beyond the control of their guilds.[87] What we find in such towns is not resistance to men in holy orders, but to men in holy orders exercising oppressive and rapacious secular lordship. Such resistance was suppressed or expressed all the way across a spectrum from daily negotiations and bargaining in fields, barns and workshops to more organized resistance to details of lords' 'liberties', to strikes like those at Thornbury to raids on caravans of vehicles carrying food or other commodities out of the localities and provinces, to a more focused recognition of who the enemies of the people really were. Resistance to the Church was compatible with an underlying movement of passive resistance to feudal lordship *per se*; it was indifferent to the secular or religious status of particular lords, but was most likely to be directed against monastic lords because they resisted manumission and populist vernacularization more tenaciously than their secular counterparts. 'Jack Sharpe's handbill' circulated for two decades before Sharpe had it copied and stuck up on walls around the Abingdon district. It was word for word the same document as the one presented to the Parliament of 1409, where 'the Comunes put up a bille to the kyng as for the temporaltes beyng in the handes of the spiritualtee'. This Bill, represented as the opinion of 'all the trewe Comunes saying . . . sothely' (all the true commons speaking truth), was first formulated when Lollardy was at its zenith as a national movement encompassing all ranks, but it was directed against the secular

---

[86] From c.1390 'the [Westminster] monks' treatment of their estate and their tenants betrays a change of outlook . . . demesnes were put on lease [and] the abbot and convent ceased to be intimately concerned, as producers, with labour problems . . . the fundamental change was their recognition . . . that most of the inhabitants of their manors were not of villein status but free. By the mid-fifteenth century, only those who could be shown to be of servile parentage, the *nativi de sanguine*, were unfree; these were probably a small group. But it would . . . be more appropriate to say that a revolution in concepts of status in English society at large now compelled the monks . . . to exploit their tenant-land along different lines . . . ': Barbara Harvey *Westminster Abbey and its Estates in the Middle Ages* (Oxford 1977), 5.

[87] PRO E28/62/36, 'Petition of the Weavers of Oxford', and E28/62/35 'Privy Seal Warrant transmitting Petition of the Weavers . . .' (1438): etext.lib.virginia. edu/toc/modeng/public/AnoChan.html, University of Virginia, *Anthology of Chancery English*, Texts 203–4.

wealth and power of ecclesiastical lords, not their theology.[88] If its secular estates were taken away, the Church would naturally find it difficult to sustain pompous ecclesiastical magnates like Thomas Arundel.

Jack Sharp's rebellion was another symptom of a movement that included *Piers Plowman* and that seemed to be winning over knights and even magnates in Parliament. Historians have seen urban opposition to exceptionally powerful and religious lords as isolated phenomena, local, contained by city walls and limits. It is certain that resistance to the Church as secular lord was most intense and routine in such places, but the simple ideas that gave rise to it were not so easily restricted. This most common type of anticlericalism was not about theology, ceremony and ritual at all. As the antecedents of Tyndale saw it, no matter how much they juggled with logic and propositions, the wealth and power of the Church was overwhelming. It was a constant, flagrant offence to what popular culture had come to know and imagine the real Jesus to have been. A thousand local and estate-specific resistance movements set themselves, not against the religion, but against the power and wealth, the secular 'estate', of the Church.[89] This is one reason why men who spent their lives leading popular resistance against the hegemony of a local religious house, also wished to retire to such places when they were old and alone, left generous bequests to, and were finally laid to rest in the chapels and churches of monasteries, abbeys and convents to await the Second Coming.[90] Virulent anticlericalism and passionate doctrinal conservatism existed side-by-side in the same lives and minds. Recent studies have emphasized the conservative devotion of perhaps a majority of English people well into the protestant era. The medieval English Church failed itself by failing to win the argument that it served the religious needs of the community before its own estates.

Rather than see the 'Jack Sharpe' movement as an episode in the history of Lollardy, we should see it as the latest episode in a conflict that

---

[88] 'To the which bille atte that tyme was noone answere yoven For the kyng wolde be avysed.' *Chronicle of London*, ed. Thomas and Thornley.

[89] For the case of Cirencester, see above, n. 51; R.H. Hilton, 'Towns in English Feudal Society', in *Class Conflict and the Crisis of Feudalism*', 109, describes Bury St Edmunds and St Albans as 'well-known examples'. It is notable, in view of the pro-monastic sentiments of the Northern rebellion of 1536, that most of them seem to have been south of the Trent.

[90] 'In order to make its voice effective [the Church] resorted to those very attributes of wealth and exclusiveness which removed it further and further from the gospel on which is was founded. As a consequence, by the end of the twelfth century it was less and less able to compete with the claims of Cathars, Arnoldists, Humiliati, and Waldensians, that they were the true Christians in their pursuit of poverty and simplicity': Gordon Leff, *Heresy in the Late Middle Ages* (Manchester 1967), 15; England's was a variant response to this contradiction.

was centuries older than Lollardy. It was probably as old as the Abbey's lordship, which existed before 1066. 'The Abingdon Chronicle tells us that before the time of Abbot Faritius it was held lawful on the manors of the Abbey to drive the peasants away from their tenements':

The stewards and bailiffs often made free use of this right, if anybody gave them a fee out of greed, or out of spite against the holder. Nor was there any settled mode of succession, and when a man died, his wife and children were pitilessly thrown out of their home in order to make place for perfect strangers. An end was put to such a lawless condition . . . by Faritius's reforms: he was very much in want of money and found it more expedient to substitute a settled custom for the disorderly rule of stewards. But he did not thereby renounce any of his manorial rights: he only regulated their application. The legal feature of base tenure – its insecurity – was not abolished on the Abingdon estates.[91]

The earliest recorded protests took place in the reign of Henry II.[92] The half-century before the Black Death was marked by 'a series of revolts against the abbey'. As was the case in other monastic towns like Cirencester and Bury St Edmunds, their 'primary objective was to gain control of the market and fairs, but they also desired to obtain some voice in their own government'. 'The base of all the actions', according to one account of the situation in the first half of the fourteenth century, was the fraternity of the Holy Cross at St Helen's parish church. In May 1327 the townspeople, assisted by neighbouring villages and 'the commonalty of Oxford headed by their mayor' attacked the abbey, entered and burnt houses, assaulted and beat the monks and abbey servants, killing some and detaining others in prison until they paid fines for their release. Damage was estimated to have exceeded a thousand pounds.[93] Smaller scale revolts occurred in 1348 and 1370. Abbey estates in the Abingdon district were involved in the 'great rumour' of 1377, when the men of the manor of Warfield requested from the crown a copy of the Domesday entries for the hundred of Ripplesmere, in the belief that this would show their freedom from the abbot's yoke. The hundred included the manor of Winkfield, held by Abingdon Abbey.[94] This historical background explains why, in *Piers Plowman*, Langland represented the abbot of Abingdon as the archetype of monastic tyrants.[95] In August 1391

[91] P. Vinogradoff, *Villainage in England* (Oxford 1892), 165, quoting from G.G. Coulton, *The Medieval Village* (Cambridge 1926), 121–2.

[92] *VCH Berks* vol. 2 (London 1907) 'Religious Houses: Abingdon'.

[93] C.F. Slade and Gabrielle Lambrick (ed.), *Two Cartularies of Abingdon Abbey* (Oxford 1995), 327–9; *VCH Berks* vol. 1 (London 1972), 56.

[94] Rosamund Faith, 'The Great Rumour of 1377 and Peasant Ideology', in R.H. Hilton and T. Aston (ed.), *The English Rising of 1381* (Cambridge 1984), 72.

[95] Langland, *Piers the Ploughman*, trans. J.F. Goodridge (Harmondsworth 1959), p. 160 and n. 36, p. 338.

'certain malefactors and disturbers of the king's peace armed and arrayed in warlike mode...entered the precincts and houses of the abbot of Abingdon...by force and armed might...and [took], consumed and removed goods, objects, rents and other profits there'.[96] The tradition of rebellion against Abingdon Abbey preceded Lollardy by several generations.

No matter how assiduously religious houses cultivated appropriate disciplines on the part of their members (and none was ever successful in doing this without scandal for long), too many of them were undone in popular opinion by their obvious thirst for wealth and power over the people of this world. It is an interesting but entirely speculative question, whether Henry VIII would have been able to suppress English monastic houses in the 1530s had there not been a very widespread sense that, in the final analysis, they got only what they deserved. It may be that wealthy and powerful houses existed, in the north perhaps, that were not viewed by locals with deep suspicion and reservation. In most cases abbots went into their Henrician retirements with a pensioned whimper rather than a bang. Their demise was welcomed by local populations, even (or especially) the local 'big men' who had been their trusted middlemen and stewards.

As had been the case in 1381, when so many local insurrections had been directed against abbeys, a monastic writer attempted to have the last, definitive word about the character of Jack Sharpe's rebellion:

> Yf heretike ought kouthe pike him fro
> Yf Sharpe or Wawe hadde of the lawe a feste
> Yf right was fond in al this londe vnto
> Hit to gouerne he doon the sterne unto

This attempt to stamp Sharpe as both a heretic and a common brigand is from a verse composed in honour of duke Humphrey of Gloucester, probably by a monk of St Albans Abbey.[97] Wawe led a gang of robbers who terrorized Hertfordshire and Buckinghamshire in the 1420s.[98]

And in passing let us note this tendency, evident as early as 'The Song of the Flemish Insurrection', and forming the entire substance of Jack Sharpe's Handbill, to *count* the ruling class, lay and clerical, as well as to *write* their abuses. It strengthened awareness of just how small a proportion of the English population the lords were.

---

[96] *Two Cartularies*, doc. L657, 27 August 1391, p. 449.
[97] Quotation from R.A. Griffiths, 'William Wawe and his Gang', in Griffiths, *England and Wales in the Fifteenth Century* (London 1991), 227.
[98] G.O. Sayles (ed.), *Select Cases in the Court of King's Bench under Richard II, Henry IV and Henry V* (London 1971).

5.6 The crisis continues: rising for the commonweal, 1450–1549

And in that furynys they went, as they said, for the comyn wele of the realm of England.

The discourse of the commonweal emerged out of the 'furynys' of the decades from 1381 to 1450. Cade's Rebellion has a critical place in the new constitutional history of fifteenth-century England. New research, derived from the hermeneutic theories of J.G.A. Pocock and Quentin Skinner, rejects the idea that politics in general, and fifteenth-century politics in particular, can be analysed and understood effectively in terms of the 'cynicism and self-interest' of the actors. 'Ideas influence politics,' writes John Watts, 'because in order to promote and defend their activities in a particular public environment, politicians are forced to explain themselves with reference to its "accepted principles", and this consideration, in turn, shapes their behaviour.' Conventional ideas and climates of opinion *necessarily* structure discourse and discourse shapes actions. Without reference to conventionally real and rhetorical contexts, discourse will be incomprehensible, strange, or in some other way incompatible with the prejudices and preconceptions of the contemporaries who must be persuaded. Watts argues that constitutional 'principles' decisively influenced the ways fifteenth-century politics were conducted. *Contra* Stubbs and Maitland, 'the Wars of the Roses' *were* about ideas. It was not politicians' cynicism that 'wrecked the thirteenth-century achievement and opened the way to despotism.'[99]

Behind these new ideas lurked the spectre of the commonalty, a spectre that regularly but unpredictably manifested itself in resistance and rebellion. In Watts's view, 'the crisis of 1450 . . . entirely changed the nature of Henry VI's polity'. 'So broad and deep was the failure of government,' he writes, 'that the authority of king and lords momentarily, but entirely, collapsed'. The outcome, for Watts, was unprecedented: 'into the breach stepped the commons of England, both the people themselves and their *soi-disant* representatives in parliament. For the next year or two, it was they who dictated the political agenda, leaving the nobility little choice but to represent them and to respond to their concerns.'[100] 'Besides the

---

[99] F.W. Maitland, *The Constitutional History of England: a Course of Lectures*, ed. H.A.L. Fisher (Cambridge 1961), 194, summed up the anti-ideas and anti-class consensus: 'So far as I can understand it, the confusing struggle which we call the Wars of the Roses is not to any considerable extent a context between opposite principles – it is a great faction fight in which the whole nation takes sides.' John L. Watts, 'Polemic and Politics in the 1450s', in Margaret Lucille Kekewich, Colin Richmond, Anne F. Sutton, Livia Visser-Fuchs, John L.Watts (ed.), *The Politics of Fifteenth-Century England: John Vale's Book* (Stroud 1995), 3–4.

[100] John Watts, *Henry VI and the Politics of Kingship* (Cambridge 1996), 205.

interests of the king and the common interest of the lords, the two factors which had so far governed the manufacture of central authority, there was now a third factor to be considered: the common interest of the realm, brought to the fore in 1449–50 by dissidents, rebels, the commons in parliament and the duke of York.' Watts shows that the ideological 'wars of the Roses' differed from the more muted and ambivalent populism of Henry of Lancaster, in 1399–1400, in that the field of forces was clearer and more articulated. In this sense, the political presence of the commonalty in all its manifestations became part of 'the traditional pattern of authority' in 1450.[101]

Never in recorded history had the English been so at odds with each other about what exactly 'traditional patterns of authority' were, and how they applied in contingent circumstances. Uncertainty began with the throne. In place of the idea that the English monarchy was political or constitutional from *Magna Carta* forward, Watts describes a public opinion that fluctuated mercurially between Fortescue's alternatives, *dominium regale* and *dominium politicum*.[102] There was a divided discourse, all the way from the constitutions of Clarendon, through the deaths of Edward II, Richard II, Edward V and Richard III to the execution of Charles I. The issue was only ever resolved in practice. Similarly, early vernacular sources testify to the existence of several different models of how a perfectly cooperating commonwealth would be ranked and ordered, from the egalitarian commune implied in the rebel letters of 1381 to Thomas Wimbledon's three mutually dependent estates (1387) and the Digby poet's detailed anatomy of the body politic of c.1400.[103] Uncertainty pervaded everything, from the prescribed role and make-up of the commonalty to the nature of the eucharist.[104] In short, Watts describes an enduring legitimacy crisis that went well beyond dynastic struggles: 'kingship, lordship, justice, the social structure, the economy, history, law, religion, morality had never before been opened up to such searching and extensive comment'. Watts describes an 'information explosion' that 'cannot have been without political and social

---

[101] Watts, *Henry VI*, 254. Watts writes that 'the king' and 'the company of true lords' constituted 'the traditional pattern of authority'. Yet by their violent actions rather than by their moderating words, the rebels of 1450 established a continuity with 1381, a tradition of communes intervention that implied a challenge to the 'traditional authority' of the king and the lords' counsel. (Watts, 'Polemic and Politics', 10.) It is a confusing struggle, as Maitland observed, yet Watts is surely right to emphasize the crucial importance of ideas and the importance of public opinion and commons rebellion.

[102] Fortescue, *The Difference*, ch. 1, f. 1.   [103] Wimbledon; 'Mannes membres', 64–8.

[104] Watts, 'Polemic and Politics', 39.

consequences'.[105] This *furynys* tempered the emerging discourse of the English commonweal.[106]

In May and June of 1450 'the commons (*comyns*) of kent arose with certain other shires, and they chose them a captain, the which captain compelled all the gentry to arise with them.' The first of the Kent manifestoes (distributed in May or early June 1450), evokes the role of 'murmuring' in the early stages of rebellion. The rising was justified, not by poverty, but by the law of self-defence and a disagreement about foreign affairs. It had been 'openly noised that kent should be destroyed with a royal power and made a wild forest for the death of the duke of Suffolk of which the commonalty therof was never guilty'. Murmuring voices and noise, a hubbub just out of earshot, was where commotions began. The London chronicler, William Gregory, took up the tale after the voices had converged into an army. That army arose with the demand that the slanderers of Kent be searched for 'through all the realm'. Likewise, 'common voices... noised that the king landed in France [had] been alienated and put away from the crown... with untrue (disloyal) means of treason'. They demanded that these reports be investigated, 'and if such traitors may be found guilty, they are to have execution of law without any pardon, in example of other'.[107] It was a rebellion of but one province, but 1381 had demonstrated that provincial rebellions could converge and merge. All it took was a general milieu of uncertainty and disillusion with government, a scattering of local disputes, an argument in a market place, the visit of an itinerant preaching friar, an attempt on the part of a local lord to collect his dues, unemployment in industrial districts. Crowds gathered in market towns. People were present who knew that crowds were gathering in neighbouring districts and their market towns. The crowds began to move from the market towns of a region to its provincial capital: Beverley or Maidstone, say, Colchester or Cirencester. At such times the spectre of the commonalty became a mysterious, many-headed beast, a river flowing along the lanes and highways of Kent, Essex or the Thames Valley, towards London. This was how contemporaries viewed and recorded it. The landscape rose against the forces designed to keep it settled.

---

[105] John L. Watts, 'Conclusions', in *The End of the Middle Ages: England in the Fifteenth and Sixteenth Centuries* (Stroud 1998), 270.

[106] For the radicalism of the *comuynes* of Sussex in the months following Cade's death, see Mavis Mate, 'The Economic and Social Roots of Medieval Popular Rebellion: Sussex in 1450–1451', *Economic History Review*, new series, 45:4 (November 1992).

[107] *John Vale's Book*, 204–5.

Rebellions made use of existing constitutional arrangements. Constables organized, or were persuaded to organize musters at traditional gathering-points. How it worked varied from place to place, but the common pattern is a spectral, ranked army. Certain people, families and households were known from long experience as good organizers and leaders of small groups of local people. Often they had acted as soldiers or were trained men. Murmuring districts nominated corporals to make contact with the sergeants. District and regional sergeant majors were informed. The troops came together at their traditional hundredal and provincial capitals. In these ways, and through these institutions, 'In the last weeks of May 1450, the power of the county of Kent assembled in arms under its elected constables and thereby set in motion Jack Cade's Rebellion.'

the Kentishmen joined together as a 'host' and selected a captain to lead them. They drew up petitions to explain their purposes and swore oaths to obey their leaders and stand with each other . . . Then . . . the host marched towards London, gathering in contingents as they went. By June 11 [they] were at Blackheath . . . By the 18th [they] withdrew . . . pursued by a royal army. On that day, an advance party of the royal force encountered and was destroyed by the Kentish rearguard at Sevenoaks . . . . [This] convinced the king to retreat . . . to Kenilworth. By the 27th, the road to London was clear . . . In the early days of July, London was occupied by the army of Kent, reinforced by men from Essex and elsewhere. The occupation was not gentle, and by the 5th the Londoners had had enough: throughout the nights of the 5th and 6th of July, the militia of kent fought the militia of London . . . for possession of London Bridge. Having failed in this battle to gain control of the bridge . . . Jack Cade negotiated a general pardon for his followers. By the 9th, the host of Kent seems to have disbanded itself: most of the men headed home . . . [108]

As in 1381, so in 1450 'they came with a great might and a strong host unto the Black Heath, beside Greenwich, the number of 46,000'. Contemporaries noted the rebels' military discipline. At Blackheath, 'they made a field, ditched and staked well about, as it would be in the land of war, save only they kept order among themselves'. They kept military order, but not rank, 'for as good was Jack Robin as John at the Nook, for all were as high as pigs feet'. They elected their leader, and oaths were sworn to act 'for the weal of him our sovereign lord, and of all the realm, and for to destroy the traitors being about him, with other diverse points

---

[108] Montgomerie Bohna, 'Armed Force and Civic Legitimacy in Jack Cade's Revolt', *English Historical Review* 118:471 (June 2003), 563.

that they would see that it were in short time amended'. 'Now is time', as John Ball had put it in 1381.[109]

The next day Captain Cade 'came with a great host to Southwark, and at the White Hart he took his lodgings'. On the evening of Friday 3 July they 'smote asunder the ropes' across London Bridge and entered the city. After these first forays, 'they went with their simple captain to his lodgings'. Gregory imagined them talking deep into the night about what they had achieved and what they should do next. 'Certain of his simple and rude men abode there all the night, saying to each other that they had wit and wisdom for to have guided or put in guiding all England, as soon as they had got the city of London.' They convinced themselves that they had the nation in their hands, and they knew why: they were one or two provinces only, it is true. But now they had the City of London at their mercy. The next step would be Westminster.

Gregory never forgot the July Days, when rebellion came to his doorstep. Not just the realm, but Gregory's own oligarchic world, 'the city' was threatened. This aroused emotions and coloured his prose.[110] 'Many a man was murdered and killed in that conflict', he wrote. For all that he could see the justice in much of what the rebels enacted, they were not his people or class.[111] He knew what he was, but not what *they* were. We hear no more of military discipline. As always happened when writers witnessed the multitude in action, Gregory was lost for words: 'I wot not what name [to write] for the multitude of *ryffe raffe* . . . They entered into the city of London as men that had been half beside their wits.'

What was most painful to Gregory was that as soon as the rebels crossed London Bridge they were immediately joined by the converging 'ryffe raffe' of London. Now 'they had other men with them, as well of London as of their own party'. The crossing of London Bridge had been a meeting 'by them of one part' (Kent) 'and of that other part' (London),

---

[109] 'John Ball seynte marie prist greteth wele alle maner men . . .', transcribed in Stephen Justice, *Writing and Rebellion: England in 1381* (Berkeley 1994), 14.

[110] David Grummit, 'Deconstructing Cade's Rebellion: Discourse and Politics in the Mid-Fifteenth Century', in *The Fifteenth Century*, vol. 6 (2006), 12, writes that 'it would be naïve to describe events such as "Gregory's Chronicle" as eyewitness accounts'. Gregory's account is certainly not dispassionate or 'objective'.

[111] The Treasurer, Lord Sayle, *ressayvyd hys jewys and hys dethe*. His death was no more than he deserved. 'At the comyng of the camptayne yn to Sowthworke, he lete smyte of the hedde of a strong theff that was namyhd Haywardyn.' Gregory gave no reason why Cade 'lette to be heddyd a man of Hampton, a squyer, the whyche was namyd Thomas Mayne', but his account suggests strongly that it wasn't only actual rebels who saw the justice in what they did: *The Historical Collections of a Citizen of London in the Fifteenth Century*, ed. James Gairdner, (London 1876) (henceforth *Gregory's Chronicle*), 192.

and between them 'they left nothing undone'. No-one could be sure that similar movements were not approaching from Essex, Hertfordshire and the Thames Valley. Popular rebellions were convergent movements that drew upon conditions found in most districts of England. Thus began the six-day rule of Captain Cade. On Saturday he executed three men, a lord (and state official), a squire (a provincial official), and a looter from his own ranks, and ordered that 'all the 3 heads that day smitten off were set upon London Bridge'. These were the rebel flags: as long as they stood on spikes on London Bridge, rebellion was ascendant. London belonged to 'that sorry and simple and rebellious captain with his many men'.

It took the 'true commons' a week to marshal its resources and plan the ejection of the rebels. These were Gregory's men, the elders and citizens. They, for Gregory, were 'the city', not this 'ryffe-raffe' rabble of the commonalty. 'That same evening London did arise . . . and from that time unto the morrow eight of bell they were ever fighting on London Bridge.' Six days after they were put up, 'the Saturday at evening, the three heads were taken down off London Bridge . . . and the bodies with heads were buried at the Grey Friars at London'. The rebels were 'voided' from London.[112] Rebellion was over, the repressions and myths could begin. Gregory saved the most shocking aspect of the rebellion until last. 'And in that furiousness they went, as they said, for the *comyn wele* of the realm of England.' The riff-raff rascability had presumed, not for the first time, to speak for the nation. In doing so, they institutionalized their word for what the whole struggle was about.

The spectre of popular rebellion haunted every generation from 1381 to 1649. Like parliamentarians in 1376 and the rebels of 1381 and 1450, the leader of a rising in 1469 'denounced the "covetous rule" of "sedicious persones" and called for "reformacioun". The stated object of the [1469] rebellion,' writes Wood, 'was to protect the "comonwele of this lond" against the "singular loucour" of its rulers.' Taxes, evil advisers and the duty of the 'trewe commons' to rise for the commonweal were, by now, traditional themes.[113] The Northern Rising of 1489 began with bands of 'rebel commoners' gathering in the North and East Ridings of Yorkshire 'in the first days of May'. The commons rose and were joined by discontented magnates and gentry. 'What turned out to be a rather small-scale plebeian revolt prompted an extraordinarily powerful response' from the nervous Henry VII, another king whose legitimacy was, to put it mildly, questionable. Michael Bennet warns against too

---

[112] *Gregory's Chronicle*, 193.   [113] Wood, *1549 Rebellions*, 3.

easily dismissing 'the danger posed by plebeian unrest' in 1489 and sees the rebellion as symptomatic of 'a changing political climate'.[114]

In 1497 an army of redressers marched out of Cornwall, through Devon to Wells, Somerset, where they recruited the seventh baron Audley, yet still remained under the command of Michael An Gof, a blacksmith from Keverne. Thomas Flamank, a lawyer, was clearly aware of the traditions of popular rebellion; to him was attributed the strategy of marching across the south of England to Blackheath, where, it was hoped, they would unite with the commons of Kent.[115]

The Cornish rebellion was fresh in Edmund Dudley's mind when, in 1509, he formulated the theory that the English commonalty was habitually subject to visits from two truthful but dangerous 'messengers'. The first messenger was 'discontention and murmur', the second 'Arrogancy, near cousin of pride'. For over a century these messengers had inspired common people to follow the 'banner of Insurrection'. 'The commynaltie of this realm of England,' wrote Dudley, 'often tymes smartyd righte sore for such lewd enterprise.' 'Behold [well whether] ye commyners of the west parte of this land wan any honestie or profytt by there lewde enterprise with ther capten the Black Smithe?' He prayed to God to save 'this realme from any suche captain herafter'. Notable in his theory that 'insurrection' was the 'perilous core of [the commons'] fruite', was that it should be avoided, not because the messengers were false but because the commons never 'profit' from them. In place of insurrection, Dudley advised the commons to 'well and substancially imprincte [the messages] in the hartes of the nobles'. As long as they stopped short of insurrection, reminding the nobles of their duty would do 'no harme; peradventure yt wold cawse [the nobles] at seasons to haue the more compassion, marcy and charitie on [over] the poore commyners'. The commons were to 'eschew this perilous core of your fruite', that is to say insurrection; 'yet cast not away this enterprise of your core for it may fortune to be to you a chief frind. Therfore kepe hym close within you vnto the tyme ye may lawfully vse hym.'[116] But what more effective way was there to 'imprincte' their 'discontentment' in the 'hartes of the nobles' than by insurrection?

Dudley's first 'messenger' was active in April 1523, and made itself heard by the government in the form of sporadic resistance arising from

---

[114] Michael J. Bennet, 'Henry VII and the Northern Rising of 1489', *English Historical Review* 105:414 (January 1990), 40, 45, 55 and *passim*.

[115] Anthony Fletcher and Diarmaid MacCulloch, *Tudor Rebellions*, 5th ed. (Harlow 2005), 19–21.

[116] *The Tree of Commonwealth: a Treatise written by Edmund Dudley* (1509–10), ed. D.M. Brodie (Cambridge 1948), 91–3.

rumours that an unprecedentedly heavy tax was in the offing. The wealthy shires of 'East Anglia, Berkshire, Wiltshire and Kent' were restive and clothmaking districts in Suffolk were close to violence.[117] Insurrection did not follow on this occasion because taxation was the only issue. Thirteen years later, however, this was not so. As Fortescue's theory predicted, the northern rebellion of 1536 was, in its beginnings, 'overwhelmingly popular'.[118] 'In the late commotion,' wrote one witness, 'the busiest were the poorest.'[119] In 1536 'commons' (like 'commonwealth') was a 'portmanteau term' that carried variable meanings. The many-headed image was foreshadowed in an observer's report that 'the people, being of divers sorts, diversly take the matter'. Modern studies have shown us that the commonalty was indeed a much fractured, many-headed beast, but 'the majority of writers [in 1536] simply used "the commons" to describe an undifferentiated, apparently homogeneous, body of men'. When the movement was over and everyone had gone home, the Justices turned to the '"honest men" of the neighbourhood(s) . . . to exercise some influence in calming the revolt'. The point is not that the commonalty arisen ceased to be structured and ranked, 'divided' according to the official doctrine of degree into third and fourth 'sorts', and, beyond the 'sorts', into a multitude of vocations, degrees of wealth, age, physique, 'conceits and capacities', but that everyday forms of authority, status and organization were commandeered for other purposes.

The rebels of 1536 saw themselves in Fortescue's terms. 'Master Poverty' was an NCO in the platoon of 'Captain Poverty', in a battalion led by 'Lord Poverty', under the general command of the 'Earl of Poverty'.[120] All were served by 'Poverty's Chaplains'. Taxes and religious discontent fuelled but did not spark rebellion, which exploded 'from below' and was caused by poverty. Robert Aske was 'the architect of the movement's image'.[121] The image he did not want the rebellion to be associated with was stated in the first injunction of the oath he administered to the rebels: 'Ye shall *not* enter into this our Pilgrimage of Grace for the Commonwealth.' Aske's intention was to redirect a rebellion that was under way before he became involved. He insisted on it not being 'for the commonwealth', because that was exactly how the rebels had justified their actions up to that point.[122]

---

[117] Fletcher and MacCulloch, *Tudor Rebellions*, 21–5.
[118] R.W. Hoyle, *The Pilgrimage of Grace and the Politics of the 1530s* (Oxford 2001), 17.
[119] Quotation from Hoyle, *Pilgrimage of Grace*, 427.   [120] *Ibid.*, 'Poverty', Index, 484.
[121] *Ibid.*, p. 207.
[122] The earlier articles have a realistic, pragmatic bias. The 'suppression of so many religious houses' was regretted not only because 'the service of our God is not well maintained but also the commons of your realm unrelieved'. They were also affected

For Ethan Shagen, the decision of Lord Darcy and the northern nobility to join the rebels 'allowed the commons to wield real power in public affairs even though their elite allies were no more enamoured of popular politics than were their enemies'.[123] In the thirteenth century common people signed up for a common enterprise inaugurated by lords. From 1381 to 1549 the dynamic was reversed: common rebels took the initiative and lords reacted. Like Sir Thomas Elyot and other educated men of their generation, Aske felt that 'commonweal' terminology could not be used innocuously. As we saw, Elyot was alarmed at the way in which Tudor counsellors had appropriated the term as a synonym for 'republic' and 'state', when in his view it was popularly understood to mean, and actually *did* mean, *Res Plebeia*, implying the existence of a powerful 'plebeian public sphere'.[124] Elyot's argument was that the state and its counsellors should stop using a word which meant one thing at court but quite another amongst the commonalty. Everything the state did, the usage proclaimed, was not in the interests of the ruling classes, but for the commonwealth.[125] Trevisa had stated the official position in the 1380s: 'Ye shulde knowe that al that governours of the comynte doth, thei doth hit al for profit of the comynte to fore her owne savacioun.'[126] With such formulae, ruling classes acknowledged that government was supposed to be for the commonweal. What then, if, as Dudley assumed, 'governours of the comynte' manifestly did not put the profit of their community before their own salvation? What was then the duty of their subordinates? The principle of commonweal was not just applied to kings, barons and counsellors, but to relations between every rank and class. Elyot shared Fortescue's fears of the term's communist meanings: in common ears,

---

by what Hoyle ('Taxation and the Mid-Tudor Crisis', *Economic History Review* 51:4 (1998), 649–75) shows to have been a series of the most crippling taxes endured in England since the wars of Edward III. They were concerned with the king's appointment of 'persons that be of low birth and small reputation', at the expense of the Commonwealth. Finally, they objected to the king's promotion of 'divers bishops . . . that hath not the faith of Christ'. Aske noticed the secular thrust of the original motivations of the Lincolnshire Commons, associated them immediately with Commonwealth ideology, and made it his business to define the purposes of the movement more carefully: Hoyle, *Pilgrimage of Grace*, p. 206.

[123] Shagen, 'Popularity and the 1549 Rebellions Revisited', 125.

[124] 'And consequently there may appere lyke diversitie to be englisshe, between a publike weale and a commune weale, as shulde be in Latin betwene Res publica and Res plebeia.' *Thomas Elyot's "The Governor"*, A1r, A1v, A2r; Elyot also defines *publike weale* in *The Bankette of Sapience* (1534), in Lillian Gottesman (ed.), *Four Political Treatises by Sir Thomas Elyot* (Gainesville, Fla. 1967), 186–7.

[125] For the provenance of 'state', cf. Quentin Skinner, 'From the State of Princes to the Person of the State', in Skinner, *Visions of Politics* (Cambridge 2002), 368–413.

[126] John Trevisa, *Dialogus inter Militem et Clericum*, ed. A.J. Perry, Early English Text Society (London 1925), 34.

'commonweal' meant either 'the commoners only must be wealthy, and the gentlemen and nobles needy, or else excluding gentility, all men must be of one degree and sort, and a new name provided'. *Commonweal* meant *Res Plebeia*. Elyot insisted this was the *correct* meaning. That was why he wanted everyone to stop using it.

Robert Aske's oath aimed to transform aggressive 'commonwealths' into penitent, respectful petitioners, 'pilgrims' of the lowest ranks, spokesmen not for themselves but for immemorial customs and the Church of Christendom. Not understanding that the term had been officially appropriated by circles around the throne, their complaints and murmurings coalesced under the rubric of 'common weal'. Aske wanted to avoid connotations of Cade's *ryffe raffe* and Ball's *comuynes*. Yet he affirmed the popular demand that the king 'expulse all villein blood and evil counsellors against the commonwealth from his grace and his privy council'. This, as suggested above, was a common variant of the evil counsellor theme: they hated men who had betrayed their class and become 'counsellors against the commonwealth'. So it was about the commonwealth after all.

The principle from which the 'many mischiefs' always arose was disturbingly simple. Government is supposed to be for the common good. Any person and class whose government is subtly or blatantly self-serving is suspect. The *comun wele* is greater than any individual, household, rank, clan, neighbourhood, shire, class or kingdom. The power of the word was that it had become irresistibly associated with resistance and rebellion that welled up from below, as Fortescue described it, and ran out of control. By however fuzzy a logic or chain of associations, the reasons for rebellion could merge into one great reason: the abolition of all institutionalized inequalities. The question Elyot raised was not how did rebellion begin, but where would it end? He raised the spectre of communism. For Elyot, like Marx, the English popular rebel's 'foundational intellectual purpose was . . . to place historical practice in the service of a utopian abolitionist project – the revolutionary achievement of a class*less* society'.[127] Marx did not invent the theory of class-struggle, nor did he invent the spectre of communism.[128] The commonweal is greater than any of its component parts. This reflexive, second-nature,

---

[127] Christopher Tomlins, 'Out of the Cradle, Endlessly Orbiting', commentary on 'Language and Class', Conference on Class-Struggle in the Atlantic World, University of Montana (September 2003), 3.

[128] On historicizing Marx and his theory of class-struggle, cf. Rollison, *Local Origins*, 247; Keith Wrightson, *Earthly Necessities: Economic Lives in Early Modern Britain* (New Haven 2000), 10–13; and Rollison, 'Marxism', in Garthine Walker (ed.), *Writing Early Modern History* (Oxford 2005), 3–24.

collectivist, corporatist, populist, pre-liberal and pre-party state of mind was central to English vernacular politics, and above all to the 'plebeian public sphere', up to 1649. It emerged in all of the favoured metaphors – the mill or ship of state, the body politic, the *communem utilitatem regni* ('common utility of the realm') of Edward I and the *commune weal* of Cade's rebels. It defined the constitutional culture of the age.

The gentlemen, nobles, yeomen and citizens who were later tried and executed for their involvement in 1536 were not the instigators of the movement, but were drawn in more or less unwillingly, as Fortescue's formula predicted. They found themselves in the midst of that enduring nightmare, the 'fourth sort' on the move.[129] Commons rebellions reversed prescribed social order; the common people forced its social superiors to choose and act, not *vice-versa*. The accumulating tradition of autonomous popular rebellion created the condition for the high-political 'strategy' that Shagen sees as having emerged in 1536 and 1549. As we have seen, 'popularity strategy' had been a feature of the 'common enterprise' of 1258 and was employed tactically by Edward III's advisers in 1327. It had been central to Henry of Lancaster's bid for the throne in 1399–1400. As Watts has shown, it was central to Yorkist strategy in the mid-fifteenth century. 'In 1549,' writes Shagen, 'Somerset found himself riding that same tiger.'[130] The 'peasant rebels' who gathered at Norwich under the leadership of Robert Kett in 1549 'brought England closer to pitched class warfare than it had come since 1381'. Protector Somerset's decision to conduct 'an unprecedented dialogue with many of the rebel camps' raised fears among the gentry that 'monarcho-populism' was government strategy: Elyot's nightmare come true.[131]

---

[129] That this was Cromwell's view is implicit in the list of questions he formulated for Robert Aske after the rebellion was over. The first twenty-five of his questions are designed to ascertain Aske's *reactions* to the 'brutes' (rumours) that were 'spread abrode in those countreis': Mary Bateson, 'Aske's Examination', *English Historical Review* 5:19 (July 1890), 551–2.

[130] Shagen, 'Popularity and the 1549 Rebellions Revisited', 125. Shagen points out that Protector Somerset's 'political modus operandi' is extremely revealing of 'how elite politics changed in response to pressures from the commons' (121). In 'Protector Somerset and the 1549 Rebellions: New Sources and New Perspectives', *English Historical Review* 114 (1999), 48, Shagen writes that 'regardless of his true beliefs, the public face of Somerset's politics became extremely novel, using rhetoric that came dangerously close to envisaging a political partnership between government and commons'. Thus he created 'his own symbolism of authority, enacting a series of ostentatious gestures to public opinion in which he presented himself as an intellectual and godly patron and a friend to the poor commons'.

[131] Holstun, 'The Spider and the Fly', 53. Andy Wood, *1549 Rebellions*, esp. Part II, 'Political Language', describes the structure and the words and motivations of the participants in a way that no earlier study has done. Wood argues (Chapter 5, 'The Decline of Insurrection') that 1549 was 'the last medieval rebellion'. There is something

5.7   The tradition of rebellion

We have seen that reports attributing political agency to the commons first appear in English archives relating to Simon de Montfort's 'common enterprise' of the 1250s and 1260s. They recurred throughout the reigns of Edward I and Edward II and reached a crescendo immediately after Edward II's disappearance in 1327. They became a conventional pretext of House of Commons petitions throughout the long reign of Edward III. Another crescendo began with the 'Good' Parliament of 1376, exploded in 1381 and was sustained, virtually without respite, roughly from the Commons Rebellion until Jack Sharpe's minor but notorious rebellion of 1431. Another crescendo peaked during the 'furyness' of Cade's Rebellion in 1450 and became the basis of a burst of strategic magnate populism through the 1450s and 1460s. Dangerous words turned into popular rebellions again in 1469, 1485 and 1497; and rebellions approaching the scale and public consciousness of 1381 and 1450 erupted in the northern rebellions of 1536; and, once again, in several regions of England, in 1549.

In this socio-political *longue duree*, 1381 marks an obvious turning-point. It was the first time that common people rose in rebellion without the leadership and encouragement of magnates. In the period from *Magna Carta* to the deposition of Edward II, magnates led and commons followed. After 1381 the commons led and the governing ranks reacted. After 1549, renewed efforts were made by all the propertied ranks to end, or minimize, the unwonted intervention of 'common people' in affairs of state.

Michael Bush argues that while the tradition of rebellion was undoubtedly popular and bore many similarities to a class movement, it was reactionary in motivation and ideology. Although leadership often came from the wealthier villagers and marginal gentry, the driving force came from below and leadership was grounded in 'a principle of answerability to the

to be said for the idea that the 'polarization' of the third and fourth sorts may have intensified during the century 1549–1649, thus reducing the propensity for momentary alliances of the 'respectability' and 'rascability'. As I have suggested above, I see such 'polarization' as a permanent tendency of local communities from the thirteenth to seventeenth centuries. It is especially evident, for example, in the aftermath of 1381, 1450 and 1536, when the state had good reason to want to accept 'respectable' participants' appeal to Sir John Fortescue's theory that 'worthymen' were drawn in against their will. I suggest (below, Chapter 9) that the civil wars of the 1640s saw the re-articulation of most of the abiding features of the 'age of the Commonweal'. The key condition was the coincidence and 'equivalentialization' of different discontentments of the local chapters of the propertied and the rascability. In that sense the 1640s, not 1549, saw 'the last medieval rebellion'. In my revision of the periodization, each of the rebellions of 1381–1649 was 'early modern'.

commons'. Rebels were animated by a conviction that they belonged to a 'commonalty of the realm'. The tradition thus constituted 'a social force that transcended "feudal" and local allegiances'. Rebels saw themselves as members of a national class, 'the commons'; they believed they represented 'a shared identity and cause'. Yet in Bush's account the identity and the cause were far from revolutionary. The risings of 1549, like the earlier rebellions, were informed by a corporatist 'rationale'. 'Risings of the commons,' writes Bush, 'were part of the corrective machinery associated with the society of orders.' The implication was 'that the notion of orders was not a belief simply suspended from above but one upheld from below', suggesting that 'risings of the commons had derived their strength from the *weakness* of class divisions' in late medieval society.[132]

In contrast to Bush, Andy Wood argues that the tradition of rebellion is 'best understood as manifestations of a deeper popular political culture'. Wood recognizes the accumulative importance of the practice of rebellion and offers evidence of a conscious link, a chain of 'popular memory' and 'oral tradition' spanning the rebellions of 1381, 1407, 1450, 1469, 1485, 1497, 1536 and 1549. Bush held that what was handed down was a passionate commitment to the society of orders and a belief that when all the senior ranks failed to uphold the principle of commonweal that held it together, it was the commonalty's duty to restore it. Wood confirms 'the orderliness of the rebellion' but shows, crucially, that earlier accounts have 'understate[d] the significance of [the] anger, vengeance and violence [that was] apparent in rebel behaviour'. The anger was directed primarily against the gentry and, more generally, against all intermediary ranks between the king and the commons.

The class contempt that gentry and (increasingly) 'middle sorts' frequently expressed towards the labouring classes was reciprocated. Class feeling *was* manifest in the tradition of rebellion. The 'deeper political culture' that underpinned popular rebellions was centred on an alternative to the society of orders: they rose in the name of 'a polity based upon a combination of monarchical lordship and popular sovereignty'.[133]

The 'clearest expression of late medieval popular politics', writes Wood, is to be found in the Mousehold articles, drawn up by the Norfolk rebels on Mousehold Heath 'in the course of a protracted process of negotiation with Protector Somerset'. They represent 'a process of state formation from the bottom up', in which 'local inhabitants' attempted to 'create some governmental unity within their communities, taking power

---

[132] Michael Bush, 'The Risings of the Commons in England, 1381–1549', 109, 111, 112, 113–14, 117, 123–5 (emphasis added).
[133] *The 1549 Rebellions*, 4, 10, 150, 151.

from the lords and placing it instead within the village'. They envisaged 'wrest[ing] power from the lords' and excluding the gentry 'from the village economy'. 'Priests were to be chosen by the parish', allowing individual communities to select men whose views were compatible with their own. Absence of religious dogma from the articles suggests tolerance of religious differences. 'Overall', writes Wood,

The Mousehold articles spelled out a corporatist vision of an alternative social order "in which society consisted of watertight compartments, each with its own functions and each interfering as little as possible with the others." This new order was to be fostered within a dispersed polity comprised of autonomous village communities, bound together by the force of the monarch's law. It was in this reform programme that we see the logic of popular monarchism, in which the forces of legalism and orderliness within late medieval popular politics were linked to early modern processes of state formation.[134]

The implication is that the tradition of rebellion was not entirely restorationist. It encompassed something more than 'memory' of 'What Has Been'. It 'reached beyond' what was and what (in elite ideals of hierarchy, rank and degree) was supposed to be; it expressed the often denied and neglected human capacity that Ernst Bloch regarded as the *sine qua non* of the revolutionary tradition: seeing beyond what has been and what is: 'the utopian function'.[135]

In Wood's view the tradition of rebellion ended after 1549 because the 'community of common interests' in which it had been rooted was broken.[136] That community, exemplified in the Mousehold articles, envisaged a dispersed polity of autonomous local communities governed by the distant crown. The rebellions themselves, and Somerset's apparently sympathetic response, articulated a bi-polar model of the commonweal that had animated popular rebellions since 1381, a model which challenged all lordship (secular and ecclesiastical) between the localities and the crown.

It is easy to understand the attraction of this model for its two beneficiaries. From a local perspective, the crown was a distant lord, much less likely to interfere than local seigniors. For centuries the commonalty had seen the king's justice as a court of appeal against violent and rapacious local lords. At the other pole, Machiavelli's analysis of the

---

[134] *Ibid.*, 163–4; quotation from Diarmaid MacCulloch, 'Kett's Rebellion in Context', *Past and Present* 84 (1979), 47.
[135] Bloch, *The Principle of Hope*, trans. Neville Plaice, Stephen Plaice and Paul Knight (Oxford 1986), vol. 1, Part 2: 'Anticipatory Consciousness', 141 and *passim*.
[136] Wood, *Riot, Rebellion and Popular Politics*, 72.

threat posed to oligarchic republics and monarchies by traditional nobles and gentry had been anticipated by Fortescue, whose observations were informed by English history, in which many kings-cum-tyrants had been overthrown in the past. The idea that kings could only be disciplined and even deposed if the whole community, including the commons agreed, had been a virtual institution of English politics since the century of *Magna Carta*, and in particular the period from 1258 to 1327; that convention prepared the way for the later depositions of Richard II and Henry VI. As Fortescue had recognized, however, only rebellions led by great magnates aimed to depose and replace kings. In this context, rebel magnates courted popular support for their own strategic purposes. Wood argues that the tradition of popular rebellion, rooted as it was in the poorest classes of society, had an agenda of its own. Class and local identity were never so closely intertwined as in the period from the Black Death to 1549. After 1549 the common identity that had held village and small-town England together for over two centuries divided; the commonalty of agrarian England gradually polarized into two classes, those with estates and those without. Deprived of local leaders, the great tradition of medieval rebellions of the commonalty came to an end.

Against this we have seen that more or less institutionalized divisions in village society long preceded the accelerated economic, religious, educational, political, administrative and ideological changes of the later sixteenth century. Some yeomen were attracted by the communalist vision expressed in the Mousehold articles, but like gentlemen and nobles, many who joined rebellions did so, not out of any solidarity with their poorer neighbours, but in pursuit of their own strategies or in order to avoid having their property (and with it their superior status) ravaged or confiscated. Fortescue formulated his bottom-up model of popular rebellion in the aftermath of Cade's rebellion: it explained away the involvement of the richer sorts of villagers and, at the same time, neatly relieved them of any real responsibility for what, by then, was widely perceived as an institutionalized tendency of English society.

Fortescue insisted that 'the poorest men' were the 'greatest causers and doers' of popular rebellions. He was reluctant to admit that yeomen might be so alienated from the social order that they became instigators of insurrection. Men of yeoman or equivalent rank certainly became caught up in popular rebellions, not always as reluctantly as Fortescue suggested. In the wake of the 1450 rebellion a Sussex yeoman, John Merfold, allegedly said that he and his 'fellowship . . . wold leve no gentilman alyve but such as them list to have'. Mavis Mate shows that 'prosperity later touched by recession' was an underlying cause. The poor were hungry, yeomen and master-craftsmen 'found that demand for their goods and services had dried up.' Wood shows that 'rebel politics in 1549 were driven not only by ideological ferment, but also by immediate economic crisis'.[137] Economic recession remains an important part of explanations of the paradox of the great popular rebellions of 1381, 1450, 1536 and 1549: the coming together of heterogeneous households and neighbourhoods of core districts into major regional revolts that posed a potential threat to the state. Revolt was always most likely, as Fortescue implied, when young labourers and journeymen, the 'middle band' and the 'smaller sprinkling' of richer sort were all affected – in different ways – by 'prosperity later touched by recession'.[138]

Wood's account of 1549 suggests that economic recession sprang the trap of routine class hatred between village communities and the gentry, dispelling the myth that rebels were inspired to restore an organic harmony of classes, ranks, orders or parts that, while serving, as an ideal, as a constant trigger for moral fervour, had never existed. Studies of the gentry of fourteenth to sixteenth-century England reveal a culture absorbed to the point of obsession with the accumulation of estate: by law if possible, by violence if not.[139] The tradition of popular rebellion was premised on consciousness of a sharp division between what Wood calls 'the closely felt local and regional plebeian identities' of the commonalty and the violent, competitive, patriarchal gangsterism that the age

---

[137] Mate, 'The Economic and Social Roots of Medieval Popular Rebellion', 661–2, 664; Wood, *The 1549 Rebellions*, 30.

[138] Poos, *A Rural Society after the Black Death*, 229, 231, 233; Mate, 'The Economic and Social Roots of Medieval Popular Rebellion', 688, notes 'the important role played not only by yeomen and husbandmen, but by artisans as well . . . among those indicted by name [in 1450–1] were a sprinkling of agricultural labourers and husbandmen, but the majority were clearly artisans – a carpenter, skinner, mason, thatcher, and dyer, and several tailors, smiths and cobblers. So too the rebels who rose up in the Weald in the spring of 1451 included smiths, weavers, shingelers, triggers, tanners, and butchers. Such men were also prominent amongst those who had received pardons for participating in Cade's rebellion itself. In the small market town of Alfriston, for example, 22 men received pardons and they included 1 butcher, 1 baker, 1 carpenter, 2 chapmen, 3 smiths and 2 shoemakers. Moreover 10 of these men were clearly selling ale publicly and were probably running an alehouse where people came to drink and socialize. Although not everyone who sought a pardon may have been a very active supporter of Cade, it seems reasonable to assume that most of the people below the rank of the gentry did at least sympathize with his cause.'

[139] E.g. Nigel Saul, *Knights and Esquires: the Gloucestershire Gentry in the Fourteenth Century* (Oxford 1981); Helen Castor, *Blood and Roses: The Paston Family and the Wars of the Roses* (London 2004), describes in loving detail the price gentry families paid to establish and hold on to 'estate'; for more quotations illustrating mutual class hatred, see Wood, *The 1549 Rebellions*, 98–9.

demanded of men determined to achieve and maintain an estate large enough to sustain the 'estate' of gentry and nobility. After 1549 sustained economic and cultural trends brought the gentry and the yeomen and their equivalents closer together.

'An alternative social order' emerged in England and Wales from the 1560s to the 1640s, a period when national income doubled. Its distribution became 'markedly and increasingly uneven'. On one hand it became more acceptable for yeomen and their equivalents 'to acquire and to consolidate wealth'; on the other 'a larger proportion of the national population was more deeply mired in a perennial struggle for economic survival'. For Keith Wrightson, the 'alternative social order was . . . composed along lines determined by new economic fields of force'.[140] The combined and uneven effects of the great inflation remain the single most important explanation for changes in the social relations of production and distribution at the end of the middle ages. Evangelical and vocational Protestantism, literacy and bible-reading, a grammar-school and university education, a 'good accent' and gentry-aping manners, creeping aspirations to a coat of arms and so on: all these, singly or together, were tactics pursued, often across several generations, as combinations of sustained inflation and short-term crises broke smallholders and created opportunities for wealthier sorts to expand their estates – and their 'estate'.

As a result the 'middle sort' became more firmly and securely incorporated into the ruling or constitutional classes – not without much complaint and grumbling on the part of conservatives who felt that traditional prerogatives were being encroached upon. The labouring classes became more firmly *excluded*. The tradition of popular rebellion had always expressed the insistence of the smallholding and unpropertied 'fourth sort' that they should be, and by the act of rebellion were included in the decision- and policy-making apparatus of the commonweal. Wood's argument is that this demand of common people became both clear and intolerable in 1549, when the accumulating implications of the tradition of rebellion became fully articulate.

It will be argued in Chapter 9 that this division did not achieve full clarity until after the Parliamentarian victory in the late 1640s (when the dream of a plebeian commonwealth seemed achievable). Yet there is a case for saying that consciousness of a class divide between the propertied and unpropertied, associated by Marx with 'the bourgeois mode of

---

[140] K. Wrightson, *Earthly Necessities: Economic Lives in Early Modern Britain* (New Haven 2000), 198, 200, 201; *The 1549 Rebellions*, Chapter 5.

production', began to emerge as a discursive convention after, and in part as a result of, the 1549 rebellions.[141] The idea of a constitutional division between the richer and poorer sorts of commons was in no sense new. We have seen that 'village notables' and 'petty officialdom' had been institutions of local life in most parts of agrarian England for centuries: the former were probably a presence throughout the long history of agrarian England; the latter, formally, had been present since jury service was institutionalized in the twelfth century. Although there was much 'local variation', as Keith Wrightson observed nearly thirty years ago, 'the gap which separated them from their social inferiors was in some respects greater than that which removed them from their immediate superiors' long before the 'polarization' of the later sixteenth and early seventeenth centuries.[142]

Extremely variable and conflicting status conceptions aside, nobles, knights, gentlemen, freeholders and urban burgesses successively became institutions of constitutional life in the fourteenth century. The tradition of popular rebellion coincided with the rise of the 'vulgar tongue' as the language of politics and public life. It repeatedly raised the possibility that the 'deepening' of the English constitution that undoubtedly did occur from the thirteenth to fifteenth centuries *was not over*. This was what appalled William Paget in his comment in a letter to Protector Somerset, in which he referred to an implication of popular rebellion that his master seemed to be encouraging: 'The foot,' he wrote, 'taketh upon him the part of the head, and commyns is become king; a king appointing conditions and laws to the governors, saying, Grant this and that, and we wil go home.'[143] Sir Thomas Smith's response was more measured. He queried the convention that the largest class of all, the 'fourth sort', 'rascability of the popular', or '*proletarii*', was *by definition* excluded from governance, observing that in the absence of sufficient men of the 'third sort' they often served as local or hundred jurors and – a crucial institution in the organization of popular rebellions – constables.[144] My sense of Fortescue's and Smith's analysis is that both were aware of the need, somehow, to incorporate the 'fourth sort' into the constitution, thus removing its outraged sense of exclusion. If so, they anticipated a compromise offered by Oliver Cromwell during the Putney debates a century

[141] 'The capitalist era dates from the sixteenth century': Karl Marx, *Capital*, vol. 1 (1867) (Harmondsworth 1967), 876 and Part 8, 'So-called Primitive Accumulation', *passim*.

[142] Keith Wrightson, *English Society 1580–1680* (London 1982), 37.

[143] Sir William Paget to Protector Somerset, 7 July 1549, quotation from Wood, *The 1549 Rebellions*, 22.

[144] Thomas Smith, *De Republica Anglorum*, ed. Mary Dewar (Cambridge 1982), 74–7; Wood, *Riot, Rebellion and Popular Politics*, 29–30.

later. In an attempt to find a middle ground between the birthright franchise proposed by Rainsborough and the freeholder franchise on which
Ireton insisted, Cromwell appeared to concede that 'a very considerable
part of copyholders by inheritance . . . ought to have a voice'.[145] This
would only exclude the *proletarii*.

---

[145] David Wootton (ed.), *Divine Right and Democracy: an Anthology of Political Writings in Stuart England* (Harmondsworth 1986), 'Putney Debates', 306.

Part III

The English explosion

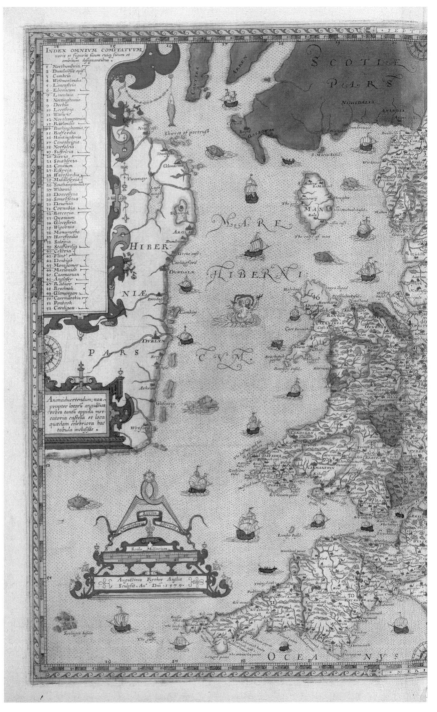

'The English Explosion': Christopher Saxton's *Anglia* (1579) from *An Atlas of England and Wales*. Reproduced by kind permission of the Syndics of Cambridge University Library, Atlas.4.57.6.

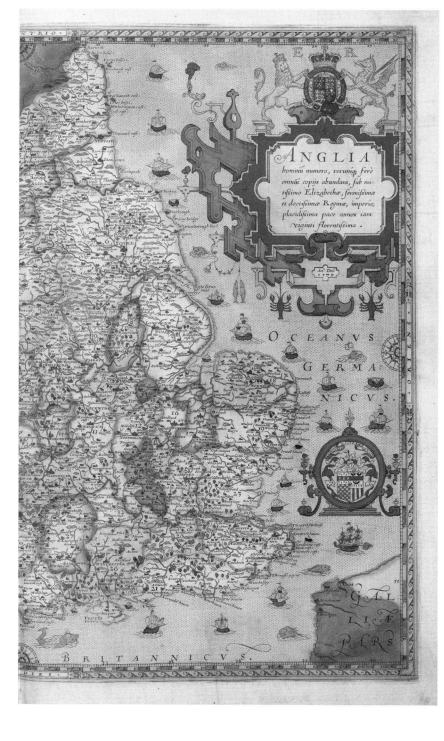

ANGLIA
hominū numero, rerumq; ferè
omniū copijs abundans, sub mi-
tissimo Elizabethæ, serenissimæ
et doctissimæ Reginæ, imperio,
placidissima pace annos iam
viginti florentissima .

Anº Dñi
1579.

OCEANVS

GERMA:

NICVS.

BRITANNICVS.

GAL-
LIÆ
PARS

Verily it is a most laudable use and profitable custome, to find means to reward the worth and acknowledge the valour of rare and excellent men, to satisfie and content them with such payments as in no sort charge the commonwealth, and put the prince to no cost at all . . . If to the prize, which ought simply to be of honour, there be other commodities and riches joyned, this kind of commixing, instead of encreasing the estimation thereof, doth empaire, dissipate and abridge it.[1]

Since all men confesse (that be not barbarously bred) that men are borne as well to seek the common commodities of their Countrey, as their owne private benefite, it may seeme follie to perswade that point, for each man meaneth so to doe. But wherein men should seek the common commoditie, and what way, and by what meane that is to bee brought about, is the point or summe of the matter, since every good man is ready to imploy his labour. This is to be done by an infinite sort of meanes, as the number of things bee infinite that may be done for common benefite of the Realme. And as the chiefe things so to bee done be divers, so are they to bee done by divers men, as they bee by wit and manner of education more fit, or lesse fit, for this and for that. And for that many things that tend to the common benefite of the State, some tend more, and some lesse, I find that no one thing, after one another, is greater then Clothing, and the things incident to the same . . . Ample and full Vent of this noble and rich commoditie is it that the common weale of this realme doeth require.[2]

The commoning of English culture was associated with an accelerating decline in the credibility of traditional aristocratic virtues. The Hundred Years War at first energized ideologies of martial chivalry and then saw them gradually discredited and displaced, in the 'Wars of the Roses', by internecine, competitive struggles within the ruling class. The discrediting of warrior nobility, long ago anticipated by John of Salisbury, opened the gates to a challenger from classical antiquity, elite republican virtue and learning: what came to be called 'renaissance humanism'. Renaissance humanism, however, was very much an elite movement. As Charles Taylor points out, the striking thing about the transformations in question here is that they affected 'the whole culture'. 'The culture of modernity' involved the 'isolation' of 'economics', a 'domain with its own laws, distinct from (even though potentially disturbed by) what happens in the domains in which humans relate to each other through politics and culture'. Taylor argues that 'this domain cannot be seen just

---

[1] John Florio (trans.), *Montaigne's Essays* (1603), Book II, ch. VII: 'Of the Recompenses or Rewards of Honour'.

[2] 'Remembrances for Master S . . . to the great profite of the Common weale of this Countrey. Written by . . . Richard Hakluyt, for a principall English Factor at Constantinople', *Hakluyt's Principall Navigations, Voyages, Traffiques and Discoveries Made by Sea or Overland to the Remote and Farthest Distant Quarters of the Earth at any time within the compasse of these 1500 Yeares* (Dent, Everyman Edition: London nd), vol. 3, 91.

as a "scientific" discovery that people stumbled on. It reflects the higher value put on this dimension of human experience, the affirmation of ordinary life'. Taylor believes that the political economy outlook drew heavily on the scientific revolution of the seventeenth century, especially in its gradual adoption of the principle that 'the events in this domain form a self-regulating system'. As a result of these earlier intellectual movements, Taylor writes, 'the eighteenth century saw the birth of political economy, with Adam Smith and the Physiocrats'.[3] This book has traced even earlier incidents and strands of what Taylor calls the 'affirmation of ordinary life' movement, locating them as ideological outcomes of a long, accumulative 'revolution of commonalty'. Without this movement the scientific revolution of the seventeenth century, and one of its most consequential corollaries, the political economy outlook, would not have begun. While it was clearly grounded in the affirmation of what, measured by authorized medieval standards, was very much 'ordinary' life, the political economy outlook actually preceded the scientific revolution by a century or more.

Its birth was assisted by well-placed genius. In Sir John Fortescue and Sir Thomas Smith we have two thinkers who reached the centre of political power in their respective ages. Fortescue's social anatomies were written in the wake of the 1450 rebellions, Smith's in the wake of those of 1536 and 1549. We see in Chapter 6 that the idea of moving the business of the commonalty (production and trade) to the centre of state policy was mooted by mercantilist propagandists of the fifteenth century. The seminal figure in the formulation of an ideology of material growth and expansion, however, was Sir Thomas Smith. Smith the statesman gave prestige to a traditional precept of the mercantile classes. His successors were the mercantilist propagandists of the generations of the two Richard Hakluyts and Edward Misselden (c.1570–c.1630). As Steve Pincus has shown, by the 1640s the 'political economy' outlook, not classical republican *virtu*, was the pragmatic median of republican debate.[4] The aim in the next two chapters is to trace the historical origin of the political economy outlook and its relationship to the birth of capitalism.

From the outset two ideas, associated respectively with merchants and manufacturers, competed for precedence in the political economy

---

[3] Charles Taylor, *Sources of the Self: the Making of the Modern Identity* (Cambridge, Mass. 1989), 286.

[4] Steve Pincus, 'Neither Machiavellian Moment nor Possessive Individualism: Commercial Society and the Defenders of the English Commonwealth', *American Historical Review* (June 1998); for discussion of republican efforts to reconcile liberty and maritime expansion, see also David Armitage, *The Ideological Origins of the British Empire* (Cambridge 2000), Chapter 5.

outlook. The first was that merchants were 'of all callings the most beneficial to the commonwealth, by setting the poorer sort of people on work'.
If poverty was the primary cause of rebellion, as Fortescue had argued,
then merchants, by alleviating it, were more profitable to the commonweal than any other class. This core of merchant or 'mercantilist' ideology
was challenged by a competing idea that the *producers* of commodities, in
particular of commodities for export, were of all classes the most profitable to the commonweal. Both ideas were premised on the idea that
utility, not absolute (theological) good was what determined the quality
of the commonweal. In this sense they represent a marked secularization
of commonweal ideologies. If the most important purpose of constitutions was to produce and distribute wealth in the material sense – if 'weal'
or 'woe' ultimately depended on it – it seemed to follow that states must,
first and foremost, look to the interests of the class or classes responsible
for production and distribution. Although wealthy merchants routinely
aspired to and purchased gentility, and members of the nobility and gentry engaged in trade and invested capital in manufacturing and mining,
the idea that production and trade were, definitively, the vocations of
the commonalty or third estate, the 'feet' and 'legs' of the body politic,
remained a dominant convention in the determination of status throughout our period. In that sense the emergence of the political economy
outlook was revolutionary. It entailed a reversal of traditional values.

From the outset, then, the political economy outlook was an argument
between two classes traditionally seen as inferior to nobles – merchants
and producers – about which of them was of greater importance to commonwealth and kingdom. We know in retrospect that this misconceived
argument between rival classes (production and trade are two sides of the
same process) resulted in the victory of mercantile or (Adam) 'Smithian'
economics. Yet Marx's alternative, valuing direct producers over all other
classes, was not original, as we shall see. Sixteenth-century propaganda
represented merchants as heroes of growth, yet never quite overcame
the taint of selfish gain. Clothiers, weavers, miners, ironworkers, soapmakers and so on were generally less wealthy and prestigious than great
merchants, but they actually made the commodities that increased the
common wealth of England. Chapter 6 traces the rise of dispersed manufacturing for export from the fourteenth to seventeenth centuries, and
argues that it was accompanied by increasing awareness of a need to influence and affect affairs of state. This completes my account of the causes
of the 'English explosion' by describing the accumulation, not only of
a significant manufacturing and mining sector, but also of a *discourse*
of industry. It focuses on the most extensive of early modern England's
industries. As throughout this book, my contention is that modes of

production are structural *and* ideological. It is never enough that certain material conditions prevail. Material conditions must be observed, analysed and synthesized by intelligent minds, and disseminated. Chapter 7 takes us inside the creative ferment that was at one and the same time a national 'explosion' and the intellectual birth of the modern capitalist world order.

Leigh Shaw-Taylor and E.A. Wrigley recently argued that 'overwhelming' evidence now supports the view that 'there was more growth in [England's] secondary sector between 1500 and 1750 than there was between 1750 and 1850'.[5] Richard Hakluyt the Elder's list of English manufactures in c.1570 (see Chapter 7.4) leaves no doubt that clothmaking was far from being early modern England's only manufacturing industry. Chapter 6 concentrates on 'pre-industrial' England's most extensive, prominent and export-oriented industry. Geographically and in terms of its impact on public consciousness, clothmaking was England's first *national* industry. It contributed to the formation of national identity and, as we see in this and the next chapter, the cloth industry was absolutely central to plans for English commercial and imperial expansion from the mid-fifteenth century to the elder Richard Hakluyt's formation of a blueprint for the English explosion in the 1570s. A properly comprehensive treatment of industrial development would include the expansion, mainly from the second half of the sixteenth century, of extractive industries like lead mining in the Mendips and the Derbyshire Peak, coal mining in the North-East and South-West Midlands, and the transition from iron to steel-smelting in the Forest of Dean and the Sussex Weald. My aim here is to trace the impact of industry on English national consciousness, and for that purpose, treatment of the cloth industry is both emblematic and essential.

---

[5] Shaw-Taylor and Wrigley, 'The Occupational Structure of England, c.1750–1871: a Preliminary Report', Cambridge Group for the History of Population and Social History, Department of Geography, University of Cambridge 2008, 2006, 1.

6 How trade became an affair of state: the politics of industry, 1381–1640

Trade was never esteemed an affair of state until the (seventeenth) century... There is scarcely any ancient writer on politics who has made mention of it.[6]

Since the time of Henry VIII the wealth and revenue of the country have been continually advancing, and, in the course of their progress, their pace seems rather to have gradually accelerated than retarded. They seem not only to have been going on, but to have been going on faster and faster.[7]

The capitalist era dates from the sixteenth century.[8]

6.1 The propensity of industrial districts for resistance, riot and rebellion

Supporting the tendency for words to spread between localities, districts and regions, fourteenth-century England was a far more commercial and industrial society than it had been in the past, and remained so through the greater and lesser mortality crises with which that century was littered. Commerce means *trafike*, in commodities, people, and ideas. Between the fourteenth and sixteenth centuries, the cloth industry probably did as much to transform the landscape and generate and routinize lines of communications as any other agency. Clothworking districts were always prominent in contemporary accounts of disorder, resistance and rebellion. Nineteen years after the earthquake of 1381, Henry IV's officials had difficulty collecting taxes in cloth-making districts: violence broke out at Dartmouth, Bristol (where a mob that included large numbers of women drove off the collectors), and at Williton and Kentsford in Somerset. At Frome an order was issued confiscating all pikes, sticks with iron heads like lances, and axes. Thomas Newton, a special officer of the king sent

---

[6] David Hume, 'Of Commerce', in Stephen Copley and Andrew Edgar (ed.), *Selected Essays* (Oxford 1993), 119.
[7] Adam Smith, *The Wealth of Nations*, ed. Andrew Skinner (Harmondsworth 1974), 192.
[8] Marx, *Capital Volume One* (Penguin Marx Library edition, 1974), 876.

to assess and collect the taxes at Norton St Philip, was set upon by a mob and 'stabbed in a hundred places'.[9] A chronicler recorded confidently that he was 'killed by the drapers'.[10] We should not see clothmaking or any other industrial activity as in any way sealed off from more traditional agrarian communities. 'Industry needed houses, food, wool and labour', writes J.N. Hare, 'while the prosperity it generated created demand for consumer goods and services'.[11]

Clothworking districts were rebellious in 1450. As I.M.W. Harvey observes, cloth workers 'suffered badly from insecurity of employment'. For this and other reasons they were 'the most persistent insurgents of mid-fifteenth-century England: in the Midlands, in Wiltshire, in East Anglia, and in Kent'. Harvey's survey of the commotions of 1450 takes in many districts that were to be hot-spots of resistance, riot and rebellion in the future. 'The southern Cotswolds' already produced 'some of the finest broadcloths in England'. Near-neighbour 'Southern Wiltshire' was industrious, a dozen or so miles south-west of another island in 'Berkshire . . . producing smaller and less heavily fulled types of cloth' like 'another equally important area . . . along the Suffolk-Essex border'. 'Kerseys and straits were manufactured in large quantities at towns such as Dedham, Sudbury, Clare, Hadleigh and Lavenham . . . (and) in certain other towns of Essex and Suffolk such as Coggeshall, Braintree, Bury St Edmunds, and Halstead.' It was already possible to travel from Cirencester (even Gloucester) to London without ever leaving weavers' country. Another area 'extended through the southern counties of England from Hampshire, through Surrey (Guildford was an important centre), to the villages of the Kentish Weald and beyond'. Harvey estimates that 'almost a quarter of the male population was engaged in the cloth industry' in the villages of Smarden and Pluckley, on the edge of the Low Weald or Vale of Kent. Maidstone was the provincial capital for this branch. 'The Wealden cloth villages nurtured a tradition of religious dissent so strong as to constitute one of the more distinctive features of this singular district – a tradition encouraged by large parishes, scattered settlements, and the weakness of the local manorial structure.'[12]

From the late fourteenth century the English cloth industry was centred on London, where the 'the business was transacted in Blackwell Hall which had been specially constructed for the purpose in the last years of

---

[9] J.H. Wylie, *History of England Under Henry the Fourth* (London 1884), 197–8.

[10] *The Chronicle of Adam Usk*, ed. and trans. C. Given Wilson (Oxford 1991), 130–1.

[11] J.N. Hare, 'Growth and Recession in the Fifteenth-Century Economy: the Wiltshire Textile Industry and the Countryside', *Economic History Review* 52 (1999), 1–26; see also Hare, 'The Wiltshire Rising of 1450', *Southern History* 4 (1982), 13–31.

[12] I.M.W. Harvey, *Jack Cade's Rebellion of 1450* (Oxford 1991), 17–19.

the previous century'.[13] Of the 126 men indicted after Percy's Rebellion, in April 1446, forty-seven were tailors, weavers, fullers or clothiers.[14] In 1450 'orchestrated and sustained attacks' on officials of church and state occurred in West Wiltshire and at Salisbury, which 'together formed one of the most intensive cloth-producing districts in England'.[15]

Such districts epitomize what L.R. Poos calls 'the destabilization of the traditional social structure' that occurred, historically, wherever the manufacture of commodities for export took root. The pattern is unmistakeable. Poos focuses on an industrious district of Essex that was an 'epicentre of many of the period's most spectacular social and agrarian revolts and uprisings' – 1381, the Lollard uprising of 1413–14 and the rebellion of 1450. He writes that the rebellions of 1381 and 1450 were related to 'many more localised and modest eruptions of discontent with authority'. In such districts 'the later 14th and 15th centuries provide the backdrop to a heritage of radicalism in the county stretching forward in time to at least the Civil War, when Essex would be the most Puritan and the most Parliamentary of constituencies'. Such episodes 'derived their immediate impetus from a variety of factors, political, fiscal, seigneurial, social and economic, and religious . . . ' The episodes and incidents emerged from a 'deeply rooted strain of anti-authoritarianism'. 'Civil turbulence was the crossroads where a volatile, stratified social structure and local economy merged with an entrenched anti-authoritarian mental culture.'[16] Most surprisingly, Poos is able to show that 'social structure and local economy' did not change from the fourteenth (possibly the thirteenth) century to the eve of the classic industrial revolution of the nineteenth century.[17]

Poos's study provides a rare opportunity to look inside one of these precocious hot-spots of change.[18] It reveals a structure that is very familiar

---

[13] Harvey, *Cade's Rebellion*, 21.   [14] *Ibid.*, 172–3.   [15] *Ibid.*, 121.

[16] L.R. Poos, *A Rural Society after the Black Death: Essex 1350–1525* (Cambridge 1991), 229, 231.

[17] Christopher Tomlins, 'Out Of The Cradle, Endlessly Orbiting', Conference on Class-Struggle in the Atlantic World, University of Montana (September 2003); Tomlins's discussion of class as 'intransitive relationships' and as consciousness, discourse and language clarified the issue: is class 'real', or just discourse and language? Which is cause, and which effect? My answer is 'either'. Sometimes the ideal appears before the real. The idea of an English *commonweal* seems to have played an enormously influential part in shaping class-relations from the fourteenth to seventeenth centuries. Ultimately, it is wrong to see intransitive social relations separately from their verbal and written epiphenomena: as Poos suggests, they are parts of the same molecule.

[18] For a summary of the bigger picture, cf. John H. Munro, 'Industrial Transformations in the North-West European Textile Trades, c.1290–c.1340: Economic Progress or Economic Crisis', in Bruce S. Campbell (ed.), *Before the Black Death: Studies in the 'Crisis' of the Early Fourteenth Century* (Manchester 1991), 134–5 and *passim*.

to historians of the sixteenth to eighteenth centuries. 'At least half the householders' were 'smallholders or landless, drawn into wage labour or artisanal by-employment'. A social structure once thought to be typical of the nineteenth century had, by then, been normal in parts of Essex and Hertfordshire (and probably in other districts elsewhere) for five hundred years. The Black Death and its aftermath reduced numbers, but social relations of production continued relatively unchanged. Assessors of the 1381 Poll Tax for seventy townships in three of the hundreds listed 426 'agriculturalists' (25.1 per cent), 884 labourers (52.2 per cent), 385 craftsmen and retailers (22.7 per cent), the latter including cloth workers (110), construction workers (76), Smiths (53), bakers/brewers (45), cobblers (27), and butchers (21). 143 years later, listings of 1524 disclose the same underlying structure. Throughout, the data is 'entirely compatible with the earlier scenario of something around or over one-half of the districts households being heavily reliant upon earnings'. A 'basic structure' in which 'wage earners with little or no land comprised the majority of the district's rural population' prevailed 'from the fourteenth century onward'. 'In 1300, 1381 and 1524 the district had high population density and a high proportion of cottagers & smallholders.' It comprised about 20,000 people in the fifteenth century, featured 'an unusually marked development of rural industry (especially textiles), a large degree of social and economic differentiation, and a propensity toward religious nonconformity and violent agrarian unrest'. After nearly two centuries of intensive enquiry into the subject, historians using 'reconstitutionalist' methods and approaches to study the local and district cultures of early modern England are finally discovering the birth-places of industrial capitalism.

Poos is cautious, admitting that his Essex communities were atypical. In 'normal' districts gentlemen reigned over deferential, even cowed, peasants. Measured against that misleading stereotype, Essex was at the 'sharp end of change'. The national average lay somewhere between rebellion and deference, but rebellion usually smouldered in these hot spots of early industrialization. Poos's study is a 'test case of the limits of chronological evolution'.[19] Wage-systems and the management of a potentially turbulent proletariat were experimented with and practised in such districts for centuries before the industrial revolution.

Density of population, relative landlessness and occupational specialization meant a high degree of market dependence. Consequently there was no sharp division between 'urban' and 'rural' parts. A busy little microcosm of the commonweal, Poos's district drew in 'a well developed

---

[19] Poos, *Rural Society*, 3–4, 9, 24, 30, 64.

network of small market centres, and also large exporting centres like Malden, Colchester and Ipswich'. Whether as cause or effect, 'rural cloth making expanded rapidly' in the fourteenth and fifteenth centuries. Early manufacturing and extraction industries always responded quickly to demand, and even more quickly to contractions and recessions. Fifty per cent of households in industrious districts like these got most of their income by working for others. The cash-nexus was far from universal as yet. 'Truck' (working for food and drink, goods or tokens) was still routine (and routinely despised) in the eighteenth century. And while Poos's Essex district may not be typical, a 'structure' in which 40–50 per cent of manorial tenants held less than five acres of land, *was* highly typical of all the parts of England that have been the subject of comparable microstudies.[20] 'Landholding and occupation were therefore intricately intertwined . . . many demographic and other aspects of life . . . differed considerably between different occupational groups.'[21] It was one of those districts of early modern England where the class-structure of capitalism began to emerge.[22]

---

[20] Poos, *Rural Society*, 10–11, 17, and n. 18: Table 1.1 analyses the distribution of tenancy size on seven manors 1288–1340, commenting that 'if 5 acres is taken as the limit for smallholders, then 48.7% fit'. 'Under a broader criterion – tenancies of no more than 5 acres, plus those consisting solely of residential property . . . nearly three-fifths (58.9%) of all the manors' tenants would be classified as smallholders. And, once again, the wholly landless are excluded from these data.' Studies of other parts of England produce a range of from 26 to 47 per cent, though nearly all are in the 40s: Kosminsky, *Studies in the Agrarian History of England in the Thirteenth Century*, ed. R.H. Hilton (Oxford 1956), 216–23 (29 per cent of villeins and 47 per cent of free tenants in six Midland counties were recorded in the 1279 Hundred Rolls as holding less than five acres); M.M. Postan, *The Medieval Economy and Society* (Harmondsworth 1978), 127–9 (at 104 manors in the home counties and southern England in the mid- and later thirteenth century, approx 45 per cent of tenants held less than a quarter-virgate; Christopher Dyer, *Lords and Peasants in a Changing Society: the Bishopric of Worcester, 680–1540* (Cambridge 1980), 299–301 (at four West Midlands manors in 1299 tenants holding less than a half-yardland ranged from 26 to 42 per cent); J.Z. Titow, *English Rural Society, 1200–1350* (London 1969), 79 (at Bishop's Waltham, Hants, 51.5 per cent of all tenants held less than ten acres in 1332). Even in other less densely populated parts of Essex tenurial fragmentation was less marked: cf. Marjorie K. McIntosh, *Autonomy and Community: the Royal Borough of Havering, 1200–1500* (Cambridge 1986), where, in 1352/3, about 38 per cent of tenancies were of less than five acres; for a synthesis: David Levine, *Reproducing Families: the Political Economy of English Population History* (Cambridge 1987).

[21] *Rural Society*, 11.

[22] On this point, see Andy Wood, 'Rethinking Class in Early Modern England', in Wood, *The Politics of Social Conflict: the Peak Country 1520–1770* (Cambridge 1999), 26–7, where he writes that 'Studies of class formation have long been hampered by modern social historians' strange obsession with the nation state. Ever since late nineteenth- and early twentieth-century European socialists linked their political project to the transformed national identities of that period, social historians have been mesmerized by that single definition of class-identity. The assumption that "true" class consciousness

As in the better-documented sixteenth to nineteenth centuries, the labouring population was highly mobile. One consequence of the Black Death was 'especially high migration rates'. In the most precociously 'advanced' districts labourers comprised about half of local households, had 'modest means and multiple pursuits', were more mobile than land-holders, 'settled later in life, and were less likely to be married than their contemporaries'.[23] One of the most brilliant reconstitutions of a district like this is Rudolf Braun's classic study of a 'proto-industrial' region of eighteenth-century Switzerland.[24] In David Levine's phrase, there were many 'precociously proto-industrial' districts in early modern England.

In gross product and exports, Essex clothworkers ranked 'second only to the south-western area of Wiltshire, Somerset & Bristol'. By 1377 tex-tile workers were outnumbered only by agriculturalists.[25] On the basis of a microstudy of Colchester, R.H. Britnell doubts whether the 'concept of industrial development as a regional phenomenon' affecting only pre-viously 'rural' districts, can cover the variety of contexts in which it took root. When she coupled together the words 'rural' and 'industry', Joan Thirsk did not mean that industry took place only in 'rural' districts.[26] Her point was that 'industry' (and all it connotes) was not restricted to towns. Pamela Sharpe's exemplary study of Colyton in Devon, another district affected by cloth (but not only cloth) manufacturing, suggests that the inherited institutional structure (parish, manor, town) is less important than the existence of large numbers of people dependent upon wages – and, she shows, a spirit of 'resourcefulness'.[27] The records of the fourteenth century are not rich enough for us to test for this – or for de Vries's equally important quality, 'industriousness'.[28] Poos is only able to show that 'the geographical boundaries of clothmaking in Essex do seem to have been fairly sharp, and the reasons for this pattern fit

can be manifest on the level of the nation-state has led historians to find in the early modern period one of the main barriers to the operations of class.' In objecting to 'The reductive connection between nation and class', Wood points out that 'the history of modern European working-class political culture has often been the history of regions and localities. Whether historians are describing the insurrectionists of the Paris Com-mune, the mining communities of the Rhondda valley or the anarchists of Catalonia, class and local identity have in many contexts been historically inseparable.'

[23] *Rural Society*, 108, 159, 163–4, 208.

[24] Rudolf Braun, *Industrialization and Everyday Life*, trans. Sarah Hanbury Tenison (Cam-bridge 1990).

[25] *Rural Society*, 58.

[26] Thirsk, 'Industries in the Countryside' in F.J. Fisher (ed.), *Essays in the Economic and Social History of Tudor and Stuart England* (Cambridge 1961), 70–88.

[27] Pamela Sharpe, *Population and Society in an East Devon Parish: Reproducing Colyton, 1540–1840* (Exeter 2002), Chapters 3–4.

[28] J. De Vries, 'The Industrial Revolution or the Industrious Revolution', *Journal of Eco-nomic History* 54 (1994), 2.

within a larger continuing debate concerning rural industry or "proto-industrialisation", not just in late medieval England but also in preindustrial Europe at large'.

Whether we call the disorderly proliferation of wage labour and the cash nexus 'proletarianization', or some other term, is a matter of taste. Poos describes the condition of the workforce in early modern Essex as 'imperfectly proletarianized'. It was a class of individuals without capital, dependent on wages earned by working for others. Six centuries later this is the condition of us all. We grow up knowing we have to work, get a job, hopefully a long-term, 'regular' one. Success in pursuit of wages makes us independent, i.e. not 'dependent' on hand-outs from others. That is proletarian pride and the proletarian way of life. The insulting view that the first modern proletarians could not be as independent as the classes with settled landholdings is quite false: there is no need to assume that fourteenth-century wage-workers were not as resourceful and individual, in their contexts, as many of those who spend their lives dependent on wages and salaries are today.

David Levine's view is that 'the proletarian component was very small' in the first half of the sixteenth century. It grew from about 125,000 adult males in c.1500 to maybe 204,000 in c.1620, rising again to 449,000 in 1688 and to 1,200,000 in 1851.[29] Since the women and children of wage-dependent families also worked, these figures must be doubled or tripled to gain an impression – and it can never be more than that – of the proportion of the total population that grew up working and depended on wages all their lives. What remains to be seen is whether the perfectly or imperfectly proletarianized part was anything more than a statistical entity produced by modern definitions and categories. Was 'it' 'conscious', and could 'it' act collectively? We have seen that Sir John Fortescue and his successors thought that in moments of stress it could and did.

Richard of Fulham spread fiery propaganda to the wage-labourers of Hertfordshire in the 1350s. The hated laws restricting workers' wages and conditions have always been considered an important ingredient in 1381. The image of workers not ashamed (or even accepting) of their low status as workers, and convinced they should be paid the going ('market') rate, is not absurd. Where Marx went wrong was not in describing the rise of the proletarian class as the most distinctive feature of 'the bourgeois mode of production', but in reducing all the individuals and groups who have belonged to it to the class as a historical agency. There are no individual proletarians in Marx's voluminous writings. 'While doubtless only imperfectly proletarianized . . . the requisite underemployed workforce was undoubtedly there', writes Poos, yet warns against positing 'one comprehensive set of circumstances influencing the development of clothmaking regions . . . In this district, it was the local particular combination of technical enablement, marketing opportunity, and an amenable social structure.'[30] As in fifteenth-century Gloucestershire, 'virtually the only people (apart from a very few genuine entrepreneurs, discernible *mainly* from the late 1400s) who might qualify as large-scale capital investors and traders within the rural Essex . . . industry were fullers'.[31]

This mixed band of entrepreneurs was equivalent to Gloucestershire's *cloathmen*. A *cloathman* could be from several trades – some began as weavers, graduating, for the successful few, to lessees and even owners of cloth-mills, dyeing plants and, best of all, mastery of a little finishing factory and marketing business linked to connections in the large provincial towns and, increasingly the monopolist from the fourteenth century on, London. What made the difference between 'entrepreneur' and 'worker' was, then as now, industriousness, resourcefulness, creditworthiness, trusty contacts (and family connections) – and a little cushion of capital. In the fourteenth as in the sixteenth and seventeenth centuries, such men took the opportunities created by existing demographic and social structures, and 'between the middle and last decade of the fourteenth century Essex clothmaking centres increased their output by a factor of at least five'. 'At a time of abrupt depopulation and agrarian contraction, the local cloth industry expanded remarkably quickly, drawing into its orbit an increasing number of workers who were otherwise economically marginal . . . The continuing, large proportion of cottagers and smallholders in the region during the century after the Black Death was thus at the same time an enabling factor and a consequence of local industrial output, for as long as there remained a buoyant demand (fuelled chiefly . . . by exports).'[32]

This 'mode and social relations of production' endured. Famine and plague had no discernible impact on it. 'There was no wholesale promotion of smallholders, proportionately speaking . . . in the century after the Black Death', writes Poos. 'There was no proportional growth of numbers of large tenancies and no corresponding decrease in the ranks of middling and lesser tenants.' The conclusion, that 'the long term persistence of a smallholding or near-landless stratum in rural society would appear to have been an integral feature of this district of Essex, where an essentially identical land distribution in the decades around 1600 was merely a continuation of an already long-entrenched phenomenon', seems inescapable.[33]

---

[30] *Rural Society*, 58.   [31] *Ibid.*, 68.   [32] *Ibid.*, 71–2.   [33] *Ibid.*, 20.

Poos describes remarkable continuities of social structure through the late medieval and early modern periods. The cloth industry was exceptional, not in its rebelliousness *per se* but in the causes and contexts of the rebelliousness. Andy Wood estimates that 'probably the most common cause of riots during the sixteenth and early seventeenth centuries was the enclosure of common land'.[34] In this part of Essex 'the absence of common fields and much in the way of communal grazing resources meant that... anti-enclosure violence, the most ubiquitous form of village revolt in much of the rest of England from the end of the middle ages onward, was largely unknown'.[35] Proto-industry went along with enclosed farms in Gloucestershire too. It transformed the settlements (hamlets, 'common' and 'waste' lands, villages, market towns) and changed the landscapes of their 'rural' hinterlands. Industrial and proletarianized districts were always in the forefront. Anti-enclosure feelings, wage-disputes and resistance to the introduction of labour-saving technology necessarily went together. They all threatened labouring peoples' incomes. The reason why craft-workers and craft-working districts were prominent in resistance and rebellion is that they usually constituted a majority of the mostly wage-dependent people who made up the rank and file. Their districts were likely to erupt because more people there had less to fall back on in bad times. They were acutely sensitive to market contractions, recessions and depressions.

Beyond that 'structural' condition, no single cause or motive can be assigned to the propensity of such districts for resistance, riot and rebellion. 'More than one distinct if overlapping factor or motive impelled different sectors of rural society to coalesce temporarily into common action', writes Poos. While every incident brought together many causes and pretexts (several, perhaps, for every rebel), what mattered was that rebels – or, more precisely, a rebellious culture – already existed: 'each episode managed, if only inadvertently, to tap into an underlying stream of more diffused anti-authoritarian unrest among ordinary rural people'.[36] In times of national crisis such communities were liable

---

[34] Wood, *Riot, Rebellion and Popular Politics in Early Modern England* (Basingstoke 2002), 82.

[35] Poos, *Rural Society*, 261–2.

[36] With regard to 1381, Poos lists 'Rapid economic restructurings of rural society in the post Black Death era...Manorial economies...transformed in some places...in others lords attempted to reinforce their traditional claims for bond labour...friction caused by attempts (in Essex at least largely futile ones) to stem geographical mobility and wage increases under the...Statute of Labourers...Political uncertainties and fiscal demands compounded tensions: when RII assumed the throne as a minor in 1377 the English war effort in France had been turning sour...the third poll tax within four years, voted by the Commons in late 1380...ignited the spark within this volatile

to apply the same standards to princes, lords and gentlemen that they applied daily in their relationships with the wealthier sorts at home. The decisive element was social-structural:

In the long-term perspective of common action by Essex people over a century or more, the welter of diverse motives, aims and irritants are likely to obscure some basic points of continuity. The core of these episodes . . . was a middling band of agriculturalists, craftsmen and retailers with a smaller sprinkling of the most well-off villagers and some labourers. Where organisation can be glimpsed it appears to have rested upon that network of village notables and petty officialdom prominent in local organisation from the outset of the period.

Revolt was when this 'middle band' and the 'smaller sprinkling' of richer sort could no longer hold back the murmuring or resist the pressure from below. Below the middle we encounter, once again, the spectre of the multitude. It was an anti-authoritarian culture with a repertoire of reasons to resist and rebel. 'A shifting calculus of grievances fuelled revolts', writes Poos. 'Groups whose discernible or imputable motivations differed . . . joined a common cause under a unifying rubric . . . As purely anti-seigneurial concerns waned, economic and social factors of different sorts, legal and political volatility (which the proximity of London doubtless helped stoke), and even religious nonconformity conspired to unite, albeit briefly, a disparate rural society.'[37] Without intending to, Poos's detailed reconstitution of the social relations of production in a precociously capitalist district affirms John Fortescue's account of the class dynamics of rebellion.

From the early fourteenth century to the civil wars, the commonalty of proto-industrial districts was a highly stratified 'class', featuring at the very least three 'strata': the servants and labourers and 'proto-proletarians' at the bottom and the 'proto-yeomanry' at the top. The largest group, that in between, was most active in revolts. Definitely not rich, destitution always hovered: injury or sickness of the main breadwinner always threatened. Without a cushion of land to fall back on when

---

atmosphere . . . in the spring of 1381 commissions were appointed to investigate and remedy the collection's shortfall.' *Rural Society*, 233.

[37] *Ibid.*, 261–1; 'Heretical attitudes meshed easily with anti-authoritarian tendencies', 264; A chaplain named William 'used books written in English to preach to the king's people, heretically and . . . against the catholic faith in Maldon and Thaxted' since 1402. A cobbler named John Smyth was 'a great Lollard' and did likewise. 'At Pattiswick, the brothers Thomas and John Cok, both weavers, organized and paid for men to go to London to support Oldcastle . . . John Abraham of Colchester, probably originally from Kent, was burned in 1428/9 for organizing a conventicle. A tailor from Mundham (Norfolk) confessed that 'before this tyme Y have be conversant, familier and hoomly with heretikes . . . in the hous of John Abraham, cordewaner of Colchester, kepying and holdyng scolwes of heresy': 266.

recession bit, resistance and insurrection brewed. The first law was that the best and strongest commonwealths judged themselves by the condition of their least fortunate neighbours and fellow-members. A succession of constitutional writers from Fortescue to Bacon affirmed this principle. Look after the poor, or they will rise up. Industrial employment was the first solution to the constitutional problem of poverty. Empire was the second, as we shall see in Chapter 7.

6.2   Industry transforms the landscape

The changes that took place in districts affected by industrial development were not and could not be restricted to those districts. Regions, districts and households employed in new 'projects', but above all in the cloth industry, became connected by routine *trafike* with many more communities and cultures than their ancestors, in ways that led to new habits of thought and life, revisions of old governmentalities and attitudes towards status, and new horizons.[38] Contemporaries did not use the word 'industry', which in modern usage tends to have a degree of abstraction that implies the development of political, economic and social discourses which arose from the process with which I am concerned here.[39] The

---

[38] Joan Thirsk has argued that to 'concentrate attention on the well-established economic activities of the sixteenth and seventeenth centuries – wool clothmaking [in particular] . . . is like viewing England through a telescope stationed half-way to the moon. Only the most conspicuous landmarks are visible . . . none of the subtle changes within the structures of innumerable local economies can be discerned . . . ': *Economic Policy and Projects: the Development of a Consumer Society in Early Modern England* (Oxford 1978), 7. I take Thirsk's point that 'industry' (or the 'mania' for 'projects') meant more than just the 'well-established' manufactures, which represented a *movement*, a widespread enterprising habit of mind, almost an ideology: on this topic, cf. Jan de Vries, 'The Industrial Revolution and the Industrious Revolution', *Journal of Economic History* 54:2 (June 1994) 249–70. This said, the cloth industry was the most widespread and prominent form which 'projects' took, and it is perhaps best seen as the 'vanguard' of the movement in that it was via clothmaking that 'industry' inserted itself into national constitutional discourse.

[39] Referring to the weak impact of the Enlightenment on British culture, Patrick Joyce writes that 'in comparison to much of Europe . . . Britain's well-developed political institutions meant that historically there was less difficulty in defining "society" in relation to the state (unlike much of Europe, where Sociology was born out of social crisis.': 'The Return of History: Postmodernism and the Politics of Academic History in Britain', *Past and Present* 158 (February 1998), 217. I would argue that it was the nascent discourse that became Political Economy that helped teach the English to think (in a particular way) about 'society', and, as I am suggesting here, Political Economy was born out of an earlier social, economic and political crisis, when the political institutions and culture that (e.g.) Voltaire so admired were not yet 'well-developed'. I am not of course suggesting that the discourse about industry, trade, the state and the common weal (i.e. early Political Economy) was the only element in the 'field of force': e.g. for the revolution in legal discourse, cf. Alan Cromartie, 'The Constitutionalist Revolution: the

politics of industry linked local, national and imperial development. The development and expansion of its manufacturing base was not the only element in the creation of English nationalism, but it was elemental. Without it, there would have been no empire.

One staple of industry theory that is now discredited is the idea that the factory (or 'the factory system') is its defining characteristic. Factories rationalized production on the basis of a much longer-evolving and all-pervasive revolution in settlement pattern, social management and administration, which began its 'take-off' between the fourteenth and sixteenth centuries. Historians (and the human sciences generally) have long regarded industrialization as an epochal conjuncture of themes and circumstances. Its 'preconditions' have been traced in reproduction, work and leisure habits, consumption, population movements, epidemiology and medicine, transport and communications, schooling, science and technology, finance . . . and so on.[40] With all the broadening and lengthening of perspective that has affected the history of industrialization in the past generation, one dimension has been neglected: the politics. The changes that made the factories and megalopolises of the nineteenth century possible were not only associated with the social structural changes described in the first section, but also with a long intensification of what Michel Foucault called 'governmentality'.[41]

The idea that just such a revolution of 'governmentality' (or shall we say, 'mentality of governance'?) occurred in England between 1300 and 1600 is supported by an important study of 267 public courts in 255 local communities or clusters of communities (hundreds) with records spanning the fourteenth to late sixteenth centuries. On the basis of a

Transformation of Political Culture in Early Stuart England', *Past and Present* 163 (May 1999), 76–120.

[40] Pat Hudson, *The Industrial Revolution*, is a useful synthesis of a massive secondary literature.

[41] Michel Foucault, 'Politics and the Study of Discourse', in Graham Burchell, Colin Gordon and Peter Miller (ed.), *The Foucault Effect: Studies in Governmentality* (London 1991), describes his 'project' as 'neither a formalization nor an exegesis, but an *archaeology* . . . as its name indicates only too obviously, the description of an *archive*'. By 'governmentality', Foucault meant: '1. The ensemble formed by the institutions, procedures, analyses and reflections, the calculations and tactics that allow the exercise of this very specific albeit complex form of power, which has as its target population, as its principal form of knowledge political economy, and as its essential technical means apparatuses of security; 2. The tendency which, over a long period and throughout the West, has steadily led towards the pre-eminence over all other forms (sovereignty, discipline, etc.) of this type of power which may be termed government, resulting, on the one hand, in the formation of a whole series of specific governmental apparatuses, and, on the other, in the development of a whole series of *savoirs*; 3. The process, or rather the result of the process, through which the state of justice of the Middle Ages, transformed into the administrative state during the fifteenth and sixteenth centuries, gradually becomes "governmentalized"': Foucault, *ibid.*, 102–3.

systematic survey and analysis of these difficult sources, Marjorie McIntosh concludes that constitutional historians need to pay closer attention to diffuse but continuous grass-roots developments. She charts the policies of the yeomen, husbandmen, clothiers, craftsmen and traders who sat on local juries and made presentments. 'Starting in the later fourteenth century', she writes, 'jurors worked to maintain a disciplined labour force, particularly in communities experiencing the transition to larger scale and more highly capitalized forms of agriculture or industrial production or craftwork'.[42] Many English communities and districts 'had a tradition of local self government' that is present in the oldest vernacular records. McIntosh 'demonstrates that new problems and solutions to them might well emerge first at the lowest level of government and courts, moving only gradually into the attention of higher authorities'. This finding 'reverses the directionality assumed by many analyses of national politics and law.' McIntosh notes that 'lags could develop between practical developments and revised ideological statements during periods of rapid change'. Pursuing the bottom-up trajectory of innovation into the world of ideology, she finds that 'the rhetoric used in the lesser courts . . . between 1460 and 1539 bears interesting resemblances to the idealistic view of society and political control advocated by the "commonwealth" approach of the mid-sixteenth century'.

In this model, influence flowed up from the NCOs and the communities to the peaks of government – out of the peripheries into the circles around the king. The local anticipated the national.[43] The experiences and experiments of the jurors created what, later, the clerks and intellectuals (often their sons) put into writing. They created the common weal long before authors of petitions of the people, propaganda, and political treatises began to incorporate the commonalty into their imaginings of the realm and common weal of England. The revolution of the commonalty was a practical reality before it was incorporated into politics and constitutional thinking in 1450. Behind the new language of politics lay a movement that was a potential alternative to the conventional chain of command.

The growth of London had a lot to do with its strategic role in the cloth industry. 'The extraordinary development of Tudor (London)', wrote Ramsay, 'owed more to the flourishing transit traffic in textiles than to occasional meetings of Parliament or the visits of rural litigants to the law courts of Westminster'.[44] London became enmeshed in this

---

[42] Marjorie K. McIntosh, *Controlling Misbehaviour in England, 1370–1600* (Cambridge 1998), 5, 7–8, 12–14.

[43] *Controlling Misbehaviour*, 15, 69.

[44] G.D. Ramsay, *The English Woollen Industry* (London 1982), 52.

national nexus in the fourteenth century, when a mutual colonization process gradually connected it directly with the districts upon which, up to then, provincial capitals like Bristol, York, Norwich, Southampton and Coventry, had built themselves. Multiple causes are difficult to unravel, but this national London-centring process cannot be ignored. Progressively, the smaller towns and rural districts to which industry, particularly the woollen cloth industry, migrated in the fourteenth and fifteenth centuries became connected more or less directly with the London merchants. The middle-men (in this case provincial towns and regional cities) fade into the background of centuries of seedy or genteel survival. These are the towns and cities tourists love today. Instead of circling around the provincial capitals and the king at Westminster, the cloth industry circled around the merchants of London.

This appears to have been well known at the time; the 'conservative gentry' who tried to restrict industrial development in the 1540s took for granted that chartered market towns formed the new centres of manufacturing activity. Following the enactment of 5–6 Edward VI, however, the clothiers had to make the court and legislature aware that while the new industrial districts were generally 'centred', organizationally, on established market towns, the landscape of manufacturing industry was more complex and ramified. Although clothiers often based themselves in market and provincial towns, this was not always the case. Even where it was, prohibiting clothmaking outside towns would leave the clothiers without their workforces in the villages, hamlets and squatters' cabins of their hinterlands. In 1608, 55 per cent of Gloucestershire clothiers, but only 36 per cent of weavers and 26 per cent of broadweavers, lived in the small towns.[45] The same form of organization was implied in a report of 1629 which declared that there were in Essex 'about twelve or fourteen towns wherein is exercised the manufactures upon wools' and estimated that in the surrounding districts 'not less than . . . fifty thousand . . . receive the livelihood and dependence upon' it.[46]

For these reasons it is misleading to think of this first phase of industrialization as the rise of industries in the countryside. Industrious

[45] Calculations derived from John Smyth of Nibley, *Men and Armour for Gloucestershire in 1608* (Gloucester 1980); closer examination suggests that even when the larger clothiers lived in parishes situating market towns, they nearly always lived at mills some distance from the town itself: e.g. Edward Halydaye 'clothmaker' of Rodborough (PCC Ayloffe 20, 1519); Roger Fowler of Bisley (PCC 34, November 1540); Thomas Sewell of Stroud (PCC Spent 23, 1540); Thomas Walworth of Dursley (PCC Fitiplace 17, 1512); Richard Halydaye complains (PRO Early Chancery Proc. 1005, 1540) that 'the hamlet of Rodborough [mainly concerned with clothmaking] is distant from their parish church of Minchinhampton two and a half miles'.

[46] Joan Thirsk and J.P. Cooper (ed.), *Seventeenth Century Economic Documents*, 224.

proletarians colonized unexploited 'waste', like the hundreds of 'cabiners' working in the steelmaking industry of the Forest of Dean in the 1620s. Yet even the forest was part of organized territory centred on one or more of the myriad market towns that were chartered in the last great phase of the Norman-Angevin reconstruction of England. Little market towns had a vested interest in the settlement of industrial workers, who, in good times, had money in their pockets to spend at the weekly markets, and, by the end of the seventeenth century, shops which opened for trading six and even (to the dismay of magistrates) seven days a week. On occasion the rise of 'rural' industry resulted in the gradual emergence of a new town, but usually industry gradually changed a medieval market town into an early modern manufacturing town.[47] Most importantly, these market towns were conduits of national stories.

E.P. Thompson suggested that 'the most common industrial configuration of the early 19th century was a commercial or manufacturing centre which served as the hub for a circle of straggling industrial villages'.[48] The complex typical of the Industrial Revolution, in his view, was neither the factory nor the new industrial megalopolis, which only gradually congealed constellations of small manufacturing towns surrounded by straggling 'suburban' development into unities like greater Manchester or Birmingham. Thompson's characterization of the landscape of industry in the nineteenth century applies with even greater force to the industrial communities of the fourteenth, fifteenth and sixteenth centuries, which were centred on medieval market towns like Malden, Wotton under Edge, Minchinhampton, Bolton or Blackburn. These, in turn, were usually the satellites of medieval provincial capitals like Cirencester, Colchester or Manchester. Between the fourteenth and sixteenth centuries such regions began to form a constellation that was centred on London. In Braudel's terminology, the cloth industry connected every 'level' (landscape, material life, the wheels of commerce, and 'the higher levels' with their 'perspective of the world') into one movement.[49] Between the fourteenth and

---

[47] 'All the outlying villages of the great parish of Manchester were given over to linen weaving.' Fustians took hold first in the hilly country between Bolton and Blackburn; by 1630 they had also become firmly established in . . . the present Oldham area': Alfred P. Wadsworth and Julia De Lacy Mann, *The Cotton Trade and Industrial Lancashire* (Manchester 1931), 25. The town of Stroud, in Gloucestershire, is somewhat exceptional in being pretty much a commercial and industrial centre from its formation in the thirteenth–fifteenth centuries: its story is told in N.M. Herbert, 'Stroud', in N.M. Herbert (ed.), *VCH Gloucestershire*, vol. XI, 4–41, 99–144.

[48] E.P. Thompson *The Making of the English Working Class* (Harmondsworth 1991), 446.

[49] Fernand Braudel, *The Structures of Everyday Life*, vol. 1 of *Civilisation and Capitalism, 15th–18th Century* (New York 1979); *The Wheels of Commerce*, vol. 2 (1982); *The Perspective of the World*, vol. 3 (1984).

sixteenth centuries, the cloth industry gradually (or in the case of Coventry, suddenly) leaked away from the medieval urban centres like Salisbury, Gloucester and Bristol, and reproduced itself more or less exactly around a larger number of suitably placed market towns in many parts of England. This movement produced a constellation of production districts connected to one national centre. Such places had many of the advantages of the old medieval centres, and far fewer of the entrenched restrictive practices. It was within this framework that the Industrial Revolution would occur. What matters is not that particular districts made the transition from proto-industry to Industrial Revolution, but that from the start they were linked into a larger, national context.[50] They were linked, practically, by *trafike*; gradually, as we shall see, they were integrated, ideologically, by an emerging scenario or 'discourse'.

What emerged was a national network, consisting of new industrial districts which, as the list of exemptions to an Act of 1555 that attempted to restrict its development showed, were scattered across the kingdom, and, in the place of the many regional outports of the medieval dispensation, just one great mercantile centre, London. How it emerged is less important than that it emerged. In the long run it meant that consciousness of the cloth industry, wherever production went on, was also national. Thus emerged England's first national industry.

6.3   A recurring theme: 'deindustrialization'

In a notable study of the origins of modern economic thought, Joyce Appleby identified the 1670s as the first time 'deindustrialization' became an item in governance, and 'the underemployment of the poor surfaced as a major problem'.[51] What Appleby calls 'deindustrialization' is related to a more general characteristic of early industry which was an item of governance as early as the fifteenth century. In 1438 the weavers of Oxford complained to the king 'that where the numbre of the said craft of weuers in the said Towne were wonede to be of lx persones and more in the tyme (of e Aiel) of the said kyng Iohn . . . And now . . . ther ben in the said Town atte this tyme but ij persones of the said craft of weuers and they ben so poure and nedi.' Oxford was still a clothmaking centre,

---

[50] J.N. Hare, 'Growth and Recession in the Fifteenth-Century Economy: the Wiltshire Textile Industry and the Countryside', *Economic History Review* 51 (1998), shows that the industrial archipelagoes invariably enriched their agricultural hinterlands, adding another reason why 'industries in the countryside' must not be studied in isolation, but always in relation to their specific wider social and economic contexts.

[51] J. Appleby, *Economic Thought and Ideology in Seventeenth-Century England* (Princeton 1980), 123–7.

but most of the workers lived outside the town. The town was suffering 'by cause that othure that ben of the same craft dwelling wyth out the said Towne comyth dayly wythynne the said towne and (.v.) mile abowte and there they purchace and taken the matere apperteynyng to the same craffte and cariene hit a way out of the said towne and werkythe'.[52] It is a theme of the history of capitalism that industry and economic prosperity always threatens to migrate elsewhere. From the fourteenth century until the Industrial Revolution labour was cheaper (and less well organized) outside city walls. Where city industries survived and flourished in the fifteenth and sixteenth centuries, it was because they took advantage of cheaper labour in surrounding 'rural' districts. At Bristol, attempts to extend urban influence into the hinterlands was stymied by powerful nobles, and then by the increasingly gentrified middle rank culture that replaced them in districts like Gloucestershire's Vale of Berkeley. The cloth industries of places like Salisbury and Cirencester survived as strategic centres for the distribution of wool and yarn, the maintenance of high standards of weaving in far-flung hill villages, and, most important of all, as the masters of 'toukers, dyers, and schermyn', the crucial finishing trades.[53] In envisaging the organization of the English cloth industry from the fourteenth to eighteenth centuries, we have to abandon notions of an urban/rural divide and think instead of a rural-urban continuum. Wherever it was maintained, town or country, Norwich or the Stroudwater Valleys, it always took advantage of cheap rural labour. As soon as labour got too well organized, capital looked elsewhere. Deindustrialization is a threat that hovers over every community and district ever visited by the spirit of capitalism.

By the mid-fifteenth century it was becoming clear that while commodity production moved around, it was a permanent feature of the English landscape. This landscape was diagnosed in *A Trade Policy*, a *lybell* distributed among parliamentarians in 1463, but written earlier, perhaps by John Lydgate. It gives us a systematic account of the ideas that influenced that parliament when it introduced legislation regulating clothmaking and introducing basic protections for wage-workers – theoretically, a national system for what the libel made clear was already England's premier industry. The *lybell* has claims to be the earliest document of English economic history. Its topic, explicitly, was 'the welth of ynglond'.

---

[52] PRO E28/62/36 Petition of the Weavers of Oxford (1438); PRO E28/62/35 Privy Seal: Warrant transmitting Petition of the Weavers of Oxford (1438); Edward Miller and John Hatcher, *Medieval England: Towns, Commerce and Crafts* (London and New York 1995), 111, suggests that the Oxford weavers had been recycling this complaint since 1230.

[53] 'A Trade Policy' (c.1460), no. 70 in R.H. Robbins, *Historical Poems of the XIVth and XVth Centuries* (New York 1959).

Axiomatically, every 'realm' in the world, and every 'manner' and 'degree' of its subjects, 'have nede to oure englysshe commodyte'. There were no exceptions, 'noothir pope, Emperowre, nor king,/ Bysschop, cardynal, or any man levyng'. All needed 'Mete, drynke, & Cloth . . . For who-so lackyth any of thyse iij thynges . . . Yt may not stonde with theym in any prosperyte'. *Wele*, a more general and perhaps spiritual condition, was, in this strategic usage, *welth* or constitutional *prosperyte*. England was self-sufficient in food and drink, and it produced a surplus (*supplusage*) of cloth for export. Everywhere clothmaking was a means by which the poor became industrious and able to support themselves and the commonweal. They produced much more than the English market could absorb. Every sort of rank, manner and degree of person in every country, 'both crystyn and hethyn', needed cloth. At present, their 'merchauntes comme oure wollys for to bye', which feeds the manu-factories of

> . . . Arteyse, pekardy, henaude, & normandy
> Bretayne, fraunse, petow, and barry,
> Gascoyne, gyon, and also aragun,
> Portingale, spayne, & nauerun;
> Castyle, Cesyle, coleyn, & swethyn,
> Pruse-londe, florence, venyse, & Iene,
> Melane, catelony, and all ytally,
> Bewme, hungry, greke, and gret turky

Engross manufactures and conquer markets. What the king lost in taxes on wool exports would be infinitely outweighed by the riches that would flow into England if it could establish itself as clothmaker to the world. It is the earliest plain statement of which I am aware that the conquest of markets could lead to the conquest of peoples. Through cloth, the author explained, 'we myght rewle and govern all crystyn kinges/ And paynymns also we myght mak theym ful tame'. When it first appeared, this argument may have seemed like futuristic bravado. In retrospect it is deeply ominous. The sale of English cloth would succeed where the crusades of feudal lords had failed.

The *lybell* assumes that there is nothing inherently virtuous about poverty. The priority, as for Langland, was 'that the comyns of thys land may wyrke at the full'. Kingdoms of beggars were defenceless against more industrious neighbours. The author of the *lybell* was proud of the vocations of industry and trade and spoke for (and to) something approximating a 'business community'. Clothmaking was a dispersed but interconnected corporation encompassing flockmasters, shepherds, shearers, sorters and combers to carders, yarn-makers, yarn-badgers and broggers, weavers, fullers, dyers, finishers, clothiers and merchants. Managing it was not like managing communities of peasant serfs and *liberi homines*. Discipline and good faith were essential. The *lybell* complained that too many of the households and families who coordinated local production, up to the great London merchants, were in it for themselves, caring neither for the poor or the commonwealth. They sucked up all the profit, leaving none for the workers. At present, 'the pore have the labur, the ryche the wynnyng'. The poor were 'defrawded in every contre' where industry settled. The *lybell* urged them, instead, 'to uoyde [avoid] fraude, and sett egallyte', meaning 'that syche wyrkfolk be payde in good mone[y]', not goods or tokens. Everyone from the king down would benefit and there would be 'a gret enscherychyng to all the comynalte'.[54] If every rank of the industry worked in their allotted vocations, for the commonwealth and not for themselves, England would be the richest, happiest and hardest-working country in the world.

As an indication of the extent of the cloth industry alone, consider the landscape implied in the following references. A century after Jack Sharpe's Rebellion, in 1429, a 'capitalist clothier' from Oxfordshire offered to restore the clothing industry at Abingdon so that the poor of the district 'schall gayn more in few yeres commynge than they have done in twenty yeres past'. And if markets for cloth abated, he would set them at work producing yarn for the well-established industry of *Strodewater*, fifty miles to the west.[55] All the arguments Appleby identifies in the pamphlet literature of the last third of the seventeenth century were implicit in a petition of grievances from the weavers of Suffolk and Essex in 1539.[56] A document of 1550 spoke of 'the multitude of clothiers lately encreased in the realm', which, if true, implied a much greater increase in the number of clothworkers generally.[57] The merchant George Nedham estimated the annual value of cloths exported to Antwerp in 1560 at £920,000, a figure that is 'not in conflict with other evidence from documents of the period'.[58] In the twelve months following 29 September 1561, 372 clothiers from twenty-two counties were fined for sending defective cloth to London for export. The leading counties were Kent

[54] 'A Trade Policy'; Robbins observes that 'these demands for regulation of the woollen trade, and, moreover, for the protection of workers, were accepted. In 1463 Parliament passed legislation . . .': *Historical Poems*, p. xliii.

[55] *SPD Elizabeth* CXIV No.5: in R.H. Tawney and E. Power, *Tudor Economic Documents* (London 1924) *(TED)*, vol. 1, 176–7.

[56] *SPD Hen VIII* vol. 151, ff. 128–31, in *TED*, 177.

[57] *Acts of Privy Council* vol. III, 19–20, in *TED*, 184.

[58] Ramsay, *English Woollen Industry*, 76.

(eighty-five cases), Gloucestershire (sixty-six), Wiltshire (forty-one), Suffolk (thirty-three) and Lancashire (fifteen).[59] Eleven years later, in 1572, 4,000 people 'about Manchester' were said to be 'for lack of worke utterlye impoverished'.[60] The activities of wool brokers were said to be responsible for 'the impoverishment of many poor people' in Gloucestershire in 1577.[61] 'Multitudes' who were 'very apt to idleness' would be 'put from their lawful maintenance' at Shrewsbury in 1582, if a Staple for Cottons and Friezes were to be established at the rival port of Chester.[62] That the function of the cloth industry was 'for keeping of a great multitude of poor people in worcke' was assumed in an agreement between the West Country Clothiers and the Merchant Adventurers in 1586.[63] The same year a petition to the government claimed that thousands of clothworkers in central Gloucestershire were reduced to eating 'oates and dog-grass', and would soon starve if several ship-loads of wheat from the Baltic did not arrive soon at Bristol. 'Thousandes of poore people (would be) utterlie undone' at Rochdale in 1588 if local wool-badgers were prosecuted, as, by custom, they should have been.[64] In Gloucestershire in 1608 a seventh of the 19,402 able-bodied men mustered were clothworkers.[65] The same year Richard Blacheford the Elder of Dorchester organized the manufacture of 'many a thousand . . . Dorset Dozens', and had done so since 'forty years past', when he transferred his business from Devon. All these cloths were sold to Normandy and Brittany, where 'the people of the country are poor and of a base disposition and will not go the price of good cloth'.[66]

A spokesman for the merchants, Edward Misselden, wrote in 1622 that 'the Principall Cities and Towns for execution of the Statute for searching and Sealing of Cloth, are . . . Wiltshire: Salisbury, Wilton, Westbury, Trubigde, Wooton-Basset, Deuizes, Malmsbury, Chipnam, Castlecomb, Calne, Bradford, Bromhil, Beckinton, Warminster; Somersetsh[ire]: Bath, Wells, Freshfor, Tauton, Philips-Norton, Frome, Somerton, Wellington, Bridgewater, Ilmister, Axbridge, Glastonbury;

---

[59] Calculated from G.D. Ramsay, 'The Distribution of the Cloth Industry in 1561–2,' *English Historical Review* 57:227 (July 1942), 362–9.

[60] *SP Ireland* XXXV, no. 149: *TED*, vol. 1, 189.

[61] *SPD Elizabeth* CXIV no. 32: *TED*, 191.

[62] *SPD Elizabeth* CLVII no. 5: *TED*, vol. 1, 191.   [63] *TED*, vol. 1, 214.

[64] Wadsworth and Mann, *Cotton Trade*, 7, where they add that 'the long controversy over the prohibition of middle men dealers in wool . . . suggests that the transition to capitalist control was well under way, and that already the large scale entrepreneur had more influence than the petitioners cared (or were free?) to admit'.

[65] R.H. and A.J. Tawney, 'An Occupational Census of the Seventeenth Century', *Economic History Review* 5 (1934).

[66] PRO E134 Jas I Easter 30: Thirsk and Cooper (ed.), *Seventeenth-Century Economic Documents*, 191–2.

Glocestersh[ire]: Glocester, Tedbury, Strowdwater, Dursley, Wotten-underhedge, Ebley, Witcomb, Winchcomb, Thornbury, Teuxbury, Cirencester; Oxfordshire: Burford, Witney; Worcesters[hire].: Worcester, Kidderminster; Herefordshire: Hereford, Lidbury; Warwickshire: War-wicke, Coventry; Devonshire: Exceter, Tanton; Hampsh[ire]: Southamp-ton, Portsmouth.'[67] Every one of them was directly connected with London by routine *trafike*.

The driving force in this multiplication and accumulation of the man-ufacturing sector was constitutional in the sense that it represented fun-damental changes in the way society was made up, interconnected and imagined. Bacon picked up the argument that had underpinned dis-course about the commonweal since the fifteenth century. 'The matter of seditions is of two kinds', he wrote: 'much poverty and much discon-tentment'. Poverty caused 'discontentments', which were 'in the body politic like to humours in the natural, which are apt to gather a preter-natural heat and to inflame'. And 'if there be fuel prepared, it is hard to tell where the spark shall come that shall set it on fire'. Bacon was not being over-dramatic about the role of resistance and rebellion in English history. His 'first remedy' was to remove its 'material cause...which is, want and poverty in the estate'. We shall see that by the time he was writing his essays, in the 1590s, the solution had been defined: 'the open-ing and well-balancing of trade (and) the cherishing of manufactures'.[68] Arguably Bacon invented 'Natural History' (Science) as an adjunct to this primal threat to peaceful and orderly commonweal. Hobbes agreed. 'They who seem to themselves to be burthened with the whole load of the commonweal, are prone to be seditious', he wrote; 'they are affected with change, who are distasted at the present state of things'.[69] Industry was supposed to be the solution to poverty, but some believed it led only to better organized 'discontentments'.

---

[67] Edward Misselden, *Free Trade or, The Meanes To Make Trade Florish. Wherein, The Causes of the Decay of Trade in this Kingdome, are discovered: And the Remedies also to remoove the same, are represented* (London 1622).

[68] Francis Bacon, 'On Seditions and Troubles', *Essays* (London 1906), 44–5; but cf. also the pamphlet 'Howe to reforme the realme in settyng them to werke and to restore tillage' (c.1535–6), in *TED*, vol. 3, 117: 'Wheras now so grete nombre of idull people ar in Englonde besyde all such that workith husbandry...havyng lyff in theym must needs have living. Ergo, yf they [by] workes of artificialitie gete no money...muste nedes bege or stele their lyvinge from them that werkith husbandrie, or otherwise by craftie meanes of beying and sellyng, or by policy to stody howe of plentie to make scarcitie, for their singulare weale to distroye the comon weale: *that is the wisdome of this worlde*' (emphasis added).

[69] Thomas Hobbes, 'Of the internal causes tending to the dissolution of government', Bernard Gert (ed.), *The Citizen; Philosophical Rudiments Concerning Government and Society* (Indianapolis 1991), ch. 12, 251–2.

George Unwin's view that the English cloth industry first flexed its muscles as a political and constitutional force in the 1540s needs to be pushed back to the 1450s, when thoughtful men were giving their attention to the relations between what are now called 'recession' and 'depression', and their early modern corollary, popular rebellion.[70] The exact number of English people whose livelihoods depended directly and indirectly on anything that would now qualify as 'secondary' production and trade in its commodities is not known, and was not known in any statistically exact sense at the time. Statistical accuracy is less important than how contemporaries perceived its relative importance in whatever grand scheme of things contemporary minds located their political and constitutional thoughts. Unwin's recognition of the seminal importance of Sir Thomas Smith's *Discourse of the Commonweal* (1549) has stood the test of time.[71] Smith's conservative Knight argued that 'it were better that there were (no clothiers) in the realm at all' than that they 'should take occasion of commotion' whenever war or other necessity of State resulted in 'stay of cloth'. 'All . . . insurrections do stir by occasion of . . . these clothiers':[72]

> For when our clothiers lack vent over sea, there is great multitude of these clothiers idle; and, when they are idle, they then assemble in companies and murmur for lack of living, and so pick a quarrel or other to stir the poor commons, that be as idle as they, to a commotion.

This gave the learned Doctor, who spoke for Smith, the opportunity to point out the flaws in the Knight's scheme to ban manufacturing projects, especially clothmaking. 'You said that wool is sufficient to bring in treasure', he replied. The ban he proposed would not benefit 'the Commonweal nor (ensure the) continuance of the realm':[73]

> For when every man would fall to breed sheep to increase wool and so at length all other occupations should be set aside . . . ; so in process of time, the multitude of

---

[70] George Unwin, *Studies in Economic History: the Collected Papers of George Unwin*, ed. R.H. Tawney, (London 1927), 187–8; Mavis Mate, 'The Economic and Social Roots of Medieval Popular Rebellion: Sussex in 1450–1451', *Economic History Review*, new series, 45:4 (November 1992), 661–2, 664; cf. also Thirsk and Cooper (ed.), *Seventeenth-Century Economic Documents*, 1.

[71] Neal Wood, *Foundations of Political Economy: Some Early Tudor Views on State and Society* (Berkeley 1994); Wood, 'Foundations of Political Economy: the New Moral Philosophy of Sir Thomas Smith', in Paul A. Fideler and T.F. Mayer (ed.), *Political Thought and the Tudor Commonwealth: Deep Structure, Discourse and Disguise* (Cambridge 1997); Keith Wrightson, *Earthly Necessities: Economic Lives in Early Modern Britain* (New Haven and London 2000), 154–6.

[72] *A Discourse of the Commonweal of this Realm of England*, attributed to Sir Thomas Smith, ed. Mary Dewar (Charlottesville 1969), 87.

[73] *Ibid.*, 89, 92.

the King's subjects none left but a few shepherds which were no number sufficient to serve the King at his need or defend the realm from enemies . . . Wherefore in my mind they are far wide of right consideration that would have either none or else less clothing within this realm because sometimes it is occasion of busyness [anxiety] and tumults for lack of vent.

It was an argument with a future. The Doctor did not question the Knight's assumption that secondary industry institutionalized insurrections of the commonalty, which were threatened or actually occurred whenever commodity markets contracted or evaporated, leaving insecurity, unemployment, makeshift and misery in their wake. Industry breeds sedition, says the Knight. Unemployed workers tried to influence government policy, which was no business of commoners.[74] Rebels should be hanged, the conditions which bred them stamped out. England should deindustrialize in order to stamp out indiscipline in the ranks and lack of respect for those who were born to rule.

It was already an old-fashioned perspective. The Knight was a vehicle for Smith's account of an idea that was becoming commonplace, a 'spin' on 'reality', a public 'myth', or 'discourse', grounded in the premise that 'the cloth industry' could mobilize – or succesfully represent itself as having the capacity to mobilize – large numbers of people. It could disrupt the realm. For the Knight, the body of clothiers, represented as the leaders of the insurrectionary clothworkers, epitomized a class of men against whom Thomas Wilson waxed angrily in 1600, disloyal sergeant-majors of the social order, selfish and ambitious yeomen-traders of the villages and the citizens of the town. Such men surreptitiously usurped constitutional functions (and pretensions) for which they had no brief, and which were 'no matter invented and sett downe by authority for the bettering of that state of the people, but rather by the substelty (sic.) of them and the simplicity of gentlemen'.[75] Clothiers had no constitutional brief to do so, but henceforth all parties to the discourse on industry would take for granted that they commanded and led large numbers of people. This, as Smith implied, was bound to offend Knights of Shires. The Knight represented 'the opinion of the average English country gentleman (who) was opposed to the expansion of the cloth industry', and whose spirit Unwin saw in the wave of restrictive legislation of the reigns

---

[74] The cloth industry was thought to provide employment for 'the fourth sort of men which do not rule . . . day labourers, poor husbandmen, yea merchants or retailers which have no free land, copyholders, and all artificers . . . (who) have no authority in our commonwealth': Sir Thomas Smith, *De Republica Anglorum* (written before 1565), William Huse Dunham and Stanley Pargellis (ed.), *Complaint and Reform in England, 1436–1714* (New York 1968), 212.

[75] Thomas Wilson, *The State of England, Anno. Dom. 1600* (London 1925), 38–9.

of Edward VI and Mary, and the first half of the reign of Elizabeth. He was as reactionary with regard to industry as his counterpart of the nineteenth century. His view was that to allow, let alone encourage industrial development, was socially irresponsible, since it would increase the numbers of the potentially and periodically poor who, all agreed, represented the most continuous threat to the peaceful, orderly life of the common weal and kingdom.[76]

The Act of 5–6 Edward VI was an attempt on the part of 'the average English country gentleman' to stop the development of rural industry dead in its tracks, by stipulating 'that no Person shall make Woolen Cloth, but only in a market town where Cloth had commonly been made . . . ten years past, or in a City, Borough, or Town Corporate'. 'The spirit that animates the Acts of Edward VI', Unwin explained, emanated from the magistrate class, a class of men who, in Thomas Wilson's constitution of 1600, were in charge of administration and justice at the local and district level. Their influence was 'still more clearly revealed in the chief Acts passed for the regulation of the cloth industry during the next reign – the Weavers' Acts of 1555 and 1558'. The movement of opposition achieved its 'finishing stroke' with the Statute of Artificers of 1563, which added further restrictions on the expansion of industry.

The point, of course, is that this powerful anti-industry lobby failed. Edward's Act was in force for only six years. In 1555 an *Act touching the making of Woolen Cloth* 'mitigated' the earlier act in a curiously ambivalent way. In its 32nd section it repeated the earlier proscription of any development outside chartered towns, boroughs and cities. Then, as if as an afterthought, its 38th section specifically excluded

All Persons which shall dwell in *North Wales*, or *South Wales*, *Cheshire*, *Lancashire*, *Westmoreland*, *Cumberland*, *Northumberland*, Bishopric of *Durham*, *Cornwall*, *Suffolk*, *Kent*, the town of *Godalmin* in *Surrey*, or *Yorkshire*, being not within 12 miles of the City of *York*, or any Towns or Villages near the River *Stroud*, in the County of *Gloucestershire*, where Cloths have usually been made.

'The places here mentioned', wrote John Smith in 1747, 'are sufficient to give another Idea of the State of the Woolen Manufacture at the time in England, than what we receive from the Generality of Writers'.[77] They are very considerable exemptions. The Act of 4–5 Philip and Mary hints at what had taken place in the six years since the passing of 5–6

---

[76] 'In France they have divers bands of men of arms in divers places to repress such tumults quickly if any should arise. If we had the like here, we might be bold to have as many artificers as they have': the Knight, in *A Discourse of the Commonweal*, 92.

[77] John Smith, *Memoirs of Wool*, 1747 (Reprints of Economic Classics: New York 1969), vol. 1, 98–101.

Edward VI, c.6. In its preamble it tries to appease the 'average English country gentleman' by stating that while 5–6 Edward was 'one good Act for the true and perfect making of Woolen Cloth', it had been necessary to heed the opinion of 'divers Clothiers (who) found themselves aggrieved' by its provisions, and made their grievances felt.

For Unwin, a progressive liberal himself, the Doctor represented 'the most progressive opinion of the time'. The Doctor did not dispute the Knight's claim that industry went with commotions and seditions. The point, for Smith, was that wise lords and princes cherished 'mysteries' and 'artificers' because 'the highest princes of them all, without such artificers, could not maintain their estate'. The Doctor saw the socially and constitutionally disruptive potential of industrial districts. In Unwin's summary, the Doctor urged 'that the government ought not to shirk the increase of responsibility involved in the expansion of the cloth industry':

> . . . if, as he argues, it is the chief means of bringing money into the country. Nevertheless, he is clearly of the opinion that the expansion ought to take place in towns, since the towns are the natural seat of industry. This was the view universally held by contemporary theorists; and, since the disinterested outsider was so favourable to their cause, it would have been surprising if the towns themselves had not seized the opportunity to protect their supposed industrial interests.[78]

If so, they failed. As the Act of Philip and Mary proscribing cloth making outside certain towns and districts demonstrated, the clothiers and merchants of the new industrial districts were, by the 1550s, powerful and articulate enough to ensure their survival against a powerful opposition movement. Unwin thought that the exemptions of 1555 very largely define the regions and districts in which industry was to develop in the future, yet it excludes all of the regions of development in the West Country except Stroudwater. The 'country party' failed in its attempt to quietly put down the upstart infant that in its view threatened the constitution. Reactionary knights and gentlemen discovered that industry was no longer an infant. The Act of 1555 proved that it could stand up for itself. In *A Discourse of the Commonweal*, the doctor affirmed the implication of an idea that had been current nearly a century earlier, when it was voiced by *A Trade Policy*. Industry was constitutionally necessary.

The power of the cloth industry to organize as a lobby was crucial to the progress of early industry, but it was just as important that it had an argument from necessity. This argument was already implicit, in that the conditions that made it so plausible were already in existence.

---

[78] Unwin, *Studies in Economic History*, ed. Tawney, 188.

Smith integrated it further into constitutional discourse. The next key figure was Richard Hakluyt the elder, the first expert on what we would call 'economy' to make the link between industry, the commonweal of England, and overseas expansion, three elements that he also saw as connected by *necessity*.[79]

6.4   The emergence of the political economy outlook

To have any chance of persuading the government to take them seriously, petitioners had to persuade it that their interests were also, as the *Discourse of the Commonweal* put it, those of 'the Commonweal [and the] continuance of the realm'. There was a sense of crisis.[80] Smith's *Discourse* set out to circumvent the problem that every rank, trade and occupation tended to blame every other group for everything that appeared to be going wrong.[81] He showed the superficiality of this view by describing the commonweal, not as a hierarchy of ranks, but as a field of force within which an alteration in the relative strength of one element entailed an alteration in all the others. What was needed was policy that took this interrelatedness into consideration. The Doctor's reply to the Knight implied that depopulating enclosures were not necessarily harmful, if work could be created and maintained elsewhere. The Knight could enclose his estate and tap into the profitability of woolgrowing, but it was illogical at the same time to oppose the development of industry, which provided employment for those who left, or were forced from the land. Enclosures were not harmful to the commonweal and crown as long as they did not 'reduce the number sufficient to serve at [the monarch's] need or defend the realm from enemies'. Individual interests must take

---

[79] Richard Hakluyt the younger printed seven of the elder Hakluyt's memoranda in his *Principall Navigations, Voyages and Discoveries of the English Nation*, Facs. of 1589 edition, ed. David Beers Quinn and Raleigh Ashlin Skelton (Cambridge 1965); cf. esp. 'Inducements to the liking of the voyage intended towards Virginia' (1582), in E.G.R. Taylor (ed.), *The Original Writings and Correspondence of the Two Richard Hakluyts*... (London 1935); 'Which way the Savage may be able to purchase our cloth', in 'Notes in writing by M. Richard Hakluyt Esquire... To M. Arthur Pet, and to M. Charles Jackman... for the discoverie of the North-east straight', in *Original Writings*, ed. Taylor, 460ff.; and 'Remembrance... for a principall English factor at Constantinople', in *Original Writings*, ed. Taylor, 161ff.

[80] For a discussion of the historiography of the crisis, and a new reading of its significance, cf. Robert Brenner, 'The Dynamics of Commercial Development, 1550–1640: a Reinterpretation,' in Brenner, *Merchants and Revolution: Commercial Change, Political Conflict, and London's Overseas Traders, 1550–1653* (Cambridge 1993), ch. 1. I think Brenner overstates the overall importance in the emerging field of force, of the Company Merchants, and that his interpretation is, as a result, too London-centred. In my interpretation the innovative force comes from the 'peripheries', i.e. the provincial industries.

[81] *A Discourse of the Commonweal*, 38–41.

second place to those of the state, because the 'weal' of all the interests depends on the integrity of the state. Throughout the sixteenth century, the strongest arguments concerning the state of England were military. When Thomas Wilson penned his sketch of the constitution in 1600, he took for granted that the main justification for the traditional ranking system was that England was, and had to be, an army, ready at all times to defend the country against invasion and conquest. In time this defensive priority would give way to a more aggressive justification – that expansion was the best form of defence; but not yet. The ranking system served the Commonweal by providing its best means of defence. It was within these conventional contexts that all interest groups had to couch their petitions.

In the second half of the sixteenth century the discourse turned to demography.[82] By the 1580s, no-one doubted that industry created districts that, relatively speaking, were swarming with people. There is nothing new in the argument of proto-industrialization theory that as long as markets could be found for its commodities it led to a multiplication of units of production. There were others in the generations between Smith, Old Hakluyt and Marx who recognized that industry was the nucleus of the English explosion that they were, in effect, advocating. It seemed perverse to insist, as did Smith, that the labour of craftworkers, artisans and journeymen was the *primum mobile* of the English commonweal. Surely, enterprising manufacturing projects were no more than sophisticated poor-relief schemes. The political economy that emerged in writers from Edward Misselden to Adam Smith emphasized the glorious exploits of *trafike*.[83] If it is human nature to barter and truck, then clearly no nation

---

[82] 'I take not (enclosures) to be the only cause of this dearth [dearness] at this time, but this I think in my mind that if that kind of enclosure do as much increase in twenty years to come as it has done twenty years past, it comes to the great desolation and weakening of the King's strength of this realm *which is more to be feared than dearth*': *ibid.*, 49 (emphasis added).

[83] Brenner's argument (e.g. p. 5, n. 6) that 'imports powered commercial expansion', is fine as far as it goes, but chronologically, in my view, it puts the cart before the horse. I argue that the developing groundswell represented by what I am calling 'the discourse of industry' (and, in turn, *its* causes) was a precondition for the eventual victory of the merchants' political economy, which was to achieve its most abstract rhetorical form in Misselden's *Circle of Commerce*. What we call 'industry', the production of commodities, Misselden called 'Projects', which, 'though they promise much, *yet the utility is commonly Contingent*, which may be, or may not be'. Against the arguments of the clothiers, who wanted the merchant monopolies abolished, Misselden argued that 'Industry' was *contingent upon Trade*. Thus 'in the mutation of the naturall course of Trade, there ought to be Perspicuity and apparency of evident utility: Else a Breach may be sooner made *in Trade* then can be repaired: and the Current once diverted, will hardly bee revolved, into it genuine Source and Course againe.' Wise governments tinkered with trade at their own peril. Industry needed governing. The great merchants knew best the crafts and mysteries of trade: Edward Misselden, *Circle of Commerce*.

in the world better exemplified it than the English, humanity in its purest form. These 'trails of progress' also lead us back to the new industrial districts of the fourteenth to eighteenth centuries, where so many seminal social, political and religious experiments were conducted, and where, whenever the unpredictable world economy that was being constructed to satisfy their need for markets went into recession, the pinch was felt first, longest and hardest.

The discourse on industry entered the field of forces that made up governance and constitutional life between 1450 and 1585. If Richard of Fulham could speak, he might stake a claim for Hertfordshire in the 1350s. From 1450 it was a rare parliament that did not discuss it. It is true that the only time anyone ever attempted to describe the scope of the industry was when a slump of trade, as petitions invariably claimed, left hundreds, or thousands of households in one or another of the districts of England, though mainly in Dorset, Devon, Somerset, Wiltshire, Gloucestershire, East Anglia, South Lancashire and the West Riding of Yorkshire, with no work and no subsistence. Were they telling the truth, or was it merely a torrent of conventional exaggeration, little white political lies designed to serve the interests of petitioners? The sum of the villages, towns, districts and regions of England which, in one petition or another, claimed that their lives and livelihoods depended on the cloth industry alone, adds up to a third of England's population or more. At the very least we can say that persons describing themselves as representatives of these communities were prepared to testify to their dependence from the sixteenth to the late twentieth century. Their testimony lends weight to the elder Richard Hakluyt's down-to-earth vision of the English commonwealth in the 1580s, when England was already an 'industrial' society, one whose health and wealth depended on industry.

By then, the new dispensation was making itself sufficiently obvious to be noticed by the upper ranks of regional and district life, the gentry and knights of the shire, who invented a tradition that is still with us: constitutional disdain for the kinds of individuals and communities bred by industry, and a deep suspicion of the invasion of constitutional life by commerce, this new and disturbing intensification of *trafike* and *trucking*. There was a half-hearted attempt in the middle years of the sixteenth century to restrain it within urban walls, but the early industrial capitalists proved stronger and better able to command and manage large numbers of people, and wield them, imaginatively, as a political tool. In the writings of Sir Thomas Smith and others, the idea emerged that industry was not an evil necessity. Exemptions to the Act of 1555 signify the power of the 'industry lobby' – by which I mean the actual multiplication of manufacturing households and districts, the associated intensification of *trafike*, and the discourse that emerged as a result of the effort to make sense of the new realities – to inflict a humiliating defeat on the conservative countryman.

6.5   Jack Winchcombe's political economy

The core of this industry lobby was the *cloathman* or 'clothier', who connected merchant capital and the industrial workforce. In the West Country, the sixteenth-century *cloathman* was as closely implicated in the organization of production as in the business of trade. It was a matter of emphasis, and a certain amount of snobbery, that merchants were seen as being of higher status than clothiers, or their equivalents in industries like steel-smelting and coal-mining. Like every corner of English society in late Tudor and early Stuart England, social relations of production and trade quivered with status ambiguities.[84] One difference between cloth-iers and merchants was that the former were more likely to be perceived as representatives of the provinces and localities, and were usually proud to be perceived as such. The clothier knew more about production than company merchants. He (occasionally she) was more intimately con-nected with trade than the workers. The organizers of production knew that the big profits were made by a quite small group of privileged mem-bers of the trade companies, and developed powerful regional networks to balance and sometimes outweigh the influence of the very rich, and well-placed, London merchants. There was class and status tension at every point between the husbanding and shearing of sheep to the ships that took the cloth to Antwerp and the world. Representation of this 'bloc' as a coherent commonweal smooths over many contradictions and competing interests. The clothiers, collectively, held it together and gave it an identity. They were an interesting group of men, the first English industrial capitalists.

Their sixteenth-century myths were given definitive form in the 1590s by Thomas Deloney, 'the balletting silk-weaver of Norwich'. Like his contemporary, Shakespeare, and Winstanley and Tom Paine after him, Deloney left the town he grew up in to try his fortune in London, work-ing as a silk-weaver, living in England's first Grub Street, where an entry in the parish register of St Giles, Cripplegate, dated 16 October 1586,

---

[84] Michael McKeon, *The Origins of the English Novel 1600–1740* (Baltimore 1988), ch. 4, 'The Destabilization of Social Categories'; Keith Wrightson traces 'the language of sorts of people [. . . an essentially *dichotomous* perception of society . . .]' to 'the second quarter of the sixteenth century': 'Sorts of People in Tudor and Stuart England', in Jonathan Barry and Christopher Brooks (ed.), *The Middling Sort of People, Culture, Society and Politics in England, 1550–1800* (London 1994), 33–4.

records the baptism of his son, Richard. Here, in the terrible 1590s, he wrote ballads and one-sheet stories and stereotypes, news-sheets and the like, which were highly ephemeral and very popular. By 1598 he was the acknowledged 'general' of the London ballad-mongers, a 'ballad-journalist' who was 'installed as the poet of the people' by the publication, in 1596, of a piece entitled *The Ballad On the Want of Corn*. Strype described him as 'vain and presumptuous', and refers to another pamphlet titled 'Book of the Silk Weavers', to which fraternity Deloney himself belonged.[85] What was 'presumptuous' about his work was that the heroes and heroines of his stories were clearly common people. As such they were not suitable for any theatrical or poetical genre except comedy, or, more correctly, bumbling, blustering farce. Who was he to presume such matters to be important enough to be represented at all? This condemnation was applied to Shakespeare's work throughout the seventeenth century.[86] Dryden thought his representations of common people were too sympathetic, and Nietzsche's view was that the artistic culture of Shakespeare's age was never free from 'the whiff of the sewer'.[87] Deloney was a pleb.[88]

Deloney's modern editor refers to a contemporary reputation for choosing 'dolorous subjects'.[89] All his best-known works were written between 1596 and 1600, when the fabric of English society was shaken by a general crisis the like of which would not be experienced again in England until the time of Paine and Wollstonecraft, exactly two centuries later. Neither the ballad on the want of corn, nor the book he wrote

[85] Francis Oscar Mann (ed.), *The Works of Thomas Deloney* (Oxford 1912), 'Introduction', ix.

[86] Gary Taylor, *Reinventing Shakespeare: a Cultural History from the Restoration to the Present* (London 1990), ch. 1.

[87] 'We enjoy (Shakespeare) as an artistic refinement reserved precisely for us and allow ourselves to be as little disturbed by the repellant fumes and the proximity of the English rabble in which Shakespeare's art and taste live as we do on the *Chiaja* of Naples, where we go our way enchanted and willing with all our senses alert, however much the sewers of the plebeian quarters may fill the air': Nietzsche, *Beyond Good and Evil*, trans. R.J. Hollingdale (Harmondsworth 1973), 134–5.

[88] C.S. Lewis, *English Literature in the Sixteenth Century, excluding Drama* (Oxford 1954), 429, wrote that Deloney wrote 'to please a coarse, kindly, thrifty, and ambitious society of urban tradesmen'. Deloney exemplifies a theory of 'plebeian realism' developed from two of the essays in Johan Huizinga, *Men and Ideas*, trans. James S. Holmes and Hans van Marle (New York 1959). In 'Renaissance and Realism', Huizinga defines 'realism' as 'a *need* to depict reality accurately' (*ibid.*, 308); in 'The Task of Cultural History', he writes that 'if one removes the sting of disdain from the word "plebeian", the term "democratic" can be reserved for political and social fields, and the concept plebeian can be placed in antithesis to aristocratic in the field of culture' (*ibid.*, 47).

[89] Mann (ed.), *Deloney*, xiii, citing *Skialetheia or the Shadow of the Truth* (1598).

for the silkweavers has survived, but their titles, and what does survive of Deloney's writings, identify him as a voice from below. He belongs to a tradition that includes obvious radicals like the Levellers, Gerard Winstanley, Mary Wollstonecraft and Thomas Paine. Less obviously, a respectable stream of scholarship has always identified more canonical figures like Chaucer, Langland, Tyndale and Shakespeare as members of this 'common' (more accurately, vernacular) tradition, which in turn represents an abiding element in that problematical field of force we call English constitutional life. Deloney was political.

London was the centre linking the manufacturing districts of England. In London, Deloney routinely mingled with artisans and traders from places as exotic as Oldham, Halifax, Norwich, Cirencester, Salisbury, Tavistock and Monmouth. London was the heart of the system. When its merchants sneezed, places like Gloucestershire's Stroudwater Valleys caught pneumonia. Ambitious provincials migrate to London – that is a law of English culture. Once there, they absorb a perspective on all else that London attracts. Deloney came from Norwich (an ancient centre of English clothmaking) but his England is centred on London, whence, in his stories of the cloth industry, he looks west, towards the boom districts of the sixteenth century. By the time he put pen to paper, London was his centre, and most of his clothiers came out of the West.

Deloney set his stories within a national cloth industry, centred on the households of great clothiers, where in the good times of the past there was natural harmony between the organizers of industry and their workers. Then as now, history was a way of commenting on the present. *Jack of Newbury* is located sixty years before the crisis of the 1590s, in the reign of Henry VIII. *Thomas of Reading* is set in the time of Henry I. *Jack of Newbury* relates a series of episodes from the life of a legendary clothier, Jack Winchcombe. The story-line is traditional: poor apprentice works hard, shows character and charm, boss dies, marries widow, assists widow with what is now her business, outlives her, inherits and expands it and his own fame to the highest level of achievement. He can hold his beer, becomes immensely rich without losing the common touch, and is fair to his workers. He certainly represents enterprise, yet his virtue lies in the fact that his enterprise is not 'private'. It is for the commonweal.[90]

He is a stereotypical provincial industrial magnate. His glory is not in his heredity, or his membership of a great company of London merchants, but in his capacity to organize, manage and lead the

---

[90] Lewis, *English Literature*, 429, adjudged that '*Jacke of Newbury* comes nearest of his works to the shape of a true novel'.

commonalty of his district, most of whom are his workers. He supplies them with raw materials and (if necessary) instruments of production, and finds markets for the commodities they produce. Every clothier was an exception to every stereotype, but all clothiers connected production and trade. In practice this meant that they connected their district with the provincial capital, and, by the sixteenth century, with the national and international networks of the merchants in London. The key to every clothier's success lay in the ability to arrange for the production of commodities that could be sold. Clothiers had to be attuned to the world of fashion and marketing, and to have the ability to persuade workers to follow his advice in ways that would not seem unduly coercive or exploitative. Such men, greater and lesser industrial capitalists of Tudor-Stuart England, appeared to their armigerous neighbours to have usurped functions of leadership which were supposed to be restricted to men of noble blood. Surely, it was the function of lords, knights and esquires to marshall and lead the people of the provinces, to employ stewards and entrust yeomen to see that the work was done. Industry, after all, was no more than an alternative to charity and poor relief, the business, in the local communities, of common churchwardens and bailiffs. There were few if any clothiers in Deloney's England who came close to the glory and stature of Jack Winchcombe, and who were capable of bringing together the diffuse and dispersed clothiers and clothworkers all over England. But there were clothworkers all over England, and the basic structures and sentiments that formed the context of his tale were in place. Deloney's anecdotes of industry contributed to the formation of a paradigm.

In one story the mature Jack has dealings with the king, very much a Bluff King Hal Henry VIII, who is shocked that a mere businessman could equip and muster as many fighting men as his greatest nobles. Jack invites the king down to his complex at Newbury, provides him with a sumptuous lunch, and takes him on a tour round the factory. This turns out to be a great hall, no doubt once the domain of a great medieval abbot, 'where he saw an hundred loomes, standing in a roome, and two men working in every one, who pleasantly sang . . . The Weavers' Song'. The king is so impressed that he pauses to listen fleetingly to the words. The song represented the weavers as devotees of a craft as old as civilization itself, participants in an epic history alongside the heroes of ruling class history. In ten verses, the king hears their enterprises linked to Hercules, Pallas, Princes and Queens, Giants, David and Goliath, Greeks, Troy, Penelope, Helen, Paris, King Priam, and the Earls of Northumberland. All through this epic history, the song implies, the great affairs of state have been sustained by the less glorious, but nonetheless fundamental business of 'cloathing of the back'.[91] The song finishes and the king makes a little speech in which he describes their Craft as one of but five pillars which hold up the kingdom, alongside 'Clergy for the Soule, the Soldier for defence . . . , the Lawyer to execute justice, (and) the Husbandman to feede the belly'.

The song had a sting in its tail:

> Yet this by proof is daily tried,
> For God's good gifts we are ingrate:
> And no man through the world so wide,
> Lives well contented with his state.

'Well sung good fellows', cries the delighted Prince. 'Light hearts and merry minds live long without grey hairs.' It is an odd response, given the clear message of the last verse that none of his subjects, including these two hundred weavers and journeymen, is contented with their lot in life. Deloney sketches in the well-known fact that weavers, 'discontentment', sedition, riot and rebellion went together and passed on, but he must have noticed it, as would any attentive listener or reader. The king hears only what he wants to hear, his attention alighting only on the heroic, pastoral references. Jack of Newbury's happy weavers are shown not only to be slightly less than happy, and capable of playing a dissembling little joke on their king, who would find out soon enough that when times were not so good . . .

The political threat posed by the cloth industry was given definitive form in Chapter 4 of *Jack of Newbery*, which describes its mobilization in a time of crisis. A slump is caused, as usual, by the king's wars 'with other countries', as a result of which 'the clothiers had most of their cloth lying on their hands, and that which they sold was at so low a rate, that the money scantly paid for the wool and workmanship'. Within a few weeks they had little alternative but to

ease themselves by abating the poor workmens wages. And when that did not prevail, they turned away many of their people, weavers, shearmen, spinsters and carders, so that where there were a hundred looms kept in one town, there was scant fifty: and he that kept twenty put down ten. Many a poor man (for want of work) was hereby undone, with his wife and children, and it made many a poor widow to sit with a hungry belly.

---

[91] 'They have in France more handicrafts occupied and a greater multitude of artificers than we have by a great deal, and for all that they have made many great stirs and commotions there before this. *Yet they will not destroy artificers for they know that the highest princes of them all without such artificers could not maintain their estate.*' *A Discourse of the Commonweal*, 89 (emphasis added).

Deloney was not the first to tell this story, only the first to give it a literary form explicitly linking the localities into a national movement which integrated the needs and interests of its poorest and wealthiest members into a single *bloc*. It is a notable (perhaps intended) irony that not until unemployment reaches fifty per cent does Jack of Newbury make 'supplication to the king'. When he acts it is with a national movement behind him.

The clothiers invite Jack to be their leader, and in response 'hee sent letters to all the chiefe cloathing towns in England', urging them that 'nothing was more needfull... than a faithfull unity among our selves'. This was the most essential, but also the most difficult task of all, for in such times 'the poore hate the rich, because they will not set them on work; and the rich hate the poore, because they seem burdensome'. They should remember what they had in common. 'Let our Art of Cloathing... perswade us to an unity... Our Trade will uphold us, if wee will uphold it.'

Unity was to be tested and expressed by a call, issued 'in every towne', for all clothworkers to assemble together at a specified time and place. The assemblies were to elect 'two honest discreet men oute of every towne to meete me at *Blackwell Hall* on *All Saints Eve*, and then wee will present our humble petition to the King'. A collection should be made, for 'Noble men's secretaries and cunning Lawyers have slow tongues and deafe ears, which must be daily nointed with the sweet oyl of Angells.' In artisans' eyes the English state was already 'Old Corruption'. And so he could grease the wheels in advance with some judiciously placed information, Jack asked the clothmakers' leaders to 'tell the number of those who have their living by meanes of this Trade, note it in a Bill, and send it to mee'. After collating the Bills, 'there were found of the Clothiers, and those they maintained, threescore thousand and six hundred persons'. An Industry that could assemble an army of 60,600 people, at 66 strategic locations throughout England, was clearly capable of constitutional devilry, should it decide to move. On All Saints Eve 'an hundred and twelve persons' representing the 66 chief towns of the English cloth industry met at Blackwell Hall. The next day they gathered in St James Park to meet the King.

The King is moved by Jack's decorous petitioners, and orders his counsellors to 'let these mens complaint be thoroughly looked into, and their griefs redressed'. A solution, the industry representatives had urged, was at hand: abolish mercantile monopolies. The king abolishes monopolies, ordering that 'Marchants should freely traffique'. Responsibility for proclaiming this and seeing to its enactment 'as well on the other side of the sea, as in our Land' is delegated to the wicked Cardinal Wolsey.

Naturally, Wolsey prevaricates, keeping the clothiers hanging around in the frosty grounds of his palace while he tries to change the king's mind. He whispers that Jack is 'an Heretike . . . infected with Luther's spirit, against whom oure kinge hath of late written a most learned book'. The clothiers are heroes of industry and religion, like the merchants in young Richard Hakluyt's *Voyages and Discoveries*. They wait patiently, for they know the King's word is his bond, not to be usurped by an evil adviser. Eventually, the wicked Cardinal gracelessly grants their suit, which is 'published through London' the following day. They return home to tell their neighbours to be patient for good times will surely return soon.

6.6   Deindustrialization again: the 1620s

Deloney gave his contemporaries a literary sketch of the political dynamics of England's first national industry, which leaned on Tudor-Stuart governments by appearing to demonstrate the facts laid out in its petitions. This was the case in 1621–2, when magistrates reported 'tumultuous assemblies' in the clothworking districts of Somerset, Devon, Dorset, Berkshire, Northamptonshire, Hampshire, Wiltshire and Gloucestershire.[92] On 24 October 1621 an order was made in Council appointing a committee to look into reports delivered by merchants explaining the current decay of the cloth trade. The following February, the committee apparently having deliberated, instructions were sent to the Justices of the Peace of the clothing counties, referring to 'the greate distresse . . . fallen upon the weavers, spinners, and fullers in various counties for want of work'. The JPs were to instruct the clothiers not to lay off their workfolk, 'who, being many in number and most of the poore sort, are . . . likely to disturb the quiet government of those parts wherein they live'.[93]

---

[92] Barry Supple, *Commercial Crisis and Change in England, 1600–1642* (Cambridge 1959), 56–7. Mary Poovey, *A History of the Modern Fact: Problems of Knowledge in the Sciences of Wealth and Society* (Chicago 1998), 71, sees the conjuncture as being of momentous significance. 'These developments', she writes, '. . . witnessed a realignment of the relations among politics, religion, economic activity, and the production of knowledge. This realignment created the idea that abstract knowledge (theory) [i.e. of society] could be value-free'. Unemployment among the clothworkers of England caused the Social Science mentality?

[93] 'State Papers Relating to the Cloth Trade, 1622', *Transactions of the Bristol and Gloucestershire Archaeological Society*, 154–62. For earlier sources indicating the same pattern: 'Negotiations between the Clothiers and the Merchant Adventurers, 1550', in Tawney and Power (ed.), *Tudor Economic Documents*, vol. 1, 184; 'An agreement between the Western Clothiers and the merchant Adventurers, December 24 1586', *Ibid.*, 214–15; Rollison, 'Exploding England: the Dialectics of Mobility and Settlement in Early Modern England', *Social History* 24, no. 1 (January 1999), 11; William Woodall (curate

In March 1622 Gloucestershire magistrates reported that the clothiers 'are generally grieved as well as the poore workmen, and . . . cannot continue their trade without vend of cloth'. A petition signed by thirty-four Gloucestershire clothiers reported that the 'deadnes(s) of trade being more than a year past', many of them had simply given up. As an example they cited 'one William Benet, a very ancient and good clothier, (who) doth offer to live by brown bread and water rather than his great number of poore people should want work, yf he had meanes to kepe them in worke'. As Jack Winchcombe had counselled, they cited numbers of workers and gave an exact estimate of the capital required to keep them in work. They estimated that there were at least 1,500 looms in Gloucestershire; it cost twenty shillings and sixteen persons and upwards to maintain one loom; thus to keep all their looms working required the labour of 24,000 men, women and children. To keep 24,000 people employed required an investment of 15,000 pounds every week, and even this left out of consideration 'all those that are releyved thereby'. They reckoned that even the wages of the few weavers they were still able to employ (12d per week) were too low to maintain a family decently.

By 3 May the Justices of Gloucestershire reported 'that the complainte of the weavers and other poor workfolkes depending on the trade of clothing . . . doe daylye encrease, in that their worke and meanes of releyf doe more and more decaye'. The masters and the middle ranks 'in these late tymes growen poore, (were) unnable to releyve the infynite numbers of poore people residing' in their districts, 'drawne hither by meanes of clothing, butt by that trade wherein they have bene browgte upp . . . ' abandoned, such that 'very manye of them doe wander, begg and steale and are in case to starve as their faces (to our grete grefes) doe manifest'.

The situation was getting out of hand. The 'infinite numbers of the poore . . . doe so farre oppress these parts wherein they live that oure abler sort of people . . . are not much longer able to connteyn the same'. 'Wee muche fear', reported the Justices, 'that the peace . . . wilbe very shortly endangered, notwithstanding all the vigilance wee use or can use to the contrary'. The clothiers and 'abler men' of the clothing districts were anxious to assure the Council that *they* were not threatening insurrection, but the fact of their 'neare dwelling among those poore people doe emboulden' them to make their betters aware of the seriousness of their situation. One of the magistrates, Sir William Guyse, reported that he had recently received a visit from one Richard Webbe, a master weaver

of Stroud 1599–1610), *A Sermon on the original and accidental causes of every dearth and famine, and especially of this dearth in England now 1608 and 1609* (London 1609): Gloucestershire Records Office (Hyett Collection) Pamphlet 351.

of Kings Stanley, to inform him that '500 persons . . . were coming unto mee such as were in want with their staves readye at their doors'. Guyse may have taken this as a threat rather than a warning, but Webbe assured him that he meant his worship 'no harm but to make their wants known'. Webbe told Guyse that it was also their intention to raid trows carrying malt down the Severn from Gloucester to Bristol. Guyse asked for names, but Webbe would only say they were 'manye poore men'. Here is where the trail we have been following ends, where the chain of cause and effect connected apprentices, journeymen, master craftsmen, mill owners, clothiers, magistrates, merchants, the government and colonial expansion. The 'infinite numbers of poor' would not die, or let their communities die, quietly.

This was the point where 'discourse' connected with 'reality'. The power of the cloth industry in the long sixteenth century was that, while not yet as ubiquitous as husbandry, it was dispersed extensively across the realm of England and, unlike agriculture, it could plausibly be represented as being interconnected and 'centred', in other words, as a coherent, or potentially coherent, national movement. And so, I have shown, it was represented. Between 1549 and 1622 the idea that industry, particularly the cloth industry, was, one way or another, essential to the common weal of England, became a commonplace of public debate – as did the idea that for it to flourish, the English nation had to conquer overseas markets.

In politics, it has been said, perception is everything. What mattered was not whether the figures and tropes accurately represented reality, but whether they were in accordance with everything else that was said and publicly 'known' about the cloth industry at the time. As we have seen, they were. The crisis of 1617–23 in fact reproduced Deloney's model exactly – except for one minor detail: in Deloney's tale, the union of the clothworkers achieved its aims.

The discourse was also mistaken in its representation of the clothiers as the source of seditious activity. Here as in all their other activities, they were middle-men. From Fortescue to Bacon, the most perceptive students of rebellion recognized that the impulses came 'from below'. The pattern was invariable. Markets contracted; hardship among the young and least secure clothworkers generated an electric current which coursed through every rank of the trade. Turned-off apprentices and turned-away journeymen abused master-craftsmen, who petitioned the stewards of their fellowships to urge clothiers to find more markets. The clothiers were a much abused race, but for all the complaints they had an impossible task, and when they were able they tried to do what they could to alleviate the hardships of the 'thousands of clothworking families' who depended on the sale of cloth. Deloney's attractive, public-spirited clothiers were not a complete myth.[94]

If direct pressure on the clothworking and merchant company buyers in London failed to get results, the clothiers petitioned Parliament and Privy Council. Tempers frayed and paper flew to agents despatched to foreign empires and lands to find new vend for English commodities. In the next chapter we shall see that the elder Richard Hakluyt made the future of the cloth industry the key to his advocacy of overseas expansion. He saw that what we call 'rural manufacturing' or 'proto-industry' now provided a livelihood, not for the odd household among dozens of husbandmen and peasants, but, in many districts, for entire villages and towns. More to the point, any contraction of demand lasting more than a few weeks exhausted the stocks of food which households saved up when they could, and which appear in the inventories of many master-craftsmen. Symptoms of crisis were legion: pinched, hungry faces; a growing stream of men, women and children passing through begging and looking for work; epidemics and resurgences of endemic diseases associated with malnutrition; thefts and fighting; murmuring about who was to blame and what might be done about it; preachers excoriating the rich; threats of collective action and hands reaching for the staves at the door. There is no evidence that 'the cloth industry' ever came together as Deloney portrayed Jack of Newbury bringing it together. What mattered was that it was taken for granted that the raw material for such a movement existed, along with routine forms of organization that could, conceivably, be transmuted into something closely resembling an army.

---

[94] Although Woodall, *Sermon*, 61, indicated a common perception within the clothing communities when he blamed 'al cruel and covetous Corn-breeders, buyers, Corne-makers, corne-mongers, *cloth-maisters*, and everie other pinching penny-father', for the crisis of 1608–9.

7   Touching the wires: industry and empire

The great decaye of our usuall trades in all places in Europe at this tyme, And the wonderfull increase of our people here in Englande and a greate nomber of them voyde of any good trade or ymployment to gete their lyving maye be a sufficient cause to move not only the marchants and clothiers but alsoe all other sortes and degrees of our nacion to seeke newe dyscoveryes of peopled regions for vent of our Idle people, otherwyse in shourte tyme many mischiefs maye ensue.[1]

It is only at a time when the mind of a people is strung to a higher tension by civil and social difficulties, so great as to threaten destruction, that isolated spirits among its individuals search more intently into the promise which the present contains, and consolidate their faith in that promise into an ideal. Then . . . thought can outstrip mechanical processes and leap to an invention.[2]

7.1   A new way of seeing the constitutional landscape: Fortescue, Smith and the political economy outlook

'Commonweal/th' entered English as a political economy concept in the generations of Sir John Fortescue, William Tyndale, Sir Thomas Smith, John Dee and the two Richard Hakluyts.[3] The strategy involved converting traditional negatives, notably 'industry' and its chief justification,

---

[1] Richard Hakluyt the Elder, 'Inducements to the liking of the voyadge to that parte of America wch lyeth betwene 34 and 36 degree of Septentrional Latytude', in E.G.R. Taylor (ed.), *Original Writings of the Two Richard Hakluyts* (London 1937), vol. ii, 343.

[2] John G. Gow, 'The Political Ideal of the English Commonwealth', *English Historical Review*, 6:22 (April 1891), 306.

[3] Neal Wood, *Foundations of Political Economy: Some Early Tudor Views on State and Society* (Berkeley 1994); Wood, 'Foundations of Political Economy: the New Moral Philosophy of Sir Thomas Smith', in Paul A. Fideler and T.F. Mayer (ed.), *Political Thought and the Tudor Commonwealth: Deep Structure, Discourse and Disguise* (Cambridge 1997); for Smith and the social-science outlook, see Arthur B. Ferguson, 'Renaissance Realism in the "Commonwealth" Literature of Early Tudor England', *Journal of the History of Ideas* 16:3 (June 1955), 287–305; Keith Wrightson, *Earthly Necessities: Economic Lives in Early Modern Britain* (New Haven 2000), 154–6; William H. Sherman, *John Dee: the Politics of Reading and Writing in the English Renaissance* (Amherst, Mass. 1995), ch. 7; Hakluyt (e.g.), 'Remembrance for Master S . . .', in Taylor (ed.), *Original Writings*, vol. 2, 184–95.

the 'necessity' or poverty of the 'rascability', into reasons for pursuing an imperial policy. Sir Thomas Smith was the seminal figure in this movement, but the portrait he painted in *A Discourse of the Commonweal* (1549) was a systematic development of Sir John Fortescue's precept that a commonweal was not a hierarchy but a working landscape. The first and second 'commodities' of England, in Fortescue's account, were its rivers and harbours. 'The third comodyte' was 'that the grounde therof is soo goode and comodyous to the shepe, that beren soo gode wooll'. The wool was no longer exported, as it had been in the past. It was worked at home, producing 'The fourth commodyte, that the comons have... wolleyn clothe redy made at all tymys to serve the merchaunts of ony two kyngdomys Chrytenye or hethenye.' Behind Fortescue's map of the actual (as against prescribed) condition of England was the crucial seventh 'comodyte', 'that the commune peple of thys londde are the best fedde, and also the best cledde of any natyon crysten or hethen'.[4]

The cutting edge of Fortescue's vision was not his favouring of political over absolute monarchy, which had been entrenched polarities of English constitutional culture since the thirteenth century. What was new was his insistence, hardly surprising in view of his theory of rebellion, on the 'harme [that] wolde come to England yff the commons there off were pouere'. 'Some men', he wrote, 'have said that it were good ffor the kyng, that the commons of England were made pore, as be the commons of Fraunce. For than thai wolde not rebelle, as now thai done oftentymes.' This was an argument of 'thai that see but few thynges... For soth theis folke consideren litill the good of the reaume off England, wheroff the myght stondith most uppon archers, which be no ryche men.'[5] The commonalty and public opinion were central to national politics in the aftermath of Cade's rebellion. The political economy outlook began to emerge in the wake of renewed debate in the aftermath of the rebellions of 1536 and 1549.

Fortescue saw the ebullient prosperity and confidence of the commonalty as a peculiarity, and a peculiar necessity, of English polity.[6] In

---

[4] 'These be the comodytes of England', *Sir John Fortescue, Works*, ed. Lord Clermont (1869), 549–54; David Starkey, 'Which Age of Reform?', in C. Coleman and David Starkey (ed.), *Revolution Reassessed: Revisions in the History of Tudor Government and Administration* (Oxford 1986), p. 14, notes 'how very untheoretical Fortescue's theory is. What he has seen is more important than what he has read; and the real views of the authors he cites are ruthlessly bent to fit the facts as he observes them'; J.G.A. Pocock, *The Machiavellian Moment: Florentine Political Thought and the Atlantic Republican Tradition* (Princeton 1975), p. 9, describes Fortescue as 'the kind of amateur of philosophy who helps us understand the ideas of an age by coarsening them slightly'.

[5] *The Governance of England: The Difference between an Absolute and a Limited Monarchy* (1471–6, Oxford 1885), ch. XII, p.137.

[6] For Fortescue's 'pragmatic test for the ultimate evaluation of the merits of a constitutional system', Neal Wood, *Foundations*, p. 47; 'comodite' meant 'benefit, profit, welfare

France, where the power of the nobility was not counterbalanced by a vigorous, independent commonalty, the king was afraid to tax his nobles 'for fear of rebellion'. 'The (French) Commons be so impoverished and destroyed that they may scarce live', he wrote. 'They drink water, they eat apples with bread very brown made of rye, they eat not flesh but if it be seldom a little lard, or of the entrails or head of beasts':

They wear no wool, but if it be a poor coat under their uttermost garment made of greate canvas, and they call it a frock. Their host be of like canvas and pass not their knee, wherefore they be gartered and their thighs bare, their wives and children go barefoot... they grow feeble and crooked, not able to fight and defend the realm, neither have they weapon, nor money to buy them weapons. But verily they live in most extreme poverty and misery, and yet they dwell in one of the most fertile realms of the world, through which the French king hath not men of his own to defend it (except his nobles)... and is compelled to make his armies (for the defence of the land) of strangers, as Scots, Spaniards, Arrogonese, Almaines and of other nations, else all his enemies must overrun him, for he hath no defence of his own except his castles and fortresses... In the realm of england under such a prince it would then be a prey to all other nations that would conquer, rob and devour it... [7]

What made the difference, it seems, was that the English commonalty did expect to eat flesh, wear wool and not live 'in the most extreme poverty and misery'. Behind this lay the precept that if English kings were to avoid rebellion and continue to defeat their enemies, they must have a stronger, healthier and more independent commonalty.

While Fortescue was careful to restrict his comments to the constitutional disruptiveness of the *French* nobility, there are many passages in his writings which suggest that, for him (as for John of Salisbury) the key constitutional relationship was between the monarch and 'the commune peple'. In a sense, and ironically given Henry VI's failure to live up to the populist rhetoric of his grandfather's coup of 1399, Fortescue was only giving more analytic force to a central theme of Henry IV's claim to the throne. Before that, the rebels of 1381 had favoured 'a popular monarchy, a state without nobles, perhaps without churchmen', in which

---

... something benefiting a community or commonwealth... income, revenue, profit, whether derived from agriculture, manufacture, trade or from an office... also crops or produce': Kurath (ed.), *Middle English Dictionary*, 435.

[7] Bodleian Library, Rawlinson MS D69, *The Difference betwene Dominus Regale and Dominium Politicum et Regale, made in the time of Edward IV*, ch. 3; on the title page is written, in a seventeenth-century hand, *per Johem ffortescue*; this manuscript is identical to John Fortescue-Aland (ed.), *The Difference between an Absolute and Limited Monarchy, by Sir John Fortescue, faithfully transcribed from the Ms copy in the Bodleian Library, and collated with 3 other manuscripts* (London 1714), except that Aland's printed version divides D69's ch. 11 (ff. 10–14) into three chapters (xi, xii and xiii).

villagers and the king are the key political nexus.[8] The idea that nobles were unnecessary was thinkable, as John Ball's legendary couplet ('when Adam delved and Eve span/ who was then the gentleman?') testified. But so was the idea that, under certain circumstances, the secular nobility could stand for and represent the 'commonalty', understood as the whole community beneath the monarch. A lord himself, albeit one who had seen and suffered personally as a result of noble rebellions against his king, Fortescue does not go that far in either direction. The key variable was the *English* king's responsibility to the commonweal. 'It is the king's honour and . . . office', wrote Fortescue, 'to make his realm rich, and it is dishonour when he has a poor realm, of which men will say that he reigneth upon beggars'.[9] Beyond honour and office, there was, as we saw in Part II, an urgent, practical reason for Fortescue's advocacy of the 'common profit' as a principle of government. The English commonalty did not suffer in silence.

As it had influenced Fortescue, the tradition of popularly inspired rebellion shaped the climate of opinion in which Protector Somerset's counsellor, Sir Thomas Smith, the most influential of the intellectual and literary 'commonwealths men' who appropriated the term, took up his pen. Sobered by the gentry's outrage at his master's apparent flirtations with common rebels, Smith set out to cleanse the term of its connotations of naked class struggle between ruling patricians and subject plebeians by grounding it in pragmatic, analytic, apparently 'value free' content.[10] In *A Discourse of the Commonweal* (1549), written in the aftermath of the rebellions, Smith created a new conception of the English commonweal. It was the first full-scale anatomy of the common *wealth* understood as that which is produced by the third estate, the commonalty, those who worked, managed the work and trafficked its commodities.

Accordingly, the first rule of Smith's commonweal was 'members unlimited'. In his view 'no man is a stranger to the Commonweal that he is in'.[11] In *De Republica Anglorum*, Smith defined 'a common wealth' as 'a society or common doing of a multitude of free men collected together and united by common accord and covenants among themselves, for

---

[8] R.H. Hilton, *Bond Men Made Free: Medieval Peasant Movements and the English Rising of 1381* (London 1977), 66–7.

[9] Fortescue, *Difference*: Bodleian, Rawlinson MS D69, ch. 11, f. 11; Fortescue-Aland (ed.) *The Difference*, 91–3.

[10] 'The foot', wrote Sir William Paget to Protector Somerset, 7 July 1549, 'taketh upon him the part of the head, and commyns is become king; a king appointing conditions and laws to the governors, saying, Grant this and that, and we wil go home'. Quotation from Andy Wood, *The 1549 Rebellions and the Making of Early Modern England* (Cambridge 2007), 22.

[11] *A Discourse of the Commonweal of this Realm of England, attributed to Sir Thomas Smith,* ed. Mary Dewar (Charlottesville 1969), 17.

the conservation of themselves as well in peace as in war'.[12] The definition occurs in the tenth of his introductory chapters in which he follows the system of Aristotle, who 'of all writers . . . hath most absolutely and methodically treated of the divisions and natures of common wealths'.[13] The inevitability of change is central to his entire oeuvre; the particular form taken by 'common wealths and government' is contingent and inevitably changes over time. 'The nature of man is never to stand still in one manner or estate, but to grow from the less to the more, and decay from the more to the less.'[14] He reiterates Aristotle's 'quality test'. There are three basic 'manners of ruling', 'by one, by the fewer part, and by the multitude or greater number'. These, however, are ideal types. They are tools of analysis, for 'never shall you find common wealths or government which is absolutely and sincerely made of any of them above names, but always mixed with another'.[15] Every constitution is a unique variant of the six-note chord. Rule of the one, the few and the many must each be divided into two, making 'the one good and just, and the other evill and unjust'. 'It is profitable to every common wealth', of course, 'to be kept in her most perfect state'. But how? What *was* the most perfect state for a commonweal?

Smith was thinking about real, not prescribed constitutions: how the 'thing publique' actually hangs or does not hang together, not how it ought to be. Every constitution is a unique and changing combination of the six basic possibilities, and thus must be studied freshly, with an open mind. The model does not tell us how the world is, only how we might find it useful to analyse it. The mixture is contingent, and will change. 'The common wealth must turne and alters as before from one to a few, so now from a few to many and the most part.' Whatever constitutional form is adopted, harmony depends on every element being 'willing to save the political body, to conserve the authority of their nation, to defend themselves against all other, their strife being only for empire and rule, and who should do best for the common wealth'.[16] Strife is fundamental, and by 'empire and rule', as we will see, Smith links domestic harmony with an expansive disposition to conquer and colonize other parts of the world.[17] The Imperial Office had not yet split from the Home Office. In accepting strife, he concedes, realistically, that government offices excite competition for places at the centres of power and largesse.[18]

---

[12] Sir Thomas Smith, *De Republica Anglorum*, ed. Mary Dewar (Cambridge 1982), 20.
[13] *Ibid.*, 17.   [14] *Ibid.*, 12.   [15] *Ibid.*, 14.   [16] *Ibid.*, 27.
[17] For the extent and limits of Smith's expansionism, see David Armitage, *The Ideological Origins of the British Empire* (Cambridge 2000), 47–9.
[18] Alston, 'Introduction' to *De Republica*, xxii, asks 'How then is our author going to treat England? Is it to be called predominantly democratic, aristocratic, or monarchical?'. Smith's response to this question in what we have come to conceive of as 'Tudor

If the parts of the commonwealth 'that do beare the rule, do command that which is profitable to it . . . it is to be accepted to be just'. If not, if the governor 'doe contrary to the Law . . . he therefore by the law is justly to be condemned.'[19] None of the characters in the *Discourse* assumes other than that the commonwealth is not in a healthy condition, that there is an epidemic of division and contention as to who is to blame. The Doctor hints that the real problem is the king, who has been badly advised with regard to recent debasements of the coinage. 'A man at the first blush', says the Doctor, 'would think that a king within this realm . . . might make coin of what estimation they would of vile metal . . . to what sum he would'. At first blush England might seem to be the absolute imperial monarchy Tudor propaganda said it was. The Doctor's explanation contains a moral for theorists who place rhetoric over reality: 'But he that so thinks marks but the terms and not the things that are understood by them.'[20] What matters is not what the king intends, but what the community thinks what he says and does mean, and whether, in all the innumerable activities they engage in, they comply with his theory. Where the common weal is concerned, *commune opinioun* runs further and deeper than the king's writ. In a very tangible sense, what Smith described in the *Discourse* was the critical public sphere of early Tudor England.

For Sir Thomas Elyot, as we saw, every individual vocation corresponded to a 'degree' in a universal hierarchy. Up to a point Smith held to the vocational precept. 'The only cause sufficient to overthrow a whole common weal', he wrote, 'is . . . when [people] take on them the judgement of things to whom it does not appertain, as youth of things belonging to old men, children over their fathers, servants over their masters and private men over magistrates'.[21] But when he describes the commonweal within which all the vocations were distributed it becomes clear that his vision differed markedly from Elyot's. His characters demonstrate the problem: they all agree that the commonwealth is sick, but everyone has a different explanation and a partial solution. In such times, who speaks for the commonwealth? The Doctor's answer is humanist. Only learned men have the knowledge and dispassion for this task.[22] His companions protest that no vocation was guiltier of formulating and spreading the many different and apparently incompatible ideas that fed

---

England' is astonishing: Smith seems to have hesitated. Alston's explanation was that Smith had 'not thought the question of sovereignty out to its logical issues' (xxiii), but it is clear that he had thought it out within the terms of Aristotle's system; he wavered because he was uncertain as to exactly how the contingencies of England's circumstances at the time could be expressed in terms of a mixture of Aristotle's types.

[19] *De Republica*, 10–11.   [20] *Discourse*, 70–1.
[21] *Ibid.*, 31.   [22] *Ibid.*, 25–32.

the eternal disputatiousness of the times. The proliferation of ideas and ideologies, the Doctor objects, are the result of pseudo-learning. For one thing, too many fathers sent their sons to university just to learn enough to make them vocationally qualified: they learn languages, logic, rhetoric and law, but this, the Doctor insists, is not learning. It suffices to get a job as a lawyer, a scrivener or a clerk, that is all. The Knight contends that experience is more important than learning, since it teaches men to know their own world. The Doctor agrees that the task is to know and understand the world in order to govern it harmoniously. But individual experience, however necessary, is a minute resource compared to the knowledge of humanity recorded in books. 'Where it is denied man to live above an hundred years', he suggests, 'by the benefit of learning he has the commodity of a thousand years, yes, two or three thousand years, by reason he sees the events and occurrences of all that time by books'. So far so classically humanist, but the emphasis on learning was only his point of departure.

The knight knows his shire, the merchant his markets and the husbandman his fields, but only long immersion in history and moral philosophy enables us to see beyond the limited, local experience that characterized *every* vocation, from the king and court down to the humblest labourer. Vocational education was fine in its place. Like his successor, Bacon, Smith took a utilitarian view of academic disciplines. 'May we not through cosmography,' he asks, 'see the situation, temperature, and qualities' not only of our own, but 'of every country in the world'? Husbandmen can learn much from the classical horticultural writings. 'Arithmetic', he says to the Knight, is surely vital 'in disposing and ordering of your men': the military forerunner of William Petty's 'Political Arithmetic'. Astronomy, geometry, building, architecture, have practical value to the husbandman, the artisan, the architect, the lawyer, merchant and knight. Yet moral philosophy is the monarch of disciplines, enquiring into and teaching how the individuals, families, households and communities that make up the whole commonweal should be disposed and governed, regardless of its many striving elements and interests. 'What part of the Commonweal is neglected by moral philosophy', the Doctor asks. 'Does it not teach how every man should guide himself honestly? Did it not show 'how he should guide his family wisely and prophetically, and . . . how a city or realm or any other Common Weal should be well governed both in peace and war?'[23]

A little learning, however, is a dangerous thing. The Doctor protects his own (and Smith's) status, reminding his fellow disputants that the

---

[23] *Ibid.*, 29.

knowledge required by learned counsellors to commonwealths and king-doms is not acquired easily or quickly. With regard to religion, Smith seems to have anticipated the scepticism later expressed by Bacon and Petty. Theology reaches too high for the minds of men: they should leave it alone and concentrate on what they can know, understand and change. The Doctor complains that 'Divinity' should be the last, not the first body of ideas picked up by young university students. The mysteries of religion should not be contemplated until all the other bodies of learning, our 'disciplines', had been mastered. At the very least students should be qualified Bachelors of Arts before they study Divinity.[24] The Doctor pointed out that 'Pythagoras to his scholars that came to learn his pro-fane sciences commanded silence for seven years that by all that space they should be hearers only and not reasoners.'[25]

Only after his ostensibly humanist defence of learning, and his estab-lishing of the special significance of moral philosophy, does the *Discourse* take a novel turn. It is his learning, conceded by the Knight, which establishes the Doctor's special qualifications for dealing with contem-porary problems. Now he must offer a vision that all can agree with, a commonweal that transcends all the differences. The remainder of the *Discourse* propounds the social and economic perspectives that have attracted scholars to it ever since.

In the towns and cities of England in 1549, the ranks of the com-monalty were dominated by the merchant class. They can look after themselves. 'If any sort of men have licked themselves whole', he says to the Merchant, 'you be the same, for what odds soever there happen to be in exchange of things, you that be merchants can espy it anon'.[26] 'Strangers and all merchants bring things that be best cheap to them and dearest to us.'[27] Merchants are 'them', the commonwealth is 'us'. Mer-chants are necessary, but by definition they are driven by profit motive. Above the merchants, in Smith's estimation, came the petty merchants, or retailers, the mercers, grocers, vintners, haberdashers, milliners. These Smith classifies as 'the second sort . . . who do sell wares growing beyond the seas and do fetch out our treasure . . . I reckon them tolerable and yet not necessary in a Common Weal.' They *fetch out* the wealth of the nation. Above them were the old trades, the 'shoemakers, tailors, carpen-ters, masons, tilers, butchers, bakers and victuallers'. In Smith's scale of values they were more valuable to the commonwealth than the great

---

[24] Smith follows his own prescription, leaving his own recommendations for the reform of Church discipline until last: 'except we reform ourselves first', he says, 'I can have no great trust to see this general schism and division in religion utterly taken away': *Discourse*, 127–37.

[25] *Ibid.*, 31.   [26] *Ibid.*, 33–4.   [27] *Ibid.*, 45.

and petty merchants and retailers, because as 'they get their living in the country, so they spend it'. They add commodities and take nothing away. At the very bottom of the social scale of mid-Tudor England were the manufacturing artisans, above all the clothiers and the workers in the cloth industry. Typically, Smith assigns them the highest utility. 'Therefore', says the Doctor, 'we must cherish well the third sort, and these be clothiers (which is as it were our natural occupation), tanners, cappers and worsted makers; only that I know which by their mysteries and faculties do bring in any treasure'.[28] Like Marx, Smith puts production before trade.

The Knight grumbles at this. 'All these insurrections do stir by occasion of these clothiers', he says. When they lack markets, 'they . . . assemble in companies and murmur for lack of living and so pick one quarrel or other to stir the poor commons, that be as idle as they, to a commotion'. That may be true, the doctor concedes, but the tradition of rebellion related to a deeper truth, that 'the highest princes of them all without such artificers could not maintain their estate'. Properly governed, the plebeians constitute far less of a threat to the commonwealth (including the prince) than the armigerous classes: 'And some wise men have said and written that . . . men of arms may be the destruction of their kingdom at length.'[29] At times the Doctor seemed to take an almost perverse delight in turning the established hierarchy upside down.

The perversity fits Mary Dewar's perceptive study of Smith's character. He lived long enough to develop his barely concealed, and highly unfashionable, distaste for 'Gloriana' and her court.[30] His stress on the constitutional contingency of commonwealths, expressed most clearly in the later *De Republica*, might be seen as a simple recapitulation of Aristotle's theory, except that it so clearly and logically follows from the Doctor's insistence, in the *Discourse*, that 'the third sort' of men are those who bring in the most treasure to England, and therefore contribute more than any other group to the common profit. This 'bottom up' perspective was no mere gesture, and may mean that for all his academic and political success, Smith never forgot where he came from. If Marjorie McIntosh is correct in her conjecture that in the same year

---

[28] *Ibid.*, 90–1; the hierarchy is repeated and expanded on 123.   [29] *Ibid.*, 93.

[30] Mary Dewar, *Sir Thomas Smith: A Tudor Intellectual in Office* (London 1984), 7, notes that 'Smith could perhaps have been a typical Elizabethan but for two things. He lacked the virile touch of Elizabethan self-confidence and he thoroughly disliked the Queen. He looked at the throne and was neither dazzled by Gloriana nor bewitched by Eliza. He never even saw the point of behaving as if he were. He had little use for women and none whatsoever for the Queen.' It is clear that he did not admire or respect 'Elizabeth the Great', as Dewar repeatedly shows; but the *Discourse* suggests he was as indifferent to the institution as he was to the person who, in this case, happened to occupy it.

that he was writing the *Discourse* he also formulated the 1549 ordinances of incorporation for his industrious little home town, the Essex market of Saffron Walden, we have another clear example of his down to earth humanism. These ordinances, writes McIntosh, 'make clear that older social values were being appropriated and modified, not discarded'.[31]

We must not be misled by this reference to 'older social values'. McIntosh's study of the juror class in English local communities from the fourteenth to the early seventeenth century 'demonstrates that new problems and solutions to them might well emerge first at the lowest level of government and courts, moving only gradually into the attention of higher authorities, an observation that reverses the directionality assumed by many analyses of national politics and law'.[32] McIntosh suggests that local communities were not ignorant of, nor were they merely indifferent to insensitive and even, at times, disdainful, national governance and policy, but that (as in James C. Scott's model[33]) they were often hostile to it. Manufacturing communities like Saffron Walden were 'characteristic of the transition to early capitalism', and 'contributed to special regulation in several ways'. 'The presence of manufacturing... artisans and traders... a rising number of wage labourers' entailed in the increasing 'scale of production and degree of specialization' was, in McIntosh's view, a key variable determining a responsiveness to change that was characteristic of districts affected by 'new forms of craftwork or industry', and which was well in advance of national movements and policy.[34]

Smith did not invent the labour theory of value. John of Salisbury had observed that twelfth-century nobles and princes lived 'in the breath of other men', and advised them to govern with that in mind. He also wrote that the vocations of the Third Estate were not susceptible to government, but had to be left to self-management. 'Economics', in John's world, was household business, beyond the grasp of precepts of state. Smith was the first English writer to view politics as the state management of economic activity.[35] In the *Discourse*, he discovered that viewing politics as the management and maximization of production and profit led logically

---

[31] Marjorie K. McIntosh, *Controlling Misbehaviour in England 1370–1600* (Cambridge 1998), 203; Essex Record Office RO T/A 104/1.

[32] McIntosh, *Controlling Misbehaviour*, 15.

[33] James C. Scott, *Domination and the Arts of Resistance: Hidden Transcripts* (New Haven 1990).

[34] McIntosh, *Controlling Misbehaviour*, 161–2.

[35] Neal Wood, *Foundations of Political Economy: Some Early Tudor Views on State and Society* (Berkeley 1994); Wood, 'Foundations of Political Economy; Arthur B. Ferguson, 'Renaissance Realism in the "Commonwealth" Literature of Early Tudor England', *Journal of the History of Ideas* 16:3 (June 1955), 287–305; Wrightson, *Earthly Necessities*, 154–6.

to a reversal of traditional social values. In this sense he restated the proverbial idea that the higher people were in status, the less they actually contributed to the common wealth of the kingdom. This led him to the decidedly radical conclusion that the most useful members of the commonwealth were clothmakers, low in status and bad in reputation, ever to the fore of sedition, heresy and rebellion. They increased the common wealth more than any other vocation, including husbandmen. Their commodities brought not just necessity, stasis, but profit, *growth*. This was the seed of the idea, taken up by Old Richard Hakluyt, that to maintain itself, the English commonwealth had to expand. The *weal* of England depended upon the sale abroad of what its households produced. Manufactures employed the numbers necessary for England to be able to defend itself against invaders.[36] This was Smith's decisive spin on what was already an old word.

Like all his contemporaries, Smith knew that England was never far from crises that always fell hardest on households that were unable to 'live of their own' and had to depend on wages. The *Discourse* is essentially a debate within the parliamentary ranks: Knights, Cappers and Merchants were typical members of the Commons at Westminster. Much of their talk in Smith's lifetime had concerned the fate of the fourth character, 'Husbandman'. Enclosures, Smith suggested, were beside the point. These four of Smith's five characters ignored or regarded with contempt what would one day be called 'industry', the mass production of commodities. The role of the Doctor was to remind the others that the greatness of commonwealths depended upon the lowest, landless, wage-dependent workers who processed locally-produced or imported raw materials into commodities for export. Alongside this increasing consciousness of the importance of industry was the spectre of a shifting multitude of wage-dependent men, women and children that coalesced into a mobile, rebellious *proletarii*, drew in discontented middle ranks and, on occasion, appeared for a week or two to be capable of taking the kingdom by force.

'An alternative social order' emerged in England and Wales between the writing of the *Discourse* and the 1640s, a period when, in spite of the fact that national income doubled, its distribution became 'markedly and increasingly uneven'. Class relations were affected. It became more acceptable for the wealthier sort, including yeomen and their equivalents, 'to acquire and to consolidate wealth'; yet 'a larger proportion of the national population was more deeply mired in a perennial struggle for economic survival'. For Keith Wrightson, the 'alternative social order

---

[36] *Discourse*, 87–92.

was ... composed along lines determined by new economic fields of force'.[37] The combined and uneven effects of the great inflation remain the single most important explanation for changes in the social relations of production and distribution at the end of the middle ages. What Fortescue and Smith initiated was not economic growth but acceptance of economic growth as a moral and, especially, a political good in itself. The rebellions of 1536 and 1549 had initiated a murderous debate about the role of the commons, especially the 'lowest' (landless) commons, in national politics. Fortescue and Smith recognized that at least one of the factors driving the tradition of rebellion was the resentment of the 'fourth sort' or 'rascability' at their continuing, systematic exclusion from the politics of the realm. Smith incorporated them, but not into the polity. In effect he created a new, as yet unnamed realm in which, as the producers of commodities upon which England's common wealth rested, the *proletarii* did have an important role. Not far in the future it would be called 'economy'.

Capitalism is not only a system for coordinating national life. It is, as Marx insisted and history shows, inherently expansive. The earlier chapters of this book have shown that up to the mid-sixteenth century England was, as it were, an obsessively introverted culture, concerned above all with what kind of a community it was. The down to earth intelligence, imagination and enterprise of Sir Thomas Smith evidenced a shift in world view that the next generation turned into a lucid, world-changing blueprint. Ideologically, Smith began bringing the elementary particles together, preparing the nucleus of the English explosion.

7.2   Old empire and new: the battle of Pantalarea

In the middle decades of the sixteenth century the word 'empire' referred to 'an absolute Imperiall Monarchy held neither of Pope, Emperor but God alone', as a public servant phrased it in 1600. This original sense of 'empire', brought in by Henry VIII's original Reformation statutes, 'called to mind the relative isolation of England ... rather than its dominion over foreign territories', writes Nicholas Canny. The fact that they had not yet come to use the word 'empire' in its later, expansive sense reflected 'the poor performance of the English' in colonial enterprises, relative to Spain, Portugal and even France. Separate themes of contemporary discourse had to come together with contingent secular trends before England could acquire an imperial mission, and for most of the sixteenth century 'no ... connection' existed in English minds between

---

[37] Wrightson, *Earthly Necessities*, 198, 200, 201; Wood, *The 1549 Rebellions*, ch. 5.

'discovery' and 'the establishment of overseas empire'.[38] This began to change in the early decades of Elizabeth, when Sir Thomas Smith turned his mind to the plantation of a colony in Ireland.[39] Until the 1570s, 'English minds' were concentrated on the condition of England. The rest of this chapter focuses on the group of intellectuals and propagandists who touched the wires that ignited the slow-burning English explosion. The significance of the Hakluyt project was that it developed a coherent explanation for England's current difficulties, and, on the basis of this explanation, made 'dominion over foreign territories' the solution to England's domestic difficulties.

The Hakluyt world view incorporated the political economy outlook developed by Fortescue and Smith, which, in turn, signified growing public awareness of the relationships between economic change, rebellion and the defence of England against invaders. The 1580s marked a decisive shift in intellectual and public interest in the idea of England as an international, expansive power. Sir Francis Drake's exploits against Spain in the 1570s stirred public excitement. His return from a 'secret' circumnavigation in September 1580 caused something of a sensation, when news of his successful voyage reached London.[40] By way of a preface to discussion of the Hakluyt enterprise I focus on a typical piece of public propaganda reporting a little sea-battle that took place off the coast of Sicily, between a Spanish fleet and five English merchantmen, in July 1586. It was probably published as a news-sheet in late 1586, but its survival is due to its having been reprinted, in January 1590, in a book that a great nineteenth-century patriot and historian, Froude, described as 'the epic of the modern English nation', the younger Richard Hakluyt's *Voyages and Discoveries of the English Nation*.[41]

---

[38] Nicholas Canny, 'The Origins of Empire: an Introduction', in Nicholas Canny (ed.), *The Origins of Empire: British Overseas Enterprise to the Close of the Seventeenth Century*, vol. 1 of William Roger Louis (ed.), *The Oxford History of the British Empire* (Oxford 1998), 1, 3, and *passim*; but for 'the Edwardian conception of an "empire of Great Britain"', see Armitage, *Ideological Origins*, 46 and ch. 2 *passim*.

[39] David Beers Quinn, 'Sir Thomas Smith (1513–1577) and the Beginnings of English Colonial Theory', *Proceedings of the American Philosophical Society* 89:4 (1945). Referring to the French colonization of Florida, Thomas Hacket wrote in 1563 that 'I cannot but . . . reioyce to see the forwardness in these late years o Englysshe men for the lyke enterprises. And what good successe GOD have geven them for their travil. For albeit that such attempts seme painfull and harde to achieve to yet in the end they be most pleasant and profitable. As well, for the enlarging of the Christian faith as the enriching of kingdomes': Jean Ribaut, *The whole & true discouerie of terra Florida*, ed. J. T. Connor (1563, Facs. ed., Florida 1927), 550.

[40] Samuel Bawlf, *The Secret Voyage of Sir Francis Drake* (London 2004), 1–2.

[41] James A. Froude, 'England's Forgotten Worthies', in Froude, *Short Studies on Great Subjects* (1853, repr. New York 1967), 153.

The story told in the news-sheet was as follows. In November 1585, 'Five tall and stoute shippes' sailed out of London for the eastern Mediterranean, bound on a journey that was partly exhibition of bravado, partly an expedition of trade. The king of Spain had recently formed an alliance with outlying islands and colonies of the Mediterranean empire of the 'Great Turk', the purpose of which was to 'arrest ... and hinder the passage of all English shippes ... to intercept, take, and spoil them, their persons and goods'.

The ships were owned by a select group of English merchants 'being of the incorporation of the Turkie trade'. They were on their way to test the mettle, and tap into the wealth of two of the greatest empires of their day. In the only full contemporary account of this expedition, the equation was five English merchantmen *versus* the might of Spain.[42]

The *Marchant Royall, Tobie, Edward Bonaventure, William and John* and the *Susan* sailed without incident as far as Sicily. There, 'each shippe began to take leave of the rest', setting off for the 'several portes ... whereunto they were privately appointed ... (for) the lading of their goodes' – Venice, Tripoli and Constantinople. Before parting, they agreed to complete their business and gather again at Zante, an island off the south-eastern coast of Greece. The first ship to reach Zante was to 'stay and expect the coming of the rest of the fleet, for the space of 20 days'. If any ship had not returned within twenty days of the arrival of the first ship, it would be considered sunk or lost to the enemy.

The *Tobie* made good time in its journey to Constantinople, and was the first to reach Zante, followed by the *Marchant Royall* and the *William and John*, each arriving from Tripoli within the twenty-day limit. Though two ships appeared lost, the English celebrated by 'discharging of their ordinance, the sounding of their drummes and trumpets, the spreading of Ensignes, with other warlike and joyfull behaviours, expressing by these outward signes, the inward gladness of their mindes, being all as ready to joyne together in mutuall consent to resist the cruell enemie'. At that very moment, as if a sign from God, the *Edward Bonaventure* and the *Susan* arrived from Venice, and the intact fleet celebrated all over again 'in the maner of the seas'.

In port the locals were friendly, and warned the English 'of two severall armies, and fleetes, provided by the king of Spain, lying in wait to intercept them'. One fleet of '30 strong gallies' awaited them in the

---

[42] BL 683 h.5: 'A true report of a worthie fight, performed in the voyage from Turkie, by five shippes of London, against eleven gallies, and two frigates of the King of Spaines ..., Anno 1586. Written by Philip Jones', 227–231, of Richard Hakluyt the Preacher (ed.), *The Voyages, Navigations, Traffiques and Discoveries of the English Nation*, vol. 1 (London 1589–90).

Straits of Gibraltar. Another, composed of twenty gallies from Sicily and Malta, commanded by the Spanish Admiral John Andreas Dorea, had been sent to 'wait and attend in the Seas for none but the English shippes'. The people of Zante feared 'that not a shippe should escape their furie'. 'Being but few, and little in comparison with them', they advised, it was 'in humane reason impossible, that (the English) should passe either without spoiling, if (they) resisted, or without composition at least, and acknowledgement of dutie to the Spanish king'. How could five little English merchantmen resist the might of fifty warships of the king of Spain?

They steeled themselves by 'grounding themselves upon the goodnes of their cause, and the promise of God'. 'But least they should seeme too careless, and too secure of their estate', and too dependent upon 'God's providence', they 'deliberated advisedly for their best defence'. The *Marchant Royall* was appointed Admiral of the Fleet, the *Tobie* Vice-Admiral, and the five ships agreed not to break from each other 'whatsover extremity should fall out, but to stand to it to the death, for the honour of their Countrey'. Their cargoes loaded, the English ships sailed out to meet their 'ambitious and proud enemie'. It was early July 1586, eight months since they sailed from home.

At 7 a.m. on 13 July, they sighted the sails of thirteen enemy galleys on the horizon, and began to prepare themselves. Two small frigates came forward, carrying emissaries to 'expostulate' with the English fleet. What were they doing in these waters? Why had they not come first 'with their captaines and pursers to . . . their Generall, to acknowledge their dutie and obedience to . . . the Spanish king'? Surely, this was not too much to expect. As long as they submitted to the Spanish king, they would be granted all the courtesies due to those who properly acknowledged his rightful supremacy in those waters.

With quiet reassurances, the Captain of the *Marchant Royall*, Edward Wilkinson, thanked the emissaries for their courtesy, and persuaded them to come aboard his ship for wine and civil conversation. In the quieter atmosphere of Wilkinson's cabin it became clear that the blustering messages did not represent the true feelings of the Sicilian and Maltese lieutenants of the Spanish admiral; the conversation was friendly and promising. All talk was of how to avoid battle. Negotiations, however, eventually foundered in the face of the 'outrageous pronounciations' of the Spanish General, who swept aside the willingness of his Sicilian and Maltese subalterns to let the English ships pass. He delivered his own speech. 'Thou Englishman', he said, disdainfully, 'from whence is your fleet, why stand ye aloof off, know ye not your dutie to the Catholike king, whose person is heere represent?'

Where are your bills of lading, your letters, pasports, and the chief of your men? Think ye my attendance in these seas is in vain, or my person to no purpose? Let all these things be done out of hand as I command, upon paine of my further displeasure and the spoil of you all.

Calm in spite of insult, Master Rowit of the *Tobie* framed one final attempt to avoid bloodshed. '(We are) all merchantmen', he replied, 'using traffike in honest sort, and seeking to passe quietly if (we are) not urged further than reason'. But '(we) would be loath to take an abuse at the hands of any, or sit downe to (our) losse, where (our) abilitie is able to make defence'. The English did not wish to rule the seas (or the world) in the manner of a Spanish despot. They simply wished to be allowed to go about their business, wherever it took them, without hindrance.

As for the odds, the sides were manifestly unequal. David was small, Goliath large.[43] The Philistine's forces outnumbered God's. During the 'hot and terrible' battle that ensued, 'each English shippe matched itself . . . against two Spanish gallies, besides the . . . frigates on the Spanish side'.

The news-sheet made clear that the English had only one enemy in the Mediterranean. At Pantalarea they were opposed very reluctantly by Maltese and Sicilian vessels, whose captains bore no enmity towards England, a nation they in fact greatly admired. One of the Maltese emissaries told Captain Rowit that he had been to London, where the people were, on his own account, very nice to him. They said they were only at Pantalarea because the Spanish made them come. The English ships visited Tripoli, Venice and Constantinople, and were received (and behaved) with courtesy and respect. If these sturdy and honourable merchants and sailors were representative of their race, the report made clear, the Mediterranean would have more trade with England.

After Pantalarea, the English visited Algiers to replenish their supplies. Once more they were warmly received. One night in port a gang of Spanish soldiers attacked and stabbed an isolated English sailor who tried to defend the honour of an Algerian maiden from their drunken attentions in a bar. The Mayor of Algiers was outraged, and had the guilty Spaniards summarily executed, even though the English sailor's wound was barely a scratch (he in fact arrested them single-handedly, and handed them over to the local authorities). If the truth were known, the English would be doing the peoples and cities of the Mediterranean a favour by introducing a little protestant civilization into these parts.

---

[43] Geoffrey Parker, 'David or Goliath? Philip II and his World in the 1580s', in R.L. Kagen and G. Parker (ed.), *Spain, Europe and the Atlantic World: Essays in Honour of John H. Elliott* (Cambridge 1995), 245–66.

One implication of the news-sheet was that English merchants and seafarers were not only pursuing their own interests and those of their nation, but also the interests of all the good people of the Mediterranean except the tyrannical and unpopular Spaniard. It was not necessary for the author to spell this out, for it was the only possible conclusion to the facts as presented. The English bent over backwards to avoid bloodshed; the Spanish general alone really wanted to fight, and thoroughly deserved his shameful defeat.

God was on their side because the English were more pious than the Spanish forces. Throughout their battle against incredible odds, they 'ceased not... to make prayer to Almighty God the revenger of all evils'. The author reported that the 'foolish Spaniards', as they would, 'cryed out not to God, but to our Lady (as they term the virgin Mary)'. Only once did the automatic response-word 'Catholike' occur. It can be assumed that this Spanish nobleman represents not only the king of Spain, but also the would-be assassin of the queen of England, the murdering antichrist of Rome.

The article is good propaganda. Professor David Beers Quinn describes it as 'a fully assimilated news pamphlet'. He thinks it was 'either based on a lost publication, or composed directly from Levant Company Records and from interviews with the seamen and merchants involved'. It tells a good story, somewhat wordily to modern taste, and it may help to know that the author was an accomplished, heterodox and fiery preacher.[44] It is perhaps hurriedly, but nonetheless carefully composed and fluently written. There is never any doubt as to who are the good and bad guys, but the reporter's sketches of calm, patient, determined Englishmen and unstable, blustering Spaniards, while clearly coloured, is not more laboured than its English audience would wish. The pamphlet is presented as a historical narrative, in which the events and characters speak for themselves. No English person could read or hear it read without being moved by sympathy with fellow countrymen who went down to the sea in ships, risking their lives to open up the world for the benefit of those who stayed at home.

Behind the heroic little fleet was a small corporation of merchants of the Turkey Company, formed under Crown patent in 1581, and, between September 1582 and September 1587, the sponsor and financier of at least 27 voyages to the Levant. One of its key supporters was

---

[44] Philip Jones, *Certaine Sermons Preached of late at Ciceter*... (London 1588); Rollison, 'Only the Poor will be Saved: a Theology for the Artisans of Elizabethan England', in Ellen Warne and Charles Zika (ed.), *God, The Devil and a Millennium of Christian Culture* (Melbourne 2005), 39–60.

Sir Francis Walsingham, to whom the younger Richard Hakluyt dedicated his *magnum opus*. It was a very select corporation indeed, comprising a mere twelve of the wealthiest and most powerful citizens of London. Robert Brenner sees them as the historical nucleus of one of the most dynamic new forces in English commercial development from 1581 to 1660.[45] These circumstances bear directly on certain things that Philip Jones, the author of the news-sheet, does not say about the battle. The theme of Jones's account is Big Spain versus Little England. Ostensibly, Spain was still, at this moment of time, an infinitely greater power than England. Only hindsight tells us that in reality England already had better strategy, tactics, ship-designers and builders, metallurgists and gunfounders, and, as we shall see, better 'intelligencers'. The Hakluyt mission was to convince the English state and public that all the required qualities and conditions were in place. The battle of Pantalaria took place at a time when the master-plans for the English *mission civilisatrice* were being drawn up.

The tiny but powerful band of Turkey merchants who financed the expedition were 'among the leading shipowners of the period: proprietors of a growing fleet of great armed vessels, their boats could hold their own against all comers'. Not only could they 'directly manage their own private coercive force; they could command, as well, the state's support for their commercial initiatives'. Their ships, on his account, were state of the art. Improvements in English ship design set in motion by Sir John Hawkins in 1570 gave English ships 'an increase of about one knot in speed and (a huge advantage in battle) an ability to lie one compass point closer to the wind when sailing close-hauled'. Only under the calmest weather conditions on the flattest of seas would a fleet of Mediterranean galleys stand any chance at all against five fast and highly manoeuvrable English 'merchantmen'. Add the fact that English culverins and demi-culverins could propel a 17lb shot 'with reasonable accuracy to a range of about 2,700 yards', where Spanish guns could achieve nothing like that range, and the odds of the battle begin to look distinctly different from the way the news-sheet presents them.[46] Behind the Turkey merchants stood a highly volatile, creative and industrious nation. The news-sheet was part of a crescendo of public propaganda aimed at making the English

---

[45] Robert Brenner, *Merchants and Revolution: Commercial Change, Political Conflict and London's Overseas Traders, 1550–1653* (Cambridge 1993), ch. 1; David Harris Sacks, *The Widening Gate, Bristol and the Atlantic Economy, 1450–1700* (Berkeley 1991), pp. 43–8, identifies the same trend in the profitability of imports vis-à-vis exports in the activities of the Bristol merchants in the same period: if anything, the trend took hold a year or so later than London.

[46] Geoffrey Parker and Caroline Martin, *The Spanish Armada* (London 1988), 29.

conscious of a superiority they already, potentially, possessed. It was part of a worked-out analysis of the state of the English economy, a strategy to solve its problems, and a range of motives that would make it seem *necessary* to hundreds of thousands of English people of all stations, ranks and classes.

In 1586, the Armada had not yet been assembled and defeated. English sailors quickly discovered the technical advantages they enjoyed, and learned to exploit them. It took time for the main message to sink in. The author of the news-sheet was a writer and preacher, not a sailor or a merchant. He may not have known the significance of technical advances in ship-building and gun-founding, and was thus unable to evaluate the exaggerations of his informants. He was not in a position to understand the historical significance of the battle because, like everyone else, he could not see into the future. He touched very lightly on the economic motives of the expedition. The Turkey Company's plan was to sell English manufactures (especially cloth[47]) at the best price it could get at various ports, sail empty to Zante, where ships were loaded with a commodity the English public could not have enough of: currants.[48] The outward trip to sell English commodities was the duty part. The return trip was the profitable leg. It was possible to sell English manufactures at less than cost, because losses would be insignificant compared to profits from the sale of currants to a voracious English public. In his account of the aftermath of the skirmish, Jones reports that the English ships did not pursue the fleeing Spanish General because of 'their deep lading'. Their bellies were fat with millions of little sugar-pills.[49]

There was an inexhaustible market in England for the little sweeteners, which went, in the 1580s, from luxury to item of mass consumption. Dearth and famine haunted England for most of Elizabeth's long reign, not least at this time. Yet merchants could sell as many tons of currants as they could bring home. The more restricted supply, the higher the price. The Turkey Company agitated for a royal charter granting its members a monopoly in the currant trade. The news-sheet was reprinted, in 1589, in Richard Hakluyt's *Principall Navigations*. That context identified Pantalarea as an episode in an epic national tradition stretching back to Roman

---

[47] Sacks, *The Widening Gate*, 44, notes that at Bristol during this period 'textile shipments became much more varied as cheap "cottons" and friezes and expensive worsteds joined the older varieties of broadcloth in the holds of Bristol ships'.

[48] Brenner, *Merchants and Revolution*, 63–6.

[49] Jones's account suggests that the Turkey company had 'largely expelled the Venetians from the Greek islands of Zante and Cephalonia and established a commercial monopoly in the lucrative currants trade' by 1585–6, somewhat earlier than Brenner suggests in *Merchants and Revolution*, 49.

times. It was also propaganda for the Turkey Company's case that they deserved a monopoly because they made the trade with Zante possible by clearing the seas of pirates and Spaniards. Victories like Pantalarea might look insignificant in comparison with the glorious recent exploits of Drake and Raleigh, but they represented an important side-show with lasting benefits. The news-sheet gave them a significant place in 'the epic of the modern English nation'.

In its original form, the news-sheet represented the ideas of an extensive network of politicians and public administrators, academics, preachers and intellectuals, courtiers and merchants and the more perspicacious clothiers and manufacturers. The printing-press had never been used so skilfully, and as a means to reach so varied an audience, as it was in the 1580s. Jones's little item also belonged to a rhetorical *genre*, the 'paradigmatic anecdote', that was favoured by every late Elizabethan writer who wanted to reach as broad and deep an audience – a *public* – as they could.[50] The technique applied most explicitly to plays, which literally enacted significant scenes. But it also applied to the writings of the immensely influential Holinshed enterprise, and was an integral part of the propagation by the Hakluyts and their associates of the English imperial mission.[51] 'Paradigmatic anecdotes' were realistically portrayed scenes or episodes which exemplified a much bigger picture. Put more simply, Jones told a story which would be read, remembered and passed on to the provinces, neighbourhoods and households where the families were raised and the work went on.[52]

On its return the fleet was welcomed back to London with patriotic celebrations, and the story of how five English merchant ships had scattered the might of Spain spread like wildfire through the city. One of the first to receive the information on which Philip Jones based his news-sheet was a man who, like a handful of men in other parts of England, was associated by his contemporaries, and by posterity, with a place: Richard Hakluyt 'of the Middle Temple'. He was a lawyer by training, but earned his living as a consultant to business corporations and government. Hakluyt

---

[50] Annabel Patterson, *Reading Holinshed's Chronicles* (Chicago 1994), 42–7.
[51] Patterson, *ibid.*, passim.
[52] Significantly, Jones preached his apocalyptic sermons in just such a town to just such a constitutency. His message gave theological force to Smith's contentions about the growth-fuelling activities of manufacturing workers. Jones's 'saint' was 'an articifer or handicraftes man, labouring diligently in his manuarie trade or science'. Of all people, the poor manufacturing worker was most beloved of God, so long as he laboured 'to releeve himselfe, and maintaine his familie honestly as a Christian, and quietly like a subject in the feare of God, and according to the qualitie of his vocation. Such a one in scripture', he concluded, 'I take to be meant by the name of a poore man': Rollison, 'Only the Poor Will Be Saved', 52.

was a leading business strategist of mid-Elizabethan England, one of the first writers to make the connection, decisive in the history of capitalism, between industry and empire. He was no abstract theorist. He was that peculiar Elizabethan phenomenon, an 'intelligencer', a collector, classifier, recorder and interpreter of 'data', which he passed on to his clients in government and the City. He was a mid-Elizabethan business guru, at his most active around 1580.

Hakluyt was born around 1530 and died in 1591. In 1530 English was spoken, in hundreds of dialects and thousands of local accents, by about two and a half million people. The archives of the time will bear very pessimistic interpretations. The Norman-Angevin empire, torn apart by the Wars of the Roses, and ransacked by the confiscations and taxations of Henry VII and his son, consisted of England and Wales, its smallest extent since the Norman Conquest. By the time Hakluyt was twenty, England was in the midst of a devastating influenza epidemic, exhausted by three decades of excessive taxation, fearful of foreign invasion, and growing cynical about state religion. Wages were falling, the coinage debased, necessities scarce and expensive, the nation's finest art had been destroyed, the altars 'stripped', the religious landscape had been permanently refashioned, dearth was a routine experience and death in an epidemic of influenza or plague was a reasonable expectation for any subject of the imperial monarchy of England. Data on harvests, prices, wages and mortality crises indicate that by the 1550s, things were getting bad, and were to get much worse.[53] Hakluyt died two years after his younger relative published *Principall Navigations, Voyages and Discoveries of the English Nation,* and six years before the worst and most general mortality crisis to have struck England since the Black Death.

In 1559 Amigail Waad wrote to the young queen Elizabeth's secretary, Sir William Cecil with a deeply pessimistic assessment of the condition of England. 'The Queen [is] poor,' he wrote; 'the realm [is] exhausted, the nobility poor and decayed.' There was a dangerous 'Want of good captains and soldiers'. The common people were 'out of order' because 'Justice [was] not executed' and 'all things [were] dear'. Among the richer sort 'Excess in meat, drink and apparel' promoted 'Divisions among ourselves' and between the classes. The nation was threatened by 'Wars with France and Scotland' and the 'French king [bestrode] the realm, having one foot in Calais and the other in Scotland.' Divisions at home were

[53] Wrightson, 'Prices and People', in *Earthly Necessities*, 116ff. and *passim*; Eamon Duffy, *The Stripping of the Altars: Traditional Religion in England 1400–1580* (New Haven 1992), esp. ch. 17; Andrew Graham-Dixon, *A History of British Art* (London 1996), ch. 1.

compounded by 'Steadfast enmity but no steadfast friendship abroad'.[54]
Modern historians have tended to agree. Norman Jones writes that 'to
thoughtful English people the future was very uncertain' in 1558, at
Elizabeth I's accession.[55]

Modern research on demography, epidemiology, taxation, economy
and social conflict suggests that Waad was not exaggerating. Demographers have calculated that there were fewer English people in the first
half of the sixteenth century than there had been at any time since the
twelfth century – perhaps as few, in 1500, as two and a half million. Parish
register data show strong recovery in the second third of the century –
more births per head of population and fewer deaths. On its own this
suggests the realm Elizabeth inherited was recovering from its 'medieval'
low point earlier in the century, but even if this later proved to be true, at
least in terms of numbers, it may not have been apparent to contemporaries. The 1550s were plagued by 'sweating sickness' and if the estimate
of one scholar that 20 per cent of the population died in the influenza
epidemics of that decade is correct, it was the worst decade since the
Black Death.[56]

Waad's 'bleak prospect' summed up the condition of England in 1559.
What was discovered over the next forty years was not that Waad's bleak
prospect was untrue but that it could be managed, dealt with and made
to serve higher purposes. Just what those higher purposes became was
symbolized in the famous 'Rainbow Portrait' of Elizabeth, probably conceived and commissioned around 1600 by Francis Bacon and Robert
Cecil with the knowledge and participation of the queen. Stephen Dedijer suggests that this portrait 'is a part of the international debate on the
role and policy of England and on the philosophy of state'.[57] Dedijer
interprets this painting in the light of contemporary iconology, 'the language of symbols and images' used by contemporary artists and learned
people. He shows that Elizabeth herself saw the Rainbow Portrait a bearer
of 'good tidings' – symbolizing 'a Golden Age Empire/ under Anglican
England's world leadership/ to be based not on war/ but on strength,
peace, compassion/ and a vigilant use of knowledge, science, intelligence,
espionage and secrecy'.

---

[54] Conyers Read, *Mr Secretary Cecil and Queen Elizabeth* (Norwich and Bungay 1965),
124; PRO SP/12/1: the summary is on f. 152.
[55] Norman Jones, *The Birth of the Elizabethan Age: England in the 1560s* (Oxford 1995), 5.
[56] John S. Moore, 'Jack Fisher's 'Flu: a visitation revisited', *Economic History Review* 46:2
(1993), 280–307; Michael Zell, 'Fisher's 'Flu and Moore's Probates: quantifying the
Mortality Crisis of 1556–1560', *Economic History Review* 47 (1994), 354–8.
[57] Stephen Dedijer, "The Rainbow Scheme: British Secret Service and Pax Britannica"
(internet article).

The new vision emerged remarkably quickly. In 1570, when Pope Pius issued his Bull depriving Elizabeth 'of her pretended title to the . . . crown [of England] and of all lordship, dignity and privilege whatsoever' and 'charg[ing] and command[ing] all . . . the nobles, subjects and others . . . that they do not dare obey her orders, mandates and laws', England seemed to be about as isolated and insecure as a nation could be.[58] Religion was in disarray. By 1580, when Hakluyt's influence was at its height, 'survivalist' catholics were coming to be seen as a fifth column. It was becoming clear that the transfer of authority in religion from the pope to the imperial monarch of England was not proceeding as smoothly as Henry VIII and his successors had hoped. By then, a large but necessarily undisclosed number of English people had acquired an evangelical position with regard to church and state. The self-oriented radical protestant conscience was growing in influence, and a growing number of people suspected the inherent corruption of 'institutions of men' in the matter of religion. Religion had been in contention for 150 years. Political and constitutional theorists from all sides of all the controversies were agreed on one thing only: unity of religion is the pillar of effective government. By the 1580s it was clear that England was not united in religion.[59] This was a revolution, if anything deserves the dubious honour of being named as such. If it was true that unity in religion was an absolute law of government, as most still believed, then England was in imminent danger of falling apart.

7.3   Touching the wires: Old Hakluyt and the conjuncture of industry and empire

Old Richard Hakluyt is sometimes called 'the lawyer', 'of the Middle Temple', or 'of Eyton' (the Herefordshire village where his family estate was principally located) to distinguish him from his younger relative and ward, also Richard, whose reputation rapidly eclipsed his. Since the first publication of the younger Hakluyt's *Voyages and Discoveries* in 1590, it has become accepted that while the elder Hakluyt was the younger's patron and guide, his ideas were unformed and piecemeal. We shall see that that was far from being the case. The ideas young Hakluyt turned

---

[58] 'Pope Pius V's Bull against Queen Elizabeth' (1570), *Statutes of the Realm*, IV, 526ff.

[59] 'Tudor Englishmen, when they thought about their society, agreed, on the whole, that it was esentially an expression of Divine Will . . . "Is this what God wants or is that?" is the language of Tudor polemic': Felix Raab, *The English Face of Machiavelli: a Changing Interpretation 1500–1700* (London 1964), 8–9. Richard Hakluyt the Elder, 'Inducements to the liking of the voyadge to that parte of America wch lyeth betwene 34 and 36 degree of Septentrional Latytude', Taylor (ed.), *Original Writings*, vol. 2, 343.

into epic propaganda had been forming for two generations, and were given definitive form and power by men a generation older than the younger Hakluyt.

Hakluyt lived and wrote before the abstractions of modern economic, social and imperial theory had been formulated. His ideas shed light on the practical nature of capitalism and imperialism as historical processes, as 'world systems'. Viewed through Old Hakluyt's eyes, there was nothing accidental (or 'absent minded') about their origins. They were planned in simple yet meticulous ways. Hakluyt drew up the first blue-prints; he was a planner, where his younger relative, who styled himself as 'Richard Hakluyt, Preacher' in the dedication of *Voyages and Discoveries* to Sir Francis Walsingham, converted the vision into effective propaganda.

When Old Hakluyt died most of the 'voyadges' of this tenacious and portentious empire still lay in the future, but the rationale that motivated it was in place. His public career began in 1557, when he sat for Leominster in Mary Tudor's last Parliament. Leominster was the main town in an area that produced the finest wool in Europe; 'Leominster Ore' was 'peerless in quality', and was used in the manufacture of 'oultrefine cloth'.[60] For much of the middle ages it had been exported to Italy and the Low Countries, but by the sixteenth century its main markets were much closer to home, in the cloth-making districts of Gloucestershire, especially Kingswood and the Stroudwater Valleys, where innovative clothiers like Benedict Webb used it in mixtures with Spanish wool to manufacture cloth for export, and in luxury hatting villages like Frampton Cotterill and Winterbourne in the southern Vale of Severn, north of Bristol.[61] These were by no means the only districts of England that lived or died by the export of their commodities, but they were among the most famous: the equivalents, in this age of 'dispersed' manufacturing enterprises, of great factory cities like Manchester or Leeds during the classic Industrial Revolution. When the foreign markets for their products collapsed – at least once in every generation from the fifteenth to eighteenth centuries – such districts experienced great suffering. Hakluyt was not exaggerating when he wrote, over and again, that loss of markets led to incomparable and potentially disastrous 'mischiefs' for the nation as a whole. Hakluyt was the first to recognize, not only that England's population was increasing, but also that the only possible employment for these extra numbers lay in manufacturing. The future of these 'projects' for the employment of the poor, and therefore, in Hakluyt's view, the future of the nation, depended on the conquest of overseas markets.

---

[60] Eric Kerridge, *Textile Manufactures in Early Modern England* (Manchester 1985), 20, 34.
[61] *Ibid.*, 38.

Hakluyt's vision of empire always bore the marks of his experiences and observations at home in Herefordshire, and developed from his expanding knowledge of how the English woollen industry, the paradigmatic English industry, worked. It is probably no coincidence that the most important legislation of the Parliament of 1557 was an Act regulating the manufacturing of woollens. Although there are no records to confirm it, it is difficult to imagine that his expertise was not called upon in the debates and drafting of the Act. That experience seems to have led him away from the role of legislator, towards that of a strategist and intelligencer in 'the mercantile aspects of cosmography'.[62]

The writings of Old Hakluyt embodied the approach of his older contemporary, Sir Thomas Smith, a pioneering planner of colonies or 'plantations' closer to home.[63] Like the Commonwealth writers of his youth, Hakluyt's imperial strategies emerged from an intense search for solutions to very real and distressing disorders. He may have been the first to recognize the implications of phenomena that were not well understood at the time, and which have been relatively ignored by historians ever since, especially historians of England's (later 'Britain's') empire. We have seen that a new phase of economic development emerged between the fourteenth and seventeenth centuries, one of the most obvious signs of which was the expansion and migration of major industries, particularly *the* major industry, clothmaking, from the medieval cities to the early modern countryside.[64] This fact was the keystone of Old Hakluyt's imperial vision.

The vision was given dramatic expression by the politicians, intellectuals, merchants, manufacturers and printers who influenced and assisted in the production of the younger Hakluyt's *Voyages and Discoveries*. Old Hakluyt's career and writings flatly contradict the idea that it is not until the 1650s that we find evidence of 'secular motives taking the place of the spiritual motives that were previously invoked to justify colonization'.[65] This misrepresents the thinking and mental worlds of both Hakluyts, but especially of the elder, who, whilst certainly a pious and patriotic protestant, was not above using the biblical gestures of his sect and age. Yet in his writings such gestures are fleeting, all but submerged in an urgent materialist rationale. One has to look hard in Old Hakluyt's writings to find a trace of anything other than 'secular motives'.[66] It is, however, in

---

[62] Taylor (ed.), *Original Writings*, 5–6.
[63] Arthur B. Ferguson, 'Renaissance Realism in the "Commonwealth" Literature of Early Tudor England', *Journal of the History of Ideas* 16:3 (June 1955), 287–305.
[64] Rollison, *Local Origins*, chs. 1–2. [65] Canny, *Origins of Empire*, 22.
[66] In his will he bequeathed his 'sowle redeemed by the mearits and passions of Jesus Christe the Saviour of the World, to the same Christe that is deyd, buried, risen, and

accord with the common assumption that the mentality of the sixteenth century was overwhelmingly religious, and that not until after 1660 do we start to see signs of the secular rationalism of a new age.[67] In practice, 'secular' rationalism is perfectly compatible with even the most messianic religiosity: the latter provides the axioms, the former the tactics. Similar assumptions are evident in accounts of early English economic development, in which consciousness of the existence of a large manufacturing sector, and fears of the social consequences of 'deindustrialization', did not emerge until the last third of the seventeenth century. The idea that it was not until 'after the Restoration . . . that colonies were [seen to be] essential to the economic well-being of the community' fails to take account of the fact that this was precisely the argument that the elder Hakluyt formulated and repeated, in his memoranda of the early 1580s, over and over again. All people who 'be not barbarously bred', he wrote in 1582, acknowledge 'that men are borne as well to seeke the common commodity of their country, as theire owne private benefite'. There was 'an infinite number of things to be done for the benefit of the common-weal', he wrote, but 'I find that no one thing . . . is greater than Clothing, and the things incident to the same.'[68]

Old Hakluyt's local origins made him acutely aware of the extent of manufacturing. He understood how crucial its 'projects' (the Elizabethan word for 'enterprises') were to the well-being, even the survival, of the English commonweal. As he developed it, the central idea was simple: for England to preserve its existing population, and thus its capacity for self defence, it was necessary to conquer markets. Overseas expansion was desirable for 'the generall enriching of this realme', but it was necessary to ensure the livings of all the people who now depended on the sale of the commodities they produced.[69] He was not the first to identify the

---

ascended, and that shall be the Judge of all Nations under heaven. My body I bequeathe to the earthe till the general resurrection [when] bodie and sowle shall joyne to everlasting salvacion': 'Will of Richard Hackluyt of Eyton (1587)', Taylor, *Original Writings*, vol. 2, 370; the younger Hakluyt's formulae was if anything even more perfunctorily orthodox: 'I commend my soule into the hands of God from whence I received the same, trusting thorow the only merits of jesus Christ and the sanctification of the blessed spirit to be both in body and soule a member of His most holy and heavenly kingdom.': 'Will of Richard Hakluyt, 1612', *ibid.*, 506.

[67] Armitage, *Ideological Origins*, 71, writes that even the younger Hakluyt's usage of religion was tactical: 'Religion shaped little, if any, of Hakluyt's corpus.'

[68] 'Remembrance for Master S . . . for a principall English factor at Constantinople' (1582), in Hakluyt the younger, *Principal Navigations, Voiages, Traffiques and Discoveries of the English Nation* (1598), vol. 1, 161.

[69] Richard Hakluyt, Lawyer to Lord Burleigh, 28 February 1571, *ibid.*, vol. 1, 90–1, is advice to Cecil of information received regarding the preparation of armed forces in Spain; Hakluyt–Burleigh, 7 November 1571, *ibid.* 93–5, is about information received regarding a case of corruption in the customs office.

importance of manufacturing, as we saw in Chapter 6. But he was the first 'business strategist' to put such emphasis on the necessary connection between the two sides of what became the capitalist world-system: industry and empire.

Old Hakluyt's intelligence came together in his rooms at the Middle Temple. In what must have been quite a large room, Hakluyt had set up a large 'boord' mounted on trestles. On this table was spread out 'an universall map (on which were shown) all the knowen Seas, Gulfs, Rivers, Empires, Kingdoms, Dukedoms, & Territories'. This was almost certainly the map published in 1564 by one of the great European cosmographers, Abraham Ortelius. Hakluyt added more information to the map as and when it was brought to him from the docks, or from other intelligencers like John Dee. Beside the map were 'certein books of Cosmographie', which he constantly up-dated on the basis of information brought to him by his agents, sea-captains and merchants.[70] The table represented the accumulating database of his advices to London trading companies and his counsel to courtiers and statesmen. He had a group of associates who passed on information from the docks and city. In 1568, he was visited by his young ward, a Queen's Scholar at Westminster School, a short walk along the Strand.[71] Thirty years later the younger man remembered the fateful moment when the intelligencer took him into his office and showed him the 'universall map'. 'Seeing (the boy) curious', the intelligencer 'began to instruct (him)...he pointed with his wand' to all the newly discovered places, and told him about the

---

[70] Richard Hakluyt, 'To the Right Honourable Sir Francis Walsingham...', Preface to *The Principall Navigations, Voiages and Discoveries of the English Nation, made by Sea of over Land, to the most remote and farthest distant Quarters of the earth at any time within the compasse of these 1500 yeeres...* (London 1589, facs. ed. Cambridge 1965), 2.

[71] The ascription of this visit to the year 1568 is made first by Taylor (ed.), Letter from Richard Hakluyt, Lawyer, to M. Ortelius, Cosmographer, in Flanders, *Original Writings*, vol. 1, 78, n. 2, and repeated in D.B. and A.M. Quinn, 'A Hakluyt Chronology', in D.B. Quinn (ed.), *The Hakluyt Handbook*, vol. 1 (London 1974), 265. Taylor thought the map in question was Ortelius's universal map of 1564, and not that which Old Hakluyt had been requesting in his letter, which like most of his writing reveals the down-to-earth character of his thought: 'For as much as men usually live in houses which are neither spacious enough nor light enough within for them to be able to place or spread out conveniently a large world map in them, it will be most gratifying to many to have a map thought out on the following lines: namely that when spread out to its full extent it is quite fit and suitable for a hall or other spacious place of that kind, and also when rolled up at each end on two smooth revolving rods it lies conveniently on a table about three or four feet square... In this way you will perform a most acceptable service to a number of English lawyers, to the students of both Oxford and Cambridge Universities, and to the citizens of London, and you will produce a map that will sell better in every European city than any other kind.' At the time of writing Hakluyt was clearly preoccupied with the search for a North-West passage: 'Nor must you omit to place before our eyes the *Strait of the Three Brethren* in its correct position, since there is always hope that at some time it may be discovered': Taylor, *Original Writings*, 81.

people and commodities that could be found there. Elizabethan space travel was more than enough to catch a schoolboy's imagination, but it was not all. There was the matter of religious duty. 'From the map he brought me to the Bible,' wrote the younger Hakluyt, and 'turning to the 107 psalm the 23 & 24 verses . . . ', he read –

> They that go down to the sea in ships,
> That do business in great waters;
> These see the works of the Lord,
> And his wonders in the deep.

Young Hakluyt was brought up to be the preacher of the old intelligencer's mission.[72]

On completion of his studies at Westminster School, the London Company of Clothworkers awarded their well-connected student, the younger Richard Hakluyt, a scholarship to Oxford. There he pursued the usual syllabus, but all his spare time was spent searching out and studying 'whatsoever printed or written discoveries and voyages I found extant in the Greek, Latine, Italian, Spanish, Portugall, French or English languages'.[73] From the outset, 'Geography' was about collecting and processing particular sources and types of knowledge in order for them to be of use in the planning and executing of imperial policy. He began to develop his uncle's vision of empire, first by compiling original sources and reports of voyages and explorations of the English. But just to establish that the English were great world explorers in the past was not enough. He made it his business, he tells us, to obtain new intelligence on the state of play in international affairs, by cultivating the company of his uncle's network of 'the chiefest Captains at Sea, the greatest Merchants, & the best Marriners of our nation'.[74]

After finishing his degree, young Richard Hakluyt lectured on Aristotle's *Politics* at Oxford, but was soon offered employment by the government.[75] From 1583–8 he was in the ambassadorial service in France with Sir Edward Stafford. In Parisian diplomatic society he 'heard in speech, & read in books other nations miraculously extolled for their discoveries . . . but the English of all others for their sluggish security, and continuall neglect of the like attempts . . . ' were a subject for contempt.[76] Nothing was more calculated to offend English sensibilities than the suggestion that the French were laughing at them. He began organizing the project that would become *The Principall Navigations*. Its aim was to persuade the English to conquer the world. That would show the French.

---

[72] *Principall Navigations*, 2–3.   [73] *Ibid.*, 3   [74] *Ibid.*
[75] For young Hakluyt's use of Aristotle, see Armitage, *Ideological Origins*, 71–6.
[76] *Ibid.*, 2–3.

Young Hakluyt's first published effort, *Divers voyages touching the discoverie of America* (1582) was 'almost as much the work of the elder Hakluyt as of the younger' and included notes on colonization that Old Hakluyt had prepared to assist Sir Humphrey Gilbert in his attempts to obtain government backing for a voyage to discover a North-West Passage, in the late 1570s.[77] He began writing *A Particular Discourse concerning the greate necessitie & manifolde commoditye that are like to growe to this realme of England by the Western Discoveries lately attempted* in July 1584, when he had consultations with another of his patrons, Sir Walter Raleigh.[78] Later in the year he was commanded to wait on the queen and hand her a copy. By now his career was well under way, and his reputation began to overtake that of his guardian and namesake, 'Old Hakluyt' of the Middle Temple.

Historians have often been dazzled by the epic side of the imperial mission formulated by Hakluyt the Intelligencer, and converted into articulate propaganda by his nephew, the Preacher.[79] Unlike his nephew, the elder Hakluyt never dwelt at length on England's mission, but occasionally, scattered in his painstakingly detailed and practical instructions and advices to voyagers, merchants, ships-captains, diplomats and commercial agents overseas, he would refer to a larger rationale. And on one occasion he defined it. If there is an Ur-text of empire, it is to be found in an obscure memorandum of 'inducements to the liking of the voyage intended towards Virginia', written about 1580. Almost in passing, the intelligencer identified the 'ends of voyages' precisely. They were:

> To plant Christian Religion
> To Traffique
> To Conquer

But *to plant Christian religion without conquest will be hard,* he wrote. *Traffike easily followeth conquest.*[80] Old Hakluyt's definition of England's mission was to echo from the pulpits and schoolrooms, and in the minds of

---

[77] David B. Quinn, *Richard Hakluyt, Editor* (Amsterdam 1967), 13; 'Notes in writing . . . to merchants of the Muscovie Company for the discoverie of the northeast strait' and 'Notes . . . to be given to one that prepared for a discovery', in *Divers voyages* (London 1582, facs. ed. Amsterdam 1967), 101–18.

[78] Taylor (ed.), *Original Writings*, ii, 211–326.

[79] For example, there is not even an entry for the elder Hakluyt in the index (vol. 20) of Samuel Purchas's seventeenth-century expansion of *The Principall Navigations, Hakluytus Posthumus or Purchas His Pilgrimes* (Glasgow 1907), even though the work includes most of his writings; Young Hakluyt calls himself 'Richard Hakluyt Preacher' in signing the *Epistle Dedicatorie to Lord Howard of Effingham* to the second, two-volume edition of the *Principall Navigations* (London 1598).

[80] The full quote is 'To plant Christian religion without conquest will be hard. Traffique easily followeth conquest: conquest is not easy. Traffique without conquest seemeth possible, and not uneasie. What is to be done, is the question': 'Inducements to the

English people of all classes, for the next three centuries. It would become an axiom of foreign policy, driving all else before it. This mission would make life meaningful, and bearable for the first nation to experience the sweeping aside of an agrarian way of life that was thousands of years old. Hundreds, perhaps thousands of human cultures in every part of the world would have reason to curse it. Hakluyt's definition was the proverb from which the grand narratives of empire would grow.

'Young Hakluyt' was the propagandist (or 'Preacher') of Old Hakluyt's vision, which could not begin without persuading large sections of the English public that it had to be done – that if the nation did not expand aggressively, it would necessarily shrink, and even conceivably lose its independence as well. Young Hakluyt was never more derivative of his mentor than when he wrote of 'the swarming of beggars', and indicated his solution. 'Fooles for the swarminge of beggars alleage that the realme is toto populous', he wrote in 1584; but as 'Salomon saieth . . . the honour and strengthe of a Prince consisteth in the multitude of the people'. Writing his *Description of England* at around the same time, William Harrison also felt obliged to counter the growing idea that 'we have already too great a store of people in England'. He pointed out that Christian scripture required the faithful to go forth and multiply.[81] Sanction for this 'development' or 'growth' model was to be found in scripture and in the classical political philosophy of Aristotle's *Politics*, which Young Hakluyt had studied and lectured on at Oxford.[82] 'A wall of men is far better than stacks of corn and bags of money to defend the commonwealth', wrote Harrison, echoing the defensive theme. By the 1580s underlying economic and social changes, occurring in unpredictable local, national and international contexts, had begun to produce alarming symptoms of alienation and crisis, most evidently in what all contemporaries seem to have agreed was the rising tide of 'beggars'.[83] The obvious conclusion was that there were too many people. This meant the English commonwealth was teetering on the brink of a crash. Malthus's assumption that 'the preventative check' (hunger, disease, death) would always halt human population growth when it went beyond ecological limits was

---

liking of the voyage intended towards Virginia' (1585), in Taylor, *Original Writings*, vol. 2, 332.

[81] Hakluyt, 'Discourse on Western Planting', in Taylor, *ibid.*, vol. 2, 234, 238–9; William Harrison, *The Description of England*, ed. G. Edelen, (Ithaca, N.Y. 1968), 216, 256.

[82] For his autograph dedicatory letter to Queen Elizabeth, dated 1 September 1583 and prefixed to his analysis of Aristotle's *Politics*, cf. frontispiece to D.B. Quinn (ed.), *Hakluyt Handbook*; Armitage, *Ideological Origins*, 71–6.

[83] A.L. Beier, *Masterless Men: the Vagrancy Problem in England, 1560–1640* (London 1985).

firmly entrenched in private thoughts and public debate in the 1580s. It was the obvious conclusion, grounded in the experience of every generation that had lived since the Black Death. Modern demographers have shown that the population of England was indeed rising again after two centuries of decline. The current view is that the Black Death struck populations that had already reached their ecological limits. On these arguments those who thought like the Hakluyts were absolutely right. If something drastic was not done, the still-fragile 'empire of England' could indeed collapse and be taken over by a stronger empire.

The surprising thing was the emergence, in the 1570s, of a strongly argued and evidenced alternative, positive, interpretation, which saw that 'if worke may be had for the multitude' then England could 'support a population five times greater than her present one'. The solution to endemic poverty and unemployment was not to tuck in the national belt, work towards a fairer distribution of the fruits of the earth, and curtail reproduction in order to reduce numbers; the answer was to expand industry, for as young Hakluyt put it, 'the people beinge industrious, there shall be found victualls ynoughe'.[84] The answer was *growth*.

By comparison with his nephew, the elder Hakluyt is a shadowy figure. Apart from his writings (which were rescued from manuscript oblivion by Young Hakluyt), we glimpse him only in his nephew's description of the visit to his rooms at the Middle Temple, in the 1570s, and from a passing reference in the diary of the Elizabethan 'Magus', John Dee, dated June 1578. It says merely that Dee, in conversation, 'told Daniel Rogers, Mr Hakluyt of the Middle Temple being by, that King Arthur and King Maty both of them did conquer Gelindia, lately called Friesland'. His nephew, still at Oxford, had not yet taken on the task of collecting and recording the principal navigations of the English, among which an Arthurian conquest of Friesland would surely count. This meeting of like minds at the house of John Dee was a seed which, in his own practical way, the elder Hakluyt nurtured and young Hakluyt brought to flower. These were well-connected men: Daniel Rogers was the son of John Rogers, the Marian martyr, and a member of Walsingham's staff who was closely connected by marriage and shared interests to Ortelius, the

---

[84] 'For when people knowe howe to lyve, and howe to maynetayne and feede their wyves and children, they will not abstaine from mariage as nowe they doe: and the soile thus abounding with corne, fleshe, mylke, butter, cheese, herbes, rootes, and frutes, &c. and the seas that envyron the same so infinitely abounding in fyshe, I dare truly affirme that if the nomber in this realme were as greate as all Spaine and ffraunce have, the people being industrious, industrious I say, there shall be founde victualls ynoughe at the full in all bounty to suffice them all': 'Discourse of Western Planting', in Taylor, *Original Writings*, vol. 2, 239.

Flemish geographer.[85] Dee's sorting house was at Mortlake; Hakluyt's at the Middle Temple.

The first edition of Young Hakluyt's epic, published in 1590, gave the elder Hakluyt's vision a new and immensely powerful propaganda dimension. Where Hakluyt the elder thought in terms of a task that had yet to be enacted, the message of his nephew's legendary compendium of voyages, expeditions and discoveries of the 'English nation', however much it was expanded and added to in ensuing editions, always embodied one simple message. The English had an imperial *tradition*: they had *always* obeyed the injunction to 'go down to the sea in ships'. The reason for expanding empire by 'plantations' was that it was what the English, at their noblest and most pious, had always done, and should therefore always continue to do. The voyagers of the distant and recent past returned with information and maps (the real gold-dust) that made Hakluyt's contemporaries' task so much easier. The expansionist implications of Old Hakluyt's vision have obscured the domestic analysis that grounded the expansion of English empire in *necessytie*. Old Hakluyt was not just a collector, recorder, interpreter and distributor of information relating to foreign parts; he was also an authority on domestic affairs, and in particular on those aspects of life which we have learned to classify as 'economic'. For him, the imperial mission was necessary, not only because it was enjoined by the Bible and hardly at all because it was a traditional activity for the English. Old Hakluyt's writings never dwelt on these reasons for empire. He advocated empire because the kind of society England was, and the kind of economic activity in which it already engaged as a routine part of everyday life, demanded it.

7.4   Mobilizing an imperial economy

In the writings and collections of the younger Hakluyt, the devil lay in the great myth. In those of the elder Hakluyt, the devil was in the detail. The Hakluyts were active in the early decades of a period of economic expansion that involved increasing production of commodities of all kinds.[86] One of the elder Hakluyt's most characteristic specialities was the planning of voyages, beginning with the mundane business of listing the supplies that English ships and fleets of trade, exploration, discovery and colonization should take with them. His lists of tools and skills which

---

[85] George Bruner Parks, *Richard Hakluyt and the English Voyages* (New York 1930), 47; for Dee's '"Galfridian" conception of an Arthurian British empire', see Armitage, *Ideological Origins*, 46–7.

[86] Wrightson, *Earthly Necessities*, chs. 6–7.

colonisers would need simply to establish themselves in a new place, and information they should report back, are deceptively mundane. In fact, they are inventories of the contemporary English economy, the technology, the skills, the knowledge, the raw materials, the commodities – much of what Marx, centuries later, would call its 'mode of production'. Let us consider the instructions he prepared in the late 1570s for Muscovie Company merchants setting out in search of the North-East Passage; they survive because Young Hakluyt had them printed in 1582, on the grounds that they were 'not altogether unfit for some other enterprises of discoverie, heerafter to be taken in hand'.[87]

Hakluyt's list of things to take began, predictably, with 'kersies of all orient colours, brodecloth, frisadoes, motleys, bristow frices, spanish blankettes, bays of all colours, feltes of divers colours, taffeta hats, deepe caps for marriners' (which 'would turne to an infinite commodities of the common poore people by knitting'), quilted nightcaps ('of Levant taffeta of various colours'), 'poyntes of all sortes of silke, threed, and lether, of all manner of colours', 'shoes of spanish leather', 'a garnishe of Pewter, for a show of a vent of that Englishe commoditie', bottelles, flagons, spoones &c. of that metall', 'glasses of English making', 'looking glasses for women', 'spectacles of the common sort', 'linen of divers sort', 'handkerchiefs', 'glazen eyes to ride with against dust', 'knives in sheaths . . . of good edge', 'needles great and small of every kind', 'buttons greater and smaller', 'boxes with weights of gold, and of every kinde of the coyne of golde, good and badde, to shew that the people here, use weight and measure which is a certayne showe of wisedom, and of a certayne government setled here'. 'All the severall silver coynes of our Englishe moneys [were] to be carried . . . to bee showed to the governours at Cambalu, which is a thing that shal in silence speake to wise men more than you imagine.' 'Lockes and keyes, hinges, boltes, halves etc of excellent workemanshippe, whereof if vent may be hereafter, we shall set our subjectes in worke, which you must have in great regarde: for in finding ample vente of anything that is to be wrought in this realme, is more worth to our people besides the gaine of the marchant, than Christchurch, Bridewell, the Savoy, and all the Hospitals of England.'[88]

Besides these English manufactures, the merchants should also take along a supply of 'the sweetest perfumes to set under hatches to make the place sweet against (persons of credit) coming aboard', for 'banketing

[87] D.B. Quinn (ed.), *Divers Voyages*, 101.
[88] 'Notes in writing besides more privie by mouth given by (Hakluyt) to M. Arthur Pette and to M. Charles Jackman, sent to the merchants of the Muscovie Company for the discoverie of the northeast strayte, not altogether unfit for some other enterprises of dicoverie, heereafter to be taken in hande', in Quinn (ed.), *Divers Voyages*, 105–12.

on shipbord' on such delicacies as 'Marmelade, Sucket, Figges bar-
relled, Reysings of the sunne ('raisons'), comfets of divers kinds, prunes
damaske, dried peres, walnuttes, almondes, smallnuttes, olives to make
them taste their wine, the Apple John that dureth two yeeres to make
showe of our fruites, bullocke, sacke, Vials of good sweet waters & casting bottels of glasses to besprinckel the gests withal, after their coming
aborde, sugar to use with their wine, if they will.' They were to take 'the
mappe of England and of London . . . and let the river be drawne full of
shippes of all sortes, to make more shewe of your greate trade and trafficke
in trade of merchandise', in addition to 'Ortelius booke of mappes' and
'the book of the attyre of all nations' which 'woulde be much esteemed,
as I persuade myself'. The expedition should take 'bookes' (including
'the newe herbal'), 'the book of rates to the end you may pricke all those
commodities there specified that you shall chance to find in Cambalu,
in Quinsey, or in any part of the East', Parchment, Glew, Red Oker for
painters ('because we have great mines of it, and have no vent'), 'sope
of both kindes', 'Saffron . . . because this realme yeeldes the best of the
worlde, and for the tillage and other labours, may sett the poore greatly
in worke to theire relief', 'Threade of all colours . . . the vent thereof may
set our people in worke', 'copper spurres and hauks belles . . . for it may
set our people in worke', 'seedes', 'leadde of the first melting, leadd of
the second melting', 'English iron, Brymstone . . . because we abounde
of it in the realme, Antimony . . . for that we may lade whole navies of
it, and have no use of it unlesse it bee some smalle portion in founding
of belles, or a little that the Alcumistes use', 'tinder boxes with steele,
flint and matches', 'a painted bellows', 'a pot of cast iron . . . for that it is
a naturall commoditie of this realme', 'all maner of edge tools . . . to be
sold there or to the lesse civill people by the way'.

Hakluyt junior inherited the distinction between 'civill' and 'less civill'
peoples and cultures from his mentor, and, like him, he took a long
view with regard to both, never losing sight of the axiomatic purpose
of and reason for colonization. 'If you find any Island or maine land
populous', wrote Old Hakluyt, and 'that the same people hath neede of
cloth, then are you to devise what commodities they have to purchase
(it)'. Merchants would naturally 'indeavour to learne what commodities
the countrie there hath. For if you bring thither velvet, taffeta, spice, or
any such commodities that you yourself desire to lade yourselfe home
with, you must not sell yours dear, least hereafter you purchase theirs
not so cheap as you would.' With regard to 'civill' peoples, trade might
be fostered without conquest, but merchants should not neglect military
intelligence. They should take 'a speciall view' of their navy, note 'the
force of the walles and bulwarkes of their cities, their ordinaunce, and

whether they have any calivers, and what powder and shot, what armour they have, what swords, what pikes, halbertes and billes, what horses of force, and what light horses, and so throughout, to note the force of the countrey, both by sea and by lande'. But if 'the Savage . . . be poore, then you are to consider of the soile, and how by any possibilitie the same may be made to inrich them, that heerafter they may have something to purchase the cloth withall'.[89] If they currently enjoyed a way of life which had never felt need for cloth or any other English commodities, their mode of production was to be changed in such a way as to create in them such needs.[90] Here is the difference between capitalism and empire: capitalism is when conversion and trade can be effected without undue violence and expensive occupation; empire is when they cannot.

Young Hakluyt would also urge the founders of English colonies to enjoy and maintain good relations with the people found in control of the territories, islands and oceans that had been and would be 'discovered' – if they could. But the natives of foreign countries, in general, were not to be trusted. 'For all their fair and cunning speeches', he wrote, 'they are great liars and dissemblers':

To handle them gently, while gentle courses may be found to serve, it will be without comparison the best: but if gentle polishing will not serve, then we shall not want numerous and rough masons enough, I mean our old soldiers trained up in the Netherlands, to square them to our Preachers' hands.[91]

In Young Hakluyt's analysis, the people found in possession of the territories conquered by the English, savages, heathens and catholics, may not subject themselves willingly. They may have to be coerced into adopting the mental world that would make them willing consumers of the commodities that drove the wheels of English capitalism. The practical implications of Old Hakluyt's master-plan were becoming clearer. The

[89] 'Which way the Savage may be made able to purchase our cloth and other their wants', *ibid.*, 104.

[90] 'Yf they will not suffer us to have any Commodieites of theres without Conqueste which doeth require long time, yet may we maynteyn our first voyadges by the sea fishing on the Coasts there. Yf we fynde any kinges readye to defende their Tirratoryes by warre and the Countrye populous desiering to expell us that seeke but just and lawfull Traffique, then by reason the Ryvers be lardge and deepe and we lordes of navigacion, and they without shipping, we armed and they naked, and at continuall warres with one another, we maye by the ayde of those ryvers joyne with this kinge here or that kinge there at our pleasure and soe with a few men be revenged of any wronge offered by them and consequentlye maye yf we will conquere fortefye and plante . . . And in the end to bringe them all in subjection or scyvillitie . . . ': 'Pamphlet for the Virginia Enterprise ascribed to Richard Hakluyt Lawyer', Taylor (ed.), *Original Writings*, vol. 2, 342.

[91] R. Hakluyt the younger, *Epistle Dedicatorie to the Council of Virginia* (1609), in Taylor (ed.), *Original Writings*, vol. 2, 503.

first generations of English colonization were the rational savages, armed with a plan so simple and elegant it could not be forgotten: *conquer, convert, trafike*. All that remained was to do it.

If cloth could even be sold to the 'savages' of 'Virginia', how much more important were markets which were already civilized, but were at present served by the manufactures of England's rivals. Nor was it just a matter of immediate transactions. When the voyagers arrived in China, they were 'to remember to note especially what excellent dying they use in these regions, and therefore to note their garments and ornaments of houses: and to see their die houses and the materialles, for that it may serve this clothing realme to great purpose'. The same year (1582) Hakluyt issued a 'briefe remembraunce of things to be indevoured at Constantinople, and other places in Turkey, touching our clothing and dying . . . and touching ample vent of our naturall commodities, & of the labour of our poor people withall, and of the generall enriching of this Realme'.[92] His correspondent had just been appointed to serve the Turkey Company as their agent in Constantinople, capital of the Eastern Mediterranean.

Hakluyt's instructions were as detailed as his inventories. The agent was to get hold of seeds or roots of 'Anile, wherewith we colour Blew'. These were to be brought back to England, where experiments would be conducted in growing it. The agent should find out how the Turkish dyers 'compounded' the colours for which they were famous, and obtain 'all other herbes used in dying, & their naturall places, to be brought into this realm . . . and all trees, plants and bushes serving this use'. No detail should escape him, down to all the 'earths and minerals forren used in dying, and their naturall places, for possibly the like may be here [i.e. in England] be found upon sight'. The objective was clear enough: 'to bring in [to England] the excellency in the art of dying' in which Turkish clothmakers then led the world.

As he wrote in another memorandum, probably written later the same year,[93] there were a number of reasons why England could and should lead the world in the manufacture and marketing of woollens. England 'naturally' (though not yet in fact) produced the softest, strongest, most durable and 'most apte of nature to receive Die' fine wool in the world. 'No wool is less subject to moths.' And lest the main point was missed he

---

[92] His nephew the Preacher included it in the second, two-volume edition of the *Principall Navigations* (1598–1600, repr. in Taylor (ed.), *Original Writings*, vol. 1, 182–3).

[93] 'Remembrance for Master S to give him the better occasion to inform himself of some things in England, and after of some other things in Turkie, to the greate profite of the common weale of this country, written . . . for a principall English factor at Constantinople, 1582', Taylor (ed.), *Original Writings*, vol. 2, 184–95.

added that 'there is no commoditie of this Realme that may set so many poor subjects on worke . . . , that doeth bring in so much treasure, and so much enrich(es) the merchant . . . as this commodity of wool doeth'. It was the factor's patriotic duty to do everything in his power to further it, for 'the common weale of England requiers ample vent of this noble and rich commodity'.

The English cloth industry had very significant natural advantages over its competitors:

But if forren nations turne their wools, inferior to ours, into truer and more excellent made cloth, and shall die the same in truer, surer, and more excellent, and more delectable colours, then shall they sell and make ample vent of their clothes when the English cloth of better wool shall rest unsold, to the spoyle of the Merchant, of the Clothier and the breeder of the wooll, and to the turning to bag and wallet [beggary] of the infinite number of poor people imployed in clothing in several degrees of labour here in England.[94]

Thus in addition to his invaluable activities in the realm of industrial espionage, when it came to marketing English cloth, the agent should take care that only the finest, most assiduously crafted material should be exported, so that it would build a deserved reputation for excellence. To be assured of the finest cloth, it was necessary to have a detailed understanding of the labour process and its potential corruptions. Before he left, he should 'know wooll, what kinds of cloths and all other imployments of wooll, home or forren'. Then he should perfect his knowledge of the manufacture of cloth, and, above all, of 'all the deceits in clothmaking; as the sorting together of wools of severall natures, some of nature to shrink, some to hold out, which causeth cloth to cockle and lie uneven'. He should watch out for any hint of 'the evil sorting of good and bad wool, some tootoo [sic] hard spun, some tootoo soft spun, delivered to be woven' in the same cloth.

Like many other Elizabethan governors, Old Hakluyt was gravely concerned about the quality of English commodities. With regard to cloth, he observed, self-defeating corruption went on at every stage in the manufacturing process: in weaving, walking (fulling), rowing and burling (removing knots and lumps), and, particularly notorious, 'in Racking the Clothes above measure in the Teintures' (overstretching). The Factor could learn of these corrupt practices from honest craftsmen or merchants, and cloth that was even faintly suspicious was 'to be shunned'. This was Hakluyt's passion, and he may have allowed himself to become a little prolix. The basic point was pretty obvious: give us the means to

[94] 'Remembrance for Master S', 185–6.

make better cloth than the Turks make, and show us how to sell it to them.

The agent should learn from English dyers in order to 'discerne all kinds of colours' made in England already. There was a double purpose in discovering the names of all the substances 'used in dying in this Cittie (London) or in the Realme . . . which are good, which bad and what colours they die, what prices, which are naturall here, and the forren materials used':

These things superficially learned in the Realme before you go, you are the fitter in forren parts to serve your Countrey, for by this means you have an enterie into the things I wish you to travell in.

Only by knowing the quality, type and colour of cloth that was currently manufactured in England, could the Factor recognize what the English cloth industry could not yet do, but might achieve by the efforts of men like him. He was to send home 'mowsters' (samples) of dyed Turkish cloth to be analysed at Dyers Hall, in London. This was a salutary exercise, for it would 'remove out of their heads, the tootoo great opinion [English Dyers had of] themselves', in order 'to moove them to shame to indevour to learn more knowledge to the honour of their countrey'.

He was willing to concede that English dyers were expert in the manufacture of green and yellow cloths, but even here there was a lesson to be learned. 'Olde' and 'Greenweed', sources of these colours, grew 'naturally' in England and as a result some ill-informed fellows thought that green and yellow were England's natural colours. But what they thought were indigenous resources, were in fact nothing of the kind, like Saffron, which was brought to Saffron Walden by a medieval pilgrim who risked his life to smuggle it home. Nearer to their own time was the enterprise of one of Elizabethan England's great holy men, archbishop Grindal, currently in disgrace with the queen and under house arrest for refusing to suppress preaching and other forms of evangelical protestant 'prophecying'.

Hakluyt seems to have assumed that his correspondent would be impressed by a story about the economic initiative enterprise of this hero of evangelical reformation. At the death of Mary Tudor Grindal 'returned out of Germany' whence he 'brought into this realme the plante of Tamariske'. An even more recent example was 'the seed of Tobacco, (which) hath bene brought hither out of the West Indies'. Potatoes would not arrive until later in the decade, when successful experiments in growing it were conducted on Sir Francis Drake's Irish estates.

If the point of the exercise was still unclear, the Factor was to remember the example of the greatest of all imperialists, the Romans, who 'brought from all the coasts of the world into Italie all arts and sciences, and all kinds of beasts and fowles . . . that might doe the realme good':

And if this care had not been heretofore in our ancestors, then had our life bene savage now, for we had not Wheat nor Rye, Peaze nor Beanes, Barley nor Oates, Peare nor Apple, Vine nor many other profitable and pleasant plants.

The Hakluyts wanted a free international trade in goods and information, centred on London, to make life better for all English people – for hundreds of thousands of clothworkers, or for merchants, or gentry: in short, for 'all sortes and degrees of our nacion'. He saw beneath the glorious façade of Roman civilisation to the industry and *trafike* that it had sustained, and that had sustained it.

If Turkey produced any commodity 'not made in this realme, that is there of great use', a sample should be sent back, 'that our people may fall into the trade, and prepare the same for Turkie'. And of course this was true above all of cloth:

for the more kinds of cloth we can devise to make, the more ample vent of our commoditie we shall have, and the more sale of the labour become idle and burdenous to the common weale, and hurtful to many: and in England we are in our clothing trade to frame our selves according to the desires of foreign nations . . . But with this proviso alwayes, that our cloth passe out with as much labour of our people as may be had . . . [95]

Finally, the most subtle and decisive mysteries of manufacturing were in the mind, eye and hand of craftworkers bred up with the working of special materials which required special, intuitive (or second nature) skills. Importing samples and treatises on the theory of 'arts and sciences', and the raw materials to which they were applied, was not enough. Turkish artisans alone possessed the secrets, not only of ingredients, but their own special 'mysteries' of mixing, preparing and dying. Thus the Factor must 'carry (back to England) an apte young man brought up in the Arte . . . one for Silkes, and another for Wooll'. And if he was unable to perform this essential task 'by ordinary meanes', then he was 'to work it by some great Bassa's (Pasha's) means (or through the French ambassador)'. At any rate, he was to 'leave no meane unsought that tendeth to this end'. It is not clear that this instruction excluded kidnapping. Or the agent might consider purchasing a slave bred up in the mysteries of clothmaking and dyeing.

The English cloth industry had many natural advantages, which Hakluyt drew to his correspondent's attention. It had 'great and blessed

---

[95] *Ibid.*, 190–1.

abundance of victuals' to breed up and sustain its labouring population. Its temperate climate, he pointed out, made it possible to work hard all the year round. 'The clothiers in Flanders by the flatness of their rivers cannot make Walkmills (fulling mills)...but are forced to thicken and dress all...by the foot and by the labour of men, whereby their clothes are raised to an higher price.' England had an abundance of raw materials like fuller's earth. But none of this justified complacency. 'We need...oyl', he reminded his correspondent, to replace olive oil, which had to be imported from the Mediterranean. The task facing his correspondent was to increase England's comparative advantages by replacing imported goods. 'It is written by one that wrote of Afrike', he wrote, 'that in Egypt...there be many milles imployed in making of oyl of the seede of an herbe called Sesamun'. The Factor was to obtain seeds for planting, and learn the exact details of the production of sesame seed oil.

Old Hakluyt's principles of political economy were very simple. 'Our cloth', and all commodities, he wrote, must always 'pass out (of the country) with as much labour of our people as may be'.

For...as it were greatest madness to vent (sell) our wooll not clothed, so it were madness to vent our wool in part or in the whole turned into broadcloth, if we might vend the same in kerseys (dyed and finished cloths): for there is great...profit to our people between the clothing of a sack of wooll, (and) I wish the merchants of England to have as great care as they may for the universall benefit of the poore; and the turning of a sack of wool into bonnets is better than both...

Hakluyt's Law was that domestic manufactures hold the key to prosperity and power. This has become an axiom of economics, exerting incomparable influence today on national and international politics. To trade, it was necessary to have something to sell; manufactures employed more people than the production of raw materials; a nation with more people is a more powerful nation. Empire was dependent on industry, and vice versa.

7.5   England is not bounded by its horizon: the 'theorick part of commerce'

Even as early as 1582, the point of all this detailed planning was to ameliorate, and if possible to banish altogether, that very modern obsession, unemployment. Hakluyt's purpose was to encourage his correspondent 'to do your country good'. 'If you have any inclination to such good, [you will] do more good to the poor ready to starve for reliefe, then ever any subject did in this realme by building of Almshouses, and by giving of lands and goods to the reliefe of the poore.' The successful completion of the tasks Old Hakluyt set his agent would be 'of more worth then all the golde of Peru and of all the West Indies'.[96]

Old Hakluyt's writings show him to have been one of the first to recognize the importance of manufacturing industry to the common weal of England. Improving the manufacture of English woollen cloth, and finding new overseas markets for it, was his main obsession. His strategy assumed that the livelihoods of significant numbers of English people depended on manufacturing. Their very survival depended on the sale, or 'vend' as they put it, of their commodities. If vend failed, people died. If vend failed completely, as happened at least once in every generation between the reigns of Henry VI and Charles II, a third of England's people were threatened. This was catastrophic for all English people, rich or poor, and if markets were not found soon population would decline, even to the extent, eventually, that they might lose the capacity to defend their territory. This was a very potent argument in the 1580s, when rumours and intelligence of Spanish invasion forces were routine. At a pinch, it could be argued that England's fragile independence depended on its manufacturing sector. Therefore everything should be done to create and maintain markets for English manufactures.

Like every part of the English economy not involved in the production of food and drink, the many districts and regions of England involved in the cloth industry were poised on the brink of deep crisis in the 1580s.[97] Precise estimates of the proportion of England's population that was directly affected by any failure of markets mattered less than the fact that Hakluyt could take for granted a certain public awareness of what the cloth industry was all about. It meant, first, all the people with occupations and interests that depended on the trade in cloth, wool and all the other raw and processed materials involved in the industry from the breeding and farming of sheep to the spinners and carders, weavers and journeymen, fullers, dyers, finishers, clothiers, agents, factors and immensely wealthy London merchants who served as middlemen between the manufacturing districts and the national and international markets. As with the mining industry of the twentieth century, whole districts of Elizabeth's kingdom depended on the cloth trade. If the cloth they made could not be sold the communities (and many of the workers and their families) would die. Thousands of farming families grew rich feeding these 'industries in the countryside'. Old Hakluyt

---

[96] *Ibid.*, 195.   [97] See above, Chapter 6.

believed that England's fragile prosperity could not survive the collapse of its cloth industry.

Men at the pinnacle of the English status hierarchy, nobles as caricatured in the character of *Coriolanus* (1609), the bastard feudal courtiers whose companionship at court the queen preferred, had difficulty grasping the economic priorities and perspectives employed by counsellors like Old Richard Hakluyt. There was no shortage of voices willing to offer knowledgeable advice about industry and trade, but England was, in the reign of Elizabeth, and perhaps for the last time, governed by a monarchy and aristocracy, for whom industry was an inherently servile occupation – perhaps the most servile of all. Commercial advice reached them via the stewards of their own estates, and as courtiers via the intelligence networks of Secretary Walsingham. The English business community was beginning to conduct publicity campaigns, and to formulate measured and rational accounts of the importance, in foreign and domestic affairs, of the manufacturing and extractive industries. But the average courtier's world view was not, finally, able to comprehend that as servile a vocation as trade really mattered in the final scheme of things. Underlying it all was the nagging fear that the world of the commonalty was invading the realm of rule, for which nobility was the necessary qualification. This matter of commoners trespassing on the ground of the nobility 'was no matter invented and sett downe by authority for the bettering of that state of the people, but rather by the substelty [sic] of them and the simplicity of gentlemen'.[98]

The queen prided herself on her knowledge of and sympathy with the common people, and was always interested in projects that would make them more prosperous. In order to get to the queen a subject had first to pass the scrutiny of a courtier. Old Hakluyt's scheme had natural supporters at court. Elizabeth's courtiers were an unusually talented, glory-loving, and above all pugnacious breed, who loved to hear plans which involved falling upon and inflicting defeats on over-mighty foreign enemies, especially Spaniards, and (in this decade in particular) above all, Catholics. There were not many foreigners Elizabeth's courtiers were not in favour of attacking, should favourable circumstances arise. Any plan that involved systematically defeating and robbing foreign enemies would have their ear, even if (after much expostulating and breast-beating) they had to admit to its impracticality. Old Hakluyt's plans appealed to the pugnacious glory-seeking side of Elizabeth's courtiers, and to the piety of English protestants in the population at large, who sought comfort in

---

[98] *The State of England Anno Dom. 1600 by Thomas Wilson*, ed. F.J. Fisher (London 1925), 38–9 and *passim*.

the idea that no matter how bad things were for them, they were God's chosen people and had a mission to perform.

In Old Hakluyt's vision, the advancement of industry was more worthwhile than anything the merchants could bring back. The object of the exercise was to conquer markets for the products of English industry. In essence, Old Hakluyt's priorities were exactly those which Marx affirmed as the basis of industrial capitalism, except that like the seventeenth-century political economists from whom he worked out his periodization of the stages of capitalist development in England, Marx tended to underestimate the degree to which industrial production in the modern (though not the 'factory') sense, had penetrated into the fabric of sixteenth-century England. The early mercantilists' pamphlets are in fact propaganda deriving from the epic vision of England's mission propagated by Old Hakluyt's nephew, the Preacher, whose career was financed from start to finish by the London Clothworkers Company. It was the heroic side that appealed to the London merchants' monopolies, and this was the side that their propagandists emphasized in their tracts. Dudley Digges probably had Hakluyt in mind when, in 1615, he wrote that 'stories can shew us which we may reade in the Courses of Common Weales, how tolerable, nay how laudable it is in all States, to enlarge Commerce'.[99] In Digges, and in Thomas Mun's *A Discourse of Trade* (1621), there are only the briefest passing references to 'the sale of oure owne Staple merchandise . . . Cloth, Lead, Tin'. For Mun, only what merchants brought in from outside resulted in 'encrease of the common-stocke'. 'Cloth, Lead, Tin, or any of our own Merchandize', i.e. production, merely provided what was necessary to obtain what mattered. England had what its producers produced already. What mattered was what was added to what England had already. What they took from the Hakluyt blueprint was the tale of heroic and historic English merchant-explorers probing seas unknown for continents and commodities – 'Drugges, Spices, Indico, Raw-Silkes and Callicoes'[100] – imagined and, as yet, unimagined. 'Nor is England bounded by our horizon,' proclaimed Digges, 'to goe noe further than we see'. It is hardly necessary to emphasize the attraction of this side of the equation, for the vanity of merchants, and for the glory of God and the English nation. Compared to this, industry was a rather squalid business.

The merchants, urged Digges and Mun, should fly the English flag on every ocean and let the people of the world know the English are not

[99] Dudley Digges, *The Defence of Trade* (London 1615, facs. ed. New York 1968), 7.

[100] Thomas Mun, *A Discourse of Trade* (London 1621, facs. ed. New York 1969), 'Briefe Notes . . .'.

a people to mess with. This was the privateering merchant's vision of capitalism, Braudel's 'higher levels', yet we should not assume from the merchants' disdain for it that industry did not exist, or that Old Hakluyt's more balanced 'economics', in which industry was the motive power of all the rest, is not, in fact, the most realistic view. The early political economists, carried away by Young Hakluyt's propaganda, forgot Old Hakluyt's broader picture, which took in the small things that made the grand design necessary. He understood, as it were, that cloth came before currants, and that domestic policy and international relations were aspects of the same problem. It is possible that Old Hakluyt was the first Englishman to discover the fundamental law of empires, which is that for the core to maintain currently existing standards of living, it must continue to expand. I would suggest that the most important aspect of capitalism is not whether it is driven by merchants or industrialists, or by the state or by something called 'free enterprise', the 'free market', or any of the thousand abstractions trotted out by economists since Edward Misselden first defined economics as an arcane mystery, in 1623.[101] Whether or not the early modern mercantilist community saw itself as such or not, it was joined to what would one day be called 'industry' by an unbreakable connection.

Misselden's adventure in what he called 'the theorick part of commerce' was altogether more sophisticated and intellectually exciting than those of his predecessors, and carried the Hakluyt vision to a new level of abstraction. Misselden was the first to envisage reducing 'the circle of commerce' to a geometric and mathematical system, 'the balance of trade', that rested on a single axiom: exchange. 'Surely', wrote Misselden, 'it is in this kinde of *Exchange*, that one Country maketh with another in the *Balance of Trade*. All the mysteries of other Exchanges are hidde in this mystery. All the knowledge of Commerce, is presented and represented to the life in this story, in this history. All the rivers of Trade spring out of this source, and empt themselves againe to this *Ocean*. All the waight of Trade falle's to this *Center*, & come's within the circuit of this *Circle*'. This was an attempt to describe a circle encompassing the entire world, with England at its centre. At the centre, 'every *County*, yea every *City* if it will, may have the mannaging and disposing of their owne adventures, without any General or promiscuous confusion with others, and with such Immunities, priviledges, and encouragements conferr'd upon them from the fountaine of his Majesties grace, as may at last bring that to action and execution, which we have so long had in discourse

---

[101] Edward Misselden, 'To the Right Honorable, the Earle of Middlesex, Lord High Treasurer of England, &c.' Epistle Dedicatorie to *The Circle of Commerce* (London 1623; facs. ed. New York 1969).

and contemplation'. Misselden spelled out that his 'theorick part of commerce' was no more than a tighter formulation of a plan and a vision for England's future that had been unfolding for two generations since Old Hakluyt laid the groundwork of the grand theory around 1580.[102]

'A brave design it is', he continued,

> as Royall as Reall: as honourable as profitable. It promiseth Renowne to the King, Revenue to the Crowne, treasure to the Kingdome, a purchase for the land, a prize for the sea, ships for Navigation, Navigation for ships, Mariners for both: entertainment of the rich, employment for the poore, advantage for the adventurers, and encrease of Trade to all the Subjects. A Mine of Gold it is: the Mine is deepe, the veines are great, the Ore is rare, the Gold is pure, the extent unlimited, the wealth unknowne, the worth invaluable. And this is also another meanes, not inferiour unto any, for the recovery of our *Exportations*, in the *Balance of Trade*.

Every so often, historians come across words which echo. Misselden's glorious vision of *the Balance of Trade* within *the Circle of Commerce* continues to haunt the thinking of governments of the early twenty-first century.

'The theorick part of commerce', the abstract, mathematical, harmonious system as it is supposed to be, 'all other things being equal', was to become an increasingly important theme in England's attempt to convince itself that it was not out conquering the world in its own interests, and for its own reasons, but was merely enacting its part in a universal scheme. In the early seventeenth century England was still under the influence of that massive and complex millenarian movement, the Reformation. English Bibles still exerted greater influence than the cool, learned and godless prose of Edward Misselden. In the reigns of James I and Charles I, England's mission was most likely to be understood as a variant of the God's chosen people theme. Misselden's vision of mathematically interacting free trade within the circle of the world was in advance of its time. As Old Hakluyt pronounced, the goal was *Trafike*, but it was not yet time to forget completely that for trade to be really free for the English, it would be necessary to conquer and convert its peoples. Only when the peoples of the world had been conquered and/or converted, would they be able to understand that 'free trade' was good for them.

7.6   Global interdisciplinarity: Elizabethan intelligence

The utility of geography in reading and remembering histories are too apt and well known for them to need proof or recommendation from me. But geography has another

---

[102] Misselden, *Circle of Commerce*; Wrightson, *Earthly Necessities*, 204.

and much more eminent dignity (if it is rightly directed . . .), namely, in that it will contribute greatly to the knowledge of political regimes . . . (Gerard Mercator)

The fundamental premise of Old Hakluyt's strategy was to ensure that English voyagers, soldiers, sailors, explorers, missionaries, merchants, agents, diplomats, indeed all English travellers abroad, collected and brought back information about the places and countries they visited. Once it had been established that it was necessary for England to conquer, convert and trade with the world, it became a matter of practical necessity to accumulate accurate intelligence about its peoples. Elizabethan England saw the birth of a mighty impulse to discover, know, classify, and disseminate everything about the world and its peoples, those at home and those abroad, usually in vernacular English, but over time more and more frequently in the arabic numerals that were just then becoming fashionable among the university-trained men who have always been the nucleus of official intelligence-gathering in the English-speaking world.[103]

The Elizabethan discourse on method was an intellectual movement generated by an avalanche of documented evidence and discussion concerning the exact nature of the world. This new information, to be useful, had to be classified, stored and distributed to people who could use it. English people of the generation of Shakespeare, Bacon and the Hakluyts did not think about 'humanity' in universal terms. They took for granted that their information should be useful to England. If it proved useful to England, it would be copied by (or imposed upon) everyone else. What was needed was a new filing system. 'Intelligence' was flooding in. How could it be recorded in ways that made it quickly retrievable? The Hakluyt circle had clearly begun to address this issue, and its suggestions were summarized in a little pamphlet published in London in January 1589, under the title of *Certaine briefe and special Instructions for Gentlemen, merchants, students, souldiers, marriners etc. Employed in service abroad or anie way occasioned to converse in the kingdomes and governments of forren princes*.[104] The pamphlet took for granted that the English secret

---

[103] Andrew McRae, *God Speed the Plough: the Representation of Agrarian England 1500–1660* (Cambridge 1996), 58, writes that 'the Elizabethan state consistently distanced itself from moral complaint, in favour of an increasingly empirical and rationalist approach to social and economic problems'. See also Richard Helgerson, *Forms of Nationhood: the Elizabethan Writing of England* (Chicago 1992).

[104] By Philip Jones: BL; compare Bodleian Library: Rawlinson MS C878 (2), 'The polliticke Survey of a kingdom' (unsigned and undated, but written for the earl of Dunbar, a member of James I's Privy Council), which offers a guide to 'the observations . . . to be wayed by him that would be acquainted with the condition of a kingdom and the state of a princes government' that is more 'polliticke' in the sense of focused on the form of the state to be observed.

service was every English traveller abroad. It sketched out a programme for intelligence gathering that remains in place to this day, a framework of disciplines and a method still used in the training of special reconnaisance troops in modern armies, including our SAS. It was a little book of method that told every English intelligencer how to observe, what to look for, what information to bring back, and what category to put it in.

The dedication to Sir Francis Drake called it 'a small, but sweete book of Method, for men intending their profite and honour by the experience of the world . . . composed by one M. Albertus Meier . . . of Sleswike Holstein'. Followers of the method would 'enrol themselves in the Catalogue of Homer his "seers of many Regions, and of the maners of many Nations"', to which illustrious company the great circumnavigator and recent vanquisher of the Spanish Armada, Sir Francis, already belonged.

The manual was 'long-term advance publicity' for the more momentous project in which the author, Philip Jones, had been engaged since he met Richard Hakluyt at Oxford in the late 1570s. Jones was a member of the small inner sanctum of associates and printers, who helped Hakluyt to write, collect and assemble the material for his epic of English imperial traditions, the long awaited *Principal Navigations*. Professor Beers Quinn suggests that Jones 'may have played a significant part in the search for materials while Hakluyt was in France' in the early 1580s, as well as contributing his own news-sheet account of the 'worthie fight' of the Turkey Company Merchants, which Professor Quinn suggests was 'composed directly from Levant Company Records and from interviews with the seamen and merchants concerned'.[105] The 'swete book of method' outlined an essential theme, or requirement, of the strategic plan. The *Principal Navigations* would provide a vast and definitive compendium of English overseas experience; Jones's pamphlet provided English travellers with a framework for the gathering and storage of information when they were overseas.

It classified information under twelve headings – Cosmography, Astronomy, Geography, Chorography, Topography, Husbandry, Navigation, Political State, State Ecclesiastical, Literature, History and, finally, 'Chronicles'. These were the human sciences of the late sixteenth century. They aimed at constructing a rich and many-layered representation of foreign societies, for the material and cultural benefit of the home country. The Hakluyts' discipline, 'Cosmography', or 'the description of

---

[105] Professor Quinn thinks the *Principall Navigations* came out in December 1589 or January 1590, based on dating derived from *Certaine Briefe Instructions*, which he dates a year earlier, to January 1589: 'Preface' to David Beers Quinn and Raleigh Ashlin Skelton (ed.), *Principall Navigations, Voyages and Discoveries of the English Nation*, facsimile of 1589 edition (Cambridge 1965), xviii–xx.

the world', was strategic. It was the cosmographer who put all the bits and pieces of information in lucid relationship to each other. But like all the disciplines, it was conceived for practical purposes. Cosmographers identified the exact location of a place (longitude and latitude etc.), its ascription to a climatic zone ('temperate or intemperate'), the length of the day and night and so on. This was the kind of information that enabled the intelligencers of the age to locate it on their evolving maps of the world. All other information was useless if the place to which it referred could not be located again.

Under 'Astronomy', travellers were instructed to find out their host's achievements in 'the art of skill in the course of the stars'. Had their astronomers made any discoveries which English navigators could add to their maps of the skies? Maps of the stars were of even greater value to navigators than maps of the world, for beyond the sight of land they provided the only way a sailor could work out roughly where on the earth's surface his ship was in relation to its home port. Sir Francis Drake, to whom the curriculum was dedicated, would have agreed that it had its priorities right. Cosmography and Astronomy came first. Travellers should always give first priority to knowing exactly where they were.[106]

'Geography' was concerned with 'the drawing of the Earth'. Travellers abroad were specifically instructed to collect maps which might fill in gaps in their knowledge of the coasts and islands of the world. Maps were the most prized objects of international espionage, although the great English cartographers have always concentrated on mapping England itself. 'Chorography', 'the demonstration of Regions and Citties', involved defining borders, mapping the size and internal settlement of the territory – 'to what parts of the erthe it stretcheth', and 'whether (it) be much or little frequented of travellers and merchants'. It was also useful to know 'whether it be of any name or fame for power, welthe, force, multitude of people'. These were important variables, for they would determine how best to make them serve English purposes. A powerful empire like China, for example, would require different strategies than the acquisition of land from peripatetic hunters and gatherers. How developed was the country's commerce? Visitors were to ascertain if they had market towns, 'places of resort and trafike', where they were, and what goods they habitually dealt in.

'Topographie' invited the traveller to carry a sketching-pad, and provide a 'portraiture of particular places'. Under 'Husbandrie' he was instructed to analyse the country's agriculture. Under this heading, travellers would record information ranging from the times of seasons,

---

[106] See Dava Sobel, *Longitude* (London 1996).

prevailing winds, chief places and dwellings of health, 'unwholesome airs' and 'ill winds', the longevity of the people, the quality and elevation of land, the composition of soils, arboriculture and orcharding, 'wild beasts', 'parks and warrens', to the type and availability of fish. They might have information on 'Navigation' that English navigators did not yet possess; assessing their knowledge in this field would also signal whether a country was likely to provide serious competition for English shipping and trade.

The method emerged from certain fundamental questions: what do they know that we do not? What can they do and make that we cannot? The aim was to borrow unashamedly, reproduce the source's goods more cheaply using English labour, and drive out local industry by selling its workers English goods. The second task involved discovering everything there was to know about new people and new lands – 'intelligence' in the more conventional sense – which would clearly be useful in infiltrating the country with English commerce, and, if the opportunity was there, colonizing it.[107] Knowledge of this sort, combined with the adventurous spirit embodied in Hakluyt's *Voyages*, was a recipe for global power. It would not guarantee it, but without it, overseas trade and empire were, literally, unthinkable.

Information on 'Political State' and 'State Ecclesiastical' was classified under no less than fifty different sub-headings, many of which have entire modern disciplines associated with them. Traditional (Aristotelian) categories were useful in preliminary classification. Was the country 'a monarchie... as in England, France, Spain, Scotland etc.'; or 'an Aristocracy, that is the government of the better sort, as of old in Athens and Lacedemon'; or was it a 'Democratie, that is a popular regimen as among the cantons of Zurich'? Was it corrupt? Did it resemble any of Aristotle's 'contraries... whether a tyranny or an oligarchie which is a tumultuous and disordered confusion'? It is assumed that the reader has read Aristotle's *Politics*. If not, perhaps he should do so before setting out on his travels.

The pamphlet anticipates a highly complex polity that conformed to English expectations and prejudices. Exotic cultures were only beginning to encroach upon the English imagination twenty years before the first staging of *The Tempest*. The author and translator assume that any society an English intelligencer might visit would be rather like a European

---

[107] But the impulse to conquer foreign markets without the fuss and expense of 'plantations' was foremost in the Hakluyt circle: for early contemporary discussions of 'plantations', cf. David Beers Quinn, 'Sir Thomas Smith (1513–1577) and the Beginnings of English Colonial Theory'; Francis Bacon, 'On Plantations', *Essays*.

society. Is its monarchy elective or successive? Does it live by Common or Civil Law, or by some amalgam of both? How are its cities and towns governed, under what offices and titles, 'of what names, state, number, continuance in office and manner of election'? To understand its constitution it was necessary to know 'the multitude of the people, wherein consisteth much of the strength of the realme'. The first task was to estimate the total population of the country. In the next section ('State Ecclesiastical'), a method is suggested for testing more general impressions: count 'the number of churches and congregations in every city or town, whereby the populousness may be known'. This was the best available method of counting the people at a time when demography and statistics were in their infancy. But Elizabethan intelligencers were to ask questions that future political economists would put at the centre of their enterprise. The questions they were asking would be asked again.

Travellers were instructed to observe the everyday lives of the populace, the 'commonalty'. The pamphlet was not condescending to the 'multitude', as Elizabethan graduates sometimes were; it urged a more dispassionate, even empathetic point of view. Health was critical. 'Diet' and 'Clothing' would offer clues. The traveller should assess the 'wits and conceits of the people, whether quick and sharp or blunt'. A sharp, intelligent working class was more to be desired than a stolid, stupid one. What of the 'industry, studies, manners, honesty, humanity, hospitality, love and other moral virtues of the inhabitants'? This would involve a good deal of participant research, and left some questions for future anthropologists to ask. 'Industry' was worth a closer look. The traveller should pay particular attention to 'the special manuarie artificers and handicrafts of the place'. These, especially, offered the possibility of assessing the relative health and decadence of a society.

Where there is law, there is crime. What offences were most common, which were most heavily punished and which were relatively tolerated? An increasing flow of printed books now advised English people about 'the kindes and varieties of malefactors' who were likely to cross their path. Travellers should notice these things when they were abroad. They should do some criminology. Popular culture should not be neglected. Travellers (like modern and even post-modern scholars) should study the 'manners, rites and ceremonies of espousals, marriages, feasts and banquets' and their funerary customs. Sport was relevant. It couldn't hurt to know 'the variety and manner of their exercises for pastime and recreation'. The traveller must also be a social psychologist, assessing 'the disposition and spirit of the people'. This was the heart of the matter. Were they 'warlike and valiant, or faint hearted and effeminate'? Were they well or badly equipped for modern warfare: what was 'their store of military furniture and provision'? Were 'their ancestors famous for victories or infamous for cowardliness and overthrows'?

This was a very broad and deep conception of 'Political State' which anticipated a highly complex polity. Monarchy (England's state) was there at the head of the list, but as one reads on it becomes clear that much more mattered in constitutional life than its symbolic head, and other forms of government than monarchy were possible and existed. However, we should also note another potential implication of this elaborate 'method' for assessing complex polities and societies. Many of the cultures English navigators were encountering and were yet to encounter lacked the institutional forms of such societies. In fact, the recommended programme was really designed for the analysis and interpretation of European societies. These, by and large, were the questions the most powerful European nations were going to be asking about themselves, as well as of other parts of the world, for the next four centuries, during which time there would be a common tendency to assume that societies which failed to live up to this level of complexity were not societies at all.

The assumption under 'State Ecclesiastical', that the number of well-preserved churches in a kingdom was an accurate measure of its populousness, took for granted that religion was the soul of a well-regulated nation. Travellers should observe and record 'preaching, prayers and holy exercises'. How often did they take place, and, even more importantly, 'with what devotion'? The traveller should note carefully 'the greatnes or smalness of auditories, assemblies and concourse to sermons'. What was 'the number of godly preachers and ministers in the greatest cities'? How well (or badly) were the pastors of the people paid? This question was close to the heart of many graduates of Oxford and Cambridge. What were 'the disciplines of Church government'? Who were the great 'Ministers, Divines, Preachers and Clergymen of greatest pains, account, learning and judgement'? Who were the 'Archbishops and Bishops with their fees and churches, Deans, Abbots, Priors, Monks and Priests'? Was their religion 'true and reformed or Romish and superstititous'? Did 'hereticks spring up'? What were their 'names, errors, absurdities, false opinions and punishments'? Did they have 'public fasting, alms giving (and) pilgrimages'?

Modern societies have devoted an ever increasing stock of resources to the discovery, classification and conceptualization of information of this type, relating to foreign countries and to themselves. In this context, the information was to be collected by travellers overseas. But as the elder Richard Hakluyt had advised his merchants in the early years of the decade, to make the best of one's intelligence about other countries, it was first necessary to know one's own. Governments and public interest groups of all kinds today, including business interests, rely on information fed to them by a wide range of graduates in the human and social sciences: sociologists, social psychologists, students of law and politics, and historians are prominent among them. Jones's book of method foreshadows the national departmentalization of knowledge, and the expansion of the intelligence-gathering and interpretation sectors: the modern mind industry.[108]

Beginning, roughly, in the seventeenth century, European states began collecting more and more information about their subjects, and developed new (conceptual and statistical) ways of interpreting the data. Historians of late medieval and early modern England have shown that from the fifteenth century at the latest, local elites adopted an efficient and innovative approach to local government, involving new ways of managing and administering the everyday lives of the working population. The central-state perspective is not the most valuable one for understanding the complex political and governmental revolution that took place in England between the late middle ages and the Industrial Revolution (c.1300–1850). The most significant advances in government and social management took place in the localities, many of them centred on the provision and management of 'projects' by which the labouring poor could support themselves, thus not becoming a burden on their neighbours. R.H. Tawney once wrote that the most important issue in democratic politics was not the government of the state, but the government of economic enterprises. This administrative, or managerial revolution, what Foucault called a revolution in 'governmentality', had its origins among the yeomanry and citizens of the fifteenth century, who, in the absence of any sustained sense of responsibility for the common weal on the part of the king, nobles and Church, took to managing the affairs

---

[108] For Hans Magnus Enzenburger, 'The Industrialization of the Mind', *Raids and Reconstructions* (London 1973), the process 'cannot get under way until the rule of theocracy . . . is broken'; for Mary Poovey, *A History of the Modern Fact*, ch. 2, the process begins by 'accommodating merchants', but with adaptations of double-entry bookkeeping; James C. Scott, *Seeing Like a State: How Certain Schemes to Improve the Human Condition Have Failed* (New Haven 1998), 45, cites John Norden, *The Surveyer's Dialogue* (1607) as a seminal text in the emergence of the 'cadastral' approach to governmentality; Francis Bacon, *The Advancement of Learning* (New York 2001), aims to put knowledge in the service of 'human utility and power', but in a somewhat more abstract framework than in the 'politic surveys' genre, which seem to anticipate what Benedict Anderson, *The Spectre of Comparisons*, 20, calls 'country studies'. One significant difference between the 'social science' implied by the 'swete boke of method' and Enlightenment social science is that geographical (landscape) perspectives frame the disciplines: for the absence of which in modern political and social sciences, see Adam T. Smith, *The Political Landscape: Constellations of Authority in Early Complex Polities* (Berkeley and Los Angeles 2003).

of the localities as if the ruling classes did not exist. Various statutes of Henry VIII gave legitimacy to these plebeian enterprises, but, chauvinist though he was, he was also a rapacious and insensitive tyrant, which tended to weaken any impulses that may have existed at the time towards genuinely popular absolutism. On the whole, Henry VIII's reign left the yeomen and citizen classes more independent than ever.

The tide of local and district administrative documentation began to rise. Documentation relating to the government of the common people, most of it in parochial and manorial archives, greatly increased in the second half of the sixteenth century. Local collections increase in size considerably with the routinization of the poor and settlement laws that takes place after 1660 on the back of a very intense period of reform and improvement of local systems under the Commonwealth. What is a trickle of information in the sixteenth century has become, at the time of the first national census in 1801, a deluge. It is at this point that the central state began to come back into the picture, mainly by addressing itself to changes that had already taken place in the localities where the work went on. The state tried to manage and direct a commonwealth that was already in place.

The Hakluyt network was in the forefront of a great information revolution. Jones's translation of the 'book of method' sprang from the idea of new bureaucracy of knowledge. In order to become an effective instrument of state and commonwealth, the information had to be filed in strategic categories. The book of method left until last three disciplines, 'Literature', 'History' and 'Chronicles', which it saw as the core of national identity. Literature covered a very broad range of subjects, including the collection of 'ingenious epigrammes, sonets, epitaphs, orations, poems, speeches, verses, adages, proverbs and other scholastical and learned exercises'. Jones had no difficulty at all with the notion that national 'Literature' had a hard-edged practical purpose, in that it taught disciplines of language designed to make men good speakers. Because of all the research on literacy, historians are at risk of underestimating how firmly still sixteenth-century English people were rooted in oral and aural culture. As men who carried the title of 'Preacher' proudly, neither Jones nor Hakluyt was ever likely to underestimate the power of the spoken word to inspire a spirited people.

The discipline of Literature, as envisaged here, included all 'manner and kind of studies in liberall artes', but it also covered 'public and private lectures'. It was during this generation that the more secular-sounding 'lecture' and 'lecturer' began to displace sermons and preachers. Travellers were urged to evaluate the degree of excellence foreign cultures had achieved in 'the faculty of Imprinting' by counting 'the number of

Printers and Stationers', and assessing the 'degree of exactness' of their work. Jones held up the publication, in 1588, of a book of sermons, in order to include reference to six printer's errata. His work was carefully composed, and he did not want it marred by a comma in the wrong place, or a word fatally misspelled. Three printing workshops worked on Hakluyt's *Navigations*, and produced very impressive 'imprinting'. Since the printers generally shared the world view of the Hakluyt circle (and were indeed part of it), they had an added incentive to make their scholarly propaganda precise, 'exact'.

Literature included accounts of 'Alphabets', the number of 'common or publike libraries', 'persons renowned for vertue, knowledge, learning and judgement', 'ancient epitaphs and inscriptions cut, graven and carved or painted upon tombes, pillars, gates and churches', 'ancient coynes', instruments of music, geometry and 'excellent and rare articifers'. 'Diligence in government and other good partes' meant that any half-way civilized country would have a network of 'publike schools and scholemasters', and universities to teach 'discipline, wit and degrees'. They would have 'men of special learning in Divinitie, Philosophie, Arithmetick, Geometrie, Astronomie, Astrologie, Musick, Poetrie, Grammar, Hebrew, Greek, Rhetorique, Law, Physicke and (last but not least) Histories'. Item 15 under 'Literature' instructed travellers to find out how much academics were paid. Hakluyt's research assistant was trying to earn a living without a sinecure, a fate which was to affect the outlook of an increasing proportion of two more generations of potentially unemployed graduates before the civil wars, and remains an issue today.

Seekers of 'Antiquaries' also belonged to the disciplines of Literature: 'men excellently seen in antiquities and ancient monuments'. This would grow into archaeology and palaeoanthropology among other disciplines. It is not overstating the matter to say that Elizabethan England began a massive inventory of its own ancient monuments, signalling the birth of a passion for national heritage that is still with us. How did foreign countries compare? Were their landscapes littered with signs of ancient glories?

It is a strange discipline until we see the common element. Literature, in this account, includes *all* the ways a society represents itself: on coins, in massive architecture, in verse, inscriptions, long barrows and Roman milestones. The field that most resembles it today is cultural studies, but it is even broader than the modern discipline in that it does not exclude the study of 'men of special learning' and canonical figures. Travellers were encouraged to 'read the signs' of foreign cultures. In societies in which it was assumed that at least two-thirds of people could neither read nor write, it would be a puny national 'Literature' that included only printed books.

Knowledge about the past was divided into two disciplines. 'Histories' were 'to be searched' for accounts of the states men made, whereas 'Chronicles' lumped popular rebellions with other unpredictable interveners in and disrupters of the courses of secular states like plagues and earthquakes. 'Histories' were dignified, formal, official accounts of the lives of great men and narratives of great events. Histories asked who the 'first inhabitants' were and what were the 'antiquities and originalls of the cities, towns and kingdom'? Were they Christian? When were they converted to Christianity? Who were the first builders of great towns and cities? Travellers should report on the 'Prince now living', recite his 'royal line', describe 'the fortitude, behaviour, magnanimity, discipline and fame of the ancient nobility', and give the names of 'ancient families'. If other countries were like England, the technical rulers, the ancient nobility and gentry, wouldn't always provide 'the chiefest men of policy'. It was a blueprint for a magisterial historiography that studies elites and assumes that the history of statecraft is all. It included international relations and diplomacy – the study of 'old wars' and 'affinities and alliances'.

'Chronicles', on the other hand, recorded forces and agencies which disrupted the orderly processions of state: 'seditions, rebellions, conspiracies, insurrections and tumults', 'mischiefs, losses, and detriments by accident of fire', 'dearthes, famines and extremities of want of corne and graine, and how long the scarcity endured', 'sickness and pestilence that have happened in any countrey, cittie or towne: the beginning and cause of them, their continuance, end, and mortality of the people'. Chronicles covered political interventions by the commonalty and what we still call 'acts of God': natural disasters like bush fires, famines, climatic disasters, epidemics and mortality crises. They recorded what governments, as yet, could neither predict nor control, but only endure. The odd man out here is rebellion. On this account, the age saw rebellions as interventions of divine providence, signs from God that his will and the common good were not being served. One of the reasons the regimes of that epoch were so intensely preoccupied with rebellions of the people was that the people were seen as agents and signs of God. The distinction between chronicles and history suggested that they dealt with subjects that were different in type. History was about leaders and ruling classes, who governed and how. It dealt with a special class or caste of people whose function was to govern. They differed by heredity and learning from the common people, the subject population. For the subject population to intervene in matters of government and policy was against nature, and could thus only be explained as an intervention of supernatural powers. The power of states to resist or cope with public murmuring, riot and rebellion, was, like vagaries of climate and earthquakes, known to be limited. Rebellion belonged in the same category as 'great frosts, deep snows, thick and monstrous yce', 'hot and burning summers', 'lightnings and thunders', 'storms and tempests', 'inundations, deluges, overflowings, breakings in of the seas, when, where, by what occasions or negligence'. All were interventions in human affairs of inexplicable and unpredictable supernatural forces. The more there were, the angrier God was with the state in question. 'Strange and memorable events', 'births of monsters', 'prodidgious signs and apparitions in the ayre', 'comets, blazing stars, great and extraordinary eclipses', 'earthquakes and their consequences' were all clues to the mind of God. Chronicles were about the forces which states had to contend with or propitiate, the forces of change. The horsemen of the apocalypse still rode in England in the 1580s, and one of their instruments was rebellion.

Wicked peoples were punished by 'social diseases'. 'Notable pyracies' and 'egregious theeveries and robberies' (as it were 'internal' and 'external' crimes) would be met 'with the judgements of God and the Law upon such persons'. Travellers should chronicle 'the horrible and just ends of malefactors'. How frequent were executions, and what methods were used? Chronicles included, finally, 'the perpetual care of the Prince to withstand all the policies, inventions, invasions, violences, hostilities and indignities of other princes and to preserve the realme and people in peace, tranquillity, security and prosperitie'. We have seen that English chronicles did not always show this. They contained many examples when this was not seen to be the case, and suggested that this was the real reason for rebellion.

With the little book of method in their pockets, Jones's Englishmen travelled with an impressive array of intellectual disciplines, beginning with the subjects of greatest certainty (cosmographie to literature) and ending with those of greatest uncertainty (history and chronology), where the fallibility of human ingenuity stumbled against the unpredictable contingency of realms Elizabethans thought could not be understood and controlled because they were beyond nature and history. When 'the sword of the Lord was upon the land', it was the task of divine preachers to read the signs, and teach the people what to do. 'Euerie true Minister is the Lords watch-man, and therupon bound by the hand of obedience towards God, to blow the Trumpet, and warne the people, when he seeth the sword of the Lord come uppon the land, that is, the Plague of Pestilence, dearth, Famine, War.' Thus spoke another voice of the movement in 1609.[109]

---

[109] GRO Hyett Collection, Pamphlet 351: *A Sermon Upon the XII, XIII, and Verses of the XIII Chapter of Ezechiel, Wherein are chiefly shewed both the original and accidental causes*

If the task of the soon to be published book on which he was working with the younger Hakluyt at this time was to inspire the English people to continue a great tradition of voyaging expeditions, explorations and overseas conquests that went back to the days of king Arthur, the book of method told them what intelligence to gather when they got there. It envisaged a much vaster body of yet to be accumulated knowledge that would follow in the wake of the voyages. The physical, human and social sciences (not yet seen as inherently different and unrelated bodies of knowledge) are still struggling to come to terms with the vast information flows that schemes like that envisaged by the Hakluyt circle set in motion.

This gathering tide of documented information represents one of the most remarkable and significant movements in the history of the early modern state. Familiarity with this overflowing archive should make us at least sceptical about suggestions that England was the least governed and most free society in Europe. For the middle and upper ranks a case might be mounted. The revolution in governmentality, if that is what the widening flood of archival evidence does in fact represent, was principally if not exclusively concerned with the government of the labouring and mechanic classes, who, by the end of the seventeenth century, constituted a good half of the population. As Marx claimed in the famous appendix to *Capital*, Volume 1, the labouring classes of England had never been monitored and governed in more routine and detailed ways than they were, progressively, from the sixteenth to the late eighteenth centuries. And as Foucault maintained, the discourses which became the modern Human and Social Sciences were deeply implicated in this intensification of governmentality which marks the history of the modern state.

The book of method called for systematic collection of data about foreign societies, but it was impossible to read it in the 1580s without immediately seeing that it was tailor-made for the comprehension of English society. The disciplines of modern knowledge began as instruments of states and commonwealths and only later mutated into supposedly 'universal' disciplines.

A revolution was taking place in the organization and collection of 'intelligence', and in its dissemination, via the increasingly ubiquitous written and printed word. The existence, perhaps for the first time in so systematic a fashion, of the intriguing government espionage networks of Elizabethan England is a symptom of the larger movement in England of

of euerie dearth and famine, and especially of this dearth in England now 1608 and 1609. With the effects and fruit of the same, as also the helpes & remedies therof, if they may be speedily and effectually practised. Preached at Strowd in the Countie of Glocester and published for the good of the church melitant By William WOODALL, Minister and Preacher of the Word. 1609: London. Printed by EA for Ed. White, & are to be solde at his shop neere the little North doore of St Paules Church at the Signe of the Gunne, 1609.

information about itself and the rest of the world.[110] The conjuncture of all this information includes the activities of Tudor chroniclers, chorographers, mapmakers, writers of histories and news-sheets, the skills and perspectives of whom, in Jones's book of method, were to be learned by all English travellers and applied to the analysis and registering of information about every place and society they found themselves in. In the immediate future, problems would arise not in the availability and collection of information, of which there would be too much. The solution was the evolution of systematic disciplines and methods for recovering and interpreting the data, and experts with time to devote to every specialist field. This discourse on method was a manifesto for what were to become the modern Humanities and Social Sciences. Before then, they just exploded – following the maxim laid down by the elder Richard Hakluyt in the early 1580s: *conquer, convert, trafike.*

The blueprints for a new age of information began to appear in the sixteenth century, were sifted and synthesized by the generations of Bacon, Hobbes and Petty in the seventeenth, and came to a head in the late eighteenth century, in the rising tide of documents containing data about the population individually, and as an aggregate. Stage two, building on Bacon and Hobbes and organized under the auspices of the Royal Society, began in the second half of the seventeenth century with the efforts of men like Petty, Graunt and Gregory King, to create a new discipline called Political Arithmetic. Stage three encompassed the creation of state and other organizational bureaucracies (including schools and universities) whose main or exclusive function was to propagate and interpret data and synthesize it into reports which the powerful could translate into action – or not, as the case may be. Stage four, characteristic of the 'post-modern' state, involves the supplementation of police with electronic surveillance, bureaucrats with cross-linked electronic data-processing machines, and lecturers on television. The choice remains: no matter how much and how good one's information, it has to be interpreted. Decisions have to be made about what, if anything, to do with it. No-one offered a more devastatingly simple answer to this question than the two Richard Hakluyts.

---

[110] Cf. John Bossy, *Giordano Bruno and the Embassy Affair* (New Haven 1991); Charles Nicholls, *The Reckoning: the Murder of Christopher Marlowe* (London 1992).

Part IV

The empowered community

8 'The first pace that is sick': the revolution of politics in Shakespeare's *Coriolanus*

> *His nature is too noble for the world...*
> *His heart's his mouth.*
> *What his breast forges, that his tongue must vent.*
> (*Coriolanus* III, i, 257–8)

8.1 'Take but degree away'

Elizabethan and Jacobean England offered other new ways of assimilating and interpreting information. Shakespeare's *Coriolanus* represents a world where politics explode out of narrow, institutional, prescribed limits, and engulf the whole community. The play gives us another way of looking at the revolutionary transition from elite to popular politics. Its setting is ancient Rome and its context is early modern England. Shakespeare feared that something that we might call 'politics' was happening in Jacobean England. The play's motif is that hoariest of all political metaphors, the body politic. It transports its audience to the legendary source of a metaphor that had been a reflex of popular and learned political discourse for centuries. According to Livy, Shakespeare's ultimate source, the oracle was a certain Roman Senator, Menenius Agrippa, in 493 BCE. *Coriolanus* pursues the primeval political idea further than any of his learned or popular predecessors, perhaps to the point of absurdity. The body politic described in the play is not just limbs and organs, as it was for John of Salisbury and his 'sources', Plutarch and Pope Adrian, or for the earliest surviving version in English, written c.1400. Shakespeare's body politic has mercurial emotions, sexual proclivities, and stinks. On the evidence of the poetic imagery, the mood of the author seems to have been one of disgust. That would make Shakespeare's political position neither Left, nor Right, but 'a plague on both your houses'. Or even better, why not both at once? The popular and noble parties were evenly balanced in early Stuart England. Shakespeare clearly felt a strong attraction for the dialectics of noble virtue and popular debunking. Can noble honour survive plebeian contempt and mockery?

Shakespeare's attention was not on the decline of nobility alone or the *res plebeia* alone, but on the field of forces, how the very existence of the one constantly affected and undermined the other. It was in Shakespeare's generation that the evolving field of forces explored in this book began to take sharp intellectual form. *Coriolanus* was Shakespeare's book of 'politick counsell'.

The location of the play is the birth of the Roman Republic. *Coriolanus* complements *Julius Caesar*, describing the beginning to Caesar's ending of a type of government – a senatorial and later a popular republic – that had lasted half a millennium. If Rome could be a republic, England could be too. No matter how often theologians, nobles and monarchs insisted that the social order of Tudor England was divinely ordained, experience suggested otherwise. The idea that constitutions were divinely ordained had been summarily dismissed by Sir John Fortescue over a century before Shakespeare was born. As we have seen, Fortescue's successor Sir Thomas Smith took the contingency and changeability of human constitutions for granted.

Shakespeare defined Elizabethan England's 'world we have lost' in what has become the definitive English elegy on the universe as Sir Thomas Elyot had defined it: the infinite hierarchy of 'degree'. The words are spoken by Ulysses in Act I, Scene iii of *Troilus and Cressida*.

> *Take but degree away, untune that string,*
> *And hark what discord follows. Each thing meets*
> *In mere oppugnancy. The bounded waters*
> *Should lift their bosoms higher than the shores*
> *And make a sop of all this solid globe;*
> *Strength should be lord of imbecility,*
> *And the rude son should strike his father dead;*
> *Force should be right, or rather right and wrong,*
> *Between whose endless jar justice resides,*
> *Should lose their names, and so should justice too;*
> *Then everything include itself in power,*
> *Power into will, will into appetite.*
> *And appetite, an universal wolf,*
> *So doubly seconded with will and power,*
> *Must make perforce an universal prey*
> *And last eat himself up. Great Agamemnon,*
> *This chaos, when degree is suffocate,*
> *Follows the choking.*
> *And this neglection of degree it is*
> *That by a pace goes backward with a purpose*
> *It hath to climb. The general's disdain'd*
> *By him one step below, he by the next,*
> *That next by him beneath; so every step,*

Exampled by the first pace that is sick
Of his superior, grows to an envious fever
Of pale and bloodless emulation...

That Ulysses is able to describe its effects with such tragic lucidity means, in itself, that the principle of degree is doomed. It is testimony to the truth of its own propositions. Ideology only works when its axioms are taken for granted. Envy and social mobility invade an epic world that is held together only by degree.[1] The pyramid is shaken to its foundations by an 'envious fever of pale and bloodless emulation'. The spell of degree is broken, the fever spreads: 'The general's disdain'd by him one step below, he by the next, that next by him beneath . . .' and so on, until the whole great hierarchy disintegrates from within. *Coriolanus* is about what happens when the principle of degree, finally, loses its grip on the minds of the English (or any) people; the moment when, for whatever reasons, they no longer believe in it. Shakespeare gives his version of the moment when politics began, and the force-field from which they emerged.

Take degree (or *virtu*) away, and you get politics as Bernard Crick defined it.[2] The lying noble, Ulysses, like Nietzsche, sees it as a tragic degeneration into anarchy, universal competition. Mindless and Godless appetite (self-interest), loosed upon the world, becomes 'a universal wolf' doomed, at last, to eat himself up. This, on a global scale, is capitalism as Marx and twenty-first century ecologists conceive it. The principle of degree is the eternal centre of a constitutional cosmos that may, at times, deviate from it, but to which it must tend, and, eventually, return. When it collapses it is not replaced by another centre, but by eternal change and relativity. What Ulysses's speech implies is a transformation of the political universe that is exactly analogous to the transformation that Copernicus's (and Einstein's) system implied in the nature of the physical universe. 'The centre cannot hold', wrote Yeats centuries later: 'Mere anarchy is loosed upon the world.'

The principle of degree was grounded in formal ideology and in folk wisdom. People should know their place, not try to 'rise'. The 'suffocation' of degree is a social-psychological phenomenon, with constitutional consequences. It is also individual and emotional. Chaos is the constitutional result, unhappiness the personal. Another idea Shakespeare shared with Machiavelli was the hypothesis of a direct link between a constitutional state and the mental states experienced by those who constitute it.

---

[1] John Bossy, *Christianity in the West 1400–1700* (Oxford 1985), 36, writes that for Chaucer's Parson, envy 'was the worst of all sins, since the most directly opposite to solidarity and charity, and the source of back-biting, rancour and discord'.

[2] For Crick's account of the force-field of 'politics', see above, Introduction, Section 3.

Coriolanus was Shakespeare's attempt to imagine and represent how nobility died and politics were born.

We have seen that Elizabethan intellectuals took for granted that, state and church prescriptions notwithstanding, political and constitutional metamorphoses (our 'revolutions') happened. Dynasties fell; nations and localities were invaded and conquered, what was once considered low, even the lowest, could become the high. Thinkers of Shakespeare's generation took for granted that if England was ever to be a centre of civilization comparable to Greece and Rome, it would probably be subject to the kinds of epochal political revolutions that they had endured. Fortescue's syntheses of *dominium regale et politicum* offered hope that monarchy was not incompatible with republican culture. They implied a social rather than institutional reading of the constitution. Whatever else it may have been, the Renaissance was a body of thought that took for granted the contingency of political forms. A social revolution had taken place in England that the epic ego- and court-centred images of Plantagenets, Lancastrians and Yorkists, Tudors and Stuarts and histories of Parliament alike have tended to obscure. Like so many sixteenth-century political thinkers before him, Shakespeare saw the potential, even the immanence, within Tudor polity, of all the political systems imagined and created by the classical world. He could see the republic in the aristocratic monarchy that Elizabethan and Jacobean England were supposed, officially, to be. And in retrospect the least profound prophecy contained in *Coriolanus* is the assassination of its princely protagonist and the defeat of nobility.

The mood of *Coriolanus*'s wordplay is that of Maurizio Viroli.[3] It is Shakespeare's account of the revolution of politics. It is not Viroli's classical vision of statecraft and *virtu*, however, that has lost its legitimacy. What is lost is a universal hierarchy in which every person is assigned to a specific degree or rank. The framework of an entire civilization is crumbling. The world transcended by the revolution in politics was not that of classical humanism, it was that of aristocratic blood.

8.2   Mocking the body politic

We have seen that since 1381, even earlier, popular insurrection was the sign of all signs for system-collapse. An insurrection of the plebs precipitates the action of *Coriolanus*. In the opening scene 'a company of mutinous citizens, with staves, clubs and other weapons' gather and fill

---

[3] See Introduction, Section 3.

the stage. Their cause, like that of the Hakluyts, was *necessyte*. Their spokesman, the First Citizen, steps forward. 'We are accounted poor citizens,' he says, 'the patricians good'.

What authority surfeits on would relieve us. If they would yield us but the super-fluity while it were wholesome, we might think they relieved us humanely; but they think we are too dear. The leanness that afflicts us, the object of our misery, is as an inventory to particularise their abundance; our suffrance is a gain to them. Let us revenge this with our pikes before we become rakes; for the gods know I speak this in hunger for bread, not in thirst for revenge.

It is reasoned talk, with ethical concerns. We will suffer willingly for the common good, if our suffering is shared equally by all ranks and classes, but it is not shared. The rich grow fat, the poor lean and hungry. Shakespeare enacted Sir John Fortescue's theory of popular insurrection grounded in poverty and dearth; it affected the rascability first and all the other classes consecutively: the 'third sort' (their neighbours) were the first to succumb. Insurrection involved the formation of an army from below: first the rank and file, then the NCOs followed, on occasion, by discontented and/or intimidated gentlemen. It came to seem that rebellion was capable of articulating the whole social order against the state. When order was restored it was convenient to explain insurrection by poverty, thus ascribing it to the lowest ranks. Ascription to poverty neatly avoided too many prosecutions of men who were needed to restore and maintain the institutions of government.

As E.P. Thompson said of retrospective accounts of eighteenth-century moral economy riots, the rebellion of the belly idea obviates the possibil-ity that labourers and artisans actually had a reasoned point of view of constitutional matters. Everyone except the rascability and a handful of misguided leaders could plead not guilty. In 1450 and 1536 especially, the causes of popular insurrection had meshed – become 'equivalential', as Laclau puts it – with those of discontented magnates. The point was that no-one could tell where the articulation of the commonweal would stop until it was over. This was exactly the process in the early 1640s, except that, for reasons that are well known, the articulation was not halted and accelerated alarmingly to the end that Shakespeare had pre-dicted: the death of the highest form of nobility, monarchy. The play begins with an insurrection of the people, and ends with the death of a prince. In between, Shakespeare provided Jacobean audiences with a paradigm of the constitutional force-field of the English commonwealth of their day. The play is an exploration of the field of force of republi-can politics, featuring a story written by Livy and Plutarch seen through the prism of the political philosophy of Machiavelli's *Discourses*, which Shakespeare may not have read, but probably heard of and discussed with his contemporaries.[4]

The play opens with an enactment of one of the deepest constitutional obsessions of the age of the commonwealth. Tudor and Stuart writers continued to stress the constitutional significance of what they called *necessyte*, of its bitter impact upon individuals, and of its potentially disastrous impact upon kingdoms and commonwealths. 'Skantnes and derthe of victuall and other necessaries...,' wrote an anonymous 'economic adviser' to the young Edward VI in 1549, 'hath ofte tymes cawsede as wel in this realme as also in meny other places great discorde and tumultes to ryse betwein the comonaltye and the majestrates'.[5] The Roman Republic, in 493 BC, is a fledgling power not unlike Shakespeare's England, fearful of enemies abroad and fractured by fissures within. The workforce is chronically insecure, resentful and insurrectionary. The city is on the verge of famine, as England was throughout Shakespeare's lifetime. The common view, spoken from innumerable pulpits, in pamphlets and in parliamentary petitions and speeches, is that the 'leanness' of the poor is in direct proportion to the 'surfeits' of the 'patricians'. The historian of agricultural prices identifies the period as one of the worst fifty years through which England has ever passed.[6] In 1596, and again in 1607, Shakespeare's home country in Warwickshire was rife with rumours that men precisely like these were about to execute a rising of the people.[7] 'Mutinous citizens' were common rumour, any remote hint of actual insurrection became headline news.

Shakespeare knew 'the people' too well, being one of them, to place too much credence on loose talk and wild rumours; yet he does not caricature his populist demagogue, giving him good words: much depends on how the character is played. The first citizen is balanced as he would have been in real life, by a second, more moderate citizen, who warns against

[4] For the publication history and the reception of Machiavelli in Elizabethan England, see Felix Raab, *The English Face of Machiavelli: A Changing Interpretation, 1500–1700* (London and Toronto 1965), 51–76.

[5] R.H. Tawney and Eileen Power (ed.), *Tudor Economic Documents* (London 1924), vol. 3, 315.

[6] Peter Bowden, 'Agricultural Prices, Farm Profits and Rents', in Joan Thirsk (ed.), *Agricultural History of England and Wales*, vol. 4, (Cambridge 1967), 593–695.

[7] John Walter, 'A "rising of the people"? The Oxfordshire rising of 1596', *Past and Present*, 107, 90–143; Steve Hindle, 'Imagining Insurrection in Seventeenth-Century England: Representations of the Midland Rising of 1607', *History Workshop Journal*, 66:1 (September 2008), writes that 'the scale and duration of the Rising, and the volume of blood shed at Newton Field and on the gallows of Northampton, undermine the common historiographical assumption that the Tudors had successfully pacified the commons of England'.

expressions of class hatred: 'Nay', he says, 'but speak not maliciously'.[8] The moderate citizen does not attempt to refute his comrade's arguments, only warns him against expressing them too violently. The plebeian public sphere has elements of civility and reason.

The opening discussion between the radical citizens is not presented as Martius will later characterize it, leaderless, indecisive, fickle. It is a rational discourse between equals. In Act II, Scene iii, 'several citizens' discuss their attitude to the disdainful general. The First Citizen is offended by the fact that Martius 'stuck not to call us the many-headed multitude'. The Second Citizen, discriminating, argues that the real offence in this description lies not in the words or the idea, but in the contempt behind them. No-one, he urges, could deny 'that our heads are some brown, some black, some auburn, some bald'. There is a real problem in 'that our wits are so diversely coloured; and truly I think, if all our wits were to issue out of one skull, they would fly east, west, north, south; and their consent of one direct way should be at once to all points of the compass'. The commonalty, he insists, *is* a 'many-headed multitude'. The art of politics is to mould this anarchic plurality into a unified force, to get it somehow to run in the same direction; or, to use a metaphor that Shakespeare plays intensively with in the play, to make the limbs, organs and attributes of the body politic work in harmony. The Second Citizen recognizes that Martius's insult is based on a truth that must be addressed and solved if the collective power of the commonalty is ever to be given constitutional reality.

The field of force is sketched with deft economy in the first scene. The politic Senator, Menenius, joins the mutinous citizens and invents the body politic idea. But something is not right. The oracle, Menenius the Senator, voices a rather incompetent version to a disrespectful audience. Shakespeare's Senator steps forward to tell what is supposed to be a moral fable teaching that every class has its appointed function, like the limbs and organs of the body. The crowd quietens, respectfully, but the First Citizen refuses to defer to the Senator's rank: 'You must not think to fob off our disgrace with a tale', he warns Menenius. It had better be convincing: 'But, an't please you, deliver.' Menenius begins: 'There was a time when all the body's members rebell'd against the belly.' They accused it of being a gulf in the midst of the body, idle and unactive, engrossing all the food but doing none of the work. The First Citizen thinks he's heard this before, and grows impatient. 'Well . . . , what answer made the belly?' The interruption irritates Menenius, and he loses track, his speech degenerating momentarily to bluster

[8] Philip Brocklebank (ed.), *Coriolanus* (London 1976), I, i, 34 (p. 97).

about 'discontented members', 'mutinous parts' and their 'envy' of worthy 'Senators'. 'Your belly's answer?', insists the First Citizen, and provides it, showing that he knows this old tale too, has heard it many times before:

> ... what?
> The kingly crowned head, the vigilant eye,
> The counsellor heart, the arm our soldier,
> Our steed the leg, the tongue our trumpeter...

Menenius is furious at the First Citizen's sarcastic recital. He blusters: 'What..., 'Fore me this fellow speaks..., What!' The First Citizen still has the argument, and turns to his fellows and asks, 'Should the cormorant belly be restrained, Who is the sink o' the body... What could the belly answer?' He chides Menenius for his long-windedness. Come to the point. By now the parable has gone limp. The belly, Menenius says, is the first receiver of the 'general food', the 'storehouse and the shop of the whole body', to every extreme of which, high and low, it sends sustenance 'through the rivers of your blood'. As in most of Shakespeare, much depends on how the parts are played.[9]

Menenius's moral is that 'the Senators of Rome are this good belly, And you (the Citizens) the mutinous members'. Very poetic, is the First Citizen's response, but essentially bulldust. We've heard it all before. The belly (i.e. the Senate) is the welfare state of the body. How else to know of what the people's welfare consists, but to consult the people, who are gathered to demand food, for they are hungry? All Menenius offers them are artificially sweetened words. The First Citizen seems to have encountered the rhetoric of 'learned' politicians before.

If the crowd will not be appeased by rhetoric, is there another way to bring them to heel? Enter the noble Caius Martius, who sweeps aside this mealy-mouthed nonsense. 'Hang 'em!', is his policy. 'They said they were an-hungry, sighed forth proverbs – That hunger broke stone walls, that dogs must eat, that meat was made for mouths, that the gods sent not corn for the rich men only...':

> ... 'Sdeath!
> The rabble should have first unroof'd the city
> Ere so prevailed with me; it will in time
> Win over power, and throw forth greater themes
> For insurrection's arguing.

These are prophetic words. The rabble did unroof the city, 'win over power, and throw forth greater themes for insurrection's arguing'.[10]

---

[9] Brocklebank (ed.), *Coriolanus*, I, i, 113–20.   [10] *Coriolanus*, I, i, 189–219.

The absolutist warrior-prince, Caius Martius, would be the last of his breed. The *res plebeia* had arrived. In Shakespeare's reading, its birth was messy.

The citizens are ready to leap at the throats of the patricians, and Martius is eager to take them on, alone if he has to. Everyone is terrified of him, and he's dying for a fight. But just as class violence is set to explode, a foreign enemy comes to the rescue. News arrives that a Volscian army has invaded Rome's rural hinterlands. Martius has a rival worth fighting and the plebs must drop their differences with the ruling classes to defend the territory. The Volscians' champion, Aufidius, 'is a lion that (Martius is) proud to hunt'. Like prince Diponegoro's Dutch enemies, he has name and rank.[11] The senator tells the now no longer mutinous citizens to go home. 'Nay', sneers Martius, 'Let them follow, the Volsces have much corn. Take these rats hither to gnaw their garners. Worshipful mutineers . . . pray follow.' National emergency quells class conflict. War revives the principles of degree and rank so necessary for defence of the realm; it suppresses internal divisions and resentments. In Shakespeare's account it does not quite happen like that. By Scene iii the Volsces have been forced to retreat and the Romans are camped outside the gates of their capital, Corioli. The battle-scenes that follow ought to show Martius at his most noble, but in fact Shakespeare has us observe and hear about his martial feats through the eyes, words and jokes of his soldiers, common people who are shown to be deeply sceptical about his heroism. Shakespeare shows us warrior nobility through the eyes of men and women who no longer believe in it.

The siege begins, the Romans are beaten back from the walls, and the Volsces chase them back to their trenches. Enter Martius, 'cursing', even hysterical. 'You shames of Rome!', he shrieks at the enlisted citizens, 'you herd . . . boils and plagues plaster you o'er . . . '. This doesn't work, so he offers rape as their reward if they will follow him. 'Come on! If you'll stand fast we'll beat them to their wives!' A point often missed about Martius is that he really is an appalling leader. This is a point of some significance, since the *raison d'etre* of the warrior aristocracy is to lead the people in war. If, as is manifestly the case with Martius, he cannot lead, he has no function. Contempt fully expressed, he screams 'Follow me!', leaps from the trench and charges alone through the yawning gates of Corioli.[12]

Still in their trenches, the soldier-citizens are not impressed. 'Fool-hardiness, not I', says the first to address what he clearly regards as no more than an expression of normal Martius-type behaviour. 'Nor I', says

---

[11] For the significance of Diponegoro, see Introduction, Section 3.
[12] Brocklebank (ed.), *Coriolanus*, I, iv, 30–42.

a second, just as a third cries, in confirmation, 'See, they have shut him in!'. Loud alarums tell us that on the other side of the gate the Volsces are giving Martius a right battering.[13]

The men are joined by their general, Titus Lartius, trying to find out what is going on. 'What is become of Martius?', he asks them. 'Slain sir, doubtless', the soldiers agree. Lartius moves effortlessly into an impromptu funeral speech, but is interrupted by the reappearance at stage right of Martius 'bleeding, assaulted by the enemy'. 'O! tis Martius', cries the startled general. Martius and his assailants move across the stage with sound and fury. No sooner have the alarums moved offstage than three Roman looters creep in from stage right. The soldiers drift away and the stage is momentarily empty as the alarums of Martius's lone battle continue.[14]

The dust and smoke slowly clear to reveal bloodied Martius and completely unscathed Lartius, accompanied by a trumpeter. Martius wants to make an announcement. He wants more fight and rages once more against the citizens. Lartius tries to calm him down. 'Worthy sir, thou bleed'st. Thy exercise hath been too violent for a second course of fight.' We know perfectly well what is going to happen. Bloody Martius charges off once more, looking for someone to fight. We are impressed with Martius's valour, but feel there is a screw loose somewhere. Something is not quite right. The historically interesting question is whether reading this crucial scene as farce is anachronistic, possible in the epoch of Brecht, Schweik, Charlie Chaplin, Buster Keaton, Spike Milligan and Monty Python, but not possible when Shakespeare wrote it. Recent work on seditious speech suggests that it was perfectly possible when Shakespeare wrote it.[15]

The battle surges through several scenes, establishing that Martius is indeed the greatest fighter of his age, the last true noble of ancient Rome. He finally fights his way through the Volsces to where his quarry, Aufidius, awaits. They exchange polite words of endearment before hurling themselves at each other in single combat. Martius has the better of Aufidius, and is only finally beaten back by the intervention, once more, of the entire Volscian army. In the face of this awesome display of valour, Aufidius admits defeat. Martius returns to Rome in triumph and is acclaimed by the ruling patricians, assembled in Senate. They acclaim Martius's victory, award him the city's name, and elect him as Consul. He has only to stand before the assembled plebeians, displaying the wounds

---

[13] *Coriolanus*, I, iv, 30–49; I, v, 14.   [14] *Ibid.*, I, iv–v.
[15] For discussion of seditious speech and the plebeian public sphere, see below, Chapter 9, pp. 437–41.

he has sustained for their defence and glory, to be acclaimed likewise by the *vox populi*.

They all look nervously at the now even more pompous 'Coriolanus'. Will he respect the forms? He baulks, as by now we know he must. Why should he justify himself before the dregs of society? His acclamation by the patricians is unanimous. What part, he asks, did the mob play in his victory? In battle they were useless, but still the Senate rewarded them with doles of grain. This is more than they deserve, and more than he would give. Under no circumstances will he display his sacred wounds to them. The people are beneath his contempt. He will not allow them any legitimacy at all.

His patrician advisers, led by the publically paternalistic but privately cynical and class-conscious aristocrat, Menenius Agrippa, try to resolve the conflict. We are back where we began. Martius is once again spitting venom at the plebs and their tribunes. The patricians beg him to make the gesture, flatter the mob. Coriolanus retorts that a state with many heads and many voices is a weak state. It is clear that he is more than a great general. He is the very embodiment of aristocratic resistance to any hint of populism, marshalled and led by self-seeking magistrates or tribunes. None of his patrician advisers disagree with his contempt. Their concern is that Martius will precipitate violence, kill dozens or scores of baseborn commoners, go down fighting, thus leaving the more politic patricians at the mercy of an insurrectionary mob with its blood up. All he needs to do, they wheedle, is to bare his wounds before the assembled citizens. To Martius their policy seems like an acknowledgement of popular sovereignty. They suggest it is a token acknowledgement, a ritual transaction in which the shell of power is handed to the citizens and plebs in order that they may immediately hand back its substance. We know by now that Martius will not dishonour his nobility by dissembling in such a way. 'Politics' in Machiavelli's sense is beyond him.

Coriolanus, the patricians insist, takes it too personally. Politics, they counsel, is the art of the possible. The people are powerful because of their numbers. The tribunes are a power because they sway the people. The Senators have to negotiate with the tribunes. In general, the populace is moderate, and accepts the need for an orderly social hierarchy. The balance is easy to maintain. As long as the forms are respected, the power of the patriciate is assured. Coriolanus plays into the hands of the tribunes because his unbalanced pride leads him to overestimate their importance. Their unwillingness to accept his authority unconditionally is too much for him. He refuses to stand before them to receive their assent. Advised by the tribunes, the people reject his consulship. He is exiled from Rome.

The qualities of the warrior are different from the statesman's, and Martius's fatal flaw is his inability to move, as Martius's assassin puts it by way of a final judgement, 'from th'casque to th'cushion'. In peace he tries to command 'even with the same austerity and garb as he controlled the war'.[16] Rejected, he travels to the court of his erstwhile enemies, the Volscians, and offers them his services for a renewal of the war against Rome. He is deaf to appeals by his friends in Rome. He places himself above the common good of Rome. His person is above the state. The Volscians, led by Coriolanus, defeat and occupy Rome, but by now their leaders have come to fear his arrogance and power. There is a conspiracy among the victors and it becomes clear that Coriolanus, at the peak of his power, is friendless. He is assassinated. The play ends with his body being carried away amidst regretful talk of a noble funeral.

Shakespeare takes the body politic metaphor further than anyone before him, conveying through poetic devices the invasion by politics of the very *mores* and emotions of the commonalty. Body imagery, much of it very gory, provides a subliminal bass theme of the play, and pervades the language when the language seems to be talking about something else. The first allusion to cannibalism is in Act I, Scene ix, which sets the scene for Martius's triumph through the streets of Rome. Martius's language in this scene discloses the awful realization that he is about to become a human sacrifice, with hints that the people want to eat him. We are taken to the borders of ancient myths and legends about the sacrifice of princes, and ritual cannibalism. 'Diet' and 'sauce' (l. 51–2), the 'butchery of sons' (l. 87) prepare the way for Menenius's spelling out of the theme in the next scene. He is discussing the politics of Martius's triumphal march to the market place, where the people await to pronounce on his elevation to the Consulship. The tribune, Sicinius, tells Menenius that the people do not love Martius because 'Nature teaches beasts to know their friends.' 'Who does the wolf love?' asks Menenius. 'The lamb', replies Sicinius. 'Ay', replies the Senator, 'to devour him, as the hungry plebeians would the noble Martius'.

Martius's march through the streets is truly triumphal. The crowd cheers him all the way. We do not see it on stage, but overhear it described by the plotting tribunes, Sicinius and Brutus. Their descriptions are pervaded with sexual imagery. 'Prattling nurses' neglect their children because of their 'rapture' at the sight of the handsome hero. There is a very obscure reference to 'seld-shown flamens' rising in the crowd, 'priests who seldom appear' – a reference with phallic possibilities. 'Veiled dames commit the war of white and damask (references to purity and

---

[16] Brocklebank (ed.), *Coriolanus* iv, vii, 43–5.

musky sexuality) in their nicely-gawded cheeks to the wanton spoil of Phoebus's burning kisses.' The many heads and upturned faces of the flushed and adoring crowd are overwhelmingly female. Nurses, nannies, matrons and serving-wenches found Martius very attractive. Powerful and unstable emotions underlie Martius's reception, and the plotting tribunes know it. Martius *is* the Body Politic. But not for long.

They are preparing the lamb for the slaughter. They will wait patiently for Martius's disdain for the commonalty, and for the 'politics' that its collective power entails, to show itself. Then:

> At some time when his soaring insolence
> Shall touch the people – which time shall not want,
> If he be put upon't, and that's as easy
> As to set dogs upon sheep – will be his fire
> To kindle their dry stubble; and their blaze
> Shall darken him forever.
> (II, i, 243–8)

The people will provide the faggots and stake to roast him; Martius will light the fire himself. Shakespeare probably observed public executions. There were several burnings at the stake in London in the 1590s. This imagery was more immediate then than it is now. The 'darkening' of Martius, in this context, is a horrifying image.

But the imagery serves a deeper, more sinister message. Martius's triumphal march through Rome is watched, not by eyes, but devouring mouths. When Menenius becomes angry, he calls the First Citizen the 'big toe' of the body politic, but foot images are swept aside by repeated allusions to the plebs as mouths. In John of Salisbury's original, peasants are the feet of the body politic. Since the late fourteenth century it had become more and more common to think of the commonalty as the speaking, murmuring mouth. Allusions to the indiscriminately devouring quality of the public realm are obsessive. In telling his story, Menenius forgot that the senatorial belly must feed through the mouth. Brutus refers to 'The people, beg their stinking breath (II, i, 225).' The people breathe out a repulsive miasma that engulfs order and civility – but what is its source? Over and again, in the private conversations of the tribunes, the Senators, the aristocrats, the plebs are referred to with contempt, as 'voices'. Nobility, virtue and educated rhetoric are engulfed by the babbling, murmuring voices and stinking mouths of the masses, but the corruption lies elsewhere. We must note in passing, however, that this is not the way the people see themselves.

Martius develops the mouth imagery furthest, as Shakespeare plants consciousness of the people's devouring passion in his speech. The first reference is to the breath of the commonalty, whence we move quickly into the 'mouth' and on to the tongue (II, iii). There are no less than fourteen mouth references in Martius's speech in this scene.

In the first scene of Act III, the metaphorical context is once more spelled out by Martius. He will go to the market place to meet, but not submit, to the people. There await the 'voices', 'tongues' – and now also the 'teeth', 'taste' and 'palates' of 'the many-headed monster' (III, i, 32, 36, 37, 38). The subliminal imagery is Shakespeare's effort to breathe cynical life into a tired old phrase, 'the tongues of the common mouth', in use for centuries for the media of public opinion and vehicle of revolt. The metaphor of the devouring popular mouth is the subliminal form taken by Marcius's judgement on the political situation. 'It is a purpos'd thing that grows by plot, to curb the will of the nobility' (III, ii, 38–9). But he never quite puts the two levels of discourse together, and fails to realize that the combined moral is that if they are not fed on other viands – his speeches also use agrarian metaphors: 'corn' (62), 'plough-ing, sowing and scattering' (71) – the people will devour nobility. The 'market place' to which Martius insists on going is repeated too, echoing Sicinius's discussion of 'What stock (Martius) springs from', comparing the lineages of nobility and beef cattle, Martius and the proverbial town bull. It would be 'against the grain to voice (Martius) Consul'. Martius goes to the market place to meet 'the horn and noise of the monster'(95). He senses the mood, which Shakespeare gives us in metaphors: primitive agrarian myths, dying princes, human sacrifice and cannibalism (made explicit later). 'At once pluck out the multitudinous tongue', Coriolanus cries. 'Let them not lick the sweet that is their poison' (156). 'The crows (will) peck the eagles'(139), he prophecies. The devouring metaphor is not accidental. It underlies the whole of Martius's discourse in these scenes.

The imagery takes us closer than any other source to the horror that popular insurrection inspired. It connected primitive collective sacra-ments like cannibalism and human sacrifice with the Jesus of Nazareth story.[17] Shakespeare had to be careful with it, for the reference to this family of myth and ceremonial, if pursued and recognized in all its impli-cations, could lead to allegations of atheism such as those made against Marlowe when Shakespeare was first in London. He can play with pagan themes as long as they are firmly placed in a past pagan world, but *Cori-olanus* evoked intense contemporary emotions and ideas, of which the most powerful was hunger. There is a lot of paganism in Shakespeare,

---

[17] 'Suggestions of deification', writes Philip Brocklebank, 'may owe something to a distant recollection of Christ at Galilee': *Coriolanus*, II, ii, 260–6 (p. 168n).

as well as a lot of populism. It is easy to understand why the war and politics-weary Restoration elite was uncomfortable with him.[18]

Martius escapes being captured by the populace and thrown ritually from the Tarpeian Rock by the skin of his teeth, and escapes to the court of Aufidius. Explaining his presence in the city he had crushed not long before, he tells Aufidius he is no longer the Roman Caius Martius, now he is but 'Coriolanus'. 'Only that name remains . . . The cruelty and envy of the people . . . hath devoured the rest.' 'Caius Martius' has been sacrificed and eaten. Only 'Coriolanus' remains, and by non-noble standards he is a traitor to commonwealth and state. Shakespeare now has the cannibalism theme at the surface of his mind, and introduces the word into a speech by one of the servingmen at the Volscian court: 'And he (Aufidius) had been canibally given, he (Martius) might have boiled and eaten him too'. He does in fact threaten to 'devour' Aufidius's authority. His uncompromising nature quickly establishes his authority as war leader in the Volscian camp, and is prepared to lead his erstwhile enemies against Rome. But he is soon up to his old tricks. 'He waged me with his countenance', complains Aufidius, 'as if I were a mercenary'. He must die. In the end 'All the people' cry 'Tear him to pieces! Do it presently!', and all the conspirators 'Kill, kill, kill, kill, kill him'.

Politics is universal savagery barely controlled, a war of each against all. For the republic or commonwealth to exist, nobility in its traditional form, embodied in the warrior-prince, an heir of royal blood, must be sacrificed. The tragedy of *Coriolanus* is in Shakespeare's inkling that if ever nobility and the commonwealth were seen as adversaries, nobility (and Shakespeare meant this word in all its senses) would be the loser. Martius embodied the qualities of nobility that Nietzsche was to identify, when noble culture was in its death-throes everywhere in Europe: total, egoistic self-absorption such that the noble *was* the commonwealth. Whatever he willed was for the common good by dint of being willed by him. Informed by Christian or pagan *virtu*, his will is always for the common good. 'Ye shulde knowe that al that governours of the comynte doth, thei doth hit al for profit of the comynte to fore her owne savacioun', as John Trevisa had written in an earlier dynastic crisis.[19] Thus was degree and harmony maintained. The people could be noble too, keeping to the place God had willed for them, as servants and foot-soldiers to be schooled and disciplined to the lord of blood's will. Otherwise they are worthless rebels

[18] Gary Taylor, *Reinventing Shakespeare: a Cultural History from the Restoration to the Present* (London 1990), ch. 1, 'Restoration'.

[19] John Trevisa, *Dialogus inter Militem et Clericum*, ed. A.J. Perry, Early English Text Society (London 1925), 34.

fit only for execution. It is a simple idea that carries conviction only as long as the men of blood show themselves to be capable of asserting it, or of convincing the people that their government really is for the common good. The idea that people need to be persuaded is anathema to the noble point of view represented by Martius.

8.3   The spectre of comparison: Shakespeare's prophecy

Shakespeare was a man for possibilities, for starting a thought or play with 'what if . . . ?' He saw his own culture re-enacting the whole span of human history as he understood it. He had done with English history and moved on to the present and future. The epoch of *Troilus and Cressida* preceded that of the Greek polis of *Timon*, the lover of money, and the universe of the Aristotelian polis which provided one part of the political wisdom of his age. It preceded the birth of Rome, and of the birth there of politics, with which *Coriolanus* is concerned. Roman republicanism was another part of the political wisdom, the new 'ancestral constitution' of his culture. The politics of the Greek city-state grew out of the decay of degree which was the order of the world of Agamemnon and Ulysses. Rome too began as a monarchical and aristocratic state. *Coriolanus* is a re-enactment of the rebirth of republican politics in Rome that was difficult not to see as an anatomy of the spectre of politics abroad in his own society.

Shakespeare's educated contemporaries took these metamorphoses for granted, and were beginning to assume, in many cases to fear, that if England was a centre of civilization comparable to Greece and Rome, it would necessarily be subject to the kinds of epochal political revolutions that they endured. This would happen regardless of whatever the official constitutional form happened to be. Monarchy might survive, but the culture of nobility was over. Renaissance humanists took the contingency of political forms for granted. A long political revolution was taking place that the magnificent ego- and court-centred propaganda of the Tudors has tended to conceal from posterity. It is very likely that like Tyndale before him, Shakespeare was not taken in by it. Like vernacular writers before him, he could see the potential, even the immanence, within Tudor polity, of all the political systems imagined and created by the classical world. Like so many of his thoughtful contemporaries, he could see a republic in the aristocratic monarchy that Elizabethan and Jacobean England were supposed, officially, to be.

Shakespeare's culture had an ingrained sense of constitutional life as collective sensibility and subjectivity and a highly developed sense of the collective nature of the words, proverbial expressions and sayings, anecdotes, legends, myths, fairy-tales, murmurings and stories he retailed in his plays. In *Coriolanus* he described the state of a commonwealth which has lost faith. The verities of preachers no longer ring true. Coriolanus is awesome, the last nobleman. He will not truck with dissemblance: he is one thing to all men (though not the same to his wife and mother). No matter how frightened the people are of his physical power, they cannot take him seriously as a governor. He was born to rule a state that no longer existed.

Shakespeare was a realist with regard to the commonalty. There is a limit to the number of heads that can be adequately presented in a play or a history book. He had to make a small group of leaders represent the many-headed multitude, but I do not detect fear and loathing of the *plebs*, the snobbery of a new gentleman, in Shakespeare's treatments of the *comynalte*. The town he grew up in was a common place. We must assume that it represented a world in which Shakespeare had learned to survive, as infant, child and young man. He knew it. His father was of it. His parents mingled commonalty and gentry: for him as for so many provincial English families of his era, this was not the great divide, the point where nobility and commonalty met and mingled. Knights of Shires and gentlemen of localities were very often counted with the commonalty in medieval thought, because they shared a 'House' at Westminster. They were the *Communes*. Yet *Coriolanus* does depict class-struggle. Very clearly, all is precipitated by a rebellion of the belly. His contemporaries had not yet lost the medieval habit of thinking of rebellions of the common people as Acts of God, like epidemics and the weather. They were assigned, not to 'Histories', but to 'Chronicles'. The idea of oppressed, poverty-stricken masses rising up and overthrowing their masters was the dynamic of his culture's most sacred text, the Bible. There was not a wise counsellor of his generation that failed to place revolution at the very core of their political thought.

Coriolanus was prophecy: the execution of its princely protagonist prefigured that of Charles I in 1649. The idea that men of blood must die for a commonwealth to flourish has proven to be a lasting theme of the European revolutionary tradition. *Coriolanus* can be read as Shakespeare's judgement, at the birth of modern 'politics', on revolutions past and revolutions to come.

9 'Boiling hot with questions': the English revolution and the parting of the ways

> It so happened... that my country, some few years before the civil wars did rage, was boiling hot with questions concerning the rights of dominion and obedience due from subjects, the true forerunners of an approaching war.[1]

> [It] was because English society in 1642 was already different from that of other ancien regimes that the issue of radicalism came so quickly to the fore.[2]

> It is only necessary to think of Thomas Hobbes, the philosopher of absolutism, the Levellers, Gerrard Winstanley the Digger – a kind of pantheistic Christian communist – James Harrington – the agrarian classical republican – or the secular-minded defenders of the Commonwealth, to become aware that most of the truly original ideas were produced by people in varying ways out of step with prevailing orthodoxies – Anglican, Puritan, royalist, parliamentarian. Such exciting new theories about the individual, the State, and society were in the fullest sense the product of their time, yet produced as it were against the grain.[3]

9.1 To defend God's empire of England: 'the empowered community'

We have noted the constancy of an underlying, taken for granted precept that the most essential function of a constitution was to defend the territory. Myths and records of past conquests were continuously reinforced by generations of raiders and traders from the west (Wales and Ireland), north (Scotland) and south (France, Spain and the Mediterranean world).[4] What did change in the generations of Fortescue, Tyndale, Sir

---

[1] Thomas Hobbes, *De Cive*, 'Authors Preface' <www.constitution.org/th/decive00.htm>.
[2] David Wootton, 'From Rebellion to Revolution: the Crisis of the Winter of 1642/3 and the Origins of Civil War Radicalism', *English Historical Review*, 105:416 (July 1990), 657–8.
[3] G.E. Aylmer, *Rebellion or Revolution: England from Civil War to Restoration* (Oxford 1987), 103–4.
[4] The author of Bodleian: Rawlinson MS C878 (2), 'The polliticke Survey of a kingdom' (unsigned and undated, but written for the Earl of Dunbar), distinguished between three

Thomas Smith and William Shakespeare was that dominant intellectual models of England's constitution became less abstract as a result
of the incorporation of the idea that it was not constituted by stereotypical limbs, members or parts of a metaphorical 'body' or 'ship', or
arranged as a hierarchy in an abstract void defined by the will of God. It
was constituted by the *trafike* of real people and vocations in an increasingly structured, surveyed, mapped and quantified landscape of localities
and interconnected jurisdictions. These premises underlay a memorandum that was probably intended to provide James VI of Scotland, the
man it (tacitly) nominated to succeed the heirless but, as yet, still-living
Elizabeth Tudor, with counsel as to the nature of the realm he would
inherit.

It is possible that James Stuart read Thomas Wilson's *State of
England, Anno Dom. 1600*,[5] or, at least, that his understanding of what
was entailed in its governance corresponded very closely to the 'maps'
provided by Wilson and his great predecessor Sir Thomas Smith.[6] It
is also certain that he (and his son, Charles I) took Wilson's conventional but potentially dangerous definition of England as 'an absolute
Imperiall Monarchy held neither of Pope, Emperor but God alone' too
literally, and, in this respect at least, failed to follow John of Salisbury's
wise advice that a reader 'who follows everything in the text syllable by
syllable is a servile interpreter who aims to express the appearance rather
than the essence of an author'.[7] As Steve Hindle's elegant synthesis of
contemporary thinkers, modern social theory and the research of political and social historians demonstrates, the early modern English 'state'
was a 'palpable presence' at every level of society, from the localities to
the court. The Elizabethan 'settlement' was informed by a remarkable

---

types of princes: those like 'Pope Julyan, Salmon the Turke . . . and Philip II' who were
'unnaturall always striving to add to their estate', 'moderates', and a third type, 'in cases
where ye Diminucion of ye State is threatened, such a one was Queen Elizabeth & such
is nowe King James'.

[5] *The State of England Anno Dom. 1600 by Thomas Wilson*, ed. F.J. Fisher (London 1936).
(Henceforth *State of England*.)

[6] As is strongly suggested by Steve Hindle's quotations from James's letter to sheriffs and
justices of the peace (1609) expressing concern 'to prevent the growing evills which may
ensue for lacke of good distribucion in causes that concerne publique services which are
often carried so confusedlie or executed soe remisslie as the vulgar sorte of people will in
tyme gett a custome of disobedience'; Hindle writes that 'the state relied upon inferior
officers for a palpable presence in the localities, as James I well understood': *The State
and Social Change in Early Modern England, c. 1550–1640* (Basingstoke 2000), 1, 21.

[7] *Policraticus*, Book V, Chapter 2, 'According to Plutarch, what a republic is and what place
is held in it by the soul of the members', 67.

'vision of England as "simultaneously a community and an organization – a commonwealth and a state".'[8]

Maintaining the illusion of 'absolute imperial monarchy' was, necessarily, a process of negotiation. The process required the good will and, therefore, the respect, trust and loyalty of every 'sort' of English person, down to the husbandmen, artisans and labourers who, as constables and, very often, jurymen, were as essential, collectively, to its harmony as the monarch herself. The great lesson of English history was that monarchs whose upbringing and personal inclinations naturally inclined them to promote and associate with refined, learned and rhetorical souls who flattered their absolutist conceits, failed to cultivate the love of the 'vulgar' commonalty, the yeomen, citizens and (as Fortescue and Smith had insisted) the 'rascability'. Monarchs who achieved that next-to-impossible balancing act, historically, survived the most intractable crises, as Elizabeth's monarchy had survived many, including the terrible 1590s. Absolutist conceits and popularity were not easy to reconcile. The events of the 1640s would prove once again that without popularity, absolutist conceit was unsustainable. Wilson's sketch of England's constitutional landscape provided a useful mnemonic point of departure, but only if the reader read between the lines of the parts that were bound to be less attractive to a person with absolutist preconceptions.[9]

The idea that England was an 'empire' acquired and maintained by an armed population ranked like an army, was axiomatic. For Wilson

---

[8] Hindle, *The State and Social Change*, ch. 1 and *passim* is essential reading for theorists and historians of the state in general and of the English state in particular; the quotation is on p. 22, where Hindle quotes D.H. Sacks, 'Private Property and Public Good: the Problem of the State in Elizabethan Theory and Practice,' in Gordon J. Schochet (ed.), *Law, Literature and the Settlement of Regimes* (Washington DC 1990), 141.

[9] Where 'absolutism' is concerned, I follow the propositions of J.P. Sommerville, 'Absolutism and Royalism', in J.H. Burns (ed.), *Cambridge History of Political Thought 1450–1700*' (Cambridge 1994), 348–9 and *passim*, that 'in England there was no single settled idea of absolute monarchy' but that while 'there was no agreement on the nature of absolutism, . . . 'absolutist' *does* usefully describe a distinctive set of ideas' (emphasis in original). Also that it is 'unwise to impose any great intellectual consistency on English royalists of the Civil War period . . . royalism is best defined as a tendency to support the king in the political controversies of the day'. The implication is that 'royalists' were by no means bound to be dogmatic 'absolutists' and could have many reasons and motives for their loyalty. Mark Kishlansky, 'Charles I: a Case of Mistaken Identity', *Past and Present* 189 (November 2005), 41–80, describes a more accommodating character than the historiography would suggest; Charles, he writes (48), 'inherited a monarchy filled with challenges and he failed to meet them'. The point, of course, is that he was far from being the first to have 'failed'; the tendency of English grand narratives to assign crises and depositions to the personal weaknesses of the kings in question fails to do justice to the accumulating constitutional culture.

as for his prolific contemporary William Camden, 'England' was a historically constructed landscape encompassing '52 provinces which are called countyes or shires'. Scattered unevenly across the provinces were '25 cittyes, 641 markets and shire townes, 186 castles, 554 rivers, 900 forests, chases and parks, 9,725 parish churches and 26 bishoprics'. 'Of the 641 great townes', he wrote, 'there are 289 which are not inferior to most of these cittyes, being most walled towns and every one of them having voice in the Parliament by 2 burgesses'.[10] It was an England that any inhabitant or traveller could observe at first hand. The cities, market and shire towns, provincial capitals, forests, chases, parks and parish churches constitute his acknowledgement that England was first and foremost an aggregate of many communities spread across a landscape and held together by a geographically dispersed hierarchy of ranks.

The state had to be an army. The territory had been invaded before; regimes had come and gone. Wilson noted that Caesar conquered England and Wales for Rome, and after him came 'three other conquests'. It was a matter of historical record that the sovereignty of the states they established ceased to exist 'when they were no longer able to defend it'. States (and monarchies) survived only as long as they could hold and defend the territory. Their polities were threatened from without and within. Control of England meant control of great wealth and power. It was worth having. The military imperative was closer to the surface of the minds of Wilson's generation than it is to ours.

Possession achieved and maintained, as it had been since 1066, Wilson came to the occasion of his memorandum. 'The nexte and most principall that must be found by feeling the pulse', he wrote, 'is to know how it standeth for the point of succession'.[11] In Elizabeth's last years, there was intensifying anxiety about whether any of the twenty-nine possible claimants Wilson listed were at all satisfactory. Wilson went through each of them, finally settling on the flawed legitimacy of the succession of James VI of Scotland. Wilson took for granted that the only real consideration was which candidate would best serve England's interests. The election of James, he argued, 'could not be prejudicial to England, being the greater and better part, but rather beneficial as that it would draw Scotland to it, and so conjoyn both together'.[12] It would simultaneously remove a traditional enemy and increase *England's* 'empire'. The point in danger of being missed by recent conceptions of a British monarchy with its 'four kingdoms' is that 'Britain' was an essentially English plan.

---

[10] *State of England*, 11.   [11] *Ibid.*, 2.   [12] *Ibid.*, 9.

Of the four countries of the Atlantic Isles, only England had the power to make it happen. If Charles I had not so deeply offended the English commonwealth, if he had had England on his side, he could have imposed his will on the other three kingdoms had he so wished. The Stuarts never understood that the English commonwealth was greater than the state and that the state is there to serve it.

Wilson did not represent England as an abstract 'state', 'society' or 'economy', but as a geographically dispersed army capable of being mustered and conscripted for the defence of the realm. He followed tradition and the established view of the elite by dividing the army into five 'ranks': *nobiles, cives, yeemani, artisani* and *opifices rusticorum*. Each rank had a clearly defined economic, political and military and constitutional function. The nobles were the officers, divided into 'major' and 'minor', at the peak a handful of marquises, dukes and earls, descending to the non-hereditary fringes of nobility occupied by ministers of the Church and the bottom rank, graduates of Oxford and Cambridge without benefices and sinecures. In descending degree of authority, these ranks were responsible for 'matters of Estate', divided into 'politicall government' (policy) and 'administration of justice'. This was the ruling class as it was supposed to be, the peak of a three-dimensional pyramid comprising perhaps 15–20 per cent of the entire population.

At the local and district level, administration and justice was in the hands of 'Esquires...fitt to be called for office and authority in their Country where they live'. Their task was to ensure that 'matters of estate' were passed down to the officers of the commonalty in the localities. It was at this point in their visualization of England society that the attention of the Stuarts habitually turned off: the plebeian *cives* of the boroughs and the *yeemani* of the market towns and villages. They belonged to the 'commonalty', and Wilson acknowledged their vital functions as 'non-commissioned officers', whose task it was to supervise the everyday lives of ordinary people, and to execute and administer 'matters of Estate' in the localities, where the work went on. He estimated that there were 10,000 'great yeomen...in country villages, besides Cittizens', and 80,000 'yeomen of meaner ability'. 'The rest are Copyholders and Cottagers...some of them men of as great ability as any of the rest; and some poore, and lyve cheefly upon country labor working by the day for meate and drinke and some small wages.' The lowest, subsistence and wage-working class, drawn from the small tenantry, landless or land-poor artisans and labourers, 'are they which are thrust out to service in war'. They were considered expendable in overseas expeditions. Their leaders, however, 'the richer sort of yeomen and their sons', were the key to the defence of the realm, 'being trayned but not sent out of the land, but kept to defend against invasion att home unless they will go voluntary as many doe'.[13] As Fortescue had suggested, rebellions were precipitated by the rank and file of the constitutional army. The puritan John Corbet and the royalist Thomas Hobbes would later assert that it was the 'fourth sort' that precipitated the first actions of the civil wars and that would determine its outcome.[14]

Wilson's constitutional sketch has two main dimensions. With geographic realism, it sketched a constitutional landscape comprised of provinces, towns and villages. Upon this territory was superimposed a pyramidal ruling class composed of the armigerous and their non-hereditary subalterns, graduates of Oxford and Cambridge. Upon a portrait of how his society was 'constituted', in the sense of 'made up', 'constructed' or (as it were) 'laid out' (i.e. in provinces, towns and rural districts), and by whom it was inhabited, he imposed a hierarchy. For Wilson, England had to be organized in this way because it had to be an army capable of defending itself from usurpers and would-be conquerors. He was not interested in metaphysical or religious justification, only with the practical business of holding and maintaining the territory. It is instructive to read his account of how the imperial monarchy of England was constituted alongside the attendance records of musters of Gloucestershire held by order of Cardinal Wolsey in 1522, or those prepared for John Smyth of Nibley in 1608.[15] What the muster records show is a heavily armed populace. If only half of the men from the Vales of Gloucester and Berkeley and the Forest of Dean who carried long-bows to the musters of 1522 were proficient archers, it would be wise for governors to ensure that they never gave them cause to band together in a common interest. The lower ranks were everywhere under the effective command of the men of the middle ranks, who alone could ensure that

---

[13] *Ibid.*, 20.

[14] Hobbes, *Behemoth: the History of the Causes of the Civil Wars of England*, ed. William Molesworth (London 1840), 146, was sure that underlying the civil wars was a propaganda struggle 'for the common people, whose hands were to decide the controversy' yet who 'understood not the reasons of either party'. Corbet, *An Historicall Relation of the Military Government of Gloucester* (London 1645), 8–9, referred to 'the fury that took hold on the ignoble multitude, in whom not always the deep sense of their owne interests doth provoke this extasie of passion'; Fortescue's theory (see above, Chapter 2.4) had anticipated that of Machiavelli, e.g. *The Discourses* (ed. Crick), 238–42, 'The Populace, misled by the false appearances of advantage, often seeks its own ruin, and is easily moved by splendid hopes and rash promises.' Rollison, *The Local Origins of Modern Society: Gloucestershire 1500–1800* (London and New York 1992), ch. 7, offers a social-historical critique of Corbet's analysis.

[15] R.W. Hoyle (ed.), *The Military Survey of Gloucestershire, 1522* (Stroud 1993); Peter Gwyn, *The King's Cardinal* (London 1990), ch. 9; John Smyth, *Men and Armour for Gloucestershire in 1608* (Gloucester 1980).

the able-bodied men of their districts turned out on parade, and who they turned up to fight.[16]

Like all armies, Thomas Wilson's England could only function if every rank remained loyal to the pyramid as a whole, and performed its allotted tasks. Like most of his contemporaries, Wilson drew attention to a dangerous weak link in the chain of command, in the liminal territory between gentility and commonalty, where descending gentry met rising yeomen and citizens, at the district and local level.[17] He warned, first, that 'younger brothers' of the gentry (of whom Wilson was one), were a potential source of 'discontentment'. He was bitter about the way the system disadvantaged 'younger brothers' of gentry families like himself who, where inheritances were concerned, got 'that which the catt left on the malt heap'. His warning that such men were liable to feel the system as it existed did not serve their interests became a commonplace. Their alienation could, however, work in the interests of the court 'for it makes us industrious to apply ourselves to letters or to armes, whereby many times we become my master elder brother's masters'.

The greatest challenge, however, smouldered among the *cives* and *yeemani*, in the senior ranks of the commonalty. Wilson's stress on the military importance of the senior ranks of the commonalty or third estate was a view that, as we have seen, was first spelled out nearly 150 years earlier in Fortescue's comparisons of the 'commodities' (important common properties or qualities) of England, and those of its traditional enemy, France. The English middle ranks were armed and dangerous. Militarily they had to be, but it also meant that they could – and in fact

---

[16] The fundamentally military character of Wilson's constitution should also be read in the context of the contemporary debate about what specific qualities constituted a gentleman. There seems to have been a split between those who, like Thomas Churchyard, supported 'armes' [*A Generall Rehearsal of Wars* (1579)], and others who supported, variously or together, learning, estate or a more vague and comprehensive *virtu*; J.P. Cooper, 'Ideas of Gentility', in G.E. Aylmer and J.S. Morrill (ed.), *Land, Men and Beliefs: Studies in Early Modern History* (London 1983), is circumspect, saying only that 'it is tempting to speak of the evolution of ideas' (from 'armes' to broader conceptions of *virtu* in which learning, good reputation, estate and so on are inextricably [if ambiguously] combined). In my view, ambiguity is the key to the discourse, for if gentlemen were no longer legitimated by their leadership and skills in war, their traditional claim, they were on increasingly thin ice: learning and estate were clearly not exclusive to armigerous gentry. For a passionate defence of learning as the pivotal quality, cf. Sir Thomas Smith, in Mary Dewar (ed.), *A Discourse of the Commonweal of this Realm of England, attributed to Sir Thomas Smith* (Charlottesville 1969), 25–30.

[17] Rollison, 'Neighbourhood to Nation: the Trotmans: a Middle-Rank Kin-Coalition 1512–1712', in *The Local Origins of Modern Society*, 97–122, is a study of the 'conquest of space' involved in the transition from the upper ranks of the commonalty to gentry and minor nobility in the period under review.

did – lead rebellions against the government. At the very least they had long been regarded as a very real check against monarchical, aristocratic and ecclesiastical tyranny. In more peaceful times the citizens of the towns and the yeomen of the villages were supposed to translate the politics and administration of state into action at the local level, where the wealth of the nation was produced and the armies of the kingdom were bred up. In keeping with the prejudices of the intended recipients of his counsel, Wilson suggested that these ranks had surreptitiously usurped constitutional functions (and pretensions) for which they had no brief. Their independency 'was no matter invented and sett downe by authoritye for the bettering of that state of the people', he wrote, 'but rather by the substelty [sic] of them and the simplicity of gentlemen'.[18]

Viewed from the perspective of a would-be absolutist monarch who conceived himself as the embodiment of God's empire of England, Wilson mapped an army that could be mobilized against foreign enemies. Read between the lines it was also, inescapably, a commonwealth that could be, and many times in the past had been, mobilized for the chastising of the state by which it was supposed to be governed. The Stuarts failed to notice that, regardless of theory, a commonwealth that, on the face of it, was identical with the state, could be mobilized against the 'state'.

9.2 The middle sort: Elizabethan incorporation or recurring pattern?

Modern social historians have been rather more sanguine than Thomas Wilson about the constitutional attitudes of the English middle classes before the civil wars. 'It is axiomatic', writes Steve Hindle, 'that the prosperous farmers who took their turn as churchwardens, bailiffs, jurors and guildholders throughout the middle ages had been the natural leaders of the communities in which they lived.' In his account what changed after the mid-sixteenth century was that in fulfilling their time-honoured duties 'they also took on the additional obligations and duties implied by service within a national political culture'. 'National political culture' only drew in the 'middle sorts' during 'the late Tudor and early Stuart period'.

Hindle is undoubtedly right to insist that there was an 'increase of governance' in the 1549–1649 period and that this emergence of the 'early modern state' entailed 'the incorporation of the middling sort'. Tudor absolutism was an effort to absorb (and tame) the commonweal by

---

[18] *State of England*, pp. 38–9.

promoting the equivalents of that very extensive class of the thirteenth and early fourteenth centuries, the *liberi homines*. 'Until the mid-sixteenth century,' Hindle writes, 'local leadership might well have implied opposition to the policies of the regime.'

In the century after 1560, however, the notables of rural parishes in particular seem increasingly to have identified themselves with the priorities of order and reformation. To take only those places discussed in detail . . . , the inhabitants of Braintree, Cranbrook, Mildenhall, Sherborne and Swallowfield had all been involved in various episodes of late medieval disorder. It is therefore all the more striking that their early seventeenth-century successors should be precisely those men who used the law courts so enthusiastically, who policed the morals of their inferiors, who in many ways exhibited a greater respect for justice even than the regime itself. The ringleaders of late medieval and mid-Tudor rebellions were drawn from the same social strata as the conscientious vestrymen of Restoration England. The reorientation of their political attitudes owes much to the ethos of national political service created by Elizabethan legislation. Especially in the administration of social policy, central government policy took account of the interests of a much wider cross-section of society than the political nation as traditionally construed.[19]

The idea that the governance of England was, to a greater or lesser extent, transformed in the Elizabethan and Jacobean periods has become virtually an axiom of the new social and political historiography.[20] If true, it contradicts the argument of this book – that the underlying structures and dynamics of English constitutional culture show remarkable continuities from the late thirteenth century to the execution of Charles I, and that the outbreak of civil war in the early 1640s saw a reprise of the social and political dynamics that had been instrumental in the popular rebellions of 1381–1549. We need to consider the extent to which the elements of Hindle's summation represent a recurring pattern.

'The incorporation of the middle ranks' into the state had been a continuing theme of English governance since the twelfth and thirteenth centuries. It became a matter of urgency after the Commons Rebellion of 1381, when, on the one hand, the regime needed the middle sort to play a key role in restoring and maintaining order in the affected communities and, on the other, the commons in parliament were anxious to distinguish themselves from those who, in 1450, Gregory called the 'ryffe-raffe'. Once rebellions were over, it was in the interests of courtiers, gentry and

---

[19] Hindle, *The State and Social Change*, quotations 225, 226–7.

[20] For the social, economic, cultural and political reasons for 'the decline of insurrection in later sixteenth-century and early seventeenth-century England', see Andy Wood, *The 1549 Rebellions and the Making of Early Modern England* (Cambridge 2007), ch. 5, esp. 195–202.

rural and urban 'worthymen' (Wilson's *yeemen* and *cives*) to reimpose order on the *proletarii* who, in Fortescue's classic analysis, had been the first movers of rebellion. Once a regime regained the upper hand, it was in the interests of householders who had something to lose to deny or excuse their involvement by claiming to have been drawn into rebellion by mobs composed of their poorer neighbours and country people.

We saw that it was in the period of endemic social conflict following the 1381 rebellion that the term 'yeoman' began to be used as the term for those who had previously been referred to, generically, as *liberi homines*, a term which distinguished those who, by then, were seen as the parliamentary class and who, on the face of it, had nothing to gain from the abolition of serfdom. The incorporation of these 'middles' had been a strategy of the ruling classes, and of the state, since the reign of Henry II. The long term implication of the governance of the commonalty was that to short-circuit rebellions, crown and central government had to ensure that they did not pursue policies that offended the respectability and the rascability at the same time. This was where the regimes of Edward II, the senescent Edward III, Richard II, Henry VI and, finally, Charles I, came unstuck. As we have seen, tyranny, the law of the commonweal, was routinely applied at all levels of society from the localities and countries to the court. 'National political culture' – a potential, realized in consecutive crises, created by the emergence, by c.1300, of a tradition of magnate rebellion, a commercial landscape, and the vernacular revolution of the fourteenth century – was articulated as popular rebellion when all the different complaints and demands came to be directed at the court and, in the most extreme cases, the monarch. This point, however, requires further discussion of the dynamics of 'common opinion' and the public sphere, which will be reconsidered below.

The 'ringleaders of medieval rebellions' were, in Fortescue's account, the same men as Hindle's 'conscientious vestrymen' and jurors. When, in 1357, Richard of Fulham informed Hertfordshire labourers that God supported their demands for higher wages, the small employers of the county naturally turned to the national justice system for assistance. It is also clear enough that 'prosperous farmers' and the burgesses of towns had been consistent, indeed enthusiastic, users of local courts to police and reform their communities for as long as records permit any insight into the governance of the localities. In one sense this was inevitable. Lords needed men like these to administer and police their estates. The national taxation and mustering systems also needed 'non-commissioned officers' for grass-roots administration. Middle-men of this order are essential to the efficient running of any highly centralized yet geographically dispersed polity.

Prosperous farmers, master-craftsmen and petty merchants had the resources to fill these roles. Other things being equal, they were always the likeliest candidates for local government offices. That much seems to be common sense; scholars like R.B. Goheen and Marjorie McIntosh have presented persuasive evidence suggesting that the 'reform of popular culture' was an abiding, if uneven and episodic, movement of English constitutional culture at the local level. Protestantism, office-holding and literacy combined to intensify the consciousness of local elites of being part of the 'state' as well as the commonwealth during Elizabeth's reign, as Hindle suggests. Tyndale's theology – grounded in a long tradition of vernacular religion – dispersed authority into the households of local elites. The dissolution of the monasteries increased the influence and authority of the settled, substantial yeoman and citizen elites of villages and small towns. The administrative authority of the parish was incorporated by the state – incompletely, as the 1640s would show – between the Henrician Reformation and the civil wars. Conceptions of the state and the commonwealth were changing, as we have seen. Elizabeth's recognition of the importance of popularity was not new; yet it was both more conservative and more consistent than the strategies of Henry IV, the Yorkists in the 1450s and Protector Somerset in the 1540s.

Yeomen and citizens – the upper ranks of the commonalty – were bound to be the main beneficiaries of the uneven but continuing desire to absorb a truculent commonalty into the *regnum*. Smaller freeholders and larger tenants had been the most persistent victims of gentry lawlessness for centuries: their best defence was a reliable and impartial justice system. Yet like the 'polarization' of local elites from the rascability, courtly pursuit of popularity was not new. It was a recurrent tendency, built into the social relations of production and everyday forms of government. As we saw, recent work on medieval local records suggests strongly that state-level Tudor commonwealth reformism, often the initiative of counsellors with middle-rank backgrounds, was the application by the state of persistent earlier local initiatives.[21] The period from c.1550 to 1640 witnessed a more systematic, conscious, lucid and confident articulation of the collective movement examined in this book. It was premised on relentless vernacularization, the tradition of rebellion, the rise of a manufacturing economy and the quest to guarantee foreign markets for its commodities, increasing proletarianization and associated mobility, the

---

[21] Marjorie K. Macintosh, *Controlling Misbehaviour in England 1370–1600* (Cambridge 1998), 69: 'The rhetoric used in the lesser courts when describing problems... between 1460 and 1539 bears interesting resemblance to the idealistic view of society and political control advocated by the "commonwealth" approach of the mid-sixteenth century.'

weakening prestige and changing functions and definitions of nobility, a strong crown and parliament, and sharpened conceptions of the autonomy, even autarchy, of the English commonwealth. These structures of the age of the commonweal became aligned in 1640–3 at the expense of the monarchical state, in ways that the rest of this chapter will explore.

9.3   One-way traffic: the fallacy of court-centred history

Wilson's framework represented a traditional mind-set in two important ways. Firstly, the constitutional landscape as he represented it was static: its dynamics had to be 'read between the lines'. Earlier thinkers like Fortescue and Sir Thomas Smith had more dynamic, economic and decentred views. Like Wilson, they took for granted that the loyalty of the middle ranks was crucial to the maintenance of the empire of England. The ruling classes were most violently threatened at times when the 'middles' were, themselves, subjected to pressures from below, in the form of unemployment and poverty. Fortescue, Smith, John Dee and the Hakluyts built their theory of imperialism from the observation that, in times of economic or political crisis, the commons suffered, but not in silence. It had long been common knowledge that in times of crisis Wilson's *yeemani* and *cives* often sided, not with their superiors or the state, but with their lesser neighbours, the 'rascability'. The orthodox view of a hierarchy whose apex was monarchy existed alongside more lateral and decentred conceptions of a commonwealth in which authority always threatened to retreat into the households and neighbourhoods of the commonalty, where, in moments of crisis, it was capable of being reconfigured into movements against established authority. Where Wilson saw the landmarks of the old regime – parish churches, market crosses, provincial and regional capitals – the advocates of an expanding English empire saw routine circuits of *trafike* that articulated productive local and regional communities into a national political economy with 'imperial' possibilities.

Recent scholars of Stuart England have used its rich archives to tease out a quite detailed portrait of a landscape that was articulated by constant, unpredictable discourse. This was the 'public sphere' that anyone who wished to govern had to 'read between the lines' of relatively static portraits of the constitutional landscape like those of John of Salisbury or Thomas Wilson. It is not easy for social scientists and historians to capture the dynamic acoustics of public opinion, let alone to predict and control its fluctuations in response to contingent events and processes. The whole 'publique thing' was and is, inescapably, an imagined community. It was possible to spy on and experience it at all levels and to 'reconstitute' it on the basis of analysis, 'experienced intuition'; it was less easy to police and repress it on the basis of punishment and censorship derived from hierarchical prescription, the latter always being the simplistic option of absolutists, authoritarians and reactionaries. Complementing the reconceptualization of the early modern state described in the last section, it is in the field of public opinion that scholars of Stuart England have produced some of the most interesting work in recent decades.

One of the essential features of Jurgen Habermas's now classic conception of the 'public sphere' is that it nurtured and expressed a consistently critical view of the state. A 'public sphere', in his conception, is 'a sphere which mediates between society and state, in which the public organizes itself as the bearer of public opinion'.[22] As we have seen, 'the public' never 'organizes itself'; for it to be politically effective it has to be recognized and incorporated into the strategy of individuals, groups and classes. But as Habermas insisted, it is premised on the existence of an all-pervasive state.[23] As for the additional precept that this condition did not exist before the eighteenth century and the presumption that it could not exist without print technology, widespread literacy and secular rationalism, medievalists and early modernists have shown otherwise. Scholars of early Stuart England have been especially active in drawing attention to the temporal and conceptual limitations of Habermas's original theory. In April 1986, for example, Kevin Sharpe drew attention to the importance of 'the processes of communication' by which, before the civil wars of the 1640s, government won 'compliance' and the 'points of contact' (notably patron–client relations) which he saw as the principle agencies of the process.

In the new view that is emerging from the work of these historians, the turning-point was 1640–2. Sharpe believes that something resembling a 'public sphere' existed, but that before the civil wars English

---

[22] Geoff Eley, 'Nations, Publics, and Political Cultures: Placing Habermas in the Nineteenth Century', in Craig Calhoun (ed.), *Habermas and the Public Sphere* (Cambridge, Mass. 1992, repr. 1996), 290.

[23] 'The story of a state-structure built around the English monarchy and its effective successor, the Crown in Parliament' and 'the development from a feudally structured society to a politically integrated one' are central themes of Gerald Harriss, *Shaping the Nation: England 1360–1461* (Oxford 2005), vii, 650. John Walter, 'The English People and the English Revolution,' *History Workshop Journal* 61 (2006), 174, writes that 'the deep structures of the English state actively promoted popular participation. A state that had limited forces of repression placed a premium on anticipating and ameliorating problems in order to preempt protest... This was achieved in large part by securing popular consent to the exercise of power as a legitimate authority... seen in this context, crowd actions were necessarily political.'

collective consciousness was uncritically and dogmatically court-centred. Not even members of parliament, he claimed, had ever shown any 'desire to participate in government, nor to tell the king how to govern.'

> They only expected that the monarch should govern responsibly, with justice and for the good of his subjects – in the manner, as Aristotle put it, that defined a monarchy as opposed to its corruption, tyranny. The king, of course, could not govern alone. Monarchical government, it was perceived, required good advisers who could inform the king and honest and efficient officers who would execute his decisions . . . In other words, communication to the king and from the king was the binding thread of government.'[24]

In a more recent 'remapping' of collective opinion in seventeenth-century England, Sharpe clarified his position. 'The state as an artifice which needs to be justified [is] essentially alien to early Stuart thinking', he wrote. For Sharpe, the civil wars of the 1640s, and, following them, the writings of Thomas Hobbes, 'shattered' the earlier mentality, in which 'the state was seldom conceived as an "other".' As for the common-wealth, it was 'represented as a natural organism, like the family from which it grew. Man fulfilled himself as a man in so far as he was part of the commonweal, and had no social existence . . . outside it. Everything good in the created world . . . was ordered and under government: celestial bodies, beasts, men . . . the government of the commonweal reflected the divine plan and government of all nature.'[25] Against this central 'revisionist' (anti-Whig, anti-Marxist, anti-evolutionist) hypothesis, this book has argued that the idea that 'the government of the commonweal reflected the divine plan' was *not* widely believed for long at any time or in any place in late medieval and early modern England. The idea that government was often, even invariably, corrupt, serving self-, class- or sectional interests, sometimes conspiratorially, against the common good, was, by the 1640s, nothing less than proverbial.

We have seen that it is hard to find a single reign or period of English history since the Norman Conquest when 'reverence for government' was the dominant, passive mood of the English political community. Between 1215 and 1415 'five out of eight kings fought wars with their subjects; four out of eight were captured and/or deposed, and two were killed'. When Charles I was executed in 1649 he was the fifth monarch since *Magna Carta* to be deposed and killed by his subjects. Revolts significant

---

[24] Kevin Sharpe, 'Crown, Parliament and Locality: Government and Communication in Early Stuart England,' *English Historical Review* 349 (April 1986), 323–4.
[25] Kevin Sharpe, *Remapping Early Modern England* (Cambridge 2002), pp. 47–8.

enough to merit extensive treatment in the chronicles occurred in 1381, 1439, 1450, 1470, 1485, 1487, 1497, 1536, 1549, 1554 and, of course, 1642–9.[26]

Thus to the observation that most people before the 1640s believed that society and state ought to conform to such a plan we must add the recorded observation of succeeding generations that it seldom lived up to the common expectation. Authors and popular movements since John of Salisbury had repeatedly stated or implied that courts and counsellors rarely satisfied the expectation that their devotion to the common good be transparent. Then as now, the actions of governors often looked as if they were motivated by personal or sectional interests, not those of the community as a whole, and certainly not those of its lower orders. As we shall see, research on the new theme of 'dangerous words' shows that sixteenth- and seventeenth-century England was never lacking in common people incautious enough to express sceptical, even cynical sentiments about the legitimacy and efficacy of their governing institutions and classes.

A second problem with revisionist accounts is that at no point in the history of England from the fourteenth to seventeenth centuries was there only one idea of divine and secular order in circulation, there were many variations on several different themes. If, as historians of the thirteenth to sixteenth centuries have suggested, stories and ideas in 'middle' English often spread quite rapidly throughout the kingdom – that 'common opinion' was just that – it implies that what Andy Wood calls the 'semi-secret' discourse of the common people of all regions, most villages and market towns and all provincial capitals, cultivated awareness of the many different discourses and traditions. This being the case, 'the spectre of comparison' was never restricted to classically-trained counsellors like Sir Thomas Smith. For this reason it may be helpful to classify the constitutional culture of early modern England, not in terms of alternatives, but as a fluid spectrum ranging between two poles, the 'imperial' and 'populist'. Imperial versions of Christianity, for example, prescribed centralized notions of governance in which it was the duty of states and ruling classes to maintain orthodox beliefs and doctrines. In populist visions (widely used by late medieval preachers and early modern radicals) Jesus was a carpenter, his disciples were common men and women, peasants, artisans, publicans and sinners, and the arts of being saved had little or nothing to do with inevitably corrupt states and empires. How people responded to these different accounts varied greatly. We note

---

[26] Claire Valente, *The Theory and Practice of Revolt in Medieval England* (Aldershot 2003), 1, 249–50.

temporal, contingent, local, district and provincial variations. Yet we must not lose sight of underlying commonalities.

One thread of commonality emerges from a continuous stream of evidence of many kinds, dating from the second half of the thirteenth century, witnessing that the ways kings, courts, counsels, judges, juries, magistrates, manorial officials and constables went about their business were obsessively scrutinized for signs of corruption. From 1381 to 1549 this scrutiny was routinely attributed to the middle and lower ranks of society. By the 1450s it was taken for granted that when corruption, incompetence and injustice in high places was observed or suspected, word spread fast to all corners and classes of the kingdom. A highly commercialized society (by the standards of the age) trafficked not just in goods and services, but in 'news' stories, snatches of chronicles, emblematic tales of holy plebeians like Piers Plowman and Julian of Norwich, anecdotes of kings, proverbs and sayings.

Because medieval and early modern regimes very often did fall short of public expectations, often behaving as if public expectations were irrelevant, resentment smouldered constantly somewhere in society. When a regime offended men and women from too many classes and communities for too long, many 'sparks' became 'equivalential' and burst into flame in many places at the same time. The government of late medieval and early modern England was notoriously subject to all-too-human interventions. They ranged from conspiracies of nobles to gatherings (even 'covens' – groups and communities who swore oaths – 'covenants' – to stick together) of *communes* to talk taxes, foreign wars, corrupt officials, venal churchmen, magnate rebellions and the deposition and murder of tyrants. These activities often offended religious (and other) conceptions of how society ought to be conducted, but actual government, as observed, heard about or experienced, was most often bluntly mundane.

Criticism of the state was a feature of English public opinion long before 'state' became a reflexive abstraction and 'politics' became a word for a narrow, institutionalized *milieu* in which ambitious men intrigued and conspired for self-glory and the spoils of office, for the 'state' as an instrument of place and promotion, but not (demonstrably) for the common weal.[27] Sharpe writes that 'For those ambitious for place . . . absence

---

[27] The idea that affairs of state were and ought to be protected 'mysteries' was commonplace and came in various forms. In *The confutatyon of Tyndales answere made by Sir Thomas More knyght lorde chancellor of Englonde: The seconde boke whych confuteth the defence of Tyndale's boke, why he translateth the worde chyrche in to this worde congregacyon* (London 1530) Sir Thomas More haughtily accused William Tyndale of making 'a speciall shewe of hys hygh worldely wytte and that men should have sene therein that there were nothynge done among prynces, but that he was fully advertysed of all

from court, even on the king's business, gave rise to anxiety.' 'Ambition for place' is a meritorious business in this conception, but that was not the popular view in early modern England. As we saw, popular suspicion of the worlds of 'place' and 'promocion' was the basis of Tyndale's critique of the actually existing Church. In his conception the Church was not the ideal, moderating form of the whole community but a foreign conspiracy driven by sordid careerist ambition. The underlying question was intuitive and universal: were they seeking place and promotion for the common good, or only for selfish or otherwise partial motives? Were they concerned only with identifying and pleasing patrons who could further their careers, or were they true conduits of honest counsel, without which England could not function? Did they put on airs and graces, insult the commonalty, and lose their roots? Were they of or against the people?

Sharpe's view that 'the Court formed the first vital link in a chain which connected the king to the localities' is a truism; it ignores a necessary corollary, conceptions of tyranny and questions of what should be done if the court was corrupt and therefore spread corruption throughout the realm and commonwealth. The court 'was meant to bear, not break under, the contrary pressures and strains produced at times by the momentum of political life . . . This the Court of the early Stuarts clearly failed to do.' The organological conceptions that, as Sharpe says, were taken for granted by all classes before and during the civil wars, implied two-way traffic. The blockage that occurred under the Stuarts was not of information and instructions that were passed 'down' through the hierarchy or 'out' through the 'circles of the state'; the 'contrary pressures' were constituted by traffic in the other direction, from the commonwealth to

---

ye secretes and that so farre forth, that he knew the pryvy practyse made betwene the kynges hyghnes' and his counsellors. For Raleigh, at the end of the sixteenth century, 'mysteries or sophismes of State are certain secret practizes, either for the avoiding of danger; or averting such effects as tend to the preservation of the present State as it is set or founded'. 'For as in civil actions he is the greater and deeper politique, that can make other men the instruments of his will and ends, and yet never acquaint them with his purpose, so shall they do it and yet not know what they do,' wrote Bacon in *The Advancement of Knowledge* ed. G.W. Kitching (1861), 98: Political Science, for Bacon, was reading the mysteries of politics, divining the motives behind the stratagems. God's affairs were too lofty for men's understandings, and should be 'confined to his proper place' (i.e. the state). Fifty years later, John Warr was among those who turned this logic on its head: 'To advance their interest,' he wrote, 'Kings and Princes have politiques, and Principles of their own, and certain state-maxims, whereby they soare aloft, and walk in a distinct way of opposition to the Rights and Freedomes of the People; all of which you may see in Machiavil's Prince. Hence it is that Kings have been always jealous of the people, and have held forth their own interests, as a Mystery or Riddle, not to be pried into by ordinary understandings': *The Privileges of the People of England, or, Principles of Common Right and Freedom* . . . (London, February 1648), 1.

the court. Stories of Edward II, the aged Edward III, Richard II, Henry VI, Richard III and, in 1536, Henry VIII's 'evil counsellors', all preceded the Stuarts in positing a monarchy and court that had lost touch with the 'commonweal'. As Sharpe observes, echoing John of Salisbury, for monarchical government to work the king had 'to be well advised and his wishes effectively executed'. For this to happen 'the organs of advice and execution (the Court, the Council and the aristocracy) needed to maintain open communications – to the king from the country, and from the king to the locality'. Sharpe adds that 'the language of "evil counsellors" is too often dismissed by historians as mere rhetoric... In fact it was a rational and understandable analysis.'[28] Rational and understandable or not, the spectre of evil advisers had been conjured up in every public crisis since the 1250s, such that it had become a convention of public discourse and rebellion to avoid blaming the king if that proved at all possible.

Commonwealth ideology as it had developed in England during the fourteenth and fifteenth centuries was premised on preternatural suspicion of the state, whatever its form and personnel. Love of the ideal form implied hatred of its corrupters. In this conception lines of authority and communication radiating out from the centre formed 'circles' or ripples of presence at every level of society. This is what Smith had meant when he acknowledged their penetration into the worlds of the 'rascability' or 'fourth sort'. In other words, the state was an all-pervading presence in the lives of the English long before the modern era. The strength of commonweal ideology and movement was in direct proportion to the omnipresence of this tentacular state.

It is not the duality between vicious state and virtuous commonweal that requires explanation. As Steve Hindle shows, the very duality of 'state' and 'commonweal' is misleading, except in moments of crisis. Everywhere and at all times people subject to power and authority naturally consider the motives, words and instructions of those placed, by whatever means, in authority over them. They wonder and judge (usually in private) because it is natural for human beings to do so, even when prescribed authority forbids. Are those in authority motivated by service to the commonweal or by personal or other partial interests? Are they, as Tyndale wrote of More, motivated by desire for promotion and estate? In this conception, ringingly expressed in Tyndale's proverbial expressions, the state easily became 'foreign', 'Other'.

This way of looking at the world is likely to be present in all communities because, as is also proverbial, people (being all too human) cannot be

---

[28] Sharpe, 'Crown, Parliament and Locality', 325, 327, 339–40.

trusted because they are capable of dissimulation. The critical presence is the idea that falseness to certain simple, basic but far-reaching principles is both wrong and remediable. The principle of commonweal is probably universal. What must be explained is the formidable intensity, agency and effectiveness of that principle in early modern England, such that the duality between a corrupt state and a virtuous commonweal was, long before the seventeenth century, an abiding potential of a constitutional culture in which 'state' authority became a 'palpable presence' from top to bottom.

To conclude this book, I will show how the elements of constitutional culture as it had been evolving for centuries were re-articulated and came together in the 1620s, 1630s and 1640s. In those decades the model of corruption and conspiracy that Tyndale's generation so effectively projected onto the Catholic Church came to be projected, as had happened so often in the past, on the malign upper echelons of the state. Henry VIII and his children escaped conviction as tyrants because, during their reigns, opposition was, for the first time since the fourteenth century, not focused primarily on the court and corrupt counsellors etc., but on an even more foreign body, the Church and a greater tyrant, the Antichrist in Rome, and his imperial allies. As far as I know no English monarch-become-tyrant, however unpopular, was ever accused of being the Antichrist.[29]

The court-centred interpretation of English constitutional culture fails to locate successive English courts in the context of an instinctive, institutionalized but often repressed or suppressed collective idealization of the commonweal and the suspicion and critique of the state that ensued from it. Court-centred revisionists rightly emphasize the causal significance of contingent events and failures of government as precipitants of the crises of the 1640s. The events and failures, however, must be seen in the context of the genesis of a society and constitutional culture that had accumulated over many centuries, for it was that collective *longue durée* that made England such a potent force that what happened in the 1640s became a revolution with global consequences.

What remained largely unchanged and what, if anything, was different? What new ingredients, if any, made the public culture of Jacobean and

---

[29] For an exhilarating account of what and who were identified with Antichrist, see Christopher Hill, *Antichrist in Seventeenth-Century England* (1971, repr. London and New York 1990). However, David Wootton, 'Leveller Democracy and the Puritan Revolution', in Burns (ed.), *Cambridge History of Political Thought 1450–1700*, 421, observes that 'From 1639 [John] Lilburne had been one of those few sectarians arguing that the church of England was part of the Beast, one of the limbs of Antichrist. It was a small step from this view to the conclusion that the king was an agent of Antichrist, and that the struggle against royal absolutism formed part of an eschatological drama.'

Caroline England different from the situation in 1327, 1376, 1381, 1399–1400, 1450, 1497, 1536 and 1549?

9.4 The explosive public sphere

Habermas located the emergence of a 'bourgeois public sphere' amongst the reading classes of Britain, France and Germany in the eighteenth and early nineteenth centuries. This 'relatively dense network of public communication' involved a 'considerable expansion in the production of books, journals, and papers, an increasing number of authors, publishers, and book-sellers, the establishment of lending libraries, reading rooms, and especially reading societies as the social nodes of a literary culture revolving around novels'.

The societies for enlightenment, cultural associations, secret freemasonry lodges, and orders of *illuminati* were associations constituted by the free, that is, private, decisions of their founding members, based on voluntary membership, and characterized internally by egalitarian practices of sociability, free discussion, decision by majority, etc.

The result, in Habermas's view, was 'a politicization of associational life' that led quite rapidly to 'the rise of a partisan press, the fight against censorship and for freedom of opinion'.[30] Against this theory, we have seen that a 'relatively dense network of public communication' involving 'a politicization of associational life' had been a decisive feature of English constitutional culture from the fourteenth century on.

What could have been more 'public' than the great commons rebellions of 1381–1549? Those popular rebellions had been regional, but always a region or regions rose in the name of commonweal against the state. Equally, by 1640 there were not many regions, perhaps even towns, villages and households that had not been touched by popular rebellion at one time or another. The 'tradition of rebellion' is not only a phrase invented by historians: it was part of English collective memory – every rebellion was a mnemonic exclamation mark in the chronicles of kings, queens, great storms and heroic battles.[31] As we have seen, bill-posting

---

[30] Jürgen Habermas, 'Further Reflections on the Public Sphere', trans. Thomas Burger, in Calhoun (ed.) *Habermas and the Public Sphere*, 423–4.

[31] Wood, *The 1549 Rebellions*, p.10 and ch. 6: 'Memory, Myth and Representation: the Later Meanings of the 1549 Rebellions', describes the processes of memorialization and incorporation. Wood's question, 'how far rebels were conscious of these centuries-long continuities', leads him into a very subtle examination of what might be termed the 'mechanics' of popular memory which, in turn, enables him to identify evidence that elucidates the question. His use, in particular, of court depositions and other local records (see 208–16) to tease out the process of *popular* 'memory and forgetting' in the years immediately following the rebellions of 1549, before the various 'impositions

featured in every crisis from the fourteenth to seventeenth centuries. The rise of 'middle' English was of far greater consequence in the emergence of public opinion than the slow spread of secular literacy or the invention of moveable type: it was the language of the English public sphere, uniting classes in harmony or opposition, in all the crises discussed in earlier chapters. The English public sphere was above all a phenomenon of vernacularization.

Studies of the composition and dynamics of seventeenth-century England are studies of a phase of a much longer collective process. That process was episodic and uneven, but in the long run it was combined and accumulative. In qualification of the new view that the emergence of 'the public sphere' took place in seventeenth-century England, we have seen that references to something closely resembling such a phenomenon are surprisingly prominent in the archives of England from the 1250s forward. Debate tends to circle around whether the chronicle and literary references are real or rhetorical. Do the references we have considered in earlier chapters merely represent and repeat a discursive, linguistic convention or do they point to a very real, if usually widely dispersed and conceptually inchoate, process?

I will now suggest that as a result of three decades of research on prerevolutionary England, historical reconstitutions of its 'public sphere' are considerably less inchoate and allusive, much more substantive, than they used to be. It follows from what has gone before that events of the reigns of James I and Charles I articulated a public sphere that was already an institutionalized condition of English constitutional culture. What the increasingly rich documentation of this period offers is a more substantive picture of the forms of this centuries-old public sphere.

Scholars have focused on 'the whole phenomenon of scribal publication and the dissemination of news and rumours amongst the gentry and middling sort', demonstrating 'that anonymous squibs and libels, more formal newsletters and separates, all circulated in manuscript and at high speed around early Stuart England'.

The result . . . was clearly some sort of nascent public opinion, consisting of audiences in London and the provinces eager for news of political events and rumours [concerning] centrally placed figures at court and council, as well as leading parliament men and ambitious local gentry, aspiring patriots or commonwealths men, all sought to create identities or images for themselves in this *semi-public arena*.

of ideology' by interested parties, is especially important. Wood's treatment is also emblematic in the sense that it raises questions that need to be asked of the 'tradition' of rebellion, in memory, as agency.

The 'public' or 'semi-public sphere' of early Stuart England included written and oral communications and integrated literate and illiterate people.[32] It included written messages like statutes and bills posted in public places but its primary medium was the spoken word; it was not premised on literacy. As we have seen, in the view of many scholars of fourteenth- and fifteenth-century England it long preceded the invention of the printing press. The notion of a 'semi-public sphere' is a useful point of departure in that it allows for many substantive differences between the contexts of fourteenth- to sixteenth-century England and those of the eighteenth and nineteenth centuries.

Understanding of the public sphere of early Stuart England has been greatly advanced in recent years by scholarly marriages of political and social history. In a remarkable survey published in the same year as Sharpe's court-centred vision of the emergent public sphere, Richard Cust took his point of departure from a relatively new 'institution' of public communication: 'news-sheets'. These news media of late Tudor and early Stuart England, he wrote, 'presented politics as a process involving division, struggle and the need to oppose disruptive influences . . . a continuing stress on conflict . . . counterbalanced the emphasis on consensus'.[33] However, Cust found that news-sheets were only the tip of a social iceberg. In keeping with its state of very partial literacy, this public sphere integrated 'written material' and its most common form, 'word of mouth'. Cust wrote that 'opportunities for oral exchange were growing with the development of internal trade and increasing resort to London'. Efforts by Privy Council to censor the Press and prosecute 'seditious words' were largely fruitless: 'the publicity given to clashes at the centre, and the way these were presented in the news, contributed to undermining faith in the established order'. Underlying Cust's account was a map of the communications system that underpinned the public sphere. London, for example, was not just a disseminator of news from the capital and Westminster; as it had been in the 1380s and 1390s, it was a transformer, disseminating news between provinces. In news-sheets 'material was . . . worked together and retransmitted to the shires as part of a connected sequence of events, generally set alongside what

---

[32] Kenneth Fincham and Peter Lake, 'Popularity, Prelacy and Puritanism in the 1630s: Joseph Hall Explains Himself', *English Historical Review* 111:443 (September 1996) 857 (emphasis added); James Holstun, *Ehud's Dagger: Class Struggle in the English Revolution* (London and New York 2000), 17, uses the phrase 'semi-public sphere'; see also David Cressy, *England on Edge: Crisis and Revolution 1640–1642* (Oxford 2006), 320–9: 'Discourse, Opinion and the Making of a Revolutionary Culture'.

[33] Richard Cust, 'News and Politics in Early Seventeenth-Century England', *Past and Present* 112 (August 1986), 75.

was happening at the centre'. This enabled local people to 'bring out the national significance' of what was happening in specific localities, districts and shires. Provincial capitals and market towns conducted news into the localities.

Cust describes a fluid and incessant movement of information and gossip between printed, handwritten and oral forms. A Suffolk clergyman, John Rous, was in the habit of travelling to a nearby town, Thetford, where, like many generations of market-goers before him, he would read proclamations that had been 'pinned to the corner-post of the Bell inn', and talk to his companions about what they were reading. If the information contained was innocuous, undramatic and appeared not to touch local concerns, not much more would be said, but this was rarely the case in the 1620s and 1630s. While taking refreshment Rous would hear (and record) 'verses and ballads recited in alehouses', sometimes by specialists like Thomas Cotton of Colchester, who was 'accustomed to reading out the latest news on market-day with locals flocking around him "as people use where ballads are sung".' However, the most significant of Cust's conclusions was that 'the source [Rous] most frequently indicates is local talk, variously described as "some say", "it is commonly said", "great talk", "it was tould us", "a rumour there was" [and] "country intelligence".'[34]

Once again we encounter a phenomenon that, because it was so distant from their operational contexts, had sounded in the ears of generations of monastic chroniclers and highly placed apologists for hierarchy like Sir Thomas Elyot and Sir Thomas More, as an incessant, irrational 'murmuring'. Out of the earshot of authorities the words were often much clearer. Rous thought the verses he heard recited in alehouses originated with the 'vulgar multitude'.[35] Elite and popular cultures were part of a continuum, but the notion that the 'plebeian public sphere' had an especially crude, irreverent, sceptical, even cynical attitude towards government and ruling classes was virtually a truism of Tudor and Stuart England. A correspondent of Robert Cecil wrote in April 1601 that the vulgar multitude 'ar[e] carried more by rumours without an head, then by the truth of things'.[36] John Rous recorded in his diary in 1629 that he 'was particularly worried by the "vulgar multitude", which tended always "to speake the worst of state businesses and to nourish discontente as if there were a false carriage in these things"'.[37] The distinction made by

[34] Quotations from Cust, 'News and Politics', 65, 86, 70–1, 66, 65.

[35] Cust, 'News and Politics', 66.

[36] Quoted from Adam Fox, 'Rumour, News and Popular Political Opinion in Elizabethan and Early Stuart England', *Historical Journal* 40:3 (September 1997), 599.

[37] Cust, 'News and Politics', 84.

Habermas between a *bourgeois* public sphere that played 'a constitutive role' in the formation of a broadly critical civil society and a distinctive "plebeian" public sphere – a distinction between respectability and rascability, literacy and orality, rationality and religiosity or superstitition – fails to describe the capacity of words, phrases and ideas to cross class, status and technological boundaries, yet it does point to a qualitative difference between the attitudes of elite groups and the rascability.

In a revision of his original account, Habermas conceded that the 'culture of the common people' as described by Mikhail Bakhtin in *Rabelais and His World*, and in E.P. Thompson's celebrated *The Making of the English Working Class*, 'was by no means only a backdrop, that is, a passive echo of the dominant [i.e. bourgeois, 'middle class'] culture; it was also the periodically recurring violent revolt of a counterproject to the hierarchical world of domination, with its official celebrations and everyday disciplines'.[38] Habermas's revision of his original conception is entirely compatible with Fortescue's account of the 'bottom-up' impetus of earlier popular rebellions. Fortescue analysed the articulation of a 'semi-public sphere' (a public sphere not premised on literacy, writing and print, nor on critical enlightenment rationalism) in such a way as to suggest that not only the *plebs* or commonalty, but its poorest members, were the precipitants, the causal agents in the articulation of collective resistance to the state. What recent accounts suggest is that the 'counterproject' of the rascability was defined by wholesale scepticism and cynicism with regard to elites and government. Records of literate 'levels' of the early modern public sphere reveal belief in many different doctrines, nearly all of them grounded in some kind of theology. We must consider the possibility that 'below' those levels, amongst those who suffered first and hardest in crises and were regarded as most likely to begin rebellions, were many who believed in no doctrine at all except that principle of commonweal which asserted that their 'betters' ought to have their welfare at heart and almost never did.

Jerome Friedman and, more recently, Peter Lake have shown that the bulk of the literature – and, by inference, the more prevalent verbal and theatrical storytelling – that circulated in post-Reformation and Revolutionary England was sensationalist. On the face of it, much of this outpouring of the 'pulp press' was entirely innocent of political and ideological content. Yet as Friedman observes, it offers many insights into the 'emotional images, gut sentiments, and intellectual architecture by which ordinary [people] . . . understood contemporary events'. Lake notes, for example, that the 'moral obloquy' and 'gloatingly self-righteous' tone

---

[38] Habermas, 'Further Reflections', 427.

of Elizabethan and Stuart crime fiction implied 'an image of an utterly stable social and political hierarchy, of moral patriarchs, loyal and obedient wives and servants, univocally pious and obedient Christians, all bent industriously over the callings into which God had placed them, discharging their social duties towards one another without greed or personal rancour.' This 'secular utopia', he observes, 'was precisely [the] sort of view of the social order' that many scholars have 'identified behind the variety of "stirs", the plebeian revolts and disturbances, that disrupted Tudor rule'.[39]

Conclusions vary according to the type of literature under analysis. In an important study of the military literature of the pre-revolutionary decades, for example, Barbara Donegan describes a range of material and a topic that may well have been more popular than the mass of 'true' crime stories, tales of witchcraft and providential miracles combined. 'Intellectually,' she writes, 'the country was prepared [for the civil wars] by a literature that had little to do with chivalric romance and much to do with the professional practice of modern soldiers, with the latest theory of the "science of war" . . . and with the social and moral dangers that attended war.' War appealed to all classes, from 'the eminent and visible' heroes of the various continental 'nurseries of soldiery' down to the 'shoal of junior officers and common soldiers' that fought overseas, very often for international protestantism. Donegan shows that the combination of returned soldiers and the literature, letters and words of mouth that circulated their stories and described the wars in which they participated, 'conditioned' England for its own civil wars. She suggests that when civil war came it was not the terrible shock that scholars have sometimes supposed.[40]

Richard Cust's seminal account of political news reveals that the topics of public discourse – court favourites, heterodox queens and corrupt courtiers with more influence over the king and kingdom than they should have, foreign wars, conspiring factions, mooted insurrections, sexual and other scandals involving prominent people – were exactly those that had fascinated and exercised the moral obloquy of medieval

---

[39] Jerome Friedman, *Miracles and the Pulp Press During the English Revolution: the Battle of the Frogs and Fairford's Flies* (London 1993), xii; Peter Lake with Michael Questier, *The Antichrist's Lewd Hat: Protestants, Papists and Players in Post-Reformation England* (New Haven 2002), 130. Lake's observation that literary texts 'represent sites on which contemporaries could imagine, play with, act out and question the ideological and cultural contradictions and concerns of the day' (693) is an important one, and probably applies to much of the material that circulated in written and verbal forms in the 'semi-public sphere'.

[40] Barbara Donegan, 'Halcyon Days and the Literature of War: England's Military Education before 1642,' *Past and Present* 147 (May 1995), 68, 71–2, 76–7 and *passim*.

publics. The court, parliamentary debate, expensive news-sheets, London and the provinces, university men, literate merchants and gentlemen, semi-literate yeomen and master-craftsmen, print-shops, market gossip, tavern talk and street-protests, only differed in the detail and quality of the information, and the degree of habitual 'reverence for governance' with which it was received. His examples show that 'the separation often made between popular and elite culture was in practice sometimes non-existent'. As far as market- and tavern-talk was concerned, 'the literate and the illiterate shared the same medium'. National news flowed easily into the everyday milieus of the commonalty.

Adam Fox's studies take us inside these worlds. In a path-breaking study of popular 'libels' Fox described a typical case in which a group of illiterate men of Evesham hired three traveling artisans to write and produce multiple copies of a libel against a local gentleman in 1605. They 'cast abrode, divulge[d], publish[ed] and sang [them] in divers and sundry open and publicke places, and dyd sett upp and fix the same upon divers and sundry doors, walls and posts to the intente that the same might be made knowne unto all manner of persons whatsoever, to the utter infame, scandale and disgrace' of the gentleman. Often, as in this case, the episodes were local, but the same means were turned 'to publish disgraceful or false speeches against any eminent man or public officer'. Libels were a veritable genre of plebeian public spheres which, in Fox's view, were, 'like so much oral culture, inherently subversive and irreverent, implicitly running counter to the norms and values of society's elite and sometimes challenging them explicitly'.[41]

'To penetrate beneath the letters, news-diaries and commonplace books' used by Cust and others, Fox also reached 'into the world of everyday gossip' by examining state and private prosecutions of people for speaking seditious words. Note, first, that laws against seditious words were as old as records of resistance and rebellion. Statutes of 1275, 1352, 1378, 1388 occurred in the wake of earlier explosions of *commune opinioun* and were 'extended in scope by acts of 1534, 1552, 1554, 1571 and 1585'. Cust's evidence is insufficiently detailed for him to ascertain just

---

[41] Cust, 'News and Politics', 69; Cust anticipated the interest in libels, which, he wrote, 'were the products of an environment in which literacy was not expected, but was, nevertheless, relied on in order to get the message across.' This 'combination of oral and literate dissemination' (63) was 'intended to be read aloud to those who could not read' (66). Adam Fox, 'Ballads, Libels and Popular Ridicule in Jacobean England', *Past and Present* 145 (November 1994), 56, 66. Andy Wood, *Riot, Rebellion and Popular Politics in Early Modern England* (Basingstoke 2002), 131, concludes that 'between about 1580 and 1640, such libels developed into a small, burlesque literary genre' that reveals 'something of the anonymous, semi-secret nature of social critique within many towns and villages . . . '

how knowledgeable the 'alehouse audience' was about national politics, but leaves no doubt that, knowledgeable or not, they certainly expressed and discussed opinions. 'Whenever two or more met together', writes Fox, 'the conversation was likely to turn to the state of the nation'. 'Talk of foren or domesticall news' was a favourite topic of conversation among the common people, as it had been in 1327, 1381, 1399–1400, 1450, 1536 and 1549. 'Unflattering references to the king were by no means untypical', wrote Cust, and there was a tendency to polarize 'relatively extreme positions on the political spectrum'.[42] A similar observation might be made of chronicle accounts of the crisis of 1327.[43] In the 1640s as, perhaps, in the 1250s, 'news' was transmitted by carriers, chapmen, travelling traders, gossiping neighbours, vagrants and wandering beggars. The employed, underemployed and unemployed, men, women and children exchanged words seditious and non-seditious across the garden fence, in the streets, at hostelries and other routine meeting places, where libels, ballads and even the occasional news-sheet also circulated. What is striking in all these accounts is the intensity of sociability and the readiness to engage with national issues.

As had been the case for many centuries, 'rumours about the death of the monarch were an endemic feature of popular political discussion in early modern England'. So too was endemic gossip about 'the fortunes and the conduct of royal persons and their ministers'. 'People everywhere might be furnished with up to date information on events in the kingdom . . . and on this basis they were able to form quite knowledgeable opinions on important issues', writes Fox. Most importantly, the richer evidential base of seventeenth-century social and political history reveals the journeys of stories, rumours and ideas much more clearly than is the case for any earlier crisis. The new historiography of the public sphere of early Stuart England also gives us insight into what I have suggested was a recurring pattern. It describes the re-articulation, in a time of intensifying political controversy, of fluctuating but permanent channels of *trafike* and the resurgence of an existing repertoire of recurring topics of complaint, mockery and resistance.

Cust shows that in periods of conflict at the centre written and printed material increased in quantity. Fox confirms that 'the greater amount and quality of news in circulation' in the 1620s and 1630s 'begins to be reflected in the content of seditious conversations.' Links between national politics and local gossip and movements, direct and implied, are another continuing theme.[44] Cust also perceives an improvement in the

---

[42] Cust, 'News and Politics', 72, 79.   [43] See above, Chapter 2.9.
[44] E.g. Chapter 4, above.

quality of the information, 'a rising level of subtlety of political consciousness which was probably a direct result both of these improved communications channels and of the constitutional debates of the day'. Fox
concludes that 'people at the lowest levels of provincial society... were
by no means cut off from the flow of information and news'.[45]

9.5   Behemoth versus Leviathan: the revolutionary public sphere

Though I reverence those men of ancient time, that either have written Truth perspic-
uously, or set us in a better way to find it out ourselves; yet to the antiquity itself I
think nothing due: For if we reverence the age, the present is the oldest. If the antiquity
of the writer, I am not so sure, that generally they to whom such honor is given, were
more ancient when they wrote, than I am that am writing: But if it bee well considered,
the praise of ancient authors, proceeds not from the reverence of the dead, but from the
competition, and mutuall envy of the living.[46]

Your calling the people silly things, obliged me by this digression to show you, that
it is not want of wit, but want of the science of justice, that brought them into these
troubles... [They] wanted not wit, but the knowledge of the causes and grounds upon
which one person has the right to govern, and the rest an obligation to obey; which
grounds are necessary to be taught the people, who without them cannot live long in
peace amongst themselves.[47]

The new historiography of a heterogeneous, mercurial, early modern
public sphere, enriched by a growing number of reconstitutions of the
politics of neighbourhoods and districts, is important because it illuminates a collective phenomenon that conditioned the writing and reception of all of its sources without being explicitly present in any of them.
It describes a milieu that contemporaries took for granted. The work of
historians like Wendy Scase, John L.Watts, Kevin Sharpe, Richard Cust,
Peter Lake, Adam Fox, Barbara Donegan and others cited throughout
this book adds not only to the contexts of established texts and traditional
historiographies, it changes their meanings. The politics of parishes and
of the national public sphere can now be 'read into' more canonical
landmarks and literatures of constitutional history. It is appropriate that
a history of the long-term nature and causes of the English Revolution

---

[45] Adam Fox, 'Rumour, News and Popular Political Opinion', 588, 599, 600–1, 613–
14, 616, 620; I have omitted Fox's qualifier 'in Elizabethan and Early Stuart England'
because the statement could be made of the English public sphere in all the constitutional
crises since 1327. Cust, 'News and Politics', 73, wrote that in the 1620s – as always –
'news' focused on 'court scandals, state trials, disputes in parliament, attacks on the
duke and almost anything else of unusual interest'.

[46] Thomas Hobbes, *Leviathan*, ed. C.B. Macpherson (Harmondsworth 1968), 727.

[47] Hobbes, *Behemoth*, 201.

should conclude with a study of a work written by one of its greatest thinkers. By any standard, Thomas Hobbes's *Behemoth: the History of the Causes of the Civil Wars of England* is a seminal landmark in the historiography of the English Revolution. I will show that the 'Behemoth', 'great and monstrous beasts' which came together and rose up against 'Leviathan', singular embodiment of 'the science of justice' and perfect form of the state, was precisely what modern historians and social scientists, somewhat more abstractly, have called 'the public sphere'.[48]

The Behemoth was a beast born from centuries of English history. In a very real sense, Hobbes believed that history and, above all, a historical mentality, caused the 'revolution' (his word).[49] As he rightly perceived, the past as embodied in histories, historical memories, exemplars, customs and precedents framed and shaped the moral, legal and political sensibilities of all classes and communities of English people. Their justification for Protestantism was that it derived from precepts that were prior to the foundation of the Catholic Church, those of Jesus and the apostles; and that it went back, in English history, to Wyclif and the Lollards. Young Richard Hakluyt used his contemporaries' sense of the 'deep time' embodied in their nation to persuade them to go out and conquer the world: in his account, it was what the best of English people had been doing since the days of Arthur and Merlin. Representative government and the liberties of free-born Englishmen had precedence over Norman 'tyranny' because they derived from the Anglo-Saxon

[48] 'Behemoth' is of Hebrew origin (Job 40.15), the plural of *b'hemah*, probably derived from Egyptian *p-che-man*, 'water ox' or 'hippopotamus'. First used in the Lollard bible; Milton wrote, 'Behemoth, biggest born of earth'. The *OED* suggests that it is used in modern literature to mean 'one of the largest and strongest animals'. Hobbes was undoubtedly likening the sufferings of England to the proverbial sufferings of Job, and used it to refer to the 'beast' who overthrew *Leviathan*, which is singular, originally the Semitic 'name of some aquatic animal (real or imaginary) of enormous size, frequently mentioned in Hebrew poetry', e.g. Job 41. Thus 'Behemoth' referred to the *many* beasts, or 'many-headed monster', sealed against nature into one, that overthrew the *unity* of the perfect, monarchical commonwealth.

[49] Christopher Hill, 'The Word "Revolution"', in Hill, *A Nation of Change and Novelty: Radical Politics, Religion and Literature in Seventeenth Century England* (London 1990), 100–20; for Hobbes the events of 1640–60 constituted a 'revolution' in the literal sense: 'I have seen in this revolution a circular motion of the sovereign power through two usurpers, from the late King to this his son. For (leaving out the power of the council of officers, which was but temporary, and no otherwise owned by them but in trust) it moved from King Charles I to the Long Parliament; from thence to the Rump; from the Rump to Oliver Cromwell; and then back again from Richard Cromwell to the Rump; thence to the Long Parliament; and thence to King Charles II, where long may it remain' (*Behemoth*, 256). That it should have followed this circular pattern was probably inevitable, in his view, since it had taken place in defiance of his 'political science' or 'geometry'.

constitution. The past – mythical or otherwise – had been a reflexive measure of the present in movements against serfdom, labour disputes, lordly encroachments, enclosures, boundary disputes, debates about the prerogatives of parliamentarians, lords and kings since (as it were) 'time out of mind'. Far enough back, the past was good. Somewhere in the temporal distance was an ideal world that could be recovered and used to measure and judge the decay and corruption of the present. Hobbes stood the historical reflex of English constitutional culture on its head. The monstrous 'Behemoth', in Hobbes's account, embodied the collective effects of recorded English history, humanist obsessions with ancient republics and the English deification of past events. 'Leviathan', the only *true* form of a commonwealth, was ahistorical, timeless and derived from what he conceived as 'geometric' reasoning.

The single, fundamental cause of the 'revolution' of 1640–60 was, indeed, historical. It was that the 'whole nation', even 'the king's counsellors, lords, and other persons of quality and experience', had been convinced by their history that 'the government of England was not an absolute, but a mixed monarchy'. From this tragic error, as Hobbes conceived it, they deduced 'that if the king should clearly subdue this parliament . . . his power would be what he pleased, and theirs as little as he pleased: which they counted tyranny'.[50] We have seen repeatedly in these pages that theories of tyranny had underpinned every English rebellion since the thirteenth century. They were central to the discourse of the commonweal, and as pivotal to early modern English constitutional culture as any other single element. 'As if', wrote Hobbes in the conclusion to *Leviathan*, 'the Right of the Kings of England did depend on the goodnesse of the cause of *William* the Conquerour, and upon their lineall, and directest descent from him; by which means, there would perhaps be no tie of the Subjects obedience to their Sovereign at this day in all the world':

wherein whilest [Sovereigns] needlessely think to justifie themselves, they justifie all the successful Rebellions that Ambition shall at any time raise against them, and their Successors. Therefore I put down for one of the most effectuall seeds of the Death of an State, that the Conquerors require not only a Submission of mens actions to them for the future, but also an Approbation of all their actions past; when there is scarce a Common-wealth in the world, whose beginnings can in conscience be justified.

---

[50] Hobbes, *Behemoth*, 144; Kishlansky, 'Charles I', 41 and n. 6, describes the view that 'the king's overthrow . . . [was] a moment in the history of freedom . . . a stand against tyranny by defenders of the liberties of a freeborn people' as 'the current textbook line from which there are few dissenters'.

That Hobbes chose to keep his denial of the theory of tyranny until last –
his *coup de grace*, as it were – shows that he knew it to have been the
great underlying legitimation of all rebellions, past and present. Hobbes
was never more heterodox than in his view that 'the name of Tyranny,
signifieth nothing more, nor lesse, than the name of Sovereignty, be it
in one, or many men, saving that they that use the former word are
understood to be angry with them they call Tyrants;'

> I think the toleration of a professed hatred of Tyranny, is a Toleration of hatred
> to Common-wealth in general, and another evill seed, not differing much from
> the former. For to the justification of a Conqueror, the reproach of the Cause
> of the Conquered, is for the most part necessary: but neither of them necessary
> for the Obligation of the Conquered.[51]

This 'error' was rooted in a virtually unquestioned precept, that the
rights of a people and their constitution can be derived from historical
precedent. For Hobbes, it made no difference how often kings had been
deposed and even murdered in the past for upholding their absolute
sovereignty. History revealed only what people had done. It had nothing
at all to say about the rightness or wrongness of what they had done.
That 'Henry IV [or any other usurper] came to the crown by the votes
of a parliament', was of no constitutional significance whatsoever. The
Parliament of 1399–1400, in Hobbes's opinion, had been 'not much
inferior in wickedness to this Long Parliament, that [also] deposed and
murdered their lawful king'.[52] The history of constitutions was a catalogue of 'wickedness' derived from the erroneous belief that the number
of people and historical examples that can be marshalled to a cause bears
any relation at all to its truth or falsity.

Hobbes believed that the 'revolution' occurred because the sovereignty
of monarchy as he conceived it had *already* broken down. As long as
Charles I continued to insist on his prerogatives – his duty, in Hobbes's
conception – civil war and, given the way Hobbes calculated the division
of powers in *Behemoth*, the king's defeat was inevitable. Quentin Skinner
recently affirmed that the Behemoth's fundamental precept, as Hobbes
saw it (that kingly and noble prerogatives reduced the rest of the nation
to 'slavery') had first broken the surface during the debates about the
Petition of Right in 1628, when 'Sir John Scudamore asked his fellow
members seriously to consider "whether we were slaves or bondmen",
and whether "our vital liberties did in a manner want life".' Another
supporter of the Petition, Sir John Strangeways, agreed: 'the great work of

---

[51] Hobbes, *Leviathan*, 721–2.   [52] Hobbes, *Behemoth*, 131.

this day', he said, 'is to free the subject'. 'The same commitments', writes Skinner, 'surfaced with a vengeance as soon as Parliament reconvened [on Tuesday 3 November] 1640'.[53] Strafford was impeached the next day and as a result of his analysis of the situation, Hobbes immediately knew what was coming and fled for France. 'The reason I came away was that I saw words that tended to advance the prerogative of the king began to be examined in Parliament', he wrote:

And I knew some that had a good will to have had me troubled, and might for anything I saw in their honesties make both the words and the witnesses. Besides, I thought if I went not then, there was nevertheless a disorder coming on that would make it worse being there than here.[54]

Hobbes was convinced by the events of November 1640 that the kind of legitimacy crisis that had hedged in and toppled kings and regimes in England so often before, could no longer be resisted. From the belief that kings were 'political', not 'absolute', flowed the belief that they could be denied the means to govern. Hobbes was sure that if the king could have obtained the money to pay them, he could have had an army of sixty thousand men. 'But the king's treasury was very low,' he tells us, 'and his enemies, that pretended the people's ease from taxes, and many other specious things, had the command of the city of London, and most of the cities and corporate towns of England, and of many particular persons besides.'[55]

Apart from parliamentarians' sense of English historical precedent, many streams of history had conditioned the burgeoning of Behemoth. 'An exceedingly great number of men of the better sort,' he wrote, had been influenced by 'the glorious histories and the sententious politics of the ancient popular governments of the Greeks and Romans, amongst whom kings were hated and branded with the name of tyrants'. The

---

[53] Quentin Skinner, 'Rethinking Political Liberty', *History Workshop Journal* 61 (2006), 158. Noel Malcolm, 'Hobbes, Sandys, and the Virginia Company', *Historical Journal* 24:2, shows that Hobbes's first encounters with 'politicians such as [Sir Edwin] Sandys, [Sir Dudley] Digges and [Sir John] Danvers, whose sympathies lay, in general terms, with Country against Court, Common Law against Chancery, and parliamentary privilege against royal prerogative' occurred several years before Charles I became king, in the early 1620s, when he sat with those men in the Court of the Virginia Company. Malcolm warns against exaggerating the immediate effects on him of these encounters, but writes that 'Hobbes surely did react against their political ideas, which were based, at times, quite explicitly, on "natural rights" which were thought to be both prior to and independent of political society, and derivable intuitively from natural law.' (300–1).

[54] *The Correspondence of Thomas Hobbes*, ed. Noel Malcolm, 115, quotation from A.P. Martinich, *Hobbes: a Biography* (Cambridge 1999), 162.

[55] *Behemoth*, 4–5.

result was that 'popular government (though no tyrant was ever so cruel as a popular assembly) passed by the name of liberty'.[56]

The classical republicanism that was part of the elite education system was one of many streams feeding into the conjuncture. The nascent 'republicanism' of the City of London derived from a desire to imitate the prosperity of the Dutch republic, which had overthrown 'their monarch, the king of Spain'. Hobbes was in no doubt at all that commercial republicanism was an important cause of the legitimacy crisis and that it decisively shaped its outcome.[57] Moreover, classical and commercial republicanism were only two of many historical chains of cause and effect that had corrupted the populace to such a degree that the whole nation was 'so ignorant of their duty, as that not one perhaps of ten thousand knew what right any man had to command him, or what necessity there was of King or Commonwealth.'[58] Hobbes did not share the conviction of many of his contemporaries that constitutions could be deduced from theology, but like Machiavelli, Hobbes's one-time employer Sir Francis Bacon, and his amanuensis, William Petty, he did still cling to the idea that unity in religion was a *sine qua non* of unity in a commonwealth.[59]

---

[56] 'And out of these men were chosen the greatest part of the House of Commons, or if they were not the greatest part, yet by advantage of their eloquence, were always able to sway the rest': *Behemoth*, 6, 30–1. Denis Glover, 'The Putney Debates: Popular versus Elite Republicanism', *Past and Present* 164 (August 1999), 57, writes that 'Hobbes was to claim that the cause of the Civil Wars in England was the reading of translations by poorly educated fanatics who learned the wrong lessons.' The passage referred to (*Behemoth*, 56) does not mention translations or fanatics, but refers to men who, 'studying Greek and Latin, became acquainted with the democratical principles of Aristotle and Cicero . . .' *Behemoth* is not particularly useful for Glover's argument about the influence of classical republicanism on the Levellers: Hobbes invariably associated it with university men and members of parliament. In *Behemoth* elite parliamentarians' reading of classical republicans was *one* 'cause' of many that came together in the 1640s; for an account of the limitations of classical republicanism in the English revolution, see Ellen Meiksins Wood, 'Why it Matters', review of Quentin Skinner, *Hobbes and Republican Liberty* (Cambridge 2008), in *London Review of Books*, 25 September 2008.

[57] *Behemoth*, 6; *Leviathan*, 368: 'I doubt not, but many men, have been contented to see the late troubles in *England*, out of an imitation of the Low Countries.' Steve Pincus, 'Neither Machiavellian Moment nor Possessive Individualism: Commercial Society and the Defenders of the English Commonwealth', *American Historical Review* (June 1998), 720 and *passim*, has shown the predominance of commercial over classical republicanism, and the significance of the Dutch paradigm, in contemporary debate. Malcolm, 'Hobbes, Sandys, and the Virginia Company', traces Hobbes's belief in the commercial-republican tendencies of London merchants to his direct experiences of the early 1620s. BL E260/2, *A Discourse Consisting of Motives for the Enlargement and Freedom of Trade* (London, 11 April 1645), 3, arguing against monopolies, envisaged a global, universal 'republic' of free trade. Its author was aware that 'this is not a new complaint, but an old grievance, having been petitioned against above 150 years ago' (49).

[58] *Behemoth*, 4.

[59] Francis Bacon, 'Of Unity in Religion', *Essays* (London 1906); 'As for religion,' wrote Petty in his will, 'I die in the profession of that faith, and in the practice of such worship as I find established by the law of my country.' Where Hobbes's treatment of

First among the inculcators of 'ignorance' in the population at large, therefore, were schismatics, amongst whom Hobbes named Papists, Presbyterians, Independents, Anabaptists and other sectaries. Hobbes was as unconvinced by Catholic theology as he was by the constitutional claims of the papacy, yet he was far more tolerant of the 'abundance of people . . . that still retained the religion of their ancestors', than he was of protestant 'schismatics'. The problem faced by passive 'survivalists' was that notorious 'emissaries of the Roman Church' had brought about a situation in which 'the papists of England [were] *looked upon* as men that would not be sorry for any disorders that might possibly make way to the restoring of the Pope's authority'. Hobbes counted catholic 'survivalists' amongst his friends, and did not buy this slander. Nevertheless, it had contributed to 'the distempers of the state'.[60]

Another compounding cause was Bible-translation. 'After the Bible was translated into English, every man, nay, every boy and wench, that could read English, thought they spoke with God, and understood what he said.' Then, shortly after the accession of Queen Elizabeth, university men and Presbyterians (Hobbes often suggests they were both) 'went abroad preaching in most of the market-towns of England, as the preaching friars had formerly done, upon working-days in the morning; in which sermons, these and others of the same tenets, that had charge of souls, both by the manner and matter of their preaching, applied themselves wholly to the winning of the people to a liking of their doctrines and good opinion of their persons'. Hobbes's contempt for capitalists was nearly as great as his disdain for Presbyterians; he anticipated Max Weber's idea that Calvinism greased the wheels of commerce. 'The power of the Presbyterians was so very great, that, not only the citizens of London were almost all of them at their devotion, but also the greatest part of all other cities and market-towns.' Hobbes identified Presbyterians as agents of *trafike*: 'they did never in their sermons, or but lightly, inveigh against the lucrative vices of men of trade or handicraft; such as are feigning, lying, cozening, hypocrisy, or other uncharitableness, except want of charity to their pastors and to the faithful: which was a great ease to the generality of citizens and the inhabitants of market-towns, and no little profit to themselves.'[61]

'schismatics' was vitriolic, Petty's was ironic: 'He can be excellent droll', wrote John Aubrey, 'and will preach extempore incomparably, either the Presbyterian way, Independent, Capucin friar, or Jesuit': Petty's will (May 2, 1685) and Aubrey's Life of Petty repr. in Wilson Lloyd Bevan, *Sir William Petty: a Study in English Economic Literature*, American Economic Association 9:4 (1894).

[60] *Behemoth*, 27. The term 'survivalist' is from John Bossy, *Christianity in the West 1400–1700* (Oxford 1985).

[61] *Behemoth*, 28, 30–1.

This theme immensely strengthened the 'Dutch' republicanism of merchants because in Hobbes's view 'Presbyterians' owed their sinecures to businessmen. He also disliked their 'puritanism'. They wanted to ban plays, but 'no tragedian in the world could have acted the part of a right godly man unacquainted with such art'. They banned plays because they wanted to be the only theatrical act in town. The great psychologist also detected a more sinister art of repression that he was one of the first to identify as the essence of 'puritanism': 'They did in their sermons and writings,' he wrote,

maintain and inculcate, that the very first motions of the mind, that is to say, the delight men and women took in the sight of one another's form, though they checked the proceed thereof so that it never grew to be a design, was nevertheless a sin, they brought young men into desperation and to think themselves damned, because they could not (and no man can, and is contrary to the constitution of nature) behold a delightful object without delight. And by this means they became confessors to such as were thus troubled by their consciences, and were observed by them as their spiritual doctors in all cases of conscience.[62]

Streams of classical-humanist and schismatic rhetoric combined with historical memories of past resistances, classically inspired fears of 'slavery' to a constitutionally distant king and court, commercial opportunism, sexual repression, news and stories of wars against 'papist' tyranny overseas, a parliamentarian franchise expanded by inflation and, not least, no fewer than seventeen specific 'pretended faults' or occasions that had been specifically charged against the king, feeding the crescendo of disorderly and 'erroneous' public opinion that, in Hobbes's view, had been building since Charles had dissolved his first Parliament little more than a decade earlier.[63] The crescendo became a roaring hubbub in the months before he fled the kingdom, probably on the weekend of 14/15 November

---

[62] *Ibid.*, 33–4.
[63] *Ibid.*, 106–7. They were: 1. The dissolution of his first Parliament at Oxford. 2. The dissolution of his second Parliament, being in the second year of his reign. 3. The dissolution of his Parliament in the fourth year of his reign. 4. The fruitless expedition against Calais. 5. The peace made with Spain, whereby the Palatine's cause was deserted, and left to chargeable and hopeless treaties. 6. The sending of commissions to raise money by way of loan. 7. Raising of ship-money. 8. Enlargement of forests, contrary to Magna Charta. 9. The design of engrossing all the gunpowder into one hand, and keeping it in the Tower of London. 10. A design to bring in the use of brass money. 11. The fines, imprisonments, stigmatizings, mutilations, whippings, pillories, gags, confinements, and banishments, by sentence in the Court of Star-chamber. 12. The displacing of judges. 13. Illegal acts of the Council-table. 14. The arbitrary and illegal power of the Earl Marshal's Court. 15. The abuses in Chancery, Exchequer-chamber, and Court of Wards. 16. The selling of titles of honour, of judges, and serjeants' places, and other offices. 17. The insolence of bishops and other clerks, in suspensions, excommunications, deprivations, and degradations, of divers painful, and learned, and pious ministers.

1640.[64] The archaeological surface of the public sphere is represented by the surviving products of the 'unprecedented media storm' that took off in the months preceding his departure. 'The explosion of print in the opening years of the Long Parliament', writes David Cressy, 'was one of the most revolutionary features of the English Revolution'. Cressy's figures describe a startling explosion of printed opinion. 'From just six or seven hundred known items a year in the 1630s, the numbers of known publications rose dramatically to almost 900 in 1640, over two thousand in 1641, and over four thousand in 1642.'[65] *A Discourse upon Questions in Debate between the King and Parliament* (1643) was not exaggerating in its claim that the proceedings of the Short Parliament and its aftermath 'begat universal dissidence in the people of his majesties personal promises'. By then, public opinion held that Charles's 'best resolutions were easily overthrown by the counsel of others . . . Which opinion, true or false, whenever it got belief, hath proven fatale to the Princes or the People of this kingdom.'[66] The die was cast in the years immediately *before* the outbreak of the wars between Crown and Parliament.

9.6   Rascability rising: precipitating rebellion

Hobbes would have agreed with David Cressy that the civil wars were the *result* of the crisis of 1640–2. After listening patiently to Hobbes's catalogue of long-term causes and circumstances, his interlocutor (*Behemoth* is a dialogue) drew an apparently inescapable conclusion. 'In

---

[64] Brian Manning, *The English People and the English Revolution* (Harmondsworth 1978), chs. 3–4, remains the classic account of popular involvement at this point.

[65] David Cressy, *England on Edge: Crisis and Revolution 1640–1642* (Oxford 2006), 292–3. As Cressy writes, 'the quantity, character, and impact of these publications constituted an unprecedented media storm . . . There were more items published in 1641 than in any year in the previous history of English printing (2,177 in the English Short-Title Catalogue, of which the bookseller George Thomason collected 721). More appeared in 1642 than at any time again before the eighteenth century (4,188 in ESTC, including 2,134 in Thomason).' Cressy's sources (47: 292) are as follows. 'Figures from the online English Short-Title Catalogue, September 2003'; Alain Veylit, 'Some Statistics on the Number of Surviving Printed Titles for Great Britain and Dependencies from the Beginnings of Print in England to the year 1800, http://www.cbsr.ucr.edu/ESTCStatistics.html'; G.K. Fortescue (ed.), *Catalogue of the Pamphlets, Books, Newspapers, and Manuscripts Collected by George Thomason, 1640–1661* (2 vols., 1908), 1, xxi. The effect of Thomason's collecting should not be underestimated, though he had only a third of the publications of 1641 and half those of 1642. For similar figures based on the Wing catalogue, see D.F. McKenzie, 'The London Book Trade in 1644', in John Horden (ed.), *Bibliographia: Lectures 1975–1988 by Recipients of the Marc Fich Prize for Bibliography* (Oxford 1992), 152; John Barnard and D.F. McKenzie (ed.), *Cambridge History of the Book in Britain IV* (Cambridge 2003); Joad Raymond, *Pamphlets and Pamphleteering in Early Modern Britain* (Cambridge 2003), 163–70, 194–5.

[66] BL: E69/26.

such a constitution of people, methinks, the King is *already* ousted from his government', he says. He 'cannot imagine how the King should come by any means to resist them', and suggests that 'they need not have taken arms for it'.[67]

Cressy's *England on Edge* is a landmark production of research conceived and conducted on early modern England since the 1970s. Hobbes's realization that 'there was ... a disorder coming' was, to put it mildly, prescient. Cressy lists sixteen more 'shocks and repercussions' experienced by the English body politic 'between the spring of 1640 and the summer of 1642'.[68] Never had the words *commonweal* and *commonwealth* been more furiously bandied about and argued over. Printed records including pamphlets, handwritten news-sheets and libels, broadsheets, cartoons, sermons, public lectures and propaganda were, we now know, only the tip of the iceberg. Cressy and other students of the archives of everyday life have shown that 'dangerous words' were routinely spoken and heard by all ranks and classes of English people. Where the revolution differed from rebellions of the past was not in its causes and social dynamics but in the explosion of printed argument and, perhaps the decisive element, its political geography. Westminster and London were the epicentres of the storm. Classical republican rhetoric in the House of Commons mingled with the commercial or 'Dutch' republicanism of the City, provincial capitals and market towns; national news was interwoven by preachers and gossip with a legion of personal resentments, local issues and the immemorial irreverence and the hand-to-mouth desperation of the 'rascability'.

The pattern of recruitment for rebellion was as it had been in earlier rebellions. It was set by the London riots of May 1640, when 'the vile rabble of prentices and other discontented scum of the people', as a conservative churchman put it, ranged through the City making 'horns with their fingers' and 'other rude and base gestures of disgrace'. Cressy's analysis in fact shows that the participants 'were broadly representative of the metropolitan male population'. As Larry Poos showed was the case in Essex before the rebellion of 1381, and as Fortescue's theory predicted, 'most members of the crowd belonged to those strata below the "political nation" whose occupations, youth, or dependent status denied them a political voice'.[69] The 'turmoils' of 1640–2, like the 'news' that fed them, spread rapidly. Cressy describes and analyses 'parish turmoils' in Somerset, Northamptonshire, Norfolk, Herefordshire, Cambridge, Essex, Hertfordshire, Kent, Durham, Exeter, Shropshire,

---

[67] *Behemoth*, 7 (emphasis added).   [68] Cressy, *England on Edge*, 424–6.
[69] *Ibid.*, 116–7.

Birmingham, Hertfordshire, Staffordshire, Bristol, Suffolk, Warwickshire and Cheshire.[70] Cressy's telling synthesis of archival material leaves little doubt that Hobbes's diagnosis was correct. In the light of his evidence, the conceit that England was 'on edge' from 1640–2 is ironic understatement. By the time the Long Parliament came together in London in November, everybody knew they were living through nothing less than a wholesale crisis of the body politic.

Richard Baxter's view that 'the Warre was begun in our streets before the King or Parliament had any Armies' was the common memory of observers on all sides. Hobbes agreed that from start to finish it was 'the common people whose hands were to decide the controversy', and that they 'understood not the reasons of either party'. The puritan John Corbet's well-known analysis of the 'moment of decision' in Gloucestershire, and its military aftermath, was just another illustration of the common view. The 'multitude' precipitated resistance and its continuing support was the *sine qua non* of parliamentarian success. The efforts of George Brydges, lord Chandos, to serve the king's Commission of Array, Corbet explained, were 'stifled in the birth, and crusht by the rude hand of the multitude'. In this sense what happened at Cirencester was emblematic of the whole conjuncture. It was Brydges's fear of the 'fury' of the 'meanest of the people' that 'constrained' him to sign an agreement to withdraw the king's Commission, and it was the 'vulgar multitude' that tore his coach to pieces the next morning, after discovering that Brydges had made a humiliating escape through the back door of a local gentleman's house. The episode was virtually an exact reprise, in exactly the same place, of the proceedings that had brought the Epiphany plot to a violent and dramatic close in January 1400, except that in August 1642 the noble target of the 'common people' escaped.[71] As for their motives, Corbet echoed Hobbes's view that 'common people know nothing of right or wrong by their own meditation' and he was himself active in ensuring that 'our rebels were publicly taught rebellion in the pulpits'.[72] The 'ignoble multitude' was subject to 'extasie of passion', wrote Corbet; 'they glory to vent their humours by reason of their usuall restraint and subjection'. The 'unexplicable [irrational] selfe-ingagement' that came 'upon the common people' was channelled by 'a more undescerned guidance of superiour agents' to turn them 'to the terrour of the enemy'. As had happened in January 1400, a few 'prudent men' placed themselves judiciously amongst the crowd and guided its actions, 'yet', as Corbet put it, 'no further than themselves can over-rule and moderate it'.

---

[70] *Ibid.*, 192–202. [71] See above, Chapter 5.4. [72] *Behemoth*, 181.

David Underdown's description of the hanging of Hugh Green at Dorchester on 18 August 1642, provides a perhaps more realistic vignette of what was implied by the 'undescerned guidance' of 'prudent men' on such occasions. When the Catholic Green 'refused to play the condemned man's customary penitential role, and steadfastly insisted that he was no traitor' it 'inflamed the already excited crowd, and Sir Thomas Trenchard's chaplain screamed "He blasphemeth! Stop the mouth of the blasphemer!".' Few doubted the obvious, numerical fact that in the final analysis the 'common people . . . were to decide the issue'.[73] All depended on who they could be persuaded to fight for, but their indispensability did not persuade many of the persuaders to form any higher opinion of their ultimate worth.

I will suggest in my final section that earlier conceptions of class structure *hardened* as a result of the civil wars. This may be reflected in Andy Wood's observation that the term 'middling sort . . . seems scarcely to have been used before the English Revolution'.[74] My impression is that use of the phrase 'common people' to refer to the landless labouring poor also became more frequent in the course of the wars, indicating that participants were forced to think harder about the social implications of the struggle against the king. John Corbet's uses of the phrase as a synonym for 'vulgar multitude', as distinct from his own more 'discerning' middle rank, are only a little more discriminating than the usages of medieval chroniclers. Hobbes's usages are more thoughtful, as we might expect. Like Corbet, he generally used the phrase 'common people' to mean the labouring poor, but he was less taken in by the claims to superiority that were implicit in propertied parliamentarians' usages.

Unlike Corbet, who regarded the 'common people' as inherently irrational, Hobbes was capable of contemplating exceptions. On one occasion he wrote that 'there were *very few* of the common people that cared much for either of the causes, but would have taken any side for pay or plunder'. The implication is that some of them, at least, may have reasoned about the causes and did indeed care. But in general, Hobbes thought, the common people followed those who paid their wages. Artisans followed the petty capitalists who provided them with their raw materials and found markets for the commodities they produced. Tenants followed their local lords – or not, depending on whether they thought

---

[73] Richard Baxter, quoted from Andy Wood, *Riot, Rebellion and Popular Culture*, 129; Hobbes, *Behemoth*, 3, 146, 181; 'A letter sent to a worthy member of the House of Commons, concerning the Lord Shandois coming to Ciceter to execute the Commission of Array. Read in the House of Commons and ordered to be forthwith printed. August 22 1642'; Corbet, *Historicall Relation*, 8–9, 14–18, 104, 121; Underdown, *Fire from Heaven: Life in an English Town in the Seventeenth Century* (London 1993), 197–8.

[74] Wood, *Riot, Rebellion and Popular Politics*, 122.

it would get them what they wanted. The employer classes, explained Hobbes, 'must needs be of the rebel party: because the grievances are but taxes, to which citizens, that is, merchants, whose profession is their private gain, are naturally mortal enemies'. Hobbes was in no doubt about the perfidy of middle men whose profits came from 'making poor people sell their labour to them at their own prices'.

So that poor people, for the most part, might get a better living working in Bridewell, than by spinning, weaving, and other such labour as they can do; saving that by working slightly they may help themselves a little, to the disgrace of our manufacture.[75]

Hobbes's point was that 'poor people' living in manufacturing districts and commercial towns and cities were 'cozened' into accepting the leadership of the very men who most exploited them.

Later, when Hobbes was considering the authority of the Rump parliament after the execution of the king, he put his position with regard to the relative stupidity of the classes who had been lumped together by the cause of parliament more clearly. 'What silly things are the common sort of people, to be cozened as they were so grossly', says his interlocutor. Hobbes's reply describes what he considered to be the 'ignorance' of *all* parties in the civil wars. 'What sort of people, as to this matter, are not of the common sort? The craftiest knaves of all the Rump were no wiser than the rest whom they cozened.'

For the most of them did believe that the same things that they imposed upon the generality, were just and reasonable; and especially the great haranguers, and such as pretended to learning. For who can be a good subject in a monarchy, whose principles are taken from the enemies of monarchy, such as were Cicero, Seneca, Cato and other politicians of Rome, and Aristotle of Athens, who seldom spake of kings but as of wolves and other ravenous beasts? You may perhaps think a man has need of nothing else to know the duty he owes to his governor, and what right he has to order him, but a good natural wit; but it is otherwise. For it is a science, and built upon sure and clear principles, and to be learned by deep and careful study, or from masters who have deeply studied it.[76]

9.7 The constitutional landscape redefined: settlement versus mobility

I do hear nothing at all that can convince me why any man that is born in England ought not to have his voice in election of burgesses.[77]

---

[75] *Behemoth*, 3, 158–9.   [76] *Behemoth*, 200–1.
[77] Colonel Rainborough, 'The Putney Debates: the Debate on the Franchise', in David Wootton (ed.), *Divine Right and Democracy: an Anthology of Political Writings in Stuart England* (Harmondsworth 1986), 288–9.

*I would have an eye to property . . . if a man have not a permanent interest, he can have
no claim . . . I mean by permanent, local, that is not anywhere else; but he that has no
permanent interest, that is here today and gone tomorrow, I do not see that he has such
a permanent interest.*[78]

Since the end of the fourteenth century, no precept had been more 'orthodox', in Professor Aylmer's sense, than the idea that the commonwealth
was constituted by a monarch's court and the households of nobles, gentry, great merchants, yeomen and urban burgesses, and a smallholding
and landless class of artisans, labourers and servants. Controversies and
crises were not about the validity of these ranks of secular society, but
about the roles each of them was supposed to perform for the preservation and prosperity of the whole and the qualities and political agency
that should be attached to them. The emergence of this class structure
was not a result of theory but of historical agency, the repeated observation and assertion of the constitutional significance of the 'class' in
question, to a point where 'it' became institutionalized, first as observation, then as rhetoric and strategy, then as a taken-for-granted 'fact
of life'. Norman-Angevin conceptions and practices of monarchy were
challenged by movements led by barons in the twelfth and thirteenth
centuries. By the time of de Montfort's 'common enterprise' it was taken
for granted that, in times of crises, kings and barons had to compete for
the loyalty and service of 'bachelors' and 'middle people', the lesser *liberi
homines* who, along with greater merchants and barons, were formally
incorporated into the counsels of governance between 1327 and 1376.

During the fourteenth century it became a reflex for the knights and
burgesses who constituted the House of Commons to defend their intran-
sigence with regard to the king's financial demands by claiming to be
under pressure from the 'lesser people' of their towns and provinces. A
growing tradition of local 'rebellions' of various kinds added plausibility
to their contention that the 'commonalties' (their 'constituencies') were,
alas, not as passive as they ought to be. The first great commons rebellion of 1381 confirmed that the 'commonalty' was capable of forming
itself into an army and acting without gentry or noble leadership. In the
aftermath it became obvious that governments needed the support of the
'middle ranks' (or as I have characterized them, the non-commissioned
officers of the social order) in order to restore and maintain order. For
their part, burgesses in the Commons and the big men of the towns and
villages were also keen to disassociate themselves from what had happened in order to avoid confiscation of their estates. The formation of

[78] Commissary General Ireton, *Ibid.*, 290–2.

'Lollardy' in the decades after 1381 consolidated this 'spectre of com-monalty' by suggesting that, regardless of prescribed authority, it was in the process of imposing its language and populist ideas on religious thought and practice. Henry of Lancaster's strategy in 1399–1400 artic-ulated all of these agencies for his own purposes. It did not take him long to learn that summoning the commonalty was, in fact, a danger to everything he really stood for.

It was in the decades after 1381 that conceptions of a commonalty divided into two sorts of people were consolidated. Before c.1400 a 'yeo-man' was a soldier below the ranks of knight and esquire. The new associations of the word reflected the functions they had performed and the ways such men had always been perceived in the localities they gov-erned as larger landholders, independent craftsmen, jurors, officials and employers of labour. We first come across vernacular literary references defining their role in the body politic (or 'political nation') in the first decade of the fifteenth century. Henceforth the yeoman was represented less and less as the lowest rank of the military ruling classes, more and more as the leader of what Sir Thomas Smith would later call 'the fourth sort of men' or 'rascability'. If John Smyth of Nibley's research on the records of the Hundred and Barony of Berkeley (where Trevisa spent his adult life and Tyndale grew up) have general applicability, the yeo-manry became renowned for their 'independency' vis-à-vis the gentry and aristocracy (but not the monarch, whoever he or she happened to be) during the Wars of the Roses. It was during this prolonged struggle within the ruling classes, in the wake of Cade's rebellion, that Sir John Fortescue formulated his influential conceptions of the yeoman's pivotal importance in English military and constitutional life. Fortescue's theory of rebellion gave authoritative form to what men of this class had argued in most of Edward III's parliaments and had proclaimed, with under-standable anxiety, in the wake of the rebellions of 1381 and 1450: 'the "ryff-raffe" made us do it.' Sir Thomas Smith's theory of a common-alty divided into two 'sorts' – independent (propertied, 'self-possessing') yeoman 'respectability', as it were, and dependent (landless) proletarian 'rascability' – gave lucid form to what was, by then, the standard ranking system that constituted the commonwealth of England.

Smith was an original thinker in the sense that he was not afraid to follow observation and reasoning beyond the conventional class preju-dices of his day. We have observed that with regard to the 'fourth sort of men', for example, he allowed himself to stretch the now conventional view that governance only extended to the yeomen and citizens. The standard view was that 'artificers, as Taylors, Shoomakers, Carpenters, Brickemakers, Bricklayers, Masons, &c . . . have no voice or authorities in our common wealth, and no account is made of them but onelie to be ruled, not to rule other'. At that point in his discourse, however, he remembered an inconvenient observation, that in fact if not in theory such men 'be not altogether neglected', since in many localities they were needed to perform offices of the commonwealth like jurors, constables and tithingmen.[79] This conception still left the bulk of the '*capite censii proletarii* or *operae*' without 'voice or authority in our common wealth', of course, yet it almost certainly reflected his sense that habitually regarding some 70 per cent of English householders as 'inferior humans' who cared nothing and contributed even less to the commonweal was part of the reason why rebellions were such a routine phenomenon. This was almost certainly part of the reason he made such a point of reminding his peers that the mobile and despised manufacturing workers actually contributed more to the commonweal than they did.

Social historians have shown that if these were Smith's intentions, they were not heeded. In the century after 1549 the great divide between what had become the junior ranks of the constitution (the 'middles' – 'sorts', 'ranks', 'people', 'class', whichever word is preferred) and the rest intensified. The 'polarization' of the two great classes of the medieval commonalty was no new impulse. Yet it was undoubtedly nurtured, in the second half of the sixteenth century, by underlying economic, demographic, state-political and intellectual movements. The 'reform of popular culture' was given renewed force by protestant vocationalism and, somewhat paradoxically in the light of their emphasis on the critical importance of manufacturing workers, the arguments of the proto-political-economists. The abundant evidence for this polarization has persuaded Andy Wood that the rebellions of 1549 were 'the last medieval rebellions'. I have suggested that the ideas and social dynamics that brought England to boiling point in the early 1640s were those that had been sparking rebellions of the commonalty since 1381.[80]

Continuous observation and remembrance of how the civil wars had begun and been conducted, and in particular of the critical role, as precipitants and then as common soldiers, of the 'vulgar multitude', shaped the controversy that arose when the wars against the king had been won. By the time of the Putney Debates (October 1647) what Hobbes regarded as the unholy alliance that had made the war possible (propertied 'middle ranks' and the landless multitude) was becoming ragged. It was in

---

[79] Smith, *De Republica*, Part I, ch. 24.
[80] The one novelty in the conjuncture of the 1640s, as noted by Ellen Meiksins Wood, 'Why it Matters', 4–5, was that 'Inflation had made basic property qualifications [for the franchise] less exclusive, thus widening the base of the electorate.'

the army that the two classes had been in constant association, and it was there that the traditional fall-back position of the propertied middle ranks was clarified with unprecedented lucidity.

It has usually been assumed that the central issue at Putney was whether 'the basis of political rights', including the right to vote, should be grounded on 'property ownership or birthright'. Quentin Skinner recently made the arresting suggestion that this was not 'the issue dividing [Henry] Ireton and [Oliver] Cromwell from the main body of Leveller opinion'. For Skinner, the problem for Ireton and the more conservative Levellers was not ownership of property *per se*, but his belief 'that only those with sufficient property to give them *independence from the will of others* will be *capable* of casting a genuinely free vote'. Skinner's interpretation is that Ireton's position derived from 'the contrast between the figure of the *liber homo* and that of the slave'. Ireton's 'essentially Roman way of thinking' (as Skinner sees it) descended from the contrast between freemen and slaves that, as we saw, had informed parliamentary debates about the Petition of Right in 1628 and debates about the king's prerogative in the Short and Long parliaments. This distinction between freedom and its opposite, slavery, was, in turn, 'embedded in English common law' by Bracton, who got it from 'the law of Rome, and in particular... the rubric *De statu hominis*' in Justinian's *Digest*. When, after the war had been won, conservative Levellers like Petty and Reade, like Ireton and Cromwell, rejected birthright as a criterion for the franchise they were not 'simply [plumping] for property ownership as the alternative'. 'The reason why [Ireton] equates this condition with property ownership', writes Skinner, 'is because, as he expresses the point, only someone with property may be said to have "a permanent interest" in the kingdom, an interest "upon which he may live, and live a freeman without dependence". It is not the mere fact of owning property, but the distinctive ability of those with property to "live upon it as freemen", *and hence to act without servility*, that gives them the entitlement to vote.'[81]

It seems to me that this was not the basis of Ireton's argument. It may have been one of the reasons he had for arguing the way he did, but it is not what he stated. It certainly encapsulates the patronizing contempt for the 'vulgar multitude' expressed by men like John Corbet. Yet the point Ireton repeats is simply that only 'fixed men, and settled men' should vote. This related to what, in earlier sections on *Piers Plowman* and on William Tyndale's world view, I described as '*landschap*-thinking'. The populist Thomas Rainborough immediately spotted the basic, entirely traditional and conventional precept of Ireton's reasoning. Ireton was

---

[81] Skinner, 'Rethinking Political Liberty', 157–8, 163–4.

merely restating the fear of the 'mobility' (the multitude in motion) that had animated Fortescue and Elyot generations earlier: that its victory would result in the confiscation, in effect the abolition, of property.[82] It came to be accepted during the debate that freeholders constituted no more than a fifth of the adult male population.[83] That convinced Ireton that 'if you admit any man that has breath and being [to the franchise] . . . It may destroy property thus . . . those that have interest in the land may be voted out of the land'.[84] His chief opponent, Rainborough, argued that this will not happen because 'the law of God says it . . . thou shalt not steal'.[85] Ireton responded that constitutions are not God's business. 'The law of God does not give me property, nor the law of nature, but property is of human constitution . . . *Constitution founds property*.'[86] It followed that property can only be defended by human laws. The human laws that created the political community Ireton had in mind were historical, but they were not Roman. In defence of Quentin Skinner's 'classicist' argument, Rich did cite the example of Caesar's dictatorship, which came about as a result of a plebeian franchise, whence 'the people's voices were bought and sold'. Cowling immediately qualified Rich's classical exemplar with one nearer home. The forty-shilling freeholder rule, he pointed out, was established by 'the commons of England' when they 'were overpowered by the lords'. To 'make their laws good against encroaching prerogatives . . . they did exclude all slaves'. But 'now the case is not so; all slaves have bought their freedoms'.[87] This was an argument for starting afresh.

Ireton very clearly saw the task ahead as the settlement of an existing constitutional landscape. For him, property was not, first and foremost, an individual or personal attribute. The landscape *is* 'property', and therefore only those classes of people who are 'fixed and permanent' as a result of freehold land have to do with its 'settlement'. Freehold land, for Ireton, is not an abstraction or a legal concept but a permanent place in a settled landscape. It is the land plus that class of people (freeholders), literally, who make it settled. Note, again, that land and specific location, not money, is the measure. 'A man that has no permanent interest in the kingdom, if he has money, his money is as good in another place as here; he has nothing that does *locally fix him* to this kingdom. If that

---

[82] See above, Chapter 5.1, 5.2.

[83] Rich: 'you have five to one in this kingdom that have no permanent interest': Wootton (ed.), *Divine Right and Democracy*, 'Putney Debates', 296; my estimate for Gloucestershire, a county with many freeholders and burgesses, is that 72 per cent of householders were excluded by freeholder franchise: Rollison, *Local Origins*, 151–2.

[84] Wootton, 'Putney Debates', 296.

[85] *Ibid.*, 292.   [86] *Ibid.*, 301–2 (emphasis added).   [87] *Ibid.*, 297.

man will live in this kingdom, or trade among us, that man ought to subject himself to the law made by the people who have the interest of the kingdom in us.'[88] 'Property', for Ireton, is not property in the capitalist sense, it is constituted territory in Leland's, Camden's, or Wilson's sense. It is agreed that the army had fought against slavery imposed by monarchical and aristocratic privilege and prerogative. It is kings' and lords' political prerogatives that the bulk of the leaders of the Parliamentarian cause wished to see them deprived of, not their estates, which, on this reasoning, they should retain. 'I hope that they may live to see the power of the king and the lords thrown down, that may yet live to see property preserved', says Petty.[89] To allow the 'mobility' into the constitution, on these arguments, would dissolve all constitutional settlement and introduce 'anarchy'. My point is that these were not abstract, classical reflexes in the minds of men like Ireton. They pointed to an already constituted landscape.

What Ireton and his propertied contemporaries saw in their minds' eyes when they thought about the constitution was very much what Wilson had seen: a landscape that had been settled, over many centuries, by freeholders. They literally constituted the territorial community of England. Cromwell raised the possibility of a compromise in which 'a very considerable part of copyholders by inheritance . . . ought to have a voice' – in other words, he could only contemplate incorporating the most 'fixed' and 'settled' portion of the 'mobility'.[90] Social historians have shown that these arguments (whether or not we agree with them) were at least grounded in fact. Yeomen and citizens were more settled; the *proletarii* were mobile.[91] It was out of this contrast between the settled political community and the migrant multitude that the eighteenth-century usage, 'mobility', which meant both a 'mob' and 'the lower classes', was formed.[92] These usages emerged, as I have argued throughout this book, out of a very distinctive way of seeing that owed little or nothing to the classical abstractions of ancient authors or the modern abstractions that became part of the modern social-science outlook.[93] In the minds

---

[88] *Ibid.*, 299–300.   [89] *Ibid.*, 294.   [90] *Ibid.*, 306.

[91] Peter Laslett with John Harrison, 'Clayworth and Cogenhoe', in H.E. Bell and R.L. Ollard, *Historical Essays presented to David Ogg* (Cambridge 1963); Keith Wrightson and David Levine, *Poverty and Piety in an English Village, Terling 1525–1700* (London 1979); David Levine and Keith Wrightson, *The Making of an Industrial Society: Whickham 1560–1765* (Oxford 1991), 179; F. Leeson, *Travelling Brothers* (London 1979); Rollison, 'Exploding England: the Dialectics of Mobility and Settlement in Early Modern England,' *Social History* 24:1 (January 1999), 1–16.

[92] *OED*, 'Mobility', which dates the first literary usages in this sense to the 1690s.

[93] See above; John Bossy, 'Some Elementary Forms of Durkheim,' *Past and Present* 95, 12–13 writes of a shift from a mental and linguistic world in which 'society' was an activity

of those who presented them, the foundations of these arguments were neither classical nor modern. They were grounded in a conception of a landscape settled by history and always threatened by the mobile multitude. What they saw in their minds when they thought of their political community was pretty much the timescape and landscape unfolded in this book.

The difference between Rainborough and Ireton, and between the two classes for whom, respectively, they spoke, was that the former thought of the commonwealth as the *people* who had fought the king for control of it, whereas the latter thought of it, like Wilson, as a landscape of dispersed *settlement*. The former was, in this sense, more 'modern' than the latter in anticipating constitutions grounded in a genuinely popular sovereignty. The class distinction between propertied citizens and unpropertied multitude had been implicit for centuries. The civil wars clarified it by forcing both sides to think hard about what rebellions of the past, including their own, had implied. For David Wootton, the originality of the radical Levellers did not rest in their view of the franchise. 'In fact', he observes, 'they were seeking to extend to the country as a whole the franchise which already existed in those urban constituencies where the electorate was most broadly defined'.[94] In this sense, they too were 'thinking backwards' and emphasizing settlement. As we have seen, that was radical enough to strike fear into the hearts and to sharpen the minds of Cromwell, Ireton, Presbyterians, Independents and the vast majority of the 'yeomen and citizens' who had formed the established constituency of the House of Commons since the fourteenth century. To grant the franchise to the unpropertied 'mobility', Ireton assumed, would be to 'take away all property . . . which if you take away, you take away all by that'.[95] The 'revolution in political thought' begun by the

of 'companionship' or 'fellowship', and 'the laws of society' were 'laws for getting on with other people' 'our most general term ['society'] for the body of institutions and relationships within which a relatively large number of people live', and 'Society with a capital S, a kind of sublimated essence of all examples' did not emerge until after 1650. For alternative views of the 'paradigm shift', see Steven Shapin, *A Social History of Truth* (Chicago 1994); Mary Poovey, *A History of the Modern Fact: Problems of Knowledge in the Sciences of Wealth and Society* (Chicago 1998); Thomas Kuhn, *The Structure of Scientific Revolutions*; Michel Foucault, *Society Must Be Defended*, trans. David Lacey (London 2003); Adam T. Smith, *The Political Landscape: Constellations of Authority in Early Complex Polities*, Part I.

94 Wootton, 'From Rebellion to Revolution', 432; Ireton seems to have recognized this: 'And so there's a corporation, a place which has the privilege of a market and trading, which if you should allow to all places equally, I do not see how you could preserve the peace in the kingdom, and that is the reason why in the constitution we have but some few market towns': 'Putney Debates', 291.

95 Wootton, 'Putney Debates', 290.

Levellers shared at least one of Hobbes's precepts, even if, as Wootton presents them, they derived their originality from theology rather than secular, 'geometric' reasoning. Central to the Leveller world view 'was the idea of starting a state *de novo*, which had simply never been considered by previous thinkers, who had assumed that legitimacy derived from past undertakings'.[96] The idea that the past could be swept aside *was* a departure that would echo in revolutions to come.[97]

The division between the two great classes of the early modern commonalty, whose alliance had made the victory of Parliament possible, was revised and sharpened in the years before the king was charged 'as a Tyrant, Traytor, Murtherer, and a publike and Implacable Enemy to the Common-wealth of England' and, ultimately, executed.[98] As for their justification for executing the king, let us allow Hobbes to have the last words. After the king had been brought to the bar, he wrote, 'the president [of the Court] began a long speech in justification of the Parliament's proceedings'. He produced

examples of many kings killed or deposed by wicked Parliaments, ancient and modern, in England, Scotland, and other parts of the world. All of which he endeavoured to justify from this only principle; that the people have the supreme power, and the Parliament is the people. This speech ended, the sentence of death was read; and the same upon Tuesday after, January 30th, executed at the gate of his own palace of Whitehall.[99]

---

[96] Wootton, 'Leveller Democracy and the Puritan Revolution', in Burns (ed.), *Cambridge History of Political Thought*, 435 and *passim*.

[97] John Warr, *The Privileges of the People of England, or, Principles of Common Right Against Freedom* (London 1649), BL E541 (12), 10, however, wrote that 'to persuade and endeavour the alteration of government from one form to another, hath been the subject of the discourse and action of wisemen'; and Warr, *The Corruption and Deficiency of the Lawes of England* (1649), 7: 'for what, I pray you, is fundamentall law, but such customs as are of the eldest date, and longest continuance'. Christopher Hill, 'Introduction' to Stephen Sedley and Lawrence Kaplan (ed.), *A Spark in the Ashes: the Pamphlets of John Warr*, xi, wrote that 'Warr links the Leveller theory of the Norman Yoke with radical religious ideas of God within us, but unlike Winstanley, this does not lead him to advocate communism.' The idea that every generation has a right to reject the past and reconstitute it as it considers convenient became the basic proposition of Tom Paine's revolutionary tract *Common Sense* (Philadelphia 1776).

[98] BL E 540/5, *The Charge of the Commons of England Against Charles Stuart, King of England* (London, 20 January, 1648/9); Sean Kelsey, 'The Death of Charles I', *Historical Journal* 45:4 (December 2002), 727–54, suggests, against the view of Jonathan Scott, *England's Troubles: Seventeenth-Century English Political Instability in European Context* (Cambridge 2000), 45, that the king's death was not, even at this late stage, determined, but that he died because he attempted, successfully, to exploit divisions on the constitutional settlement amongst the trial commissioners.

[99] *Behemoth*, 193–4.

After the defeat of the radical Levellers and the execution of the king, England was formally constituted as a commonwealth of landed households. The words 'commonwealth' and 'commonweal' would continue to be keywords of elite (usually classical-republican) political discourse, but never again would they inspire popular resistance and rebellion. The age of the commonweal was over. A new world had been born.

Index

Abingdon, Abbey of, 267–72
Africa, 378
Anderson, Benedict, 22, 23, 207
Antichrist, 261, 434, 434 n. 29
Anticlericalism, 268, 270
Appleby, Joyce, 316
Archaeology, genetic, 5
Aristotle, 3, 18, 19 n. 28, 26, 44, 343, 347, 387
Armada, Spanish, 357
Artisans, 266, 288 n. 138, 304, 358 n. 52, 388
Arundel, Thomas, 46, 200, 270
  'constitutions' of, 172, 184, 186, 192
  Tyndale on, 198 n. 186
Aske, Robert, 246, 280–2
Astronomy, 386
Aubrey, John, 44, 46, 129
Australia, Commonwealth of, x–xi, 9, 14
Aylmer, G.E., 416

Bacon, Sir Francis, 7, 119, 130, 144, 205, 311, 321, 360, 396, 448
Ball, John, 132, 156, 158, 261 n. 64, 263, 342
Barons' Wars, 107
  See 'Common enterprise'; Henry III
Bill-posting, 141, 268, 435, 437
Birmingham, 315
Black Death, 216, 219, 220, 304, 306, 308
Bowmen, 102
Braudel, Fernand, 315
Braun, Rudolf, 306
Brenner, Robert, 326 n. 80, 327 n. 83, 356
Brinton, Thomas, Bishop of Rochester, 227
Bristol, 301, 317, 320, 362
Britain, English empire, 419
Britnell, R.H., 71–2, 306
Bury St Edmunds, 271
Bush, Michael, on the tradition of popular rebellion, 284–5

Campbell, Bruce M.S., on free and servile tenures, 95–7
Canny, Nicholas, 350
Carpenter, Christine, on political and constitutional history, 121 n. 8
Carpenter, D.A., 87–91, 100
Catto, Jeremy, 120, 120 n. 6
Cecil, Robert, 360, 438
Cecil, Sir William, 359
Charles I, king of England, 415, 417, 420, 429, 436, 446, 451, 452
Chaucer, Geoffrey, 120, 125, 129, 131–2
Cheshire, 320
China, 371
Christ, Jesus, popular representation of, 157, 165–6, 171–2, 430
Church, 148, 389
  Accumulation of wealth, 270 n. 90
  Corporate character of in late fourteenth century, 167, 178–9
  Fear of vernacular revolution, 171, 187
  Magnates, unpopularity of, 152–4
  Movement to appropriate the estates of, 267–72
  Policing of vernacular religion, 179
  Reactionary aspects, 177
  Response to 1381 rebellion, 178
  Terminology to describe rebels of 1381, 232–4
Cirencester, 254–6, 256 n. 51, 271, 453
Clanchy, Michael, 121, 121 n. 9, 125
Class, classes, 241, 454, 456
  Capitalist, emergence of, 305
  Commons or Commonalty versus Nobles, 22–3, 108
  In Norman England, 42–7
  In *Piers Plowman*, 152
  Prejudice, 285
  Struggle, 21 n. 33, 251, 285–6, 405, 407
  Struggle, c.1381–1450, 180, 252–66

465